TEACHING AND LEARNING:
Achieving quality for all

TEACHING AND LEARNING:

Achieving quality for all

UNESCO

UNESCO Publishing

United Nations
Educational, Scientific and
Cultural Organization

This Report is an independent publication commissioned by UNESCO on behalf of the international community. It is the product of a collaborative effort involving members of the Report Team and many other people, agencies, institutions and governments.

The designations employed and the presentation of the material in this publication do not imply the expression of any opinion whatsoever on the part of UNESCO concerning the legal status of any country, territory, city or area, or of its authorities, or concerning the delimitation of its frontiers or boundaries.

The EFA Global Monitoring Report team is responsible for the choice and the presentation of the facts contained in this book and for the opinions expressed therein, which are not necessarily those of UNESCO and do not commit the Organization. Overall responsibility for the views and opinions expressed in the Report is taken by its Director.

First edition
Published in 2014 by the United Nations Educational, Scientific and Cultural Organization
7, Place de Fontenoy, 75352 Paris 07 SP, France

Graphic design by FHI 360
Layout by FHI 360
Cover photo by Poulomi Basu

Library of Congress Cataloging in Publication Data
Data available
Typeset by UNESCO
ISBN 978-92-3-104255-3

Foreword

This 11th *EFA Global Monitoring Report* provides a timely update on progress that countries are making towards the global education goals that were agreed in 2000. It also makes a powerful case for placing education at the heart of the global development agenda after 2015. In 2008, the *EFA Global Monitoring Report* asked – 'will we make it?' With less than two years left before 2015, this Report makes it clear that we will not.

Fifty-seven million children are still failing to learn, simply because they are not in school. Access is not the only crisis – poor quality is holding back learning even for those who make it to school. One third of primary school age children are not learning the basics, whether they have been to school or not. To reach our goals, this Report calls on Governments to redouble efforts to provide learning to all who face disadvantages – whether from poverty, gender, where they live or other factors.

An education system is only as good as its teachers. Unlocking their potential is essential to enhancing the quality of learning. Evidence shows that education quality improves when teachers are supported – it deteriorates if they are not, contributing to the shocking levels of youth illiteracy captured in this Report.

Governments must step up efforts to recruit an additional 1.6 million teachers to achieve universal primary education by 2015. This Report identifies four strategies to provide the best teachers to reach all children with a good quality education. First, the right teachers must be selected to reflect the diversity of the children they will be teaching. Second, teachers must be trained to support the weakest learners, starting from the early grades. A third strategy aims to overcome inequalities in learning by allocating the best teachers to the most challenging parts of a country. Lastly, governments must provide teachers with the right mix of incentives to encourage them to remain in the profession and to make sure all children are learning, regardless of their circumstances.

But teachers cannot shoulder the responsibility alone. The Report shows also that teachers can only shine in the right context, with well-designed curricula and assessment strategies to improve teaching and learning.

These policy changes have a cost. This is why we need to see a dramatic shift in funding. Basic education is currently underfunded by US$26 billion a year, while aid is continuing to decline. At this stage, governments simply cannot afford to reduce investment in education – nor should donors step back from their funding promises. This calls for exploring new ways to fund urgent needs.

We must learn from the evidence as we shape a new global sustainable development agenda after 2015. As this Report shows, equality in access and learning must stand at the heart of future education goals. We must ensure that all children and young people are learning the basics and that they have the opportunity to acquire the transferable skills needed to become global citizens. We must also set goals that are clear and measurable, to allow for the tracking and monitoring that is so essential for governments and donors alike, and to bridge the gaps that remain.

As we advance towards 2015 and set a new agenda to follow, all governments must invest in education as an accelerator of inclusive development. This Report's evidence clearly shows that education provides sustainability to progress against all development goals. Educate mothers, and you empower women and save children's lives. Educate communities, and you transform societies and grow economies. This is the message of this *EFA Global Monitoring Report*.

Irina Bokova
Director-General of UNESCO

Acknowledgements

This Report would not have been possible without the contributions of numerous people. The EFA Global Monitoring Report team would like to acknowledge their support and thank them all for their time and effort.

Invaluable support has been provided by the Global Monitoring Report Advisory Board. Amina J. Mohammed, chairperson of the board, has continuously backed us in our work. Special thanks go to the funders without whose financial support the Report would not be possible.

We would like to acknowledge the role of UNESCO, both at headquarters and in the field, as well as the UNESCO institutes. We are very grateful to numerous individuals, divisions and units in the Organization, notably in the Education Sector and External Relations, for facilitating our work daily. As always, the UNESCO Institute for Statistics has played a key role and we would like to thank its director Hendrik van der Pol and his dedicated staff, including Redouane Assad, Sheena Bell, Manuel Cardoso, Amélie Gagnon, Friedrich Huebler, Alison Kennedy, Elise Legault, Weixin Lu, Albert Motivans, Simon Normandeau, Said Ould Ahmedou Voffal, Pascale Ratovondrahona and Weng Xiaodan.

A group of experts, including Beatrice Avalos, Christopher Colclough, Ricardo Fuentes-Nieva and Andreas Schleicher, helped us during the initial phase and we would like to thank them warmly.

The Report team would also like to thank the researchers who produced background papers and provided other input that informed the Report's analysis: Nadir Altinok, Massimo Amadio, Allison Anderson, Nisha Arunatilake, Monazza Aslam, Julie Beranger, Sonia Bhalotra, Michael Bruneforth, Amparo Castelló-Climent, Yekaterina Chzhen, Damian Clarke, Elizabeth Clery and Rebecca Rhead, Santiago Cueto, Marta Encinas-Martin, Brian Foster, Emmanuela Gakidou, Julián José Gindin, César Guadalupe, Kenneth Harttgen, Frances Hunt, Priyanka Jayawardena, Sophia Kamarudeen, Stephan Klasen, Simon Lange, Juan León, Ken Longden, Anit N. Mukherjee, Sandra Nieto, Yuko Nonoyama-Tarumi, Lee Nordstrum, Moses Oketch, Raúl Ramos, Caine Rolleston, Ricardo Sabates, Spyros Themelis, William Thorn, Kristen Weatherby and Jon Douglas Willms. The students from the London School of Economics who prepared a paper for the Report as part of their Capstone Project are to be thanked as well.

We are also grateful to several institutions, including the Annual Status of Education Report (ASER) India, ASER Pakistan, the Organisation for Economic Co-operation and Development, Pôle de Dakar, Understanding Children's Work, the United Nations Children's Fund and the United Nations Girls' Education Initiative.

Special thanks to all those who worked tirelessly to support the production of the Report. This includes Rebecca Brite, Erin Crum, Kristine Douaud, FHI 360, Imprimerie Faber and Max McMaster. Many colleagues within and outside UNESCO were involved in the translation and production of the Report and we would like to thank them all.

Several people have contributed to the Global Monitoring Report work in the area of communication and outreach, including Rachel Bhatia, Nicole Comforto, Rachel Palmer, Liz Scarff and Salma Zulfiqar. For the images, infographics and quotes from teachers, the Report team has benefited from the support of Schools of Tomorrow (Brazil), the Pratham Education Foundation (India), Eneza Education (Kenya), the Gauteng Primary Literacy and Mathematics Strategy team (South Africa), the Legal Resources Centre (South Africa), Class Act Educational Services (South Africa), Morpeth School (United Kingdom), Education International, Information is Beautiful, Voluntary Service Overseas and Wild is the Game.

Finally, we would like to thank the interns who have supported the team in various areas of its work: Stephie-Rose Nyot, Vivian Leung and Yousra Semmache on communication and outreach; Sarah Benabbou and Matthieu Lanusse on production and distribution and Ming Cai, Marcela Ortiz and Rafael Quintana on research.

The EFA Global Monitoring Report team

Director: Pauline Rose

Kwame Akyeampong, Manos Antoninis, Madeleine Barry, Nicole Bella, Erin Chemery, Marcos Delprato, Nihan Köseleci Blanchy, Joanna Härmä, Catherine Jere, Andrew Johnston, François Leclercq, Alasdair McWilliam, Claudine Mukizwa, Judith Randrianatoavina, Kate Redman, Maria Rojnov-Petit, Martina Simeti, Emily Subden, Asma Zubairi.

The *Education for All Global Monitoring Report* is an independent annual publication. It is facilitated and supported by UNESCO.

For more information, please contact:
EFA Global Monitoring Report team
c/o UNESCO, 7, place de Fontenoy
75352 Paris 07 SP, France
Email: efareport@unesco.org
Tel.: +33 1 45 68 07 41
www.efareport.unesco.org
efareport.wordpress.com

Previous EFA Global Monitoring Reports

2012. Youth and skills: Putting education to work
2011. The hidden crisis: Armed conflict and education
2010. Reaching the marginalized
2009. Overcoming inequality: Why governance matters
2008. Education for All by 2015 — Will we make it?
2007. Strong foundations — Early childhood care and education
2006. Literacy for life
2005. Education for All — The quality imperative
2003/4. Gender and Education for All — The leap to equality
2002. Education for All — Is the world on track?

Any errors or omissions found subsequent to printing will be corrected in the online version at www.efareport.unesco.org.

Contents

List of figures, infographics, tables and text boxes

Figures

Infographics

Tables

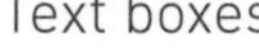

Text boxes

Overview

With the deadline for the Education for All goals less than two years away, it is clear that, despite advances over the past decade, not a single goal will be achieved globally by 2015. This year's *EFA Global Monitoring Report* vividly underlines the fact that people in the most marginalized groups have continued to be denied opportunities for education over the decade. It is not too late, however, to accelerate progress in the final stages. And it is vital to put in place a robust global post-2015 education framework to tackle unfinished business while addressing new challenges. Post-2015 education goals will only be achieved if they are accompanied by clear, measurable targets with indicators tracking that no one is left behind, and if specific education financing targets for governments and aid donors are set.

The *2013/4 EFA Global Monitoring Report* is divided into three parts. Part 1 provides an update of progress towards the six EFA goals. The second part presents clear evidence that progress in education is vital for achieving development goals after 2015. Part 3 puts the spotlight on the importance of implementing strong policies to unlock the potential of teachers so as to support them in overcoming the global learning crisis.

Monitoring the Education for All goals

Since the Education for All framework was established in 2000, countries have made progress towards the goals. However, too many will still be far from the target in 2015.

Goal 1: Early childhood care and education

The foundations set in the first thousand days of a child's life, from conception to the second birthday, are critical for future well-being. It is therefore vital that families have access to adequate health care, along with support to make the right choices for mothers and babies. In addition, access to good nutrition holds the key to developing children's immune systems and the cognitive abilities they need in order to learn.

Despite improvements, an unacceptably high number of children suffer from ill health: under-5 mortality fell by 48% from 1990 to 2012, yet 6.6 million children still died before their fifth birthday in 2012.Progress has been slow. In 43 countries, more than one in ten children died before age 5 in 2000. If the annual rate of reduction for child mortality in these 43 countries between 2000 and 2011 is projected to 2015, only eight countries will reach the target of reducing child deaths by two-thirds from their

© Amina Sayeed/UNESCO

1990 levels. Some poorer countries that invested in early childhood interventions, including Bangladesh and Timor-Leste, reduced child mortality by at least two-thirds in advance of the target date.

Progress in improving child nutrition has been considerable. Yet, as of 2012, some 162 million children under 5 were still malnourished; three-quarters of them live in sub-Saharan Africa and South and West Asia. While the share of children under 5 who were stunted – a robust indicator of long-term malnutrition – was 25%, down from 40% in 1990, the annual rate of reduction needs to almost double if global targets are to be achieved by 2025.

The links between early childhood care and education are strong and mutually reinforcing. Early childhood care and education services help build skills at a time when children's brains are developing, with long-term benefits for children from disadvantaged backgrounds. In Jamaica, for example, infants who were stunted and from disadvantaged backgrounds receiving weekly psychosocial stimulation were earning 42% more than their peers by their early 20s.

Since 2000, pre-primary education has expanded considerably. The global pre-primary education gross enrolment ratio increased from 33% in 1999 to 50% in 2011, although it reached only 18% in sub-Saharan Africa. The number of children enrolled in pre-primary schools grew by almost 60 million over the period.

In many parts of the world, however, there is a wide gap in enrolment between the richest and poorest. Part of the reason is that governments have yet to assume sufficient responsibility for pre-primary education: as of 2011, private providers were catering for 33% of all enrolled children, rising to 71% in the Arab States. The cost of private provision is one of the factors that contribute to inequity in access at this level.

No target was set at Dakar in 2000 to guide assessment of success in early childhood education. To gauge progress, this Report has set a pre-primary education gross enrolment ratio of 80% as an indicative target for 2015. Of the 141 countries with data, 21% had reached the target in 1999. By 2011, the number had risen to 37%. Looking ahead to 2015, it is projected that 48% of countries will reach the target.

An 80% target is modest, leaving many young children, often the most vulnerable, out of pre-school. Any post-2015 goal must provide a clear target to make sure all young children have access to pre-primary education, and a way to track the progress of disadvantaged groups to be sure they do not miss out.

Goal 2: Universal primary education

With just two years until the 2015 deadline for the Education for All goals, the goal of universal primary education (UPE) is likely to be missed by a wide margin. By 2011, 57 million children were still out of school.

There is some good news: between 1999 and 2011, the number of children out of school fell almost by half. Following a period of stagnation, there was a small improvement between 2010 and 2011. But that reduction of 1.9 million is scarcely more than a quarter of the average between 1999 and 2004. Had the rate of decline between 1999 and 2008 been maintained, UPE could almost have been achieved by 2015.

Sub-Saharan Africa is the region that is lagging most behind, with 22% of the region's primary school age population still not in school in 2011. By contrast, South and West Asia experienced the fastest decline, contributing more than half the total reduction in numbers out of school.

Girls make up 54% of the global population of children out of school. In the Arab States, the share is 60%, unchanged since 2000. In South and West Asia, by contrast, the percentage of girls in the out-of-school population fell steadily, from 64% in 1999 to 57% in 2011. Almost half the children out of school globally are expected never to make it to school, and the same is true for almost two of three girls in the Arab States and sub-Saharan Africa.

The top three performers in the last five years have been the Lao People's Democratic Republic, Rwanda and Viet Nam, which reduced their out-of-school populations by at least 85%. There has been little change in the list of countries with the highest numbers of children out of school. The top 10 was unchanged over the period with one exception: Ghana was replaced by Yemen.

Some countries that might have been in the list with the largest out-of-school populations are not there simply because they have no recent reliable data. Using household surveys, this Report estimates that 14 countries had more than 1 million children out of school in 2011, including Afghanistan, China, the Democratic Republic of the Congo, Somalia, Sudan (pre-secession) and the United Republic of Tanzania.

Around half the world's out-of-school population lives in conflict-affected countries, up from 42% in 2008. Of the 28.5 million primary school age children out of school in conflict-affected countries, 95% live in low and lower middle income countries. Girls, who make up 55% of the total, are the worst affected.

Often children do not make it to school because of disadvantages they are born with. One of the most neglected disadvantages is disability. New analysis from four countries shows that children at higher risk of disability are far more likely to be denied a chance to go to school, with differences widening depending on the type of disability. In Iraq, for instance, 10% of 6- to 9-year-olds with no risk of disability had never been to school in 2006, but 19% of those with a risk of hearing impairment and 51% of those who were at higher risk of mental disability had never been to school.

Children are more likely to complete primary schooling if they enter at the right age. However, the net intake rate for the first year of primary school increased only slightly between 1999 and 2011, from 81% to 86% – and it rose by less than one percentage point over the last four years of the period. Some countries have made great progress in getting children into school on time, however, including Ethiopia, which increased its rate from 23% in 1999 to 94% in 2011.

Dropout before completing a full primary cycle has hardly changed since 1999. In 2010, around 75% of those who started primary school reached the last grade. In sub-Saharan Africa, the proportion of those starting school who reached the last grade worsened from 58% in 1999 to 56% in 2010; by contrast, in the Arab States this proportion improved from 79% in 1999 to 87% in 2010.

Universal participation in primary school is likely to remain elusive in many countries by 2015. Of 122 countries, the proportion reaching universal primary enrolment rose from 30% in 1999 to 50% in 2011. Looking ahead to 2015, it is projected that 56% of countries will reach the target. In 2015, 12% of countries will still have fewer than 8 in 10 enrolled, including two-thirds of countries in sub-Saharan Africa.

Assessing whether UPE has been achieved should be judged not by participation alone, but also by whether children complete primary education. Among the 90 countries with data, it is expected that at least 97% of children will reach the last grade of primary school by 2015 in just 13 countries, 10 of which are OECD or EU member states.

Goal 3: Youth and adult skills

The third EFA goal has been one of the most neglected, in part because no targets or indicators were set to monitor its progress. The 2012 Report proposed a framework for various pathways to skills – including foundation, transferable, and technical and vocational skills – as a way of improving monitoring efforts, but the international community is still a long way from measuring the acquisition of skills systematically.

The most effective route to acquiring foundation skills is through lower secondary schooling. The lower secondary gross enrolment ratio increased from 72% to 82% over 1999–2011. The fastest growth was in sub-Saharan Africa, where enrolment more than doubled, albeit from a low base, reaching 49% in 2011.

In low income countries, only 14% of the poorest complete lower secondary school

Children need to complete lower secondary education to acquire foundation skills. Analysis using household surveys shows that completion rates had only reached 37% in low income countries by around 2010. There are wide inequalities in completion, with rates reaching 61% for the richest households but 14% for the poorest.

The number of out-of-school adolescents has fallen since 1999 by 31%, to 69 million. However it has all but stagnated since 2007, leaving many young people needing access to second-chance programmes to acquire foundation skills. Slow progress towards reducing the number of adolescents out of school in South and West Asia resulted in the region's share of the total number increasing from 39% in 1999 to 45% in 2011. In sub-Saharan Africa, the number of adolescents out of school remained at 22 million between 1999 and 2011 as population growth cancelled out enrolment growth.

Given that universal lower secondary education is expected to become an explicit goal after 2015, it is vital to assess where the world is likely to stand in 2015. An assessment of progress based on 82 countries finds that only 26% achieved universal lower secondary education in 1999. By 2011, 32% of countries had reached that level. By 2015, the proportion of countries reaching that level is expected to grow to 46%.

The number of illiterate adults fell by just 1% since 2000

This assessment is based on information from only 40% of all countries. It includes two-thirds of the countries in North America and Western Europe but only a quarter of sub-Saharan African countries, so it is not representative. Taking into account the countries that have not yet achieved universal primary enrolment, the percentage of countries that could achieve lower secondary enrolment by 2015 would be much lower.

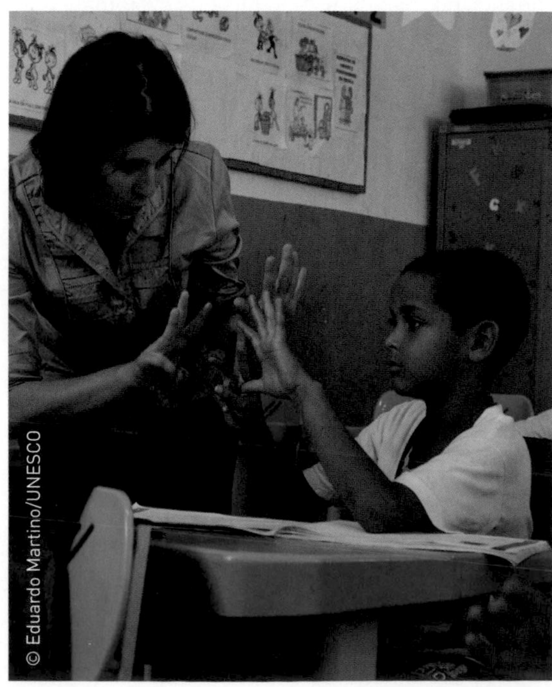
© Eduardo Martino/UNESCO

Goal 4: Adult literacy

Universal literacy is fundamental to social and economic progress. Literacy skills are best developed in childhood through good quality education. Few countries offer genuine second chances to illiterate adults. As a result, countries with a legacy of low access to school have been unable to eradicate adult illiteracy.

The number of illiterate adults remains stubbornly high at 774 million, a fall of 12% since 1990 but just 1% since 2000. It is projected only to fall to 743 million by 2015. Ten countries are responsible for almost three-quarters of the world's illiterate adults. Women make up almost two-thirds of the total, and there has been no progress in reducing this share since 1990. Of the 61 countries with data, around half are expected to achieve gender parity in adult literacy by 2015, and 10 will be very close.

Since 1990, adult literacy rates have risen fastest in the Arab States. Nevertheless, population growth has meant that the number of illiterate adults has only fallen from 52 million to 48 million. Similarly, the region with the second fastest increase in adult literacy rates, South and West Asia, has seen its population of illiterate adults remain stable at just over 400 million. In sub-Saharan Africa, the number of illiterate adults has increased by 37% since 1990, mainly due to population growth, reaching 182 million in 2011. By 2015, it is projected that 26% of all illiterate adults will live in sub-Saharan Africa, up from 15% in 1990.

Slow progress means that there has been little change in the number of countries achieving universal adult literacy. Of 87 countries, 21% had reached universal adult literacy in 2000. Between 2000 and 2011, the number of countries that had reached this level increased to 26%. By contrast, 26% of countries were very far from this level in 2011. In 2015, 29% of countries are expected to achieve universal adult literacy, while 37% will still be very far.

The 15 countries of West Africa are among those with the worst adult literacy rates globally, and include the five countries with the world's lowest literacy rates, below 35%. Those five countries also have female literacy rates below 25%, compared with an average for sub-Saharan

Africa of 50%. These trends are not likely to improve soon. In 12 out of the 15 countries, fewer than half of young women are literate.

Goal 5: Gender parity and equality

Gender parity – ensuring an equal enrolment ratio of girls and boys – is the first step towards the fifth EFA goal. The full goal – gender equality – also demands appropriate schooling environments, practices free of discrimination, and equal opportunities for boys and girls to realize their potential.

Gender disparity patterns vary between countries in different income groups. Among low income countries, disparities are commonly at the expense of girls: 20% achieve gender parity in primary education, 10% in lower secondary education and 8% in upper secondary education. Among middle and high income countries, where more countries achieve parity at any level, the disparities are increasingly at the expense of boys as one moves up to the lower and upper secondary levels. For example, 2% of upper middle income countries have disparity at the expense of boys in primary school, 23% in lower secondary school and 62% in upper secondary school.

Reaching parity at both the primary and secondary levels was singled out to be achieved by 2005, earlier than the other goals. Yet, even by 2011, many countries had not achieved this goal. At the primary level, for 161 countries, 57% had achieved gender parity in 1999. Between 1999 and 2011, the proportion of countries that had reached the target increased to 63%. The number of countries furthest from the target, with fewer than 90 girls for every 100 boys enrolled, fell from 19% in 1999 to 9% in 2011.

Looking ahead, it is projected that by 2015, 70% of countries will have reached the goal and 9% of countries will be close. By contrast, 14% of countries will still be far from the target, and 7% will be very far, of which three-quarters are in sub-Saharan Africa.

A move towards gender parity does not always mean more children in school. Burkina Faso, for example, is projected to achieve parity in primary school by 2015, but it still has the seventh-lowest gross enrolment ratio in the world. And in Senegal, where progress has been made in narrowing the gender gap, this is due to improvement in female enrolment while the male enrolment ratio has not increased since 2004.

At the lower secondary level, of 150 countries, 43% had achieved gender parity in 1999. It is projected that by 2015, 56% of countries will have achieved the target. At the other extreme, 33% of countries were far from the target in 1999, of which three-quarters had disparity at the expense of girls. It is expected that by 2015, 21% of countries will still experience gender disparity in lower secondary school, in 70% of which the disparity will be at girls' expense.

Fast progress is feasible, as the example of Turkey shows: it has almost achieved parity at both lower and upper secondary levels, even though the gender parity index in 1999 was 0.74 in lower secondary and 0.62 in upper secondary. But there is no room for complacency. Traditional perceptions of gender roles that permeate society filter down to schools.

Goal 6: Quality of education

Improving quality and learning is likely to be more central to the post-2015 global development framework. Such a shift is vital to improve education opportunities for the 250 million children who are unable to read, write, or do basic mathematics, 130 million of whom are in school.

The pupil/teacher ratio is one measure for assessing progress towards goal 6. Globally, average pupil/teacher ratios have barely changed at the pre-primary, primary and secondary levels. In sub-Saharan Africa, with teacher recruitment lagging behind growth in enrolment, ratios stagnated and are now the highest in the world at the pre-primary and primary levels. Of the 162 countries with data in 2011, 26 had a pupil/teacher ratio in primary education exceeding 40:1, 23 of which are in sub-Saharan Africa.

By 2015, 70% of countries are expected to reach gender parity in primary enrolment

Between 1999 and 2011, the pupil/teacher ratio in primary education increased by at least 20% in nine countries. By contrast, it fell by at least 20% in 60 countries. Congo, Ethiopia and Mali more than doubled primary school enrolment and yet decreased their pupil/teacher ratios by more than 10 pupils per teacher.

In a third of countries, less than 75% of primary school teachers are trained

However, many countries have expanded teacher numbers rapidly by hiring people to teach without training. This may serve to get more children into school, but jeopardizes education quality. In a third of countries with data, less than 75% of teachers are trained according to national standards. The pupil/trained teacher ratio exceeds the pupil/teacher ratio by 10 pupils in 29 of the 98 countries, of which two-thirds are in sub-Saharan Africa.

At the secondary level, in 14 of 130 countries with data the pupil/teacher ratio exceeds 30:1. Although the vast majority of the countries facing the largest challenges are in sub-Saharan Africa, the region nevertheless managed to double the number of secondary teachers over 1999–2011. Of the 60 countries with data on the share of trained secondary teachers, half had less than 75% of the teaching force trained to the national standard, while 11 had less than 50% trained.

The proportion of teachers trained to national standards is particularly low in pre-primary education. Although the number of teachers at this level has increased by 53% since 2000, in 40 of the 75 countries with data, less than 75% of teachers are trained to the national standard.

In some contexts, the presence of female teachers is crucial to attract girls to school and improve their learning outcomes. Yet women teachers are lacking in some countries with high gender disparity in enrolment, such as Djibouti and Eritrea.

Teachers need good quality learning materials to be effective but many do not have access to textbooks. In the United Republic of Tanzania, only 3.5% of all grade 6 pupils had sole use of a reading textbook. Poor physical infrastructure is another problem for students in many poor countries. Children are often squeezed into overcrowded classrooms, with those in early grades particularly disadvantaged. In Malawi, there are 130 children per class in grade 1, on average, compared with 64 in the last grade. In Chad, just one in four schools has a toilet, and only one in three of those toilets is reserved for girls' use.

With 250 million children not learning the basics, it is vital for a global post-2015 goal to be set which will monitor whether, by 2030, all children and youth, regardless of their circumstances, acquire foundation skills in reading, writing and mathematics. Meeting this need requires countries to strengthen their national assessment systems and ensure that they are used to inform policy. Many national assessment systems are lacking in this respect. Governments often consider their public examination system as equivalent to a national assessment system, even though it is mainly used to promote students between levels of education. National assessments should be a diagnostic tool that can establish whether students achieve the learning standards expected by a particular age or grade, and how this achievement changes over time for subgroups of the population.

Regional and international assessments are critical for monitoring a global learning goal after 2015. Just as improved global monitoring of access has helped maintain pressure on governments to ensure that each child completes primary school, better global monitoring of learning can push governments to make certain that all children not only go to school but are achieving the basics.

For these assessments to facilitate monitoring post-2015 global learning goals, three key principles need to be adhered to. First, all children and young people need to be taken into account when interpreting results, not just those who were in school and took part in the assessment. Disadvantaged children may already be out of the school system, and therefore unlikely to have reached minimum learning standards, by the time the assessment is administered. Not counting them means that the scale of the problem is understated. Second, better information on background characteristics of students is needed to identify which groups of students are not learning. Third, information on the quality of education systems should also be included as part of the assessments.

Leaving no one behind — how long will it take?

After 2015, unfinished business will remain across the six EFA goals, while new priorities are likely to emerge. Analysis of the time it will take to achieve universal primary and lower secondary school completion and youth literacy paints a worrying picture.

While rich boys are expected to reach universal primary completion by 2030 in 56 of 74 low and middle income countries, poor girls will reach the goal by that date in only 7 countries, just one of which is low income. Even by 2060, poor girls will not have reached the goal in 24 of the 28 low income countries in the sample. In sub-Saharan Africa, if recent trends continue, the richest boys will achieve universal primary completion in 2021, but the poorest girls will not catch up until 2086.

Spending time in primary school is no guarantee that a child will be able to read and write. Among 68 countries with data, the poorest young women are projected to achieve universal literacy only in 2072.

The situation is even more dire for lower secondary school completion. In 44 of the 74 countries analysed, there is at least a 50-year gap between when all the richest boys complete lower secondary school and when all the poorest girls do so. And, if recent trends continue, girls from the poorest families in sub-Saharan Africa will only achieve this target in 2111, 64 years later than the boys from the richest families.

While these projections are extremely disconcerting, they are based on recent trends that can be changed if governments, aid donors and the international education community take concerted action to make education available to all, including the marginalized. The projections also show how vital it will be to track progress towards education goals for the most disadvantaged groups after 2015 and to put policies in place that maintain and accelerate progress by redressing imbalances.

Monitoring global education targets after 2015

Since the six Education for All goals were adopted in Dakar, Senegal, in 2000, a lack of precise targets and indicators has prevented some education priorities from receiving the attention they deserve.

The shape of new goals after 2015 should be guided by the principles of upholding education as a right, making sure all children have an equal chance of education and recognizing the learning stages at each phase of a person's life. There should be one core set of goals aligned with the global development agenda, accompanied by a more detailed set of targets that make up a post-2015 education framework. Each goal must be clear and measurable, with the aim of ensuring that no one is left behind. To achieve this, progress should be tracked by the achievements of the lowest performing groups, making sure the gap between them and the better-off is narrowing.

In sub-Saharan Africa, the poorest girls will not achieve universal primary completion until 2086

The number of years young people spend in school is one measure of overall progress in access to education. To achieve a goal of universal lower secondary completion by 2030, young people will need to stay in school about nine years. By 2010, the richest urban young men had already spent more than 9.5 years in school in low income countries, on average, and more than 12 years in lower middle income countries. But the poorest young women in rural areas had spent less than 3 years in school in both low and lower middle income countries, leaving them well below the 6-year target that is associated with universal primary completion, which is supposed to be achieved by 2015. In sub-Saharan Africa, the gap between the time the poorest rural females and the richest urban males spent in school actually widened between 2000 and 2010, from 6.9 years to 8.3 years.

Over the past decade there has been more progress in getting children into primary school than in ensuring that children complete primary or lower secondary education. And extreme inequality persists and in some cases has widened. In sub-Saharan Africa, for example, almost all the richest boys in urban areas were entering school in 2000. By the end of the decade, their primary school completion rate

Only 8 of 53 countries plan to monitor inequality in learning

had reached 87%, and their lower secondary school completion rate 70%. By contrast, among the poorest girls in rural areas, 49% were entering school at the beginning of the decade and 61% by the end of the decade. Only 25% were completing primary education and 11% lower secondary education in 2000; furthermore, these rates had fallen by the end of the decade to 23% and 9%, respectively. Inequality in South and West Asia is also wide and largely unchanged: by the end of the decade, while 89% of the richest urban males completed lower secondary school, only 13% of the poorest rural girls did so.

A goal on learning is an indispensable part of a future global education monitoring framework, but focusing only on learning assessments can be misleading if large numbers of children never make it to the grade where skills are tested. In the United Republic of Tanzania, for example, the proportion of children in grade 6 who achieved a minimum standard in reading in 2007 ranged from 80% of the poorest rural girls to 97% of the richest urban boys. However, while 92% of the richest urban boys of grade 6 age had reached that grade, only 40% of the poorest rural girls had done so. If it is assumed that children who did not reach grade 6 could not have achieved the minimum standard, then the proportions among children of that cohort who learned the basics were 90% for the richest urban boys and 32% for the poorest rural girls.

To make sure inequality is overcome by 2030, country plans need to include specific targets so that education participation and learning can be monitored for individual population groups. Very few currently do so. Gender is the disadvantage most frequently covered in education plans, yet only 24 of 53 country plans reviewed for this report included gender equality targets in primary and lower secondary education.

Four plans included indicators on participation of particular ethnic groups. Only three specifically targeted disparity in access between rural and urban areas in primary and lower secondary education. Moreover, only three plans had an enrolment indicator that differentiated between poorer and richer children. Bangladesh's plan included a monitoring framework for tracking progress in enrolment ratios across wealth quintiles, and Namibia's included a target of making sure 80% of orphans and other vulnerable children in each region were enrolled in primary and secondary education by the final year of the plan.

Even fewer countries plan to monitor inequality in learning outcomes. Only 8 of the 53 countries did so at the primary level and 8 at the lower secondary level, and in most cases monitoring was restricted to gender inequality. Sri Lanka is one exception, with targets for achievement scores in mathematics and native language in the lowest performing regions.

The failure over the past decade to assess progress in education goals by various population subgroups has concealed wide inequality. Its invisibility is further reflected in country plans' lack of national targets for assessing progress in narrowing gaps in access or learning. Post-2015 goals need to include a commitment to making sure the most disadvantaged groups achieve benchmarks set for goals. Failure to do so could mean that measurement of progress continues to mask the fact that the most advantaged benefit the most.

Monitoring progress on financing Education for All

Insufficient financing is one of the main obstacles to achieving Education for All. The finance gap to achieve good quality basic education for all by 2015 has reached US$26 billion, putting the goal of getting every child into school far out of reach. Unfortunately, donors seem more likely to reduce their aid than increase it in coming years. Unless urgent action is taken to change aid patterns, the goal of ensuring that every child is in school and learning by 2015 will be seriously jeopardized.

With little time left before 2015, closing the financing gap might seem impossible. But analysis in this Report shows that the gap could be filled by raising more domestic revenue, devoting an adequate share of existing and projected government resources to education and sharpening the focus of external assistance.

If, as expected, new education goals after 2015 extend to lower secondary education, the finance gap will rise to US$38 billion. The post-2015 framework must include explicit financing targets, demanding full transparency, so that all donors are accountable for their commitments, and finance gaps do not thwart our promises to children.

Many countries far from EFA need to spend more on education

Domestic spending on education has increased in recent years, particularly in low and lower middle income countries, partly because of improvements in economic growth. Government spending on education increased from 4.6% to 5.1% of gross national product (GNP) between 1999 and 2011, on average. In low and middle income countries it rose faster: 30 of these countries increased their spending on education by one percentage point of GNP or more between 1999 and 2011.

The Dakar Framework for Action did not establish how much countries should commit to education. The failure to set a common financing target for the EFA goals should be addressed after 2015, with a specific goal set: that countries should allocate at least 6% of GNP to education. Of the 150 countries with data, only 41 spent 6% or more of GNP on education in 2011, and 25 countries dedicated less than 3%.

It is widely accepted that countries should allocate at least 20% of their budget to education. Yet the global average in 2011 was only 15%, a proportion that has hardly changed since 1999. Of the 138 countries with data, only 25 spent more than 20% in 2011, while at least 6 low and middle income countries decreased their education expenditure as a share of total government expenditure by 5 percentage points or more between 1999 and 2011.

This situation is not expected to improve in coming years. Of 49 countries with data in 2012, 25 planned to shrink their education budget between 2011 and 2012. Of these, 16 were in sub-Saharan Africa. However, some countries, including Afghanistan, Benin and Ethiopia, are resisting this negative trend and are expected to increase their education budgets.

To tap into the potential for economic growth in many of the world's poorest countries, governments need to expand their tax base and devote a fifth of their budget to education. If governments in 67 low and middle income countries did this, they could raise an additional US$153 billion for education in 2015. That would increase the average share of GDP spent on education from 3% to 6% by 2015.

Few poor countries manage to raise 20% of their GDP in taxes, as needed to achieve the Millennium Development Goals. Only 7 of the 67 countries with data both generate 20% of GDP in taxes and allocate the recommended 20% of the revenue to education. In Pakistan, tax revenue is just 10% of GDP and education receives only around 10% of government expenditure. If the government increased its tax revenue to 14% of GDP by 2015 and allocated one-fifth of this to education, it could raise sufficient funds to get all of Pakistan's children and adolescents into school.

Ethiopia is one of 11 among the 67 countries that have been successful in prioritizing education in the government budget but could do far more to maximize revenue from taxation. In 2011, the government received 12% of GDP from taxes, on average. If the proportion were to increase to 16% by 2015, the sector would receive 18% more resources – enabling US$19 more to be spent per primary school age child.

67 countries could increase education resources by US$153 billion through reforms to expand the tax base

Tax revenue as a share of GDP is, however, growing far too slowly in poorer countries. At present rates, only 4 of the 48 countries currently raising less than 20% of GDP in tax would reach the 20% threshold by 2015.

A well-functioning taxation system enables governments to support their education system with domestic finance. Some middle income countries, such as Egypt, India and the Philippines, have far greater potential to mobilize domestic resources for education through improved taxes. Higher levels of tax revenue in Brazil help explain how it spends ten times as much as India per primary school child.

Some countries in South Asia grant large tax exemptions to strong domestic interest groups, resulting in some of the lowest tax-to-GDP ratios in the world. In Pakistan, the tax/GDP ratio of 10% can be partly explained by the political influence of the agricultural lobby. While the agricultural sector makes up 22.5% of Pakistan's GDP, its share in tax revenue is just 1.2%. In

Reforms to expand domestic resources could meet 56% of the annual financing gap in basic education

India, the majority of tax revenue forgone is due to exemptions from custom and excise duties. The revenue lost to exemptions came to the equivalent of 5.7% of GDP in 2012/13. If 20% of this had been earmarked for education, the sector would have received an additional US$22.5 billion in 2013, increasing funding by almost 40% compared with the current education budget.

Some governments sell concessions to exploit natural resources for less than their true value. The Democratic Republic of the Congo lost US$1.36 billion from deals with mining companies over three years in 2010 to 2012, equal to the amount allocated to education over two years in 2010 and 2011.

For many of the world's poorest countries, tax evasion results in the elite building personal fortunes, rather than strong education systems for the majority. If the trillions of dollars estimated to be hidden away in tax havens were subject to capital gains tax, and 20% of the resulting income was allocated to education, it would add between US$38 billion and US$56 billion to funding for the sector.

Illegal tax practices cost African governments an estimated US$63 billion a year. If these practices were halted and 20% of the resulting income spent on education, it would raise an additional US$13 billion for the sector each year.

While governments must lead the drive to reform taxation, donors can play an important complementary role. Just US$1 of donor aid to strengthen tax regimes, for example, can generate up to US$350 in tax revenue. Yet less than 0.1% of total aid was spent supporting tax programmes between 2002 and 2011. In addition, donor country governments should demand transparency from corporations registered in their countries.

Increasing tax revenue and allocating an adequate share to education could raise considerable extra resources for the sector in a short time. The EFA Global Monitoring Report team estimates that 67 low and middle income countries could increase education resources by US$153 billion, or 72%, by 2015 through reforms to raise tax/GDP ratios and public expenditure on education.

On average across the 67 countries, spending per primary school age child would increase from US$209 to US$466 in 2015. In the low income countries among the 67, the average amount spent per primary school age child would increase from US$102 to US$158.

Fourteen of these 67 countries have already reached the proposed target of spending at least 6% of GDP on education. Of the 53 yet to reach the target, 19 could achieve it if they expanded and diversified the tax base and prioritized education spending by 2015.

These additions to domestic resources could meet 56% of the US$26 billion average annual financing gap in basic education for 46 low and lower middle income countries, or 54% of the US$38 billion gap in basic and lower secondary education.

Such reforms are not without precedent. Ecuador renegotiated contracts with oil companies, widened its tax base and made education a higher priority, tripling its education expenditure between 2003 and 2010.

To achieve Education for All, it is necessary not only to increase domestic resources for education but also to redistribute these resources so that a fair share reaches those most in need. More often, however, resources are skewed towards the most privileged. To shift education spending in favour of the marginalized, many governments have introduced funding mechanisms that allocate more resources to parts of the country or groups of schools that need greater support to overcome educational deprivation and inequality. Countries have different methods of redistributing resources. Brazil, for example, guarantees a certain minimum spending level per pupil, giving priority to schools in rural areas, with greater weight on highly marginalized indigenous groups. The reforms have led to improvement in enrolment and learning in the disadvantaged north of the country.

Other redistribution programmes have been less successful, however. One reason is that allocations per child still do not adequately reflect the costs of delivering quality education to the marginalized. In one of India's wealthier states, Kerala, education spending per pupil was about US$685. By contrast, in the poorer state of Bihar it was just US$100.

Poorer countries can find it difficult to identify and target the groups most in need. As a result, many base allocations on enrolment figures, to the detriment of areas where large numbers of children are out of school. In Kenya, for example, the capitation grant is distributed on the basis of number of students enrolled, a disadvantage for the 12 counties in the arid and semi-arid areas that are home to 46% of the out-of-school population.

To realize the full potential of redistributive measures, governments need to ensure that such resources cover the entire cost of a quality education for the most vulnerable and that far-reaching reforms strengthen education systems' capacity to implement such measures.

Trends in aid to education

With improvement in the numbers of children out of school stagnating, a final push is needed to ensure that all children are in school by 2015. Even before the economic downturn, donors were off track to fulfil their education finance promises. A more recent decline in aid to basic education increases the difficulty of this task.

While aid to education rose steadily after 2002, it peaked in 2010 and is now falling: total aid to all levels of education declined by 7% between 2010 and 2011. Aid to basic education fell for the first time since 2002, by 6%: from US$6.2 billion in 2010 to US$5.8 billion in 2011. Aid to secondary education declined by 11% between 2010 and 2011 from an already low level. This puts at risk the chance of meeting Education for All goals and any hope of more ambitious goals to include universal lower secondary education after 2015.

Low income countries, which only receive around one-third of aid to basic education, witnessed a larger decrease in aid to basic education than middle income countries. Aid fell by 9% in low income countries between 2010 and 2011, from US$2.05 billion to US$1.86 billion. As a result, the resources available per child dropped from US$18 in 2010 to US$16 in 2011.

In sub-Saharan Africa, home to over half the world's out-of-school population, aid to basic education declined by 7% between 2010 and 2011. The US$134 million reduction in basic education aid to the region would have been enough to fund good quality school places for over 1 million children.

In some countries, aid has been falling for more than a year. Aid has played a key part in supporting efforts to get more children into school in the United Republic of Tanzania, but it fell by 12% between 2009 and 2010 and by a further 57% in 2011.

The world's poorest children, who are the most likely to be out of school, live not only in low income countries but also in some lower middle income countries. Since 2000, 25 countries have graduated to this group, which now comprises 54 countries, while 36 are classified as low income. In 1999, 84% of the world's out-of-school children lived in low income countries and 12% in lower middle income countries; by 2011, 37% lived in low income countries and 49% in lower middle income countries. This shift was largely due to the graduation to lower middle income status of some large-population countries, such as India, Nigeria and Pakistan. While these countries could do far more to raise their own resources for education and distribute them to those most in need, such reforms will take time. In the meantime, donors should direct aid to the areas in lower middle income countries where poverty is concentrated to make sure another generation of children in these countries is not denied its right to education.

Direct aid to education fell slightly more than overall aid to other sectors between 2010 and 2011, and thus the share of aid to education declined from 12% to 11%. The fall in aid to education reflects the changing spending patterns of a large number of donors. Canada, France, the Netherlands and the United States, in particular, cut spending on education more than they reduced overall aid. Between 2010 and 2011, 21 bilateral and multilateral donors reduced their aid disbursements to basic education. The largest decreases in volume terms were by Canada, the European Union, France, Japan, the Netherlands, Spain and the United States, which together accounted for 90% of the reduction in aid to basic education.

In 2011, aid to basic education fell for the first time since 2002

The United States moved from being the largest bilateral donor to basic education in 2010 to second place in 2011. The United Kingdom is now the largest donor to education. The Netherlands' aid to basic education fell by over a third between 2010 and 2011; it had been the largest donor to basic education in 2007, but by 2011 was in 11th place.

Australia, the IMF and the World Bank increased their overall aid to basic education between 2010 and 2011 but reduced their spending in low income countries. World Bank aid to basic education increased by 13% overall, but fell by 23% in low income countries. The United Republic of Tanzania saw World Bank disbursements fall from US$88 million in 2002 to less than US$0.3 million in 2011.

The Global Partnership for Education (GPE) is an important source of financing for some low income countries. In 2011, the GPE disbursed a record US$385 million to basic education, making it the fourth largest donor to low and lower middle income countries that year. For the 31 countries with a programme implementation grant in 2011, 24% of basic education aid was disbursed by the GPE. It is unlikely, however, to have made up for the reduction in World Bank spending. The United Republic of Tanzania became a GPE partner in 2013 with a US$5.2 million grant for its education plan. All this, however, is allocated to Zanzibar, and the amount is small compared with what the country received from the World Bank early in the 2000s. To improve monitoring of its contributions, the GPE needs to report its aid flows to the OECD-DAC, just as global health funds such as the GAVI Alliance and the Global Fund to Fight AIDS, Tuberculosis and Malaria do.

Education receives just 1.4% of humanitarian aid

There is no sign that overall aid will stop declining before the 2015 deadline. From 2011 to 2012, total aid decreased by 4%, with 16 DAC donors decreasing their aid: 13 DAC donors made aid a lower priority by decreasing aid as a proportion of gross national income (GNI). Less developed countries are expected to bear the brunt of these reductions, with cuts to their bilateral aid of 12.8% from 2011 to 2012. In 2013, aid is expected to fall in 31 of 36 low income countries, the majority of which are in sub-Saharan Africa.

In addition, only five of the fifteen members of the European Union that agreed to increase their aid to 0.7% of GNI by 2015 are expected to meet their commitment. If these countries met their promises, they would raise US$9 billion more for education in 2015.

Education in conflict-affected countries should be a priority for donors. These countries house half of the world's out-of-school children. Currently education receives just 1.4% of humanitarian aid, far from the 4% called for by the UN Secretary-General's Global Education First Initiative. In plans for 2013, education's share of overall humanitarian aid is likely to reach no more than 2%.

In Mali, where most schools in the north remained closed due to conflict, education made up 5% of appeal requests for 2013, but just 15% of the requested funds had been pledged by September 2013. Similarly, 36% of the resources requested in 2013 for education in the Syrian Arab Republic had actually been pledged. While these countries might receive more of the requested funds later in 2013, they would come too late for the millions of children who have had to drop out of school due to conflict.

It is not only the amount of aid that counts but also whether it is used to target the most disadvantaged. These children do not receive all the aid available, however: a quarter of direct aid to education is spent on students studying in universities in rich countries. Even though scholarships and imputed student costs may be vital to strengthen human resource capacity in low income countries, most of this funding actually goes to upper middle income countries, with China the largest recipient, receiving 21% of the total.

On average over 2010–2011, donors – primarily Germany and Japan – disbursed US$656 million per year to China for scholarships and student imputed costs, which was 77 times the amount of aid disbursed to Chad for basic education over the same period. The total funding in the form of imputed student costs and scholarships received annually by Algeria, China, Morocco, Tunisia and Turkey was equivalent to the total amount of direct aid to basic education for all 36 low income countries in 2010–2011, on average.

Aid can also be delivered on unfavourable terms for poorer countries: 15% of aid is in the form of loans that countries have to pay back at concessional interest rates. Without funding from bilateral donors, poorer countries risk becoming dependent on these loans, leading to debt that could restrict their ability to fund education from their own resources.

Removing imputed student costs, scholarships and loans, Germany would drop from being the largest donor in direct aid to education to being the fifth largest; the World Bank would fall from third to fourteenth place. The United Kingdom and United States, by contrast, would jump from sixth and seventh position to first and second.

Information on the whole spectrum of education financing – including aid, domestic resources and household spending – is often insufficient and fragmented, resulting in only partial analysis and diagnosis of how much money is needed and where. New analysis from seven countries shows that households bear up to 37% of education expenditure in primary education and up to 58% in secondary education, which places a particular burden on the poorest households. In addition, it shows how vital aid is to education financing in some of the poorest countries: it accounts for almost a quarter of education spending in Malawi and Rwanda. These findings highlight the importance of building a comprehensive national education accounts system, which could be modelled on the experience in health.

To avoid failing another generation of children due to lack of resources after 2015, national governments aid donors need to be held to account for their commitments to provide the resources necessary to reach education goals. Drawing on analysis included in *EFA Global Monitoring Reports* over the years, the Report team proposes that a target should be set for national governments to allocate at least 6% of their GNP to education. Targets for governments and aid donors should also include commitments for them to spend at least 20% of their budgets on education. Setting these targets, and making sure governments and aid donors keep to them, will be an important contribution to the education opportunities of children and young people in the future.

Education transforms lives

Treaties and laws worldwide recognize that education is a fundamental human right. In addition, education imparts knowledge and skills that enable people to realize their full potential, and so it becomes a catalyst for the achievement of other development goals. Education reduces poverty, boosts job opportunities and fosters economic prosperity. It also increases people's chances of leading a healthy life, deepens the foundations of democracy, and changes attitudes to protect the environment and empower women.

Educating girls and women, in particular, has unmatched transformative power. As well as boosting their own chances of getting jobs, staying healthy and participating fully in society, educating girls and young women has a marked impact on the health of their children and accelerates their countries' transition to stable population growth.

To unlock the wider benefits of education and achieve development goals after 2015, it needs to be equitable and to extend at least to lower secondary school. And the schooling that children receive needs to be of good quality so that they actually learn the basics.

Education reduces poverty and boosts jobs and growth

Education is a key way of helping individuals escape poverty and of preventing poverty from being passed down through the generations. It enables those in paid formal employment to earn higher wages and offers better livelihoods for those who work in agriculture and the urban informal sector.

If all students left school with basic reading skills, 171 million people could be lifted out of poverty

EFA Global Monitoring Report team calculations show that if all students in low income countries left school with basic reading skills, 171 million people could be lifted out of poverty, which would be equivalent to a 12% cut in world poverty. An important way education reduces poverty is by increasing people's income. Globally, one year of school increases earnings by 10%, on average.

Education can help people escape from working poverty. In the United Republic of Tanzania, 82% of workers who had less than primary education were below the poverty line. But working adults with primary education were 20% less likely to be poor, while secondary education reduced the chances of being poor by almost 60%. It is not just time in school, but skills acquired that count. In Pakistan, working women with good literacy skills earned 95% more than women with weak literacy skills.

In the formal sector, higher wages reflect the higher productivity of more educated workers. But many of the poorest are involved in informal sector work, running small businesses. Educated people are more likely to start a business, and their businesses are likely to be more profitable. In Uganda, owners of household enterprises with a primary education earned 36% more than those with no education; those with a lower secondary education earned 56% more.

In rural areas, farmers with good literacy and numeracy skills can interpret and respond to new information, making better use of modern inputs and technologies to increase the productivity of traditional crops and diversify into higher value crops. In Mozambique, literate farmers were 26 percentage points more likely than non-literate ones to cultivate cash crops.

For each additional year of mothers' education, a child spends an extra 0.32 years in school

Education also helps people in rural areas diversify their income by involvement in off-farm work. In rural Indonesia, 15% of men and 17% of women with no education were employed in non-farm work, compared with 61% of men and 72% of women with secondary education.

One of the benefits of increased education is that educated parents are likely to have more educated children. Analysis of household surveys from 56 countries finds that, for each additional year of the mother's education, the average child attains an extra 0.32 years, and for girls the benefit is slightly larger.

By benefiting women in particular, education can help narrow gender gaps in work opportunities and pay. In Argentina and Jordan, for instance, among people with primary education, women earned around half the average wage of men, while among those with secondary education, women earned around two-thirds as much as men.

Education helps protect working adults from exploitation by increasing their opportunities to obtain secure contracts. In urban El Salvador, only 7% of working adults with less than primary education had an employment contract, compared with 49% of those with secondary education.

Education not only facilitates individuals' escape from poverty, but also generates productivity that fuels economic growth. A one-year increase in the average educational attainment of a country's population increases annual per capita GDP growth from 2% to 2.5%.

Education can help explain differences in regional growth trajectories. In 1965, adults in East Asia and the Pacific had spent 2.7 more years in school than those in sub-Saharan Africa. Over the next 45 years, the average growth rate was more than four times faster in East Asia and the Pacific.

Comparing experiences within regions further illustrates the importance of education. In Guatemala, adults had 3.6 years of schooling, on average, in 2005 and the average level increased by only 2.3 years from 1965 to 2005. If the country had matched the average for Latin America and the Caribbean, where the average number of years that adults spent at school rose from 3.6 in 1965 to 7.5 in 2005, it could have more than doubled its average annual growth rate between 2005 and 2010, equivalent to an additional US$500 per person.

Only by investing in equitable education – making sure that the poorest complete more years in school – can countries achieve the kind of growth that banishes poverty. Equality in education can be measured by the Gini coefficient, which ranges from zero, indicating perfect equality, to one, indicating maximum inequality. An improvement in the Gini coefficient by 0.1 accelerates growth by half a percentage point, increasing income per capita by 23% over 40 years. If sub-Saharan Africa's education Gini coefficient of 0.49 had been halved to the level in Latin America and the Caribbean, the annual growth rate in GDP per capita over 2005–2010 could have risen by 47% (from 2.4% to 3.5%) and income could have grown by US$82 per capita over the period.

Comparing Pakistan and Viet Nam illustrates starkly the importance of equitable education. In 2005, the average number of years adults had spent at school was similar: 4.5 in Pakistan and 4.9 in Viet Nam. Education levels, however, were very unequally distributed in Pakistan: Pakistan's Gini coefficient for education inequality was more than double the level in Viet Nam. The difference in education inequality between the countries accounts for 60% of the difference in their per capita growth between 2005 and 2010. Viet Nam's per capita income, which was around 40% below Pakistan's in the 1990s, not only caught up with Pakistan's but was 20% higher by 2010.

Education improves people's chances of a healthier life

Education is one of the most powerful ways of improving people's health. It saves the lives of millions of mothers and children, helps prevent and contain disease, and is an essential element of efforts to reduce malnutrition. Educated people are better informed about diseases, take preventative measures, recognize signs of illness early and tend to use health care services more often. Despite its benefits, education is often neglected as a vital health intervention in itself and as a means of making other health interventions more effective.

There are few more dramatic illustrations of the power of education than the estimate that the lives of 2.1 million children under 5 were saved between 1990 and 2009 because of improvements in the education of women of reproductive age. However, the challenge remaining is enormous. In 2012, 6.6 million children under 5 died, most of them in low and lower middle income countries. If all women completed primary education in these countries, the under-5 mortality rate would fall by 15%. If all women completed secondary education, it would fall by 49%, equal to around 2.8 million lives a year.

Around 40% of all under-5 deaths occur within the first 28 days of life, the majority being due to complications during delivery. Yet the most recent estimates suggest there were no skilled birth attendants present in over half the births in sub-Saharan Africa and South Asia. Across 57 low and middle income countries, a literate mother was 23% more likely to have a skilled attendant at birth than an illiterate mother. In Mali, maternal literacy more than tripled this likelihood.

Educated mothers are better informed about specific diseases, so they can take measures to prevent them. Pneumonia is the largest cause of child deaths, accounting for 17% of the total worldwide. One additional year of maternal education can lead to a 14% decrease in the pneumonia death rate – equivalent to 160,000 child lives saved every year. Diarrhoea is the fourth biggest child killer, accounting for 9% of child deaths. If all women completed primary education, the incidence of diarrhoea would fall by 8% in low and lower middle income countries; with secondary education, it would fall by 30%. The probability of a child being immunized against diphtheria, tetanus and whooping cough would increase by 10% if all women in low and lower middle income countries completed primary education, and by 43% if they completed secondary education.

If all women completed primary education, there would be 66% fewer maternal deaths

A mother's education is just as crucial for her own health as it is for her offspring's. Every day, almost 800 women die from preventable causes related to pregnancy and childbirth. If all women completed primary education, there would be 66% fewer maternal deaths, saving 189,000 lives per year. In sub-Saharan Africa alone, if all women completed primary education, there would be 70% fewer maternal deaths, saving 113,400 women's lives.

Some countries have seen considerable gains. Thanks to education reforms in the 1970s, the average amount of schooling young women received increased by 2.2 years in Nigeria. This accounted for a 29% reduction in the maternal mortality rate.

Improving education is a powerful way to help reduce the incidence of infectious diseases such as HIV/AIDS. Education helps increase awareness about HIV prevention, for example. In South and West Asia and sub-Saharan Africa, literate women were as much as 30 percentage points more likely than those who were not literate to be aware that they had the right to refuse sex or request condom use if they knew that their partner had a sexually transmitted disease. Knowing where to get tested for HIV is a first step to receiving treatment if needed. But only 52% of women who were not literate in sub-Saharan Africa knew where to get tested for HIV, compared with 85% of the literate.

Malaria is one of the world's deadliest diseases, killing one child every minute in Africa. Improved access to education is crucial in ensuring the effectiveness of preventative measures, such as the use of drugs or bed nets treated with insecticide. In the Democratic Republic of the Congo, where a fifth of the world's malaria-related deaths occur, the education of the household head or the mother increased the probability that the family slept under a bed net. Such changes result in fewer infections, especially in areas of high transmission risk. In these areas, the odds of children having malaria parasites were 22% lower if their mothers had primary education than if they had no education, or 36% less if they had secondary education.

Education – especially education that empowers women – is key to tackling malnutrition, the underlying cause of more than 45% of child deaths. Educated mothers are more likely to know about appropriate health and hygiene practices at home, and have more power to ensure that household resources are allocated so as to meet children's nutrition needs. In low and lower middle income countries, providing all women with a primary education would reduce stunting – a robust indicator of malnutrition – by 4%, or 1.7 million children; providing a secondary education would reduce stunting by 26%, or 11.9 million children.

By age 1, adverse effects of malnutrition on life prospects are likely to be irreversible. Infants in Peru whose mothers had reached lower secondary education were 60% less likely to be stunted than children whose mothers had no education.

Education promotes healthy societies

Education helps people understand democracy, promotes the tolerance and trust that underpin it, and motivates people to participate in politics. Education also has a vital role in preventing environmental degradation and limiting the causes and effects of climate change. And it can empower women to overcome discrimination and assert their rights.

Education improves people's understanding of politics and how to participate in it. Across 12 sub-Saharan African countries, 63% of individuals without formal schooling had an understanding of democracy, compared with 71% of those with primary education and 85% of those with secondary. People with higher levels of education are more interested in politics and so more likely to seek information. In Turkey, for example, the share of those who said they were interested in politics rose from 40% among those

Credit: Nguyen Thanh Tuan/UNESCO

with primary education to 52% among those with secondary education.

Education increases people's support for democracy, particularly where there have been recent democratic transitions. Across 18 sub-Saharan African countries, those of voting age with primary education were 1.5 times more likely to express support for democracy than those with no education, and twice as likely if they had completed secondary education.

Educated people are more likely to vote. In 14 Latin American countries, turnout was five percentage points higher for those with primary education and nine percentage points higher for individuals with secondary education compared to those with no education. The effect was larger in countries where average levels of education were lower, such as El Salvador, Guatemala and Paraguay. Education also encourages other forms of political participation. In Argentina, China and Turkey, citizens were twice as likely to sign a petition or boycott products if they had secondary education than if they just had primary education.

Education has an indispensable role in strengthening the bonds that hold communities and societies together. In Latin America, people with secondary education were 47% less likely than those with primary education to express intolerance for people of a different race. In the Arab States, people with secondary education were 14% less likely than those with only primary education to express intolerance towards people of a different religion. In sub-Saharan Africa, people with primary education were 10% less likely to express intolerance towards people with HIV and 23% less likely if they had a secondary education. In Central and Eastern Europe, those with secondary education were 16% less likely than those who had not completed secondary education to express intolerance towards immigrants.

Education also helps overcome gender biases in political behaviour to deepen democracy. In India, reducing the gender literacy gap by 40% increased the probability of women standing for state assembly election by 16% and the share of votes that they received by 13%.

Education lowers tolerance towards corruption and helps build accountability. In 31 countries, those with secondary education were one-sixth more likely than average to complain about deficient government services.

Increasing access to school for all generally reduces feelings of injustice in society that have fuelled many conflicts. But it needs to increase equally for all population groups; otherwise, perceived unfairness can reinforce disillusionment. In 55 low and middle income countries where the level of educational inequality doubled, the probability of conflict more than doubled, from 3.8% to 9.5%.

By improving knowledge, instilling values, fostering beliefs and shifting attitudes, education has considerable potential to change environmentally harmful lifestyles and behaviour. A key way in which education can increase environmental awareness and concern is by improving understanding of the science behind climate change and other environmental issues. Students with higher science scores across 57 countries reported being more aware of complex environmental issues. Similarly, across 29 mostly high income countries, 25% of people with less than secondary education expressed concern for the environment, compared with 37% of people with secondary education and 46% of people with tertiary education.

Education is also critical for helping people adapt to the consequences of climate change, especially in poorer countries, where threats to livelihoods are being felt most strongly by farmers dependent on rain-fed agriculture. In Ethiopia, six years of education increased by 20% the chance that a farmer would adapt to climate change through techniques such as practising soil conservation, varying planting dates and changing crop varieties.

Education can empower women to claim their rights and overcome barriers that prevent them from getting a fair share of the fruits of overall progress. Having the freedom to choose one's spouse is one such right. Women in India with at least secondary education were 30 percentage points more likely to have a say over their choice of spouse than their less educated peers.

Likewise, ensuring that girls stay in school is one of the most effective ways to prevent child marriage. If all girls completed primary school

In Argentina, China and Turkey, citizens are twice as likely to sign a petition if they have secondary education

in sub-Saharan Africa and South and West Asia, the number of girls getting married by age 15 would fall by 14%; with secondary education, 64% fewer girls would get married.

Staying in school longer also gives girls more confidence to make choices that avert the health risks of early births and births in quick succession. Currently one in seven girls have children before age 17 in sub-Saharan Africa and South and West Asia. In these regions, 10% fewer girls would become pregnant if they all had primary education, and 59% fewer would if they all had secondary education. This would result in around 2 million fewer early births.

Women with more education tend to have fewer children, which benefits them, their families and society more generally. One reason for this is because education allows women to have a greater influence on family size. In Pakistan, only 30% of women with no education believe they have a say over how many children they have, compared with 52% of women with primary education and 63% of those with lower secondary education.

In some regions, education has been a key factor in bringing forward the demographic transition. Other parts of the world are lagging, however, particularly sub-Saharan Africa, where women average 5.4 live births. In the region, women with no education have 6.7 births. The figure falls to 5.8 for those with primary education and to 3.9 for those with secondary education.

Education's power to transform lives should secure it a central place in the post-2015 framework

Conclusion

The striking evidence laid out in this chapter demonstrates not only education's capacity to accelerate progress towards other development goals, but also how best to tap that potential, most of all by making sure that access to good quality education is available to all, regardless of their circumstances. Education's unique power should secure it a central place in the post-2015 development framework, and in the plans of policy-makers in poor and rich countries alike.

Supporting teachers to end the learning crisis

A lack of attention to education quality and a failure to reach the marginalized have contributed to a learning crisis that needs urgent attention. Worldwide, 250 million children – many of them from disadvantaged backgrounds – are not learning even basic literacy and numeracy skills, let alone the further skills they need to get decent work and lead fulfilling lives.

To solve the learning crisis, all children must have teachers who are trained, motivated and enjoy teaching, who can identify and support weak learners, and who are backed by well-managed education systems.

As this Report shows, governments can increase access while also making sure that learning improves for all. Adequately funded national education plans that aim explicitly to meet the needs of the disadvantaged and that ensure equitable access to well-trained teachers must be a policy priority. Attracting and retaining the best teachers as a means to end the learning crisis requires a delicate juggling act on the part of policy-makers.

To ensure that all children are learning, teachers also need the support of an appropriate curriculum and assessment system that pays particular attention to the needs of children in early grades, when the most vulnerable are in danger of dropping out. Beyond teaching the basics, teachers must help children gain important transferable skills to help them become responsible global citizens.

The learning crisis hits the disadvantaged hardest

Despite impressive gains in access to education over the past decade, improvements in quality have not always kept pace. Many countries are not ensuring that their children achieve even the most basic skills in reading and mathematics. The disadvantaged are the most likely to suffer because of insufficient numbers of trained teachers, overstretched infrastructure and inadequate materials. Yet it is possible for countries to extend access to school while also improving equitable learning.

The global learning crisis: action is urgent

Of the world's 650 million primary school age children, at least 250 million are not learning the basics in reading and mathematics. Of these, almost 120 million have little or no experience of primary school, having not even reached grade 4. The remaining 130 million are in primary school but have not achieved the minimum benchmarks for learning. Often unable to understand a simple sentence, these children are ill equipped to make the transition to secondary education.

There is a vast divide between regions in learning achievement. In North America and Western Europe, 96% of children stay in school until grade 4 and achieve the minimum reading standards, compared with only one-third of children in South and West Asia and two-fifths in sub-Saharan Africa. These two regions account for more than three-quarters of those not crossing the minimum learning threshold.

The learning crisis is extensive. New analysis shows that less than half of children are learning the basics in 21 out of the 85 countries with full data available. Of these, 17 are in sub-Saharan Africa; the others are India, Mauritania, Morocco and Pakistan.

This learning crisis has costs not only for the future ambitions of children, but also for the current finances of governments. The cost of 250 million children not learning the basics is equivalent to US$129 billion, or 10% of global spending on primary education.

Global disparities mask huge inequalities within countries

While average figures on learning achievement provide an overall picture of the scale of the learning crisis, they can conceal large disparities within countries. Poverty, gender, location, language, ethnicity, disability and other factors mean some children are likely to get less support from schools to improve their learning.

How much a child learns is strongly influenced by family wealth. Analysis of 20 African countries for this year's Report shows that children from richer households are more likely not only to complete school, but also to achieve a minimum level of learning. By contrast, in 15 of the countries, no more than one in five poor children reach the last grade and learn the basics.

In Latin America, where performance is higher in general, children from disadvantaged backgrounds also lag far behind their wealthier peers. In El Salvador, 42% of children from the poorest households complete primary education and master the basics, compared with 84% of those from richest households.

Girls in poor households face some of the worst disadvantages, indicating that there is an urgent need to tackle gender gaps through education policies. In Benin, for example, around 60% of rich boys stay in school and attain basic numeracy skills, compared with 6% of poor girls.

Living in a disadvantaged area – especially rural ones, which often lack teachers and teaching resources – is a huge barrier to learning. In the United Republic of Tanzania, only 25% of poor children in rural areas learn the basics, compared with 63% of rich children in urban areas. In some Latin American countries, including El Salvador, Guatemala, Panama and Peru, achievement gaps in mathematics and reading between rural and urban students exceed 15 percentage points.

The cost of 250 million children not learning the basics is equivalent to US$129 billion

Location-related disadvantages begin in the early grades and widen. In Ghana, urban students were twice as likely as rural students to reach minimum levels of English in 2011 in grade 3, and more than three times as likely by grade 6.

Geographical disadvantage is often aggravated by poverty and gender. In Balochistan province, Pakistan, only 45% of children of grade 5 age could solve a two-digit subtraction, compared with 73% in wealthier Punjab province. Only around one-quarter of girls from poor households in Balochistan achieved basic numeracy skills, while boys from rich households in the province fared much better, approaching the average in Punjab.

The discrimination some indigenous or ethnic groups face is reinforced by the fact that the language used in the classroom may not be one that they speak. In Peru in 2011, Spanish speakers were more than seven times as likely as indigenous language speakers to reach a satisfactory standard in reading.

Well-designed bilingual programmes taught by qualified teachers can help children overcome this challenge.

Children who learn less are more likely to leave school early. In Ethiopia, India, Peru and Viet Nam, children who achieved lower scores in mathematics at age 12 were more likely than others to drop out by age 15. In Viet Nam, for instance, almost half the poorer performers at age 12 had dropped out by age 15, compared with around one in five of the stronger performers.

Less than 60% of immigrants in France passed the minimum learning benchmark

The disadvantages children face in gaining access to school and remaining there will stay with them into secondary school. In South Africa, for example, there is a vast gap in learning between rich and poor, with only 14% of poor adolescents achieving the minimum standard in mathematics, comparable to the performance of poor students in Ghana, a country that has less than one-fifth South Africa's wealth. Such gaps are not inevitable. Botswana has achieved much higher levels of learning thanks largely to its much narrower gap between rich and poor.

In some countries, the gap between rich and poor becomes more apparent in later grades. In Chile, for example, while the gap is narrow at grade 4, 77% of rich students achieve the minimum standards by grade 8, compared with 44% of poor students.

Rich countries are also failing to ensure that the marginalized can learn

While rich countries' achievement levels are generally higher, their education systems also fail significant minorities. For example, over 10% of grade 8 students in Norway and England performed below minimum learning levels in mathematics in 2011.

While East Asian countries, including Japan, the Republic of Korea and Singapore, have shown it is possible to overcome the disadvantages those living in poverty face, the same cannot be said for some OECD countries and for wealthy countries in the Arab States. The chance of a poor student in Oman achieving minimum learning standards, for example, is similar to that of a student in less wealthy countries, such as Ghana. In New Zealand, only two-thirds of poor students achieved the minimum standards, compared with 97% of rich students.

Immigrant students face a high risk of marginalization in education, resulting in lower levels of learning achievement. In France, Germany and the United Kingdom, over 80% of 15-year-old students achieve minimum benchmarks in reading. But immigrants perform far worse: in the United Kingdom, the proportion of immigrants making it above the minimum benchmark is no better than the average for Turkey, while Germany's immigrants are on a par with students in Chile. Immigrants in France face particular problems, with less than 60% passing the minimum benchmark – equivalent to the average for students in Mexico.

Indigenous children in high income countries often face disadvantage, and the gap in learning outcomes with the rest of the population has been persistent. In Australia, around two-thirds of indigenous students achieved the minimum benchmark in grade 8 between 1994/95 and 2011, compared with almost 90% of their non-indigenous peers.

Improving learning while expanding access

It is often claimed that expanding access to primary school in poorer countries means lowering the quality of education. Yet, although vast numbers of children are not learning the basics, some countries have been able to get more children into school while ensuring that they learn once there. This balance is particularly impressive given that new entrants are more likely to come from marginalized households. Even so, far more needs to be done to bridge the learning gap more quickly, even in richer countries.

The United Republic of Tanzania made great strides in the numbers of students reaching the end of primary school, partly because primary school fees were abolished in 2001. Between 2000 and 2007, the proportion of children who completed primary school rose from half to around two-thirds, while the proportion learning the basics in mathematics increased from 19% to 36%. This is equivalent to around 1.5 million additional children learning the basics. While it is unacceptable that 27% were in school but not learning the basics, the fact that the problems with quality were already apparent in 2000 suggests that they were more inherent in the education system than directly associated with education expansion.

In Malawi and Uganda, access and quality did not improve significantly between 2000 and 2007, and the learning gap between rich and poor widened. These countries face a triple challenge, needing to strengthen access, quality and equity.

At secondary level, too, efforts to increase access have not always succeeded in increasing learning and reaching the disadvantaged. In Mexico, as access increased, the share of students performing above minimum benchmarks also increased, from one-third in 2003 to one-half in 2009. Targeted social protection programmes aimed at disadvantaged families helped improve learning outcomes for the rich and poor alike. In Ghana, by contrast, while secondary enrolment increased from 35% in 2003 to 46% in 2009, and performance in numeracy also increased by 10 percentage points, gender gaps in learning more than doubled and the poorest barely benefited at all.

Malaysia experienced a particularly worrying trend of worsening learning outcomes coupled with widening inequality and an increasing number of adolescents out of school. In 2003, the vast majority of adolescents passed the minimum benchmark, whether rich or poor. However, only around half the poorest boys reached the minimum benchmark in 2011, compared with over 90% in 2003. Poor boys in Malaysia went from being similar to average performers in the United States to being similar to those in Botswana.

Poor quality education leaves a legacy of illiteracy

The quality of education during childhood has a marked bearing on youth literacy. New analysis for this Report, based on direct assessments of literacy in household surveys, shows that youth illiteracy is more widespread than previously believed: around 175 million young people in low and lower middle income countries – equivalent to around one-quarter of the youth population – cannot read all or part of a sentence. In sub-Saharan Africa, 40% of young people are not able to do so.

Young women are the worst affected of all, making up 61% of youth who are not literate. In South and West Asia, two out of three of young people who cannot read are young women.Comparisons among countries expose the widespread problems of illiteracy. In 9 of the 41 low and lower middle income countries in the analysis, more than half of 15- to 24-year-olds are not literate. All these countries are in sub-Saharan Africa.

In low and lower middle income countries, one-quarter of youth cannot read a sentence

The analysis confirms the assumption that children need to spend at least four years in school to become literate: among those who have spent four years or less in school, around 77% are not able to read all or part of a sentence. In 9 of the 41 countries analysed, more than half of young people have spent no more than four years in school, and almost none of them are literate.

Spending five or six years in school, equivalent in some systems to completing a full cycle of primary schooling, does not guarantee literacy, however. In the 41 countries in the analysis, around 20 million young people still cannot read all or part of a sentence – equivalent to one in three of those who leave school after grade 5 or 6.

Young people from poorer households are far less likely to be literate. Among the countries analysed, more than 80% of those from rich households can read a sentence in 32 countries, but 80% of the poor can do so in only 4 countries. At the other end of the scale, less than half of poor youth can read a sentence in 22 countries, while the rich fall below this threshold only in Niger. In several countries, including Cameroon, Ghana, Nigeria and Sierra Leone, the difference in youth literacy rates between rich and poor is more than 50 percentage points.

Disadvantages in acquiring basic skills are further compounded by a combination of poverty, gender, location and ethnicity. In Senegal, only 20% of rural young women could read in everyday situations in 2010, compared with 65% of urban young men. In Indonesia, almost all rich young women in Bali province have literacy skills, while just 60% of poor women in Papua province are literate.

These outcomes may reflect the combined effects of poverty, isolation, discrimination and cultural practices. However, they also echo failures of education policy to provide learning opportunities for the most disadvantaged populations, and they indicate an urgent need to provide these people with a second chance.

Ethiopia's youth literacy rate increased from 34% in 2000 to 52% in 2011

There are some signs of improvement in youth literacy that offer hope. Thanks to the expansion of primary schooling over the past decade, the youth literacy rate increased in Ethiopia from 34% in 2000 to 52% in 2011. Youth literacy has also improved in Nepal, especially among the most disadvantaged, who started with very low levels of literacy. Literacy among poor young women increased from 20% in 2001 to 55% in 2011.

Information on how much children with disabilities are learning is so scarce that analysis is difficult. Uganda provides a rare example where information is sufficient to compare literacy rates of young people according to types of impairment. In 2011, around 60% of young people with no identified impairment were literate, compared with 47% of those with physical or hearing impairments and 38% of those with mental impairments.

Striving for equal learning, including for children and youth with disabilities, requires identifying the particular difficulties children and young people with various types of disadvantage face, and implementing policies to tackle them.

Making teaching quality a national priority

Strong national policies that give a high priority to improving learning and teaching are essential to ensure that all children in school obtain the skills and knowledge they are meant to acquire. Education plans should describe goals and establish benchmarks against which governments can be held to account, as well as ways to achieve the goals. Improving learning, especially among the most disadvantaged children, needs to be made a strategic objective. Plans should include a range of approaches to improve teacher quality, devised in consultation with teachers and teacher unions. They also need to guarantee that strategies will be backed by sufficient resources.

Quality must be made a strategic objective in education plans

The global learning crisis cannot be overcome unless policies aim to improve learning for the disadvantaged. Of 40 national education plans reviewed for this Report, 26 list improved learning outcomes as a strategic objective. While the plans of all 40 countries address the needs of disadvantaged groups to some extent, learning is often only addressed as a by-product of increased access.

To improve learning for all, national education plans must improve teacher management and quality. Only 17 of the 40 plans include strategies for improving teacher education programmes, and only 16 envisage further training of teacher educators.

It is even less common for plans to recognize explicitly that improving teaching quality can enhance learning outcomes. In Kenya, in-service training is aimed at substantially boosting the learning of primary school leavers in poorly performing districts. South Africa and Sri Lanka link recruitment of teachers with improvements in quality and learning.

Governments need to get incentives right to attract and retain the best teachers. Of the 40 plans reviewed, 10 include reforms to improve teacher pay and 18 emphasize better career paths and promotion prospects.

Only some of the plans target teacher reforms at improving learning for disadvantaged students, mainly by getting teachers into disadvantaged areas. Among the 28 plans that aim to send teachers to disadvantaged areas, 22 aim to provide incentives, such as housing benefits and salary supplements. In 14 countries, education plans include incentives to promote deployment to rural areas, while 8, including Afghanistan, actively encourage female teachers. Cambodia's plan is notable for strategies to recruit teachers from target areas and ethnic groups and deploy them where they are most needed. In remote areas, where student numbers are often small, teachers may have to teach more than one age group at the same time. In Cambodia, Kenya and Papua New Guinea, there are plans to provide training in multigrade teaching.

Few plans highlight the need for support to students who are falling behind. Guyana's is one exception; it gives a high priority to building teachers' capacity to deliver targeted programmes.

For plans to be successfully implemented, they need to be backed by sufficient resources, but only 16 of the 40 policy documents reviewed include a budget breakdown. Countries assign different levels of importance in their budgets to policies aimed at improving education quality: they amount to over a fifth of the budget in Papua New Guinea, but to 5% or less in Palestine, for example. Few plans earmark expenditure for the disadvantaged, however.

Policies can only be effective if those responsible for implementing them are involved in shaping them. However, a survey in 10 countries showed that only 23% of teachers thought they had influence over policy and practice. Given their reach, teacher unions are key partners for governments. In some countries, engaging teacher unions has improved policies aimed at helping disadvantaged groups. In the Plurinational State of Bolivia, for example, teacher unions campaigned to ensure that indigenous rights were enshrined in the constitution.

Overall, teachers and their unions can help make sure policies are effective. Thus it is important to include them from the early stages in designing strategies aimed at tackling learning deficits.

Getting enough teachers into classrooms

The quality of education is held back in many of the poorest countries by a lack of teachers, which often results in large class sizes in early grades and in the poorest areas. Future teacher recruitment needs are determined by current deficits, demographics, enrolment trends and numbers of children out of school. Analysis by the UNESCO Institute for Statistics shows that, between 2011 and 2015, 5.2 million teachers – including replacement and additional teachers – need to be recruited to ensure that there are sufficient teachers to achieve universal primary education. This amounts to over 1 million teachers per year, equivalent to about 5% of the current primary school teaching force.

Most initial teacher education programmes last at least two years. With 57 million children still out of school, it is unlikely that countries with a lack of teachers will be able to meet the 2015 Education for All deadline for achieving universal primary education. Nevertheless, countries must start planning now to make up the shortfall. If the deadline were extended to 2020, accounting for projected increases in enrolment, the number of teachers required would rise to 13.1 million over 9 years. If it were extended to 2030, 20.6 million teachers would be needed over 19 years.

Of the teachers required between 2011 and 2015, 3.7 million are needed to replace teachers who retire, change occupations or leave due to illness or death. The remaining 1.6 million are the additional teachers needed to make up the shortfall, address expanding enrolment and underwrite quality by ensuring that there are no more than 40 students for every teacher. Thus, around 400,000 additional teachers need to be recruited each year if there are to be sufficient teachers by 2015.

Sub-Saharan Africa accounts for 58% of the additional primary teachers needed, requiring approximately 225,000 per year between 2011 and 2015. However, over the past decade the average annual increase in the region has been only 102,000.

Nigeria has by far the largest gap to fill. Between 2011 and 2015, it needs 212,000 primary school teachers, 13% of the global total. Of the 10 countries needing the most additional primary teachers, all but one are in sub-Saharan Africa, the exception being Pakistan.

The challenge of recruiting teachers becomes even greater when the needs of lower secondary education are taken into account. To achieve universal lower secondary education by 2030 with 32 students per teacher, an additional 5.1 million would be needed, or 268,000 per year. Sub-Saharan Africa accounts for half of the additional lower secondary school teachers needed over this period.

It is unlikely that the countries with the most severe teacher gaps can recruit the numbers needed by 2015. Of the 93 countries that need to find additional primary school teachers by 2015, only 37 will be able to bridge the gap; 29 will not

In Bolivia, teacher unions campaigned to ensure that indigenous rights were enshrined in the constitution

even be able to fill the gap by 2030. Meanwhile, 148 countries need more teachers for lower secondary schools by 2015; 29 countries will not have filled this gap by 2030.

To fill the teacher gap by 2015, some countries need to speed up expansion of their teacher force. Rwanda and Uganda would need to expand recruitment by 6%, on average, compared with a current average increase of 3% per year. In Malawi, the teaching force is growing by just 1% per year, which is far from sufficient to reduce the pupil/teacher ratio from 76:1 to 40:1. For Malawi to meet the universal primary education goal by 2015, it would need to increase its teaching force by 15% annually between 2011 and 2015.

29 countries will not be able to fill the primary school teacher gap by 2030

Many poor countries will not be able to fill their teacher gap simply because they do not have enough upper secondary school graduates – the minimum qualification for primary teacher trainees. In 8 out of 14 countries in sub-Saharan Africa, at least 5% of all upper secondary school graduates in 2020 would need to be drawn into teaching to fill the teacher gap, rising to almost 25% in Niger. By comparison, just over 3% of those in the labour force with at least secondary education are primary school teachers in middle income countries.

Teachers need not only to be recruited, but also to be trained. Many countries, especially in sub-Saharan Africa, also need to train existing teachers. Mali, for example, recruited teachers at a rate of 9% per year over the past decade, which helped lower the number of pupils per teacher from 62 in 1999 to 48 in 2011. However, many of these teachers are untrained. The result is that Mali's ratio of pupils per trained teacher, 92:1, is one of the world's highest. On its past trend of trained teacher recruitment, Mali would not achieve a ratio of 40 pupils per trained teacher until 2030.

Countries that have many untrained teachers need to find ways to train them. In 10 out of 27 countries with available data, this challenge is greater than that of recruiting and training new teachers. In Benin, 47% of teachers were trained in 2011. The country needs to expand teacher recruitment by just 1.4% per year to achieve UPE by 2020, but the number of existing teachers who need to be trained would have to grow by almost 9% per year, well above Benin's 6% average annual growth rate since 1999 for trained teachers.

The shortage of trained teachers is likely to affect disadvantaged areas in particular. In the northern state of Kano, one of the poorer parts of Nigeria, the pupil/trained teacher ratio exceeded 100 in 2009/10, with at least 150 pupils per trained teacher in the most disadvantaged 25% of schools.

Children in the early grades who live in remote areas often face a double disadvantage. In Ethiopia, for example, where 48% of teachers are trained, only around 20% of teachers were trained in grades 1 to 4 in 2010, compared with 83% in grades 5 to 8.

Countries that require additional teachers will have to increase their overall budgets for teacher salaries. New analysis by the UNESCO Institute for Statistics for this Report finds that US$4 billion annually is needed in sub-Saharan Africa to pay the salaries of the additional primary school teachers required to achieve UPE by 2020, after taking into account projected economic growth. This is equivalent to 19% of the region's total education budget in 2011. Nigeria alone accounts for two-fifths of the gap.

While the required increases may seem vast, most countries should be able to meet them if their economies grow as projected and if they dedicate a larger share of their GDP to education while staying within the benchmark of 3% allocated to primary education. On average, sub-Saharan African countries would have to increase the share of the budget they allocate to education from 12% to 14% in 2011 to close the teacher gap by 2020.

The financing challenge is inevitably greater for lower secondary school. In sub-Saharan Africa, recruiting enough teachers to achieve universal lower secondary education by 2030 would add US$9.5 billion to the annual education budget.

While many countries should be able to meet the cost of recruiting and paying the required additional primary teachers from their national budgets, they will also need to pay for teacher training, as well as school construction and learning materials, to ensure that children receive an education of a good quality. Expanding the lower secondary teacher workforce will place a further burden on national budgets. Some of the poorest countries are therefore likely to face a substantial financing gap and will require the support of aid donors. This need is likely to be even greater when the cost of expanding teacher education programmes is taken into account.

However, between 2008 and 2011, donors spent only US$189 million per year, on average, on pre-service and in-service teacher education programmes, equivalent to 2% of the education aid budget. While the countries most in need are in sub-Saharan Africa, the largest country recipients of this aid included richer middle income countries such as Brazil, China and Indonesia.

Four strategies to provide the best teachers

Policy-makers need to give teachers every chance to put their motivation, energy, knowledge and skills to work in improving learning for all. This Report describes the four strategies that governments need to adopt to attract and retain the best teachers, improve teacher education, allocate teachers more fairly and provide incentives in the form of appropriate salaries and attractive career paths. It then highlights the areas of teacher governance that need to be strengthened to ensure that the benefits of these four strategies are realized.

Strategy 1: Attract the best teachers

I chose to be a teacher because I believe that education has the power to transform the society we live in. What motivates me to be a good teacher is to be an active agent in this change that is so necessary for my country to fight against discrimination, injustice, racism, corruption, poverty.
– Ana, teacher, Lima, Peru

The first step to getting good teachers is to attract the best and most motivated candidates into the profession. Many people who decide to become teachers are driven by the satisfaction of helping students learn, fulfil their potential and develop into confident, responsible citizens.

It is not enough just to want to teach. People should enter the profession having received a good education themselves. They need to have at least completed secondary schooling of appropriate quality and relevance, so that they have a sound knowledge of the subjects they will be teaching and the ability to acquire the skills needed to teach.

Teaching does not always draw the best candidates, however. In some countries, teaching is seen as a second-class job for those who do not do well enough academically to enter more prestigious careers, such as medicine or engineering. The level of qualification required to enter teaching is a signal of the field's professional status. To elevate the status of teaching and attract talented applicants, for example, Egypt has introduced more stringent entry requirements, requiring candidates to have strong performance in secondary school as well as a favourable interview assessment. Once selected, candidates also have to pass an entrance examination to establish whether they match the profile of a good teacher.

Donors spend only US$189 million per year on teacher education

Making sure there are enough female teachers and recruiting teachers from a wide range of backgrounds are important factors in providing an inclusive, good quality education. Flexible policies for entry qualifications may be required to improve diversity of the teaching force. In South Sudan, women make up about 65% of the post-war population, yet less than 10% of all teachers are women. To increase the number of female teachers, financial and material incentives have been given to over 4,500 girls to complete secondary school and to women trainees to enter the teaching profession.

Recruiting teachers from under-represented groups to work in their own communities guarantees that children have teachers familiar with their culture and language. Flexible policies on entry requirements can help increase the number of candidates recruited from ethnic minority groups. In Cambodia, where teacher trainees normally have to have completed grade 12, this requirement is waived for remote areas where upper secondary education is unavailable, increasing the pool of teachers from ethnic minorities.

Strategy 2: Improve teacher education so all children can learn

Initial teacher education should impart the skills needed to teach – especially for teaching the disadvantaged and those in early grades – and lay the foundation for ongoing training. But initial teacher education is not always effective in preparing teachers to deliver good quality, equitable education.

Trainees need a good understanding of the subjects they will be teaching. In low income countries, however, teachers often enter the profession lacking core subject knowledge because their own education has been poor. In a 2010 survey of primary schools in Kenya, grade 6 teachers scored only 60% on tests designed for their students. In such circumstances, teacher education programmes need to start by ensuring that all trainees acquire a good understanding of the subjects they will be teaching.

Teacher education institutions often do not have time to upgrade weak subject knowledge, partly because of competing curriculum demands. In Kenya, teacher trainees are required to take up to 10 subjects and participate in teaching practice in the first year. This leaves little time to fill gaps in subject knowledge. Ghana has addressed this problem by making trainees pass an examination on subject knowledge in their first year.

In Turkey, a pre-service course on gender equity had a significant impact on female teachers' gender attitudes

Teachers need not only sound subject knowledge but also training in how to teach, particularly in the early grades. However, teachers are seldom trained in these skills. In Mali, few teachers were able to teach their pupils how to read. Teachers had been inadequately prepared to apply the required teaching methods and did not give sufficient attention to supporting pupils' individual reading. This is no doubt an important reason why nearly half the pupils in Mali could not read a word in their own language at the end of grade 2. Teachers are also rarely prepared for the reality of multilingual classrooms. In Senegal, for example, only 8% of trainees expressed any confidence about teaching reading in local languages.

As a result of inadequate training, including overemphasis on theory rather than practice, many newly qualified teachers are not confident that they have the skills necessary to support children with more challenging learning needs, including those with severe physical or intellectual disabilities, in mainstream classrooms. To address this, teachers in Viet Nam create individual education plans for all learners, designing and adapting activities for children with different learning needs, and assessing learning outcomes of children with special needs.

Teacher education should also prepare teachers for remote or under-resourced schools, where some teachers need to teach multiple grades, ages and abilities in one classroom. In some countries in sub-Saharan Africa, including Burkina Faso, Mali, Niger, Senegal and Togo, at least 10% of students study in such classrooms. A small project in Sri Lanka trained teachers to develop lesson plans and grade-appropriate tasks for classes combining grades 4 and 5. Results indicated that such methods had a positive impact on pupils' achievement in mathematics.

Countries with high student learning outcomes require trainees to receive practical training in classrooms before teaching. This is especially important for teachers who teach in under-resourced and diverse classrooms, but is rarely provided. In Pakistan, trainee teachers only spend 10% of their training time in classrooms. To address this need, an NGO teacher education programme in Malawi includes a full year of practice teaching in rural districts. Some 72% of the participants said the school practice component was the area of study that most prepared them for teaching in rural areas. In addition, 80% of them gained experience in providing remedial support to students, compared with 14% in government colleges.

Teachers also need training in how attitudes to gender can affect learning outcomes. In Turkey, a one-term pre-service course on gender equity had a significant impact on female teachers' gender attitudes and awareness.

All teachers require continuing support once they reach the classroom to enable them to reflect on teaching practices, to foster motivation and to help them adapt to change, such as using a new curriculum or language of instruction.

Ongoing training can also provide teachers with new ideas about how to support weak learners. Teachers who have received some in-service training are generally found to teach better than those who have not, although it depends on the purpose and quality of the training.

Ongoing training is even more important for teachers who enter classrooms with little or no pre-service teacher education, or whose training has not sufficiently exposed them to the reality of the classroom. In Benin, many teachers have been hired as community or contract teachers with no pre-service teacher education. A programme designed in 2007 offers them three years of training to give them qualifications equivalent to those of civil service teachers.

Teachers in conflict zones are among those most in need of a coherent strategy to upgrade their skills. In the Dadaab refugee camps in northern Kenya, 90% of teachers are hired from the refugee community, only 2% of whom are qualified. Refugee teachers are ineligible for admission to higher education institutions in Kenya, and so require alternative qualification options. A teacher management and development strategy for 2013–2015 aims to provide them with training, including school-based practice. The strategy also recommends qualification and certification options for teachers who meet minimum higher education admission requirements, as well as options for the majority who do not meet the requirements.

Ongoing training can bridge gaps in the quality and relevance of pre-service teacher education, but often fails to foster the skills teachers need to respond to particular learning needs, especially in the early grades. An Early Grade Reading Assessment in Liberia found that around one-third of grade 2 students were unable to read a word. As a result, in 2008, the Ministry of Education launched a new programme consisting of teacher education and support, structured lesson plans, teaching resource materials, and books for children to take home. Teachers participated in an intensive one-week course in early grade reading instruction and how to use formative and diagnostic assessment to identify and support weak learners. This was followed up with classroom-based support from trained mentors over two years. Pupils in this programme increased their reading comprehension scores by 130%, compared with 33% for non-participants.

In many low income countries, teaching relies on traditional approaches such as lecturing, rote learning and repetition, rather than fostering transferable skills such as critical thinking. A school-based teacher development programme in Kenya has shown that training can be effective in helping teachers adopt learner-centred methods. The programme, involving self-study using distance-learning materials and meetings with tutors at cluster resource centres, led to teaching becoming more interactive, with improved use of lesson plans and resources.

The key role that teacher educators play in shaping teachers' skills is often the most neglected aspect of teacher preparation systems, particularly in developing countries. Many teacher educators seldom set foot in local schools to learn about the challenges prospective teachers face. Analysis of six sub-Saharan African countries found that teacher educators helping train teachers how to teach reading skills were rarely experts in approaches used in the field.

Reforms aimed at helping disadvantaged students need to ensure that teacher educators are trained to give teachers appropriate support. In Viet Nam, many teacher educators had limited awareness of how to deal with diversity until training was provided for teacher educators from universities and colleges to act as experts on inclusive education in pre-service programmes.

Not only is the quality of teacher education often insufficient, but many teacher education institutions also lack the capacity for the huge numbers of people needing to be trained, and expanding capacity is costly. Using technology to provide training from a distance is one way to reach larger numbers of trainees. Distance education programmes must be of adequate quality, and should be complemented by mentoring and face-to-face support at key stages.

The extent to which information and communication technology (ICT) is used in distance learning for teacher education is dictated by ICT infrastructure and resources, and the needs of target audiences. In South Africa, where surveys revealed that only 1% of teachers had regular Internet access but the vast majority had access to mobile phones, a teacher education programme supplements paper-based distance learning with text messaging. In Malawi, battery-powered DVD players and interactive instructional DVDs are used to assist with training.

Distance teacher education programmes could reach more future teachers at lower cost than programmes in teacher education institutions. Costs per student graduating from distance programmes have been estimated at between one-third and two-thirds of conventional programmes.

Strategy 3: Get teachers where they are most needed

Teachers are understandably reluctant to work in deprived areas, which lack basic facilities such as electricity, good housing and health care. If the best teachers seldom work in remote, rural, poor or dangerous areas, however, the learning opportunities of children who are already disadvantaged suffer further as a result of larger class sizes, high rates of teacher turnover and a scarcity of trained teachers.

In South Sudan, pupil/teacher ratios reached 145:1 in Jonglei

Governments need to devise strategies to ensure that teachers are equally allocated, but they rarely do so. In Yemen, schools with 500 students were found to have between 4 and 27 teachers. In South Sudan, average pupil/teacher ratios varied from 51:1 in Central Equatoria to 145:1 in Jonglei.

Unequal distribution of teachers is one reason some children leave school before learning the basics. In Bangladesh, only 60% of students reach the last grade of primary school in subdistricts where there are 75 students per teacher, compared with three-quarters where there are 30.

The unequal allocation of teachers is affected by four main factors:

Urban bias: Weak infrastructure in rural areas means teachers are less keen to teach there. In Swaziland, for example, remote rural schools are mostly staffed with newly recruited, inexperienced teachers and teachers with low qualifications.

Ethnicity and language: Because education levels of ethnic minorities are often lower, fewer can apply to be teachers. In India, states cannot fill their caste-based quotas for recruitment of teachers unless teachers with lower levels of qualifications are hired.

Gender: Women are less likely than men to work in disadvantaged areas. In Rwanda, only 10% of primary school teachers were female in Burera district, compared with 67% in wealthier Gisagara district.

Subjects: In secondary schools, in particular, there are often teacher shortages in specific subjects. In Indonesia, for example, at junior secondary level there is a surplus of teachers in religion, but a shortage in computer science.

To achieve a balance of teachers across the country, some governments post teachers to disadvantaged areas. One reason for the Republic of Korea's strong and more equitable learning outcomes is that disadvantaged groups have better access to more qualified and experienced teachers. Over three-quarters of teachers in villages have at least a bachelor's degree, compared with 32% in large cities, and 45% have more than 20 years of experience, compared with 30% in large cities. Teachers working in disadvantaged schools benefit from incentives such as an additional stipend, smaller class sizes, less teaching time, the chance to choose their next school after teaching in a difficult area and greater promotion opportunities.

Providing incentives is a way to encourage teachers to accept difficult postings. Safe housing is particularly important in encouraging women to teach in rural areas, as in Bangladesh. The Gambia introduced an allowance of 30% to 40% of their base salary for positions in remote regions. By 2007, 24% of teachers had requested a transfer to hardship schools.

Alternatively, countries can recruit teachers from within their own communities. In Lesotho, a system of local recruitment allows school management committees to hire teachers, who apply directly to the schools for vacant posts. As a result, there is relatively little difference in pupil/teacher ratios between rural and urban areas.

Some countries are opening alternative pathways into teaching to attract highly qualified professionals with strong subject knowledge. One approach is exemplified by the Teach for All programmes in a range of countries, which recruit graduates with strong subject-level degree qualifications to teach in schools that predominantly serve disadvantaged students. Evidence from evaluations of Teach for America suggests that, once they have gained some experience, these teachers help improve students' learning, provided they receive some training.

Strategy 4: Provide the right incentives to retain the best teachers

Salaries are just one of many factors that motivate teachers, but they are a key consideration in attracting the best candidates and retaining the best teachers. Low salaries are likely to damage morale and can lead teachers to switch to other careers. At the same time, teacher salaries make up the largest share of most education budgets, so they need to be set at a realistic level to ensure that enough teachers can be recruited.

The level of teacher salaries influences education quality. In 39 countries, a 15% rise in pay increased student performance by 6% to 8%. However, teachers in some countries do not even earn enough to lift their households above the poverty line. A teacher who is the main breadwinner, and has at least four family members to support, needs to earn at least US$10 per day to keep the family above the poverty line of US$2 per day per person. However, average teacher salaries are below this level in eight countries. In the Central African Republic, Guinea-Bissau and Liberia, teachers are paid no more than US$5, on average. Teacher salaries are similarly low in the Democratic Republic of the Congo, where communities often have to supplement their pay. Communities that are too poor to do so suffer from further disadvantage, losing good teachers.

In some countries, few teachers can afford basic necessities without taking a second job. In Cambodia, where a teacher salary did not cover the cost of basic food items in 2008, over two-thirds of teachers had a second job. National data on average teacher pay disguise variations in pay among different types of teachers: salaries are often considerably less than average for teachers at the beginning of their career, unqualified teachers and those on temporary contracts. In Malawi, those entering the profession, or lacking the academic qualifications needed for promotion, earn less than one-third of teachers in the highest pay category. Their salary was equivalent to just US$4 per day in 2007/08.

Average teacher salaries are below US$10 per day in 8 countries

When teachers are paid less than people in comparable fields, the best students are less likely to become teachers, and teachers are more likely to lose motivation or leave the profession. In Latin America, teachers are generally paid above the poverty threshold, but their salaries do not compare favourably with those working in professions requiring similar qualifications. In 2007, professionals and technicians with similar characteristics earned 43% more than pre-school and primary school teachers in Brazil, and 50% more in Peru.

In sub-Saharan Africa and South and West Asia, policy-makers have responded to the need to expand education systems rapidly by recruiting teachers on temporary contracts with little formal training. Contract teachers are usually paid considerably less than civil service teachers; some are hired directly by the community or by schools.

In West Africa, contract teachers made up half the teaching force by the mid-2000s. At the end of the decade, there were far more teachers on temporary contracts than on civil service contracts in some of these countries: the proportion reached almost 80% in Mali and Niger and over 60% in Benin and Cameroon. In Niger, contract teachers earn half as much as civil service teachers.

In some countries, governments eventually hire contract teachers as civil service teachers. In Benin, for example, contract teachers, with the support of teacher unions, campaigned to obtain more stable employment conditions and better pay. In 2007, the government issued a decree absorbing into the civil service contract all teachers who had achieved the required qualifications. Thus, despite the share of contract teachers having increased dramatically, the average teacher salary in Benin rose by

45% between 2006 and 2010 as the salaries of contract and civil service teachers converged.

In Indonesia, where contract teachers made up over a third of the primary school teaching force in 2010, regular teachers earned up to 40 times their salary. The government ensured that contract teachers would eventually attain civil service status, with implications for the education budget: giving all contract teachers permanent status would increase the salary bill for basic education by 35%, to about US$9 billion.

Where contract teachers are paid by the community, sustaining their services depends on parents' ability to mobilize funding, putting considerable financial pressure on poorer communities. In some cases this can lead to the government taking over some of the responsibility, ultimately adding to the budget. In Madagascar, community teachers, who made up around half of all teachers in 2005/06, are hired directly by parent-teacher associations and generally receive less than half of regular teachers' salaries. Since 2006, the government has increasingly taken on the responsibility for paying community teachers.

In the Republic of Korea, an experienced teacher can earn more than twice as much as a new teacher

While hiring contract teachers to alleviate teacher shortages can help in the short term, it is unlikely to meet the long-term need to extend quality education. Countries that rely heavily on contract teachers, notably in West Africa, rank at or near the bottom for education access and learning.

Teachers' salaries – and the rates at which they increase – are conventionally determined by formal qualifications, the amount of training and years of experience. But pay structures based on these criteria do not necessarily lead to better learning outcomes. Relating teachers' pay to the performance of their students is an alternative approach that has intuitive appeal. This appeal is supported by PISA data from 28 OECD countries: the countries where teachers' salaries are adjusted for student performance have higher scores in reading, mathematics and science. However, a closer look at the evidence on performance-related pay from around the world does not show clear-cut benefits.

It is difficult to find reliable ways to evaluate which teachers are the best and add the most value, as experience from the United States shows. Performance-related pay can also have unintended side effects on teaching and learning. In Portugal, it has led to competition between teachers in ways that can be harmful for the weakest students. In Mexico, many teachers are excluded from participating in such programmes, with those teaching in schools with low achievement at a disadvantage. Experience in Brazil suggests that rewarding schools with collective bonuses may be a more effective way to improve learning outcomes.

In poorer countries, performance-related pay has rarely been tried on a large scale, but experience suggests there is a risk of it encouraging teachers to teach to the test, rather than promoting wider learning. In an experiment in Kenyan primary schools, teachers were rewarded for good student test scores and penalized if students did not take end-of-year examinations. Test scores and examination attendance increased, but test scores did not go up in subject areas that were not taken into account in the teacher pay formula.

A more appropriate way of motivating teachers is to offer an attractive career path. In some OECD countries, the difference in pay between a more experienced teacher and a new teacher is small and there is little scope for promotion. In England, for example, a beginning teacher earns US$32,000 while the most experienced teacher can receive, at most, US$15,000 more. By contrast, the Republic of Korea has a considerably steeper pay structure: a new teacher earns a similar salary to new teachers in England, but an experienced teacher can earn more than twice that. In France, insufficient career management and other inadequate teacher policies are contributing to poor learning.

In many developing countries, teachers' career structures are not sufficiently linked to prospects of promotion that recognize and reward teacher effectiveness. In 2010, Ghana began reviewing its teacher management and development policy to address such concerns.

Strengthening teacher governance

Better teacher governance is vital to reduce disadvantage in learning. If days are lost because teachers are absent or devote more attention to private tuition than classroom teaching, for example, the learning of the poorest children can be harmed. Understanding the reasons behind these problems is crucial for the design of effective strategies to solve them. Strong school leadership is required to ensure that teachers show up on time, work a full week and provide equal support to all. Gender-based violence, which is sometimes perpetrated by teachers, damages girls' chances of learning. Strategies to prevent and respond to teacher misconduct, and take action against perpetrators, require advocacy and support from head teachers, teachers and their unions, as well as communities, if girls are to be protected.

The scale of absenteeism is evident from surveys carried out in a range of poor countries over the past decade: in the mid-2000s, teacher absenteeism ranged from 11% in Peru to 27% in Uganda. Absenteeism exacerbates the problem of teacher shortages. In Kenya, where the typical primary school faces, on average, a shortage of four teachers, 13% of teachers were absent during school visits. Absenteeism can also affect disadvantaged students in particular. Across India, absenteeism varied from 15% in Maharashtra and 17% in Gujarat – two richer states – to 38% in Bihar and 42% in Jharkhand, two of the poorest states.

Teacher absenteeism harms learning. In Indonesia, a 10% increase in teacher absenteeism was estimated to lead to a 7% decrease in mathematics scores, on average, and absenteeism was most likely to harm weaker students: the teacher absence rate was 19% for the quarter of students with the highest mathematics scores, and 22% for the quarter with the lowest scores.

Head teachers themselves are sometimes absent, impeding effective monitoring of teacher attendance and demonstrating inadequate leadership regarding the problem. A 2011 survey of schools in Uganda found that, on average, 21% of head teachers were absent on the day the schools were visited.

Policy-makers need to understand why teachers miss school. In some countries, teachers are absent because their pay is extremely low, in others because working conditions are poor. In Malawi, where teachers' pay is low and payment often erratic, 1 in 10 teachers stated that they were frequently absent from school in connection with financial concerns, such as travelling to collect salaries or dealing with loan payments. High rates of HIV/AIDS can take their toll on teacher attendance. Zambia has introduced strategies to improve living conditions for HIV-positive teachers, including greater access to treatment, provision of nutritional supplements and loans.

Gender-based violence in schools is a major barrier to quality and equality in education. A survey in Malawi found that around one-fifth of teachers said they were aware of teachers coercing or forcing girls into sexual relationships.

Programmes and policies addressing gender discrimination and gender-based violence need to protect and empower girls, challenge entrenched practices, bring perpetrators to light and take action against them. Legal and policy frameworks that provide general protection for children need to be strengthened and publicized, and teachers need to be made aware of their own roles and responsibilities. In Kenya, for example, a range of penalties is available to discipline teachers in breach of professional conduct, including suspension and interdiction; new regulations state that a teacher convicted of a sexual offence against a pupil is to be deregistered.

Advocacy and lobbying constitute an important first step in seeing that policies tackling gender-based violence are in place and enforced. In Malawi, a project lobbied successfully for revisions to codes of conduct and stronger reporting mechanisms. When it ran an awareness campaign, the number of teachers who said they knew how to report a code violation rose by over one-third.

In Egypt, rich students are almost twice as likely as poorer students to receive private tuition

Working directly with teacher unions is a way to build support for taking action against teachers who violate codes of conduct. In Kenya, the National Union of Teachers collaborated with the Teachers' Service Commission, Ministry of Education and Children's Department to help draft a parliamentary bill that would reinforce procedures for reporting abuse or violence by teachers and prevent convicted teachers from simply being transferred to other schools.

Private tuition is another outcome of poor teacher governance. If unchecked or uncontrolled, it can be a detriment to learning outcomes, especially for the poorest students who are unable to afford it. Private tutoring by teachers is often a symptom of badly functioning school systems and low pay that forces teachers to supplement their income. In Cambodia, teacher salaries are small and often paid late. One consequence is that 13% of primary school teachers and 87% of secondary teachers provide private tuition. This reinforces disparities between those who can afford fees and those who cannot. In urban areas, grade 9 students scored 8.3 points out of 10 in Khmer with tutoring and 3.8 points without.

In Egypt, the situation has become extreme, partly due to a decline in the quality of education and partly because teachers need to supplement their low income. The amount spent annually on private tutoring is reported to be US$2.4 billion, equivalent to 27% of government spending on education in 2011. Private tuition is a significant part of household education spending, averaging 47% in rural areas and 40% in urban areas. Children from rich households are almost twice as likely as poorer students to receive private tuition. Teachers may be their own students' private tutors, and thus responsible for their grades. Students complain that teachers do not cover the curriculum during the school day, forcing them to take private tuition to cover the syllabus to enable them to pass exams. Strategies should at least be in place to prevent tutoring of pupils by teachers who are responsible for teaching them in their daily classes. This would ensure that full curriculum coverage is available to all students, even those unable to afford tutoring.

Private schools that charge low fees are seen by some as a way of expanding access to better quality education for disadvantaged children where government schools are failing. In Pakistan, a child in a low fee private school performs better than the average child in the top one-third of children in government schools. However, even in private schools, many pupils barely reach expected competency levels. According to analysis by the Annual State of Education Report team in Pakistan, 36% of grade 5 students in private schools could not read a sentence in English, which they should have been able to do by grade 2.

Learning outcomes may be better in low fee private schools in part because lower salaries enable these schools to hire more teachers and keep pupil/teacher ratios low. In private schools in parts of Nairobi, there are 15 students per teacher, compared with 80 in government schools. Small class sizes also enable teachers at private schools to interact more with their students. In Andhra Pradesh, India, 82% of teachers regularly corrected exercises given to children, compared with only 40% in government schools.

Private school teachers are generally thought to work under conditions of greater accountability. In India, only one head teacher in 3,000 government schools reported dismissing a teacher for repeated absence. By contrast, 35 private school head teachers, out of 600 surveyed, reported having dismissed teachers for this reason.

The benefits of low fee private schools do not mean they are better per se; often their students face far fewer disadvantages than students in government schools. In Andhra Pradesh, over 70% of students attending government schools belong to the poorest 40% of households, compared with 26% in private schools. Around one-third of teachers in government schools are teaching students of different ages in multigrade classrooms, compared with 3% in private schools.

There are no excuses for students not having the right conditions to learn: ultimately, it is vital that all children, regardless of their background and the type of school they attend, have the best teachers to offer them this opportunity.

Curriculum and assessment strategies that improve learning

To improve learning for all children, teachers need the support of curriculum and assessment strategies that can reduce disparities in school achievement and offer all children and young people the opportunity to acquire vital transferable skills. Such strategies need to build strong foundation skills by starting early, moving at the right pace, enabling disadvantaged pupils to catch up, meeting the language needs of ethnic minorities and building a culture of reading.

Ensuring all children acquire foundation skills

The key to ensuring that children succeed at school is to enable them to attain critical foundation skills, such as reading and basic mathematics. Without these basic skills, many children will struggle to keep up with the prescribed curriculum, and learning disparities will widen for disadvantaged children.

The quality of pre-school education makes a crucial difference to children's learning in early primary grades. In Bangladesh, primary school children who had attended pre-school performed better than children without any pre-school experience in skills relating to reading, writing and oral mathematics.

It is crucial that primary school pupils master the foundation skills of basic numeracy and literacy in the early grades so they can understand what is taught in later grades, but they sometimes fail to do so because curricula are too ambitious. Viet Nam's curriculum focuses on foundation skills, is closely matched to what children are able to learn and pays particular attention to disadvantaged learners. By contrast, India's curriculum, which outpaces what pupils can realistically learn and achieve in the time given, is a factor in widening learning gaps. In Viet Nam, 86% of 8-year-olds answered grade-specific test items correctly. Similarly, 90% of children aged 8 in India did so. However, when 14- to 15-year-olds were asked a two-stage word problem involving multiplication and addition, 71% of children in Viet Nam answered correctly, while in India the percentage was 33%.

For children from ethnic and linguistic minorities to acquire strong foundation skills, schools need to teach the curriculum in a language children understand. A bilingual approach that combines continued teaching in a child's mother tongue with the introduction of a second language can improve performance in the second language as well as in other subjects. To reduce learning disparities in the long term, bilingual programmes should be sustained over several years. In Cameroon, children taught in their local language, Kom, showed a marked advantage in achievement in reading and comprehension compared with children taught only in English. Kom-educated children also scored twice as high on mathematics tests at the end of grade 3. However, these learning gains were not sustained when the students switched to English-only instruction in grade 4. By contrast, in Ethiopia, children in regions where local language instruction extends through to upper primary school performed better in grade 8 subjects than pupils taught only in English.

Language policies may be difficult to implement, particularly where there is more than one language group in the same classroom and teachers are not proficient in the local language. For bilingual education to be effective, governments need to recruit and deploy teachers from minority language groups. Initial and ongoing programmes are also needed to train teachers to teach in two languages and to understand the needs of second-language learners.

For early grade literacy and bilingual education to be successful, pupils need access to inclusive learning materials that are relevant to their situation and in a language they are familiar with. Open licensing and new technology can make learning materials more widely available, including in local languages. In South Africa, open source educational materials are being developed and made available in several African languages. Digital distribution is increasing the number of districts, schools and teachers with access to curricular resources.

Providing appropriate reading materials may not be enough on its own, however, to improve children's learning; children and families must also be encouraged to use them. In poor or remote communities where there is little access to print media, providing reading materials and supporting activities to practice reading can improve children's learning. Save the Children's Literacy Boost programme aims to improve early grade reading skills in government schools through interventions such as training teachers to teach core reading skills and monitor pupils' mastery of them. In addition, communities are encouraged to support children's reading. Evaluations in Malawi, Mozambique, Nepal and Pakistan all showed greater learning gains by children in Literacy Boost schools than by their peers, including a reduction in the number of children whose scores were zero, suggesting that the programme benefited low achievers.

In India, schools with trained female community volunteers helped increase children's learning

Support outside school hours is one reason for such success. In Pakistan, children who had attended after-school reading camps coordinated by community volunteers showed greater learning gains in reading fluency and accuracy in both Pashto and Urdu than classmates in the same schools. In Malawi, pupils whose parents had received training to support their children's reading made greater vocabulary gains than those whose parents had not.

Curricula need to address issues of inclusion to enhance the chances of students from marginalized backgrounds to learn effectively. Where gender-responsive curricula have been developed, as in projects in Mumbai, India, and in Honduras, test scores measuring attitudes on several gender-related issues improved. In Honduras, adolescents who participated in the project also demonstrated better problem-solving skills and higher test scores.

More needs to be done to design curricula that pay attention to the needs of disabled learners. In Canberra, Australia, curriculum reform aims to help teachers improve student attitudes regarding students with disabilities, improve the quality of interactions between students with and without disabilities, and enhance the well-being and academic achievement of students with disabilities.

Classroom-based assessment tools can help teachers identify, monitor and support learners at risk of low achievement. In Liberia, the EGRA Plus project, which trained teachers in the use of classroom-based assessment tools and provided reading resources and scripted lesson plans to guide instruction, raised previously low levels of reading achievement among grade 2 and 3 pupils.

Assessments need to be aligned with the curriculum so that they do not add significantly to teachers' workloads. In South Africa, well-designed assessments with clear guidelines on how to interpret results helped teachers with little training who were working in difficult conditions: 80% of teachers were able to use them in class.

Students can make considerable gains if they are offered opportunities to monitor their own learning. In the Indian state of Tamil Nadu, primary students learn at their own pace, using self-evaluation cards that can be administered alone or with the help of another child; teachers strategically pair more advanced learners with less advanced ones for certain exercises. Overall, children's self-confidence has grown as a result of the approach, and learning achievement in the state is high.

Targeted additional support for students via trained teaching assistants is another way of improving learning for students at risk of falling behind. An initial early reading intervention delivered by teaching assistants in London schools in the United Kingdom was found to improve reading skills and have longer-term positive effects for children with poor literacy skills. In India, schools with trained female community volunteers helped increase the proportion of children able to do two-digit addition. While only 5% of pupils were able to carry out simple subtraction at the start of the study, 52% could by the end of the year, compared with 39% in other classes.

Interactive radio instruction can lead to improvement in learning outcomes for disadvantaged groups by addressing barriers such as distance and poor access to resources and quality teachers, as identified in a review of 15 projects. The use of interactive radio can be particularly beneficial in conflict contexts. Between 2006 and 2011, the South Sudan Interactive Radio Instruction project enrolled over 473,000 pupils, providing half-hour lessons linked to the national curriculum and including instruction in English, local language literacy, mathematics and life skills elements such as HIV/AIDS and land mine risk awareness. In locations that were out of range of any radio signal, the project distributed digital MP3 players to be used by trained teachers.

Digital classrooms can complement classes given by less qualified teachers. In India, the Digital Study Hall project provides digital video recordings of live classes taught by expert teachers, which are shown by DVD in rural and slum schools. An evaluation of four schools in Uttar Pradesh found that, after eight months, 72% of pupils had improved test scores.

Innovation in the use of technology can help improve learning by enriching teachers' curriculum delivery and encouraging flexibility in pupil learning. Greater access to computers in schools can also help reduce the digital divide between low and high income groups. However, new technology is not a substitute for good teaching.

Teachers' ability to use ICT as an educational resource plays a critical role in improving learning. A study in Brazil found that the introduction of computer laboratories in schools had a negative impact on student performance, but that teachers' use of the Internet as a pedagogical resource supported innovative classroom teaching and learning, resulting in improved test scores.

Children from low income groups are less likely to have experience of ICT outside school and may thus take longer to adapt to it and need additional support. In Rwanda, 79% of students who used computers in secondary school had previously used ICT and the Internet outside school (primarily in Internet cafés). However, girls and rural children were at a disadvantage because they were less likely to have access to Internet cafés or other ICT resources in their communities.

One promising way of increasing the accessibility of ICT for teaching and learning is 'mobile learning' – the use of mobile phones and other portable electronic devices, such as MP3 players. In rural India, an after-school programme for children from low income families used mobile phone games to help them learn English. This resulted in significant learning gains in tests of the spelling of common English nouns, particularly for children in higher grades who had stronger foundation skills.

Where children are learning little and dropping out early, second-chance programmes can teach foundation skills through a shorter cycle of learning, which is one way of accelerating children's progress and raising achievement for disadvantaged groups. Several such accelerated learning programmes raise achievement for disadvantaged groups in less time than formal government schools, allowing them the opportunity to catch up and to re-enter formal schools. They usually benefit from small classes and teachers speaking the local language recruited from surrounding communities. In northern Ghana, for example, 46% of those who had attended an accelerated learning programme and re-entered primary school attained grade-appropriate levels in grade 4, compared with 34% of other students.

Formal primary schools can also use accelerated learning programmes in situations where large proportions of students are over-age for their grade. In Brazil, over-age students in grades 5 to 8 were taught a substantially modified curriculum, covering more than one grade in a year. Overall, schools' share of students with a two-year age grade gap was reduced from 46% in 1998 to 30% in 2003. Once the students were restored to the right grade for their age, they were able to maintain their performance and their promotion rates in secondary school were comparable with those of other students.

Beyond the basics: transferable skills for global citizenship

Curricula need to ensure that all children and young people learn not just foundation skills, but also transferable skills, such as critical thinking, problem-solving, advocacy and conflict-resolution, to help them become responsible global citizens. An interdisciplinary approach involving hands-on, locally relevant educational activities can also develop students' understanding of the environment and build skills to promote sustainable development.

The Philippines has integrated disaster risk reduction into education

Between 1999 and 2004, Germany introduced an interdisciplinary programme that fostered participatory learning and provided opportunities for students to work together on innovative projects for sustainable living. An evaluation found that participants had a greater understanding of sustainable development than their peers, and up to 80% of the students said they had gained transferable skills. In South Africa, an initiative links the curriculum to practical actions such as adopting recycling systems and water harvesting in schools, using alternative energy sources for cooking, cleaning up public spaces, creating indigenous gardens and planting trees. Participating schools have reported increased environmental awareness and improved sustainability practices at school and in homes.

Empowering children through communication and advocacy can help them reduce their vulnerability to environmental risk. In the Philippines, which is prone to environmental disasters, a strong commitment to integrating disaster risk reduction into education has led children to take an active role in making their communities safer.

Programmes that emphasize inclusion and conflict resolution can also help bolster individuals' rights and build peace. In Burundi in 2009, secondary schools taught communication and conflict mediation skills to help returning refugees. After two years, trained teachers had abandoned corporal punishment, issues of sexual abuse and corruption were more easily debated, relationships had improved among pupils, their peers and their teachers, and pupils were acting as mediators in the resolution of minor conflicts at school and in the community.

© Karel Prinsloo/ARETE/UNESCO

Unlocking teachers' potential to solve the learning crisis

This Report identifies the 10 most important teaching reforms that policy-makers should adopt to achieve equitable learning for all.

1 *Fill teacher gaps*

On current trends, some countries will not be able to meet their primary school teacher needs by 2030. The challenge is even greater for other levels of education. Thus, countries need to activate policies that begin to address the vast shortfall.

2 *Attract the best candidates to teaching*

It is important for all children to have teachers with at least a good secondary-level qualification. Therefore, governments should invest in improving access to quality secondary education to enlarge the pool of good teacher candidates. This reform is particularly important if the pool of better-educated female teachers is to increase in disadvantaged areas. In some countries, this will mean introducing affirmative measures to attract more women into teaching.

Policy-makers also need to focus their attention on hiring and training teachers from under-represented groups, such as ethnic minorities, to serve in their own communities. Such teachers, familiar with the cultural context and local language, can improve learning opportunities for disadvantaged children.

3 *Train teachers to meet the needs of all children*

All teachers need to receive training to enable them to meet the learning needs of all children. Before teachers enter the classroom, they should undergo good quality pre-service teacher education programmes that provide a balance between knowledge of the subjects to be taught and knowledge of teaching methods.

Pre-service teacher education should also make adequate classroom teaching experience an essential part of training to become a qualified teacher. It should equip teachers with practical skills to teach children to read and to understand basic mathematics. In ethnically diverse societies, teachers should learn to teach in more than one language. Teacher education programmes should also prepare teachers to teach multiple grades and ages in one classroom, and to understand how teachers' attitudes to gender differences can affect learning outcomes.

Ongoing training is vital for every teacher to develop and strengthen teaching skills. It can also provide teachers with new ideas to support weak learners, especially in the early grades, and help teachers adapt to changes such as a new curriculum.

Innovative approaches such as distance teacher education, combined with face-to-face training and mentoring, should also be encouraged so as to extend both pre-service and ongoing teacher education to greater numbers of teachers.

4 *Prepare teacher educators and mentors to support teachers*

To ensure that teachers have the best training to improve learning for all children, it is important for those who train teachers to have knowledge and experience of real classroom teaching challenges and how to tackle them. Policy-makers should thus make sure teacher educators are trained and have adequate exposure to the classroom learning requirements facing those teaching in difficult circumstances.

To enable newly qualified teachers to translate teaching knowledge into activities that improve learning for all children, policy-makers should provide for trained mentors to help them achieve this transition.

5 *Get teachers to where they are needed most*

Governments need to ensure that the best teachers are not only recruited and trained, but also deployed to the areas where they are most needed. Adequate compensation, bonus pay, good housing and support in the form of professional development opportunities should be used to encourage trained teachers to accept positions in rural or disadvantaged areas. In addition, governments should recruit teachers locally and provide them with ongoing training so that all children, irrespective of their location, have teachers who understand their language and culture and thus can improve their learning.

6 *Use a competitive career and pay structure to retain the best teachers*

Governments should ensure that teachers earn at least enough to lift their families above the poverty line and make their pay competitive with comparable professions. Performance-related pay has intuitive appeal as a way to motivate teachers to improve learning. However, it can be a disincentive to teach students who achieve less well, have learning difficulties or live in poor communities. Instead, an attractive career and pay structure should be used as an incentive for all teachers to improve their performance. It can also be used to recognize and reward teachers in remote areas and those who support the learning of disadvantaged children.

7 *Improve teacher governance to maximize impact*

Governments should improve governance policies to address the problems of teacher misconduct such as absenteeism, tutoring their students privately and gender-based violence in schools. Governments can also do more to address teacher absenteeism by improving teachers' working conditions, making sure they are not overburdened with non-teaching duties and offering them access to good health care. Strong school leadership is required to ensure that teachers show up on time, work a full week and provide equal support to all. School leaders also need training in offering professional support to teachers.

Governments need to work closely with teacher unions and teachers to formulate policies and adopt codes of conduct to tackle unprofessional behaviour such as gender-based violence. Codes of practice should refer clearly to violence and abuse, making penalties consistent with legal frameworks for child rights and protection.

Where private tutoring by teachers is prevalent, explicit guidelines, backed up with legislation, so that teachers do not sacrifice classroom time to teach the school curriculum privately are needed.

8 *Equip teachers with innovative curricula to improve learning*

Teachers need the support of inclusive and flexible curriculum strategies designed to meet the learning needs of children from disadvantaged groups. Equipped with the appropriate curriculum content and delivery methods, teachers can reduce learning disparities, allowing low achievers to catch up.

Policy-makers should ensure that early grade curricula focus on securing strong foundation skills for all and are delivered in a language children understand. It is important for curriculum expectations to match learners' abilities, as overambitious curricula limit what teachers can achieve in helping children progress.

Getting out-of-school children back into school and learning is vital. Governments and donor agencies should support second-chance accelerated learning programmes to achieve this goal.

In many countries, radio, television, computers and mobile technologies are being used to supplement and improve children's learning. Teachers in both formal and non-formal settings need to be given skills to maximize the benefits of technology in ways that help narrow the digital divide.

It is not sufficient for children to learn foundation skills in school. A curriculum that promotes interdisciplinary and participatory learning, and fosters skills for global citizenship, is vital for teachers to help children develop transferable skills.

9 *Develop classroom assessments to help teachers identify and support students at risk of not learning*

Classroom-based assessments are vital tools to identify and help learners who are struggling. Teachers need to be trained to use them so that they can detect learning difficulties early and use appropriate strategies to tackle these difficulties.

Providing children with learning materials to evaluate their own progress, and training teachers to support their use, can help children make great strides in learning. Targeted additional support via trained teaching assistants or community volunteers is another key way of improving learning for students at risk of falling behind.

10 *Provide better data on trained teachers*

Countries should invest in collecting and analysing annual data on the number of trained teachers available throughout the country, including characteristics such as gender, ethnicity and disability, at all levels of education. These data should be complemented by information on the capacity of teacher education programmes, with an assessment of the competencies teachers are expected to acquire. Internationally agreed standards need to be established for teacher education programmes so that their comparability is ensured.

More and better data on teacher salaries in low and middle income countries are also needed to enable national governments and the international community to monitor how well teachers are paid and to raise global awareness of the need to pay them well.

Conclusion

To end the learning crisis, all countries, rich and poor, have to ensure that every child has access to a well-trained and motivated teacher. The 10 strategies outlined here are based on the evidence of successful policies, programmes, strategies from a wide range of countries and educational environments. By implementing these reforms, countries can ensure that all children and young people, especially the disadvantaged, receive the good quality education they need to realize their potential and lead fulfilling lives.

Part 1 Monitoring progress

With the deadline for the Education for All goals less than two years away, it is clear that despite advances over the decade, not a single goal will be achieved globally by 2015. This means millions of children, young people and adults will have been let down by the signatories of the Dakar Framework for Action. It is not too late, however, to accelerate progress in the final stages. It is also vital to put in place a robust global post-2015 education framework to tackle unfinished business while addressing new challenges.

One of the starkest reminders that EFA is not attainable is the fact that 57 million children were still out of school in 2011. If progress continues to be as slow as in recent years, 53 million children will remain out of school in 2015. Maintaining the speed of progress between 1999 and 2008 would have left just 23 million children out of school.

This Report projects that universal primary enrolment (goal 2) will be reached by just over half the world's countries by 2015 (Figure I.1). In one out of eight countries, less than 80% of primary school age children will be enrolled. For primary school completion, less than one in seven countries has achieved this target.

The world will be much closer to ensuring that equal numbers of boys and girls are enrolled in primary education (goal 5). By 2015, 7 in 10 countries will have reached the target. Gender parity in lower secondary education, however, will have been achieved in fewer than 6 in 10 countries. And gender parity should have been achieved by 2005. Moreover, parity is only the first step towards full gender equality.

Some countries have made fast progress towards improving adult literacy (goal 4), reaping the benefits of having expanded their basic education systems. In some regions, however, the rate of improvement has not kept pace with population growth. As a result, the number of illiterate adults worldwide remains stubbornly high at 774 million, a fall of just 1% since 2000. The number is projected to fall only to 743 million by 2015, when the adult literacy rate will still be below 80% in more than one in three countries.

Other goals established in 2000 have been difficult to monitor because clear targets were not set. For the first EFA goal, early childhood care and education, we assume for this Report that at least 80% of young children should be enrolled in pre-primary education programmes by 2015,

Figure I.1: By 2015, many countries will still not have reached the EFA goals
Percentage of countries projected to achieve a benchmark for five EFA goals by 2015

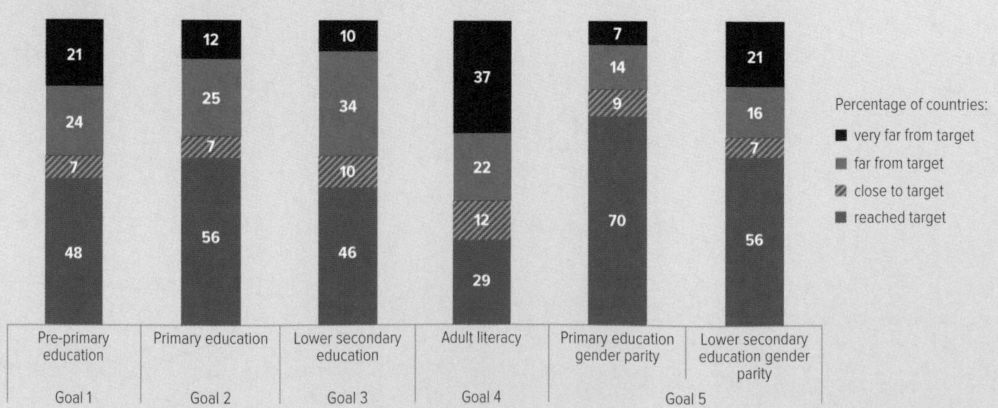

Notes: Countries are assessed as having reached the target if they have achieved a pre-primary education gross enrolment ratio of 80% (goal 1); a primary education adjusted net enrolment ratio of 97% (goal 2); a lower secondary education adjusted net enrolment ratio of 97% (goal 3); an adult literacy rate of 97% (goal 4); a gender parity index between 0.97 and 1.03 at primary and lower secondary education respectively (goal 5). The analysis was conducted on the subset of countries for which a projection was possible.
Source: Bruneforth (2013).

towards the EFA goals

but only 5 in 10 countries are likely to reach this target. For the third EFA goal, skills for young people and adults, universal lower secondary education can be taken as one measure of progress towards ensuring that all young people have foundation skills, but fewer than 5 in 10 countries will have reached this level by 2015.

It is even more difficult to estimate the number of countries still to achieve the sixth EFA goal, improving the quality of education to ensure that all are learning. To help give education quality the greater focus that it deserves after 2015, this Report proposes ways to strengthen international and regional assessments so that progress towards a global learning goal can be measured.

New analysis for this Report vividly underlines the fact that the most marginalized have continued to be denied opportunities for education over the past decade. In 62 low and middle income countries, the richest urban young men had spent more than 9.5 years in school by 2010 in low income countries and more than 12 years in lower middle income countries. But the poorest rural young women had spent fewer than 3 years in school in both low and lower middle income countries, leaving them well below the 6-year target that is associated with universal primary completion, which is supposed to be achieved by 2015.

Although the percentage of girls from the poorest rural households entering school in sub-Saharan Africa grew over the decade, their primary school completion rate fell from 25% in the early 2000s to 23% in the late 2000s. Similarly, the rate of lower secondary school completion fell from 11% to 9% for this disadvantaged group.

Unless special efforts are urgently taken to extend educational opportunities to the marginalized, the poorest countries may take several generations to achieve universal completion of primary and lower secondary education as well as universal youth literacy, according to new analysis for this Report. In sub-Saharan Africa, if recent trends continue, the richest boys will achieve universal primary completion in 2021, but the poorest girls will not catch up until 2086 – and will only achieve lower secondary school completion in 2111.

The gap between the EFA goals and what has actually been achieved shows that additional resources must be better targeted at those most in need. Many of the success stories of the past few years can be traced back to a strong commitment by some of the poorest governments to invest in education. The global share of public expenditure devoted to education increased from 4.6% to 5.1% of gross national product (GNP) between 1999 and 2011, with the largest increases in low income countries.

Many low and middle income countries have the opportunity to expand their education spending still further. This Report estimates that a modest increase in tax-raising efforts, combined with growth in the share of government budgets allocated to education, could help raise education spending by US$153 billion by 2015 in 67 countries, a 72% increase from 2011 levels.

The Dakar Framework for Action included a commitment that no country should be left behind due to lack of resources. A failure by donors to keep this promise has left an education financing gap of US$26 billion per year in some of the world's poorest countries. There are signs that this gap will widen further. Between 2010 and 2011, aid to basic education declined for the first time, by 6%, with low income countries bearing the brunt. It is forecast that many low income countries will see their levels of aid cut further by 2015.

Experience over the past decade of monitoring progress towards the EFA goals offers vital lessons for designing a post-2015 education framework. Goals must be accompanied by clear, measurable targets and indicators. The progress of subgroups must be measured to make sure the most disadvantaged not only advance, but also narrow the gap between them and the more privileged. Post-2015 education goals will only be achieved if governments and aid donors also set specific targets for education financing, with a focus on the poorest, and demonstrate the leadership and political will necessary to keep their commitments.

Tough conditions: At a primary school in Baqir Shah, a village in Sindh, Pakistan, classes take place outside because the buildings collapsed years ago.

Credit: Amina Sayeed/UNESCO

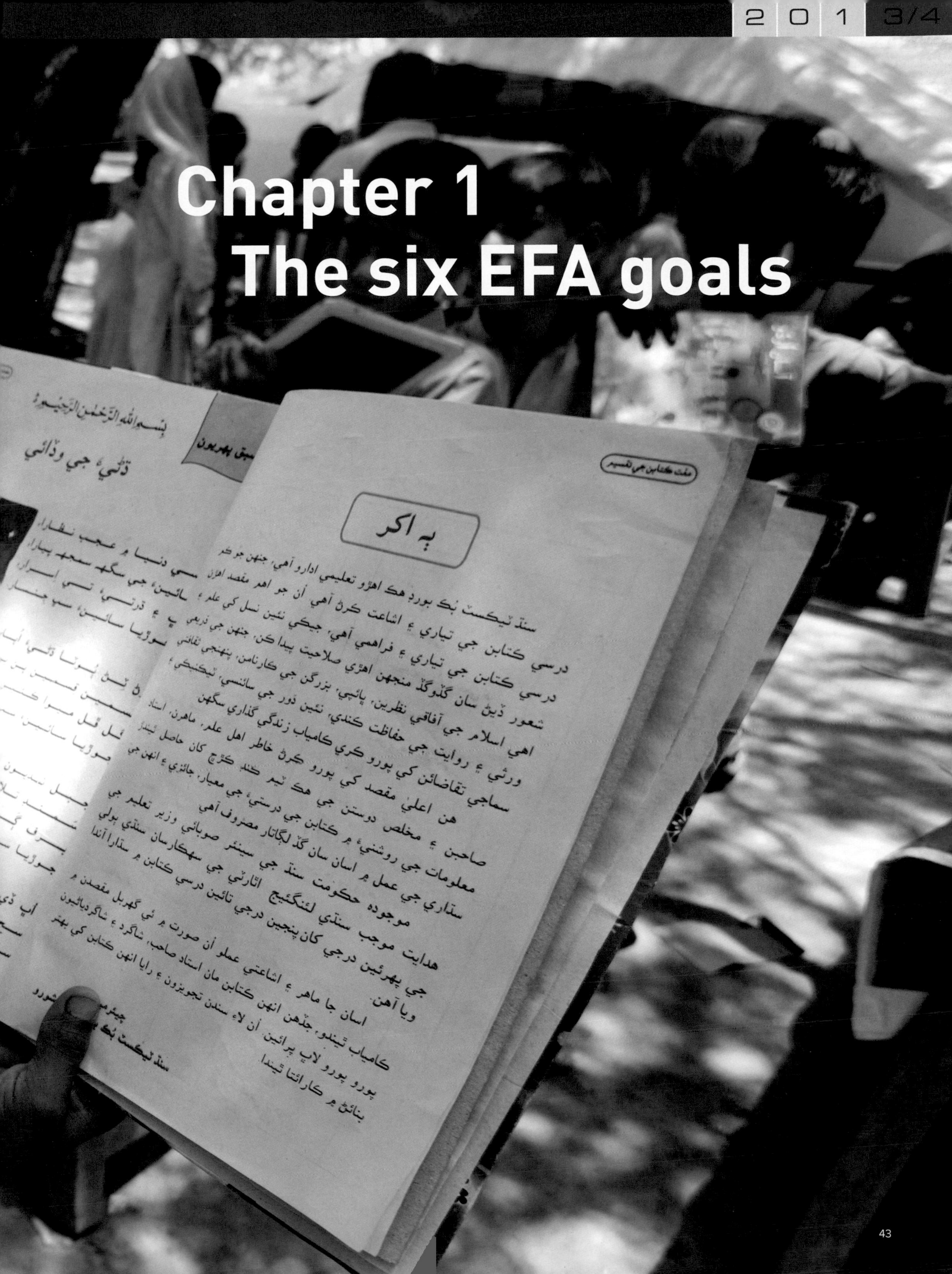

Chapter 1
The six EFA goals

More children than ever are going to school, but it is now a certainty that the EFA goals will not be met by the 2015 deadline, in large part because the disadvantaged have been left behind. This chapter, which presents evidence-based analysis of progress, should serve as an indispensable guide for the shape of post-2015 education goals. It shows that, unless special efforts are urgently taken to reach the marginalized, the poorest countries may take several generations to achieve universal completion of primary and lower secondary education, as well as universal youth literacy.

Goal 1 Early childhood care and education

Expanding and improving comprehensive early childhood care and education, especially for the most vulnerable and disadvantaged children.

Highlights

- Despite major improvements, an unacceptably high number of children suffer from ill health: under-5 mortality was 48 deaths per 1,000 live births in 2012, equivalent to 6.6 million deaths. Of the 43 countries where child mortality was greater than 100 deaths per 1,000 live births in 2000, 35 are not expected to reach the target of reducing child deaths by two-thirds from the 1990 level by 2015.
- Progress in improving child nutrition has been considerable. Yet, as of 2012, the share of children under 5 who were short for their age – a sign of chronic deficiency in essential nutrients – was 25%. Sub-Saharan Africa and South and West Asia account for three-quarters of the world's malnourished children.
- Between 1999 and 2011, the pre-primary education gross enrolment ratio increased from 33% to 50%, although it reached only 18% in sub-Saharan Africa. It is projected that by 2015, only 68 out of 141 countries will have a pre-primary education gross enrolment ratio above 80%.
- In many parts of the world, governments have yet to assume responsibility for pre-primary education: as of 2011, private providers were catering for 33% of all enrolled children. The cost of this provision is one of the factors that contribute most to inequity in access.

Table 1.1.1: Key indicators for goal 1

	Care			Education					
	Under-5 mortality rate		Moderate or severe stunting (children under age 5)	Total enrolment		Gross enrolment ratio (GER)		Gender parity index of GER	
	2000 (‰)	2012 (‰)	2012 (%)	2011 (000)	Change since 1999 (%)	1999 (%)	2011 (%)	1999 (F/M)	2011 (F/M)
World	**75**	**48**	**25**	**170 008**	**52**	**33**	**50**	**0.97**	**1.00**
Low income countries	134	82	37	10 743	88	11	17	0.98	0.99
Lower middle income countries	93	61	35	65 195	112	22	46	0.93	1.01
Upper middle income countries	38	20	8	64 164	29	43	67	1.00	1.02
High income countries	10	6	3	29 906	17	72	82	0.99	1.01
Sub-Saharan Africa	156	97	...	12 222	126	10	18	0.95	1.00
Arab States	53	33	...	4 142	72	15	23	0.77	0.94
Central Asia	62	36	...	1 713	35	19	32	0.96	1.00
East Asia and the Pacific	39	20	...	47 603	29	39	62	1.00	1.01
South and West Asia	92	58	...	49 539	130	22	50	0.93	1.02
Latin America and the Caribbean	32	19	...	20 999	31	54	73	1.02	1.01
North America and Western Europe	7	6	...	22 341	17	76	85	0.98	1.01
Central and Eastern Europe	24	11	...	11 448	21	51	72	0.96	0.98

Note. Gender parity is reached when the gender parity index is between 0.97 and 1.03.
Sources: Annex, Statistical Tables 3A and 3B (print) and Statistical Table 3A (website); UIS database; Inter-agency Group for Child Mortality Estimation (2013); UNICEF et al. (2013).

The total number of children dying before their fifth birthday fell by 48% between 1990 and 2012

The foundations set in the first thousand days of a child's life, from conception to the second birthday, are critical for the child's future well-being. Hence it is vital for women of reproductive age to have access to adequate health care so that they are well prepared for the risks of pregnancy and the postnatal and infanthood periods. Families need support to make the right choices for mothers and babies. And access to good nutrition holds the key to ensuring that children develop strong immune systems and the cognitive abilities they need in order to learn.

Realization of the significance of early childhood has led to a stronger monitoring system and a better understanding of the scale of the problems in this area, as well as the progress made, which has been considerable.

A decline in the child mortality rate is a key indicator of child health. Between 1990 and 2000, global child mortality fell from 90 deaths per 1,000 live births to 75, and it fell further to 48 in 2012. However, it is still well above the 2015 target of reducing child mortality by two-thirds from the 1990 level to 30 deaths per 1,000 live births (Inter-agency Group for Child Mortality Estimation, 2013).

The total number of children dying before their fifth birthday fell by 48% from 12.6 million in 1990 to 6.6 million in 2012. However, it fell by only 14% in sub-Saharan Africa, the region with the highest mortality rate. On the positive side, the rate of progress in sub-Saharan Africa reached 3.8% per year between 2000 and 2012, compared with 1.4% in the 1990s.

Out of the 43 countries where the child mortality rate was in excess of 100 deaths per 1,000 live births in 2000, all but seven were in sub-Saharan Africa. Two countries had achieved the target by 2011: Liberia and Timor-Leste. If the annual rate of reduction between 2000 and 2011 is projected to 2011–2015, only six more countries reach the target: Cambodia, Ethiopia, Madagascar, Malawi, Niger and Rwanda. By contrast, child mortality has fallen by less than 1% per year in seven countries, including Cameroon, the Democratic Republic of the Congo and Somalia (Figure 1.1.1).

Figure 1.1.1: Despite progress, few countries are expected to meet the target for child survival
Under-5 mortality rate, selected countries, 2000–2015 (projection)

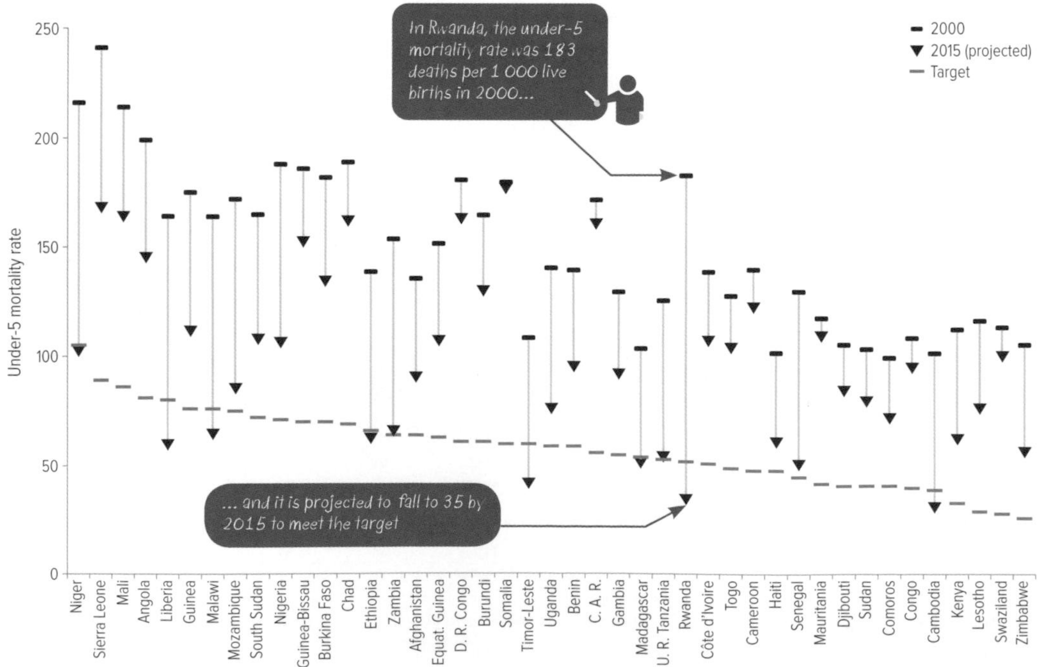

Notes: The countries shown are those where the child mortality rate exceeded 100 in 2000. The projection from 2011 to 2015 is based on the average rate of reduction between 2000 and 2011.
Source: EFA Global Monitoring Report team calculations (2013), based on the Inter-agency Group for Child Mortality Estimation (2012).

Figure 1.1.2: Despite improvements, over 40% of young children are malnourished in many countries
Moderate or severe stunting rate, selected countries, 1987–1995 and 2008–2011

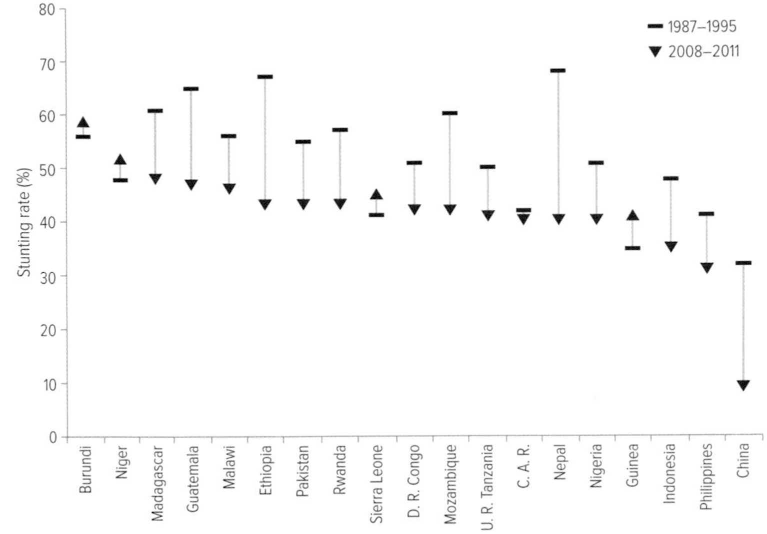

Source: UNICEF (2013a), based on Demographic and Health Surveys, Multiple Indicator Cluster Surveys or other national surveys.

Among the 41 countries that had reached the target by 2011, most were in North America and Western Europe or Central and Eastern Europe, or were high income countries in other regions. Nevertheless, some of the world's most populous developing countries, which invested in early childhood interventions, also reduced child mortality by at least two-thirds well in advance of the target date, including Bangladesh, Brazil, China, Egypt, Mexico, and Turkey. Other countries reduced child mortality by more than 70% in the short space of two decades, including El Salvador, the Lao People's Democratic Republic, Maldives and Mongolia.

Nutrition has improved in recent years, yet, in 2012, it is estimated that 162 million children under 5 were moderately or severely stunted – that is, short for their age, a robust indicator of long-term malnutrition. The proportion of children who were malnourished reduced from 40% in 1990 to 25% in 2012 (UNICEF et al., 2013). This means the annual rate of reduction needs to increase from 2% to 3.6% if the global target adopted by the World Health Assembly in 2012, to reduce the number of stunted children to 100 million (equivalent to a stunting rate of 15%), is to be achieved by 2025. Achieving the target could, if anything, become more difficult in coming years as a result of factors such as the impact of climate change on agriculture and the increasing volatility of food prices.

The global burden of malnutrition is unequally distributed, with 38% of children in sub-Saharan Africa and in South Asia suffering from malnutrition in 2012. These two regions account for three-quarters of the total population of malnourished children.

Progress has so far also been unequal. China reduced its stunting rate by two-thirds. As a result, upper middle income countries reduced stunting at twice the rate of low and lower middle income countries. Ethiopia and Nepal reduced stunting by more than one-third over little more than 15 years, albeit from excessively high levels. By contrast, in Burundi and Sierra Leone, the proportion of malnourished children slightly increased (Figure 1.1.2).

A lesson from the countries that have made the most progress is that their policies saw malnutrition as a social problem that required an integrated approach, rather than as an isolated challenge to be addressed through technical solutions. In Guatemala, despite some progress over the last 20 years, almost half of all children are still stunted. The signing of the Pacto Hambre Cero (Zero Hunger Pact) in 2012 exemplifies the government's resolve to accelerate progress, especially for indigenous communities. The government's aim is to reduce chronic malnutrition among children under 3 by 10% by 2016 as a first step towards a reduction of 25% by 2022. The implementation plan, which is part of the National Food Security and Nutrition System Law, envisages measures to promote breastfeeding and folic acid and micronutrient supplements to combat chronic malnutrition, along with support for subsistence agriculture and temporary employment programmes to deal with seasonal malnutrition (Guatemala Government, 2012).

Nepal reduced stunting by more than one-third over 15 years

The links between early childhood health care and education are strong and mutually reinforcing. Educated mothers adopt better practices that lead to better health outcomes for their children (see Chapter 3). Healthy and well-nourished children, in turn, are more likely to spend more years at school. In one of the most comprehensive studies of the long-term impact of a healthy start to life, groups of children in Brazil and India were followed from birth to adulthood. Boys and girls who were born 500 grams heavier attained 0.3 to 0.4 more years of schooling than their peers. Likewise, boys and girls who had grown faster than expected by the age of 2 attained 0.4 to 0.6 more years of school and were more likely to complete secondary school (Adair et al., 2013).

Early childhood care and education services help build cognitive and non-cognitive skills at a time when children's brains are developing, with long-term benefits for children from disadvantaged backgrounds. In Uganda, a cash transfer programme conditional on pre-school attendance, funded by UNICEF and the World Food Programme, led to an improvement in visual reception skills, fine motor skills and receptive or expressive language (Gilligan and Roy, 2013). In Jamaica, a survey tracked young adults from disadvantaged backgrounds who, as infants, had received psychosocial stimulation through weekly visits by community health personnel. By their early 20s, individuals who had taken part in the programme were earning 42% more than other disadvantaged youth (Gertler et al., 2013).

In Chad, hardly any poor children attended early childhood education in 2010

Since 2000, early childhood education services have expanded considerably. The pre-primary education gross enrolment ratio increased from 33% in 1999 to 50% in 2011. Almost 60 million more children have been enrolled in pre-primary schools over the period. The enrolment ratio more than doubled in South and West Asia, from 22% in 1999 to 50% in 2011. Low income and sub-Saharan African countries lag behind, however, with gross enrolment ratios of 17% and 18%, respectively.

Governments face significant challenges in expanding pre-primary education. As a result, the proportion of enrolment in private sector institutions increased from 28% in 1999 to 33% in 2011. In the Arab States, it was as high as 71% (Box 1.1.1). Constraints in collecting data from unregulated non-state providers mean these figures are likely to be an underestimate in some countries.

As private providers tend to serve households who can afford fees, generally those who are better off and concentrated in urban areas, the network of public nurseries and pre-schools needs to expand if more disadvantaged groups are also to be reached. The absence of such provision is a key reason why poorer children are unable to benefit from early childhood education services. In Chad and the Central African Republic, for example, hardly any poor boy or girl attended any form of early childhood education in 2010, but one in six richer children did so. Even in middle income countries with better coverage on average, such as Ghana, Mongolia and Serbia, there is a wide gap in access between the richest and poorest boys and girls (Figure 1.1.3).

Box 1.1.1: In the Arab States, the private sector is the main provider of pre-primary education

The pre-primary gross enrolment ratio in the Arab States increased from 15% in 1999 to 23% in 2011, but remains the second lowest among the regions. Moreover, this region has the highest share of private provision, with more than two-thirds of total enrolment in private pre-schools and nurseries.

Algeria stands out as the country with the highest share of government provision in the region, at 86%. In addition, it achieved the largest expansion in pre-primary education, from just 2% in 1999 to 75% in 2011. This was the result of a reform that introduced a pre-primary curriculum in 2004 and aimed to increase the gross enrolment ratio to 80% by 2010. At the same time Algeria undertook this rapid expansion of the public system, it encouraged private provision in urban areas. An inspection system monitors implementation of the curriculum in both types of institutions.

In Jordan, the construction of almost 400 kindergartens under a World Bank loan resulted in the share of enrolment in government institutions increasing from zero in 1999 to 17% by 2010. However, enrolment levels remained almost constant over the period, reaching 38% in 2012 despite a target of 50% for that year. It is likely that the continuing predominance of private sector provision is an obstacle to universal access. The share of expenditure on pre-primary education in the education budget was just 0.3% in 2011. As a result, many commendable initiatives taken as part of the national early childhood development strategy – which are unique for the region, including programmes aimed at improving teacher qualifications, setting and monitoring standards, and raising parental participation – have yet to benefit the majority of the population.

Sources: Benamar (2010); Jordan Ministry of Education (2013); UNICEF (2009).

Figure 1.1.3: Few poor 4-year-olds receive pre-primary education
Percentage of children aged 36 to 59 months who attended some form of organized early childhood education programme, by wealth, selected countries, 2005–2012

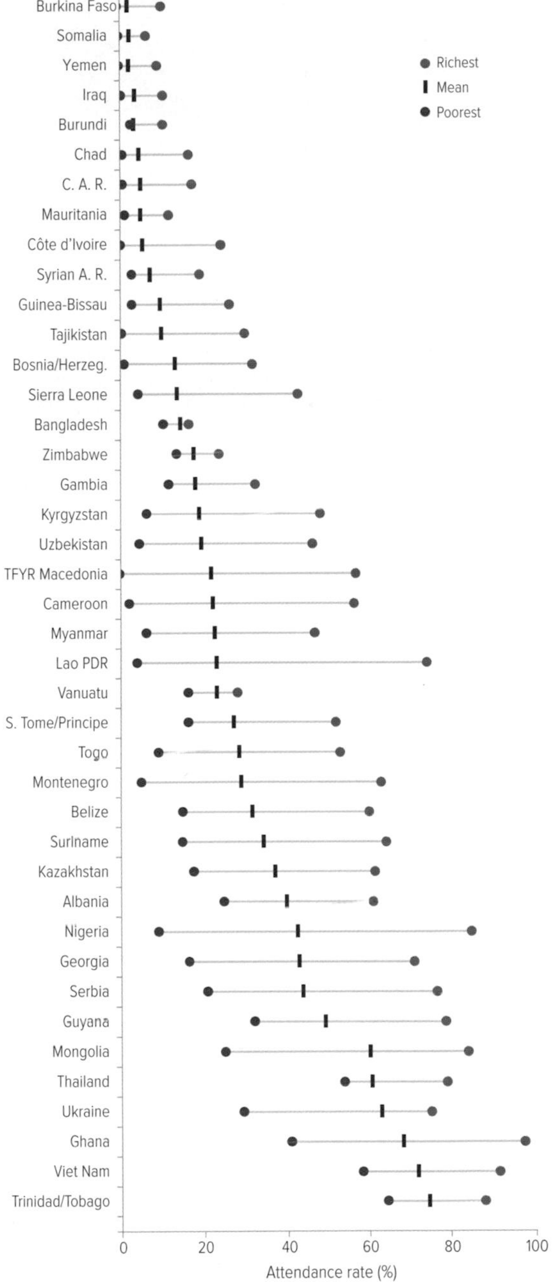

Source: World Inequality Database on Education, www.education-inequalities.org.

How many countries are likely to reach the pre-primary education goal by 2015?

While the Millennium Development Goals were a clear guide towards the early childhood health components of the first Education for All goal, no target was set at the World Education Forum in Dakar in 2000 to guide assessment of success in promoting early childhood education. To gauge comparative progress across countries over the decade, this Report has set an indicative pre-primary education gross enrolment ratio of 80% as a target, which should be realistic for countries to reach by 2015. The analysis, which looks at how close countries are to achieving the target, not only takes stock of the situation as of 2011, but also examines whether countries have a realistic chance of reaching the target by 2015.

By 2015, 68 countries are expected to have reached pre-primary enrolment of 80%

Out of the 141 countries for which there are data, in 1999 just 30 had a gross enrolment ratio above 80%, while 11 were close. Between 1999 and 2011, the number of countries that reached the target increased to 52, and 17 had come close (Figure 1.1.4). Looking ahead to 2015, it is projected that 68 countries will reach the target, including Costa Rica, Lithuania and South Africa, and 10 will come close (Table 1.1.2).

The number of countries with a gross enrolment ratio of less than 30% fell from 53 in 1999 to 33 in 2011. Of the 20 countries that moved out of this group, Angola and Mongolia have since

Figure 1.1.4: Goal 1 – pre-primary education will need to grow faster after 2015
Number of countries by level of pre-primary gross enrolment ratio, 1999, 2011 and 2015 (projected)

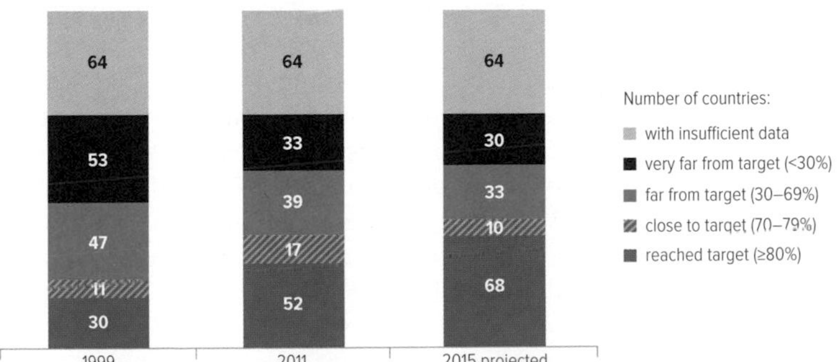

Note: The analysis was conducted on the subset of countries for which a projection was possible; therefore, it covers fewer countries than those for which information is available for either 1999 or 2011.
Source: Bruneforth (2013).

A stronger role for the state calls for clear plans on the objectives of the system, including paying attention to the preparation of teachers and caregivers to address the particular learning needs of young children.

Table 1.1.2: Likelihood of countries achieving a pre-primary enrolment target of at least 70% by 2015

Level expected by 2015		Strong relative progress (41)	Slow progress or moving away from target (22)
Target reached or close (≥70%)	78	Algeria, Angola, Antigua and Barbuda, Argentina, Aruba, Australia, Austria, Barbados, Belarus, Belgium, Brunei Darussalam, Bulgaria, Canada, Cape Verde, Chile, Cook Islands, Costa Rica, Cuba, Cyprus, Czech Republic, Denmark, Dominica, Ecuador, El Salvador, Equatorial Guinea, Estonia, Finland, France, Germany, Ghana, Greece, Grenada, Guatemala, Guyana, Hungary, Iceland, India, Israel, Italy, Jamaica, Japan, Latvia, Lebanon, Lithuania, Luxembourg, Malaysia, Maldives, Malta, Mexico, Mongolia, Nepal, Netherlands, New Zealand, Nicaragua, Norway, Panama, Peru, Poland, Portugal, Qatar, Republic of Moldova, Romania, Russian Federation, Saint Kitts and Nevis, Seychelles, Slovakia, Slovenia, South Africa, Spain, Suriname, Sweden, Switzerland, Thailand, Ukraine, United Kingdom, Uruguay, Venezuela (Bolivarian Republic of), Viet Nam	
Far from target (30–69%)	33	Armenia, Belize, Cameroon, China, Croatia, Egypt, Honduras, Indonesia, Iran (Islamic Republic of), Kazakhstan, Lesotho, Montenegro, Philippines, Sao Tome and Principe, Solomon Islands, Turkey	Albania, Bermuda, Bolivia (Plurinational State of), Cayman Islands, Colombia, Dominican Republic, Jordan, Kenya, Marshall Islands, Morocco, Palestine, Paraguay, Saint Lucia, Samoa, Serbia, United States, Vanuatu
Very far from target (<30%)	30	Azerbaijan, Bangladesh, Benin, Bhutan, Burkina Faso, Burundi, Cambodia, Congo, Côte d'Ivoire, Democratic Republic of the Congo, Djibouti, Eritrea, Ethiopia, Guinea-Bissau, Kyrgyzstan, Lao People's Democratic Republic, Madagascar, Mali, Myanmar, Niger, Nigeria, Rwanda, Senegal, Togo, Yemen	Fiji, Syrian Arab Republic, Tajikistan, The former Yugoslav Republic of Macedonia, Uzbekistan
		Change between 1999 and 2011	

Countries not included in analysis because of insufficient data	64	Afghanistan, Andorra, Anguilla, Bahamas, Bahrain, Bosnia and Herzegovina, Botswana, Brazil, British Virgin Islands, Central African Republic, Chad, Comoros, Democratic People's Republic of Korea, Gabon, Gambia, Georgia, Guinea, Haiti, Iraq, Ireland, Kiribati, Kuwait, Liberia, Libya, Macao (China), Malawi, Mauritania, Mauritius, Micronesia (Federated States of), Monaco, Montserrat, Mozambique, Namibia, Nauru, Netherlands Antilles, Niue, Oman, Pakistan, Palau, Papua New Guinea, Republic of Korea, Saint Vincent and the Grenadines, San Marino, Saudi Arabia, Sierra Leone, Singapore, Somalia, South Sudan, Sri Lanka, Sudan, Swaziland, Timor-Leste, Tokelau, Tonga, Trinidad and Tobago, Tunisia, Turkmenistan, Turks and Caicos Islands, Tuvalu, Uganda, United Arab Emirates, United Republic of Tanzania, Zambia, Zimbabwe

Source: Bruneforth (2013).

achieved the target, while Algeria and Equatorial Guinea have come close. It is projected that, by 2015, 30 countries will still be very far from the target, of which 16 are in sub-Saharan Africa, including Côte d'Ivoire, Ethiopia and Mali.

In assessing performance, it is important to recognize how quickly some countries have moved towards the target even if they have not yet made it. Of the 72 countries that were far or very far from the target in 2011, 50 had nevertheless made strong progress since 1999, increasing their gross enrolment ratio by at least 33%. Eight countries expanded access by more than 25 percentage points, including India (from 19% to 55%), the Islamic Republic of Iran (from 14% to 43%), Nicaragua (from 28% to 55%) and South Africa (from 21% to 65%).[1]

By contrast, enrolment ratios stagnated in some countries, including the Plurinational State of Bolivia, which remained at 46%, Morocco (58%) and Serbia (53%). Of the 53 countries that were furthest from the target in 1999, only 5 did not rapidly increase their gross enrolment ratio, remaining below 30% by 2011: Fiji, the Syrian Arab Republic, Tajikistan, the Former Yugoslav Republic of Macedonia and Uzbekistan. Countries in Central and Eastern Europe have experienced different trajectories. Their speed of progress towards achieving universal pre-primary education depends on their political commitment towards equality (Box 1.1.2).

Not only is it a cause for concern that 63 countries are likely to be far or very far from the 80% target by 2015, but this excludes the 64 countries without data. Moreover, 80% is a modest target, leaving some young children without access to pre-primary education. Given that those excluded are often the most vulnerable, it is vital for any post-2015 goal to provide a clear target to ensure that all young children have access to pre-primary education.

1. In such comparisons it is important to recognize that differences between countries are sometimes due to variation in age groups: the chances of a country with a one-year target age group (e.g. 5-year-olds in Angola) are higher than those of a country with a three-year target age group (e.g. 3- to 5-year-olds in India).

Box 1.1.2: In Central and Eastern Europe, the quest for universal access to pre-primary education continues

Access to pre-primary education increased rapidly in Central and Eastern Europe between 1999 and 2011, from 51% to 72%. This region, together with Central Asia, has the highest share of government provision at more than 97%. However, countries in Central and Eastern Europe have progressed at different paces, reflecting the varying degree of attention that governments have paid to this level of education.

In the Republic of Moldova, where there has been a concerted effort to expand pre-primary education, the gross enrolment ratio of children aged 3 to 6 increased from 43% in 2000 to 77% in 2011. Strong political commitment led to pre-primary education's share of the education budget reaching as much as 20% in 2011. Education already receives a high share of the government budget, at 22%, or 7.9% of GNP. The national strategy aims to achieve enrolment ratios of 78% by 2015 for children aged 3 to 6 and 98% for those aged 6 and 7 while reducing inequality between urban and rural areas by 5%. The strategy focuses on both access – targeting lagging areas and disadvantaged groups – and quality, expanding the training systems of educators and nurses.

The Former Yugoslav Republic of Macedonia appears to have a very low enrolment ratio, at 25% in 2010 – placing it in the group of countries most off track – but this figure is partly the result of a reform in 2005/06 that converted the final year of pre-primary education into a compulsory preparatory first year of primary education. In addition, early childhood education enrolment ratios are calculated for all children aged 6 and under, a much wider age group than other countries in the region.

Evidence from household surveys suggests that there has been progress in recent years but that inequality is high and increasing. Between 2005 and 2011, the percentage of 3- and 4-year-olds who attended some form of organized early childhood education programme doubled from 11% to 22%. However, the beneficiaries were almost exclusively children from the wealthiest 40% of families.

To improve access, the cost to households needs to be reduced. Families have to contribute 30% of the cost, restricting the access of the poorest. Children from the country's minorities also benefited far less, with attendance ratios for members of the Albanian and Roma communities at less than 4%. In the case of the Roma, this is despite initiatives to promote their inclusion in pre-primary schools.

Sources: Open Society Foundations et al. (2011); Republic of Moldova Ministry of Education (2010); TFYR Macedonia Ministry of Health et al. (2011); TFYR Macedonia Ministry of Labour and Social Policy (2010); UNESCO IBE (2011).

Goal 2 Universal primary education

Ensuring that by 2015 all children, particularly girls, children in difficult circumstances and those belonging to ethnic minorities, have access to and complete, free and compulsory primary education of good quality.

Highlights

- The goal of universal primary education is likely to be missed by a wide margin, as 57 million children were still out of school in 2011. Half of these children live in conflict-affected countries.
- If the global rate of reduction of the out-of-school population observed between 1999 and 2008 had been maintained, the target could have been achieved by 2015.
- The region lagging the most is sub-Saharan Africa, where no progress has been made since 2007, leaving 22% of primary school age children out of school in 2011. No progress was made in the region on preventing children from dropping out of school over the decade: of those who entered school, the proportion who reached the last grade fell from 58% in 1999 to 56% in 2010.
- Girls make up about 54% of the global population of children out of school. The proportion rises to 60% in the Arab States, a share that has remained unchanged since 1999.
- Of the 57 million children out of school, nearly half are expected never to make it to school. In the Arab States and sub-Saharan Africa, almost two-thirds of girls who are out of school are expected never to go to school.
- It is projected that by 2015, only 68 out of 122 countries will achieve universal primary enrolment. In 15 countries, on current trends, the ratio will still be below 80%.
- The record is likely to be far worse for primary school completion: it is expected that only 13 out of 90 countries will achieve universal primary school completion.

Table 1.2.1: Key indicators for goal 2

	Total primary enrolment		Primary adjusted net enrolment ratio		Out-of-school children			Survival rate to last grade of primary education	
	2011 (000)	Change since 1999 (%)	1999 (%)	2011 (%)	2011 (000)	Change since 1999 (%)	Female (%)	1999 (%)	2010 (%)
World	**698 693**	**7**	**84**	**91**	**57 186**	**-47**	**54**	**74**	**75**
Low income countries	126 870	70	59	82	21 370	-46	54	55	59
Lower middle income countries	293 937	20	79	90	27 826	-49	55	68	69
Upper middle income countries	204 934	-20	95	97	6 337	-44	49	85	90
High income countries	72 951	-4	97	98	1 653	-24	46	92	94
Sub-Saharan Africa	136 423	66	59	78	29 798	-29	54	58	56
Arab States	42 771	22	79	89	4 823	-42	60	79	87
Central Asia	5 468	-20	94	95	290	-34	55	97	98
East Asia and the Pacific	184 257	-18	95	97	5 118	-50	44	84	89
South and West Asia	192 850	24	77	93	12 450	-69	57	62	64
Latin America and the Caribbean	65 686	-6	94	95	2 726	-24	45	77	84
North America and Western Europe	51 686	-2	98	98	1 249	39	45	92	94
Central and Eastern Europe	19 552	-21	93	96	732	-57	49	96	98

Sources: Annex, Statistical Tables 5 and 6; UIS database.

With just two years until the 2015 deadline for the Education for All (EFA) goals, the world is unlikely to fulfil one of the most modest promises: to get every child into primary school. More than 57 million children continue to be denied the right to education, and almost half of them will probably never enter a classroom.

There is some good news: between 1999 and 2011, the number of children out of school fell almost by half, from 107 million to 57 million. Following a period of stagnation, the number of children out of school began to fall again between 2010 and 2011. Yet that reduction, of 1.9 million, is little more than half the average annual level of decline between 2004 and 2008 of 3.4 million and scarcely more than a quarter of the average annual level of decline between 1999 and 2004 of 6.8 million. Had the rate of decline between 1999 and 2008 been maintained, the number of children out of school would be 23 million by 2015, just below the EFA target of a 97% net enrolment ratio (Figure 1.2.1). But since 2008 the rate of decline has been so slow that 53 million children are likely to be out of school in 2015.

There are wide regional variations in the fall in out-of-school numbers since 1999. South and West Asia and sub-Saharan Africa have accounted for three-quarters of the world's out-of-school population throughout the Dakar period, but have seen very different trends. South and West Asia experienced the fastest decline of all regions, contributing more than half the total reduction in the number out of school. In India and the Islamic Republic of Iran, the out-of-school population fell by more than 90%. By contrast, in sub-Saharan Africa, after three years of stagnation, there was a small reduction in the number out of school between 2010 and 2011, of 0.8 million – leaving it at the same level as in 2007. In 2011, 22% of the region's primary school age population was still not in school.

Girls make up about 54% of the global population of children out of school. In the Arab States the share is 60%, unchanged since 1999. In South and West Asia, by contrast, the share of girls in the out-of-school population fell steadily from 64% in 1999 to 57% in 2011.

Over the past five years, there has been little change in the list of countries with the highest numbers of children out of school. Among the countries with data for both 2006 and 2011, the 10 worst performers for both periods are identical, with one exception: Ghana was replaced by Yemen, whose out-of-school numbers increased (Table 1.2.2A).

Figure 1.2.1: Millions of children remain out of school in 2011
Number of primary school age children out of school, by region, 1999–2011

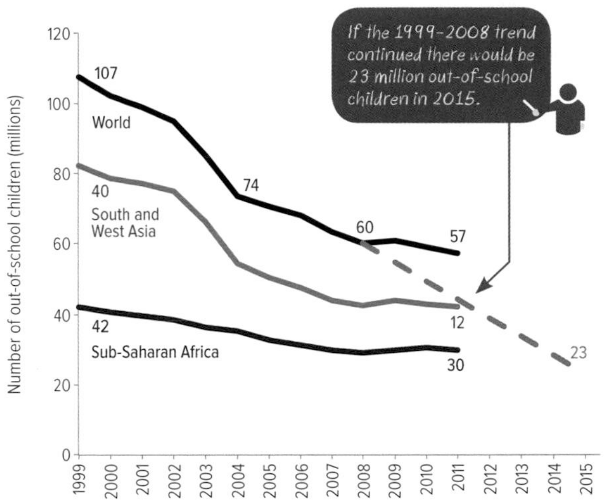

Note: The dotted line from 2008 to 2015 is based on the average annual absolute reduction in the number of out-of-school children between 1999 and 2008.
Sources: UIS database; EFA Global Monitoring Report team calculations (2013).

The top three performers since 2006 are the Lao People's Democratic Republic, Rwanda and Viet Nam, which reduced their out-of-school populations by at least 85% (Table 1.2.2B). Ethiopia and India are among the 10 countries that reduced their out-of-school populations the most in relative terms, and they also contributed significantly to the overall reduction in out-of-school numbers – by 2.2 million and 4.5 million, respectively.

Ethiopia and India have contributed significantly to the overall reduction in out-of-school numbers

Five of the 10 countries with the largest relative increases in out-of-school populations since 2004–2006 are in sub-Saharan Africa (Table 1.2.2C). Nigeria's out-of-school population not only grew the most in absolute terms, by 3.4 million, but also had the fourth highest rate of growth. In some countries, including Colombia, Paraguay and Thailand, the out-of-school population rose even though they are in regions that have been performing better on average.

Some countries that might have been on these lists are not there simply because no data are publicly available (Box 1.2.1). Half of the world's out-of-school children live in conflicted-affected countries, many of which lack data (Box 1.2.2).

Table 1.2.2: Changes in the out-of-school population, 2006–2011

A. The ten countries with the highest out-of-school populations

	Out-of-school population 2011 (000)
Nigeria	10 542
Pakistan	5 436
Ethiopia	1 703
India	1 674
Philippines	1 460
Côte d'Ivoire	1 161
Burkina Faso	1 015
Kenya	1 010
Niger	957
Yemen	949

B. The ten countries with the highest relative decreases in out-of-school populations

	Out-of-school population		
	2006 (000)	2011 (000)	Change (%)
Rwanda	273	20	-93
Viet Nam	436	39	-91
Lao PDR	123	19	-85
Congo	239	47	-81
Lebanon	58	12	-78
India	6 184	1 674	-73
Timor-Leste	61	18	-71
Morocco	419	134	-68
Cambodia	91	31	-66
Ethiopia	3 947	1 703	-57

C. The ten countries with the highest relative increases in out-of-school populations

	Out-of-school population		
	2006 (000)	2011 (000)	Change (%)
Paraguay	57	136	139
Colombia	206	435	112
Thailand	387	611	58
Nigeria	7 150	10 542	47
Eritrea	295	422	43
Gambia	65	86	33
South Africa	519	679	31
Liberia	325	386	19
Mauritania	113	131	16
Yemen	853	949	11

Note: The countries considered were those that had data for both 2006 and 2011 and an out-of-school population in the first period that exceeded 50,000.
Source: UIS database.

Box 1.2.1: Which countries have more than 1 million children out of school?

Despite improvements in the availability of education data over the past decade, it is regrettable that recent data on out-of-school numbers, one of the simplest education indicators, are not publicly available for 57 countries. Focusing only on countries with publishable data is likely to be misleading for global policy debates, particularly as many of the countries without data are likely to be the furthest from achieving UPE. Recent improvements in the availability of household survey data help better understand the global picture. However, this picture will only be complete once all countries have publishable data.

The global figure for out-of-school children includes publicly available data from 147 out of 204 countries, and unpublished estimates by the UNESCO Institute for Statistics (UIS) for the remaining countries. Countries for which the UIS publishes no data either do not have enrolment by age or population data, or these data are not considered sufficiently reliable.

The publicly available data for individual countries account for only 68% of the 57 million children out of school. For example, published data account for 95% of out-of-school children in North America and Western Europe, but only 38% in the Arab States.

The largest gaps are in sub-Saharan Africa, where 14 countries lack data. These include countries affected by conflict, such as the Democratic Republic of the Congo and Somalia, where the chances of going to school remain slim, but also countries such as Benin, Sierra Leone, Togo and the United Republic of Tanzania. While most countries in Latin America have published data, Brazil, for example, does not, due to lack of agreed population figures.

For this Report, an attempt was made to identify which countries lacking data are likely to have more than 1 million children out of school, using estimates of the primary net attendance rate from household surveys carried out between 2008 and 2011.[1]

These calculations add six countries to the eight known to have more than 1 million children out of school (Table 1.2.3). Together the 14 countries would account for around two-thirds of the global out-of-school population.

Table 1.2.3: Fourteen countries are likely to have more than 1 million children out of school

Afghanistan	Kenya
Burkina Faso	Nigeria
China	Pakistan
Côte d'Ivoire	Philippines
D. R. Congo	**Somalia**
Ethiopia	**Sudan (pre-secession)**
India	**U. R. Tanzania**

Notes: Countries in bold are estimated to have more than 1 million children out of school, according to EFA Global Monitoring Team calculations using household survey data. During the period in question, Sudan is still included in the area that is now South Sudan.
Source: EFA Global Monitoring Report team calculations, based on the UIS database, the 2010 World Population Prospects and data from Demographic and Health Surveys and Multiple Indicator Cluster Surveys.

It is probably not surprising that Afghanistan, the Democratic Republic of the Congo, Somalia and pre-secession Sudan have out-of-school populations of over 1 million. China's estimated out-of-school population of more than 1 million is consistent with its having achieved UPE – defined as a net enrolment ratio of at least 97% – because of its large population.

Among the countries added to the list, the most unexpected is the United Republic of Tanzania. The most recent publishable UIS estimate for the United Republic of Tanzania put the out-of-school population at 137,000 in 2008. According to the 2010 Demographic and Health Survey, however, the primary net attendance rate was 80%, well below the 98% net enrolment ratio estimate provided by the UIS for 2008. One reason for this discrepancy is likely to be differences in the way information is collected on child age.[2] Moreover, primary completion rates estimated by both the Demographic and Health Survey and the UIS indicate that only around 7 out of 10 children finish primary school. This supports the possibility that the out-of-school population is indeed over 1 million.

1. Somalia is an exception, with data from the 2006 Multiple Indicator Cluster Survey. Continuing conflict in the country makes it unlikely that enrolment improved significantly over the following five years.

2. See Box 2.5 in the 2010 *EFA Global Monitoring Report* for an explanation of the difference between administrative and household data (UNESCO, 2010).

Box 1.2.2: The continuing hidden crisis for children in conflict-affected areas

In many of the world's poorest countries, armed conflict continues to destroy the education chances of a whole generation of children. This Report draws on the international reporting systems used for the 2011 *EFA Global Monitoring Report* to construct an updated list of conflict-affected countries. Thirty-two countries were identified as affected by armed conflict in the period from 2002 to 2011, three fewer than in 1999–2008 (Table 1.2.4). New countries have joined the list, however, including Libya, Mali and the Syrian Arab Republic.

The analysis shows that, while the global number of children out of school fell slightly from 60 million in 2008 to 57 million in 2011, the benefits of this progress have not reached children in conflict-affected countries. These children make up 22% of the world's primary school age population, but 50% of its out-of-school children, and the proportion has increased from 42% in 2008.

Of the 28.5 million primary school age children out of school in conflict-affected countries, 12.6 million live in sub-Saharan Africa, 5.3 million in South and West Asia, and 4 million in the Arab States. The vast majority – 95% – live in low and lower middle income countries. Girls, who make up 55% of the total, are the worst affected.

Table 1.2.4: Conflict-affected countries, 1999–2008 and 2002–2011

Afghanistan	Ethiopia	Myanmar	Sierra Leone
Algeria	Georgia	Nepal	Somalia
Angola	Guinea	**Niger**	Sri Lanka
Burundi	India	Nigeria	Sudan (pre-secession)
Central African Republic	Indonesia	Pakistan	**Syrian Arab Republic**
Chad	**Iran, Isl. Rep.**	Palestine	Thailand
Colombia	Iraq	Philippines	Timor-Leste
Côte d'Ivoire	Liberia	Russian Federation	Turkey
D. R. Congo	**Libya**	Rwanda	Uganda
Eritrea	**Mali**	Serbia	Yemen

Notes: The 2002–2011 list comprises countries with 1,000 or more battle-related deaths over the period, plus those with more than 200 battle-related deaths in any one year between 2009 and 2011. Data are compiled using the Peace Research Institute Oslo and Uppsala Conflict Data Program data sets on armed conflict and battle deaths. See Box 3.1 in the 2011 *EFA Global Monitoring Report* for further information.
Countries in light blue were on the list in 2011 but are no longer identified as conflict-affected in 2013.
Countries in red joined the list in 2013.
During the period in question, Sudan still included the area that is now South Sudan.

One of the biggest disappointments since the EFA goals were established in 2000 is that nearly half of the 57 million children currently out of school are expected never even to make it to school. The percentage is considerably higher in the Arab States and sub Saharan Africa, where girls are also much more affected: in these regions almost two in three out-of-school girls are expected never to go to school. The remaining half of the out-of-school population is split almost equally between children who enrolled but dropped out and those who are expected to enter school but will be older than the official primary school age, and so are more likely to eventually drop out (Figure 1.2.2).

Figure 1.2.2: Almost half of children out of school are expected never to enrol
Distribution of out-of-school children by school exposure, gender and region, 2011

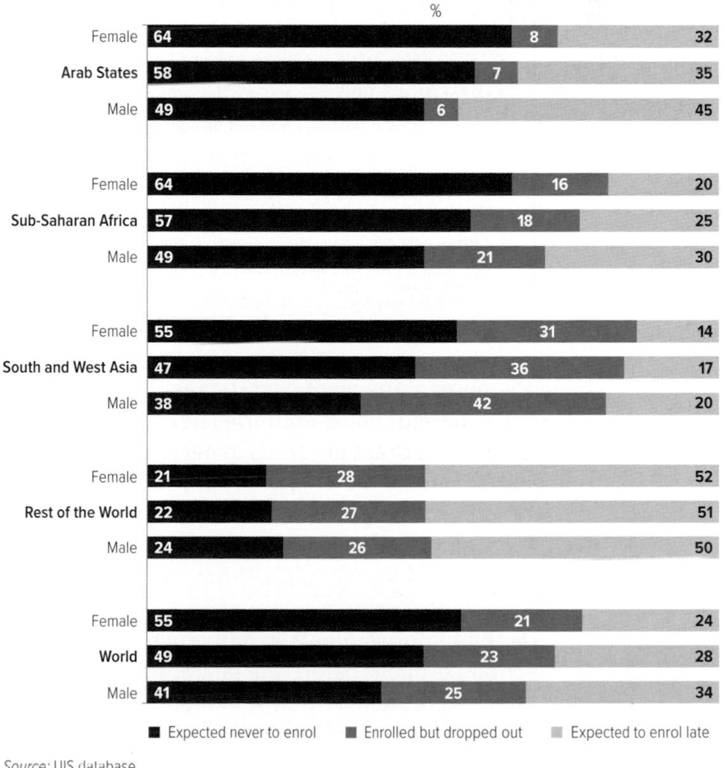

Source: UIS database.

The reasons for children not making it into school vary, but are usually associated with disadvantages children are born with – poverty, gender, ethnicity, or living in a rural area or a slum, for example. One of the most neglected of such disadvantages is disability (Box 1.2.3).

Children are more likely to complete primary schooling if they enter at the right age. The global adjusted net intake rate for the first year of primary school increased between 1999 and 2011, but only slightly, from 81% to 86% – and rose by less than

Box 1.2.3: Children with disabilities are often overlooked

Children with disabilities are often denied their right to education. However, little is known about their school attendance patterns. The collection of data on children with disabilities is not straightforward, but they are vital to ensure that policies are in place to address the constraints they face. Statistics on the education experience of children with disabilities are rare in part because household surveys, which tend to be the best source of information on access to school by different population groups, do not have sufficient information on the degree or type of disability, or their sample size is too small to make it possible to draw accurate conclusions.

By one estimate, 93 million children under age 14, or 5.1% of the world's children, were living with a 'moderate or severe disability' in 2004. Of these, 13 million, or 0.7% of the world's children, experience severe disabilities.

According to the World Health Survey, in 14 of 15 low and middle income countries, people of working age with disabilities were about one-third less likely to have completed primary school. For example, in Bangladesh, 30% of people with disabilities had completed primary school, compared with 48% of those with no disabilities. The corresponding shares were 43% and 57% in Zambia; 56% and 72% in Paraguay.

The obstacles that children face depend on the type of disability they experience. Since 2005, Multiple Indicator Cluster Surveys have used a tool with 10 questions to screen children aged 2 to 9 for the risk of various types of impairment. This information points to a risk of disability ranging from 3% in Uzbekistan to 49% in the Central African Republic. While data on the risk of disability may overestimate the number of children actually living with a disability, they throw some light on the barriers that children at risk of disability face in getting to school.

Analysis for this Report of Multiple Indicator Cluster Surveys from four countries shows that children at higher risk of disability are far more likely to be denied a chance to go to school. In Bangladesh, Bhutan and Iraq, children with mental impairments were most likely to be denied this right. In Iraq, for instance, 10% of 6- to 9-year-olds with no risk of disability had never been to school in 2006, but 19% of those at risk of having a hearing impairment and 51% of those who were at higher risk of mental disability had never been to school. In Thailand, almost all 6- to 9-year-olds who had no disability had been to school in 2005/06, and yet 34% of those with walking or moving impairments had never been to school (Figure 1.2.3).

Sources: Gottlieb et al. (2009); Mitra et al. (2011); WHO and World Bank (2011).

Figure 1.2.3: Children at risk of disability face major barriers in gaining access to school

Percentage of children aged 6 to 9 who have never been to school, by type of impairment, selected countries, 2005–2007

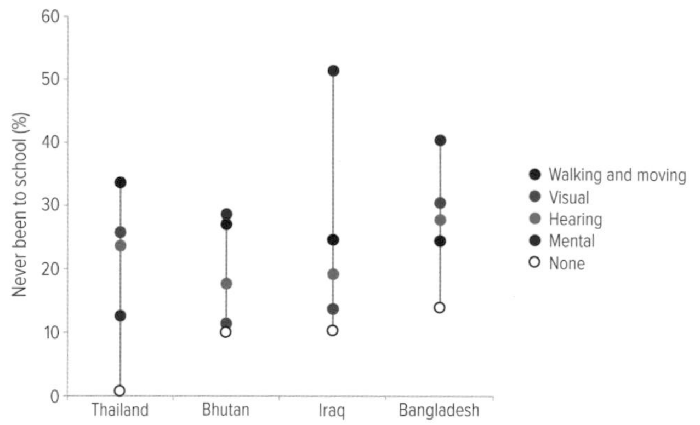

Source: EFA Global Monitoring Report team calculations (2013), based on Multiple Indicator Cluster Surveys.

one percentage point over the last four years of the period. Some countries nevertheless have made great progress in getting children into school by the official school starting age, including Ethiopia (where the rate rose from 23% to 94%), the Islamic Republic of Iran (from 46% to 99%) and Mozambique (from 24% to 71%).

Despite improvements in getting children into school, dropout before the last grade remains a serious problem in many low and middle income countries. The chances of children completing the primary cycle have hardly changed since 1999. In 2010, around 75% of those who started primary school reached the last grade. In sub-Saharan Africa, the proportion making it to the last grade even fell slightly, from 58% in 1999 to 56% in 2010. In South and West Asia, fewer than two out of three children entering school manage to reach the last grade. By contrast, in the Arab States there has been progress from 79% of students reaching the last grade in 1999 to 87% doing so in 2010.

How many countries are likely to reach UPE by 2015?

While the UPE goal has clear indicators, it is not always easy to assess overall progress towards it. The commonly used benchmark of whether at least 97% of children of primary school age are in school does not show whether children complete primary school. Nor does it account for the varied experiences of children from different backgrounds. Thus it is likely to provide an overly optimistic picture of progress.

New analysis for this Report uses data on net enrolment as well as completion to assess progress towards UPE. It also looks at the speed at which countries have moved towards the target, given their starting points. From this information, the analysis projects whether countries have a realistic chance of reaching UPE between 2011 (the latest year for which data are available) and 2015.[1]

Universal access to primary schooling is likely to remain elusive in many countries

In 1999, 37 of the 122 countries with available data had already reached the target of a 97% primary net enrolment ratio (Figure 1.2.4). By 2011, the number of countries that had reached the target had increased to 61. Looking ahead to 2015, it is projected that seven more countries will reach the target: Croatia, El Salvador, Latvia, Nepal, Nicaragua, Qatar and the United Arab Emirates. This leaves 54 countries that are not expected to meet this target by 2015, only eight of which are even close to it.

Of the countries furthest from UPE, 27 had enrolment ratios below 80% in 1999. In 2015, 15 countries are still expected to be in this situation, including 10 in sub-Saharan Africa: Burkina Faso, Côte d'Ivoire, Equatorial Guinea, Eritrea, the Gambia, Lesotho, Liberia, Mali, Niger and Nigeria. Djibouti and Pakistan are among the remaining countries in this group (Table 1.2.5). Of the 12 countries that moved out of this group, three have since reached the target (the Lao People's Democratic Republic, Rwanda and Zambia), and two are expected to come very close (Morocco and Mozambique). In addition,

1. For this analysis, the countries used are those with at least three data points since 1999, the most recent dating from 2009 or after. See Bruneforth (2013) for further information.

Figure 1.2.4: Goal 2 – progress towards achieving universal primary education by 2015 is less than usually assumed

Number of countries by level of adjusted net enrolment ratio, 1999, 2011 and 2015 (projected)

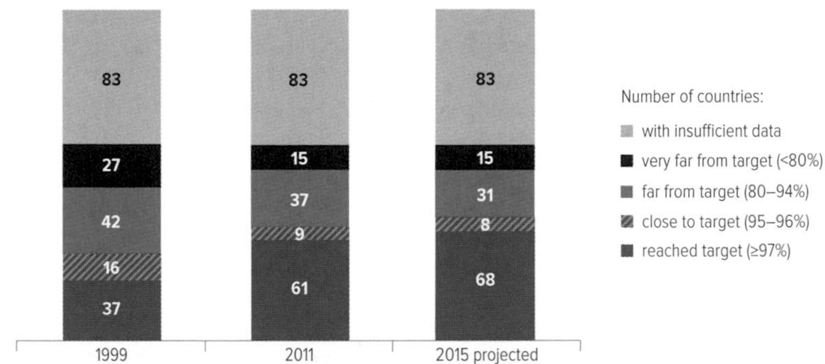

Note: The analysis was conducted on the subset of countries for which a projection was possible; therefore, it covers fewer countries than those for which information is available for either 1999 or 2011.
Source: Bruneforth (2013).

Mauritania, Senegal and Yemen will move out of the group of countries that were furthest from the target in 2011, as their net enrolment ratio is projected to exceed 80% by 2015.

While some countries are still off track, others have made considerable progress. Of the 46 countries with data that are expected to be far from UPE by 2015, 15 will have made strong progress, increasing their net enrolment ratio by at least 15% since 1999. Of the 27 countries that were furthest from the target in 1999, 20 have made strong progress; Botswana, Côte d'Ivoire and Eritrea have made weak progress, with increases between 5% and 15%, while Equatorial Guinea, the Gambia, Liberia and Nigeria have made even less progress than that, or have regressed.

By 2015, 54 countries are not expected to have achieved universal primary enrolment

Progress towards primary school completion is even more disappointing

Enrolment is a partial measure of whether UPE has been achieved, given that success should be judged with respect to whether all children 'have access to and complete' primary education. Hence this Report considers an indicator related to completion: the expected cohort completion rate (Box 1.2.4). One disadvantage of this new indicator is that fewer data are available and no trend can be established to monitor progress since 1999 or make projections to 2015.

In three-quarters of the 90 countries with data since 2008, at least 95% of children were

Box 1.2.4: Measuring primary school completion

A common measure of whether children are completing primary school is the gross intake rate to the last grade.[1] While this is relatively straightforward to calculate from existing data, over-age enrolment and insufficient data on repetition mean it exceeded 100% in 44 of the 153 countries with data for 2011, so it does not provide an accurate picture. This indicator has been used more broadly in recent years to make the case that the MDG on education has been almost achieved. A preferable measure of completion is one that avoids mixing children from different age groups, following instead a group (cohort) of children of primary school entrance age.

The expected cohort completion rate is one such measure. This new indicator measures the percentage of children of primary school entrance age expected to enter and complete primary education. It is estimated by multiplying two indicators:

- The *expected net intake rate* to the first grade of primary education, showing the probability that a child of official primary school entrance age will ever enrol in the first grade. In Senegal, for example, the expected net intake rate was 83% in 2010.
- The *survival rate to the last grade* of primary school, which shows the probability that a child who has entered primary school will ever reach the last grade. Reaching the last grade is taken as a proxy for completion because actual graduation records from primary school are not collected in many countries. In Senegal, 60% of those who enrolled in school reached the last grade. Taking account of the expected net intake rate, 49% of current 7-year-olds are expected to complete primary school.

Gross intake to the last grade in Senegal was higher, at 63% in 2011, showing that it can overestimate progress towards completion. An indicator in the spirit of the expected cohort completion rate provides a more accurate picture of completion, and so is more appropriate for measuring progress towards post-2015 goals.

1. This indicator is equal to the number of students of any age in the last grade of primary school (excluding repeaters), divided by the number of children of official graduating age.

expected to enter primary school in 2011. Yet, just four years before 2015, there were still eight countries – all in sub-Saharan Africa, and notably including Nigeria – where at least one-fifth of the children were not expected to enrol in primary school (Figure 1.2.5).

Progression remains an even greater challenge. In 26 of the 90 countries, almost three-quarters of them in sub-Saharan Africa, at least one–fifth of the children who entered school were not expected to reach the last grade. In Uganda, for example, fewer than one in three children were expected to reach the last grade.

Combining the two indicators to measure whether a given group of children will both enter primary school and reach the last grade conveys a sobering message. In only 13 out of the 90 countries with data is it expected that at least 97% of children will both enter primary school and reach the last grade. Of these 13 countries, 10 are OECD or EU members. The other three are Belarus, Kazakhstan and Tajikistan.

These findings raise the question whether assessing progress towards UPE solely on the basis of the net enrolment ratio is sufficient. Among the 70 countries that, in net enrolment ratio terms, were considered to have achieved the target in 2011 or to be close to achieving it, data on the expected cohort completion rate are available for 42. Only 15 of these would be considered to have achieved the target in 2011 or to be close to achieving it if the expected cohort completion rate to the last grade were the criterion.

For some countries, the discrepancy between the two measures is particularly large. For example, Rwanda, with a net enrolment ratio of 99% in 2010, had an expected cohort completion rate of 38% in 2009. Guatemala, with a net enrolment ratio of 98% in 2010, had an expected cohort completion rate of 79% in 2009.

Comparing the experiences of the two sub-Saharan African countries that had the largest out-of-school populations in 1999 shows what can be achieved, with strong political commitment, in improving primary school completion. Ethiopia has made good progress while narrowing inequalities, and though it remains far from the target, it is advancing towards the goal. Nigeria, by contrast, has the world's largest number of children out of school. Its out-of-school population grew by 42% between 1999 and 2010 and it is among the 15 countries that are likely to be off track in 2015. In addition the high level of inequality has remained unchanged (Box 1.2.5).

The contrasting records of two countries in East Asia further show how variable degrees of political commitment to EFA have resulted in different outcomes since 2000: while Indonesia championed access to school and is among the countries that have reached the net enrolment ratio target, the Philippines is far from the target and in danger of going backwards (Box 1.2.6).

As the 2015 deadline for the EFA goals approaches, it is disconcerting to note not only that too many countries are far from the goal, but also that data remain insufficient to enable a full global monitoring of progress towards whether children are accessing, and also completing, primary school. Nor do the available data allow assessment of progress for various population groups. Promising developments in the availability of comparable household surveys offer encouraging signs that this situation could change in the post-2015 era.

Figure 1.2.5: Goal 2 – progress towards universal primary completion is disappointing
Number of countries by level of expected net intake rate, survival rate to the last grade and expected cohort completion rate, 2011 or latest available year

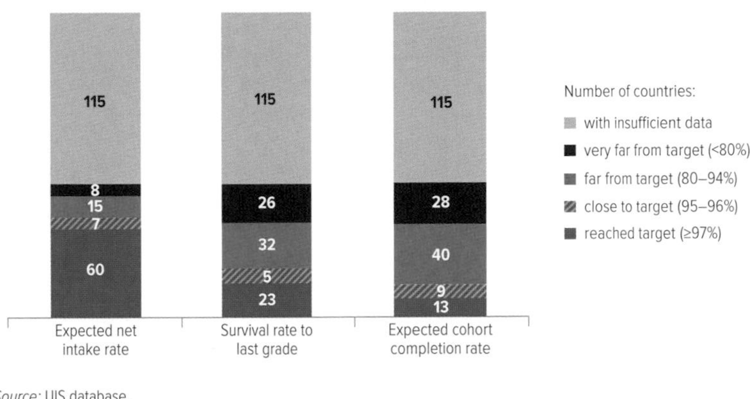

Source: UIS database.

Table 1.2.5: Likelihood of countries achieving a primary enrolment target of at least 95% by 2015

Level expected by 2015		Change between 1999 and 2011: Strong relative progress (15)	Change between 1999 and 2011: Slow progress or moving away from target (31)
Target reached or close (≥95%)	76	Algeria, Aruba, Australia, Bahamas, Belgium, Belize, Bulgaria, Cambodia, Croatia, Cuba, Cyprus, Dominica, Ecuador, Egypt, El Salvador, Estonia, Fiji, Finland, France, Germany, Greece, Grenada, Guatemala, Honduras, Hungary, Iceland, India, Indonesia, Iran (Islamic Republic of), Ireland, Israel, Italy, Japan, Kazakhstan, Kyrgyzstan, Lao People's Democratic Republic, Latvia, Lebanon, Luxembourg, Malawi, Maldives, Mexico, Mongolia, Morocco, Mozambique, Nepal, Netherlands, New Zealand, Nicaragua, Norway, Oman, Panama, Peru, Portugal, Qatar, Republic of Korea, Rwanda, Saint Vincent and the Grenadines, Samoa, Sao Tome and Principe, Slovenia, Spain, Sweden, Switzerland, Syrian Arab Republic, Tajikistan, The former Yugoslav Republic of Macedonia, Trinidad and Tobago, Tunisia, Turkey, United Arab Emirates, United Kingdom, United States, Venezuela (Bolivarian Republic of), Viet Nam, Zambia	
Far from target (80-94%)	31	Bhutan, Ethiopia, Ghana, Guinea, Kenya, Mauritania, Senegal, Yemen	Azerbaijan, Belarus, Bolivia (Plurinational State of), Botswana, British Virgin Islands, Cape Verde, Colombia, Denmark, Dominican Republic, Jordan, Lithuania, Malta, Namibia, Palestine, Paraguay, Philippines, Poland, Republic of Moldova, Romania, Saint Lucia, South Africa, Sri Lanka, Suriname
Very far from target (<80%)	15	Burkina Faso, Djibouti, Eritrea, Lesotho, Mali, Niger, Pakistan	Cayman Islands, Côte d'Ivoire, Equatorial Guinea, Gambia, Jamaica, Liberia, Nigeria, Saint Kitts and Nevis

Countries not included in analysis because of insufficient data	
83	Afghanistan, Albania, Andorra, Angola, Anguilla, Antigua and Barbuda, Argentina, Armenia, Austria, Bahrain, Bangladesh, Barbados, Benin, Bermuda, Bosnia and Herzegovina, Brazil, Brunei Darussalam, Burundi, Cameroon, Canada, Central African Republic, Chad, Chile, China, Comoros, Congo, Cook Islands, Costa Rica, Czech Republic, Democratic People's Republic of Korea, Democratic Republic of the Congo, Gabon, Georgia, Guinea-Bissau, Guyana, Haiti, Iraq, Kiribati, Kuwait, Libya, Macao (China), Madagascar, Malaysia, Marshall Islands, Mauritius, Micronesia (Federated States of), Monaco, Montenegro, Montserrat, Myanmar, Nauru, Netherlands Antilles, Niue, Palau, Papua New Guinea, Russian Federation, San Marino, Saudi Arabia, Serbia, Seychelles, Sierra Leone, Singapore, Slovakia, Solomon Islands, Somalia, South Sudan, Sudan, Swaziland, Thailand, Timor-Leste, Togo, Tokelau, Tonga, Turkmenistan, Turks and Caicos Islands, Tuvalu, Uganda, Ukraine, United Republic of Tanzania, Uruguay, Uzbekistan, Vanuatu, Zimbabwe

Source: Bruneforth (2013).

Box 1.2.5: The contrasting education fortunes of Ethiopia and Nigeria

The education experience of the 2000s for the two most populous countries of sub-Saharan Africa could not have been more different. It was a lost decade for Nigeria in terms of educational development. Despite the optimism generated by the restoration of democracy in 1999 and the introduction of the Universal Basic Education Law in 2004, the percentage of children out of school showed no improvement. By contrast, Ethiopia made major advances, with the number of children out of school falling by three-quarters between 1999 and 2011. While major challenges remain, the reforms that Ethiopia has put in place suggest that continued progress should be possible.

Household survey data confirm this divergent picture. Between 1998 and 2008, the share of children who had not completed primary school remained at about 29% in Nigeria (Figure 1.2.6). The gap between the country's two most populous areas hardly changed, with the rate of non-completers six times higher in the North-west than in the South-west. The gender gap within the two regions did not change either. As a result, 70% of young women in the North-west have not completed primary school.

By contrast, Ethiopia witnessed improvement, albeit from a low base. In 2000, 82% of children had not completed primary school, falling to 60% by 2011. While there are still fewer benefiting from education than in Nigeria, on average, it is notable that inequalities have narrowed while progress has been made overall. The gap in primary school completion between Addis Ababa and the Somali region fell from 63 to 49 percentage points. Given that there has been a large reduction in the percentage of children who have never been to school in the Somali region (from 84% in 2000 to 37% in 2011), this gap is expected to fall even further in coming years.

Since Ethiopia became a federal republic in 1994, its central government has been effective both in exercising its coordinating function and in promoting policy decisions. It more than doubled the share of the budget allocated to education between 2000 and 2010, to 25%. These resources were used to fund rapid classroom construction and teacher recruitment. At the same time, the government ambitiously devolved power to the regions and districts, while closely monitoring results in the delivery of education and other social services. An analysis of almost 200 urban and rural districts in the Oromiya region and the Southern Nations, Nationalities and People's Region showed that the introduction of formula-based funding led to declines in inequality between districts not only in terms of funding per student but also in terms of enrolment outcomes.

In Nigeria, the federal government has less control over the states. The absence of data on the share of the budget spent on education since 1999 is one sign of poor accountability. An attempt to track whether schools in Kaduna and Enugu states received allocated resources revealed that, for most basic inputs, including maintenance, textbooks and in-service training, there were not even any norms as to what each school should receive.

Sources: Garcia and Rajkumar (2008); Nigeria National Bureau of Statistics et al. (2013); World Bank (2008b).

Figure 1.2.6: Ethiopia has made progress in primary education while Nigeria has stagnated
Percentage of children who have not completed primary school, by gender and selected regions, Ethiopia 2000–2011 and Nigeria 1999–2008

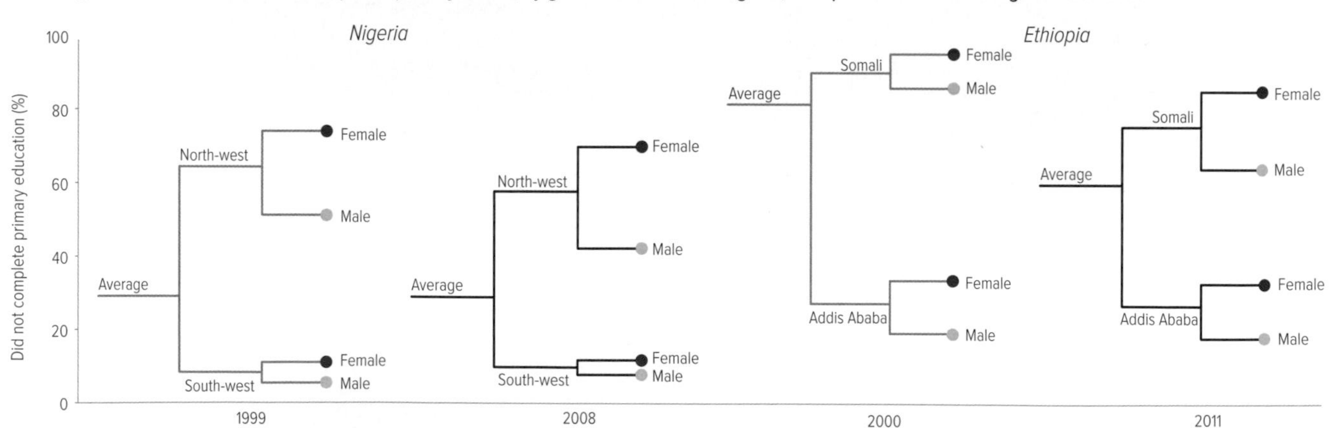

Source: EFA Global Monitoring Report team analysis (2013), based on Demographic and Health Survey data.

Box 1.2.6: The cost of delaying action for disadvantaged children – the diverging paths of Indonesia and the Philippines

The Philippines is one of 14 countries estimated to have more than 1 million out-of-school children and also one where there has been lack of progress towards UPE. By contrast, Indonesia managed to reduce its out-of-school population by 84% between 2000 and 2011.

Evidence from household surveys shows, moreover, that inequality gaps in the Philippines have remained wide. The percentage of young people who had not completed primary education slightly increased in the Philippines over 1998–2008, from 11% to 13%, with inequalities between the poorest and richest and between young men and young women remaining entrenched. In Indonesia, the percentage of youth who had not completed primary education almost halved over a similar period, 1997–2007, from 14% to 8%, while gender inequalities remained narrow (Figure 1.2.7).

Whether children in the Philippines have a chance of attending school depends strongly on where they live. In the Autonomous Region of Muslim Mindanao, which continues to suffer from conflict, 21% of primary school age children were not in school in 2008 – more than twice the national average of 9%. The share of national income invested in education, which equalled the subregional average in 1999, had fallen behind by 2009 at 2.7% of GNP, compared with an average of 3.2% for East Asia.

Indonesia, for its part, showed strong political will towards education reform. After the 1997/98 financial crisis, the country embarked on an ambitious set of reforms regarding decentralization, social protection and education, which all contributed towards the improvement of educational outcomes. Since 2005, the School Operational Assistance programme has provided grants to schools to cover their running costs so they do not have to charge fees.

In 2009, the central government fulfilled a constitutional commitment to allocate 20% of its budget to education. The increase in resources has resulted in an overhaul of the scholarship system for poor students, which was insufficient, poorly targeted and not timed well enough to prevent dropout in the last grade of primary school. The reform will improve the targeting mechanism, increase the scholarship amount and modernize the administration to ensure that households are paid in time.

Sources: Albert et al. (2012); Chaudhury et al. (2013); Indonesia National Development Planning Agency et al. (2012); Satriawan (2013); World Bank (2013e).

Figure 1.2.7: Indonesia has moved much faster than the Philippines towards universal primary education
Percentage of young people who have not completed primary school, by gender and wealth, Indonesia 1997–2007 and the Philippines 1998–2008

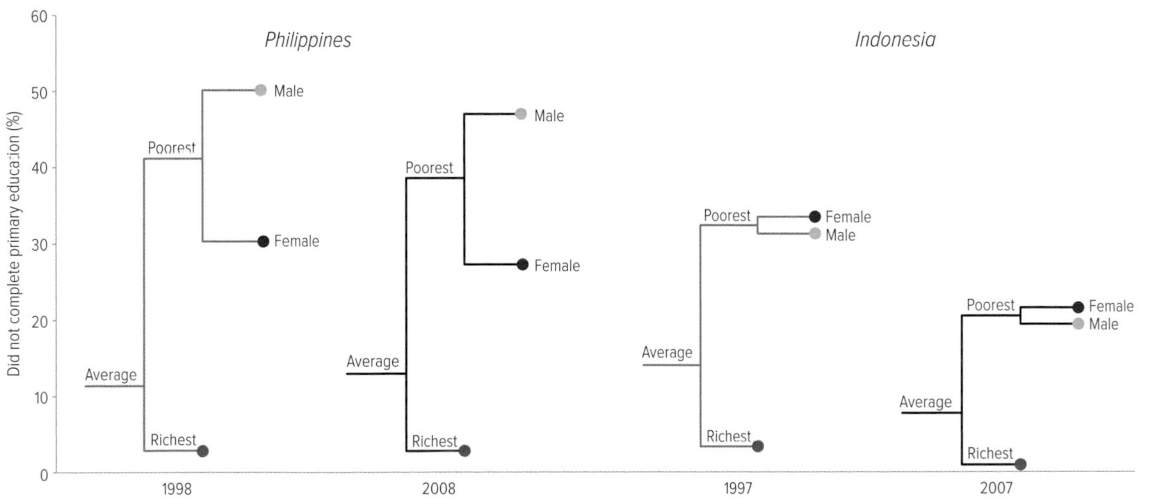

Source: EFA Global Monitoring Report team analysis (2013), based on Demographic and Health Survey data.

Goal 3 Youth and adult skills

Ensuring that the learning needs of all young people and adults are met through equitable access to appropriate learning and life skills programmes.

Highlights

- Participation in lower secondary education increased from 72% in 1999 to 82% in 2011. The fastest growth was in sub-Saharan Africa, where enrolment more than doubled, albeit from a low base, reaching 49% in 2011.
- Progress in completing lower secondary school – a prerequisite for acquiring the foundation skills necessary for decent jobs – has been more modest, with little improvement in low income countries, where just 37% of adolescents complete that level. Among adolescents from poor families in these countries, completion rates are as low as 14%.
- The number of adolescents out of school stood at 69 million in 2011. While this constituted a reduction of 31% since 1999, most of the improvement had been achieved by 2004. In sub-Saharan Africa, the number of adolescents out of school remained at 22 million between 1999 and 2011, as population growth cancelled out any improvement in enrolment growth.
- Of the 82 countries with data, 38 are expected to achieve universal lower secondary enrolment by 2015. But three-quarters of the countries in sub-Saharan Africa are not included among these 82 countries. Given most of these countries have not yet achieved universal primary completion, it is extremely unlikely that they will achieve universal lower secondary education by 2015.
- Across 19 high income countries around half of young people have poor problem-solving skills in part due to too low upper-secondary completion.

Table 1.3.1: Key indicators for goal 3

	Total secondary enrolment		Lower secondary gross enrolment ratio		Upper secondary gross enrolment ratio		Technical and vocational education as a share of secondary enrolment		Out-of-school adolescents of lower secondary school age		
	2011 (000)	Change since 1999 (%)	1999 (%)	2011 (%)	1999 (%)	2011 (%)	1999 (%)	2011 (%)	2011 (000)	Change since 1999 (%)	Female (%)
World	**543 226**	**25**	**72**	**82**	**45**	**59**	**11**	**11**	**69 413**	**-31**	**49**
Low income countries	49 393	83	36	54	23	31	5	5	18 435	-13	51
Lower middle income countries	203 179	48	61	77	31	48	5	5	42 359	-25	53
Upper middle income countries	205 015	11	88	96	52	75	13	16	7 810	-65	30
High income countries	85 640	-2	102	105	97	100	17	14	809	-52	39
Sub-Saharan Africa	46 282	114	29	49	21	32	8	8	21 832	-1	55
Arab States	30 726	37	73	88	44	52	14	9	3 757	-31	56
Central Asia	10 288	12	85	97	81	102	6	13	397	-56	57
East Asia and the Pacific	159 783	22	78	90	44	70	15	17	8 944	-64	33
South and West Asia	144 402	48	61	76	30	47	1	2	31 277	-21	50
Latin America and the Caribbean	60 525	15	95	102	62	77	10	10	1 494	-55	49
North America and Western Europe	61 433	1	102	106	97	99	14	14	583	-50	35
Central and Eastern Europe	29 787	-27	92	95	82	83	18	21	1 129	-68	48

Sources: Annex, Statistical Table 7 (print) and Statistical Table 8 (website); UIS database.

The 2012 *EFA Global Monitoring Report* put a spotlight on goal 3, which has been one of the most neglected EFA goals in part because no targets or indicators were set for its monitoring. To address this shortcoming, the 2012 Report proposed a framework for the various types of skills as a way of improving monitoring efforts. While highlighting some promising initiatives, the 2012 Report recognized that the international community was still a long way from measuring systematically the provision of skills-oriented programmes and the acquisition of skills, so monitoring progress on goal 3 is likely to remain challenging.

The framework emphasizes the crucial importance of foundation skills, including literacy and numeracy, which are essential for meeting daily needs, succeeding in the world of work and acquiring transferable skills and technical and vocational skills. While there are other pathways young people can take to acquire foundation skills, the most effective is lower secondary schooling, hence the calls for universal completion of lower secondary school to be a goal in the post-2015 framework. The global lower secondary gross enrolment ratio increased from 72% in 1999 to 82% in 2011. The largest increase was in sub-Saharan Africa, where the number of students more than doubled, although the share reaching this level was still only 49%.

Analysis by the EFA Global Monitoring Report team of household surveys shows that completion rates are significantly lower than these enrolment ratios suggest. In low income countries, completion rates increased from 27% in the early 2000s to 37% in the late 2000s. Moreover, almost all the increase was recorded among the richest fifth of the population, where the rates rose from 53% to 61%, while completion rates among the poorest increased from 11% to 14% (Figure 1.3.1). Similar patterns of stagnation for the poorest groups are apparent in countries in sub-Saharan Africa (Box 1.3.1).

In low income countries, completion rates among the poorest reached just 14% in 2010

Figure 1.3.1: Inequality in lower secondary completion is growing in poorer countries
Lower secondary school completion rate by wealth and gender, selected countries, 1997–2000 and 2007–2011

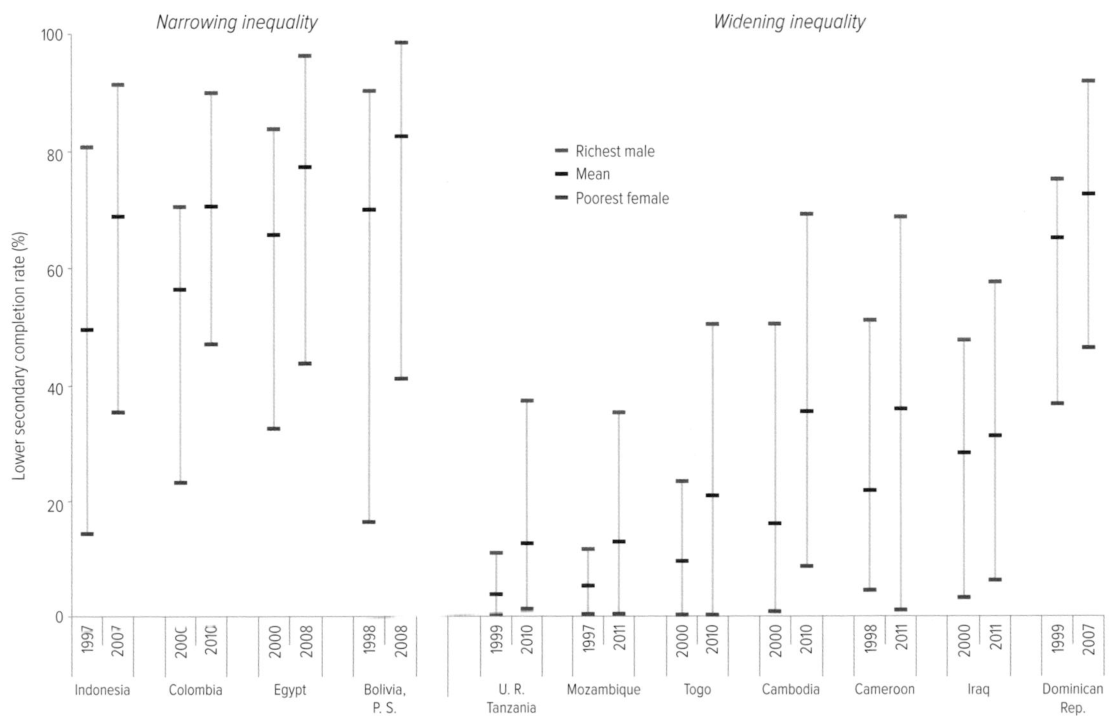

Source: EFA Global Monitoring Report team analysis (2013), based on Demographic and Health Surveys and Multiple Indicator Cluster Surveys.

Box 1.3.1: In sub-Saharan Africa, far too few young people complete lower secondary school

Many countries in sub-Saharan Africa have expanded access to lower secondary school, but it will take more time and effort to translate these gains into higher completion rates. The poorest, in particular, appear not to be benefiting from current policies. In cash-strapped secondary education systems, unplanned growth in private schooling appears to be excluding many of the continent's more disadvantaged adolescents.

Enrolment data from the education ministries in Rwanda and Malawi show the divergent paths countries can take. Rwanda has carried out a major expansion of lower secondary schooling, with the gross enrolment ratio quadrupling in about 10 years to reach 47% in 2011, overtaking Malawi, where the ratio hovered around 40% for most of the decade (Figure 1.3.2).

Information collected from households, however, shows that completion rates remain low in both countries. Between 2000 and 2010, the lower secondary school completion rate increased from 9% to 15% in Rwanda and from 16% to 25% in Malawi (Figure 1.3.2). It is of particular concern that in both countries completion is extremely inequitable, with fewer than 5% of poor, rural girls completing lower secondary school. This is partly because poorer households are obliged to spend a high share of their income to educate their children (see Chapter 2).

The approaches the two countries have taken towards expanding access to lower secondary education differ, however, and Rwanda's could improve completion rates in coming years. In 2006, Rwanda extended basic education from six to nine years, through to lower secondary level, and abolished fees for the entire cycle. In 2009, it also removed the obstacle of the primary completion examination. The share of private enrolment in lower secondary education decreased from 43% in 2001/02 to 27% in 2008.

In Malawi, by contrast, expansion of lower secondary schooling has remained limited, even though a universal primary education programme in the 1990s increased demand for secondary education. Enrolment has increased only in private schools, whose share of total secondary enrolment rose from 13% in 2001 to 23% in 2007.

Because supply has not kept pace with demand, a highly selective system has developed. Only the students who perform best in an examination at the end of primary school enter higher quality government secondary schools. Those who do not pass the exam, but can afford the cost of private school, take that option. The vast majority, however, have to settle for community day secondary schools, which are widely considered to be of poor quality. As a result, adolescents in these schools are likely to drop out or have poor learning outcomes.

Sources: Chiche (2010); de Hoop (2011); World Bank (2010, 2011).

Figure 1.3.2: Completion of lower secondary school remains elusive for many adolescents in Malawi and Rwanda

Lower secondary gross enrolment ratios and completion rates, Malawi and Rwanda, 2000–2010

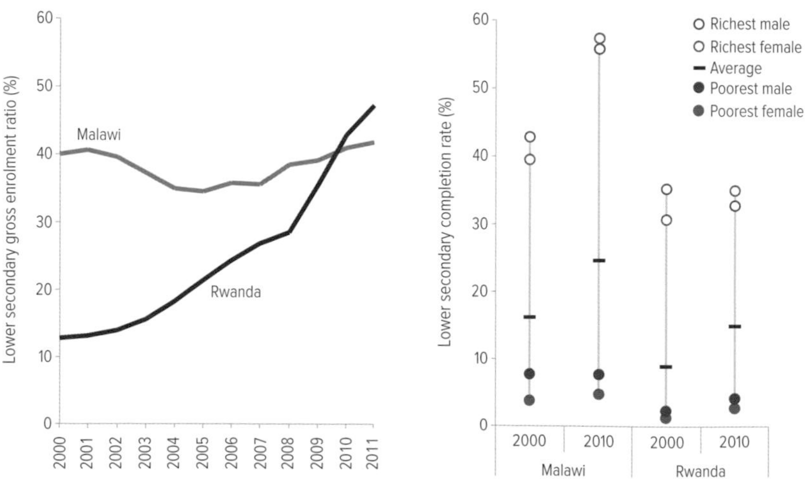

Note: The completion rate has been calculated for people aged 18 to 22.
Sources: Gross enrolment ratio: UIS database; Completion rate: EFA Global Monitoring Report team calculations (2013), based on Demographic and Health Survey data.

There is wide inequality between population groups in lower secondary completion. In poorer countries, only the most advantaged have benefited from progress. In Mozambique and the United Republic of Tanzania, for example, almost no young women from the poorest families completed lower secondary school in 2010/2011. By contrast, young men from the richest families more than tripled their completion rates, to over 35%, between the late 1990s and 2010/2011. This pattern is also apparent in middle income countries, such as the Dominican Republic and Iraq. In some countries, while poorer adolescents have benefited from progress, wide gaps remain: in Indonesia, lower secondary school completion increased from 81% to 92% for the richest males and from 15% to 36% for the poorest females (Figure 1.3.1).

Another measure of progress towards goal 3, the number of adolescents of lower secondary school age who are out of school, also shows that advances have been limited. While the number has fallen since 1999 by 31% to 69 million in 2011, progress has all but stagnated since 2007. Moreover, the reduction has been much more modest than for primary school age children (Figure 1.3.3). As a result, many young people have been denied a lower secondary education and so need access to second-chance programmes to acquire foundation skills.

South and West Asia has made great strides in reducing the number of primary school age children out of school, but progress has been slower for adolescents with progress achieved only up to 2004. The region's share of the global number of out-of-school adolescents increased from 39% in 1999 to 45% in 2011. In sub-Saharan Africa, 22 million adolescents remained out of school over the entire period. Any progress in enrolment has been cancelled by the 33% increase in the population of this age group since 1999.

Transferable skills are acquired at all education levels. But upper secondary education has a distinct role in instilling such skills (Box 1.3.2). The global upper secondary gross enrolment ratio increased from 45% in 1999 to 59% in 2011. The largest increase was in East Asia and the Pacific, where the ratio increased from 44% to 70%. In absolute terms, the largest expansion took place in sub-Saharan Africa, where the number of students doubled over the period, although the region's enrolment ratio had only reached 32% by 2011.

Data sources are fragmented for technical and vocational skills. While this kind of knowledge is often best acquired on the job, for instance in apprenticeship programmes, no systematic information on such programmes currently exists. The information that is available indicates that the share of technical and vocational education in total secondary education enrolment has remained constant at 11% since 1999, with relatively small variations in regional trends, such as a decline in the proportion of enrolment in technical and vocational education in the Arab States. Governments around the world need to pay more attention to improving the quality of these programmes and ensuring their relevance to the world of work.

In sub-Saharan Africa, 22 million adolescents remained out of school between 1999 and 2011

Figure 1.3.3: The number of adolescents out of school has hardly fallen since 2007

Out-of-school adolescents, by region, 1999 to 2011

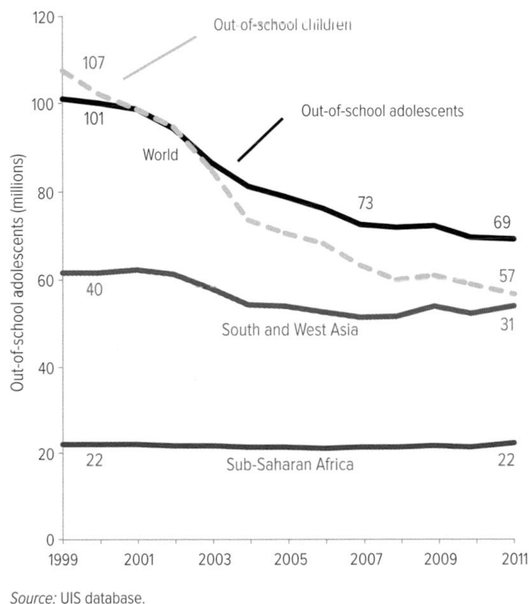

Source: UIS database.

Box 1.3.2: Upper secondary education is key to acquiring transferable skills

Transferable skills, such as problem-solving, are vital for adapting knowledge to different work contexts, but there have been few attempts to measure how many people have acquired such skills.

One important step towards filling this gap is the OECD's Programme for the International Assessment of Adult Competencies (PIAAC). The results of the 2011 PIAAC survey confirm that upper secondary education is a vital way of improving transferable skills such as analysing information. Another key finding of the survey is that low literacy, associated with lower educational attainment, is as much of a barrier to effective engagement in the online world as lack of basic information and communication (ICT) skills. The digital divide may therefore also be a literacy divide.

Twenty-four countries participated in the 2011 PIAAC survey, which assessed the literacy, numeracy and problem-solving skills of 16- to 65-year-olds. It also collected information on the acquisition of problem-solving skills in technology-rich environments.

Across the 19 high income countries and regions where problem-solving skills in technology-rich environments were surveyed, 51% of those aged 16 to 24 were proficient at the two highest levels (2 and 3). At these levels of proficiency, individuals are typically able to solve problems involving several steps, evaluate the relevance of information and use several computer applications.

This leaves around half of young adults with low levels of such skills. These young adults are at most able to use familiar applications to solve problems that involve few steps and explicit criteria, such as sorting e-mails into pre-existing folders.

Proficiency in problem-solving in technology-rich environments among young adults is strongly associated with literacy skills. On average, moving from level 1 to level 2 in terms of performance in problem-solving skills is associated with an increase in the PIAAC literacy score from 264 to 300 points. This is equivalent to the difference in literacy skills between a person who can only draw lower level inferences from a text compared with a person who can interpret information from different sources (Figure 1.3.4).

Proficiency in problem-solving in technology-rich environments is also associated with the level of education completed. Nearly 47% of 16- to 24-year-olds who had not completed upper secondary education scored at level 1 or below, compared with 39% of those who had completed upper secondary education. In England and Northern Ireland (United Kingdom) 88% of those who had not completed upper secondary education scored at or below this minimum benchmark, compared with 54% of those who had completed it.

The PIAAC results show that countries need a more effective mix of policies and practices aimed at developing the skills necessary to manage information in digital environments. Policies should ensure that young people have solid foundation skills in literacy and numeracy, and that access to upper secondary education is expanded. In economies and societies in which access to resources and information is increasingly governed by digital ability, poor problem-solving skills increase chances of exclusion in the job market and other areas of life.

Figure 1.3.4: Literacy is crucial to developing ICT skills
Mean scores of 16- to 24-year-olds on the literacy scale, by level of proficiency in problem-solving in technology-rich environments, PIAAC, 2011

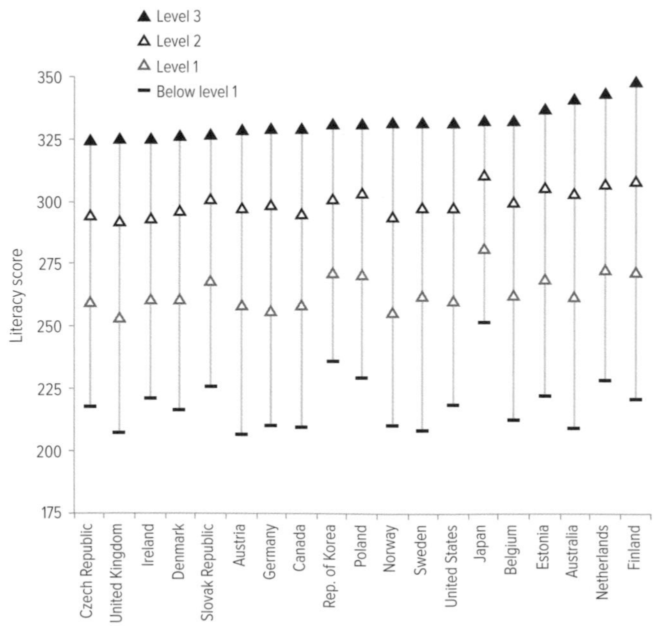

Notes: A literacy score between 225 and 275 points means respondents could paraphrase or draw low level inferences from the text. A score between 275 and 325 points means respondents could identify, interpret, or evaluate one or more pieces of information that required varying levels of inference and where competing information was often present.
The UK data refer to England and Northern Ireland. The Belgian data refer to Flanders.
Source: OECD (2013c).

How many countries are likely to achieve universal lower secondary education by 2015?

No clear target was set in 2000 to guide an assessment of global success in promoting skills development and, at that time, universal lower secondary education was not an explicit goal. Since it is likely to become one after 2015, it is vital to assess where the world may stand in 2015.

The lower secondary school completion rate would be an appropriate indicator to measure progress, but data are lacking. The adjusted net enrolment ratio for lower secondary school age adolescents is a second-best indicator which has information on trends for just 82 countries.

Figure 1.3.5: Goal 3 – of 82 countries with data, less than half will achieve universal lower secondary education by 2015

Number of countries by level of adjusted net enrolment ratio for lower secondary education, 1999, 2011 and 2015 (projected)

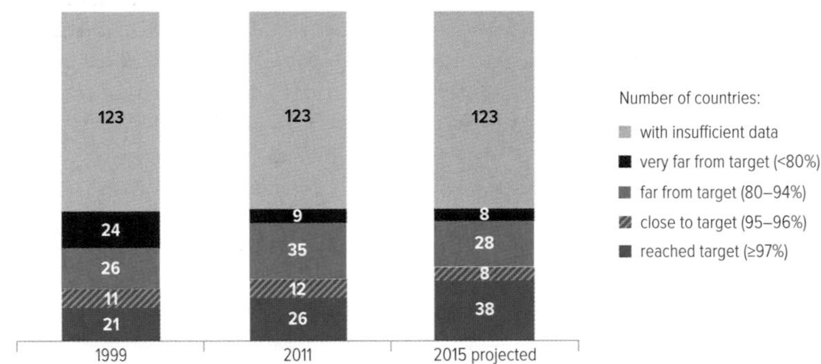

Note: The analysis was conducted on the subset of countries for which a projection was possible; therefore, it covers fewer countries than those for which information is available for either 1999 or 2011.
Source: Bruneforth (2013).

Of the 82 countries, 21 had an adjusted net enrolment ratio above 97% in 1999, and 11 were close. By 2011, 26 countries had reached the target and 12 were close. By 2015, the number of countries meeting the target is expected to grow to 38, with 8 countries close (Figure 1.3.5).

The number of countries furthest from the target, with a ratio below 80%, fell from 24 in 1999 to 9 in 2011. Of the countries that moved out of this group, Oman and Turkey have achieved the target of 97% enrolment, while Tajikistan has come close. By 2015, 8 countries are likely to have net enrolment below 80% – 7 in sub-Saharan Africa plus the Lao People's Democratic Republic – and 28 countries are expected to remain far from the target with net enrolment between 80% and 95% (Table 1.3.2).

While many countries will not have met the target of universal lower secondary net enrolment by 2015, assessing how quickly countries have moved towards the target indicates how soon they may achieve it. Of the 56 countries that had not reached the target by 2011, 14 made strong progress, increasing their net enrolment ratio by at least 15% since 1999. Eleven countries expanded access by more than 20 percentage points, including Ecuador (from 72% to 93%), Ghana (from 62% to 83%) and Indonesia (from 65% to 89%). The net enrolment ratio increased for all countries with data in Central America, including El Salvador, Guatemala, Nicaragua and Panama (Box 1.3.3).

This assessment is based on information from only 40% of all countries. It includes two-thirds of the countries in North America and Western Europe but only a quarter of sub-Saharan African countries, some of which are unlikely to have achieved universal lower primary education so will not be in a position to achieve universal secondary schooling.

After 2015, it will be vital to set a target for lower secondary education. In order to monitor progress towards such a goal, more comprehensive data will be needed on access to and completion of lower secondary education.

Between 1999 and 2011, Ecuador, Ghana and Indonesia rapidly expanded access to lower secondary school

Box 1.3.3: Latin America has made good progress in secondary education, but wide inequality remains

Secondary education has expanded in Latin America over the past decade, although at only half the speed of the previous decade. By 2011, the net enrolment ratio had reached 77%. In general, the countries that lagged behind were those that expanded secondary education fastest over the decade. Among the countries that had the lowest enrolment ratios in 1999, Ecuador and Guatemala's ratios improved faster, while Paraguay's increased more slowly.

Regardless of the speed of progress, household surveys show that the education systems of the three countries are still characterized by high levels of inequality. Ecuador appears to have made greater strides towards narrowing inequality gaps. Its gap in the secondary net attendance ratio between urban and rural males fell from 32 percentage points in 2001 to 13 percentage points in 2011. The gap between urban and rural youth fell more slowly in Paraguay, while it hardly changed in Guatemala, with the result that inequality there remained very high: only 28% of rural females attended secondary school compared to 62% of urban females in 2011 (Figure 1.3.6).

What explains this divergent performance in expanding secondary education? One factor is differences in spending priorities. Public education expenditure as a share of GNP almost tripled in Ecuador, from 2% in 1999 to 5.3% in 2011, while it fell in Paraguay from 5.1% in 1999 to 4.2% in 2010, the largest absolute decline in the subregion.

Another reason for the divergent performance is that the three countries have differed in the success of their policy approaches. In Ecuador, the Bono de Desarrollo Humano cash transfer programme, introduced in 2003, was conditional on school attendance. An evaluation at an early stage of implementation showed that the programme was having a positive effect on school attendance among children aged 6 to 17. The level of the transfer more than doubled in the second half of the decade. By 2010, it provided 44% of the beneficiaries' income. While the effects of this change have not yet been evaluated, the acceleration in the growth of enrolment after 2006 is likely to be related to the increasing availability of income to poor households.

In Guatemala, part of the increase in secondary enrolment is explained by the introduction of distance education programmes previously implemented on a large scale in Mexico. The country is however a latecomer to the social policy revolution that has taken place in many countries in the region. A major conditional cash transfer programme, Mi Familia Progresa, was introduced in 2008 and expanded rapidly to cover 23% of the population within two years. However, in 2011 it provided only 9% of beneficiaries' income, much lower than the average in the region.

In Paraguay, the main government intervention at the lower secondary level is the second phase of the Escuela Viva programme. As a means of increasing retention and learning outcomes, it aims to improve participation in school management by training stakeholders to identify school needs and then develop, implement and monitor a school improvement plan. In addition, it provides transport subsidies, scholarships and boarding school arrangements. However, the expected results are relatively modest: from a baseline of 15% in 2005, the target is to raise the lower secondary completion rate in a thousand targeted rural schools to 25% by 2014.

Since 2005, Paraguay has also had a cash transfer programme, Tekoporã, which is targeted at the poorest households in the poorest districts and is conditional on children attending school. An evaluation at the pilot stage found that it had a positive effect on school attendance. However, the level of the transfer was low, and coverage was limited until it increased in 2009. Overall, the social policies of the government, including education transfers in kind, achieved one of the lowest income redistribution rates in the sub-region in 2010, reducing inequality by only 3.5%, compared with 15% in Mexico and 19% in Brazil. Social protection policies need to be enhanced if they are to produce a stronger effect on enrolment in secondary education.

Sources: Higgins et al. (2013); Inter-American Development Bank (2007, 2013); Ponce (2010, 2011); PREAL and Instituto Desarollo (2013); SITEAL (2013a, 2013b); Stampini and Tornarolli (2012); Teixeira et al. (2011).

Figure 1.3.6: In Latin America, inequalities in secondary education remain
Secondary education net attendance rate, by gender and location, Ecuador, Guatemala and Paraguay, 2000–2011

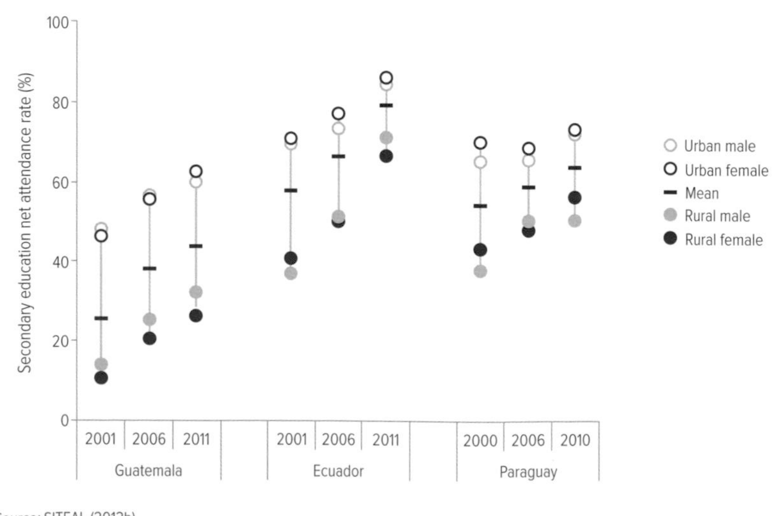

Source: SITEAL (2013b).

Table 1.3.2: Likelihood of countries achieving a lower secondary education net enrolment target of at least 95% by 2015

<table>
<tr><td rowspan="3">Level expected by 2015</td><td>Target reached or close (≥95%) 46</td><td colspan="2">Bahamas, Belarus, Botswana, Colombia, Croatia, Cyprus, Denmark, Dominica, Estonia, Fiji, Finland, France, Greece, Hungary, Iceland, Ireland, Israel, Italy, Japan, Kazakhstan, Kenya, Luxembourg, Mexico, Mongolia, Netherlands, Norway, Oman, Peru, Philippines, Qatar, Republic of Korea, Romania, Saint Kitts and Nevis, Saint Lucia, Saint Vincent and the Grenadines, Samoa, Seychelles, Slovenia, Spain, Switzerland, Syrian Arab Republic, Tajikistan, Turkey, United Kingdom, United States, Venezuela (Bolivarian Republic of)</td></tr>
<tr><td>Far from target (80-94%) 28</td><td>Bhutan, Dominican Republic, Ecuador, El Salvador, Ghana, Guatemala, Indonesia, Nicaragua, Panama</td><td>Aruba, Azerbaijan, Barbados, Bolivia (Plurinational State of), Bulgaria, Cayman Islands, Cook Islands, Cuba, Jamaica, Jordan, Lithuania, Malawi, Malaysia, Palestine, Paraguay, Poland, Republic of Moldova, Sweden, Trinidad and Tobago</td></tr>
<tr><td>Very far from target (<80%) 8</td><td>Burkina Faso, Ethiopia, Guinea, Mozambique, Niger</td><td>Eritrea, Lao People's Democratic Republic, Lesotho</td></tr>
<tr><td></td><td></td><td>Strong relative progress 14</td><td>Slow progress or moving away from target 22</td></tr>
<tr><td></td><td></td><td colspan="2">Change between 1999 and 2011</td></tr>
</table>

Countries not included in analysis because of insufficient data 123	Afghanistan, Albania, Algeria, Andorra, Angola, Anguilla, Antigua and Barbuda, Argentina, Armenia, Australia, Austria, Bahrain, Bangladesh, Belgium, Belize, Benin, Bermuda, Bosnia and Herzegovina, Brazil, British Virgin Islands, Brunei Darussalam, Burundi, Cambodia, Cameroon, Canada, Cape Verde, Central African Republic, Chad, Chile, China, Comoros, Congo, Costa Rica, Côte d'Ivoire, Czech Republic, Democratic People's Republic of Korea, Democratic Republic of the Congo, Djibouti, Egypt, Equatorial Guinea, Gabon, Gambia, Georgia, Germany, Grenada, Guinea-Bissau, Guyana, Haiti, Honduras, India, Iran (Islamic Republic of), Iraq, Kiribati, Kuwait, Kyrgyzstan, Latvia, Lebanon, Liberia, Libya, Macao (China), Madagascar, Maldives, Mali, Malta, Marshall Islands, Mauritania, Mauritius, Micronesia (Federated States of), Monaco, Montenegro, Montserrat, Morocco, Myanmar, Namibia, Nauru, Nepal, Netherlands Antilles, New Zealand, Nigeria, Niue, Pakistan, Palau, Papua New Guinea, Portugal, Russian Federation, Rwanda, San Marino, Sao Tome and Principe, Saudi Arabia, Senegal, Serbia, Sierra Leone, Singapore, Slovakia, Solomon Islands, Somalia, South Africa, South Sudan, Sri Lanka, Sudan, Suriname, Swaziland, Thailand, The former Yugoslav Republic of Macedonia, Timor-Leste, Togo, Tokelau, Tonga, Tunisia, Turkmenistan, Turks and Caicos Islands, Tuvalu, Uganda, Ukraine, United Arab Emirates, United Republic of Tanzania, Uruguay, Uzbekistan, Vanuatu, Viet Nam, Yemen, Zambia, Zimbabwe

Source: Bruneforth (2013).

Goal 4 Adult literacy

Achieving a 50% improvement in levels of adult literacy by 2015, especially for women, and equitable access to basic and continuing education for all adults.

Highlights

- The adult illiteracy rate fell from 24% in 1990 to 18% in 2000 and 16% in 2011. However, the number of illiterate adults remains stubbornly high at 774 million, a fall of 12% since 1990 but just 1% since 2000.
- In sub-Saharan Africa, the number of illiterate adults has increased by 37% since 1990, mainly as a result of population growth. This region, together with South and West Asia, accounts for three-quarters of the global population of illiterate adults.
- The number of illiterate adults is projected only to fall to 743 million by 2015. In 32 out of 89 countries, the adult literacy rate will still be below 80%.
- Almost two-thirds of illiterate adults are women. Only half of the 61 countries with data for the beginning and end of the decade are expected to achieve gender parity in adult literacy by 2015.
- West African countries account for 44% of illiterate young people in sub-Saharan Africa. Household survey data suggest that in 12 of 15 West African countries fewer than half of young women are literate, which means the quest for universal youth literacy will continue for at least another generation.

Table 1.4.1: Key indicators for goal 4

	Illiterate adults				Adult literacy rates				Youth literacy rates			
	Total		Women		Total		Gender parity index		Total		Gender parity index	
	2005–2011 (000)	Change since 1985–1994 (%)	1985–1994 (%)	2005–2011 (%)	1985–1994 (%)	2005–2011 (%)	1985–1994 (F/M)	2005–2011 (F/M)	1985–1994 (%)	2005–2011 (%)	1985–1994 (F/M)	2005–2011 (F/M)
World	**773 549**	**-12**	**63**	**64**	**76**	**84**	**0.85**	**0.90**	**83**	**89**	**0.90**	**0.94**
Low income countries	183 552	23	60	60	51	61	0.69	0.79	60	73	0.79	0.90
Lower middle income countries	470 164	2	61	65	59	71	0.71	0.78	71	84	0.80	0.88
Upper middle income countries	112 671	-57	67	67	82	94	0.86	0.96	94	99	0.96	1.00
High income countries	...	...	...	...	...	...	...	...	...	...	...	...
Sub-Saharan Africa	181 950	37	62	61	53	59	0.68	0.74	66	70	0.80	0.84
Arab States	47 603	-8	63	66	55	77	0.62	0.81	74	90	0.78	0.93
Central Asia	290	-69	77	63	98	100	0.98	1.00	100	100	1.00	1.00
East Asia and the Pacific	89 478	-61	69	71	82	95	0.84	0.95	95	99	0.96	1.00
South and West Asia	407 021	2	60	64	47	63	0.57	0.70	60	81	0.70	0.86
Latin America and the Caribbean	35 614	-16	55	55	86	92	0.97	0.99	93	97	1.01	1.01
North America and Western Europe	...	...	...	...	...	...	...	...	...	...	...	...
Central and Eastern Europe	4 919	-59	79	78	96	99	0.96	0.99	98	99	0.98	1.00

Notes: Data are for the most recent year available during the period specified. Gender parity is reached when the gender parity index is between 0.97 and 1.03.
Sources: Annex, Statistical Table 2; UIS database.

Universal literacy is fundamental to social and economic progress. Literacy skills are best developed in childhood through good quality education. Few countries have been able to build robust adult education institutions that offer genuine second chances to the majority of illiterate adults. As a result, countries with a legacy of low access to school have so far been unable to eradicate illiteracy among youth and adults.

The number of illiterate adults is estimated to have fallen by 12%, from 880 million in the period 1985–1994 to 774 million in the period 2005–2011. The pace of decline has slowed considerably. Almost all the decline took place in the 1990s. Since 2000 the number of illiterate adults fell by only 1%. In relative terms, the adult illiteracy rate fell from 24% in the earlier period to 16% in the later period. It is projected to fall further to 14% by 2015.

Women make up nearly two-thirds of the total, and since 1990 there has been no progress in reducing this share. Of the 61 countries with data on gender parity in adult literacy for the beginning and end of the decade, 22 were already at parity at the beginning and 6 have achieved it since. It is projected that only 2 more countries will reach parity by 2015, although 10 will be within 2 percentage points from parity.

Since 1990, adult literacy rates have risen fastest in the Arab States, from 55% to 77%. Nevertheless, as a result of population growth, the actual number of illiterate adults has only fallen from 52 million to 48 million. South and West Asia and sub-Saharan Africa account for 76% of the global population of illiterate adults, up from 61% in 1990.

South and West Asia has experienced the second fastest increase in adult literacy rates (from 47% to 63%). Yet it has seen its population of illiterate adults remain stable at just over 400 million. As a result, the region accounts for a higher share of the global population of illiterate adults now (53%) than in 1990 (46%).

In sub-Saharan Africa, where the adult literacy rate has only increased from 53% to 59% since 1990, the actual number of illiterate adults has grown by 37% to 182 million in 2011. By 2015, it is projected that 26% of the world's illiterate adults will live in sub-Saharan Africa, up from 15% in 1990.

In order to move towards universal adult literacy, youth literacy rates need to improve. Globally, the youth literacy rate stands at 89%, 5 percentage points higher than the literacy rate of the entire adult population. In the Arab States, the youth literacy rate of 90% exceeds the adult literacy rate by 13 percentage points. In sub-Saharan Africa, the youth literacy rate exceeds the adult literacy rate by 11 percentage points (70% versus 59%). In Mozambique the difference is 17 percentage points (67% versus 51%). However, in Angola it is only 3 percentage points (73% versus 70%), indicating that universal adult literacy is unlikely to be achieved for at least another generation.

China has reduced its number of illiterate adults by 130 million over 2 decades

The countries that appear to have higher youth literacy rates are those that have made greater progress in recent years towards UPE. However, new estimates prepared for this Report, which are based on direct assessments of literacy rather than on self-declarations, suggest that progress towards universal youth literacy may have been overstated (see Chapter 4). West Africa is of particular concern, accounting for 35% of sub-Saharan Africa's young population but 44% of its illiterate youth (Box 1.4.1).

Ten countries account for 557 million, or 72%, of the global population of illiterate adults. These countries have followed very different trajectories. China has made enormous progress, reducing its total by 130 million (or by 71%). India has by far the largest population of illiterate adults, 287 million, amounting to 37% of the global total. Its literacy rate rose from 48% in 1991 to 63% in 2006, the latest year it has available data, but population growth cancelled the gains so there was no change in the number of illiterate adults. And Nigeria had 17 million more illiterate adults in 2008 than in 1991, an increase of 71% (Figure 1.4.2).

Schooling is not the only determinant of literacy skills. The UIS Literacy Assessment and Monitoring Programme (LAMP) draws attention to the key contribution to sustained literacy made by diverse everyday reading practices (Box 1.4.2).

Box 1.4.1: West Africa accounts for almost half of the region's illiterate adults

The 15 countries of West Africa are among those with the worst adult literacy rates globally, and include the five countries with the world's lowest literacy rates, below 35%. Those five countries also have the unenviable record of female literacy rates below 25%, compared with an average for sub-Saharan Africa of 50%. Ten of the 15 countries with the lowest female literacy rates are in the subregion.

Some countries have made considerable progress. Cape Verde's literacy rate has reached 85% and Ghana's 71%. From 1988 to 2009, Senegal almost doubled its literacy rate, from 27% to 50%, and more than doubled its female literacy rate, from 18% to 39%. But Benin, Liberia and Nigeria stagnated at low levels. In Benin, the adult literacy rate increased by just two percentage points between 1992 and 2006, to 29%.

Unfortunately, these trends are not likely to improve soon. In 11 out of 14 countries, less than one in four of children complete lower secondary school. Direct assessments of literacy collected through household surveys and analysed for this Report provide further evidence that West Africa has not caught up with the rest of the world. Young women are the least likely to be literate. Twelve West African countries are among the 20 countries with the world's lowest female youth literacy rates, below 50% (Figure 1.4.1). In Mali, for example, only 17% of young women can read a sentence.

A key reason levels of youth literacy have remained low is that school systems have not expanded quickly enough. Nigeria, for example, has the highest number of out-of-school children in the world and a female youth literacy rate of just 38%. Even those who do attend school fail to acquire basic literacy skills because of the poor quality of education. Almost 80% of young people aged 15 to 24 who left school after five to six years could not read a full sentence. And conflict helps explain why youth literacy rates remain low in countries such as Liberia.

Figure 1.4.1: In 12 West African countries, less than half of young women are literate
Female youth literacy rate, selected countries, 2004–2011

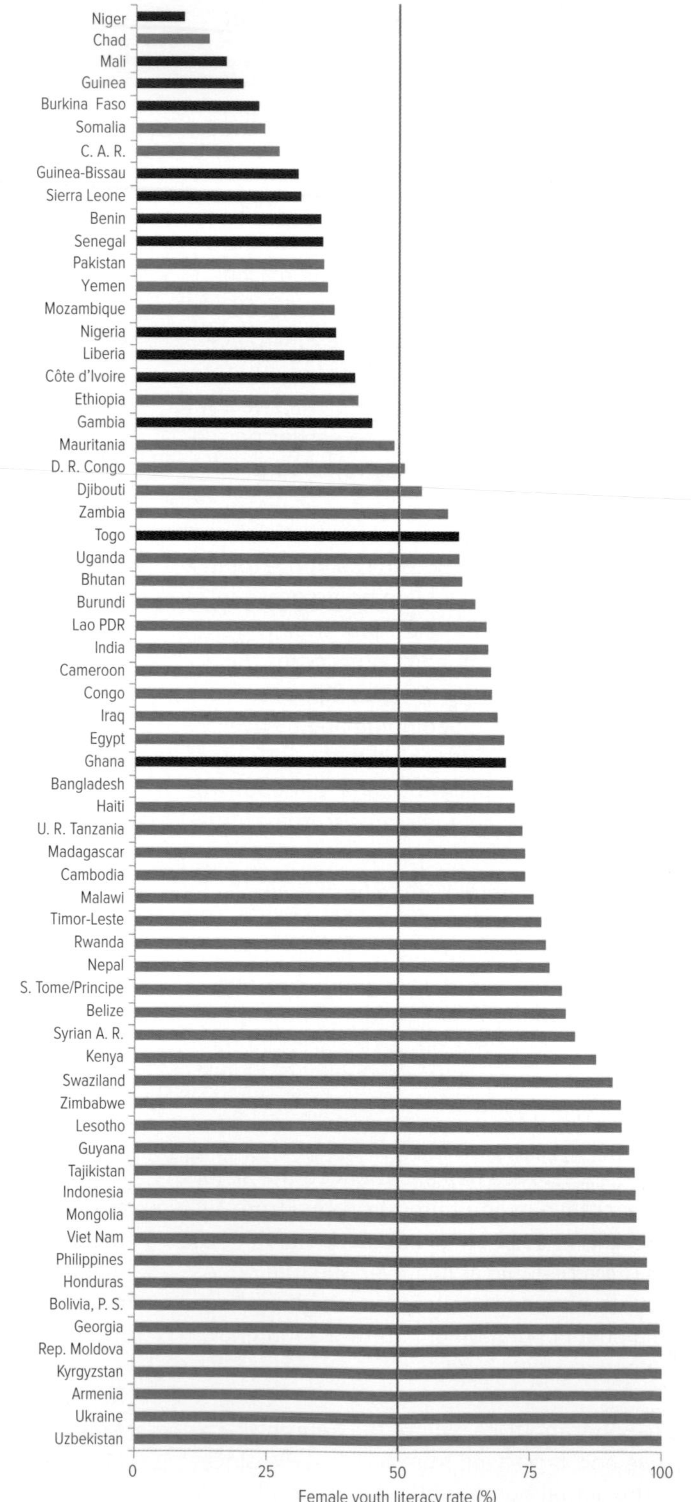

Notes: A purple bar signifies a country in West Africa. Data are unavailable for Cape Verde.
Source: EFA Global Monitoring Report team analysis (2013), based on Demographic and Health Survey data and Multiple Indicator Cluster Survey data.

Figure 1.4.2: 10 countries account for 72% of the global population of illiterate adults
Number of illiterate adults, 10 countries with highest populations of illiterate adults, 1985–1994 and 2005–2011

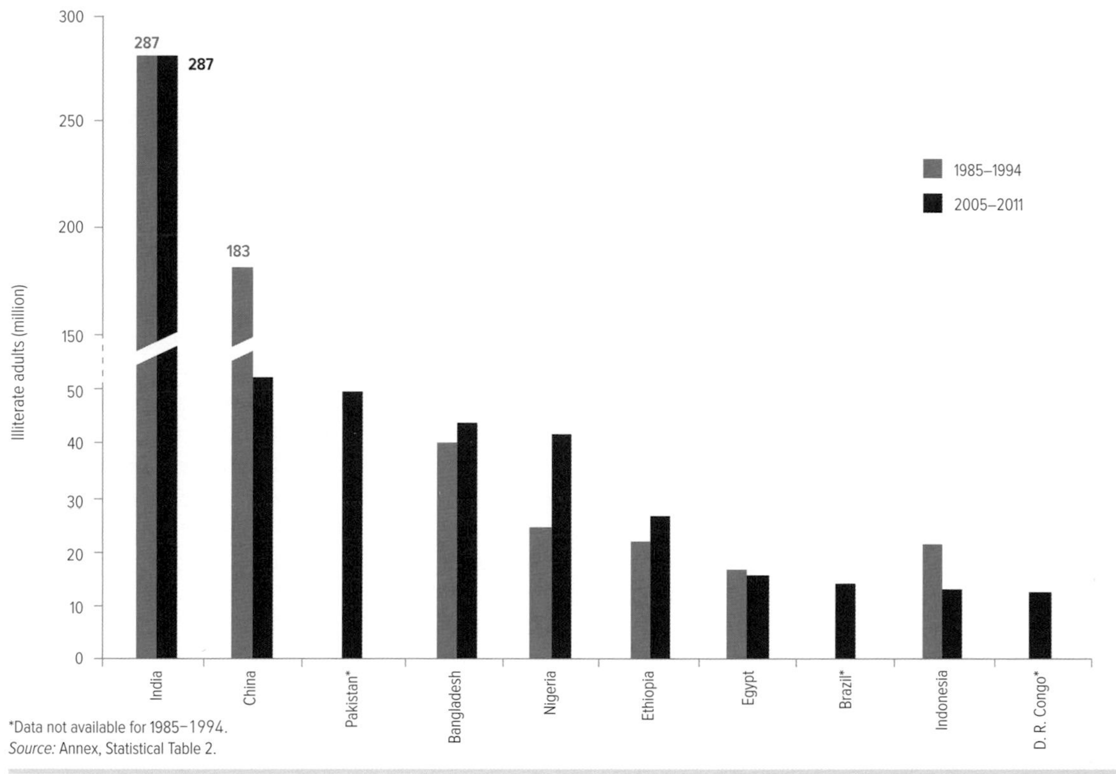

*Data not available for 1985–1994.
Source: Annex, Statistical Table 2.

Box 1.4.2: Engagement in everyday reading activities helps sustain literacy skills

The number of years spent in school is the most important predictor of literacy skills. However, everyday reading activities such as sending text messages or emails and using the Internet can sustain and extend literacy skills beyond what would be expected based on an individual's schooling history. Conversely, individuals who are unable to engage regularly in such activities may lose even the skills they acquired in their schooling.

Recognizing this, the Literacy Assessment and Monitoring Program (LAMP) collected information on everyday reading activities that could be related to literacy in four countries – Jordan, Mongolia, Palestine and Paraguay. Respondents were grouped into three levels of engagement in these activities. At the lowest level, respondents watch television, listen to the radio and use mobile phones only for talking. At the next level, respondents also use their mobile phones to send text messages. At the highest level are computer users, who also send e-mail, search the Internet and use social media. They tend to be highly educated and younger: in all four countries the vast majority of those at the highest level are under 40 years old.

Two people with the same schooling could end up with very different literacy levels depending on how much they use literacy skills in their spare time. In the four countries, at least half of the people with the least engagement in everyday reading activities perform at the lowest level of prose reading (level 1). This means they can, at best, identify a telephone number in a newspaper advertisement, or locate and copy, verbatim, the answer to a simple question in a one-paragraph text.

Those who engage more in everyday reading activities tend to be more educated. Even at a given level of education, however, these activities affect literacy skills. In Mongolia, among those with secondary schooling, only 12% of those who engage in few everyday reading activities score at the highest level in prose reading tests (level 3). The share increased to 31% among those with the highest engagement in everyday reading activities (Figure 1.4.3).

Figure 1.4.3: Literacy skills differ among people with the same education
Performance in prose reading, by level of engagement in everyday reading activities, adults with secondary education, 2010–2011

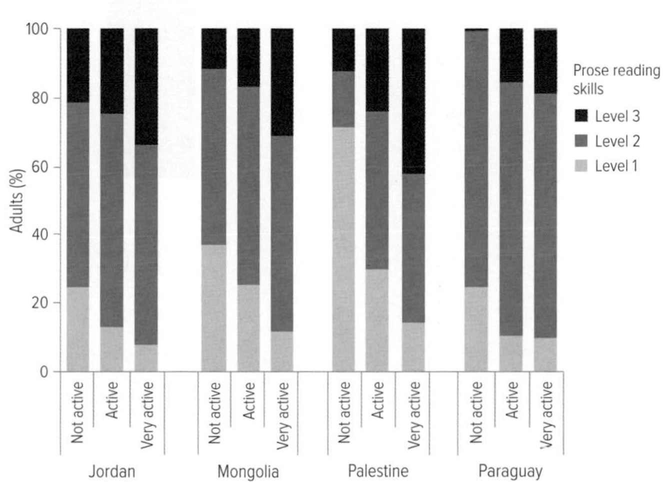

Source: UIS calculations (2013), based on Literacy Assessment and Monitoring Programme data.

How many countries are likely to achieve universal adult literacy by 2015?

The literacy goal set in 2000 at the World Education Forum in Dakar, Senegal – which restated the commitment made in Jomtien, Thailand, in 1990 – was to halve illiteracy by 2015. The EFA Global Monitoring Report team proposes that after 2015 the goal should be made more ambitious: to achieve universal youth and adult literacy. While UIS projections are available to 2015 for most countries, information is not always available for the starting point in 2000.[1]

New analysis for this Report considers how close countries are likely to get to universal adult literacy by 2015. For the 87 countries with the information, 18 had an adult literacy rate above 97% in 2000, while 7 were close. Between 2000 and 2011, the number of countries that had reached the target increased to 23, and 8 were close. It is projected that by 2015, 25 countries will have achieved universal adult literacy and 11 countries will be close.

By contrast, 34 countries were very far from the target in 2000 and 35 in 2011. Three countries moved out of this group during the period (Burundi, the Islamic Republic of Iran and Saudi Arabia) but four fell back into it (Kenya, Lesotho, Namibia and Sao Tome and Principe). It is projected that by 2015, 32 countries will be very far from the target, while 19 countries will be far from it (Figure 1.4.4).

Of the 32 countries that are expected to be very far from the target in 2015 for which information on trends between 2000 and 2011 is available, three have reduced their illiteracy rate by at least a quarter, and at least five percentage points in absolute terms: Eritrea, Ghana and Timor-Leste. Of the 19 countries that will still be far from the target in 2015, six have reduced the illiteracy rate by at least half: the Plurinational State of Bolivia, Burundi, Malaysia, Mexico, Myanmar and Viet Nam (Table 1.4.2).

Figure 1.4.4: Goal 4 – At least one in five adults will be illiterate in a third of countries in 2015

Number of countries by level of adult literacy rate, 2000, 2011 and 2015 (projected)

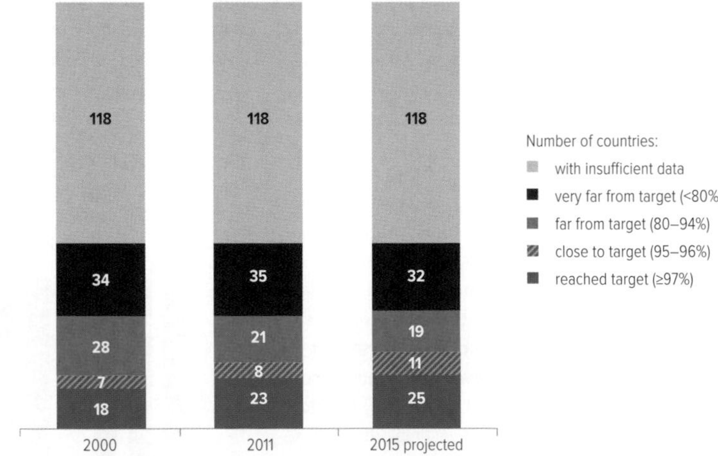

Note: The analysis was conducted on the subset of countries for which a projection was possible; therefore, it covers fewer countries than those for which information is available for either 2000 or 2011.
Source: Bruneforth (2013).

1. Note that, unlike with other indicators, almost half the 58 countries for which such projections are not provided are high income countries.

Table 1.4.2: Likelihood of countries achieving an adult literacy target of at least 95% by 2015

Level expected by 2015		Change between 2000 and 2011: Strong relative progress 13	Slow progress or moving away from target 38	No evidence on trend 34
Target reached or close (≥95%)	58	Albania, Argentina, Armenia, Aruba, Azerbaijan, Bahrain, Belarus, Bosnia and Herzegovina, Brunei Darussalam, Bulgaria, Chile, China, Costa Rica, Croatia, Cuba, Cyprus, Democratic People's Republic of Korea, Equatorial Guinea, Estonia, Georgia, Greece, Italy, Kazakhstan, Kuwait, Kyrgyzstan, Latvia, Lithuania, Macao (China), Maldives, Mongolia, Montenegro, Netherlands Antilles, Palestine, Panama, Paraguay, Philippines, Portugal, Qatar, Republic of Moldova, Romania, Russian Federation, Samoa, Serbia, Singapore, Slovenia, Spain, Suriname, Tajikistan, Thailand, The former Yugoslav Republic of Macedonia, Tonga, Trinidad and Tobago, Turkey, Turkmenistan, Ukraine, Uruguay, Uzbekistan, Venezuela (Bolivarian Republic of)		
Far from target (80-94%)	37	Bolivia (Plurinational State of), Burundi, Honduras, Iran (Islamic Republic of), Malaysia, Mexico, Myanmar, Saudi Arabia, Swaziland, Viet Nam	Algeria, Brazil, Dominican Republic, Ecuador, Mauritius, Namibia, Nicaragua, Sri Lanka, Syrian Arab Republic	Botswana, Cape Verde, Colombia, El Salvador, Gabon, Guyana, Indonesia, Jamaica, Jordan, Lebanon, Libya, Malta, Oman, Peru, South Africa, Tunisia, United Arab Emirates, Zimbabwe
Very far from target (<80%)	48	Eritrea, Ghana, Timor-Leste	Angola, Bangladesh, Benin, Cameroon, Central African Republic, Chad, Comoros, Côte d'Ivoire, Democratic Republic of the Congo, Gambia, Guatemala, Guinea-Bissau, India, Iraq, Kenya, Lao People's Democratic Republic, Lesotho, Madagascar, Mauritania, Nepal, Niger, Papua New Guinea, Rwanda, Sao Tome and Principe, Senegal, Togo, Uganda, United Republic of Tanzania, Zambia	Bhutan, Burkina Faso, Cambodia, Egypt, Ethiopia, Guinea, Haiti, Liberia, Malawi, Mali, Morocco, Mozambique, Nigeria, Pakistan, Sierra Leone, Yemen

Countries not included in analysis because of insufficient data	62	Afghanistan, Andorra, Anguilla, Antigua and Barbuda, Australia, Austria, Bahamas, Barbados, Belgium, Belize, Bermuda, British Virgin Islands, Canada, Cayman Islands, Congo, Cook Islands, Czech Republic, Denmark, Djibouti, Dominica, Fiji, Finland, France, Germany, Grenada, Hungary, Iceland, Ireland, Israel, Japan, Kiribati, Luxembourg, Marshall Islands, Micronesia (Federated States of), Monaco, Montserrat, Nauru, Netherlands, New Zealand, Niue, Norway, Palau, Poland, Republic of Korea, Saint Kitts and Nevis, Saint Lucia, Saint Vincent and the Grenadines, San Marino, Seychelles, Slovakia, Solomon Islands, Somalia, South Sudan, Sudan, Sweden, Switzerland, Tokelau, Turks and Caicos Islands, Tuvalu, United Kingdom, United States, Vanuatu

Note: This table includes a wider group of countries with projections by the UIS.
Source: Bruneforth (2013); UIS database.

Goal 5 Gender parity and equality

Eliminating gender disparities in primary and secondary education by 2005, and achieving gender equality in education by 2015, with a focus on ensuring girls' full and equal access to and achievement in basic education of good quality.

Highlights

- At the primary level, only 60% of countries with data had achieved gender parity by 2011. Among low income countries, just over a fifth have achieved parity. Of all countries, 17 had fewer than 9 girls enrolled in school for every 10 boys.
- It is projected that by 2015, 112 out of 161 countries will have achieved parity in primary education, but also that 12 countries will still have fewer than 9 girls enrolled in school for every 10 boys.
- At the secondary level, only 38% of countries with data had achieved parity by 2011. There are 30 countries with fewer than 9 girls enrolled in school for every 10 boys, but also 15 countries with fewer than 9 boys enrolled for every 10 girls.
- It is projected that by 2015, 84 out of 150 countries will have achieved parity in lower secondary education, but also that 31 countries will still have severe gender disparities.

Table 1.5.1: Key indicators for goal 5

	Primary education					Secondary education				
	Gender parity achieved in 2011		Countries with fewer than 90 girls enrolled for every 100 boys	Gender parity index (GPI)		Gender parity achieved in 2011		Countries with fewer than 90 girls enrolled for every 100 boys	Gender parity index (GPI)	
	Total number of countries	Countries with data		1999	2011	Total number of countries	Countries with data		1999	2011
World	**104**	**173**	**17**	**0.92**	**0.97**	**59**	**157**	**30**	**0.91**	**0.97**
Low income countries	7	32	10	0.86	0.95	1	27	18	0.83	0.88
Lower middle income countries	20	46	6	0.86	0.96	11	39	9	0.80	0.92
Upper middle income countries	33	48	1	0.99	1.00	17	44	1	0.98	1.04
High income countries	44	47	0	1.00	0.99	30	47	2	1.01	0.99
Sub-Saharan Africa	12	43	13	0.85	0.93	1	31	18	0.82	0.83
Arab States	7	15	2	0.87	0.92	2	15	6	0.88	0.93
Central Asia	6	7	0	0.99	0.98	5	7	1	1.00	0.97
East Asia and the Pacific	13	21	0	0.99	1.02	7	20	2	0.94	1.03
South and West Asia	5	9	2	0.83	0.98	0	8	2	0.75	0.92
Latin America and the Caribbean	17	34	0	0.97	0.97	11	31	0	1.07	1.07
North America and Western Europe	24	24	0	1.01	0.99	18	25	1	1.02	1.00
Central and Eastern Europe	20	20	0	0.97	1.00	15	20	0	0.96	0.97

Note: Gender parity is reached when the gender parity index of the gross enrolment ratio is between 0.97 and 1.03.
Sources: Annex, Statistical Tables 5 and 7.

Gender parity – equal enrolment ratios for girls and boys – is just the first step towards the fifth EFA goal of full gender equality in education: a schooling environment that is free of discrimination and provides equal opportunities for boys and girls to realize their potential. Other starting points towards gender equality include making sure the school environment is safe, improving facilities to provide, for example, separate latrines for girls and boys, training teachers in gender sensitivity, achieving gender balance among teachers and rewriting curricula and textbooks to remove gender stereotypes.

Parity in enrolment ratios at both the primary and secondary levels was singled out among all EFA goals to be achieved by 2005. With that early deadline missed, there has been progress towards this goal since, but the achievement of parity remains elusive.

At the primary education level, where disparities remain in 40% of the countries with data, disparity is at the expense of girls in more than 80% of the cases. South and West Asia is home to four of the countries with the highest gender disparities globally. Two of these have very high disparities at the expense of girls: Afghanistan, with 71 girls in school for every 100 boys, and Pakistan, with 82 girls for every 100 boys. Two other countries in the region have high disparities at the expense of boys: Bangladesh, with 94 boys for every 100 girls, and Nepal, with 92 boys for every 100 girls.

Of the 31 countries with fewer than 90 girls for every 100 boys enrolled in 1999, only about half had managed to exit that group by 2011. Others, such as Cameroon and the Central African Republic, made very slow progress towards parity. But even in some countries that made very fast progress towards parity, such as Burkina Faso and Senegal, enrolment ratios have remained among the lowest globally. In addition, gender parity is even more elusive in relation to primary school completion (Box 1.5.1).

In secondary education, gender parity trends vary by region, income group and level. Among countries with data, 38% have achieved parity in secondary education. By level, 42% of countries are at parity in lower secondary education and 22% in upper secondary education. In two-thirds of the countries with gender disparity in lower secondary education, it is at the expense of girls. But this is the case in less than half the countries with gender disparity in upper secondary education.

The most extreme cases of inequality in secondary education continue to afflict girls. Of the 30 countries with fewer than 90 girls for every 100 boys, 18 are in sub-Saharan Africa. Extreme examples from other regions include Afghanistan and Yemen, despite improvements over the decade. In Afghanistan, no girls were in secondary school in 1999. By 2011, the female gross enrolment ratio rose to 34%, increasing the gender parity index to 0.55. In Yemen, the female gross enrolment ratio increased from 21% in 1999 to 35% in 2011, resulting in an improvement in the gender parity index from 0.37 to 0.63.

Just 20% of low income countries have achieved gender parity at the primary level

There are also 15 countries with fewer than 90 boys for every 100 girls, about half of which are in Latin America and the Caribbean. In secondary school in Argentina, there were 95 boys for every 100 girls in 1999 and 90 boys for every 100 girls in 2010.

Comparisons by income group show that low income countries differ from middle and high income countries in terms of gender participation in education. Just 20% of low income countries have achieved gender parity at the primary level, 10% at the lower secondary level and 8% at the upper secondary level. In Burundi, while parity in primary education has been achieved, only 77 girls are enrolled for every 100 boys in lower secondary education, and only 62 girls for every 100 boys in upper secondary education.

By contrast, in middle and high income countries, where parity has been achieved in a higher percentage of countries, disparity is often at the expense of boys in lower and upper secondary education (Figure 1.5.3). In Honduras, while parity in primary education has been achieved, only 88 boys are enrolled for every 100 girls in lower secondary education and only 73 boys for every 100 girls in upper secondary education.

Box 1.5.1: In some sub-Saharan African countries, progress in primary school completion

Sub-Saharan Africa remains the region with the largest number of countries having severe gender disparity in access to primary education. Countries in the region have followed varying trajectories since 1999. However, even where there has been progress in gender parity, this has not necessarily meant getting more children into school, let alone improving equality in completion or learning achievement.

Burkina Faso and the Central African Republic started from the same level of extreme gender disparity, with around 70 girls enrolled for every 100 boys. Gender disparity in the Central African Republic has remained unchanged, with the result that the country now has the second highest level of gender disparity in the world, after Afghanistan. Burkina Faso has made fast progress towards parity, reaching 95 girls for every 100 boys in 2012, although it still has the world's seventh lowest gross enrolment ratio (Figure 1.5.1).

Part of the reason for Burkina Faso's progress was the successful implementation of the Ten-year Plan for the Development of Basic Education 2000–2009, which included a focus on girls' education. Measures, often carried out in collaboration with non-government organizations, included publicity campaigns, targeting girls in disadvantaged areas, and scholarships.

In addition to the government plan, other aid-supported interventions have helped move the primary education system towards gender parity. The Burkinabé Response to Improve Girls' Chances to Succeed programme provided an integrated set of interventions in rural areas, including the construction of schools equipped with boreholes and latrines, an increased number of female teachers and mobilization of community support for girls' education. An evaluation of the programme showed that it increased enrolment by 18 percentage points for boys and 23 percentage points for girls.

Cameroon and Senegal also started from similar levels of severe primary gender disparity, with around 80 girls enrolled for every 100 boys. Cameroon's disparity remained largely unchanged. But its enrolment levels rose continuously throughout the decade. Senegal made fast progress and reached parity in 2006. However, it still has the ninth lowest primary gross enrolment ratio in the world. Its move towards gender parity is a result of extremely slow progress in male enrolment – which is virtually unchanged since 2004 – rather than substantial growth in female enrolment.

Figure 1.5.1: A move towards gender parity does not always mean access for all
Primary gross enrolment ratio by gender and gender parity index, 1999–2011

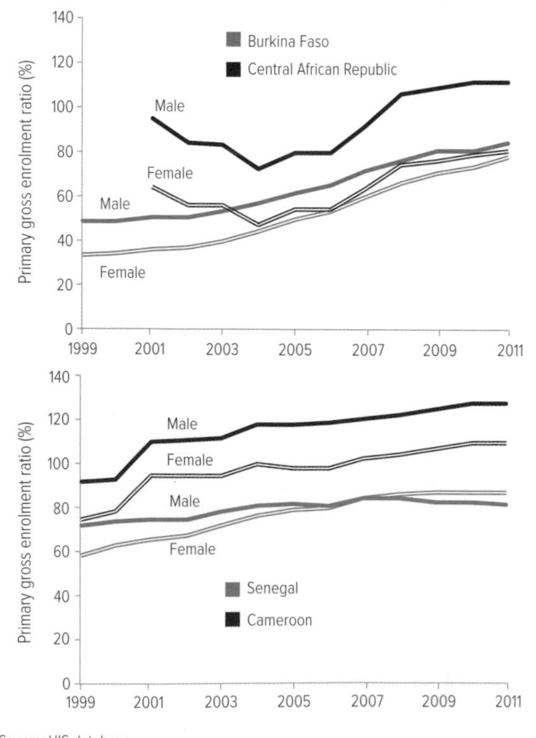

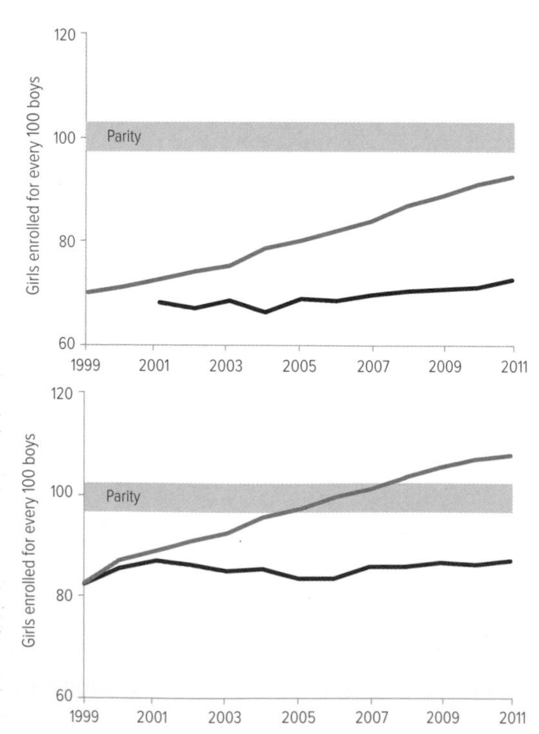

Source: UIS database.

for the poorest girls is too slow

Household survey data allow a more detailed look at trends in primary completion rates between and within these four countries, showing that, in terms of primary completion, much higher levels of gender disparity remain in all four countries.

In Burkina Faso, which has moved towards parity in enrolment, the gender gap in primary school completion remains wide, with 34% of boys and 24% of girls completing primary education in 2010. The gender gap in completion is narrow among the poorest because so few reach this stage: in 2010, just 11% of boys and 7% of girls completed primary school, only a slight increase from 1998. Greater progress in completion is evident in Senegal, but as poor boys have benefited more than poor girls, the gender gap among poor children has widened. In 2005, there was very little difference in poor children's completion rates, which were very low, but in 2010, 20% of boys completed while only 12% of girls did (Figure 1.5.2).

In Cameroon, the improvement in overall completion rates did not filter down to the poorest girls, who were even less likely to complete in 2011 than in 1998, while completion rates for the poorest boys stagnated. As a result, the gap in enrolment widened from 10 percentage points to 20 percentage points over the period.

In the Central African Republic, the effects of conflict contributed to a slight reduction in completion rates for both boys and girls, in the population on average as well as for the poorest boys and girls. As a result, by 2006, only 3% of girls were completing primary school.

While the numbers of girls and boys completing primary school give an indication of the degree of gender parity in education, what boys and girls learn in school is a better measure of equality. In the 2006/07 round of the PASEC survey, both Burkina Faso and Senegal had a considerable gender gap in learning outcomes of grade 5 students. For example, in Burkina Faso, 45% of boys and 39% of girls passed the low benchmark in reading, while 53% of boys and 45% of girls passed the low benchmark in mathematics. The gap was almost twice as large in rural areas.

At first sight, it appears that countries such as Burkina Faso and Senegal have made strong progress towards eliminating gender gaps in enrolment. However, even in these countries, policies need to be put in place to ensure that all children, regardless of their gender, both stay in school and learn.

Sources: Burkina Faso Ministry of Basic Education and Literacy (1999); Kazianga et al. (2012).

Figure 1.5.2: The poorest girls have the least chance of completing primary school
Primary school completion rate by gender, national average and poorest 20% of households

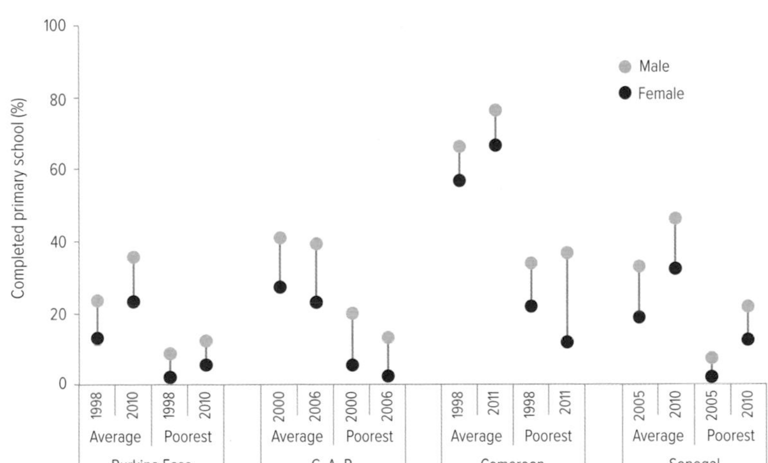

Source: EFA Global Monitoring Report team analysis (2013), based on Demographic and Health Surveys and Multiple Indicator Cluster Surveys.

Figure 1.5.3: Few low income countries have achieved gender parity at any level of education
Countries with gender parity in enrolment ratios, by country income group, 2011

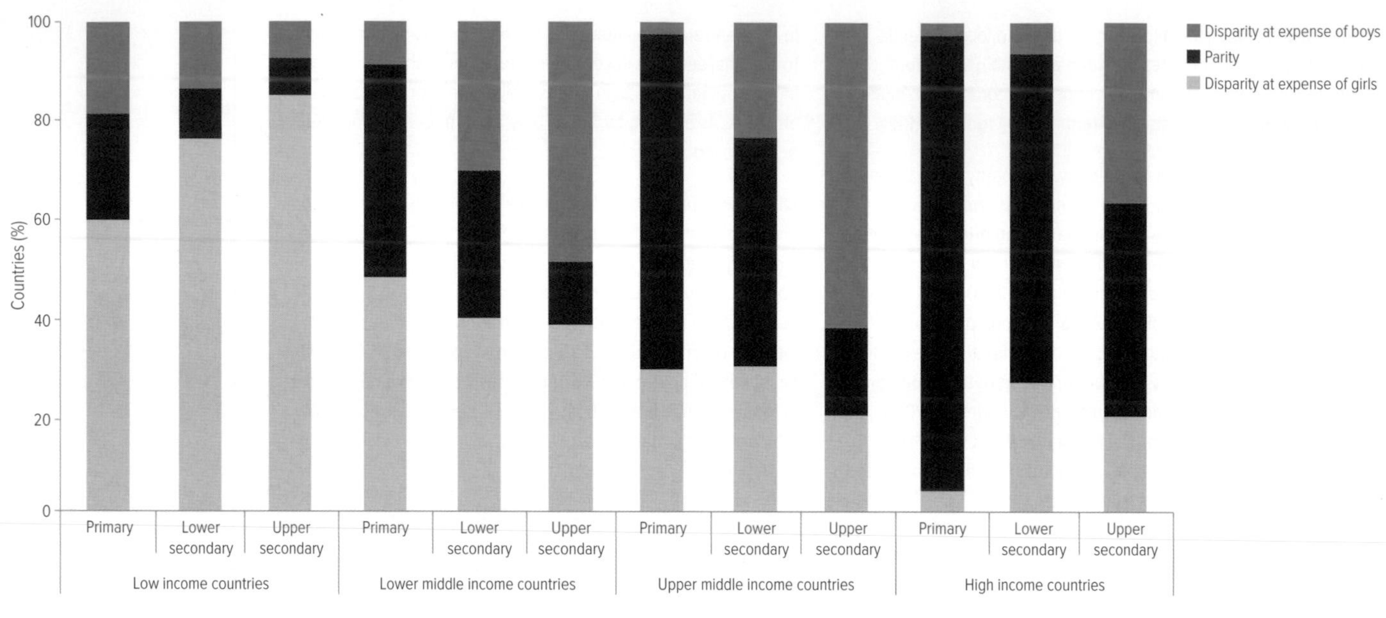

Source: UIS database.

How many countries are likely to reach the gender parity goal by 2015?

The Dakar Framework for Action established clear targets on gender parity, with a value of the gender parity index between 0.97 and 1.03 indicating parity. Values below 0.90 and above 1.11 demonstrate severe disparity.

By 2015, 84 countries are expected to have achieved gender parity in lower secondary enrolment

At the primary education level, it is possible to make projections on gender parity to 2015 for 161 countries. In 1999, 91 had achieved gender parity. Between 1999 and 2011, the number of countries that had reached the target increased to 101. It is projected that by 2015, 112 countries will have reached the goal and 14 will be close. However, 23 will be far from the target, and 12 will be very far from it. Of the 35 countries that will still be far or very far from the target, 19 are in sub-Saharan Africa. The number of countries furthest from the target, with severe disparity, fell from 31 in 1999 to 15 in 2011 (Figure 1.5.4).

In assessing the performance of countries that have not achieved parity, it is important to recognize how quickly they have moved towards the target. Of the countries that are not expected to reach or come close to the target, 8 made strong progress nonetheless, increasing their gender parity index by at least 33% between 1999 and 2011 (Table 1.5.2). In Mozambique, the female gross enrolment ratio increased from 59% in 1999 to 105% in 2012, helping to bring about an increase of the gender parity index from 0.74 to 0.91.

At the lower secondary level, it is possible to make projections to 2015 for 150 countries. In 1999, 65 countries had achieved gender parity, increasing by only one, to 66, by 2011. But many came close to the target. It is, therefore, projected that by 2015, 84 of the 150 countries will have achieved the target and 10 will be close (Figure 1.5.4).

Among the 50 countries that were furthest from the target in 1999, in 38 the disparity was at the expense of girls. Of these 38 countries, 17 had moved out of this group by 2011. Although only two achieved parity, several came close despite having started from a gender parity index below 0.75, Turkey being a notable example (Box 1.5.2). It is projected that by 2015, 31 countries will still be very far from the target, and in 22 of these the disparity will be at the expense of girls.

Figure 1.5.4: Goal 5 – despite progress towards gender parity in education, the goal will not be achieved by 2015
Number of countries by level of gender parity index in primary and lower secondary education, 1999, 2011 and 2015 (projected)

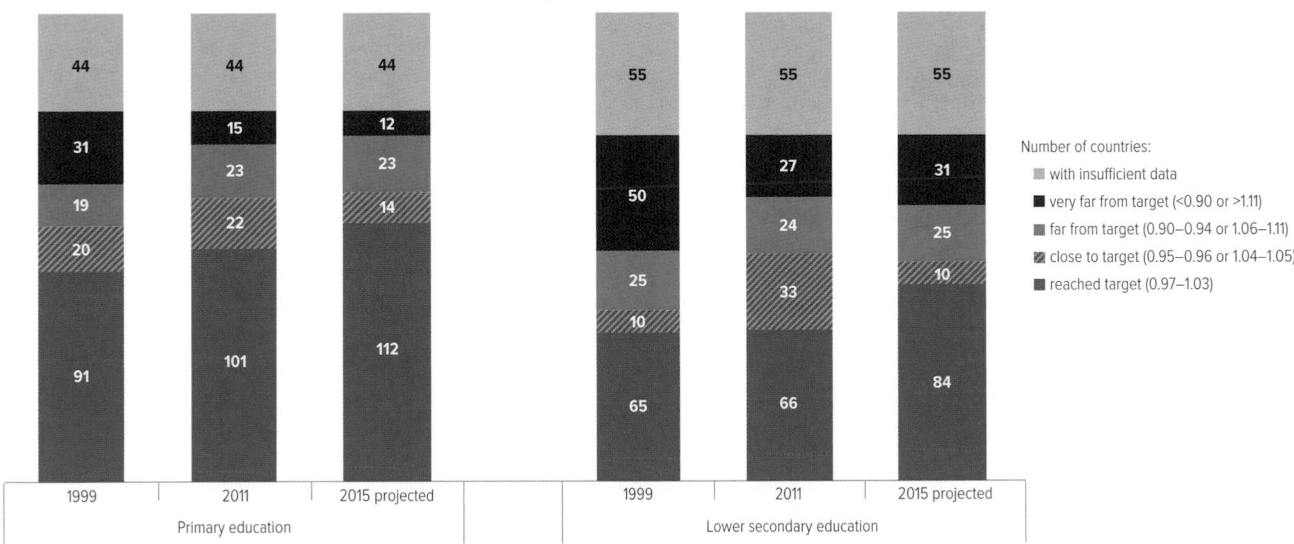

Note: The analysis was conducted on the subset of countries for which a projection was possible; therefore, it covers fewer countries than those for which information is available for either 1999 or 2011.
Source: Bruneforth (2013).

Table 1.5.2: Likelihood of achieving gender parity in primary education by 2015

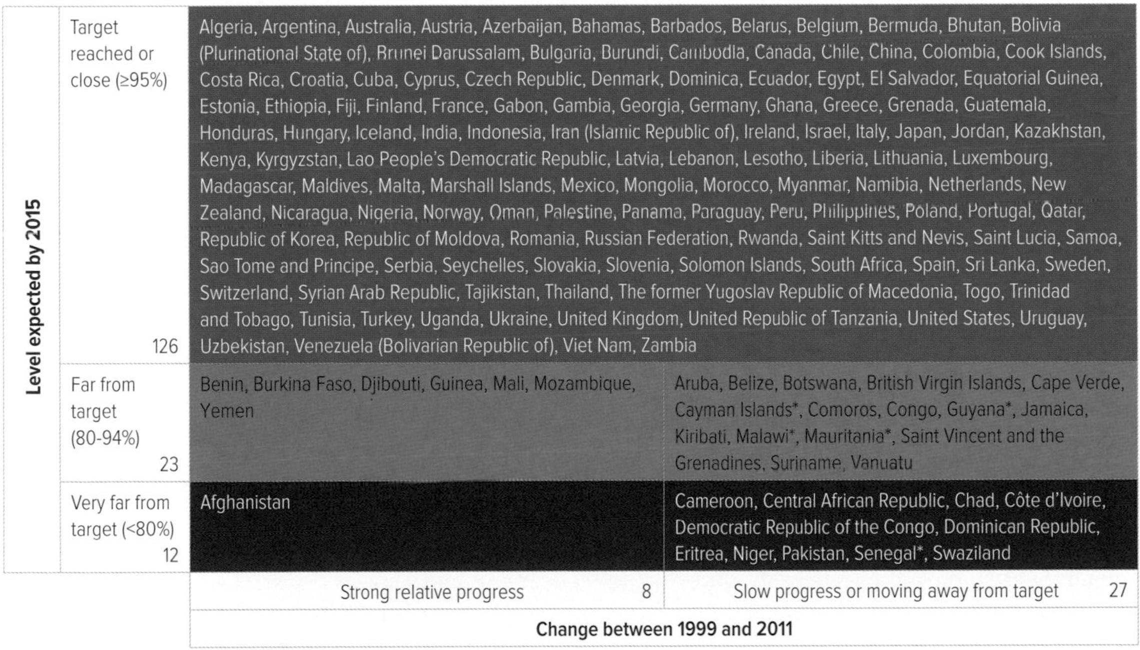

Level expected by 2015		Strong relative progress (8)	Slow progress or moving away from target (27)
Target reached or close (≥95%)	126	Algeria, Argentina, Australia, Austria, Azerbaijan, Bahamas, Barbados, Belarus, Belgium, Bermuda, Bhutan, Bolivia (Plurinational State of), Brunei Darussalam, Bulgaria, Burundi, Cambodia, Canada, Chile, China, Colombia, Cook Islands, Costa Rica, Croatia, Cuba, Cyprus, Czech Republic, Denmark, Dominica, Ecuador, Egypt, El Salvador, Equatorial Guinea, Estonia, Ethiopia, Fiji, Finland, France, Gabon, Gambia, Georgia, Germany, Ghana, Greece, Grenada, Guatemala, Honduras, Hungary, Iceland, India, Indonesia, Iran (Islamic Republic of), Ireland, Israel, Italy, Japan, Jordan, Kazakhstan, Kenya, Kyrgyzstan, Lao People's Democratic Republic, Latvia, Lebanon, Lesotho, Liberia, Lithuania, Luxembourg, Madagascar, Maldives, Malta, Marshall Islands, Mexico, Mongolia, Morocco, Myanmar, Namibia, Netherlands, New Zealand, Nicaragua, Nigeria, Norway, Oman, Palestine, Panama, Paraguay, Peru, Philippines, Poland, Portugal, Qatar, Republic of Korea, Republic of Moldova, Romania, Russian Federation, Rwanda, Saint Kitts and Nevis, Saint Lucia, Samoa, Sao Tome and Principe, Serbia, Seychelles, Slovakia, Slovenia, Solomon Islands, South Africa, Spain, Sri Lanka, Sweden, Switzerland, Syrian Arab Republic, Tajikistan, Thailand, The former Yugoslav Republic of Macedonia, Togo, Trinidad and Tobago, Tunisia, Turkey, Uganda, Ukraine, United Kingdom, United Republic of Tanzania, United States, Uruguay, Uzbekistan, Venezuela (Bolivarian Republic of), Viet Nam, Zambia	
Far from target (80-94%)	23	Benin, Burkina Faso, Djibouti, Guinea, Mali, Mozambique, Yemen	Aruba, Belize, Botswana, British Virgin Islands, Cape Verde, Cayman Islands*, Comoros, Congo, Guyana*, Jamaica, Kiribati, Malawi*, Mauritania*, Saint Vincent and the Grenadines, Suriname, Vanuatu
Very far from target (<80%)	12	Afghanistan	Cameroon, Central African Republic, Chad, Côte d'Ivoire, Democratic Republic of the Congo, Dominican Republic, Eritrea, Niger, Pakistan, Senegal*, Swaziland
		Change between 1999 and 2011	

Countries not included in analysis because of insufficient data	44	Albania, Andorra, Angola, Anguilla, Antigua and Barbuda, Armenia, Bahrain, Bangladesh, Bosnia and Herzegovina, Brazil, Democratic People's Republic of Korea, Guinea-Bissau, Haiti, Iraq, Kuwait, Libya, Macao (China), Malaysia, Mauritius, Micronesia (Federated States of), Monaco, Montenegro, Montserrat, Nauru, Nepal, Netherlands Antilles, Niue, Palau, Papua New Guinea, San Marino, Saudi Arabia, Sierra Leone, Singapore, Somalia, South Sudan, Sudan, Timor-Leste, Tokelau, Tonga, Turkmenistan, Turks and Caicos Islands, Tuvalu, United Arab Emirates, Zimbabwe

Note: An asterisk indicates disparity at the expense of boys.
Source: Bruneforth (2013).

Box 1.5.2: Challenges in improving access to secondary education for girls in Iraq and Turkey

Iraq and Turkey have moved at different speeds towards gender parity in secondary education. Turkey has made greater progress. In 1999, 87% of boys made it to lower secondary school, compared with 65% of girls. By the end of the decade, this large gap had been almost closed. Gender inequalities remain in upper secondary education but they also narrowed rapidly over the last decade (Figure 1.5.5).

The turning point was the extension of compulsory education from five to eight years in 1997, accompanied by a range of strategies aimed at widening access. A conditional cash transfer programme that provided a larger benefit for girls than for boys also helped close the enrolment gap.

Nevertheless, despite overall progress, problems remain. Girls in rural areas are more disadvantaged and some differences by region have been not only deep but also persistent: in the poor predominantly Kurdish provinces of Siirt, Mus and Bitlis, just 60 girls are enrolled in secondary school for every 100 boys, with little change in recent years.

Figure 1.5.5: Fast progress towards gender parity in secondary education is possible
Gender parity index of the secondary education gross enrolment ratio, Iraq, 1999–2007, and Turkey, 1999–2011

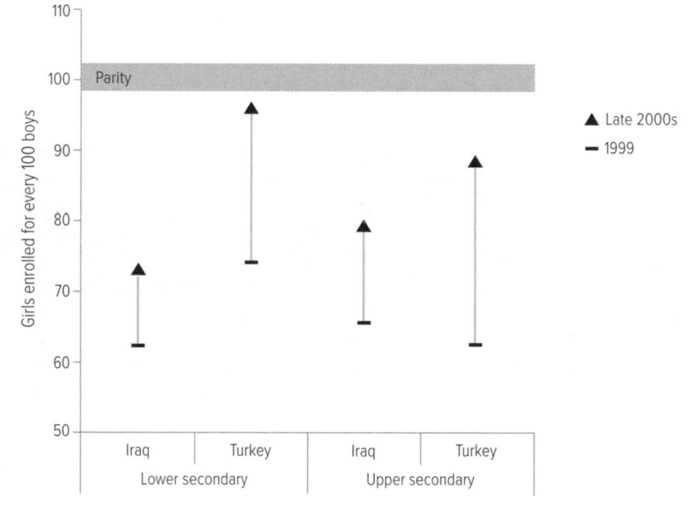

Source: UIS database.

There is continuing commitment to eliminate the remaining disparities: the 2010–2014 strategic plan of the Ministry of National Education aims to lower the gender gap in secondary education enrolment from 8.9% to less than 2%. An amendment to the Education Law introduced in April 2012 that extended compulsory education from 8 to 12 years might help further close the gap at the upper secondary level.

But there is no room for complacency. The continuing very low participation of women in the labour force and their marginalization in the labour market could deter young girls from completing secondary school. More generally, traditional perceptions of gender roles that permeate society filter down to schools. These are issues that neighbouring countries aspiring to gender equality in education need to contend with.

In Iraq, not only has progress towards gender parity been slower, but poor, rural girls have not benefited. The lower secondary completion rate was 58% for rich urban boys and just 3% for poor rural girls in 2011. Safety remains an issue for girls' schooling, particularly in areas of major instability and insecurity (Figure 1.5.6).

Sources: Turkey Ministry of National Education (2009, 2013); Uçan (2013); World Bank (2012b).

Figure 1.5.6: Poor Iraqi girls living in rural areas are far less likely to complete lower secondary school
Percentage who have ever been to school, completed primary, and completed lower secondary school, by gender, location and wealth, 2000 and 2011

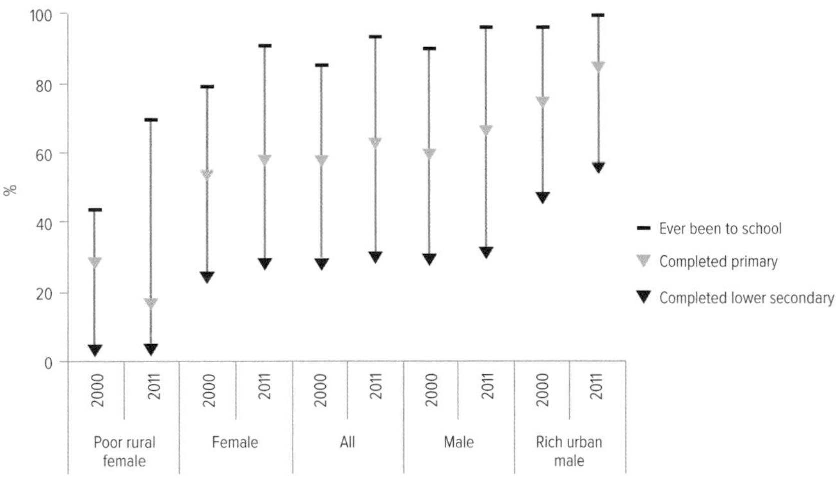

Source: EFA Global Monitoring Report team analysis (2013), based on the 2000 and 2011 Iraq Multiple Indicator Cluster Surveys.

Goal 6 Quality of education

Improving all aspects of the quality of education and ensuring excellence of all so that recognized and measurable learning outcomes are achieved by all, especially in literacy, numeracy and essential life skills.

Highlights

- At the primary education level, the pupil/teacher ratio exceeded 40:1 in 26 of the 162 countries with data in 2011. Less than 75% of primary school teachers are trained according to national standards in around a third of the countries with data.
- At the secondary education level, the pupil/teacher ratio exceeded 30:1 in 14 of the 130 countries with data in 2011. Less than 75% of secondary school teachers are trained according to national standards in half of the countries with data.
- In sub-Saharan Africa there is a lack of female teachers in primary schools that is even more accute in secondary schools. Among the countries with data, female teachers make up less than 40% of the total in 43% of countries at the primary level, in 72% of countries at the lower secondary level and in all countries at the upper secondary level.

Table 1.6.1: Key indicators for goal 6

	Pre-primary education				Primary education				Secondary education			
	Teaching staff		Pupil/teacher ratio		Teaching staff		Pupil/teacher ratio		Teaching staff		Pupil/teacher ratio	
	2011 (000)	Change since 1999 (%)	1999	2011	2011 (000)	Change since 1999 (%)	1999	2011	2011 (000)	Change since 1999 (%)	1999	2011
World	**8 230**	**53**	**21**	**21**	**28 824**	**16**	**26**	**24**	**31 473**	**28**	**18**	**17**
Low income countries	427	100	27	25	2 978	70	43	43	1 892	95	28	26
Lower middle income countries	...	...	26	...	9 589	24	31	31	9 229	61	24	22
Upper middle income countries	3 521	35	19	18	11 017	4	24	19	13 446	17	16	15
High income countries	1 990	43	18	15	5 239	10	16	14	6 906	9	14	12
Sub-Saharan Africa	439	123	28	28	3 190	62	42	43	1 788	115	26	26
Arab States	197	66	20	21	1 931	27	23	22	2 023	48	16	15
Central Asia	158	24	10	11	340	3	21	16	873	9	11	12
East Asia and the Pacific	2 262	60	26	21	10 355	13	24	18	10 000	32	17	16
South and West Asia	...	...	36	...	...	...	36	...	5 428	85	33	27
Latin America and the Caribbean	1 149	53	21	18	3 079	13	26	21	3 811	26	17	16
North America and Western Europe	1 596	50	18	14	3 801	11	15	14	4 957	10	14	12
Central and Eastern Europe	1 130	1	8	10	1 127	-17	18	17	2 694	-23	12	11

Source: Annex, Statistical Table 8.

The quality of education was at the heart of goals set at the World Education Forum in Dakar, Senegal, in 2000. Until recently, however, international attention has tended to focus on universal primary education, which is also the second Millennium Development Goal. A shift in emphasis is now discernible towards quality and learning, which are likely to be more central to the post-2015 global framework. Such a shift is vital to improve education opportunities for the 250 million children who have not had the chance to learn the basics, even though 130 million of them have spent at least four years in school.

This Report's thematic part presents analysis on learning disparities (see Chapter 4). It discusses in depth how to improve learning, in particular the vital role that teachers play supported by appropriate curricular and assessment practices (see Chapters 5, 6 and 7). This section examines progress in education quality in selected areas of the learning environment: the pupil/teacher ratio, the share of trained teachers, number of female teachers, availability of learning materials and school infrastructure. In addition, it provides an overview of the role international and regional assessments can play in monitoring progress towards a global goal on education quality and learning beyond 2015.

Pupil/teacher ratios have changed little

The pupil/teacher ratio has been a key measure for assessing progress towards goal 6 since the EFA goals were set. Globally, between 1999 and 2011, average pupil/teacher ratios have barely changed at the pre-primary, primary and secondary education levels. In pre-primary education, the average pupil/teacher ratio remained at 21:1; in primary education it improved slightly, from 26:1 to 24:1; and in secondary education, from 18:1 to 17:1.

The pupil/teacher ratio has tended to improve only in richer countries. In primary education, it fell by 13% in high income countries and 23% in upper middle income countries, but by only 3% in lower middle income countries. In low income countries it remained at 43 pupils per teacher, three times higher than in high income countries.

Pupil/teacher ratios in sub-Saharan Africa hardly changed at any level of education. In primary education, teacher recruitment grew by 62%, lagging behind enrolment, which grew by 66% over the period. At 43 pupils per teacher, this is now the region with the highest ratio at the primary level.

As of 2011, 26 out of 162 countries with data had a pupil/teacher ratio in primary education exceeding 40:1. Of these, 23 were in sub-Saharan Africa, two in South and West Asia (Afghanistan and Bangladesh) and one in East Asia (Cambodia). Of the countries that had a pupil/teacher ratio above 40:1 in 1999, nine managed to bring the ratio below 40:1 by 2011; in Timor-Leste it halved, from 62:1 in 2001 to 31:1 in 2011. But in eight of these countries, the ratio increased, often because teacher recruitment did not keep pace with increases in enrolment thanks to policies such as fee abolition. In Malawi, the ratio increased by 20% from an already high level, reaching 76:1 in 2011. In Kenya, the ratio was below 40:1 in 1999, but rose by 45% to 47:1 in 2009.

The pupil/teacher ratio in primary education increased by at least 20% in nine countries between 1999 and 2011, including the Democratic Republic of the Congo, Egypt, Pakistan and Yemen. By contrast, it fell by at least 20% in 60 countries, including Georgia, Guatemala, the Republic of Moldova, Nepal, Senegal, Tunisia and Viet Nam. Congo, Ethiopia and Mali more than doubled primary school enrolment while reducing their pupil/teacher ratios by more than 10 pupils per teacher.

In Rwanda, the share of qualified teachers increased from 49% of the teaching force in 1999 to 98% in 2011

However, many countries have expanded teacher numbers rapidly by hiring people without the qualifications of a trained teacher. Some countries have even lowered entry requirements to the profession, often out of necessity. For example, in Ghana, while there has been a 54% increase in the number of primary school teachers, keeping the pupil/teacher ratio below 40:1 over the decade, the proportion of trained teachers fell gradually from 72% in 1999 to 52% in 2012. Hiring untrained teachers may well serve to get more children into school, but it can jeopardize education quality. In Rwanda, by contrast, the pupil/teacher ratio remained high, at 58:1 in 2011, but the share of qualified teachers increased from 49% of the teaching force in 1999 to 98% in 2011.

In 34 of the 98 countries with data on trained teachers, less than 75% of teachers are trained

Figure 1.6.1: In 29 countries, there is a big gap between the number of pupils per teacher and per trained teacher

Pupil/teacher ratio and pupil/trained teacher ratio, primary education, countries where the pupil/trained teacher ratio exceeds the pupil/teacher ratio by at least 10:1, 2011

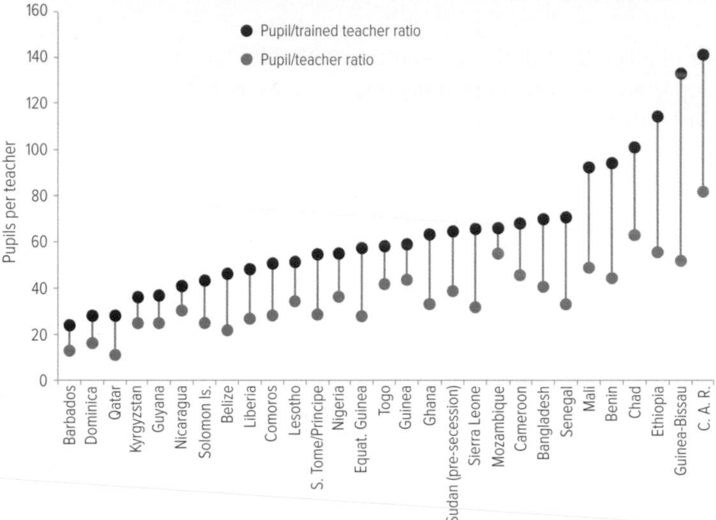

Source: Annex, Statistical Table 8.

according to national standards, with figures below 50% in Guinea-Bissau, Sao Tome and Principe, Senegal and Sierra Leone. In Guinea-Bissau, only 39% of primary school teachers have minimum qualifications, and the pupil/teacher ratio increased from 44:1 in 2000 to 52:1 in 2010. The ratio of pupils to trained teachers exceeds the pupil/teacher ratio by 10 pupils in 29 of these 98 countries, including 19 in sub-Saharan Africa and 4 in the Caribbean (Figure 1.6.1). In Sierra Leone, for example, the pupil/teacher ratio was 31:1 but the pupil/trained teacher ratio was 65:1 in 2011.

At the secondary level, in 14 of the 130 countries with data, the pupil/teacher ratio exceeds 30:1. In the Central African Republic, Ethiopia and Malawi, the ratio exceeds 40:1. Although the vast majority of the countries facing the largest challenges are in sub-Saharan Africa, the region nevertheless managed to expand the number of secondary teachers by 115% over the period to maintain the pupil/teacher ratio at 26:1.

In Niger, only 17% of teachers in secondary schools are trained

Of the 60 countries with data on the share of trained secondary teachers, half had less than 75% of the teaching force trained to the national standard, while 11 had less than 50% trained. Niger had the lowest share of trained teachers in secondary education (17%).

The proportion of teachers trained to national standards is even lower in pre-primary education. Although the number of teachers at this level has increased by 53% since 1999, the share of trained teachers remains very small. In 40 of the 75 countries with data, less than 75% of teachers are trained to the national standard. In Senegal, the share of trained pre-primary school teachers was just 15% in 2011.

Women teachers are still lacking in some regions

In some contexts, the presence of female teachers is crucial to attract girls to school and improve their learning outcomes.
In other contexts, a lack of male teachers can hinder boys' learning. The availability of male and female teachers is heavily unbalanced, however, between levels of education and between regions.

In sub-Saharan Africa, which suffers from gender disparities in schooling at the expense of girls, the lack of female teachers in primary schools is even more acute at secondary school. Among the countries with data, female teachers make up less than 40% of the total in 43% of countries at the primary level, in 72% of countries at the lower secondary level and in all countries at the upper secondary level. In Niger, the share of female teachers falls from

Figure 1.6.2: The lack of female teachers is marked in

Percentage of female teachers, primary, lower and upper secondary

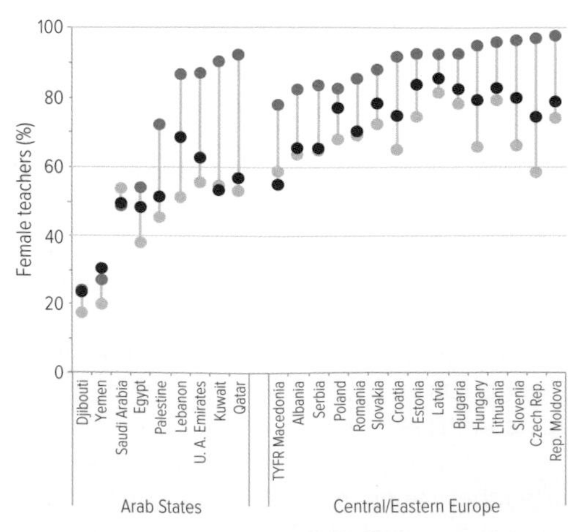

Sources: Annex, Statistical Table 8 (print) and 10B (web).

46% in primary school to 22% in lower secondary school and to 18% in upper secondary school. The same problem is encountered in South and West Asia: in Nepal, the share of female teachers falls from 42% in primary school to 27% in lower secondary school and to 16% in upper secondary school (Figure 1.6.2).

Women teachers are particularly lacking in countries with wide gender disparity in enrolment. In Djibouti and Eritrea, only about 8 girls were enrolled for every 10 boys in lower secondary school, with very limited progress since 2000. The percentage of female teachers remained at 25% in Djibouti over the period and 14% in Eritrea. By contrast, in Cambodia, where in 1999 the level of gender disparity in lower secondary enrolment was the seventh highest in the world with 53 girls enrolled for every 100 boys, gender parity had almost been achieved by 2011 and the share of female teachers had increased from 30% to 36%.

By contrast, in Latin America and the Caribbean, where more girls tend to be enrolled in school than boys, female teachers make up at least 60% of the total in 70% of countries at the lower secondary level. In Suriname, where there are 91 boys for every 100 girls enrolled, 75% of lower secondary education teachers are female

Insufficient textbooks and poor infrastructure hinder learning

Teachers need good learning materials, such as textbooks, to be effective. Factors affecting the quality of textbooks differ, from content to printing quality and timeliness of distribution. But many students suffer from a very basic problem: they do not have access to textbooks.

In the United Republic of Tanzania, only 3.5% of all grade 6 pupils had sole use of a reading textbook (SACMEQ, 2010). In Cameroon, there were 11 primary school students for every reading textbook and 13 for every mathematics textbook in grade 2. Pupils in early grades were the most disadvantaged. For example, in Zambia there were 3.5 students for every mathematics textbook in grade 2, compared with 2.3 students in grade 5 (UIS, 2012). In Rwanda, where the government target was one textbook for every two pupils, a 2007 study in two-thirds of districts revealed that there were 143 pupils for every Kinyarwanda textbook in grade 1, and 180 pupils for every mathematics textbook (Read and Bontoux, forthcoming).

In some countries, textbooks are becoming even scarcer. Between 2000 and 2007, Kenya, Malawi and Namibia experienced rapid increases in enrolment, but the availability of textbooks did not keep pace. In Malawi, the percentage of students who either had no textbook or had to

Women teachers are particularly lacking in countries with wide gender disparity in enrolment

sub-Saharan Africa
education, 2011

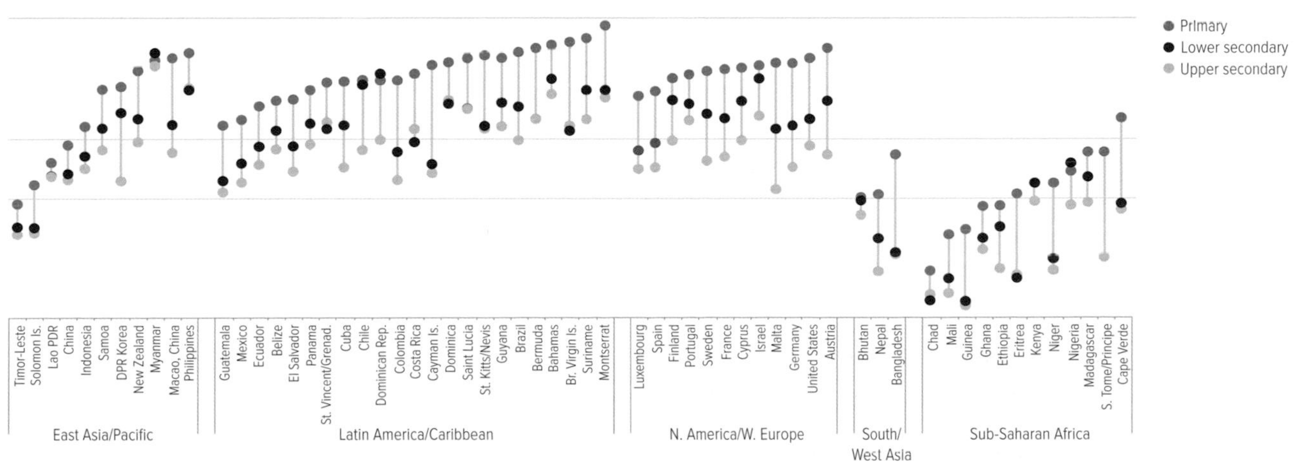

share with at least two more pupils increased from 28% in 2000 to 63% in 2007 (Figure 1.6.3).

Factors that limit textbook availability include low priority on teaching and learning inputs in countries' education budgets, high textbook costs and wastage due to wear and tear (Box 1.6.1).

Poor physical infrastructure is another problem for students in many parts of sub-Saharan Africa. Children are often squeezed in overcrowded classrooms or learning outside, with those in early grades again particularly disadvantaged. In Malawi, there are 130 children per classroom in grade 1 on average, compared with 64 in grade 6 (Figure 1.6.4). In Chad, only one in seven schools has potable water, and just one in four has a toilet; moreover, only one-third of the toilets that do exist are for girls only (UIS, 2012).

Box 1.6.1: Reducing the cost of textbooks helps increase their availability

The availability of textbooks could be significantly increased by devoting more resources to teaching and learning materials, and by reducing the cost of each book. Textbooks and other teaching and learning materials accounted for just 6.6% of education budgets in sub-Saharan Africa in 2009. Uganda allocated as little as 1.7% of its primary education recurrent budget on textbooks and learning materials in 2009, which was equivalent to US$1.30 per student. An analysis of six districts in Pakistan found that only 5% of the recurrent budget in 2009/10 was spent on non-salary items, and as little as 0.6% in one district.

After abolishing school fees, some countries introduced grants per pupil to schools to cover non-salary expenditure, including textbooks. The grants are often insufficient and vulnerable to budget cuts, however. In the United Republic of Tanzania, the government shifted the responsibility for procuring textbooks and other materials from the district to the school. It introduced a grant of US$10 per primary school pupil, earmarking 40% for textbooks and teacher guides. But this amount covered only 10% of the cost of a full set of textbooks for a grade 5 pupil. Furthermore, as a result of inflation and budget cuts, by 2011 less than US$2 per primary pupil was reaching schools. In addition, schools received their allocation several months after the school year started, so funds were not available to purchase textbooks in time.

Reducing the cost per textbook would significantly increase their availability, even within existing budgets. In sub-Saharan Africa, a primary school textbook costs around US$4. In Viet Nam, by contrast, the cost is US$0.60 because it is possible to print books in country, with competition between publishers driving prices down. Not all countries have the technical capacity to do so, however. In Timor-Leste, for example, the unit cost would double if books were printed in country rather than in Singapore or Indonesia.

Other options for reducing unit costs include higher printing quality to extend the life of textbooks, printing in black and white instead of colour or increasing print runs. On one estimate, in India if a primary school book's specifications give it a four-year shelf life rather than just one year, the cost per textbook per year falls from US$0.36 to US$0.14.

The logistics of distribution also need to be improved to reduce wastage. Costs increase because of poor security in transport and storage, and because books are stolen and resold to private schools. A tracking survey in Ghana found that 29% of English textbooks could not be accounted for in 2010, for example.

Sources: Bontoux (2012); Fredriksen (2012); Read and Bontoux (forthcoming); Twaweza (2012); UIS (2011); UNESCO (2013b); World Bank (2008a).

Figure 1.6.3: Access to textbooks in some southern and east African countries has worsened
Percentage of grade 6 pupils without access to a reading textbook or having to share with two or more pupils, selected countries, 2000–2007

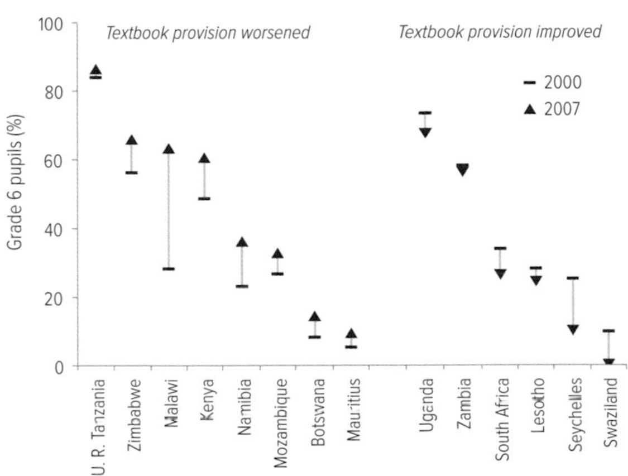

Source: SACMEQ (2010).

Figure 1.6.4: Children in early grades often learn in overcrowded classrooms
Pupil/classroom ratio in public primary schools by grade, selected sub-Saharan African countries, 2011

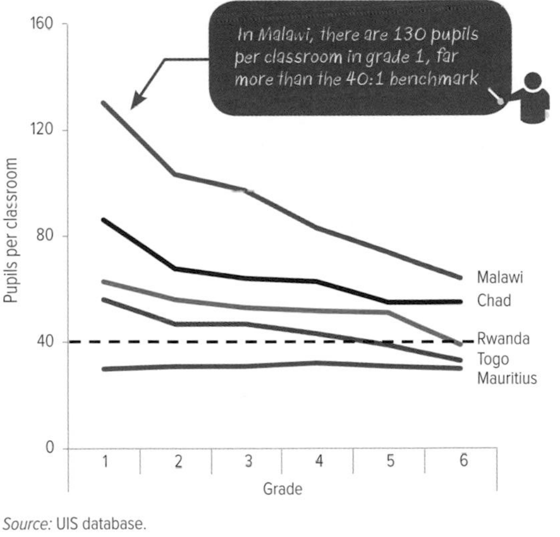

Source: UIS database.

Strengthening learning assessments to measure progress towards global goals after 2015

With 250 million children not learning the basics and the 2015 deadline for the Education for All goals fast approaching, it is vital for a global post-2015 goal to be set to ensure that, by 2030, all children and youth, regardless of their circumstances, acquire foundation skills in reading, writing and mathematics. Setting a goal is not enough on its own, however; it is also crucial to monitor progress to make sure countries are on track to achieve the goal.

A global post-2015 goal must be set to ensure that, by 2030, all children and youth, regardless of their circumstances, acquire foundation skills

International and regional assessments, which have expanded to include more countries over the past two decades, provide a good basis for tracking such progress. Beyond assessing whether children are learning the basics, the Learning Metrics Task Force promotes an expanded vision of learning (Learning Metrics Task Force, 2013). This expanded vision highlights the need for a global measure of whether all children are learning the basics to be complemented by monitoring within countries of progress towards a wider set of learning outcomes.

This section argues that meeting this need is important, but also requires countries to strengthen their national assessment systems and ensure that they are used to inform policy in ways that can help tackle the global learning crisis. In addition, this section reviews the learning assessment instruments available for monitoring progress towards a global learning goal, noting their strengths for monitoring progress in learning and for informing policy, as well as key principles that still need to be addressed to enable global monitoring of learning.

National assessments are indispensable for informing policy

Many governments in low and middle income countries have been paying greater attention in recent years to measuring learning outcomes in an attempt to assess the quality of their education systems and use the results to inform policy. However, policy-makers often consider their public examination system as equivalent to a national assessment system, even though the two serve very different purposes. Public examination systems are used to promote students between levels of education (and so set standards and benchmarks according to places available); national assessments should be a diagnostic tool that can establish whether students achieve the learning standards expected in the curriculum by a particular age or grade, and how this achievement changes over time for subgroups of the population.

Brazil has used national assessments to significantly improve education quality, especially for disadvantaged groups

The ultimate test of national assessments as a diagnostic tool is whether the results are used effectively to help education ministries strengthen the policy mix so as to improve education quality and learning outcomes. Many national assessment systems are lacking in this respect. Brazil is an exception, having used national assessments to significantly improve education quality, especially for disadvantaged groups. A national assessment system, Prova Brasil, is used to build an Index of Basic Education Development, combining measurements of students' learning and progress, including repetition rates, grade progression and graduation rates. This has been a key tool in holding schools accountable for the quality of the education they provide. Each school, working with the municipality and monitored by the state, develops a strategic plan for achieving the required improvement in learning. Schools performing poorly attract more support (Bruns et al., 2012).

Government action is not the only route to an effective assessment system for informing national policy. Some civil society organizations have drawn government attention to the need for reforms and supported local communities in their demands for better learning outcomes in schools. In India, for example, the Annual Status of Education Report (ASER) produced by Pratham, an NGO, has been influential in shaping policy and planning to improve education quality. ASER's findings contributed to India's 12th five-year plan (2012–2017), helping to place emphasis on basic learning as an explicit objective of primary education, and on the need for regular learning assessments to make sure quality goals are met. Pratham has also used ASER results to influence education policy and practice at state level. In Rajasthan, for example, ASER results have led the state government to focus on improving instruction in early grades (ASER, 2013).

International aid can be a catalyst for effective national assessment systems. In Liberia, an assessment funded by a USAID project highlighted the low reading ability of children in early grades, prompting the Ministry of Education to institute reforms. These include revising the national curriculum to provide reading as a separate subject and strengthening capacity to train and support teachers in early grade reading approaches (Davidson and Hobbs, 2013). Similarly, Zambia has been benefiting from the Russia Education Aid for Development (READ) Trust Fund, executed by the World Bank, which aims to help low income countries strengthen the capacity of institutions to assess student learning and use the results to improve the quality of education (World Bank, 2013h).

Other countries need to learn from such experiences and use national assessments to monitor learning in ways that can inform policy. To obtain a globally comparable picture of progress in learning, however, international and regional approaches are also needed.

Regional and international assessments are vital for global monitoring

Regional and international assessments have developed considerably since the 1990s, covering an increasing number of countries, subjects and levels (Table 1.6.2). Participating in a regional or international assessment helps mobilize interest in improving learning around the world. Just as improved global monitoring of access has helped maintain pressure on governments to ensure that each child completes primary school, better global monitoring of learning can push governments to make certain that all children not only go to school but are achieving the basics.

Participating in such assessments can present challenges. The need for cross-country comparability may mean that countries are asked to assess students in unfamiliar curriculum areas, so countries may re-orient their systems to fit these international assessments in ways that do not suit their circumstances. In addition, the assessments are sometimes used inappropriately to rank countries, which can discourage participation by poorer countries where fewer children are learning the basics. The cost of participation, moreover, can be substantial for poorer countries, which are likely to need support from international aid agencies.

It is vital nonetheless for all countries to engage in regional and international assessments to track whether all children, regardless of their circumstances, are learning the basics. These assessments promote a culture of transparency, evidence-based public debates on learning outcomes, and better national and international policy-making. They can also help countries develop their capacity for analysing results and assessing a wider range of skills (Bloem, 2013).

Regional and international assessments have been successfully used by some countries to inform national policy. Armenia, which has participated in three rounds of the TIMSS, has regularly and widely disseminated copies of reports on its performance and communicated key findings through press releases, television, radio and newspapers. The Ministry of Education and Science has used the results to track the impact of reforms on student achievement levels, to improve curricula and teacher training, and to inform classroom assessment activities (World Bank, 2013b).

Similarly, Namibia has used information from SACMEQ to improve learning. Namibia recorded one of the highest increases in reading and math scores of any country between 2000 and 2007. The increase of over 40 points in both scores has been attributed to policies that provided additional support for six poor-performing regions (Makuwa, 2010).

For regional and international learning assessments to facilitate monitoring post-2015 global learning goals, three key principles need to be taken into account:

All children and young people need to be included in evaluation of learning, whether they are in school or not. Regional and international assessments must increase understanding of the impact of poverty, ethnicity, location and gender on learning outcomes – and how policies can respond. To do so, they need to take into account the most disadvantaged children, who may already be out of the school system. The assessments collect information only from students without including information on children not in school, which can produce misleading results. For example, more than half of children are out of school by grade 5 in the Central African Republic, Mozambique and Niger. While it is likely that the vast majority of these children have not learned the basics, their exclusion means that the scale of the problem is understated, and can also let governments off the hook in addressing the learning needs of these children.

This issue is also relevant in assessments of older children. Even among the higher income OECD countries participating in PISA, 13% of 15-year-olds are not in school. It is difficult to determine whether adolescents of lower secondary school age who have dropped out of school by age 15 have failed to learn the basics. Only if they are included in assessments can governments form a full picture of learning achievement in the population. One way of including all children, whether they are in school or not, is to test young people's literacy as part of household surveys. This is currently done in the Demographic and Health Surveys and the Multiple Indicator Cluster Surveys (see Chapter 4 for an analysis of these data), but their purpose is only to gather very basic information on literacy.

The OECD is offering an alternative approach, redesigning its PISA surveys to be more relevant to developing countries while producing results that are comparable with the main PISA assessment. PISA for Development intends to explore how best to include out-of-school youth, and its results will help inform future approaches.

Namibia has used information from a regional assessment to improve learning

Better information from learning assessments is needed to identify children from disadvantaged backgrounds

Better information on background characteristics of students is needed to identify which groups of students are not learning. All regional and international assessments collect information on children's socio-economic background (see Table 1.6.2). However, some countries opt out of this process, such as Mexico in the SERCE study, reducing the results' comparability and hence their usefulness. Comparability also suffers when surveys fail to distinguish clearly between children from advantaged and disadvantaged households. Analysis for this Report suggests that surveys conducted as part of PASEC show children from the worst-off families in some countries doing as well as children from better-off families, a result which is likely to reflect weaknesses in how socio-economic background information is collected, rather than strong performance by students from poor households.

Collecting information on socio-economic status is not straightforward when the source of the information is a child or youth, who may not know, for example, the family's income or expenditure. Such information is better collected via household surveys. Nevertheless, some robust measures have been developed enabling comparable information to be collected using proxies for socio-economic status, such as parental education, occupation, and ownership of particular items (radios, televisions, cars, mobile phones). It should be possible to develop indicators that are comparable across countries and surveys so as to more accurately identify the most disadvantaged children.

Information on the quality of education systems should be included as part of the assessments. To inform policy, it is vital to know not just which students are not learning, but also other factors that can lead to poor learning outcomes. Collecting information on the school environment and teacher quality can help ascertain whether the right strategies are in place. The information on teacher subject knowledge that countries participating in SACMEQ have collected is useful in this respect. The experience of TIMSS could also be drawn upon, as its surveys collect data from students, teachers, principals and curriculum experts on the context of teaching and learning, allowing more in-depth analysis that links individual characteristics to the quality of education systems (Drent et al., 2013).

Existing regional and international assessments differ in many respects, including the target groups and the competencies tested. There is no strong reason to argue that countries should choose to participate in one rather than another. However, if policy-makers around the world are to have a picture of the extent of the global learning crisis and so be able to take measures to tackle it, agencies involved in administering regional and international assessments will need to collaborate to increase the comparability of their instruments. There is some evidence that this is already happening: TIMSS, PASEC and SACMEQ have been coordinating test items to ensure that there is a minimum basis for making their results comparable.

Table 1.6.2: Major international and regional learning assessment studies

General						Background data		
Assessment	Countries	Target group	Subjects	Frequency	Years	Socio-economic status	Other	Prior achievement
International								
TIMSS	76	Grades 4, 8	Mathematics Science	4-year cycle	1995, 1999, 2003, 2007, **2011**, *2015*	Books, computer, study desk, parental education, parental occupation	Language spoken at home, country of birth of student and parents	Preschool, early literacy and numeracy
PIRLS	59	Grade 4	Reading	5-year cycle	2001, 2006, **2011**, *2016*			
PISA	73	15 year-olds	Reading Mathematics Science	3-year cycle	2000, 2003, 2006, 2009, **2012**, *2015*	Index based on parental education, parental occupation and home possessions, including books	Language spoken at home, country of birth of student and parents, reading habits	Grade repetition, self-reported performance, pre-school, extra tuition
Regional								
LLECE Latin America	18	Grades 3, 6	Reading Mathematics Science	Variable	1997 **2006** (SERCE) *2013* (TERCE)	Index based on parental education, home facilities, asset ownership, house construction materials, books	Language spoken at home, child labour, reading habits	Grade repetition, age at entry, pre-school
SACMEQ Anglophone eastern and southern Africa	14	Grade 6	Reading Mathematics	Variable	1995-1997, 2000-2002, **2007**, *2014*	Index based on parental education, parental occupation, home possessions, books	Language spoken at home, child labour, distance travelled	Grade repetition, absenteeism, pre-school
PASEC Francophone sub-Saharan Africa and South East Asia	24	Grades 2, 5; (as of 2014) Grade 6	Reading Mathematics	Variable	1993-1995, 1997-2001, **2004-2010**, *2014*	Home facilities (water, sanitation, electricity), consumption of meat, parental literacy, books	Language spoken at home	Same students tested over time, grade repetition, absenteeism, pre-school

Note: Dates in bold are the most recent rounds; dates in italics are the forthcoming rounds.

Leaving no one behind — how long will it take?

After 2015, unfinished business will remain across the six EFA goals, while new priorities are likely to emerge. This section looks across three areas: universal primary school completion, universal lower secondary school completion and universal youth literacy. It assesses how long it will take to achieve these three goals, in particular from the perspective of reaching the most marginalized.[1]

This analysis paints a worrying picture. In many countries, the last mile to universal primary education will not be covered in this generation unless concerted efforts are taken to support the children who are the most disadvantaged. On recent trends, it may be only in the last quarter of this century that all of the poorest boys and girls in more than 20 countries will graduate from primary education – and only next century that they will all complete lower secondary education.

Achieving universal primary completion

By 2060, universal primary completion will not have been achieved for poor girls in 24 low income countries

Many of the world's poorest countries have made considerable progress in expanding access to primary school since 2000. This progress tends to be measured using the adjusted primary net enrolment ratio. As the analysis of goal 2 has shown, this indicator can provide a snapshot of whether children of primary school age are at school, but fails to show whether children actually complete primary education. Household survey data on the percentage of young people who have completed primary education give a clearer picture of actual progress towards the target – and whether this progress is shared across population groups.

Seventeen mostly upper middle income countries, out of the 74 analysed, have reached universal primary completion or are expected to reach it by 2015 if recent trends continue. Even by 2030, however, only 26 of these countries will have met the goal. The majority of lower middle income countries are not expected to reach universal primary completion until the 2030s or 2040s. For low income countries, the picture is even worse: on recent trends, they are only expected to start achieving the target from the 2040s onwards. Four West African countries, Burkina Faso, Mali, Niger and Senegal, will not reach it before 2070.

Disadvantaged groups face an even harsher reality. Among the low income sub-Saharan African countries in the sample, Zimbabwe and Kenya are the first expected to reach universal primary completion, by 2019 and 2026 respectively. For children in urban areas, the target has already been achieved in Zimbabwe and is expected to be reached in Kenya by 2018. But for children in rural areas of both countries, the goal will not be achieved before the late 2020s (Figure 1.7.1A). The period that will elapse between the achievement of the goal among boys in urban areas and among girls in rural areas is projected to be considerably wider in other countries: 39 years in the Lao People's Democratic Republic, 46 years in Yemen, 52 years in Ethiopia and 64 years in Guinea.

The differences are even starker when looking at the projected achievement patterns by gender and family income. While rich boys are expected to reach the goal by 2030 in 56 of the 74 countries, this is the case for poor girls in 7 countries. Even by 2060, universal primary completion will not have been achieved for poor girls in 24 of the 28 low income countries in the sample.

Lower middle income countries with large populations also face considerable challenges. In Nigeria, for example, rich boys already complete primary school, but it may be another three generations before poor girls do. In Pakistan, rich boys and girls are expected to complete primary school by 2020, but on recent trends poor boys will reach this fundamental target only in the late 2050s and poor girls just before the end of the century. In the Central African Republic, rich boys are expected to complete primary school by 2037 but poor girls only after 2100 (Figure 1.7.1B).

1. Household surveys covering 74 low and middle income countries were included in this analysis (Lange, 2013).

Figure 1.7.1: On recent trends, universal primary completion will not be achieved for the poor in some countries for at least another two generations
Projected year of achieving a primary completion rate in excess of 97%, selected countries

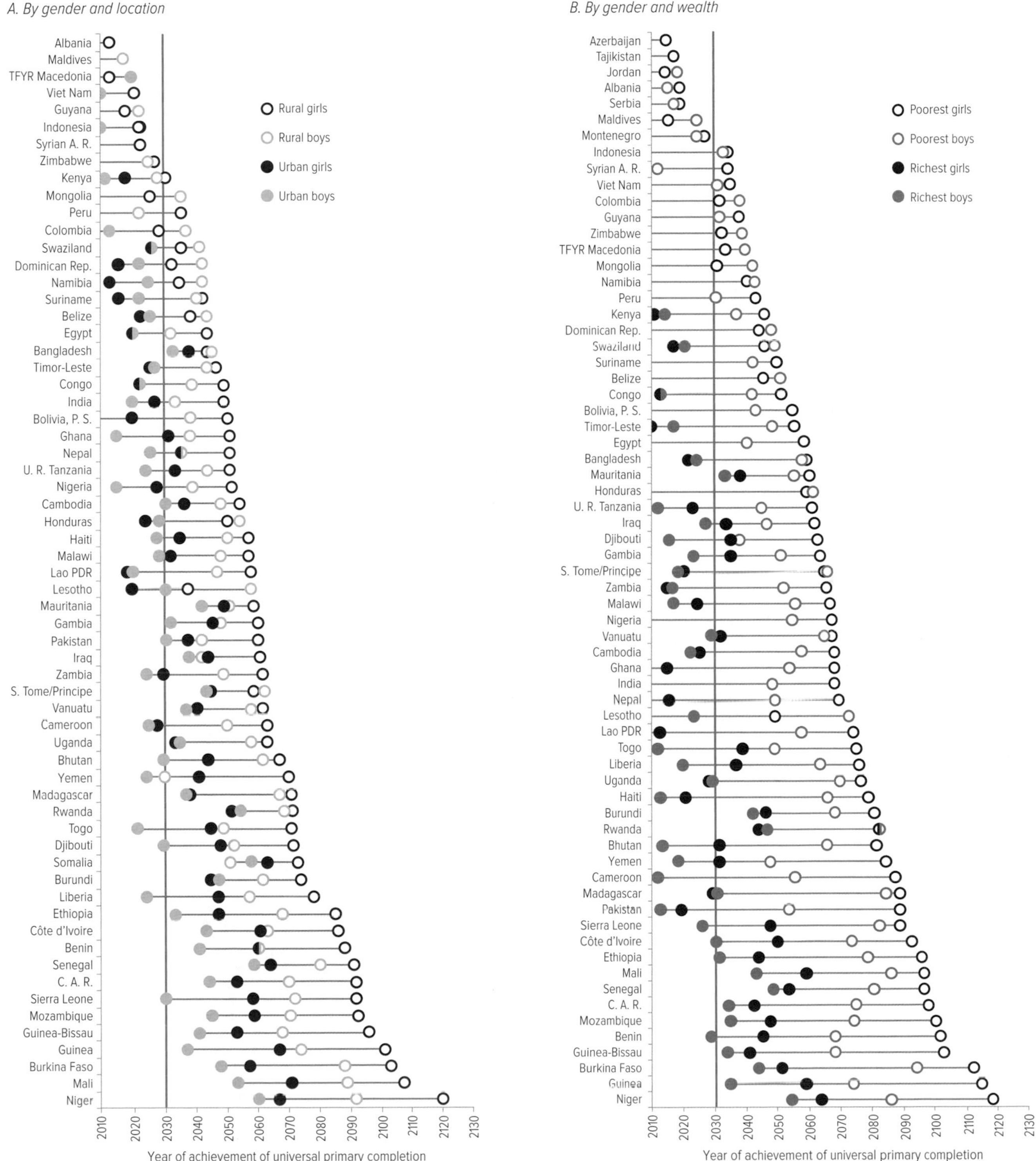

Source: EFA Global Monitoring Report team analysis (2013), based on Lange (2013).

Achieving universal lower secondary completion

Post-2015 global education goals are widely expected to include achieving universal lower secondary completion by 2030. To inform forthcoming decisions on this target, it is vital to consider the results of projections on how long it would take countries to reach it.

Of the 74 countries analysed, in only six will all children be completing lower secondary school by 2015 on recent trends. In 25 countries, less than half of adolescents will be completing lower secondary school by this date, which shows that there will be a considerable distance to travel after 2015.

Taking the projections to 2030, 11 countries in the sample, most of them upper middle income countries, are expected to have reached universal lower secondary completion by that year. Of the 31 lower middle income countries in the sample, 14 are not expected to reach universal lower secondary until 2060. And only six low income countries are expected to achieve the target before 2060. On recent trends, the average gap between achieving universal completion of primary education and lower secondary education is projected to be 19 years in low income countries and 17 years in lower middle income countries.

In 44 countries, there is at least a 50-year gap between all the richest boys completing lower secondary school and all the poorest girls doing so

The gap between better-performing and worse-performing groups is likely to be even wider for achieving universal lower secondary completion than for achieving universal primary completion. In 44 of the 74 countries, there is at least a 50-year gap between all the richest boys completing lower secondary school and all the poorest girls doing so. In low income countries, the average gap is 63 years (Figure 1.7.2).

In Honduras, it is projected that the target will be achieved in the 2030s for the richest boys and girls but almost 100 years later among the poorest boys and girls. In 2011/12, 84% of the richest but only 10% of the poorest boys and girls completed lower secondary school (Honduras Ministry of Health et al., 2013). In Niger, the gap in achievement between the most and least advantaged groups will also span a century, with a massive gender gap: all the poorest girls are projected to be completing lower secondary school almost half a century after all the poorest boys if current trends continue.

Figure 1.7.2: Achieving universal lower secondary completion will require more concerted efforts
Projected year of achieving a lower secondary completion rate in excess of 97%, by gender and wealth, selected countries

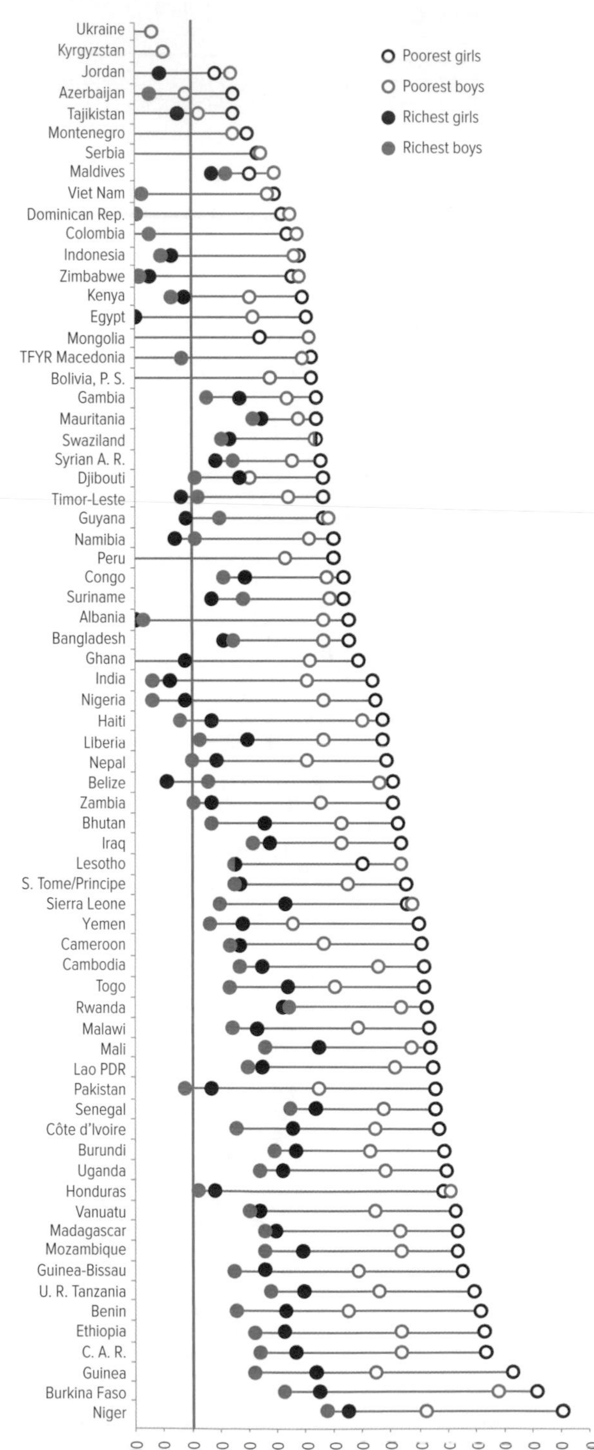

Source: EFA Global Monitoring Report team analysis (2013), based on Lange (2013).

How long will it take to achieve universal completion in sub-Saharan Africa?

Available data for primary and lower secondary completion cover more than four-fifths of the population in sub-Saharan Africa, so it is possible to project average achievement rates for different population groups for the entire region (Figure 1.7.3). On average, if recent trends continue, the region will not achieve universal primary completion until 2052, more than 35 years after the Dakar target and two decades after the likely target date for the post-2015 goals. While boys are expected to reach the target by 2046, on average, the richest boys are expected to achieve it in 2021 – before the post-2015 target – but the poorest boys only by 2069. Girls are further behind: on average they will reach it by 2057, with rich girls getting to zero by 2029. The poorest girls will, however, only reach the target by 2086.

On average, if recent trends continue, lower secondary school completion will be achieved in 2069 in sub-Saharan Africa, several decades after the target dates currently under discussion. Girls will achieve universal lower secondary completion by 2075, on average. Girls from the richest fifth of the population will reach the target by 2051, but girls from the poorest fifth of families are currently projected to achieve it only by 2111.

Overall, it is projected that, on average, all children in low income countries will be completing primary school by 2053 and lower secondary school by 2072. Lower middle income countries will achieve these targets about two decades earlier, in 2036 for primary school and in 2053 for secondary school.

Achieving universal youth literacy

Even children who complete primary school are not necessarily able to read and write (see Chapter 4). To assess how long it will take to achieve universal youth literacy, projections were made based on household survey data available in 37 countries for the whole population and in 68 countries for the female population only.

Figure 1.7.3: The achievement of universal primary and lower secondary education lies well into the future for sub-Saharan Africa
Projected year of achieving primary and lower secondary completion in excess of 97%, by population group, sub-Saharan Africa

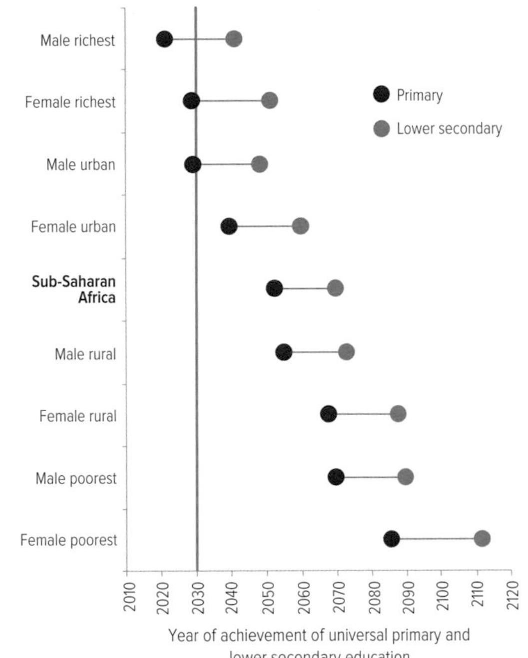

Source: EFA Global Monitoring Report team analysis (2013), based on Lange (2013).

Among the 37 countries for which information is available for the whole population, universal youth literacy may not be achieved before 2060 in 11 countries, most of them low and lower middle income countries, if recent trends continue. And among the larger group of 68 countries with only a sample of the female population, there are 22 low and lower middle income countries where universal youth literacy may not be achieved before 2060.

The poorest young women in low and middle income countries will only achieve universal literacy by 2072

The situation is worse for the poorest women: across the 68 countries, the poorest young women will only achieve universal literacy by 2072, on average. In India and the Lao People's Democratic Republic, the richest young women have already achieved universal literacy but the poorest will only do so around 2080. In Nigeria, while universal youth literacy has almost been achieved for the richest women aged 15 to 24, their poorest counterparts will need to wait 70 years to realize this fundamental right if no active steps are taken to fight illiteracy among the most disadvantaged groups (Figure 1.7.4).

Figure 1.7.4: Literacy is a distant dream for the most vulnerable young women
Projected year of achieving a female youth literacy rate in excess of 97%, by wealth, selected countries

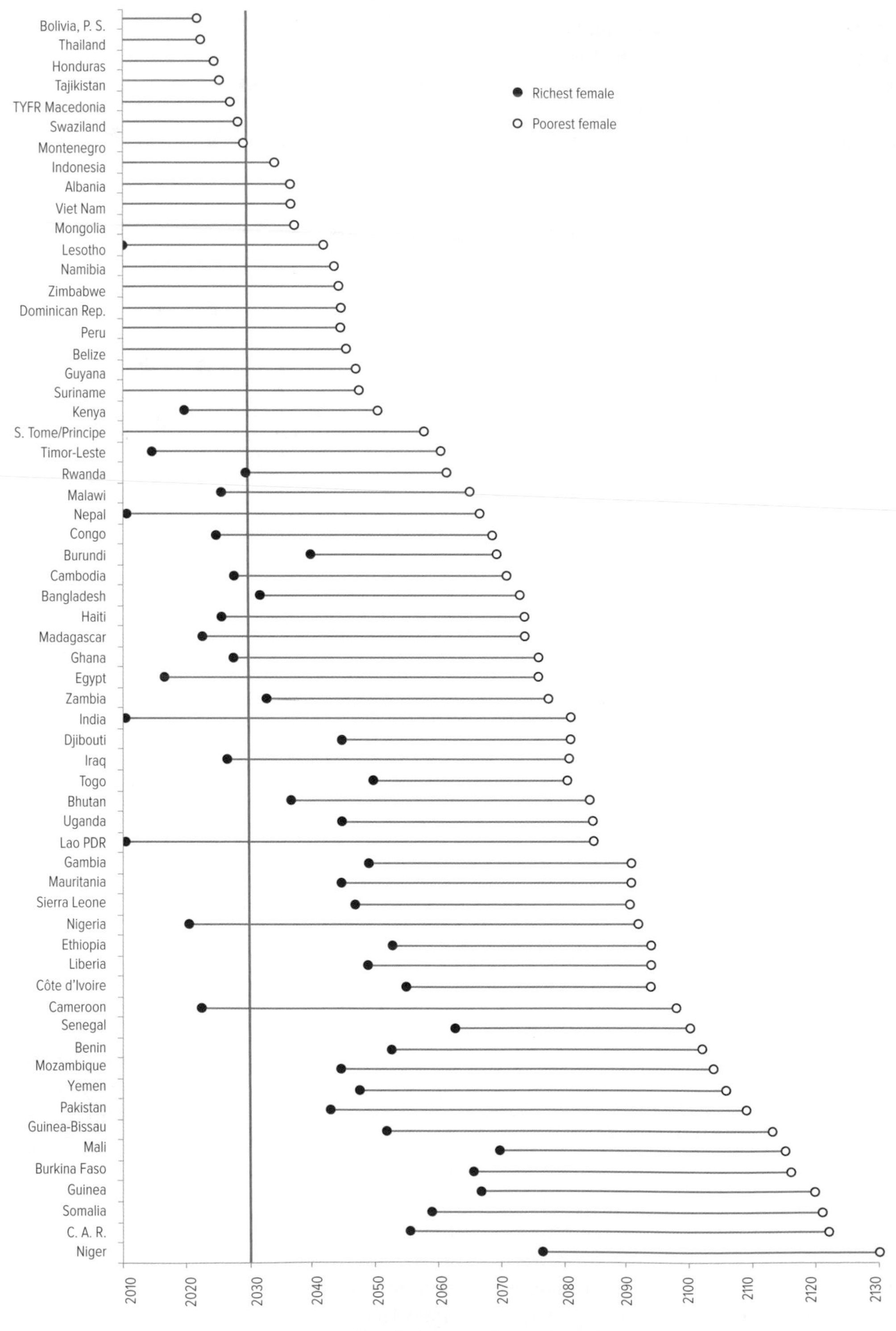

Source: EFA Global Monitoring Report team analysis (2013), based on Lange (2013).

Conclusion

These projections of the time it could take to achieve universal primary and secondary education and youth literacy are extremely disconcerting. However, they are based on recent trends that can be changed if governments, aid donors and the international education community take concerted action to make education available to all, including the marginalized. The key message that emerges from the analysis in this section is that it is vital to track progress towards education goals for the most disadvantaged groups after 2015, and to put policies in place that maintain and accelerate progress by redressing imbalances.

Monitoring global education targets after 2015

Since the six Education for All goals were adopted in Dakar, Senegal, in 2000, a lack of precise targets and indicators has prevented some education priorities from receiving the attention they deserve. To ensure that nobody is left behind after 2015, it is vital for the global framework to include targets and indicators, tracking the progress of the most disadvantaged.

As the new global development framework takes shape, a consensus is emerging over post-2015 education aims (UNESCO and UNICEF, 2013; United Nations, 2013b, 2013c). Common priorities include:

- addressing unfinished business on primary school completion;
- extending goals to include universal access to early childhood care and education programmes, and lower secondary school completion;
- ensuring that children are not only in school but are also learning;
- making sure all young people and adults have the skills needed for the world of work.

Better data are needed to help governments track progress of disadvantaged groups

These goals are a foundation on which to build more ambitious goals, including those set nationally.

The High Level Panel on the Post-2015 Development Agenda further noted the need for a data revolution to improve the quality of statistics and information available to citizens. It emphasized that data need to be disaggregated – broken down according to factors such as gender, geography, income or disability – to make sure no group is left behind due to circumstances of birth. It underlined the need for better data not only to help governments track progress and make evidence-based decisions, but also to strengthen accountability.

These issues have been at the heart of the *EFA Global Monitoring Report* over the past decade. Building on this experience, the Report team proposes five principles for setting goals after 2015 (Box 1.8.1).

Each of the EFA goals specified a commitment to equity – the basic principle of making sure every person has an equal chance of obtaining an education. Over the years, however, the *EFA Global Monitoring Report* has shown that progress in narrowing inequality in education has been limited. One possible reason is that the MDGs, which have dominated development planning, did not incorporate equity as a core principle.

Box 1.8.1: Guiding principles for setting education goals after 2015

The following five principles should guide post-2015 education goals:

- The right to an education, as guaranteed under international and national laws and conventions, must be at the core of the goals. As a right, education should be free and compulsory. It should help people fulfil their potential and should foster the well-being and prosperity of individuals and society.
- Ensuring that all people have an equal chance of education, regardless of their circumstances, must be at the heart of every goal. No person should be denied access to good quality education because of factors such as poverty, gender, location, ethnicity or disability.
- The goals should recognize the learning needs at each stage of a person's life and the fact that learning takes place in non-formal as well as formal settings.
- One core set of goals should encapsulate the overall ambition for education as part of the broader post-2015 global development framework replacing the MDGs. The goals should be universally applicable and accompanied by a more detailed set of targets and indicators that make up a post-2015 education framework.
- The goals should enable governments and the international community to be held to account for their education commitments. Each goal must have a specific deadline, be worded clearly and simply, be measurable, and have the ambition of leaving no one behind. The framework should include a commitment to independent regular and rigorous monitoring of the goals at the global and national levels.

Another is that disaggregated data were scarce when the goals were established, so targets and indicators were not developed that might have enabled national and global tracking of progress for different population groups. The growing availability of household survey data in recent years has eased the constraints on comparing groups within countries and over time. It is increasingly possible to measure equity targets, and incorporating them in post-2015 goals is now essential.

Equity is vital not just in access to education, however; it also needs to extend to education quality, so that each child has an equal chance to learn. While the sixth EFA goal focuses on education quality, an absence of concrete targets and of internationally comparable data has undermined efforts to monitor progress towards the goal. The neglect of learning outcomes in the MDGs also diminished attention to education quality. The international development agenda is now giving increasing recognition to learning outcomes, as the expansion of regional and international surveys has revealed low levels of attainment and extreme inequality in learning. While more coordination is needed before commonly agreed measures can be reached (see Goal 6), it is time to include learning outcomes in an improved global education monitoring framework.

Within this framework, goals must be simple, clear and measurable. One challenge the *EFA Global Monitoring Report* has faced over the past decade is that indicators were not identified for many of the goals and targets. As a result, progress towards the EFA goals and MDGs was measured using indicators that were not always compatible. In addition, some goals failed to receive the attention they deserved because they could not easily be measured, either with existing data or with data that could be collected within the timeframe. One example is goal 3 on skills, the focus of the 2012 *EFA Global Monitoring Report*. Such gaps need to be avoided in a post-2015 framework.

How far are we from achieving equality in education goals?

It is not acceptable for any child or adolescent to remain out of school or to be in school but not learning, or for any young person or adult to lack the skills needed to get decent jobs and lead fulfilling lives. The EFA Global Monitoring Report team proposes, therefore, that each global education goal should aim for no one to be left behind by 2030.

Targets should be set to achieve equality, taking into account that characteristics of disadvantage often interact: girls from poor households in rural areas, for example, are usually among the most marginalized. Each goal should be tracked not only overall but also according to the progress of the lowest performing groups in each country to ensure that these groups reach the target by 2030.

Collecting data on children with disabilities needs to be improved urgently

Among the lowest performing groups, children with disabilities are likely to face the most severe discrimination and exclusion, which in many contexts keep them out of school. Collecting data on children with different types and severity of impairments needs to be improved urgently so that policy-makers can be held accountable for making sure these children's right to education is fulfilled.

To inform post-2015 monitoring, this section analyses the progress made by those who were most behind in 2000 on selected goals that are likely to be set for 2030.[1] Through this analysis, several data limitations are identified that need to be overcome (Box 1.8.2).

1. For the analysis in this section, data from Demographic and Health Surveys and Multiple Indicator Cluster Surveys have been grouped into two waves: surveys undertaken between 1998 and 2003, and surveys undertaken since 2005. The reported results are based on 62 countries for which a survey is available in each period. The surveys are at least five years apart for each country.

Box 1.8.2: Data needs for monitoring education goals after 2015

Several difficulties in measuring progress in priority areas after 2015 deserve urgent attention:

- The number of children of primary school age who are not learning the basics, whether they are in school or not, is a key indicator that needs to be updated regularly. Its importance is underlined by the fact that the number is estimated at 250 million in this Report. But to measure progress, it is vital to have information from more countries on this indicator, as current surveys of learning achievement do not provide the necessary data.
- To enable better tracking of progress among the children who are the most disadvantaged – whether by poverty, gender, location or disability – comparable household surveys need to be conducted more frequently and should cover more countries, with sufficient observations to allow analysis of population subgroups.
- Despite progress since 2000, there are still major gaps for key indicators reported by the UNESCO Institute for Statistics. Extending goals, for example to include lower secondary completion, will require much better information from administrative data sources.
- For some indicators, there are still no data available systematically:
  - *Early childhood care and education programmes.* A survey should be developed that collects information on access to and quality of these programmes.
  - *Skills domains for young people and adults.* Indicators should be agreed for measuring foundation skills in literacy and numeracy, transferable skills, and technical and vocational skills, based on the analysis in the 2012 *EFA Global Monitoring Report*. Currently data are fairly widely available on foundation skills, but only from selected countries for some transferable skills, chiefly problem-solving (from the OECD PIAAC and World Bank STEP programmes). It is also vital to collect data on technical and vocational training programmes for youth and adults outside of the formal education system. The International Labour Organization collects some information on these programmes, but does not collate the data systematically.

Which young people are spending at least nine years in school?

By 2010, poor rural young women had spent fewer than 3 years in school in low and lower middle income countries

The number of years young people have spent in school is one measure of overall progress in access to education across countries.[2] For universal lower secondary education completion to be achieved, young people would need to have stayed in school for around nine years.

Between 2000 and 2010, the number of years spent in school increased from 4.8 to 6 in low income countries and from 7.1 to 8 in lower middle income countries. While this is a big achievement, the gap between advantaged and disadvantaged groups has remained wide.

In the early part of the decade, the richest urban young men had already spent 9 years in school in low income countries and 11.5 years in lower middle income countries. But the poorest rural young women had spent only 2.3 years in school in low income countries and 2.6 years in lower middle income countries.

By the latter part of the decade, the richest urban young men had spent more than 9.5 years in school in low income countries and more than 12 years in lower middle income countries, well above the 9-year target suggested for 2030. But the poorest rural young women had still spent fewer than 3 years in school in both low and lower middle income countries, leaving them well below even a 6-year target that is associated with universal primary completion, which is supposed to be achieved by 2015. This leaves a wide gap between the time they spent in school and that spent by the richest urban young men. In sub-Saharan Africa, the difference between the time the poorest rural females and the richest urban males spent in school actually widened between 2000 and 2010, from 6.9 years to 8.3 years (Figure 1.8.1).

Looking across the 62 low and middle income countries with data at the beginning and end of the decade, the lack of progress for the disadvantaged becomes even clearer. The poorest rural young women spent more than 6 years in school in 18 of the 62 countries in 2000, increasing to 21 countries in 2010. They spent more than 9 years in just 9 countries in 2000, mostly in Central and Eastern Europe and

2. The indicator used in this section measures the number of years of schooling completed among 20- to 24-year-olds and is net of years spent repeating grades. While many young people continue their education until their late 20s, the age group is sufficiently indicative of progress in the average population.

Central Asia, with no improvement by 2010. By contrast, the richest urban young men spent more than 6 years in school in all but one country, Niger, in 2000. And they reached more than 9 years in 42 countries in 2000, increasing to 51 countries in 2010. Progress has often been faster for the more advantaged group: between 2000 and 2010, the gap in years spent in school has widened by at least half a year in 29 countries of the 62 countries, and by at least one year in 19 of these countries.

Data for 11 sub-Saharan African countries confirm this general pattern: while the average number of years spent in school increased across the board, in all but two countries the progress was faster for the richest urban young men. For example, in Mozambique attainment among the richest urban young men increased by 3.5 years, to 9.6 years, while among the poorest rural young women it increased by less than a year, to 1.9 years (Figure 1.8.2).

Figure 1.8.1: Inequality in educational attainment remained unchanged over the last decade
Years of education, 20- to 24-year-olds, circa 2000 and 2010

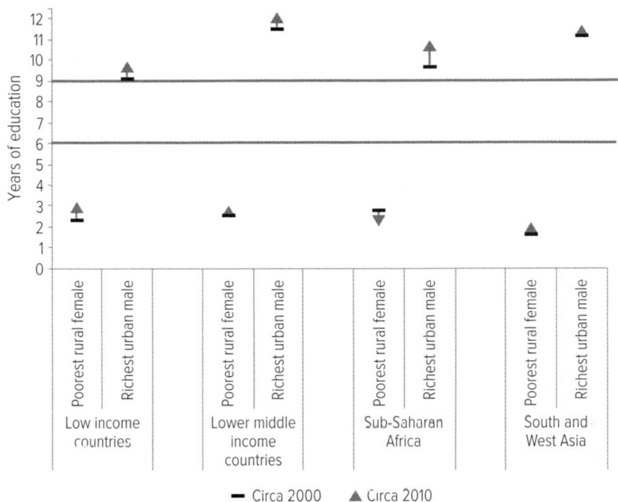

Source: EFA Global Monitoring Report team analysis (2013), based on Demographic and Health Surveys and Multiple Indicator Cluster Surveys.

Figure 1.8.2: In sub-Saharan Africa, the richest urban young men increased the number of years in school faster than the poorest rural young women
Years of education, 20- to 24-year-olds, selected countries, circa 2000 and 2010

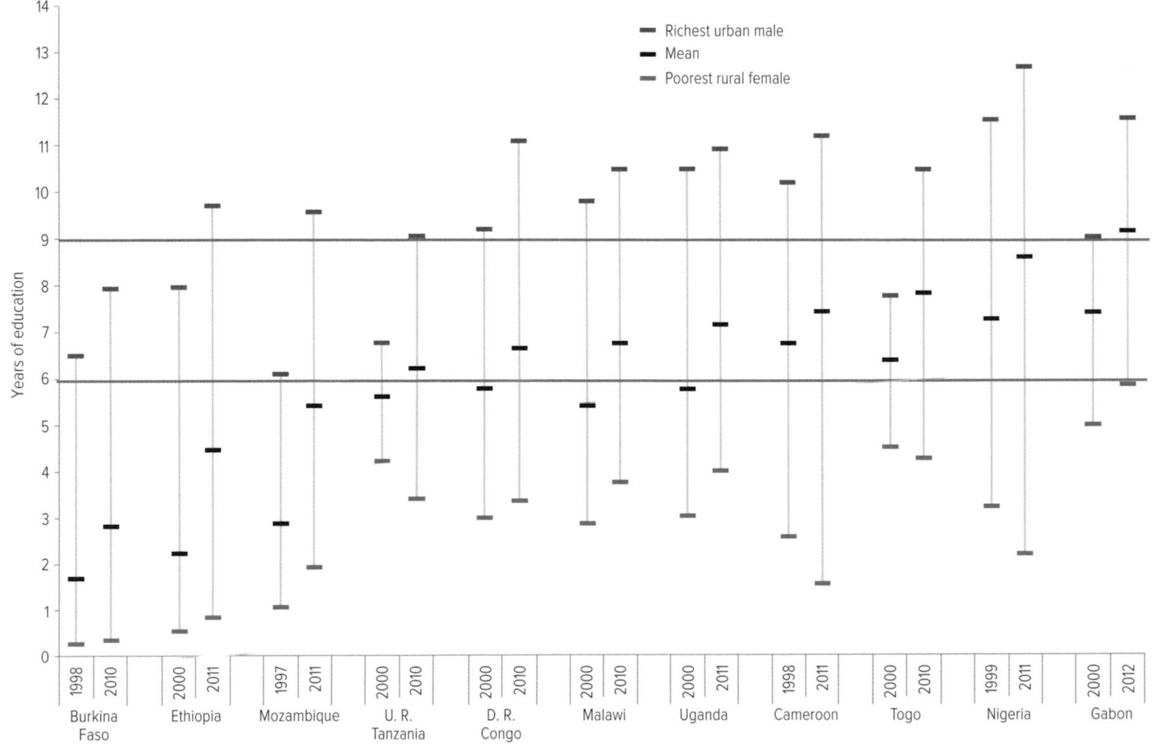

Source: EFA Global Monitoring Report team analysis (2013), based on Demographic and Health Surveys and Multiple Indicator Cluster Surveys.

Which children complete primary and lower secondary school?

Over the past decade there has been more progress in getting children into primary school than in making sure children complete primary or lower secondary education. In addition, the progress is unequally distributed; extreme inequality persists and in some cases has widened.

By 2010, only 23% of the poorest rural girls completed primary school in sub-Saharan Africa

One accomplishment since 2000 is the improvement in the proportion of children who enter school, which rose from 73% to 87% in low income countries. There is still, however, a long way to go in primary school completion, which increased from 45% to 60% in low income countries and from 72% to 79% in lower middle income countries. The proportion of adolescents completing lower secondary education increased more slowly over the decade, from 27% to 37% in low income countries and from 50% to 58% in lower middle income countries.

Insufficient attention to inequality in entry to and completion of school over the decade means that gaps remain wide. In sub-Saharan Africa, for example, almost all the richest boys in urban areas entered school in 2000. Moreover, 82% completed primary education and 62% completed lower secondary education, and these rates had improved by the end of the decade to 87% for primary school completion and 70% for lower secondary school completion.

By contrast, among the poorest girls in rural areas, 49% entered school at the beginning of the decade, increasing to 61% by the end of the decade. Only 25% completed primary education and 11% completed lower secondary education in 2000, and these rates had fallen by the end of the decade to 23% and 9%, respectively. Inequality in South and West Asia is also wide and largely unchanged: by the end of the decade, while 89% of the richest urban adolescent boys completed lower secondary school, only 13% of the poorest rural girls did so (Figure 1.8.3).

Across the 62 countries, a lack of progress in primary and lower secondary completion among the disadvantaged is clearly visible. At least half the poorest rural girls completed primary school in 2000 in only 23 countries, increasing to 29 in 2010. And at least half of them had completed lower secondary school in 2000 in just 10 countries, with no change over the decade. By contrast, at least half the richest urban boys completed primary school in 2000 in all countries except Burundi and Mozambique, and were doing so there as well by 2010. The number of countries where at least half the richest urban adolescent boys completed lower

Figure 1.8.3: Over the decade, disadvantaged groups mainly improved their access to school rather than their completion rates
Percentage of poorest rural girls and richest urban boys who have ever been to school, completed primary education, and completed lower secondary education, circa 2000 and 2010

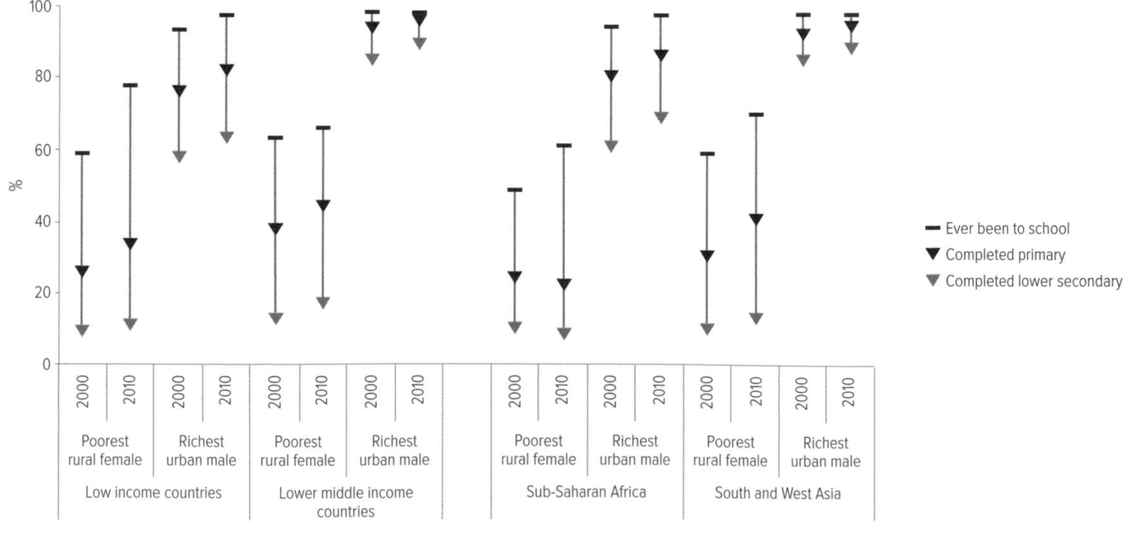

Source: EFA Global Monitoring Report team analysis (2013), based on Demographic and Health Surveys and Multiple Indicator Cluster Surveys.

secondary school increased from 39 in 2000 to 50 in 2010; the remaining 12 countries were all in sub-Saharan Africa.

Comparing these two population groups in 12 countries from five regions further shows that progress has often been slowest for the most disadvantaged. Progress in the Democratic Republic of the Congo has largely benefited the more advantaged: the proportion of the poorest rural girls completing primary school improved by only three percentage points over the decade, from 20% to 23%, while the corresponding share among the richest urban boys increased by eight percentage points, from 84% to 92%.

Similarly, among the poorest rural adolescent girls the proportion completing lower secondary school improved by seven percentage points over the decade, from 7% to 14%, while among the richest urban adolescent boys it increased by twelve percentage points, from 66% to 78%. In Burkina Faso, Ethiopia, Iraq, Mozambique and the United Republic of Tanzania, hardly any of the poorest rural females completed lower secondary school in 2010 (Figure 1.8.4).

In some countries, disadvantaged groups have made progress, albeit from a very low starting point. Countries including the Plurinational State of Bolivia, Nepal and Viet Nam achieved rapid progress for poor rural girls, showing that such change is possible. In Nepal, between 2001 and 2011, there were marked increases not only in the proportion of the poorest rural girls entering school, from 36% to 89%, but also in the share of those completing primary school, from 15% to 56%. Primary completion among the richest urban boys also increased, from 80% to 95%. There is still unfinished business, however: while nearly all the richest urban males complete primary school in the Plurinational State of Bolivia and in Viet Nam, only 72% of the poorest rural girls complete school in the Plurinational State of Bolivia and only 80% in Viet Nam.

In Iraq and Mozambique, hardly any of the poorest rural females completed lower secondary school in 2010

Which children are achieving minimum learning standards?

A goal on learning is an indispensable part of a future global education monitoring framework, but focusing only on children who take part in learning assessments can be misleading if large numbers of children never make it to the grade where skills are tested. For this reason, the EFA Global Monitoring Report team has argued that all children should be taken into account, not just those who take part in learning assessments.

Figure 1.8.4: Ensuring that the poorest girls complete lower secondary school remains a major challenge

Percentage of poorest rural girls and richest urban boys who have ever been to school, and completed primary and lower secondary education, selected countries, circa 2000 and 2010

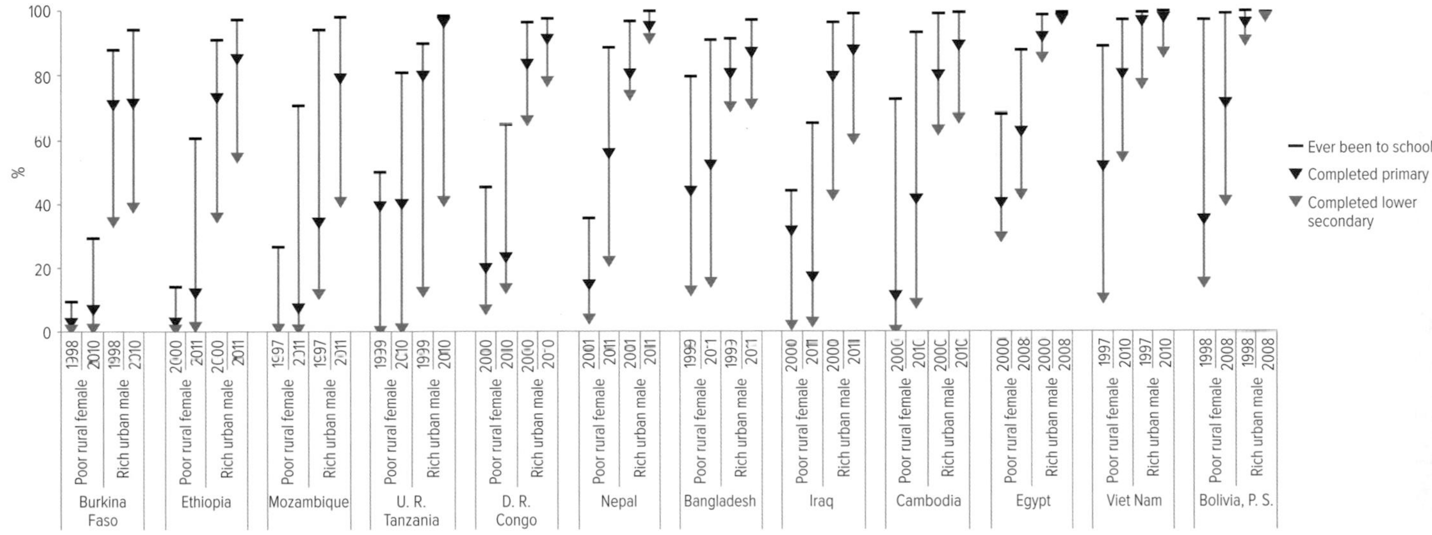

Source: EFA Global Monitoring Report team analysis (2013), based on Demographic and Health Surveys and Multiple Indicator Cluster Surveys.

Data from SACMEQ show how much difference it can make if out-of-school children are included when assessing the numbers who are learning the basics (Figure 1.8.5). In the United Republic of Tanzania, the proportion of children in grade 6 who achieved a minimum standard in reading was 90% in 2007, ranging from 97% among the richest urban boys to 80% among the poorest rural girls. However, while 92% of the richest urban boys of grade 6 age had reached that grade, only 40% of the poorest rural girls had done so. If it is assumed that children who did not reach grade 6 could not have achieved the minimum standard, then the proportions among children of that cohort who learned the basics were 90% for the richest urban boys and 32% for the poorest rural girls.

In Malawi, Uganda and Zambia, less than 10% of the poorest rural girls had learned the basics

In Malawi, Uganda and Zambia, less than 10% of the poorest rural girls learned the basics. These striking statistics emphasize the need for monitoring learning of all children, a point reiterated in Part 3 of this Report.

Figure 1.8.5: Assessing the number of children learning should not exclude those not tested

Percentage of children who achieved minimum learning standard in reading, selected countries, southern and eastern Africa, 2007

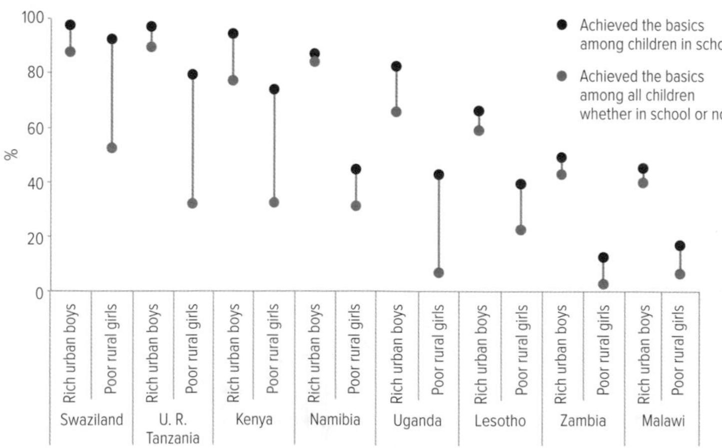

Note: The percentage of children in school was calculated using Demographic and Health Survey data from the nearest year to 2007 and projected to 2007 using a linear trend based on earlier surveys. It is assumed that children not in school have not achieved the minimum learning standards.

Source: EFA Global Monitoring Report team analysis (2013), based on Demographic and Health Surveys and SACMEQ data.

Few countries monitor education inequality

To make sure inequality in education access and learning is overcome by 2030, country plans need to include specific targets to monitor progress in education participation and learning for individual population groups. A review of the education plans of 53 countries for this Report shows that very few currently do so, although there are some encouraging exceptions (Box 1.8.3).

In terms of education participation, gender is the dimension of potential disadvantage covered best in education plans. Even so, only 24 of the 53 plans included gender equality targets on participation in primary and lower secondary education. While most of these targets were restricted to enrolment ratios, some countries included gender targets in other aspects. For example, Ghana targeted gender parity in primary and lower secondary education enrolment, attendance and completion (Ghana Ministry of Education, 2010).

By contrast, only three countries specifically aimed to reduce disparity in access between rural and urban areas in primary and lower secondary education enrolment. Indonesia, for example, sought to reduce enrolment disparity between cities and rural areas by 36% over five years (Indonesia Ministry of National Education, 2005). Otherwise, countries aimed to increase enrolment in rural areas but without setting a target or timeline. Twelve countries included indicators on primary and lower secondary education enrolment by region, but only five of these specified a target for inequality.

Of the 53 plans, only 4 included indicators on participation by particular ethnic groups. But most of these plans focused only on increases in enrolment, and no countries set specific targets on how much to reduce disparity. Only Bangladesh, Kenya and the Lao People's Democratic Republic had an enrolment indicator that differentiated between poorer and richer children.

Measures of progress in learning are not common. Of the 53 countries surveyed, 31 included indicators on learning outcomes at either the primary or lower secondary level. Of these countries, only 19 specified a target.

Even fewer countries measured inequality in learning outcomes. Only eight countries do so at the primary level and eight at the lower secondary level, and in most cases monitoring is restricted to gender inequality. At the secondary level, six countries aim to reduce gender inequality in learning to some extent, although only Rwanda had a target and timeline: 90% of boys and girls should pass the national lower secondary school grade 3 examination by 2015, compared with a baseline of 56% for boys and 44% for girls in 2009.

Box 1.8.3: Some countries take a close interest in education inequality

Some countries stand out for including indicators that pay attention to disadvantaged groups:

- In Bangladesh, the monitoring framework of the Third Primary Education Development Programme proposed monitoring enrolment ratios across wealth quintiles, using household survey data. The monitoring framework also included an index that would allow planners to assess the relative performance of the approximately 500 subdistricts. A target is set of narrowing the gap in the value of this index between the 10 top performing and 10 lowest performing subdistricts by one-third over five years. The index includes subdistrict performance in the end of primary school examination.

- In the Lao People's Democratic Republic, the 2009–2015 Education Sector Development Framework includes indicators on enrolment at the national, provincial and district levels, by gender and location. In addition, minimum learning standards are to be defined for grades 3, 5 and 9 and then assessed through sample surveys of schools.

- In Namibia, the Education and Training Sector Improvement Programme set targets on how much children should have learned by the end of primary education. Linked to SACMEQ, the targets included reducing the regional dispersion of reading scores by 4%. In terms of access, the document expressed a commitment to monitor participation for orphans and other vulnerable children as well as children from marginalized groups. For example, a target was set for 80% of orphans and other vulnerable children from each region to be enrolled in primary and secondary education by the final year of the plan.

Sources: Bangladesh Ministry of Primary and Mass Education (2011b1); Lao PDR Ministry of Education (2009); Namibia Ministry of Education (2007).

Only four countries aim to monitor inequality in learning beyond gender at the primary or lower secondary level: Bangladesh, Belize, Namibia and Sri Lanka. In Belize, scores on primary and secondary examinations are to be disaggregated by district and urban/rural location (Belize Ministry of Education, 2011). In Sri Lanka, regional targets are set for achievement scores in mathematics and native language. On average, scores are targeted to increase by four percentage points over the duration of the plan, but with higher increases envisaged for lower performing regions (Sri Lanka Ministry of Education, 2006).

Conclusion

If post-2015 goals are to be achieved, regular independent monitoring is essential

The failure over the past decade to assess progress in education goals by various population subgroups has concealed wide inequality. The invisibility of this inequality is further reflected in the lack of national targets in country plans for assessing progress in narrowing inequality gaps in access or learning.

Post-2015 goals need to include a commitment to make sure the most disadvantaged groups achieve benchmarks set for goals. Failure to do so could mean that measurement of progress continues to mask the fact that the advantaged benefit the most.

It is not enough just to set goals. If they are to be achieved, regular independent monitoring is essential so that progress can be tracked, policies that have facilitated progress can be identified and governments and the international community can be held to account for their promises. The *EFA Global Monitoring Report* has put education ahead of many other sectors in this regard. It is crucial for such independent monitoring to continue after 2015.

Chapter 2 Financing Education For All

Credit: Nguyen Thanh Tuan/UNESCO

Teaching diversity: At a school in La Pan Tân Commune, Muong Khuong county, Viet Nam, students from 10 ethnic groups are taught in groups.

Unless urgent action is taken to increase aid to education, the goal of ensuring that every child is in school and learning by 2015 will be seriously jeopardized. With little time left, closing the financing gap may seem impossible. But this chapter shows that the gap could be filled by raising more domestic revenue, devoting a fair share of existing and projected government resources to education, and sharpening the focus of aid spending.

Trends in financing Education for All

Highlights

- Many governments, particularly in poorer countries, have increased their commitment to education: 30 low and middle income countries increased their spending on education by more than 1 percentage point of GNP between 1999 and 2011.
- After 2015, a common financing target should be set for countries to allocate at least 6% of GNP on education. Of the 150 countries with data, only 41 had reached this level by 2011.
- Many countries have the opportunity to expand their tax base. For a group of 67 low and middle income countries, a modest increase in tax-raising efforts, and allocating 20% of the funds raised to education, could increase education spending by US$153 billion, or 72%, in 2015. This would raise the average share of GDP spent on education by these countries to 6%.
- Aid to basic education fell by 6% between 2010 and 2011, its first decrease since 2002.
- Low income countries were particularly hard hit by the reduction in aid to basic education: 19 of them experienced a cut, and 13 of those were in sub-Saharan Africa. The reduction was a result of 24 donors, including 9 of the 15 largest donors, reducing their spending.

Table 2.1: Public spending on education, by region and income level, 1999 and 2011

	Public education spending					
	% of GNP		% of government expenditure on education		Per capita (primary education) (PPP constant 2010 US$)	
	1999	**2011**	**1999**	**2011**	**1999**	**2011**
World	**4.6**	**5.1**	**15.0**	**15.5**	**2 149**	**3 089**
Low income	3.1	4.1	16.4	18.3	102	115
Lower middle income	4.6	5.1	15.9	16.9	356	545
Upper middle income	4.8	5.1	15.8	15.5	1 117	1 745
High income	5.3	5.6	13.3	13.2	4 752	6 721
Sub-Saharan Africa	4.0	5.0	17.1	18.7	345	468
Arab States	5.3	4.8	21.0	18.1	822	1 338
Central Asia	3.4	4.1	15.4	12.3	...	...
East Asia and the Pacific	3.9	4.4	15.0	16.6	2 216	3 245
South and West Asia	3.9	3.7	14.6	15.0	297	573
Latin America and the Caribbean	5.0	5.5	14.4	16.2	1 142	1 753
Central and Eastern Europe	4.8	5.2	12.4	12.2	1 813	3 846
North America and Western Europe	5.6	6.2	13.3	13.1	5 990	8 039

Note: World, regional and income values are means for countries with data in both 1999 and 2011, and may therefore not match what is reported in Statistical Table 9.
Source: EFA Global Monitoring Report team calculations (2013), based on UIS database.

Donors have not met their commitment to ensure that no country would be prevented from achieving Education for All due to lack of resources

Insufficient financing, particularly by aid donors, has been one of the main obstacles to achieving the Education for All goals. In 2010, the EFA Global Monitoring Report team calculated that it would take another US$16 billion per year in external financing to achieve good quality basic education for all in 46 low and lower middle income countries by 2015. Rather than increasing, however, aid has stagnated in recent years. Donors have not met the commitment they made at the World Education Forum in Dakar in 2000 to ensure that no country would be prevented from achieving Education for All due to lack of resources.

The EFA Global Monitoring Report team has calculated that, as a result of this stagnation, it would now take US$29 billion per year between 2012 and 2015, in addition to the amount that governments are spending, to achieve basic education for all. Taking into account the US$3 billion currently provided by donors to the 46 countries, this leaves an annual financing gap of US$26 billion (UNESCO, 2013c). Unfortunately, it seems that donors are more likely to reduce their aid than increase it in coming years. Unless urgent action is taken to change aid patterns, the goal of ensuring that every child is in school and learning by 2015 will be seriously jeopardized.

With little time left before 2015, closing the financing gap might seem impossible. But analysis in this chapter shows that the gap could be filled by raising more domestic revenue, devoting an adequate share of existing and projected government resources to education, and sharpening the focus of external assistance.

Post-2015 global education goals are expected to be more ambitious than the EFA goals, extending to lower secondary education. The shortfall in the financing necessary to achieve universal basic and lower secondary education by 2015 is estimated at US$38 billion annually, a gap that improvement in domestic spending alone cannot bridge.

Those who control global resources need to recommit themselves to international education goals, agree to be accountable for their financial commitments and deliver on them in a transparent way, so that they contribute to common education objectives. The post-2015 framework should therefore include explicit financing targets so that all funders can be held to account for their promises.

Figure 2.1: Most low and middle income countries have increased education spending since 1999
Public expenditure on education as percentage of GNP, low and middle income countries, 1999 and 2011

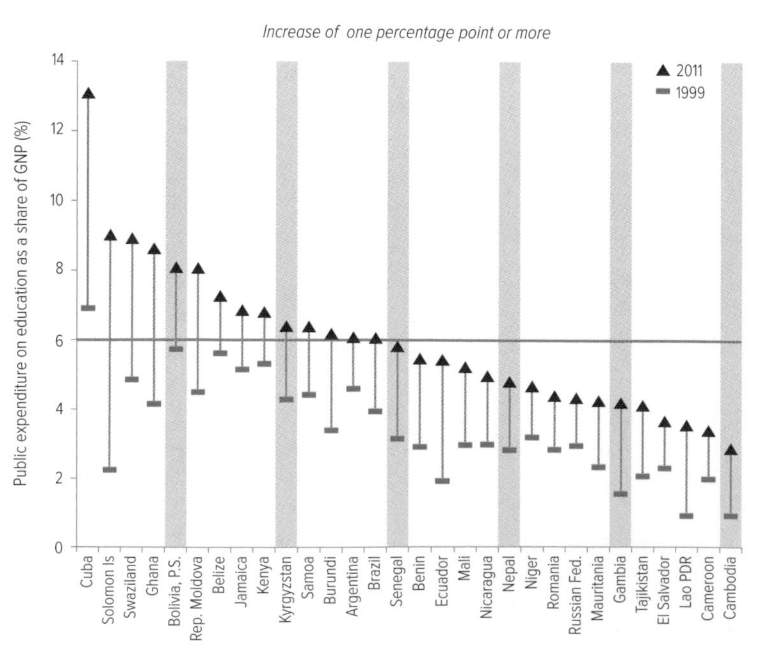

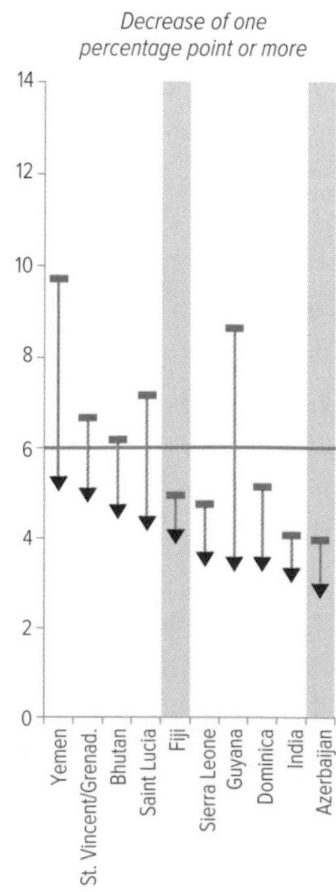

Source: Annex, Statistical Table 9.

Many countries far from EFA need to spend more on education

Domestic spending on education has increased in recent years, particularly in low and lower middle income countries, partly because their economic growth has been improving. In richer countries, by contrast, the economic downturn has hit government budgets for education.

Many governments, particularly in poorer countries, have also increased their commitment to education. Globally, the amount devoted to education rose from 4.6% of gross national product (GNP) in 1999 to 5.1% in 2011 (Table 2.1). In low and middle income countries it rose faster: 30 of these countries increased their spending on education by one percentage point of GNP or more between 1999 and 2011 (Figure 2.1).

The Dakar Framework for Action did not establish financing targets for education. This has resulted in wide differences in government spending on education, so children's chances of being in school and learning continue to depend on where they happen to be born.

The failure to set a common financing target for the EFA goals should be addressed after 2015, with a specific goal that countries should allocate at least 6% of GNP to education. Some countries, such as the United Republic of Tanzania, already spend more than 6% of GNP on education, showing that such a target is feasible. Of the 150 countries with data, however, only 41 spent 6% or more of GNP on education in 2011. It is of particular concern that 10 low and middle income countries reduced their education spending as a percentage of GNP by one percentage point or more over the decade. India, for example, decreased its spending on education from 4.4% of GNP in 1999 to 3.3% in 2010, jeopardizing the huge progress it has made in getting more children into school, and its prospects for improving its poor quality of education.

The United Republic of Tanzania spends more than 6% of GNP on education

It is unacceptable that 25 countries, including Bangladesh, the Central African Republic, the Democratic Republic of the Congo and Pakistan – most of which are still a long way from achieving EFA – dedicate less than 3% of GNP to education. It is particularly worrying that some countries that were already spending a small proportion of GNP on education, such as Bangladesh, have

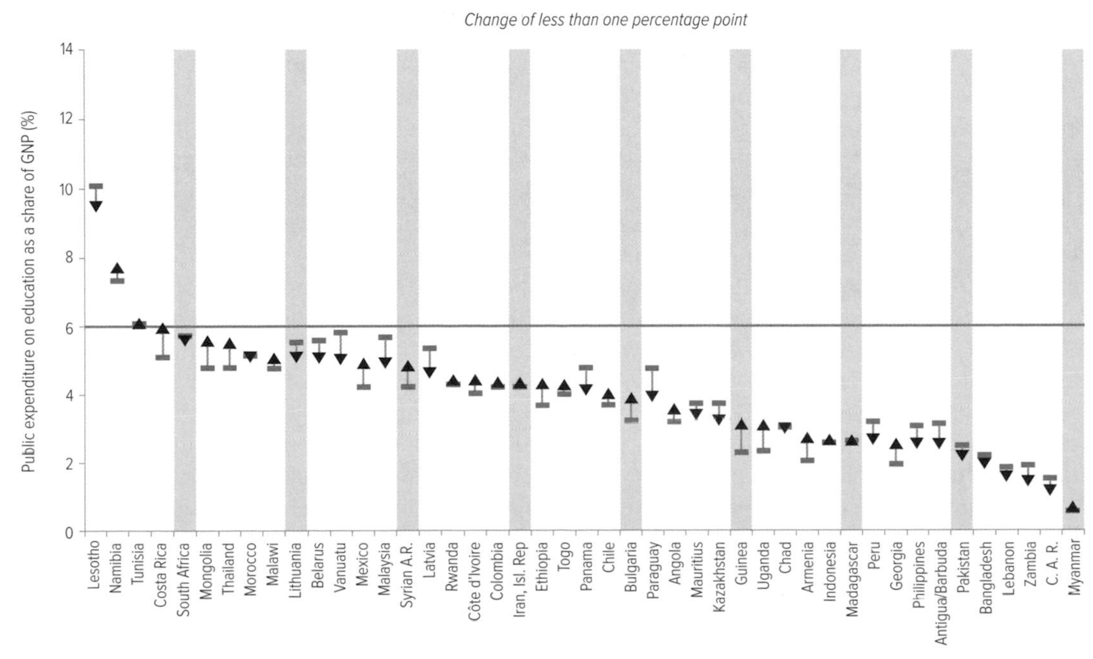

reduced their spending further. Pakistan, home to 10% of the world's out-of-school children, cut spending on education from 2.6% of GNP in 1999 to 2.3% in 2010.

If governments are to meet a target of spending 6% of GNP on education, they must not only raise sufficient revenue from tax as a share of national income, but also allocate a sufficient proportion of domestic spending to education. It is widely accepted that countries should allocate at least 20% of their budget to education, and the EFA Global Monitoring Report team recommends making this an explicit target for the goals set after 2015. Yet only 15% of government expenditure globally was directed to education in 2011, a proportion little changed since 1999.

Low income countries increased the share of government spending on education the most over the decade, having raised their spending from around 16% in 1999 to 18% in 2011. It is lower middle and upper middle income countries that are furthest from the target of 20%: while they were at a similar level to low income countries in 1999, their spending has hardly changed since. Lower middle income countries spent 17% on education in 2011 and upper middle income countries 15%. The latter, in particular, should do far more to improve children's education chances through their own spending, leaving more external funds for the countries most in need.

Only 25 countries spent more than 20% on education in 2011

Of the 138 countries with data, only 25 spent more than 20% on education in 2011, including 17 low and lower middle income countries and 8 upper middle and high income countries. Nineteen of the 25 countries spending more than 20% on education in 2011 had comparable data for 1999; of these, 12 countries, including Nepal, started below the 20% benchmark in 1999 but increased their allocation. Indeed, some of the poorest countries started from a low base in 1999 but were able to allocate more than 20% of their budget to education in 2011 (Figure 2.2). These countries have seen fast progress in education in recent years. Participation in primary schooling in Ethiopia, for instance, has achieved impressive improvement: the net enrolment ratio, which was just 37% in 1999, had increased to 87% by 2011, far above the sub-Saharan African regional average. Burundi

Figure 2.2: Only a few countries spend at least one-fifth of
Public expenditure on education as percentage of government

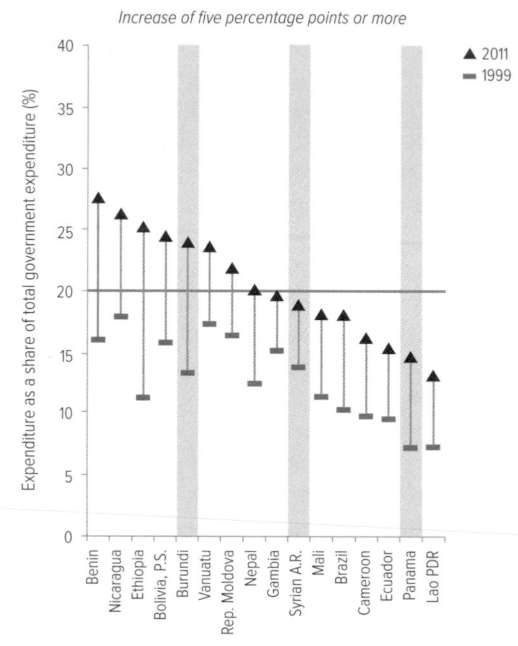

Source: Annex, Statistical Table 9.

had attained gender parity in primary school participation by 2011, in contrast to 1999 when it had only 8 girls in school for every 10 boys.

At the other extreme, it is worrying that the Democratic Republic of the Congo spent less than 9% of its budget on education in 2010, even though it is estimated to have well over 2.4 million children out of school (UNESCO, 2012). It is also of concern that at least six low and middle income countries decreased spending on education as a share of total government expenditure between 1999 and 2011 by five percentage points or more. While some of these countries had been allocating more than 20% to education, their spending has now fallen below this threshold. Chad's education spending, already below 20% in 1999, had fallen to 12% by 2011, contributing to it having some of the lowest education indicators in the world. In 2010, just 21% of children completed a cycle of primary schooling. India, which faces huge challenges in improving the quality of its education, spent 10% of its government budget on education in 2011, a reduction from 13% in 1999.

their budget on education
expenditure, low and middle income countries, 1999 and 2011

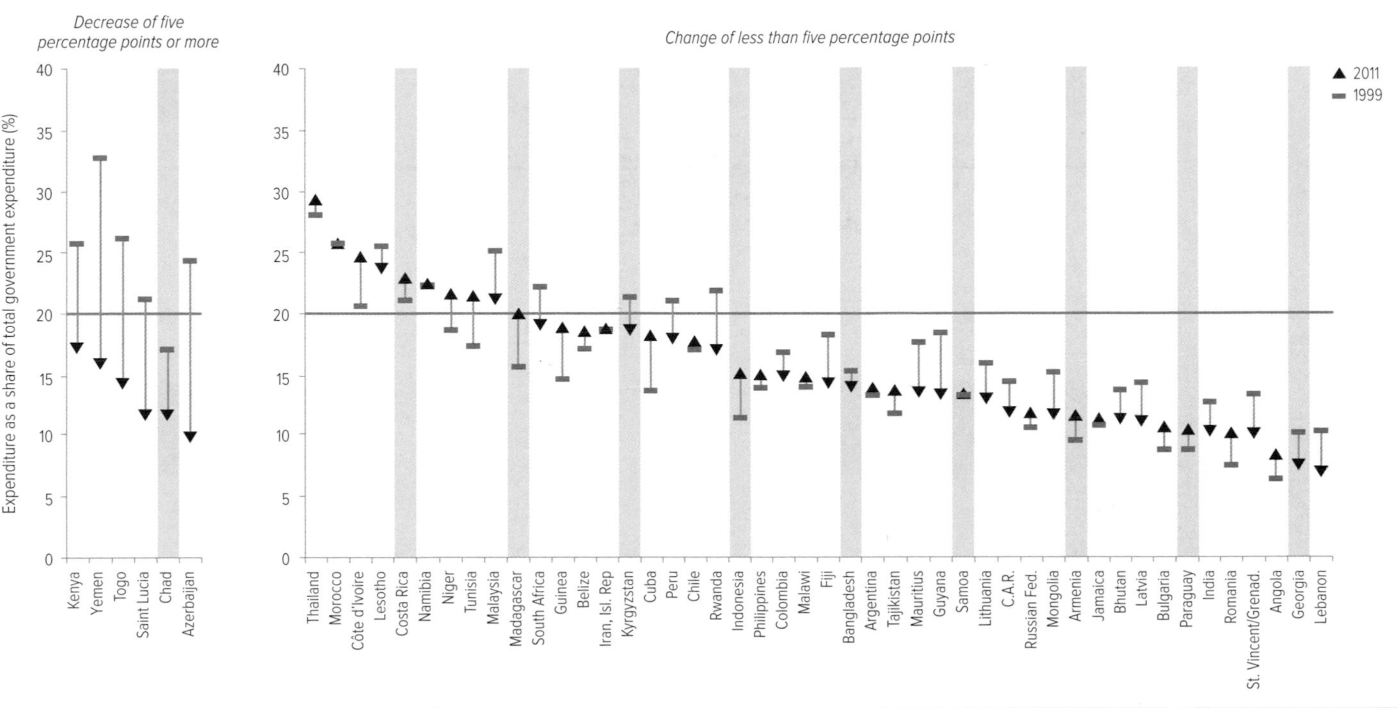

Countries' financial commitment to education can be gauged not only by looking at their education spending as a percentage of GNP and of the total government budget, but also by tracking the evolution of their education budgets in real terms – and here again there is cause for concern. Of the 49 countries with data, 25 planned to shrink their education budgets in real terms between 2011 and 2012 (Figure 2.3, Groups A and C). Of these 25 countries, 16 were in sub-Saharan Africa; they included Burundi, the Democratic Republic of the Congo, Madagascar, Malawi and Uganda – countries that are still a long way from the EFA goals. The Central African Republic's education spending was expected to decline by 13% between 2011 and 2012, resulting in it reaching just 11% as a proportion of the government budget in 2012.

Beyond sub-Saharan Africa, Bangladesh and Nepal were also expected to decrease their education budgets in real terms. Bangladesh planned to reduce its budget by 16% in 2012, resulting in its spending on education reaching only 13% of the government budget.

Some countries are resisting this negative trend, however. Afghanistan was expected to increase its spending on education by 15% in real terms between 2011 and 2012, although the share of the education budget as a proportion of government spending was likely to remain below 20% (Group D). Benin and Ethiopia are among just a handful of countries with data available where governments planned to increase resources to the education sector in real terms and where the sector is already well served by government spending (Group B).

25 countries planned to shrink their education budgets between 2011 and 2012

Figure 2.3: Many countries that are far from reaching EFA goals cut their education budgets in 2012
Percentage change in education budget, 2011 to 2012, and education as a share of government expenditure

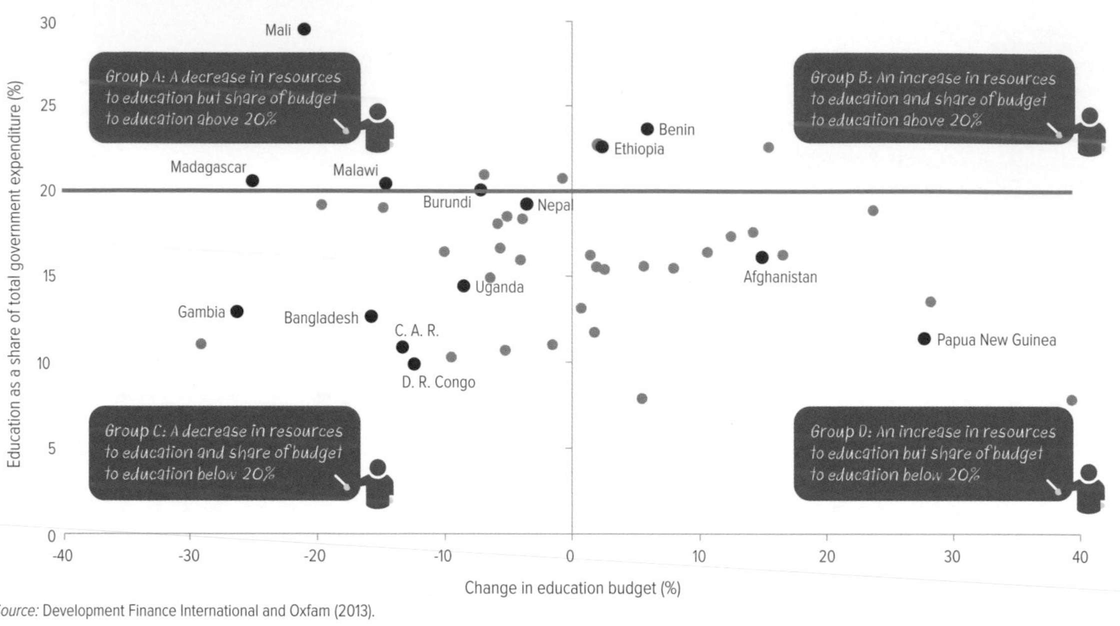

Source: Development Finance International and Oxfam (2013).

Domestic resources can help bridge the education financing gap

The benefits of Africa's growth have not yet been fairly distributed

Sustained economic growth in many of the world's poorest countries has increased the resources that governments can raise domestically to finance their education strategies. Many of the countries furthest from the EFA goals, however, do not sufficiently tap their tax base or devote an adequate share of their revenue to education.

Over the past decade, economic growth has enabled countries such as Ghana and India to cross the threshold from low income to lower middle income status, while countries such as Angola have moved to upper middle income status. Sub-Saharan Africa has achieved annual economic growth of around 5.4% in recent years, with the economies of poor countries such as Ethiopia growing by as much as 9.9% per year (World Bank, 2013c).

The benefits of this growth have not yet been fairly distributed, however. Nigeria's economy, for example, grew by at least 5% per year since 2003 but its net enrolment ratio has fallen from 61% in 1999 to 58% in 2010 (World Bank, 2013f). To guarantee their citizens' right to education and tap into education's power to transform lives, it is vital that countries put in place strong fiscal policies, backed by budget policy reforms to allocate an adequate share of public spending to education and promote equity in its distribution.

Strengthening tax systems is not only crucial for wider development but also an essential condition for achieving Education for All. This section shows that if governments in 67 low and middle income countries modestly increased their tax-raising efforts and devoted a fifth of their budget to education, they could raise an additional US$153 billion for education spending in 2015, amounting to a total of US$365 billion in 2015. This would increase the average share of GDP spent on education from 3% to 6% by 2015.

Raising taxes and allocating an adequate share to education

It is estimated that countries need to raise 20% of their GDP in taxes to achieve the Millennium Development Goals (MDGs) (IMF et al., 2011). Few low and middle income countries manage to mobilize domestic resources on this scale, however. Among those that do, many do not allocate a sufficient proportion to education. Of the 67 countries for which data are available on tax revenue as a proportion of GDP as well as on the allocation of government revenue to education, only 7 reach the 20% threshold on both indicators (Figure 2.4). Namibia, which raises 24% of its GDP in taxes and allocates 22% of its government budget to education, shows that such goals are attainable.

More commonly, countries' revenue from taxes is inadequate and education receives insufficient resources. Of the 67 countries for which data are available, 37 are below the 20% threshold on both indicators. In Pakistan, for example, tax revenue is just 10% of GDP and education receives only around 10% of government expenditure. If the government increased its tax revenue to 14% of GDP by 2015 and allocated one-fifth of this to education, it could raise sufficient funds to get all of Pakistan's children and adolescents into school.

Ethiopia is one of 11 among the 67 countries that has been successful in prioritizing education in its government budget but could do far more to maximize revenue from taxation, which would further increase the resources available for education. In 2011, the government received 12% of GDP from taxes, on average. If this proportion were to increase to 16% by 2015, and 25% continued to be allocated to education, the sector would receive 18% more resources, equivalent to US$435 million – enabling US$19 more to be spent per primary school age child.

By contrast, Angola has succeeded in converting much of its vast natural resource wealth into government revenue, with tax revenue representing 42% of GDP, but it only spends 9% of these funds on education, one of the lowest proportions in the world. Raising the share to 20% would increase resources to education almost two and a half times, or by US$7 billion. Assuming half of this is allocated to primary education, it could more than double

Namibia raises 24% of its GDP in taxes and allocates 22% of its government budget to education

Figure 2.4: Countries need to both mobilize resources and prioritize education

Tax revenue as percentage of GDP and education expenditure as percentage of total government expenditure, selected countries, 2011

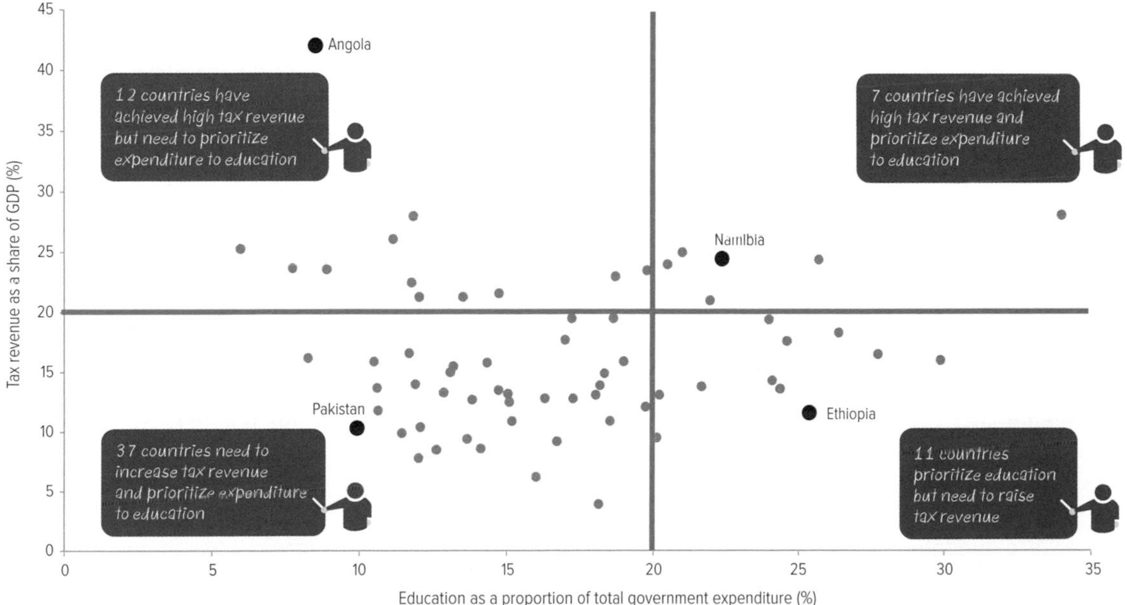

Sources: IMF (2012); Annex, Statistical Table 9.

resources spent per primary school age child. In total, 12 of the 67 countries raise 20% or more of GDP through taxes but devote less than 20% of government spending to education.

Tax revenue as a share of GDP grew by 0.44% per year in low and lower middle income countries between 2002 and 2009 (World Bank, 2013f), but many countries need to make much faster progress. At this rate of growth, only 4 of the 48 countries currently raising less than 20% of GDP through taxes would reach the 20% threshold by 2015, and Pakistan – to give one example of a country far from the target – would not reach 20% until 2034.

In some middle income countries there is far greater potential to mobilize domestic resources for education

Taxation as a pillar of development and education progress

A well-functioning taxation system enables governments to support the education system with domestic revenue instead of borrowing or relying on external finance. In high income countries in North America and Western Europe, tax revenue amounted to 27% of GDP in 2011. Most of these funds came from tax on income (13% of GDP), the majority of which is taxation of individuals.

By contrast, in sub-Saharan Africa, tax revenue accounted for 18% of GDP, with taxes on both individual and corporate income at 7% of GDP. In South and West Asia, the tax share was even lower: 12% of GDP, with revenue from individual and corporate income tax making up 4% of GDP. Unlike in North America and Western Europe, a quarter of the tax revenue in sub-Saharan Africa and South and West Asia comes from international trade and transactions (IMF, 2012).

While low and lower middle income countries are more dependent than richer countries on international and national corporate taxes for government revenue, they receive only 22% of the total annual corporation tax revenue collected globally. One study estimates that a percentage point increase could raise revenue by US$10 billion per year for these countries (Hearson, 2013).[1] If 20% of this additional income were allocated to education, an additional US$2 billion could be mobilized annually to help fill the financing gap.

1. This estimate assumes that two-thirds of corporation tax revenue comes from multinational corporations.

Many of the world's poorest countries cannot expect domestic taxes alone to provide the financing needed to meet the EFA goals in the near future. In some middle income countries, however, such as Egypt, India and the Philippines, there is far greater potential to mobilize domestic resources for education. India became the world's 10th largest economy in 2011, but tax revenue was equivalent to only 16% of GDP, and government expenditure per person was just US$409. By contrast, in Brazil – the world's sixth largest economy – tax revenue was equivalent to 24% of GDP and expenditure per person was US$4,952 (IMF, 2013).

This huge difference is a key reason Brazil has managed to go further in improving education quality and narrowing learning inequality. The levels of current spending on education as a share of total government expenditure in the two countries also reflect the greater priority that Brazil affords to the education sector. In 2011, government spending on education in Brazil was 18% of total government expenditure, with US$2,218 being spent on each primary school child. India devoted 10% of the government budget to education, with US$212 spent per primary school child. If India reduced tax exemptions, tackled tax evasion and diversified its tax base, it could greatly change this picture.

Limit tax exemptions

While low and middle income countries as a group rely heavily on tax revenue from corporations, many of them forgo considerable revenue from businesses by granting too many tax exemptions. In much of sub-Saharan Africa, these exemptions can amount to the equivalent of 5% of GDP (UK House of Commons International Development Committee, 2012). In the United Republic of Tanzania, for instance, tax exemptions were equivalent to around 4% of GDP between 2005/06 and 2007/08; it is estimated that if these taxes had been collected, they could have provided 40% more resources for education (Uwazi, 2010).

Despite committing a large share of government expenditure to education, Ethiopia has one of the lowest tax/GDP ratios of all developing countries, reaching just 12% of GDP. This is largely due to generous tax exemptions, which amounted to about 4.2% of GDP in 2008/09 (Abay, 2010). If Ethiopia eliminated these exemptions and devoted 10% of the resulting revenue to basic education, then a country with 1.7 million out-of-school children would have an additional US$133 million available, enough to get approximately 1.4 million more children into school.

Countries in South Asia have some of the world's lowest tax/GDP ratios, mainly because large tax exemptions are granted to strong domestic lobby groups, such as landowners. In Pakistan, the tax/GDP ratio of 10% can be partly explained by the political influence of the agricultural lobby in tax rate negotiations. While the agricultural sector makes up 22.5% of Pakistan's GDP, its share in tax revenue is just 1.2% (Asad, 2012). Total tax exemptions amounted to the equivalent of 3% of GDP (Pasha, 2010).

In India, the majority of tax revenue forgone is due to exemptions from custom and excise duties, and, to a lesser extent, from corporate income tax. The revenue lost to exemptions came to the equivalent of 5.7% of GDP in 2012/13 (Bandyopadhyay, 2013); if 20% of this had been earmarked for education, the sector would have received an additional US$22.5 billion in 2013, increasing funding by almost 40% compared with the current education budget.

Losses occur not only when governments grant exemptions, but also when they sell natural resource concessions for less than their true value. One analysis concluded that the Democratic Republic of the Congo incurred losses of US$1.36 billion from its dealings with five mining companies over three years between 2010 and 2012 (African Progress Panel, 2013). This is the same amount as allocated to the education sector over two years between 2010 and 2011 (Development Finance International and Oxfam, 2013).

Some governments have started reviewing the terms and conditions of concession agreements. When Liberia reviewed 105 agreements signed between 2003 and 2006, it determined that 36 should be cancelled outright and 14 needed to be renegotiated (African Progress Panel, 2013).

Fight tax evasion

For many of the world's poorest countries, tax evasion results in resources being used to build personal fortunes for the minority elite, rather than strong education systems for the benefit of the majority.

Some individuals and companies avoid taxes legally by moving money to tax havens. The Tax Justice Network estimates that between US$21 trillion and US$32 trillion is hidden by rich individuals in more than 80 tax havens. Taxing capital gains on this wealth at 30%, would generate revenue of between US$190 billion and US$280 billion a year (Tax Justice Network, 2012). If 20% of this revenue were allocated to education, it would add between US$38 billion and US$56 billion to funding for the sector. Tax avoidance by individuals is another important reason for the low amount spent on education in Pakistan. The Pakistan Federal Board of Revenue estimates that only 0.57% of Pakistanis – just 768,000 individuals – paid income tax in 2012 (Economist, 2012).

Tax avoidance practices of multinational corporations also raise grave concerns. Some companies shift profits to subsidiaries in countries with low or zero tax rates. While such tax havens are a legal way for companies to avoid paying taxes, illicit capital flight also occurs through corruption and illegal mispricing practices in some multinational companies. In 2010, developing countries lost an estimated US$859 billion through illegal practices (Kar and Freitas, 2012). This was 64 times the amount that countries received in aid for the education sector in 2011. It is estimated that African governments alone lost US$38 billion annually from such practices between 2008 and 2010. A further US$25 billion is thought to be lost annually through other tax practices related to corruption and criminal activities (African Progress Panel, 2013). If these illegal practices were halted and 20% of the resulting government income was spent on education, the sector would receive US$13 billion in additional resources each year.

In Africa, if illegal tax practices were halted education could receive US$13 billion in additional resources each year

Another stark example of the scale of the losses involved comes from the tax practices of SABMiller, a multinational drinks company, which is estimated to have deprived governments in Ghana, India, Mozambique, South Africa, the United Republic of Tanzania and Zambia of up to US$30 million in tax revenue (ActionAid, 2012).

Some governments are beginning to challenge the status quo. In Africa, 21 countries have agreed to a legal framework for the pursuit of tax avoiders and evaders across borders (Crotty, 2013). The government of India, which claims Vodafone India owes US$2.5 billion in tax (equivalent to around 4.5% of the country's education budget in 2011), recently issued a high profile tax demand against Vodafone and other multinational companies, including Shell and Nokia (Development Finance International and Oxfam, 2013; Heikkila, 2013).

Governments could raise additional revenue by increasing the amount they receive in taxes from corporations

Diversify the tax base

Governments could raise considerable additional revenue by increasing the amount they receive in taxes from corporations, particularly in the natural resource extraction industry (UNESCO, 2012). Governments need to avoid dependence on a single source of income, however, and should plan for uncertainty. It has been estimated that a 1% increase in the share of natural resource rents in government revenue lowers the fiscal capacity of a country by 1.4% because there are fewer incentives to collect taxes from other sources (Besley and Persson, 2013).

In recent years sub-Saharan Africa has relied heavily on natural resources, which represented 46% of the region's tax revenue in 2008 (Bhushan and Samy, 2012). There has been little progress made in broadening the tax base beyond these resources (AfDB et al., 2010; DiJohn, 2010). After Chad began extracting oil in 2003, tax revenue from oil surged, but other tax income fell from 6.6% to 5.2% of GDP between 2003 and 2010 (AfDB et al., 2012). Meanwhile, education expenditure, at 3% of GDP in 2011, was unchanged since 1999.

In some countries, taxes tend to penalize the poorest. In India, direct taxes, such as personal income tax, make up 5.5% of GDP while indirect taxes, such as value-added tax – which are regressive, imposing a greater burden on the poor than on the rich – account for 9.3% (Hui, 2012). Moreover, just 3.3% of GDP was converted into education spending in 2010.

By contrast, Ecuador has initiated measures to expand its tax base and reduce dependence on rents: non-oil revenue as a share of government revenue rose from 70% in 2001–2005 to 74% in 2006–2010 (Ghosh, 2012). Viet Nam, which has one of the highest tax/GDP ratios in East Asia and the Pacific, has also broadened its tax base. Direct taxes, for instance, account for 8.2% of GDP, a share that has increased primarily because of government commitment to taxing corporate income from the oil sector and foreign-owned companies (McKinley and Kyrili, 2009).

The informal sector is another potential source of tax revenue. On some estimates, the informal sector accounts for 55% of GDP in sub-Saharan Africa, and revenue forgone by not taxing it can be equivalent to at least 35% of total tax revenue (Ncube, 2013; OECD, 2012b). As the majority of the poorest work in the informal sector, governments need to ensure that taxation of the sector is not regressive. However, the sector also includes prosperous small to medium-sized businesses that often pay little or no tax. Some governments are introducing measures to register them.

The Mozambique Revenue Authority introduced a highly simplified tax regime for micro- and small enterprises in 2009 that registered 40,000 taxpayers in a year (OECD, 2012b). In the United Republic of Tanzania, the government introduced a system to register eligible small and medium-sized businesses, and 41% of new companies were registered through this system by 2009 (Joshi et al., 2012). In 2004, the Malawi Revenue Authority encouraged tax compliance by giving compliant businesses an annual certificate documenting their tax status, which banks started to use in loan transactions (OECD, 2008). Such measures can generate substantial revenue, some of which could be used for education.

External assistance is needed to strengthen tax systems

While domestic political will needs to be the main force behind tax reform and increased allocations to education, donors can play an important complementary role. Between 2002 and 2011, just 1% of total aid was directed to public financial management and less than 0.1% of total aid supported tax programmes. Yet by one estimate, every US$1 of aid to strengthen tax regimes could generate up to US$350 in tax revenue (OECD-DAC, 2013; African Tax Administration Forum and OECD, 2013).

The foundations of a long-term tax development strategy need to be put in place. It took European economies a century to increase their tax revenue from 12% to 46% of GDP by developing new taxes (Besley and Persson, 2013). There are signs of a similar shift in poorer countries. The Rwanda Revenue Authority, which has received long-term support from the UK Department for International Development (DFID), increased the share of tax revenue as a proportion of GDP from 10% in 1998 to 13% in 2011 (IMF, 2012). The additional resources mobilized through better tax collection is equivalent to recovering the full value of DFID's 10-year support programme every three weeks (Rwanda Revenue Authority, 2012). This helped raise expenditure per primary school child from US$72 in 1999 to US$81 in 2011. Similarly, the Norwegian Tax Administration assists the tax authority in Mozambique in auditing international oil companies, and the German Agency for International Cooperation has helped tax authorities in Ghana, for example, build capacity and introduce legislation on transfer pricing (Fontana and Hansen-Shino, 2012).

Part of the problem governments face in raising tax revenue is lack of transparency by companies. The support of international partners can be valuable in changing this. In June 2013, France, the United Kingdom and the United States said they intended to implement the Extractive Industries Transparency Initiative, the global standard for transparency in natural resource revenue, with which 23 countries are classed as compliant and 16 countries have been accepted as candidates. At the 2013 G8 summit, partnerships were announced with nine countries to help them support extractive industry governance and increase tax collection capacity (G8, 2013).

Similarly, while poorer countries need to strengthen their institutions to prevent tax evasion, the problem cannot be addressed without the support of the international community. The Africa Progress Panel has called for a stronger multilateral tax transparency regime to tackle unethical aspects of tax avoidance (Africa Progress Panel, 2013). In addition, governments in high income countries can put pressure on corporations registered in their countries. For example, they can require them to publish a full list of their subsidiaries and the revenue, profit and taxes paid in all jurisdictions.

The United States made a start by introducing taxation transparency requirements for 1,100 oil, gas and mineral companies in 2010. The Cardin-Lugar amendment to the Dodd-Frank law, which took effect in September 2013, requires companies listed on the stock market and their subsidiaries to make information public on profit accrued and taxes paid (Jackson, 2013). If the European Union, as expected, also starts requiring oil, gas, mining and logging companies to declare payments to governments, such legislation will cover up to 90% of the world's international extractive industries (Publish What You Pay, 2013).

67 low and middle income countries could increase education resources by US$153 billion in 2015 through tax reforms

Estimating the potential increase in domestic resources for education

Increasing tax revenue and allocating an adequate share to education could raise considerable extra resources for the sector in a short time. The EFA Global Monitoring Report team estimates that 67 low and middle income countries could increase education resources by US$153 billion, or 72%, in 2015 through reforms to raise tax/GDP ratios and public expenditure on education (Table 2.2).

These additions to domestic resources could meet 56% of the US$26 billion average annual financing gap in basic education for 46 low and lower middle income countries, or 54% of the US$38 billion gap in basic and lower secondary education.[2]

Overall, the necessary reforms would more than double resources available for education in 13 countries. The increases would be particularly important for countries that now spend very little on education per school age child, allowing

2. This assumes that 50% of the funds are allocated to basic education and 20% to lower secondary education.

Table 2.2: Countries can dig deeper to fund education from domestic resources

		Current situation (2011)			Potential situation (2015)			Unit cost (2015)	
		Education as a share of GDP	Education as a share of total government spending	Tax/GDP ratio	Education as a share of GDP	Tax/GDP ratio in 2015	Total potential additional funding in 2015	Expenditure per primary school child (stagnant)	Expenditure per primary school child (tax mobilization and education prioritized)
		%	%	%	%	%	US$ millions	US$	US$
Current tax/GDP ratio of less than 10%	Afghanistan	3.5	16.7	9.2	5.6	14.2	500	67	161
	Bangladesh	2.2	14.1	8.6	4.2	13.6	3 198	101	216
	Bhutan	4.7	11.5	9.9	7.9	14.9	94	255	924
	Central African Republic	1.2	12.0	7.8	3.6	12.8	66	44	95
	Eritrea	2.1	7.5	8.4	6.7	13.4	201	57	191
	Guinea-Bissau	2.6	12.6	8.5	5.1	13.5	28	48	101
	Madagascar	2.8	20.1	9.5	3.8	14.5	119	62	85
	Myanmar	0.8	18.1	3.9	2.3	8.9	1 000	389	513
	Sierra Leone	3.6	13.7	9.4	5.6	14.4	117	60	118
	Yemen	5.2	16.0	6.2	7.4	11.2	998	251	362
Current tax/GDP ratio of ≥10% - <12.5%	Cambodia	2.6	12.1	10.4	4.9	14.4	438	82	232
	Ethiopia	4.7	25.4	11.5	5.5	15.5	435	106	125
	Gambia	3.9	19.7	12.1	4.8	16.1	10	106	123
	Guatemala	2.8	18.5	10.9	3.8	14.9	605	365	500
	Haiti	3.6	10.6	11.8	6.9	15.8	336	65	213
	Indonesia	3.0	15.2	10.9	4.7	14.9	19 506	526	1 049
	Pakistan	2.4	9.9	10.2	5.2	14.2	7 241	62	262
Current tax/GDP ratio of ≥12.5% - <15%	Burkina Faso	4.0	18.0	13.1	5.1	16.1	157	125	154
	Burundi	6.1	24.1	14.3	6.7	17.3	19	86	94
	Cameroon	3.2	16.3	12.8	4.6	15.8	461	115	241
	Egypt	3.8	11.9	14.0	7.1	17.0	9 592	520	948
	Ghana	8.2	24.4	13.6	8.8	16.6	317	365	567
	Mali	4.8	18.2	13.9	5.9	16.9	139	81	124
	Mauritania	3.9	14.7	13.5	5.8	16.5	114	187	292
	Nepal	4.7	20.2	13.1	5.3	16.1	144	160	185
	Niger	4.5	21.7	13.8	5.1	16.8	50	92	100
	Paraguay	4.1	10.6	13.7	6.8	16.7	968	384	1 037
	Philippines	2.7	15.0	13.2	4.2	16.2	5 361	442	679
	Rwanda	4.8	17.2	12.8	6.0	15.8	116	78	137
	Sri Lanka	2.0	12.9	13.3	3.9	16.3	1 509	292	970
	Tajikistan	3.9	13.8	12.7	6.1	15.7	219	262	424
	Uganda	3.3	15.1	12.5	4.9	15.5	387	51	77
	United Republic of Tanzania	6.2	18.3	14.9	7.2	17.9	383	84	109
Current tax/GDP ratio of ≥15% - <20%	Armenia	3.2	11.7	16.6	5.8	18.6	269	1 232	2 266
	Benin	5.3	27.8	16.5	5.7	18.5	37	169	182
	Côte d'Ivoire	4.6	24.6	17.6	5.0	19.6	137	285	322
	Guinea	3.1	19.0	15.9	3.7	17.9	44	66	107
	Honduras	6.5	29.9	16.0	6.9	18.0	82	484	776
	India	3.3	10.5	15.9	6.4	17.9	70 529	157	558
	Kenya	6.7	17.2	19.5	7.9	21.5	710	181	238
	Kyrgyzstan	5.8	18.6	19.5	6.7	21.5	76	662	751
	Lao People's Democratic Republic	3.3	13.2	15.5	5.2	17.5	229	161	377
	Mozambique	6.4	17.0	17.7	7.9	19.7	274	103	137
	Nicaragua	4.7	26.4	18.3	5.1	20.3	50	526	639
	Senegal	5.6	24.0	19.4	6.0	21.4	66	188	249
	Togo	4.6	14.3	15.8	6.6	17.8	94	80	128
	Zambia	1.3	13.1	15.0	3.5	17.0	622	155	271
	Zimbabwe	2.5	8.3	16.2	6.8	18.2	588	86	221
Current tax/GDP ratio of more than 20%	Angola	3.5	8.5	41.9	8.2	43.7	6 819	588	1 534
	Belize	6.6	18.7	23.0	7.3	24.8	13	701	1 215
	Chad	2.9	11.8	22.5	5.0	24.3	317	94	171
	Democratic Republic of the Congo	2.5	8.9	23.6	6.5	25.4	885	18	59
	Georgia	2.7	7.7	23.7	6.6	25.5	734	580	2 082
	Guyana	3.6	13.5	21.3	5.9	23.1	83	544	1 415
	Lesotho	13.0	23.7	60.1	13.3	61.9	11	340	492
	Liberia	3.3	12.1	21.3	6.1	23.1	69	60	111
	Malawi	5.4	14.7	21.6	7.7	23.4	106	30	58
	Mongolia	5.5	11.9	28.0	8.9	29.8	539	953	2 391
	Morocco	5.4	25.7	24.4	5.7	26.2	431	1 428	1 490
	Namibia	8.3	22.4	24.4	8.7	26.2	50	1 093	1 406
	Nigeria	1.5	6.0	25.3	5.6	27.1	13 090	87	330
	Papua New Guinea	3.4	11.2	26.1	5.9	27.9	633	217	590
	Republic of Moldova	8.6	22.0	21.0	8.9	22.8	32	991	2 691
	Solomon Islands	7.3	34.0	28.1	7.6	29.9	4	838	1 208
	Swaziland	8.2	21.0	25.0	8.6	26.8	14	809	863
	Uzbekistan	6.4	20.5	24.0	6.8	25.8	234	1 170	1 228
	Viet Nam	6.6	19.8	23.5	7.0	25.3	750	446	732
	Total for all 67 countries	**3.4**	**13.1**	**15.7**	**5.8**	**18.4**	**153 451**	**209**	**466**

Notes: Countries were ranked in five groups according to their initial tax/GDP ratio. At one end, countries where the ratio was already at least 20% were projected to increase their effort by 0.44 percentage point per year and to allocate 20% of the budget to education if they were not already doing so. At the opposite end, countries with a tax/GDP ratio of less than 10% were projected to increase the ratio by 1.25 percentage points annually and to allocate 20% of the budget to education if they were not already doing so.

The calculations assume five different rates at which a country's tax/GDP ratio can grow, depending on its starting point. Countries starting at a tax/GDP ratio of (a) <10% should aim to increase the tax/GDP ratio by 1.25 percentage points per year, (b) ≥10% to <12.5% should aim to increase the ratio by 1 percentage point per year, (c) ≥12.5% to <15% should aim to increase it by 0.75 percentage point per year, (d) ≥15% to <20% should aim for an increase by 0.5 percentage point per year and (e) ≥20% should aim to increase the ratio by 0.44 percentage point per year.

Sources: EFA Global Monitoring Report team calculations (2013), based on UIS database; Development Finance International and Oxfam (2013); IMF (2012, 2013).

education quality to improve. Across the 67 countries, spending per primary school age child would increase from US$209 to US$466 in 2015. Of these countries which are low income, the amount spent per primary school age child would increase from US$102 to US$158. Bangladesh, for example, could allocate an extra US$3.2 billion to education in 2015, increasing the amount available to spend on each school age child from US$101 to US$216.[3]

Pakistan, where 10% of the world's out-of-school children are concentrated, spends 3% of GDP on the military (World Bank, 2013f). This is more than the amount it spends on education. If it maximized tax revenue – especially by reversing the huge exemptions it grants – and spent 20% of its budget on education, the government could add US$7.2 billion to its education budget in 2015, increasing spending per school age child from US$62 to US$262.[4]

The Central African Republic has the potential to raise an additional US$66 million in 2015 if it increased the tax/GDP ratio from its current level of 8% to 13% and at the same time prioritized the education sector within government expenditure from the current level of 12% to 20%. This could potentially more than double expenditure per primary school child, from US$44 to US$95. Such increases may seem large but are not without precedent. Through effective tax mobilization policies, Ecuador, for instance, tripled its education expenditure from US$225 million in 2003–2006 to US$941 million in 2007–2010 (Ghosh, 2012).

Tax reforms could increase spending per primary school age child from US$209 to US$466 in 2015

Calculations by the EFA Global Monitoring Report team show that it is possible for countries to spend 6% of GDP on education. Among the 67 countries analysed, 14 have already attained this target. Of the 53 countries that have not yet reached the target, 19 would be able to achieve it by expanding and diversifying the tax base and prioritizing education spending by 2015 (Figure 2.5). Such efforts would go a long way towards ensuring that children are in school and learning by 2015, and would provide a solid base for funding more ambitious goals after 2015.

Figure 2.5: Modest increases in tax effort and prioritizing education spending could significantly increase resources
Expenditure on education as percentage of GDP in 2015 if the tax/GDP ratio grew and the budget share of education increased

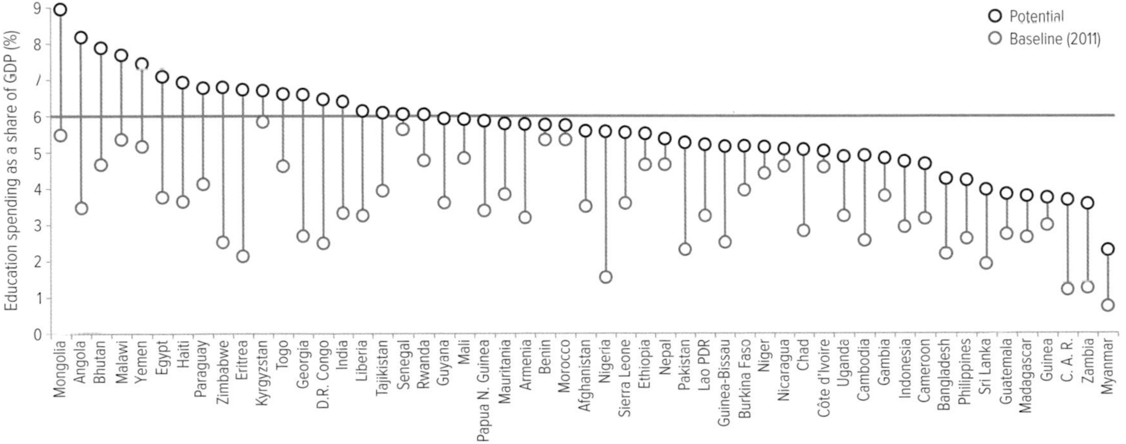

Sources: EFA Global Monitoring Report team calculations (2013), based on UIS database; Development Finance International and Oxfam (2013); IMF (2012, 2013).

3. At current levels of prioritization of education and tax effort, and with future levels of GDP and government expenditure as projected by the IMF, Bangladesh would spend US$3.9 billion on education in 2015. If it increased the share of education in its budget from 14% to 20% in 2015, the sector would have an extra US$1.6 billion at its disposal. If in addition it increased the share of tax to GDP by 1.25% per year, that ratio would rise from 8.6% in 2011 to 13.6% in 2015, making an extra US$3.2 billion, in all, available for education.

4. Expenditure on education as a share of the government budget was 10% in 2011. If the share rose to 20%, and tax as a share of GDP rose from its current rate of around 10% to 14%, the government could raise an additional US$7.2 billion for education.

Targeting the marginalized through education expenditure

To achieve Education for All, it is necessary not only to increase domestic resources for education but also to ensure that they are spent on improving education opportunities for the most marginalized. The children and young people who are hardest to reach – such as the poor, those who live in remote locations, members of ethnic and linguistic minorities, and those with disabilities – are often the last to benefit from education spending, so special efforts are needed to make sure these funds reach them. In addition, the cost of teaching these students is likely to be far higher than the average cost per student because of the expense involved in mitigating the disadvantages they face. This means redistributing domestic resources to those most in need.

In low income sub-Saharan African countries, 43% of public spending on education is received by the most educated 10%

More often, however, resources are skewed towards the most privileged. In low income sub-Saharan African countries, 43% of public spending on education is received by the most educated 10%; in middle income countries, the top 10% receive 25% of public spending on education (Majgaard and Mingat, 2012). In Malawi, where the level of public spending per primary school child is among the world's lowest, 73% of public resources allocated to the education sector benefit the most educated 10% (World Bank, 2010).

Similarly, public expenditure on education is often skewed towards urban areas, even where the majority of the school age population resides in rural areas – which are also often home to the poorest households. In the United Republic of Tanzania, for instance, nearly three-quarters of the population resides in rural areas, yet only 47% of public education resources were allocated to these areas in 2009 (U. R. Tanzania Ministry of Education and Vocational Training, 2011).

Recognizing the need to target the most disadvantaged, many countries in Latin America have established social protection programmes that transfer cash to poor households on the condition that their children attended school (UNESCO, 2010). Their success has led to similar programmes in other countries, including Malawi and the Philippines. Malawi's Social Cash Transfer Scheme provides US$14 per month to more than 26,000 households to fight poverty and hunger and help families send their children to school (UN, 2013). In the Philippines, Pantawid Pamilya, a conditional cash transfer programme, reaches 7.5 million children nationwide in an effort to keep them in school and in good health (World Bank, 2012a).

Although many social protection programmes address constraints that poor households face in getting children into school, they generally do not include strategies to improve the quality of education once children are enrolled. In addition, such programmes often represent a tiny fraction of the education budget. More effective targeting of education spending is vital for improving the education chances of the disadvantaged. For example, a cash transfer programme targeting orphans and vulnerable children in Kenya costs the equivalent of 0.12% of GDP (Bryant, 2009). By contrast, the government spent 6.7% of GDP on education in 2010.

To shift education spending in favour of the marginalized, many governments have introduced funding formulas that allocate more resources to parts of the country or groups of schools that need greater support to overcome educational deprivation and inequality. While some of these efforts have produced positive results, they have not always improved learning as much as desired, in some cases because redistribution has been too limited and in others because programmes have not focused sufficiently on improving education quality. Some programmes, moreover, have been hampered by administrative challenges and by weak capacity on the part of the lower tiers of government that are expected to implement the reforms.

How do countries redistribute education expenditure to address inequality?

Countries adopt different methods of redistributing resources to disadvantaged areas and schools, depending on their ability to identify and target those most in need. India has aimed to redistribute resources to the poorer states with the worst education outcomes. Under the Sarva Shiksha Abhiyan (Education for All) programme, districts were identified in 2006 to receive additional funding on the basis of out-of-school population, gender disparity, infrastructure conditions and minority populations (Jhingran and Sankar, 2009).

Sri Lanka, lacking sufficiently disaggregated information on poverty, took a different approach to target disadvantaged schools: in its Education Quality Input system, it skews non-salary expenditure in favour of smaller schools. These schools have higher fixed operating costs and are located in rural areas, where poverty tends to be higher, making it hard for them to mobilize their own resources. School with fewer than 100 students receive about 53% of their funding from this programme, compared with 9% for schools with more than 2,000 students, which tend to be in richer, more urban areas (Arunatilake and Jayawardena, 2013).

South Africa's redistribution reforms have aimed to reverse the legacy of the apartheid schooling system. In 2007, the National Norms and Standards for School Funding were implemented and a 'no fee schools' policy was introduced. Catchment areas were ranked according to income, unemployment and education level, and grouped into quintiles. Schools in the bottom quintile were designated as no fee schools. The policy had been extended to the bottom three quintiles by 2011. Schools in the three lowest quintiles are eligible for an allocation to cover non-salary expenditure to offset the loss of fee income. In 2009, schools in the poorest quintile received a per student allocation that was six times higher than the allocation to schools in the richest quintile (Sayed and Motala, 2012).

Indonesia's centrally funded capitation grant to schools, the School Operational Assistance programme, was found to discriminate against schools whose costs were high because of their location or the characteristics of the population they served. To address this, about half of district governments provide supplementary local grants. The majority of school funds, excluding salaries, still come from central grants, with 15% coming from local grants. In a few pilot cases, districts have attempted to favour schools that are potentially in more need of support, and there are indications that these schools have used the additional district funds to provide extra student support, along with teaching and learning materials (World Bank, 2013e).

Brazil's redistribution of funds to poorer and more marginalized parts of the country has contributed to improvements in school attendance, pupil/teacher ratios and learning outcomes (Box 2.1).

Sri Lanka skews non-salary expenditure in favour of smaller schools in rural areas

Box 2.1: Brazil's reforms reduce regional education inequality

Greater equity in national spending has been at the heart of Brazil's reforms to tackle widespread education inequality between states. In the poorer northern states, income is less than half the level in the richer southern states, so tax revenue and spending per pupil are lower.

In the mid-1990s, the government introduced the Fund for Primary Education Administration and Development for the Enhancement of Teacher Status (FUNDEF), which guaranteed a certain minimum spending level per pupil by complementing state spending with federal allocations. Schools in rural areas were generally favoured over urban schools, with greater weight given to highly marginalized indigenous groups. Of the funding distributed, 60% was earmarked for teacher salaries and 40% for school operations. The salary component allowed teachers in poor northern states to upgrade qualifications, so that by 2002 almost all teachers had acquired minimum required training, and it ensured an influx of fully qualified teachers in those areas, allowing for an increase of around one-fifth in the teaching workforce between 1997 and 2002.

In 2006, FUNDEF was replaced by the Fund for the Development of Basic Education and Appreciation of the Teaching Profession (FUNDEB), also with the aim of establishing a minimum allocation per student. Average school attendance among children from the poorest 20% of families, which had been four years in the mid-1990s, had risen to eight years.

FUNDEF led to rapid and substantial improvement in northern Brazil. Between 1997 and 2002, average enrolment increased by 61% in the North-East region and 32% in the North region. Mathematics scores for grade 4 students have increased in northern states since 2001, though they continue to lag behind those in other regions – suggesting a need for the reforms to continue and be further strengthened.

Sources: Bruns et al. (2012); OECD (2011); UNESCO (2010).

What are the lessons of redistribution policies?

Redistribution policies are vital for achieving more equal education outcomes. However, they have often not gone far enough. Experience from these initiatives offers some important lessons on how to strengthen their design to improve learning for marginalized children.

Kenya's capitation grant disadvantages arid and semi-arid areas that are home to 46% of the out-of-school population

One of the biggest criticisms of redistribution initiatives is that even these higher allocations per child often do not adequately equalize spending. In Brazil, for example, it is estimated that US$971 per pupil is required to attain a minimum level of quality for grades 1 to 4, but in 2009 the government allocated US$611 per pupil in the North-East region, about half as much as in the wealthier South-East region (PREAL and Lemann Foundation, 2009). This is one area where the reform needs to be strengthened to further narrow the gap in learning outcomes between regions.

In India, despite increased resources for Sarva Shiksha Abhiyan, allocations are still not sufficiently reaching the states most in need. In 2012/13, total expenditure per elementary pupil from both central and state funds was still much lower in states where education indicators were worse than in the states with some of the best education indicators. In one of India's wealthier states, Kerala, education spending per pupil was about US$685. Similarly, in Himachal Pradesh it was US$542. By contrast, in West Bengal it was US$127 and in Bihar US$100. Increased financial allocations are still insufficient to translate into improved learning outcomes, suggesting that far more needs to be done. In Bihar, for example, where spending rose by 61% between 2010/11 and 2012/13 but remained low, only 48% of Standard 3 to 5 students could read a Standard 1 text in 2012 (Accountability Initiative, 2013).

Another limitation of redistribution measures is that they largely focus on non-salary expenditure – often a small part of total expenditure – and thus do not allow for using the funds to implement teacher reforms that are vital to improving quality. In Sri Lanka, Education Quality Input funds amounted to just 2% of the total recurrent budget for education (Arunatilake, 2007). There are exceptions; Brazil, for instance, earmarked 60% of FUNDEF funds for teacher salaries. Salaries overall rose by 13% at the national level, but in the North and North-East they rose by 60% because all teachers were upgraded with higher education qualifications (OECD, 2011).

Rigid earmarking can prevent schools from spending funds in areas that could have greater impact on learning. In India, for example, the Sarva Shiksha Abhiyan grants are delivered to schools in the form of three separate components earmarked for maintenance, development and teaching-learning, which may not necessarily reflect the needs of a given school (Accountability Initiative, 2013).

Poorer countries can find it difficult to identify and target the groups most in need. Many base allocations on enrolment figures, to the detriment of areas where large numbers of children are out of school. In Kenya, for example, the capitation grant is distributed on the basis of number of students enrolled, a disadvantage for the 12 counties in the arid and semi-arid areas that are home to 46% of the out-of-school population. Children in these areas who do enter school tend to be first-generation learners from non-literate home environments, and so need additional support in the form of higher spending per pupil (Watkins and Alemayehu, 2012).

Similarly, in Bangladesh almost two-thirds of primary schools received a grant of about US$300 per school in 2010 to help fund improvement plans. However, the amount was the same for every school, regardless of size or location, and the grant was not directed at activities aimed at improving the quality of teaching and learning (Bangladesh Ministry of Primary and Mass Education, 2011a; Bernard, 2010).

To address the need to target out-of-school populations, Brazil complemented FUNDEB with the Bolsa Familia programme, which provides a cash transfer to compensate for the loss of children's labour, conditional on children attending school (Bruns et al., 2012).

Implementation problems also plague redistribution efforts. In many countries, schools do not receive as much funding as they expect, or do not receive it on time. In Sri Lanka in 2011, less than one-third of schools had received their Education Quality Input funds halfway through the school year.

Late arrival of funds, together with limited implementation capacity, is particularly detrimental for smaller schools, given their greater reliance on such funding. In response, the government has introduced a policy measure allowing schools to carry unspent funds into the next financial year (Arunatilake and Jayawardena, 2013).

Schools may lack the capacity to spend the resources they receive. In India, Bihar managed to spend only 38% of its Sarva Shiksha Abhiyan funds in 2011/12, while the national average was 62% (Accountability Initiative, 2013). This low spending is likely to be a reason for the continued poor learning outcomes in the state. Disbursement systems in decentralized countries can further stretch school capacity. In Indonesia, schools receive funds from eight different sources and four different budgets, making it difficult to plan (World Bank, 2013e).

In summary, redistribution measures are vital to ensure that domestic resources are used to equalize education opportunities, but they need to cover the full cost of delivering quality education to the most vulnerable. They also need to be combined with reforms that strengthen education systems' capacity to implement such measures, and they should complement other interventions aimed at making sure all children are in school and learning.

Trends in aid to education

Government spending provides the largest contribution to education, but aid is vital for many poorer countries. However, aid to basic education is declining, jeopardizing the chances of schooling for millions of children. With improvement in the numbers of children out of school stagnating, a final push is needed to ensure that all children are in school by 2015, but the fall in aid will increase the difficulty of this task.

Even before the economic downturn, donors were off track to fulfil the promise they made in 2000 at the World Education Forum in Dakar, Senegal: that no country would be left behind in education due to a lack of resources. Economic austerity should not be an excuse for donors to abandon their pledges to the world's poorest. Recipient countries need predictable financing for their national education plans. Donors urgently need to reconsider their aid cuts to ensure that they meet their commitment to the world's children.

In 2011, aid to basic education fell for the first time since 2002

Aid to education is falling

While aid to education increased steadily after 2002, it peaked in 2010 and is now falling: total aid to all levels of education declined by 7% (US$1 billion) between 2010 and 2011 (Table 2.3, Figure 2.6). Aid to basic education fell for the first time since 2002, by 6%: from US$6.2 billion in 2010 to US$5.8 billion in 2011,

Table 2.3: Total aid disbursements to education and basic education, by region and income level, 2002–2011

	Total aid to education Constant 2011 US$ millions			Total aid to basic education Constant 2011 US$ millions			Per capita
	2002	2010	2011	2002	2010	2011	2011
World	**7 799**	**14 419**	**13 413**	**3 133**	**6 174**	**5 819**	**9**
Low income	2 145	3 796	3 461	1 240	2 047	1 858	16
Lower middle income	3 012	5 407	5 371	1 290	2 451	2 607	9
Upper middle income	1 652	2 800	2 641	302	595	579	3
High income	25	36	13	6	9	6	1
Unallocated by income	964	2 379	1 926	296	1 072	769	...
Arab States	1 053	1 939	1 922	221	825	845	20
Central/Eastern Europe	305	574	517	90	80	64	6
Central Asia	130	331	346	43	99	101	18
East Asia/Pacific	1 155	2 309	2 060	253	687	552	4
Latin America and the Caribbean	560	1 110	948	226	438	381	6
South and West Asia	967	2 267	2 417	597	1 309	1 445	8
Sub-Saharan Africa	2 816	3 959	3 647	1 490	1 891	1 757	13
Overseas territories	254	523	74	127	243	26	...
Unallocated by region or country	559	1 406	1 481	86	602	648	...

Notes: The 2002 figure is an average for 2002–2003. Aid per capita refers to the amount a primary school age child received in aid to basic education in 2011.
Source: Annex, Aid Table 3.

Figure 2.6: Aid to education fell by US$1 billion between 2010 and 2011
Total aid to education disbursements, 2002–2011

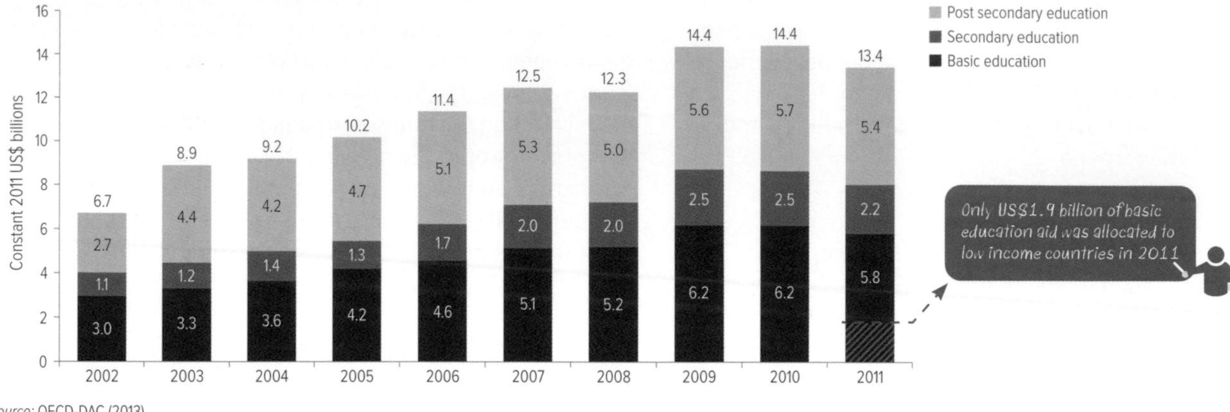

Source: OECD-DAC (2013).

The reduction in basic education aid to sub-Saharan Africa could have funded good quality school places for over 1 million children

putting at risk the chances of meeting the 2015 goals. Aid to total secondary education also declined between 2010 and 2011, by 11%, from an already low level. This means that hopes of extending global goals to include universal lower secondary education after 2015 could be difficult to meet unless this changes.

Low income countries are bearing the brunt of aid cuts

Although many low income countries are making commendable efforts to scale up domestic resources for education, a funding gap remains that needs to be addressed urgently. Aid is a crucial source of funding, equivalent to a quarter of education budgets in nine countries (UNESCO, 2012). Higher levels of education aid in the last decade have boosted enrolment (Birchler and Michaelowa, 2013).

Despite such benefits, low income countries, which only receive around one-third of aid to basic education, witnessed a larger decrease in aid to basic education than middle income countries. Aid fell by 9% in low income countries between 2010 and 2011 – from US$2.05 billion to US$1.86 billion. In sub-Saharan Africa, home to over half the world's out-of-school population, aid to basic education declined by 7% between 2010 and 2011, from US$1.89 billion to US$1.76 billion. The US$134 million reduction in basic education aid to the region would have been enough to fund good quality school places for over 1 million children.

Aid to basic education fell between 2010 and 2011 in 19 low income countries, 13 of which are in sub-Saharan Africa (Figure 2.7). In Malawi, for instance, aid to basic education almost halved over the space of one year, largely due to a political impasse between the donor community and the government at that time. While annual fluctuations in aid may not be uncommon, such changes make it difficult for countries to plan. Given that a large proportion of education spending is on teacher salaries, sudden reductions in aid can mean that teachers are not paid on time, or that teachers leaving the profession are not replaced, seriously harming the quality of education.

In some countries, aid has been falling for more than a year. In the Democratic Republic of the Congo, Mali and the United Republic of Tanzania, aid to basic education fell considerably in both 2010 and 2011. Aid has played a key part in supporting efforts to get more children into school in the United Republic of Tanzania, but it fell by 12% between 2009 and 2010 and by a further 57% in 2011, in the latter case largely because of reductions by Canada and the World Bank. These cuts endanger the progress that has been made and could thwart efforts to strengthen the quality of education.

The fall in basic education aid to low income countries has resulted in the resources available per child falling from US$18 in 2010 to US$16 in 2011. The United Republic of Tanzania received US$7 per child in 2011 – US$13 less than in 2009.

Figure 2.7: Aid to basic education fell in 19 low income countries between 2010 and 2011
Total aid to basic education in low income countries, 2010 and 2011

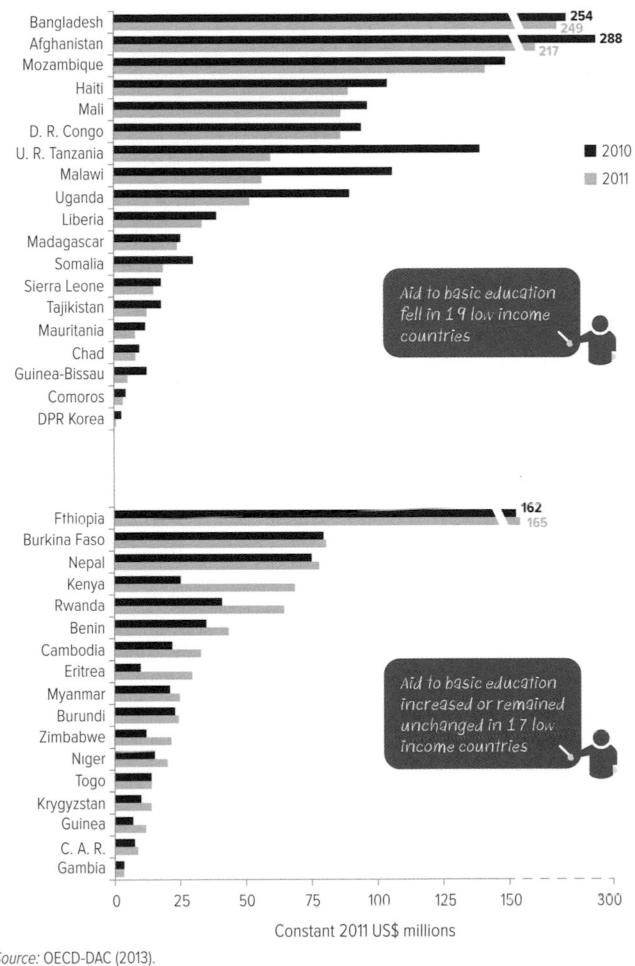

Source: OECD-DAC (2013).

Out-of-school children need the support of aid, regardless of where they live

Of the 10 countries with the most children out of school, 6 are in lower middle income countries. Of these, only two were among the top 10 recipients of aid to basic education in 2011: India and Pakistan. Nigeria, home to the world's largest number of children out of school, does not figure among the top 10 recipients of aid to basic education, and the aid it does receive decreased by nearly 28% between 2010 and 2011. While these countries need to do far more to increase their own domestic spending on education, a lack of resources should not prevent the most disadvantaged children from going to school because of where they live (Box 2.2).

Box 2.2: Poor children out of school in some lower middle income countries also need aid

The world's poorest children, who are the most likely to be out of school, live not only in low income countries but also in lower middle income countries. Since 2000, 25 countries have graduated to this group, which now comprises 54 countries, while 36 are classified as low income. In 1999, 84% of the world's out-of-school children lived in low income countries and 12% lived in lower middle income countries, but by 2011, 37% lived in low income countries and 49% in lower middle income countries, due in particular to the graduation to lower middle income status of some large-population countries, such as India, Nigeria and Pakistan.

The current income thresholds used by the World Bank to classify countries, which determine their eligibility for concessional loans and grants from the bank's International Development Association (IDA), influence heavily the allocation decisions of other major donors. The lower middle income group now comprises countries with annual income per capita between US$1,026 and US$4,035. These countries differ tremendously in the obstacles they face in reaching the Education for All goals and other development targets. They include some sub-Saharan African countries and countries affected by conflict. Their levels of income differ considerably, from Egypt, Indonesia and Morocco with higher income per capita to ones closer to the level of low income countries, such as Cameroon, Côte d'Ivoire, Senegal and Yemen. The more populous countries, India, Nigeria and Pakistan, fall at the lower end of the lower middle income group and are home to 54% of the developing world's population living below US$1.25 per day, based on 2010 population estimates.

Some lower middle income countries could do far more to raise their own resources for education and ensure that these resources reach those most in need. The necessary domestic tax reforms are likely to take time, however, so these countries will need aid in the coming years if another generation is not to be denied its right to education. In India, for example, which became a lower middle income country in 2007, there is an elite large enough to provide sufficient domestic taxes to give all those from poor households the chance to learn, but redistribution to the poorest parts of the country takes time and will not be straightforward, given its size. If each Indian state were a country, Uttar Pradesh would have the world's second largest concentration of poor people (after China), and Bihar the sixth largest. To make sure aid targets the poor, donors should direct aid to the areas in lower middle income countries where poverty is concentrated.

Sources: World Bank (2013f); Oxford Poverty and Human Development Initiative (2013).

The donor landscape is changing

The fall in aid to education reflects changing spending patterns among many donors. Direct aid to education fell slightly more than overall aid to other sectors between 2010 and 2011, and thus the share of aid to education declined from 12% to 11%. Canada, France, the Netherlands and the United States, in particular, cut spending on education more than they reduced overall aid. Between 2010 and 2011, 21 bilateral and multilateral donors reduced their aid disbursements to basic education. The largest decreases in volume terms were from Canada, the European Union, France, Japan, the Netherlands, Spain and the United States, which together accounted for 90% of the reduction in aid to basic education.[5]

Between 2010 and 2011, 24 donors reduced their aid to low income countries

The United States, formerly the largest bilateral donor to basic education in absolute terms, cut its aid in this area so much that it fell to second place. As a consequence the United Kingdom overtook the United States as the largest bilateral donor, thanks to its commitment to increase overall aid to the target agreed by European donors of 0.7% of gross national income (GNI) by 2015, as well as its prioritization of the education sector. In 2012, the United Kingdom allocated 0.56% of GNI to aid. By contrast, the United States, which has not set a similar target, devoted 0.19% of GNI to aid in 2012. Of the decline in the United States's total aid to basic education between 2010 and 2011, 94% is accounted for by large falls in its spending in Afghanistan, Iraq and Pakistan.

The Netherlands decided in 2011 that it would phase out education programmes that did not contribute directly to its foreign policy priorities. Consequently its aid to basic education fell by over a third between 2010 and 2011; it had been the largest donor to basic education in 2007, but by 2011 was in eleventh place. The Netherlands was a key funder and policy leader for education, so its shift away from the sector is cause for concern. Its reductions in aid have particularly affected Mali, Mozambique and Uganda: in all three, aid to basic education declined between 2010 and 2011, suggesting that the Netherlands did not succeed in its aim of withdrawing without harming education in affected countries, as other donors have not stepped in to fill the gap.

Australia increased its basic education aid disbursements by 49% between 2010 and 2011, though the increase was largely concentrated in lower middle income countries it considers strategically important, including Indonesia, Papua New Guinea and the Philippines. In 2011, 68% of Australia's aid disbursements to basic education went to the East Asia and the Pacific region, which is likely to continue to be a top priority. While sub-Saharan Africa received just 0.3% of Australia's total bilateral aid to basic education, the previous Australian government had committed to join the African Development Bank with initial contribution and payments for the 13th and 14th replenishment set at US$161 million for the six-year replenishment period; on average the yearly contribution to the bank would be equivalent to around 12% of its basic education aid in 2011 (Parmanand, 2013).

The United Kingdom's increase in aid to basic education between 2010 and 2011 benefited low income countries. However, 24 donors reduced their aid to these countries over this period, including nine of the 15 largest donors to low income countries. The biggest cuts were made by EU institutions, the World Bank and the Netherlands (Figure 2.8). These donors, along with Canada and Spain, were also responsible for the overall reduction in education aid to sub-Saharan Africa.

For the main donors, the cut in aid to low income and sub-Saharan African countries between 2010 and 2011 was part of an overall reduction in basic education aid. EU institutions, for example, reduced their overall aid to basic education by 31%, which resulted in a reduction of 36% for low income countries, with Bangladesh, the Democratic Republic of the Congo, Malawi and Nepal among the most affected. Australia, the World Bank and the IMF increased their overall aid to basic education between 2010 and 2011 but reduced their spending in low income countries.

World Bank aid to basic education increased by 13% overall, but fell by 23% in low income countries; the largest cuts affected Haiti and

5. The decrease in France's aid to basic education is largely due to Mayotte no longer being classed by the OECD as ODA-eligible as from 2011.

the United Republic of Tanzania. World Bank aid to basic education for lower middle income countries rose by 23%, largely due to increases in disbursements to India and Pakistan. The World Bank's aid disbursements to basic education fell or remained steady in most sub-Saharan African countries, while South and West Asia experienced an increase, reflecting a trend that has been apparent over the past decade.

Spending by the Global Partnership for Education (GPE) is unlikely to have filled the gap left by the World Bank's reduction in aid to low income countries. Uganda, for instance, was the World Bank's second largest recipient of aid to basic education in 2002, after India, receiving US$113 million for education; by 2011 disbursements were zero, even though Uganda was still classed as a low income country. Yet Uganda has not received any funding from the GPE. Similarly, the United Republic of Tanzania, another large recipient of World Bank aid disbursements to basic education in the early 2000s, saw disbursements fall from US$88 million in 2002 to less than US$0.3 million in 2011. The United Republic of Tanzania became a GPE partner in 2013 with a US$5.2 million grant for its education plan. All this, however, is allocated to Zanzibar, and the amount is small compared with what the country received from the World Bank early in the 2000s.[6] Nevertheless, the GPE is an important source of financing in some low income countries, although information is not currently publicly available in a format to enable tracking of spending patterns (Box 2.3).

Figure 2.8: Nine of the 15 largest donors reduced their aid to basic education for low income countries between 2010 and 2011
Total disbursements of aid to basic education for low income countries, 2010 and 2011

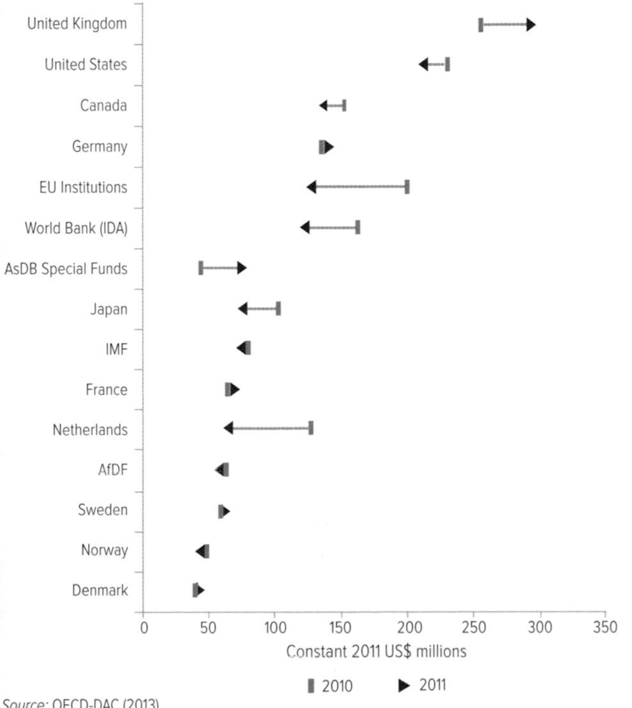

Source: OECD-DAC (2013).

Aid forecasts remain bleak

There is no sign that overall aid will stop declining before the 2015 deadline for education goals is reached. From 2011 to 2012, total aid fell by 4% in real terms. Italy and Spain accounted for most of the US$5.2 billion decrease in aid by DAC donors. The Netherlands, the United Kingdom and the United States also reported large decreases, although the UK reduction did not represent a fall in the proportion of GNI allocated to aid, as GNI also fell. It is particularly worrying that less developed countries are expected to bear the brunt of these cuts: bilateral aid to these countries fell by 12.8% from 2011 to 2012 (OECD, 2013a).

If EU countries kept their aid promises this could provide US$9 billion to fill the education financing gap in 2015

Many donors are expected to reduce their aid further in coming years (Table 2.4). In all, 16 bilateral DAC donors decreased their aid between 2011 and 2012, not only because of the economic downturn but also because they made aid a lower priority: 13 donors decreased aid as a proportion of GNI. Only five donors, including Australia and Luxembourg, disbursed more aid as a proportion of GNI in 2012 than in 2011.

The 15 countries that were members of the European Union in early 2004 agreed in 2005 to increase their aid to 0.7% of GNI by 2015, but projections by the European Commission indicate just five of the countries are expected to meet this commitment. The overall shortfall in aid due to EU donors' unmet promises is expected to be US$43 billion, the bulk of it attributed to France, Germany, Italy and Spain (European Commission, 2013). If EU countries raised their aid to the levels needed to meet their 2015 pledge, this would provide US$9 billion to fill the education financing gap in 2015 if 20% was allocated for the education sector.

6. According to the GPE, the United Republic of Tanzania is eligible to apply for a US$100 million program implementation grant (Global Partnership for Education, 2013b).

Box 2.3: How important is the Global Partnership for Education for funding basic education in poor countries?

The GPE is an important source of external financing for education for some low and lower middle income countries, although currently it only accounts for a small proportion of education aid. Between 2004 and 2011, donors paid in US$2 billion to the GPE. By comparison, donors spent US$32 billion in aid to basic education to low and lower middle income countries over the same period. However, the GPE's influence appears to be increasing over time.

In 2011, the GPE disbursed US$385 million to basic education – an all-time high – making it the fourth largest donor to low and lower middle income countries that year. For the 31 countries that had a programme implementation grant in 2011, 24% of basic education aid was disbursed by the GPE.

For three of these 31 countries, in 2011 the GPE provided at least half of external finance for basic education, either because aid from other donors was negligible or because the GPE had channelled significant volumes to some countries. GPE funding to the Central African Republic, whose grant agreement was signed in 2009, was US$13.2 million in 2011, or 60% of the country's aid to basic education that year. Eleven other donors gave small amounts. For 10 of the 28 countries receiving GPE funds in 2011, these funds constituted no more than one-fifth of aid to basic education. In Niger, whose grant agreement was also signed in 2009, the GPE disbursed US$1.5 million, less than 10% of external funding for basic education, while aid from DAC donors came to US$20.2 million (Figure 2.9).

Because of the importance of the GPE in financing education in some low income countries, it is vital for its disbursements to be timely and predictable. While much criticism was levelled at the EFA Fast Track Initiative (which the GPE replaced) for poor disbursement rates from its Catalytic Fund, the GPE committed itself to more timely and predictable disbursements.

To keep track of these commitments, the GPE needs to report its aid flows to the OECD-DAC, just as global health funds such as the GAVI Alliance and the Global Fund to Fight AIDS, Tuberculosis and Malaria do. The Global Fund also provides details such as whether funds go directly to governments or through multilateral organizations or civil society organizations, a level of disaggregation that is equally necessary for GPE disbursements.

Sources: Global Partnership for Education (2013a); OECD-DAC (2013).

Figure 2.9: In some countries, the Global Partnership for Education is a large donor for aid to basic education

Shares of the GPE and other donors in aid disbursements to basic education for countries with a programme implementation grant in 2011

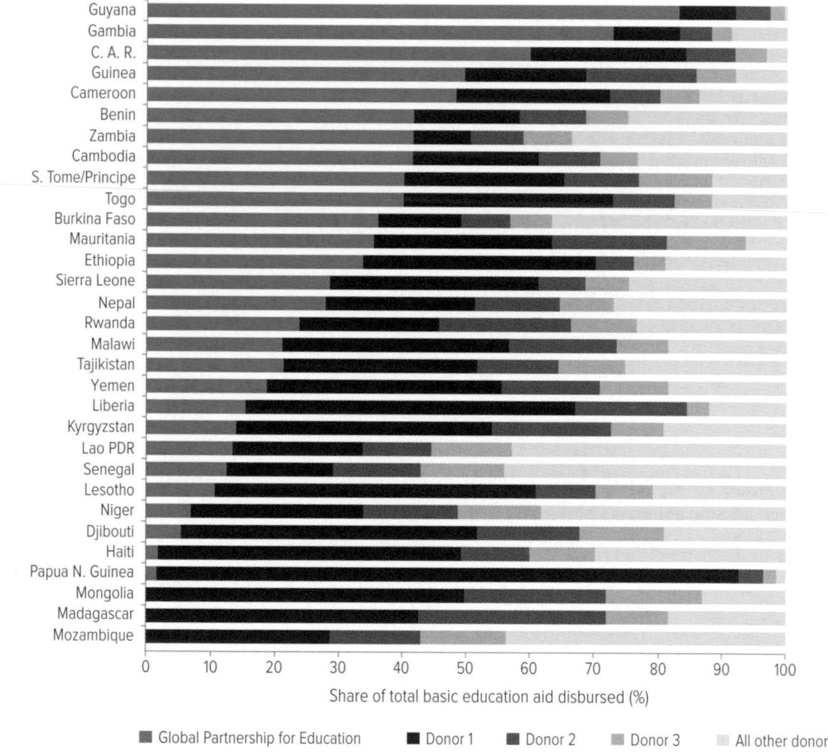

Note: Information on GPE disbursements is from the GPE; aid disbursement information for all other donors is from the OECD's Creditor Reporting System (CRS). When reporting their GPE contributions to the CRS, most donors put them in the category: 'bilateral country unspecified'. Where donors reported GPE contributions to the CRS as direct allocations to recipient countries, these were deducted to avoid double counting.

Spending projections for DAC donors' country programmable aid is also likely to decline. It is of particular concern that the countries most in need of external resources to help them meet the EFA funding gap will be hit hard: country programmable aid is expected to fall in 31 of the 36 low income countries, the majority of which are in sub-Saharan Africa, where education resources fall far short of requirements to achieve EFA (OECD, 2012a).

Projections raise further concern as to whether the remaining resources will go to the countries most in need. Any increases in country programmable aid are expected to be directed largely to middle income countries, including China and Uzbekistan, while disbursements to the countries furthest off track to reach the MDGs will fall by the equivalent of half a billion dollars. These countries include Burundi, Chad, Malawi and Niger, which depend on aid to fund education (OECD, 2013d).

Table 2.4: Many donors expect to reduce aid further in coming years

Donor	Donor's share of total aid to basic education, 2002–2011	Aid forecasts
World Bank	16%	New commitments for education totalled US$3 billion in the 2012 financial year. This is a sharp increase from US$1.8 billion in 2011, largely due to increased investment in primary and lower secondary education. South and West Asia is expected to be the main beneficiary of the additional resources.
United States	10%	The international affairs budget is expected to stay the same in 2014 as 2013. However, the bilateral aid programme is set to decrease in 58 out of 100 countries, including 17 in sub-Saharan Africa, with a shift in focus to East Asia and the Pacific. In addition, the request for basic education is 37% lower in 2014 than in 2013; total resources for basic education have been cut by half since 2010.
United Kingdom	9%	Between 2011 and 2012, bilateral aid was expected to increase from US$8.8 billion to US$8.9 billion, but aid to education was expected to fall from US$1.0 billion to US$0.8 billion.
European Union	8%	The European Development Fund budget will fall by US$4.3 billion between 2014 and 2020 as part of general cuts to the EU budget.
Netherlands	7%	Aid will fall by US$1.3 billion between 2014 and 2017, from 0.63% to 0.55% of GNI. Aid to basic education is expected to decrease from US$243 million to US$76 million between 2011 and 2014.
Japan	6%	Japan has pledged to increase funding for basic education between 2011 and 2014.
Canada	4%	After Canada decided in 2012 to cut aid by 7.5% by 2015, aid is expected to fall by US$650 million by 2013/14 and US$781 million by 2015/16. The Canadian International Aid Agency will close and aid will be managed by the Department of Foreign Affairs and International Trade.
Germany	4%	Aid in 2013 is US$159 million less than was planned and US$112 million less than in 2012. Further cuts are planned for 2014. Germany has committed to increasing aid for basic education, however, and has committed to supporting education in additional countries by 2013.
Australia	3%	The recently elected coalition government has pushed back on the country's commitment to reach the 2015 0.5% aid target pledge for an indefinite period. It has announced that, over the next four years, US$4.2 billion will be cut from the foreign aid budget. This means that aid as a share of GNI is expected to fall from a projected 0.37% in 2013 to 0.32% in 2016/17.
Denmark	1%	Bilateral aid to education is being phased out, with 11 programmes closing between 2011 and 2015. To keep to its promise of maintaining aid levels to basic education, Denmark would need to increase the levels it channels through multilateral mechanisms.

Sources: Beckett (2013); Bernard Van Leer Foundation (2013); CIDA (2013); Deutsche Welle (2012); DFID (2013); Gavas (2013); Global Partnership for Education (2012); Piccio (2013); Robinson and Barder (2013); Taylor (2013); World Bank (2013a).

It is also worrying that education's decline in importance for many donors means that cuts for education could become even more significant. At the GPE Replenishment Conference in 2011, only five donors pledged to increase aid to basic education in low income countries between 2011 and 2014 (Global Partnership for Education, 2011).

Humanitarian aid appeals neglect education needs

With half the world's out-of-school children residing in conflict-affected countries, education in these countries should be a priority for donors. Recognizing this, the UN Secretary-General's Global Education First Initiative (GEFI) set a target of 4% for education's share of short-term humanitarian aid. While this sounds modest, it is unfortunately far beyond the actual share in 2012: 1.4%, down from 2.2% in 2009. Education is the sector receiving the smallest proportion of requests for humanitarian aid, and just 26% of the amounts requested are actually covered (Figure 2.10).

The funds requested for the education sector in Yemen's consolidated appeal, for instance, was the lowest for any sector (3.2% of the total requested), and despite this just a quarter of the request was met (Figure 2.11). As a share of total funding, education received just 1.4% of the Yemen humanitarian appeal. Even in countries where requirements defined as education received a large portion of total humanitarian funding, it does not necessarily improve access to quality education. In the Central African Republic humanitarian appeal, for instance, education received 7% of total funding, a higher share than education receives in most appeals. However, 61% was for school feeding and deworming programmes administered by the World Food Programme.

In humanitarian work plans for 2013, 4.3% of total requirements were earmarked for education – matching the GEFI target – but if education receives the lowest funding relative to requests, as in previous years, its share of overall humanitarian aid is likely to reach no more than 2% once again.

Education only received 1.4% of humanitarian aid in 2012, down from 2.2% in 2009

Figure 2.10: Education's double disadvantage in humanitarian aid: a small share of requests and the smallest share of requests that get funded

Consolidated and flash appeal requests and funding by sector, 2012

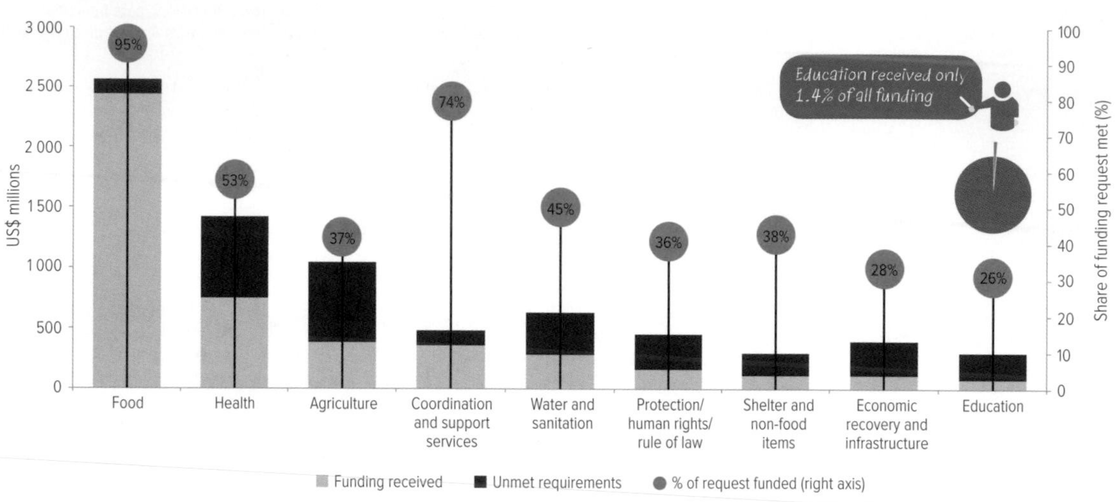

Source: OCHA (2013).

Of the 17 consolidated humanitarian appeals to the United Nations Office for the Coordination of Humanitarian Affairs for 2013, seven proposed that 4% or more of total humanitarian funds requested should be earmarked for the education sector. In Mali, where most schools in the north have been closed due to conflict, education makes up 5% of requests for the 2013 appeal, or US$21.6 million; by September 2013, however, the sector had received just 15% of the funds requested, despite the growing education crisis.

A quarter of direct aid to education is allocated to scholarships and student imputed costs

Similarly, 3% of the Syrian Arab Republic's Humanitarian Assistance Response Plan for 2013 was earmarked for education, with 36% of the resources requested for education having been pledged by September 2013 (Office for the Coordination of Humanitarian Affairs, 2013), even though one in five schools have been destroyed in some areas. In and around Aleppo, where fighting has been intense, only 6% of children were attending schools. Children comprise almost 50% of those in need of urgent humanitarian assistance in this conflict, which is in its third year (UNICEF, 2013b, 2013c). While these countries might receive more of the requested funds in the latter part of 2013, they would come too late for the millions of children who have had to drop out of school due to conflict.

Making sure education aid is spent effectively

It is not only the amount of aid that counts but also whether it is used most effectively to ensure that disadvantaged children are in school and learning. These children do not receive all the aid available, however: a quarter of direct aid to education is spent on students studying in universities in rich countries. In addition, 15% of aid is in the form of loans that countries have to pay back at concessional interest rates, depriving them of resources that could be spent domestically on education in the future (Figure 2.12).

In 2010–2011, an average of US$3.2 billion of aid was allocated annually to scholarships and student imputed costs, equivalent to a quarter of total aid to education. Of this, 81% is spent by four donors: Canada, France, Germany and Japan. Such training is no doubt beneficial, but the spending is not 'real' aid according to the OECD definition. For this reason, some countries do not register the spending as aid. The United States, for example, includes it in the Bureau of Educational and Cultural Affairs budget administered by the Department of State (US Department of State, 2013).

Figure 2.11: Conflict-affected countries receive only a tiny share of their requests for humanitarian education funding
Consolidated and flash appeal requests and funding for education, selected conflict-affected countries, 2012

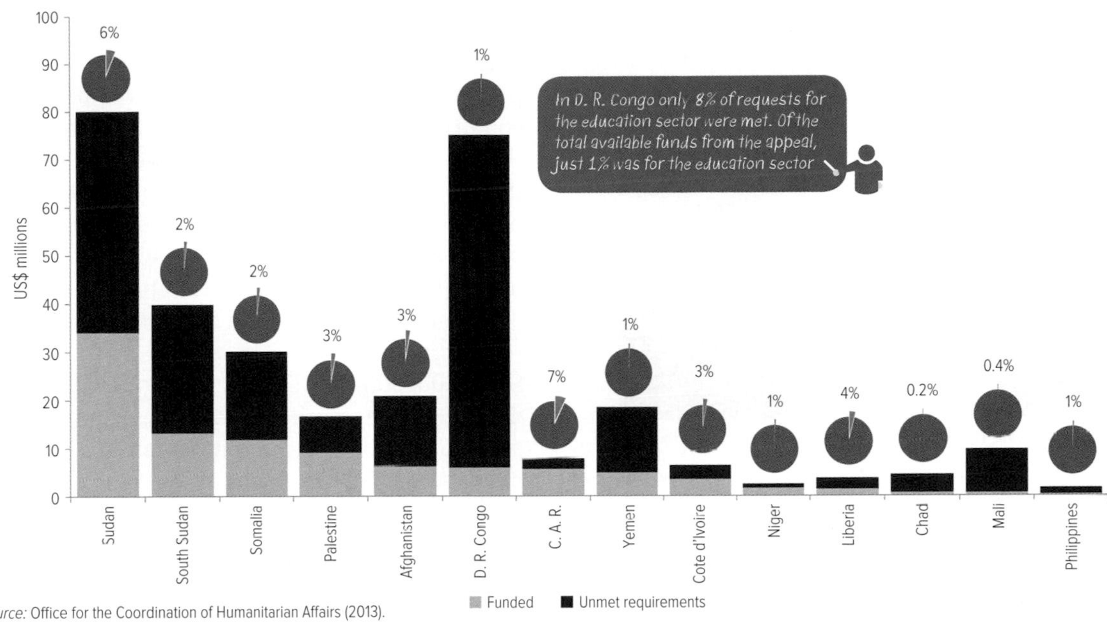

Source: Office for the Coordination of Humanitarian Affairs (2013).

Even though scholarships and imputed student costs may be vital to strengthen human resource capacity in low income countries, most of this funding actually goes to upper middle income countries, with China the largest recipient, receiving 21% of the total (Figure 2.13). Such 'aid' to China exceeds the aid received by some of the poorest countries for basic education. For instance, on average over 2010–2011, donors – primarily Germany and Japan – disbursed US$656 million per year to China for scholarships and student imputed costs, which was 77 times the amount of aid disbursed to Chad for basic education over the same period, and 37 times the amount given to Niger. The total funding in the form of imputed student costs and scholarships received annually by Algeria, China, Morocco, Tunisia and Turkey was equivalent to the total amount of direct aid to basic education for all 36 low income countries in 2010–2011, on average.

While most direct aid to education is in the form of grants, in 2011, US$2.0 billion was in the form of concessional loans, of which US$0.6 billion was spent on basic education. The overwhelming majority of such loans are disbursed by the World Bank, but some bilateral donors, notably France and Japan, also provide some education aid in this way. Japan's loans to the education sector go largely to middle income countries such as China and Indonesia, while the majority of France's have been directed to North African countries such as Morocco.

Figure 2.12: 40% of education aid does not leave donor countries, or is returned to them
Distribution of direct aid to education by type, 2010–2011

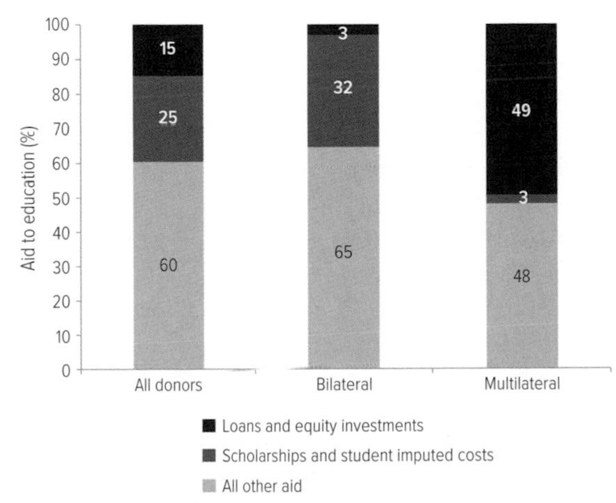

Source: OECD-DAC (2013).

Figure 2.13: Middle income countries receive almost 80% of aid to scholarships and imputed student costs
Education aid spent on scholarships and student imputed costs, 2010–2011

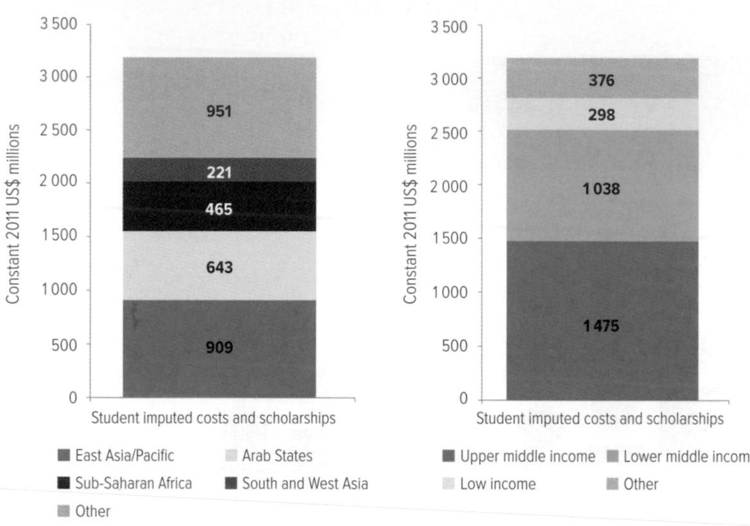

Note: For region groups, aid to 'other' includes disbursements to Central and Eastern Europe, Central Asia, Latin America and the Caribbean and aid that is geographically unallocated. For income groups, 'other' refers to high income and unallocated by income.
Source: OECD-DAC (2013).

Excluding amounts spent on students studying in donor countries and loans, Germany would drop four places from being the largest donor in direct aid to education in 2010–2011 to being the fifth largest, and France would drop two places to fourth largest. The World Bank would fall from third to fourteenth place, since a large share of its funding is in the form of loans. The United Kingdom and United States, which give negligible amounts of aid to education in the form of loans or student imputed costs, would jump from sixth and seventh place to first and second if these aid items were excluded.

The European Union, World Bank and African Development Fund are the largest multilateral donors to education, the latter two providing the majority of education aid in the form of concessional loans. Where bilateral donors are absent in providing education financing, there is a danger of low income countries becoming overdependent on concessional loans from international finance institutions, leading to indebtedness that could restrict countries' ability to fund education from their own resources.

Accounting for all education expenditure

Governments are the largest source of education financing, with donors making up a significant proportion of resources in some of the poorest countries. One important source of education finance is often overlooked, however: the amount that households themselves contribute. More broadly, information on the whole spectrum of education financing is often insufficient and fragmented, resulting in partial analysis and diagnosis of who bears the cost for education.

Since 2000, the OECD's tracking of aid from DAC donors has improved considerably, with more attention not only to commitments but also to disbursements, and to identifying 'real' aid. However, the collection of national finance data remains weak. Data on private spending from household surveys often do not provide sufficient detail on spending by level of education. To the extent that such information is available, it is not sufficiently used by policy-makers to get a comprehensive picture of education spending.

Such limitations could have consequences for the achievement of Education for All and the extension of education goals after 2015. Analysis for this Report of data from seven countries shows that the share of education expenditure borne by households ranges from 14% to 37% in primary education and from 30% to 58% in secondary education.[7] These findings highlight the importance of building a comprehensive national education accounts system, which could be modelled on the experience in health.

Learning from national health accounts

The idea of a comprehensive framework to account for all expenditure flowing into a sector is not new. It has been applied successfully in the health sector, starting with high income countries in the 1970s and spreading to middle and low income countries since the 1990s.

National health accounts systems have developed in recognition of the fact that informed decision-making requires reliable information on the quantity of financial

7. See technical note on the EFA Global Monitoring Report website for further information (www.efareport.unesco.org).

resources used, their sources and the way they are used. The systems aim to provide evidence to allow monitoring of trends in health spending, whether by government, donors or households. Drawing on this information, Eurostat, the OECD and WHO have established global standards to systematize how such information is collected, leading to the International Classification for Health Accounts. This has enabled countries to compare their performance and improve effectiveness, efficiency and equity (OECD, 2000; OECD et al., 2011; WHO et al., 2003).

Evidence from national health accounts has had far-reaching consequences for policy decisions. In Rwanda, the revelation that HIV/AIDS-related health services were starved of public funding, with households making 93% of the necessary expenditure, prompted the donor community to triple funding between 1998 and 2000 (Schneider et al., 2001). In Burkina Faso, the unequal distribution of expenditure shown by publication of national health accounts triggered the introduction of free subsidized public services, with the result that the household share of health spending fell from 50% in 2003 to 38% in 2008 (Zida et al., 2010).

The OECD has introduced a similar classification of education expenditure for OECD member states that permits useful comparisons across countries and over time. It shows, for example, that households bear the brunt of pre-primary education costs in some of these countries, such as Australia, where they account for 44% of spending, and Japan, at 38%. Even in primary and secondary education, households cover more than 20% of total expenditure in Chile and the Republic of Korea. The data also reveal that a share of education costs was shifted from government to households in the 2000s (OECD, 2013b).

Using a similar methodology, the joint OECD/UIS World Education Indicators programme provided information for 19 middle income countries, showing that a higher share of primary and secondary education costs was borne by households in these countries than in the richer OECD countries. For example, 28% of costs were met by households in India and 50% in Jamaica (UIS, 2006).

Several efforts in the last 10 years have bolstered the spread of national education accounts. Pilot accounting exercises have been carried out in El Salvador, Guatemala, Morocco and Turkey, with support in some cases from the World Bank and in others from USAID. They have lacked the common framework that has lent credibility and relevance to the national health accounts, however, and information has not yet emerged in a systematic way for poorer countries.

Piecing together the financing puzzle

Adopting a national accounts approach to education for this Report shows what is possible from existing data across a diverse set of countries. Expenditure patterns were analysed for seven countries – Albania, Bangladesh, Indonesia, Malawi, Nicaragua, Rwanda and Tajikistan – drawing on data from 2007–2011.

Three types of data sources were used. First, to estimate public expenditure by education level and type, data from ministries of education and finance or international organization reports were used. Second, the OECD Creditor Reporting System database was drawn upon to identify aid data. Third, income and expenditure data from household surveys were used to estimate private education expenditure. The analysis shows that private spending is often much higher than has been recognized, which penalizes the poorest households; and that aid provides an important contribution to education financing in some of the poorest countries.

Households in poorer countries bear a larger share of the responsibility for education spending

Across the seven countries, governments are responsible, on average, for 65% of primary education spending, 51% at secondary level and 57% for tertiary institutions, with governments responsible for a larger share of overall spending in the richer countries in the sample – Albania and Indonesia – than in the poorer countries. As a result, households in poorer countries bear a larger share of the responsibility for education spending: the share of private expenditure in primary education ranges from 14% in Indonesia to 37% in Bangladesh. Households play an even more important role at secondary level, where the share of private expenditure ranges from 30% in Indonesia to 58% in Bangladesh (Figure 2.14).[8]

8. A comparison of household education spending in 15 African countries similarly showed that, despite the abolition of fees, household expenditure amounted to 33% of government spending on primary education (Foko et al., 2012).

By comparison, the share of private expenditure in primary and secondary education in high income OECD countries is 8.5% (OECD, 2013b). Education is therefore far from free – the goal envisaged in the Dakar Framework for Action – with households in poorer countries having to devote a particularly large share of their resources to education.

In Malawi, households are responsible for 32% of secondary education expenditure

The breakdown at tertiary level is further cause for concern: because higher education is subsidized in some poorer countries, those reaching this level, predominantly the better-off, benefit from government spending more than those who do not make it this far. In Malawi, for example, households are responsible for 32% of secondary education expenditure, but 21% at tertiary level.

Closer inspection shows the degree to which poorer and richer households benefit from public expenditure and the amount of extra expenditure they incur. In the case of primary education, government expenditure is progressive. As most children in the seven countries attend primary school, and as more of the richer families send their children to private school, poorer families benefit slightly more in relative terms from public expenditure.

In secondary education, however, the picture changes considerably. As fewer children of poorer families stay in school after primary education, they benefit less from government spending at secondary level. For example, in Malawi the richest 20% of families receive a public subsidy for secondary education that is almost six times as much as that received by the poorest 20% of families. In Indonesia, the ratio is almost three times. When public spending and private spending are added, a child from the richest 20% gets four times as much as a

Figure 2.14: In low and middle income countries, families pay a heavy price for education
Share of total education expenditure borne by government, donors and households, selected countries, 2007–2011

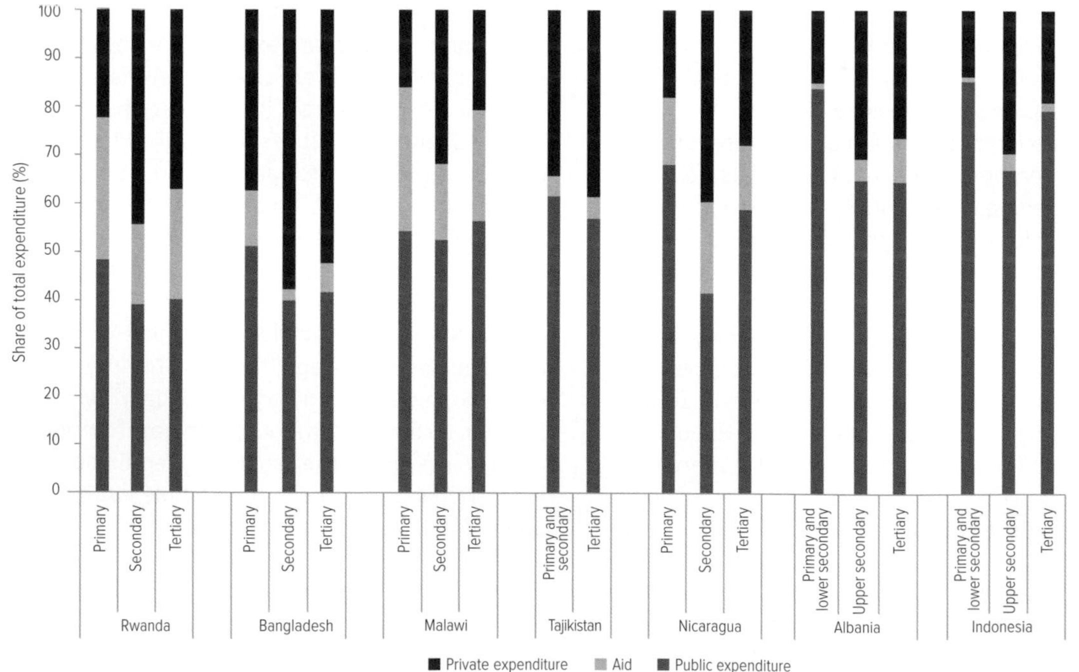

Sources: EFA Global Monitoring Report team analysis, based on data from OECD-DAC (aid), ministries of education and finance (public expenditure) and the following household surveys (private expenditure): 2008 Albania Living Standards Measurement Survey; 2010 Bangladesh Household Income and Expenditure Survey; 2009 Indonesia National Socio-economic Survey; 2010–11 Malawi Integrated Household Survey; 2009 Nicaragua National Living Standards Survey; 2011 Rwanda Integrated Household Living Conditions Survey; and 2007 Tajikistan Living Standards Measurement Survey.

child from the poorest 20% in Indonesia and Nicaragua, six times as much in Bangladesh and Rwanda and 10 times as much in Malawi.

One reason for the divergence between household contributions for primary and secondary schooling is that fees are usually still charged for secondary schools, while they have been abolished in many countries at primary level. Tuition fees in public secondary schools account for 64% of spending by the poorest households in Malawi compared with 45% spent by the richest households.

Spending by poor households on fees reduces the amount they can spend on items to improve the quality of their children's education, such as books and school supplies. In Bangladesh and Indonesia, the richest households spend four times as much on books as the poorest households in public lower secondary schools. In Bangladesh, the richest households spend 15 times as much on private tuition as poorer households for secondary education.

Analysing education spending across different sources reveals that, in the case of the two sub-Saharan African countries included, external assistance is a vital component of education financing. In Malawi, aid accounted for 23% of total spending on education in 2010/11. The share provided by donors was higher for primary education (30%) than secondary (16%) or tertiary (23%). In Rwanda, aid was equivalent to 22% of total government expenditure in 2010/11. By contrast, the share of external assistance in total education spending was 13% in Nicaragua, 9% in Albania (concentrated in tertiary education), 6% in Bangladesh, 4% in Tajikistan and less than 2% in Indonesia.

This preliminary analysis shows that a national education accounts system can be established using existing data – although improvements need to be made in terms of coverage and comparability between countries. The results can reveal whether resources are being used equitably. It is now time to build a comprehensive system to make sure that deficits in data do not thwart efforts to ensure that no child is denied the right to education after 2015. As a lead multilateral agency responsible for ensuring sufficient financing of education, the GPE could play a coordinating role in taking this forward.

Conclusion

One of the biggest failures of the EFA period has been fulfilling the pledge that no country would be thwarted in achieving its goals due to lack of resources. To avoid this happening after 2015, national governments, aid donors and other education funders need to be held to account for their commitments to provide the resources necessary to reach education goals. Post-2015 education goals must include a specific target for financing by governments and aid donors. Otherwise, children will continue to pay the price.

Post-2015 education goals must include a specific target for financing by governments and aid donors

Drawing on analysis included in *EFA Global Monitoring Reports* over the years, the Report team proposes that a target should be set for national governments to allocate at least 6% of their GNP to education. Targets for governments and aid donors should also include commitments for them to spend at least 20% of their budgets on education. Setting these targets, and making sure governments and aid donors keep to them, will be an important contribution to the education opportunities of a future generation of children and young people.

Part 2

Chapter 3 Education transforms lives

Credit: Karel Prinsloo/ARETE/UNESCO

Educating mothers: In Kenyan villages like Nagis, Turkana, educating mothers can help reduce high levels of infant mortality.

Education lights every stage of the journey to a better life. To unlock the wider benefits of education, all children need access to both primary and lower secondary education of good quality. Special efforts are needed to ensure that all children and young people – regardless of their family income, where they live, their gender, their ethnicity, whether they are disabled – can benefit equally from its transformative power. This chapter provides comprehensive evidence that progress in education is vital to achieve all new development goals after 2015.

www.education-transforms.org

Introduction

Treaties and laws worldwide recognize that education is a fundamental human right. The Education for All goals and the Millennium Development Goals acknowledge its indispensable role in imparting the knowledge and skills that enable people to realize their full potential. But the international community and national governments have so far failed to sufficiently recognize and exploit education's considerable power as a catalyst for other development goals.

As a result, education has been slipping down the global agenda and some donors have moved funds elsewhere, at the very time when education's wider benefits are sorely needed to help countries get back on track to reach other development goals. Education's power to accelerate the achievement of wider goals needs to be much better recognized in the post-2015 development framework. This chapter shows why, drawing on new analysis carried out for this Report and a thorough survey of other research to build a comprehensive overview of the numerous ways in which education advances wider development aims.

This analysis sheds new light on education's better-known benefits: the first part of the chapter examines its power to reduce poverty, boost job opportunities and drive economic growth, and the second part shows how it increases people's chances of leading a healthy life. In the third part the chapter goes beyond these questions to look in depth at education's contribution to social goals that are increasingly being recognized as vital elements of the post-2015 framework: deepening democratic institutions, protecting the environment and adapting to climate change, and empowering women.

Several common themes emerge from the evidence laid out in this chapter, each of which must be recognized and acted upon by governments and their development partners in order to realize the wider benefits of education. One persistent thread is the transformative power of girls' education. As well as boosting their own chances of getting jobs, staying healthy and participating fully in society, educating girls and young women has a marked impact on the health of their children and on accelerating countries' transition to stable population growth with low birth and death rates.

Another common thread is that universal primary education is vital – but is often not enough. To unlock the wider benefits of education, especially its power to save lives, universal access needs to be extended at least to lower secondary school. And access alone is not enough either: the education that children receive needs to be of good quality so that they actually learn the basic literacy and numeracy skills that are necessary to acquire further skills.

Above all, the evidence assembled here underlines the imperative that good quality education must be made accessible to all, regardless of their income, where they live, their gender, their ethnicity, whether they are disabled, and other factors that can contribute to disadvantage. Education's unique potential to boost wider development goals can only be fully realized if education is equitable, which means making special efforts to ensure that the marginalized can benefit equally from its transformative power.

Education's power to accelerate the achievement of wider goals needs to be much better recognized in the post-2015 framework

Education reduces poverty and boosts jobs and growth

Education is a key way of tackling poverty, and makes it more likely for men and women not just to be employed, but to hold jobs that are more secure and provide good working conditions and decent pay. It also lays the foundations for more robust and longer-term economic growth.

Education offers the poor a route to a better life

If all students in low income countries left school with basic reading skills, 171 million people could be lifted out of poverty

For the poor, education is one of the most powerful routes to a better future. As the evidence in this section shows, education enables people to escape from the trap of chronic poverty and prevents the transmission of poverty between generations. Good quality education that improves learning outcomes increases economic growth (Hanushek and Woessmann, 2012b). In turn, economic growth reduces poverty because it tends to increase wages and the amount people can earn from work in agriculture and the urban informal sector (Ravallion, 2001). Based on these two core assumptions, EFA Global Monitoring Report team calculations show that if all students in low income countries left school with basic reading skills, 171 million people could be lifted out of poverty, which would be equivalent to a 12% cut in world poverty.

The persistence of poverty makes it vital for policy-makers to take into account education's power to help reduce it. The proportion of the world's people living on less than US$1.25 a day fell from 47% in 1990 to 22% in 2010 (United Nations, 2013). However, almost 1 billion people are still likely to be living below this poverty line in 2015. In sub-Saharan Africa, almost half the population was living in poverty in 2010, and the number of poor is growing: by 2015, around 40% more people are expected to be living in poverty than in 1990. Sub-Saharan Africa's experience is in stark contrast to the experience of East Asia and the Pacific, where about 56% of the population lived below the poverty line in 1990. By 2010, the share had fallen to just 12.5%, due in part to the availability of good quality education (World Bank, 2013a).

The Millennium Development Goal (MDG) of halving the proportion of people living in poverty between 1990 and 2015 has been met, but many are proposing the eradication of poverty by 2030 as a new post-2015 goal. For the reasons outlined here, it is crucial for education to be an integral part of all plans to make poverty a thing of the past.

Education accelerates an escape from chronic poverty

For some people, poverty is transitory: they may experience brief periods of being poor or frequently move into or out of poverty. But for the more vulnerable, poverty is a chronic state: they remain poor for long periods, even all their lives, passing on their poverty to their children. For example, in Kenya three-quarters of rural households that were poor in 2000 were still poor in 2009 (Radeny et al., 2012).

Education is a key way of reducing chronic poverty, because increased levels of education not only help lift households out of poverty permanently but also guard against them falling into poverty. Evidence from diverse settings confirms that even after taking account of other factors that can have an influence, such as household land holdings and other assets, education at all levels reduces the chance of people living in chronic poverty:

- Although Ethiopia has reduced poverty by half since 1995, 31% of the population still lives in poverty (World Bank, 2013b). Raising levels of education, which are particularly low in rural areas, can make a clear difference. Between 1994 and 2009, for example, rural households where the household head had completed primary education were 16% less likely to be chronically poor (Dercon et al., 2012).

- The probability that poor households in Uganda would remain poor over a seven-year period fell by 16% for each year the household head had spent in secondary school and by a further 5% for each year the spouse had spent in primary school (Lawson et al., 2006).

- In KwaZulu-Natal province of South Africa, where education helped people escape poverty after the apartheid era, an additional year of schooling increased consumption expenditure by 11% (May et al., 2011).

- Extra years in school are more likely to help lift people out of poverty when schooling is of good enough quality to give people the basic skills they need, such as literacy. In Nepal, where more than half those in poverty remained poor over a 10-year period, 42% of adults were literate in households that remained above the poverty line throughout the period, 23% were literate in households that made a transition into or out of poverty, but only 15% were literate in chronically poor households (Bhatta and Sharma, 2011).

- Education's power to help people escape poverty even in the face of adversity is evident in a rural district in Sindh province of Pakistan, where poverty increased over a 17-year period due to drought and water shortages. The heads of households who remained poor throughout had both the lowest initial level of education (by 1 year, on average) and the lowest increase over the period (less than 1 year). By contrast, the heads of households that escaped poverty had a higher initial level of education (1.8 years) as well as the highest increase over the period (by 2 years) (Lohano, 2011).

- Getting at least as far as lower secondary school has a particularly strong effect, in a wide range of settings. Among households in rural Viet Nam, those whose heads had lower secondary education were 24% more likely not to be poor between 2002 and 2006 than households with no schooling, and likelihood for those with upper secondary education was 31% higher (Baulch and Dat, 2011). In rural Nicaragua, the chronic poverty rate was 22% for households with no educated adult, 7% for households where adults averaged three years of schooling and 1% for households where adults had six years of education or more (Stampini and Davis, 2006). In urban Brazil between 1993 and 2003, chronic poverty was 29% for those with no education, 22% for those with incomplete primary education, 12% for those with primary education and 7.5% for those with at least lower secondary education (Ribas and Machado, 2007).

- Education's power to keep people out of poverty is evident in rural Indonesia. Of all the factors making it more likely that a household would exit poverty over a seven-year period, education was the most important. Each additional year of schooling increased income growth by 6% over the seven years (McCulloch et al., 2007). Completing lower secondary education not only more than doubled the probability of escaping poverty, but also reduced by a quarter the probability of falling into poverty.

In rural Indonesia, completing lower secondary education more than doubled the probability of escaping poverty

Education prevents the transmission of poverty between generations

Children whose parents have little or no schooling are more likely to be poorly educated themselves. This is one of the ways poverty is perpetuated, so raising education levels is key to breaking the cycle of chronic poverty. The right policies can ensure that the benefits are passed on equitably. New analysis for this Report, based on 142 Demographic and Health Surveys from 56 countries between 1990 and 2009, looks at how parental education affects the number of years of education attained by household members aged 15 to 18. For each additional year of mother's education, the average child attained an extra 0.32 years, and for girls the benefit was slightly larger (Bhalotra et al., 2013b).

In Guatemala, higher levels of education and cognitive skills among women increased the number of years their children spent in school. In turn, each grade completed raised the wages of these children once they became adults by 10%, while an increase in the reading comprehension test score from 14 points to the mean of 36 points raised their wages by 35% (Behrman et al., 2009, 2010).

In poor countries parental education can even be more powerful than other possible factors, such as inheriting assets. In Senegal, for example, inheriting land or a house did not increase wealth, but children whose parents had some formal education were more likely to find off-farm employment and so escape poverty. In particular, the sons of educated mothers in rural areas were 27% more likely to find off-farm employment (Lambert et al., 2011).

How education reduces poverty

The main way education reduces poverty is by increasing people's income. It enables those in paid formal employment to earn higher wages, and offers better livelihoods for those who work in the urban informal sector or in rural areas.[1]

Education helps provide a decent wage. Globally an estimated 400 million people – or 15% of all workers – are paid less than US$1.25 per day, too little to enable them to lift themselves and their families out of poverty (ILO, 2013a). Young people are particularly vulnerable to working in poverty, with 28% in this situation (Understanding Children's Work, 2012).

In Pakistan, the wages of a literate person are 23% higher than those of an illiterate person

Education can help people escape from working poverty. In the United Republic of Tanzania, 82% of workers who had less than primary education were earning below the poverty line. By contrast, working men and women with primary education were 20% less likely to be poor, while secondary education reduced the chances of being poor by almost 60%. In Brazil, while working in poverty is less common – and almost non-existent for those with at least secondary education – 13% of those lacking primary education are consigned to this situation (Understanding Children's Work, 2013).

Better-educated individuals in wage employment are paid more to reward them for their higher productivity. On average, one year of education is estimated to increase wage earnings by 10%; in sub-Saharan Africa, as much as 13% (Montenegro and Patrinos, 2012). And, on average, returns to investment in education increase by level of education, from 8% at primary level to 13% at secondary level and 16% at tertiary level (Colclough et al., 2010).

In some countries, education has a stronger effect on the wages of the highest earners. In Colombia, for example, the return to investment in education for those whose wages are in the bottom one-tenth, or decile, is 9%, compared with 14% for those in the top decile. This may reflect the better quality of education that wealthier people receive. By contrast, in Viet Nam, where the education system is more equal, returns to education are higher for the bottom decile, with returns estimated at 10%, compared with 6% for the top decile (Fasih et al., 2012).

It is necessary to assess the returns to skills acquired in school, such as literacy and numeracy, rather than focusing only on time spent in school. Analysis in 13 richer countries showed that for every 60-point increase on a 500-point literacy skills scale, wage earnings rose from about 5% in Italy to 15% in Chile (Hanushek and Zhang, 2006).

Similarly, in Pakistan the wages of a literate person are 23% higher than those of an illiterate person. Improved literacy can have a particularly strong effect on women's earnings, suggesting that investing in women's education can pay dividends. Working women with a high level of literacy skills earned 95% more than women with weak or no literacy skills, whereas the differential was only 33% among men (Aslam et al., 2012).

Education increases earnings from informal work. In urban areas, many of the poorest are involved in informal sector work. Education can help lift these people out of poverty by increasing their earnings and enabling them to benefit more from entrepreneurial activity. More educated people are more likely to start a business, and their businesses are likely to be more profitable.

In eight sub-Saharan African countries, for example, people who had completed primary education were more likely to own household enterprises or microenterprises than those with less education. In Uganda, owners of household enterprises who had completed primary education earned 36% more than those with no education, and those who had completed lower secondary education earned 56% more (Fox and Sohnesen, 2012). In Angola, an additional year of schooling increased profits of small businesses by 7% to 9.5% (Wiig and Kolstad, 2013).

In Viet Nam, a survey of 1,400 new businesses, of which 91% were micro or small and 61% were household enterprises, showed that having at

1. Education is also linked to other factors that lead to poverty reduction. For example, it reduces fertility, which leads to fewer dependents per family.

least secondary education raised profits by 34% (Santarelli and Tran, 2013). In Thailand, a year of education increased returns to household assets by 7%, primarily because educated households tended to invest the profits (Pawasutipaisit and Townsend, 2011).

Education increases earnings from agriculture. In low and middle income countries, many of the poorest depend on farming for their livelihoods (World Bank, 2013a). Education can offer these people a crucial route to a better life.

Literacy and numeracy skills increase farmers' ability to interpret and respond to new information. Educated farmers make better use of fertilizers, seed varieties and farming technologies to increase the productivity of traditional crops. They are also more likely to diversify into higher value crops.

Examples from around the world have shown the power of education to boost farmers' productivity in ways that can help lift them out of poverty. In semi-arid areas of China, educated farmers were more likely to use rainwater harvesting and supplementary irrigation technology to alleviate water shortages (He et al., 2007). In Ethiopia, education of household members other than the household head led to increased fertilizer use (Asfaw and Admassie, 2004). In Mozambique, literate farmers were 26 percentage points more likely than non-literate ones to cultivate cash crops (Bandiera and Rasul, 2006). In Nepal, a household where a farmer had completed primary education was about 20 percentage points more likely to adopt soil conservation and erosion-control measures (Tiwari et al., 2008).

The returns to education are larger where farmers are able to make use of new technologies. In northern Nigeria, when the household head had four years of education, production of cowpeas increased by a quarter with modern technology but was unchanged where traditional methods were used (Alene and Manyong, 2007).

Education enables rural households to diversify their income sources. Many of the world's poor living in rural areas have no choice other than to work on small farms. Education allows households to respond flexibly and diversify their income-earning opportunities. It improves their chances of obtaining non-farm work – which tends to be more lucrative – as analysis of labour force survey data for this Report shows. For example, in Indonesia, where half the population lives in rural areas, the share of rural dwellers employed in non-farm work is 15% of men and 17% of women with no education, but among those with secondary education increases to 61% of men and 72% of women (Figure 3.1).

In Nepal, a household where a farmer had completed primary education was more likely to adopt soil conservation measures

Figure 3.1: Education opens doors to non-farm employment
Non-farm employment rate among people aged 15 to 64 in rural areas, by education level and gender, selected countries, 2007–2011

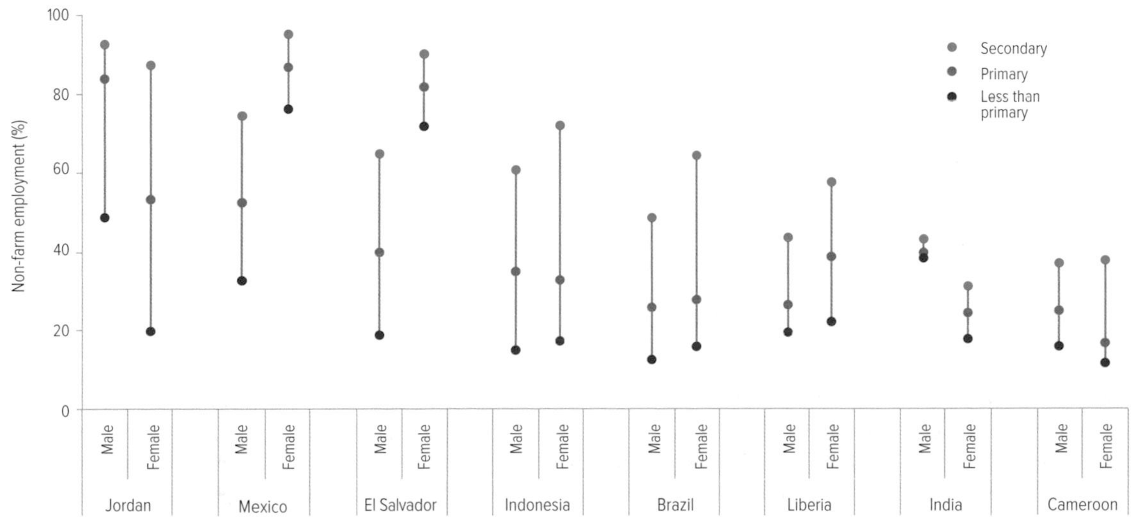

Source: Understanding Children's Work (2013).

Education transforms employment prospects

With more young people than ever entering the world of work, the poorest and most vulnerable risk being left unemployed or working below the poverty line in insecure work, because they are the least likely to have completed school. Even in richer countries, the economic downturn is leaving those with less education facing the prospect of long-term unemployment.

Education makes it more likely for men and women not just to be employed, but to hold jobs that are more secure and provide good working conditions and decent pay. Education is particularly vital for women so that they can benefit from decent jobs, becoming able to make decisions about spending resources and hence gaining more control over their own lives.

The importance of jobs in reducing poverty was recognized eight years after the MDG framework was established, when a new target was added as part of the first MDG: to achieve full and productive employment and decent work for all, including women and young people. An additional indicator for women's engagement in wage employment was also included under the third MDG, on gender equality, in recognition of the fact that better education improves women's livelihoods.

Education plays a strong role in determining women's engagement in the labour force in Latin American countries

As a way of improving people's well-being and eradicating poverty, jobs are likely to feature in the post-2015 development framework. The International Labour Organization argues that employment should be given an even stronger focus than in the MDGs, with a goal in its own right this time (ILO, 2013b). This argument is reinforced by the views of poor people, who see jobs and education as two of the most important ways to improve their lives (Bergh and Melamed, 2012).

Education protects against unemployment in rich countries

Globally, 193 million people were estimated to be unemployed in 2011, including 73 million young people – equivalent to 1 in 8 of the youth population (ILO, 2013a). Unemployment has soared in some richer countries that have borne the brunt of the economic downturn. Young people in particular have been severely hit, with their unemployment rates reaching over 50% in Greece and Spain.

Those with higher levels of education suffer less from the effects of the economic downturn: in Spain, while unemployment rates for those with less than secondary education rose from around 20% in 2007 to 60% in 2012 , they increased from 14% to 40% for those with higher levels of education (Eurostat, 2013).

Education increases women's chances of participating in the labour force

As countries develop, education becomes a passport for women to enter the labour force. When society becomes more accepting of women's formal employment, women with more education are in a stronger position to get paid work (Gaddis and Klasen, 2012). By enabling women's participation in the labour market, education contributes to their empowerment and to their country's prosperity (Kabeer, 2012).

In middle income countries in Latin America, such as Argentina, Brazil, El Salvador and Mexico, the proportion of women in paid employment increases sharply as women's education level rises, according to analysis of labour force survey data for this Report (Infographic: Job search). In Mexico, while 39% of women with primary education are employed, the proportion rises to 48% of those with secondary education.

Education plays a much stronger role in determining women's engagement in the labour force than it does for men in these Latin American countries. Men who have not even completed primary school are as likely to be engaged in the labour market as women with tertiary education in all four countries. And there is very little difference in participation between men with primary and secondary education: it is over 80% regardless of level of education achieved.

In poorer countries, cultural factors and a lack of affordable child care facilities and transport continue to prevent women from taking paid jobs. In India and Pakistan, for example, women are less likely to be counted as participating in the labour market whether they have been to

JOB SEARCH

Educated men and women are more likely to find work

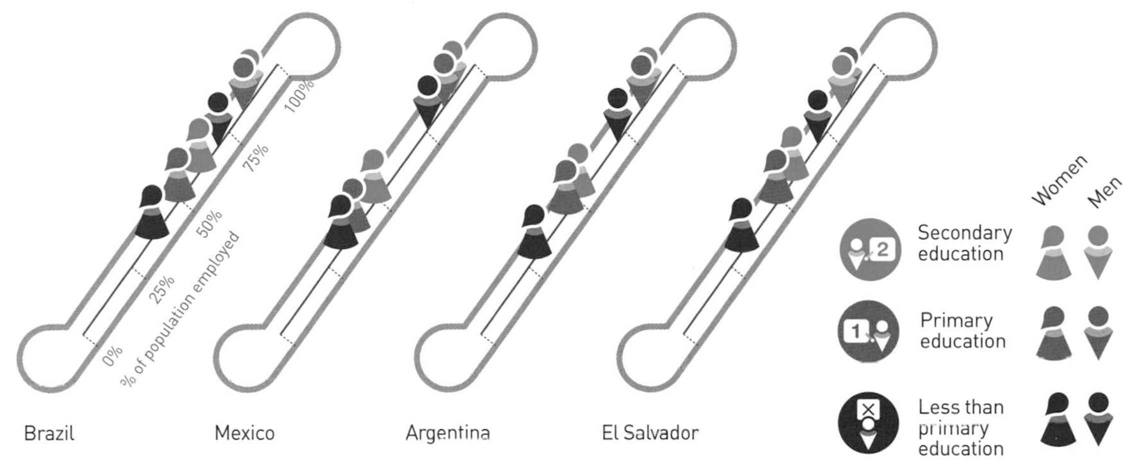

Source: Understanding Children's Work (2013).

school or not. The only exception is the extremely small numbers of women who make it to upper secondary school in Pakistan. Only around one in five make it to this level, and they are likely to be from more privileged backgrounds (Aslam, 2013). By contrast, the vast majority of men are in the labour force in the two countries, regardless of their education.

Women are kept out of the labour force not only by cultural stigma associated with taking paid employment but also by social expectations related to family size and household chores, which mean they often put in long hours in work that is less visible to policy-makers, particularly in poorer countries (Bloom et al., 2009). For example, in Jordan, 25% of rural women with only primary education work for no pay, compared with 7% of those with secondary education.

Education increases the chances of better work conditions

Those with more education tend to enjoy better work conditions, including opportunities to work full time and secure contracts. Although some choose part-time jobs, for the most vulnerable part-time work is low paid and insecure.

Education increases the chance of getting full-time work, particularly for women. Among working women in Pakistan, while one-third of those with primary education work full time, one-half of women with secondary education have full-time jobs. By contrast, almost all men work full time, regardless of their level of education.

Education helps protect working men and women from exploitation by increasing their opportunities to obtain secure contracts. In urban El Salvador, only 7% of working women and men with less than primary education have an employment contract, leaving them very vulnerable. By contrast, 49% of those with secondary education have signed a contract (Figure 3.2).

Education closes gender wage gaps

Globally, women are paid less than men for comparable work. Even though this gap has been narrowing in some parts of the world, it remains a cause for concern (OECD, 2012). The higher the level of education, the lower the gap, even in countries where discrimination in the labour force means gender differences remain entrenched, as analysis of gender wage gaps in 64 countries shows. Education makes a

In Jordan, 25% of rural women with only primary education work for no pay, compared with 7% of those with secondary education

Figure 3.2: Education leads to more secure jobs
Percentage of paid workers aged 15 to 64 in urban labour markets with an employment contract, by education level, selected countries, 2007–2011

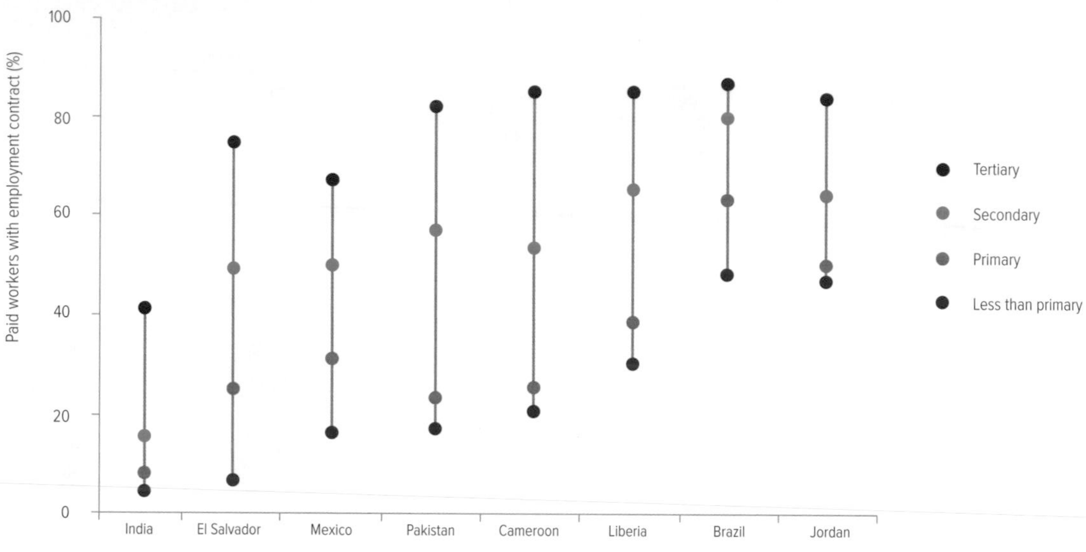

Note: The figures for Pakistan refer to both urban and rural areas.
Source: Understanding Children's Work (2013).

In the Arab States, women with secondary education earn 87% of the wages of men, compared with 60% for those with primary education

particular difference in the Arab States, where women with secondary education earn 87% of the wages of men, compared with 60% for those with primary education (Ñopo et al., 2011).
In sub-Saharan Africa, men earn twice as much as women on average, but education has a strong effect on closing the earnings gap. In Ghana, among those with no education, men earn 57% more than women, but the gap shrinks to 24% among those with primary education and 16% with secondary education (Kolev and Sirven, 2010).

These regional patterns are confirmed by analysis for this Report of data from nine countries in diverse settings. In Argentina and Jordan, among people with primary education, women earn around half the average wage of men, while among those with secondary education, women earn around two-thirds of men's wages (Infographic: Wage gaps).

Education boosts prosperity

Education not only helps individuals escape poverty by developing the skills they need to improve their livelihoods, but also generates productivity gains that fuel economic growth. For growth to reduce poverty, education needs to overcome inequality. Expanding access to education alone is not enough, however. Equitable learning for all is key to shared national prosperity for all.

Some analysts have expressed reservations about education's effect on economic growth (Pritchett, 2006). But when improved data and methods are used, and the impact of education inequality and education quality is taken into account, it is clear that education is a key force for national prosperity (Castelló-Climent, 2010; Hanushek and Woessmann, 2008; Krueger and Lindahl, 2001).

WAGE GAPS

Education narrows pay gaps between men and women

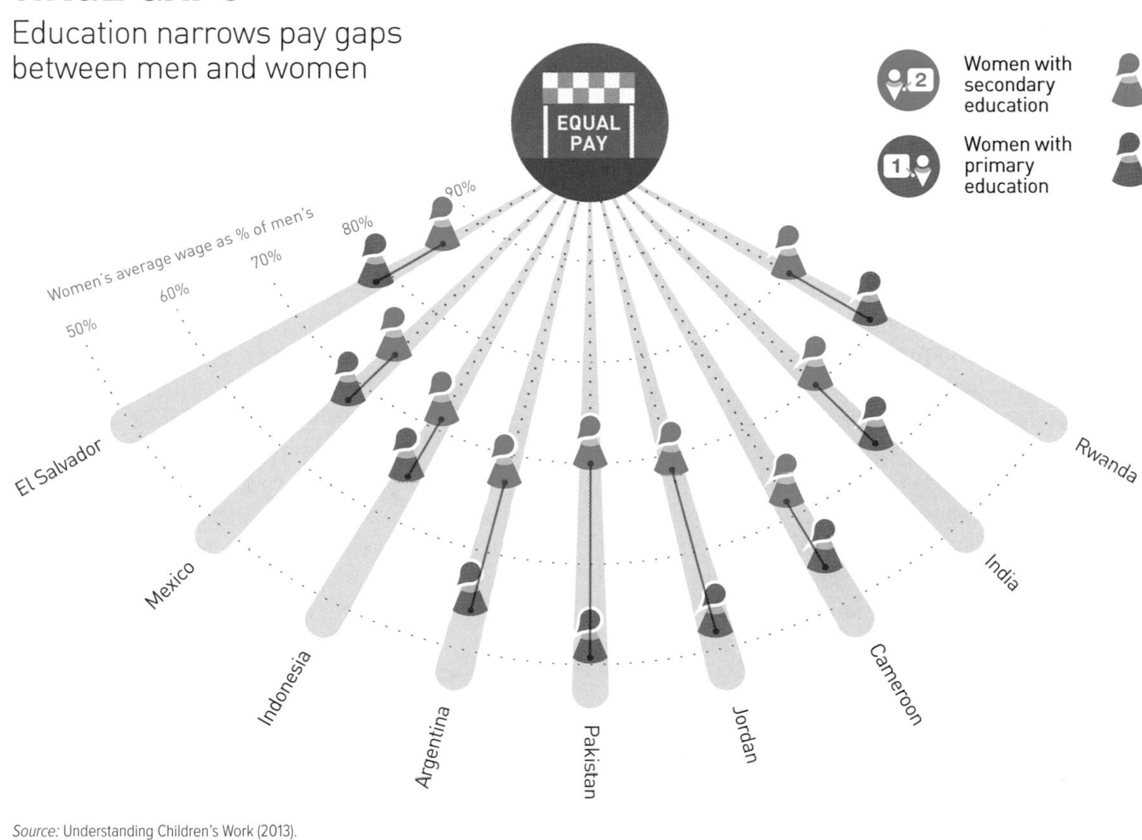

Source: Understanding Children's Work (2013).

Education can fuel economic growth ...

Education's power to boost growth substantially is underlined by new analysis for this Report. An increase in the average educational attainment of a country's population by one year increases annual per capita GDP growth from 2% to 2.5%.[2] These estimates take into account factors such as the level of income at the beginning of the period, the level of inflation, the share of the public sector in the economy and the degree of openness to trade (Castelló-Climent, 2013).

The key role of education is evident in the way it helps explain differences between regions in the pace of economic growth. In 1965, the average level of schooling was 2.7 years higher in East Asia and the Pacific than in sub-Saharan Africa. Over the following 45-year period, average annual growth in income per capita was 3.4% in East Asia and the Pacific but only 0.8% in sub-Saharan Africa. The difference in initial education levels could help explain about half the difference in growth rates.

Comparing experiences within regions further illustrates the importance of education. In Latin America and the Caribbean, the average number of years that adults had spent at school rose from 3.6 in 1965 to 7.5 in 2005. This is estimated to have contributed two-thirds of the average annual growth rate in GDP per capita of 2.8% between 2005 and 2010. But not all countries in the region kept pace. In Guatemala, adults had just 3.6 years of schooling on average in 2005, equivalent to Côte d'Ivoire in sub-Saharan Africa, and on average schooling increased by only 2.3 years in the country from 1965 to 2005, the second lowest rate in the region, after Belize. If Guatemala had matched the regional average, it could have more than doubled its average

An increase in the average educational attainment of a country's population by one year increases annual per capita GDP growth from 2% to 2.5%

2. The effect is broadly compatible with the earlier, much quoted result that each additional year of average education attainment increased per capita income by 12% among 73 countries over 1960–1990 (Cohen and Soto, 2007).

annual growth rate between 2005 and 2010, from 1.7% to 3.6%, equivalent to an additional US$500 per person (Castelló-Climent, 2013). A major reason for Guatemala's poor performance is that members of indigenous groups have historically received half as many years of schooling as non-indigenous people (Shapiro, 2006).

If Thailand had matched the regional average of years in school, its annual growth rate between 2005 and 2010 could have reached 3.9% instead of 2.9%

To take another example, average schooling attainment in Haiti lagged behind the regional average by three years throughout the analysis period. If it had been equal to the average for Latin America and the Caribbean, per capita income could have grown annually by 1.5% to almost double between 1965 and 2010, when in fact it stagnated (Castelló-Climent, 2013). This stagnation has meant that Haiti has remained the poorest country in the region, while it could have achieved the same level of income per capita as Nicaragua. Though its more recent problems are due to the effects of natural disasters, including the devastating earthquake in 2010 which destroyed much of the country's education infrastructure, its inability to invest in education adequately has meant it continues to face significant challenges in rebuilding its economy. By 2012, 51% of women and 46% of men aged 15 to 49 had no more than primary education (Institut Haïtien de l'Enfance and ICF International, 2012).

Even in East Asia and the Pacific, where growth has been high thanks to investment in education as well as economic and institutional reform, countries whose education spending has been falling – such as Thailand – risk prolonged periods of low growth (Eichengreen et al., 2013). In 2005, the average number of years that adults in Thailand had spent at school was 5.9, two years below the regional average, having increased by 2.8 years since 1965. If Thailand had matched the regional average, its average annual growth rate between 2005 and 2010 could have reached 3.9% instead of 2.9% (Castelló-Climent, 2013).

In sub-Saharan Africa, the diverging paths of Botswana and Liberia, which started at similar levels of economic and educational development and are both rich in diamonds, provide striking evidence of the benefits of education. In 1970, income per capita was about the same in the two countries. On average, adults in both countries had spent about one year in school, just below the regional average. While Botswana invested its natural resource wealth in education and other social sectors, Liberia's was until recently largely squandered, partly on financing two civil wars. The difference is reflected in spending on education: in 2009, Botswana spent 8.2% of GNP on education, twice the level of Liberia. As a result, over a 40-year period, the level of schooling increased by eight years in Botswana but only three years in Liberia, well below the average for the region. By 2010, GDP per capita was more than 20 times higher in Botswana (Figure 3.3).

Figure 3.3: Investment in education helps deliver growth

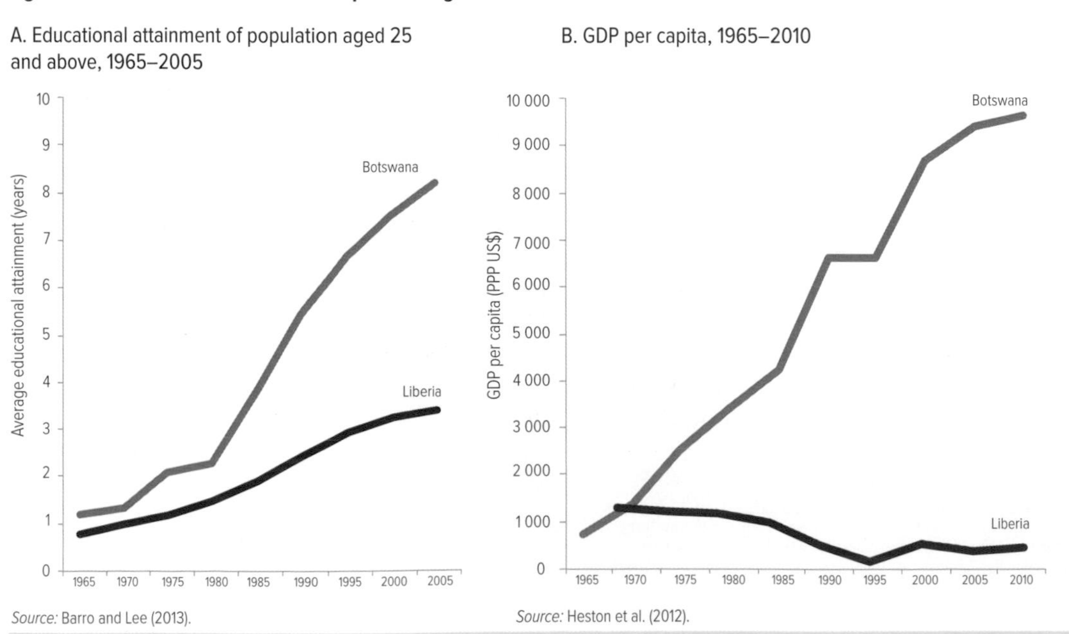

Source: Barro and Lee (2013).

Source: Heston et al. (2012).

These experiences highlight why it is a mistake for countries to reduce their investment in education, even during economic downturns. Doing so not only denies people their right to education, but also jeopardizes future prosperity. Yet countries including Greece, Italy and Portugal reduced education spending by more than 5% between 2010 and 2012, at the time when their economies needed this investment the most (European Commission et al., 2013).

... but education must be equitable to reap economic rewards ...

Poor countries cannot escape the low income trap just by increasing the average years of education. New analysis for this Report shows that only by investing in equitable education – making sure that the poorest, as well as the richest, complete more years in school – can countries achieve the kind of growth that banishes poverty. The countries that have experienced the highest levels of economic growth, including China, the Republic of Korea and Taiwan Province of China, have done so while reducing education inequality.

The new analysis shows that education inequality substantially hinders a country's growth prospects. Education equality can be measured using the Gini coefficient, which ranges from zero, indicating perfect equality, to one, indicating maximum inequality. An improvement in the Gini coefficient by 0.1 accelerates growth by half a percentage point, which increases income per capita by 23% over a 40-year period.

Education in sub-Saharan Africa is particularly unequal. If the region's education Gini coefficient of 0.49 had improved to the level in Latin America and the Caribbean (0.27), the annual growth rate in GDP per capita over 2005–2010 could have been 47% higher (from 2.4% to 3.5%) and per capita income could have grown by US$82 per capita over the period.

Differences in education inequality are one reason for the wide variations in growth rates among countries in the East Asia and the Pacific region over the past 40 years. The Republic of Korea reduced inequality in education 50% faster than countries such as the Philippines. This has resulted in very different paces of economic growth. Over the period, average annual growth in GDP per capita was 5.9% in the Republic of Korea but 1.5% in the Philippines.

Comparing Pakistan and Viet Nam illustrates starkly the importance of equitable education. In 2005, the average number of years adults had spent at school was similar: 4.5 in Pakistan and 4.9 in Viet Nam. Education levels, however, were very unequally distributed in Pakistan, where 51% of the population had no education, compared with only 8% in Viet Nam. By contrast, 33% had post-primary education in Pakistan compared with 21% in Viet Nam. The Gini coefficient for education inequality was 0.60 in Pakistan, more than double the level in Viet Nam (0.25).

The difference in education inequality between the two countries accounts for 60% of the difference in their per capita growth between 2005 and 2010. Viet Nam's per capita income, which was around 40% below Pakistan's in the 1990s, not only caught up with Pakistan's but was 20% higher by 2010, and a continued widening of the gap is seen as likely (Infographic: Educated growth).

While there are still pockets of inequality in access to education at the secondary level in Viet Nam, with ethnic minority children lagging behind the national average, almost all children complete primary school regardless of background (Viet Nam General Statistical Office, 2011). Among the poorest females aged 15 to 24, about 17% had not completed primary school and 37% had not completed lower secondary school in 2010. By contrast, in Pakistan in 2006, the corresponding figures were 89% and 96% (UNESCO, 2013).

If Pakistan were to halve inequality in access to education to the level of Viet Nam, it would increase its economic growth by 1.7 percentage points; its actual average growth in GDP per capita between 2005 and 2010 was 2.5%. This comparison highlights the urgent need for increased government investment in education in Pakistan, which devoted less than 10% of its budget to education in 2011. Spending needs to be targeted at the poorest girls in rural areas in particular, not only to benefit the girls and their families, but also for the sake of the country's prosperity.

The Republic of Korea reduced inequality in education 50% faster than the Philippines resulting in very different paces of economic growth

EDUCATED GROWTH

Education equality accelerates prosperity

Equality in education can be measured using the Gini coefficient*

Complete inequality: 1.0 Gini coefficient

Perfect equality: 0.0 Gini coefficient

Over forty years, income per capita is **23% higher** in a country with more equal education

0.1 improvement in education equality

$1,104

$1,358

+23%

	Pakistan	Viet Nam
1 The average years an adult had spent at school were very similar in 2005...	4.5 years	4.9 years
2 ...but fewer had been to school in Pakistan...	49% population with education	92% population with education
3 ...and education inequalities were more than double in Pakistan	0.6 Gini coefficient	0.25 Gini coefficient

More equality in education in Viet Nam improves economic performance

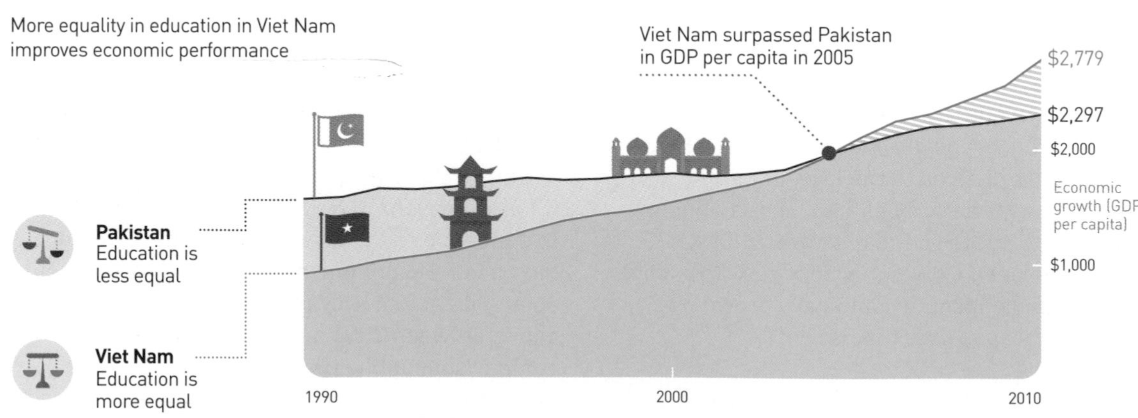

*A statistical measure of inequality. Perfect equality (where everyone goes to the school for the same amount of time) would equal 0 and perfect inequality (where only one person goes to school) would equal 1

Sources: Barro and Lee (2013); Castelló-Climent (2013); Heston et al. (2012).

... and quality of education is vital for economic growth

Spending more time in school is not enough – children need to be learning. Where quality of education is low, the skills base of the economy is low and cannot become an engine of growth.

In recent years, increases in education quality as measured by test scores have been linked to increases in annual per capita growth rates. If Mexico had raised its mathematics score in the OECD Programme for International Student Assessment (PISA) by 70 points, to reach the OECD average, this would have boosted its annual per capita growth rate by about 1.4 percentage points (Hanushek and Woessmann, 2012a). As its growth rate was 1.5% between 1990 and 2010, this means the rate would have almost doubled.

The returns to increasing learning outcomes make investment in quality very attractive. Estimates made for the Report, linking improvement in educational outcomes with economic growth, have attempted to quantify the impact of quality-enhancing investment (Hanushek and Woessmann, 2012b). The starting point is a reform in the education system costing the equivalent of 1.8% of GDP that would increase PISA scores by an estimated 50 points (or the equivalent on other assessment tests). The improved learning outcomes, in turn, would raise the per capita income growth rate by 1 percentage point per year: income per capita would rise by more than 60% over the 50 years after completion of the reform. If, as a result of the reform, 75% of students who took the PISA test passed the 400-point benchmark, rather than about 10% to 15% (which would be similar to Kyrgyzstan or Tamil Nadu, scoring at the lowest end, reaching the level of Italy or Russia, scoring just below the average), it would mean every US$1 invested in education yielded US$10 to US$15 in higher national income.

Education improves people's chances of a healthier life

Education is one of the most powerful ways of improving people's health – and of making sure the benefits are passed on to future generations. It saves the lives of millions of mothers and children, helps prevent and contain disease, and is an essential element of efforts to reduce malnutrition. But this key role is seldom appreciated. Policy-makers focusing on health often neglect the fact that education should be regarded as a vital health intervention in itself – and that without it, other health interventions may not be as effective.

The complementarity between education and health also works in the other direction: people who are healthier are more likely to be better educated. Even taking these links into account, however, there is strong evidence, presented in this section, that education consistently increases people's chances of leading a healthy life.

Investing the equivalent of 1.8% GDP on improving learning would raise the per capita income growth rate by 1 percentage point per year

Globally there has been significant progress towards the health targets laid out in the MDGs – reducing child mortality (goal 4), reducing maternal mortality (goal 5) and combating AIDS, malaria and other diseases (goal 6), as well as reducing hunger, which is part of the core goal on poverty reduction (goal 1). As this section shows, education has contributed to these advances. But more could have been achieved if education's power had been better tapped.

Education will continue to be crucial in achieving global post-2015 health targets, which are likely to go beyond the MDGs to include elimination of hunger and of preventable child and maternal deaths. 'Healthy life expectancy', the overarching post-2015 health goal preferred by many experts, implies reducing not only mortality but also the incidence of disease and disability (WHO, 2012a). These are threats that education can help hold at bay.

How education contributes to better health

Schooling increases people's chances of leading a healthy life in many different ways. Educated people are better informed about specific diseases, so they can take measures to prevent them. They can recognize signs of illness early, seek advice and act on it. And they also tend to use health care services more effectively. Education also strengthens people's belief in their ability to achieve goals, so they are likely to be more confident that they can make necessary lifestyle changes and cope with treatment of disease.

If all women completed secondary education, the under-5 mortality rate would fall by 49% in low and lower middle income countries

Educated people tend to earn more, increasing the amount they can spend on health care and on measures that help prevent illness. They also tend to be less exposed to work and living environments that can jeopardize health – not only physical factors but also psychological stress such as that caused by discrimination and exclusion (Feinstein et al., 2006; Grossman, 2006).

Most of all, educated people – and women in particular – tend to have healthier children. The education of girls and young women is a vital goal in itself, as well as a fundamental human right – but it also makes a particularly strong and effective contribution to health. Making sure that girls enter and complete lower secondary school is the key to unlocking education's health benefits.

This section shows how mothers' education improves their own health and that of their children, then explores ways in which education helps limit disease and eliminate hunger.

Mothers' education has saved millions of children's lives

There are few more dramatic illustrations of the power of education than the estimate that 2.1 million lives of children under 5 were saved between 1990 and 2009 because of improvements in the education of women of reproductive age. That is more than half the total of 4 million lives saved by reducing child mortality during the period. By contrast, economic growth accounted for less than 10% of the total (Gakidou et al., 2010).

Such progress pales beside the remaining challenge, however. The fourth MDG, which aimed to reduce the number of child deaths by two-thirds between 1990 and 2015, will probably not be achieved, even though the annual rate of reduction in under-5 deaths accelerated from 1.7% in 1990–2000 to 3.8% in 2000–2012. In 2012, 6.6 million children under 5 died, of whom 5.7 million were in low and lower middle income countries (Inter-agency Group for Child Mortality Estimation, 2013).

Many of these deaths could have been avoided through prevention and treatment measures such as making sure that there is a skilled attendant at birth, that children receive basic immunizations – which also help protect against pneumonia – and that oral rehydration treatment is given for diarrhoea (Infographic: Educated mothers, healthy children). Not only are most of these measures cheap and effective, but all are more likely to be taken when mothers are educated.

Extending girls' education could save many more lives

The scale of the impact that education – particularly of mothers – can have on child mortality is demonstrated by an analysis for this Report of 139 Demographic and Health Surveys from 58 countries. If all women completed primary education, the under-5 mortality rate would fall by 15% in low and lower middle income countries, saving almost a million children's lives every year. Secondary education has an even greater impact: if all women in these countries completed secondary education, the under-5 mortality rate would fall by 49% – an annual savings of 3 million lives (Infographic: Saving children's lives). Fathers' education has a smaller impact: if both women and men had secondary education, the under-5 mortality rate would fall by 54% in these countries.

To eliminate preventable child deaths by 2030 – which is likely to become a new global health target – urgent action is needed, and boosting secondary enrolment must be part of it. Over 9,000 children die every day in sub-Saharan Africa. The region has the lowest secondary enrolment rates in the world, and just 37% of girls are enrolled at this level. Ensuring

SAVING CHILDREN'S LIVES

A higher level of education reduces preventable child deaths

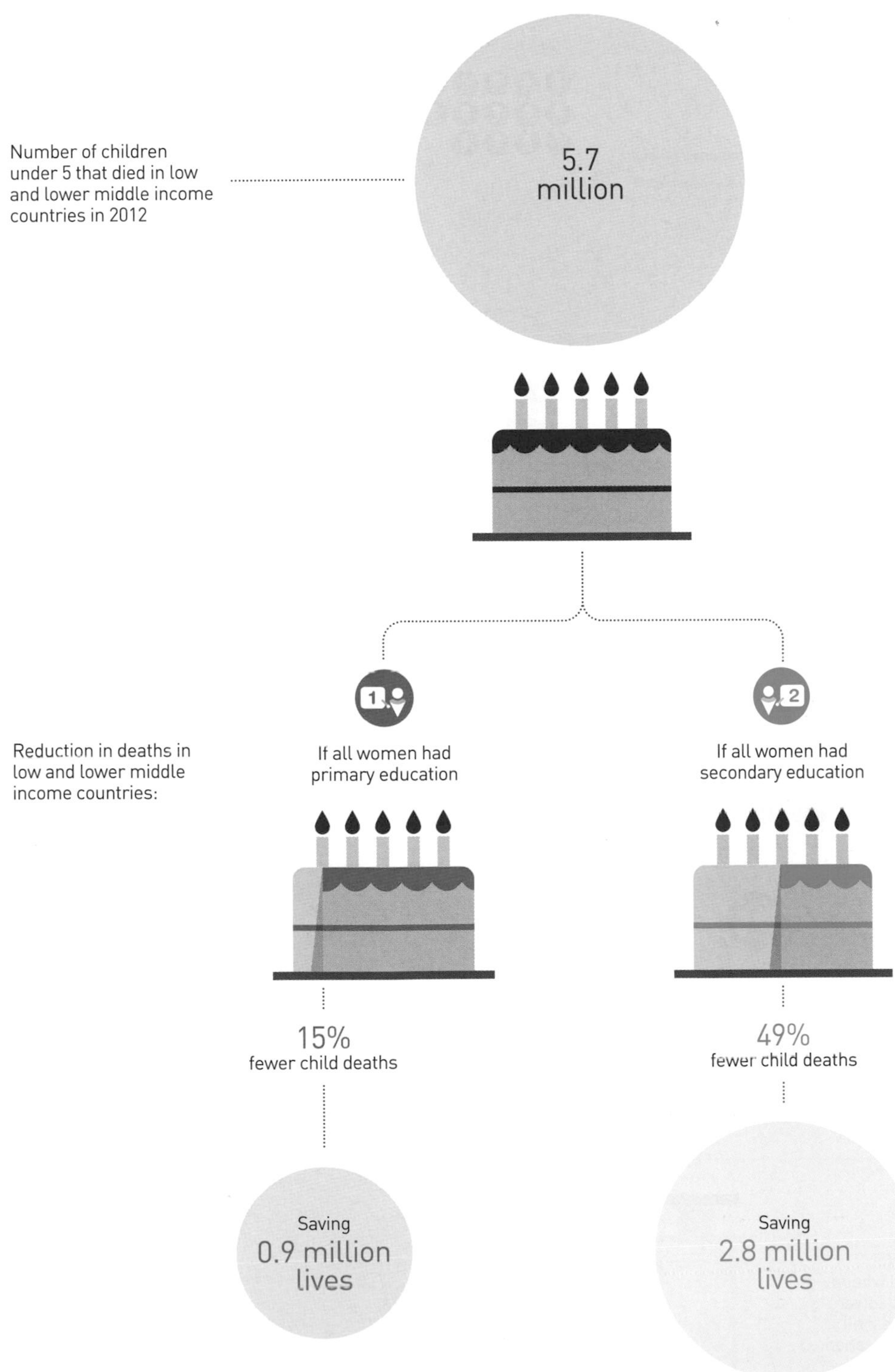

Sources: Gakidou (2013); Inter-agency Group for Child Mortality Estimation (2013).

EDUCATED MOTHERS, HEALTHY CHILDREN

Higher levels of education for mothers lead to improved child survival rates

Pneumonia

One additional year of maternal education would decrease child deaths from pneumonia by:

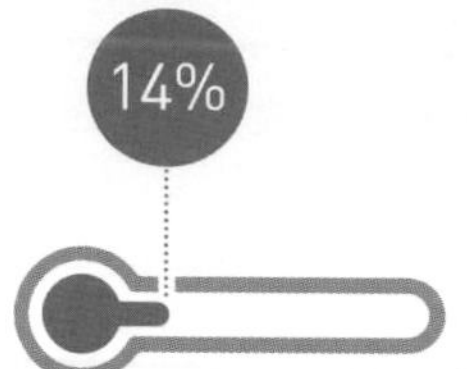

Equivalent to:

160,000
lives saved per year

Maternal education reduces factors putting children at risk of pneumonia such as:

1. malnutrition and low birth weight
2. failing to carry out measles vaccination in the first 12 months
3. burning fuel that gives off harmful smoke

Birth complications

A literate mother is on average:

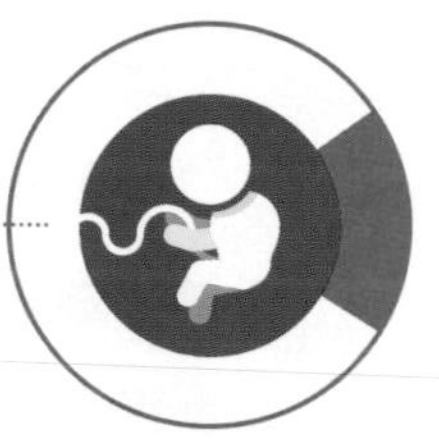

23%
more likely to seek support from a skilled birth attendant

Diarrhoea

Reduction in diarrhoea in low and lower middle income countries if all mothers had primary education:

Reduction in diarrhoea if all mothers had secondary education:

Educated mothers are more likely to:

1. properly purify water
2. seek care from a health provider when a child has diarrhoea
3. administer rehydration solutions, increase fluids, and continue feeding

Malaria

In areas of high transmission, the odds of children carrying malaria parasites is **22% lower** if their mothers have primary education than if their mothers have no education

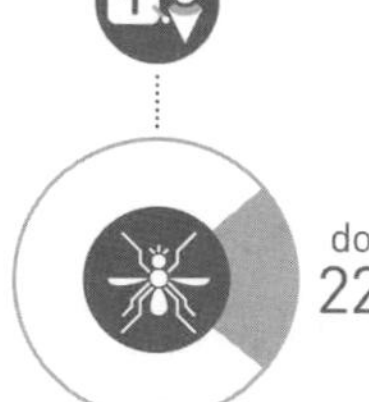

down
22%

In areas of high transmission, the odds of children carrying malaria parasites is **36% lower** if their mothers have secondary education than if their mothers have no education

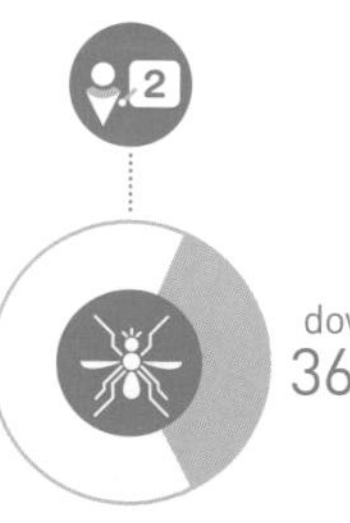

down
36%

Immunization

Increase in vaccination for diphtheria, tetanus, and whooping cough (DTP3) in low and lower middle income countries if all mothers had primary education:

Increase in DTP3 vaccination if all mothers had secondary education:

Sources: EFA Global Monitoring Report team calculations (2013), based on Demographic and Health Survey data from 2005-2011; Fullman et al. (2013); Gakidou (2013).

that all girls achieve secondary education would mean 1.5 million more children surviving to their fifth birthday. In South and West Asia, the under-5 mortality rate would fall by 62% if all girls reached secondary school, saving 1.3 million lives.

Some of the countries with the highest child mortality rates and the lowest levels of education stand to reap the greatest benefits. In Burkina Faso, the under-5 mortality rate stood at 102 deaths per 1,000 live births in 2012, while the average for all low income countries was 82 deaths per 1,000 live births. The country's secondary gross enrolment ratio for girls is one of the world's lowest, just 25% in 2012. If all women completed primary school, child mortality would fall by 46%. If they all completed secondary school, it would fall by 76% (Gakidou, 2013).

Improving access to quality education could save an enormous number of lives in India and Nigeria, which together account for more than a third of child deaths. In 2012, 1.41 million children under 5 died in India and 0.83 million in Nigeria. If all women had completed primary education, the under-5 mortality rate would have been 13% lower in India and 11% lower in Nigeria. If all women had completed secondary education, it would have been 61% lower in India and 43% lower in Nigeria, saving 1.23 million children's lives.

Education helps reduce child deaths across all groups within countries. In Ethiopia, women of reproductive age tend to have very little schooling. Even richer women have only spent two years in school, on average, while those from poorer households have not been to school at all. Projections for this Report, taking into account various child, household and community factors, show that if all women in Ethiopia were to complete eight years of schooling, equivalent to completing primary school, the under-5 mortality rate would fall by over 40 deaths per 1,000 live births for both rich and poor households (Gakidou, 2013). Since child mortality is higher among poorer households, educating the poorest mothers saves the most lives.

Education's role in reducing child mortality can be assessed by looking at individual countries in more detail. In northern India, analysis based on the Annual Health Survey and the census in 2011 showed that female literacy was strongly linked to child mortality, even after taking into account access to reproductive and child health services. An increase in the female literacy rate from 58%, the current average in the districts surveyed, to 100% would lead to a reduction in the under-5 mortality rate from 81 to 55 deaths per 1,000 live births (Kumar et al., 2012).

Education is consistently found to have a strong effect on reducing mortality before children reach their first birthday – when the majority of child deaths occur – even taking household wealth into account. An analysis using Demographic and Health Surveys showed this to be the case in 18 out of 27 countries. The odds that a child born to a mother with education above the median level would die after the first year was lower by 46% in the Plurinational State of Bolivia, 43% in Cambodia and 39% in the Democratic Republic of the Congo (Fuchs et al., 2010).

In South and West Asia, the under-5 mortality rate would fall by 62% if all girls reached secondary school

In Indonesia, the under-5 mortality rate was more than twice as high among mothers with no education than among those who had at least some secondary education. Even after controlling for wealth, region and location, maternal education helped explain child survival. By contrast, household wealth was not a determinant of child survival once the other factors were taken into account (Houweling et al., 2006).

Literate mothers are more likely to seek support from a skilled birth attendant

Analysis of the channels through which education saves children's lives reveals that mothers who are more educated are more likely to give birth with the help of a skilled birth attendant, which means their children are more likely to survive. Around 40% of all under-5 deaths occur within the first 28 days of life, the majority being due to complications during delivery (Liu et al., 2012). Yet there were no skilled birth attendants present in over half the 70 million births per year in sub-Saharan Africa and South Asia in 2006–2010 (UNICEF, 2012a).

Across 57 countries, analysis of Demographic and Health Surveys for this Report shows that a literate mother is, on average, 23% more likely to have a skilled attendant at birth (Infographic:

Educated mothers, healthy children). In Mali, where an estimated 53,000 infants died in 2012, a literate mother was more than three times as likely to have a skilled attendant on hand. In Nepal, 49% of literate mothers have a skilled attendant at birth, compared with 18% of mothers who are not literate. The effect of literacy on the presence of a skilled attendant exceeds 30 percentage points in Niger and Nigeria, countries where the infant mortality rate is around 70 children per 1,000 live births.

The benefits of being literate on having a skilled attendant at birth can be far greater for mothers from poor households. In Cameroon, 54% of literate mothers from poor households have a skilled attendant, compared with 19% of those who are illiterate or semi-literate.

One extra year of maternal education can lead to a 14% decrease in the pneumonia death rate

Educated mothers ensure their children are vaccinated

Since 2000, the GAVI Alliance has supported vaccination against preventable diseases for 370 million children in the world's poorest countries, saving an estimated 5.5 million lives (GAVI, 2013). This is a tremendous impact. There is a missing ingredient, however, in GAVI's strategy that would allow for its success to be transmitted across generations: investment in girls' education.

Analysis of data from Demographic and Health Surveys for this Report shows that if all women in low and lower middle income countries completed primary education, the probability of a child receiving immunization against diphtheria, tetanus and whooping cough – a triple vaccination known as DTP3 – would increase by 10%. If they completed secondary education, it would increase by 43% (Infographic: Educated mothers, healthy children). This is a very large potential increase, given that it takes account of other factors, including household size, household wealth, paternal education and the average community education level. The increase would be as high as 80% for sub-Saharan Africa. In Haiti, where immunization rates are low, if all women completed primary education, DTP3 immunization rates would increase from 59% to 78% (Gakidou, 2013; WHO and UNICEF, 2013).

Mothers' education helps avert pneumonia

Pneumonia is the largest cause of child deaths, accounting for 1.1 million or 17% of the total worldwide. Many pneumonia deaths could be prevented through breastfeeding, adequate nutrition, vaccination, safe drinking water and basic sanitation – and several of these factors are influenced by maternal education. UNICEF identifies pneumonia as a 'disease of poverty' (UNICEF, 2012b, p. 17). But lowering poverty only reduces pneumonia if mothers' education is improved at the same time.

As little as one extra year of maternal education can lead to a 14% decrease in the pneumonia death rate – equivalent to 160,000 child lives saved every year – according to new analysis for this Report based on estimates of under-5 pneumonia death rates from the Global Burden of Disease study in 137 countries between 1980 and 2010 (Infographic: Educated mothers, healthy children). The decrease would be 12% in South and West Asia, East Asia and the Pacific, and Latin America and the Caribbean, and 23% in the Arab States (Gakidou, 2013). In sub-Saharan Africa, however, an extra year of maternal education does not seem to reduce pneumonia death rates significantly, possibly because educated mothers do not have access to sufficient health care for their families.

Maternal education reduces all the factors that put children most at risk of dying from pneumonia, such as failure to carry out measles vaccination in the first 12 months, malnutrition and low birth weight (Rudan et al., 2008). Children's risk of pneumonia is also higher when they live in poorly ventilated homes and their families use traditional cooking stoves that burn solid fuel, giving off harmful smoke and fine particles. A review of 32 studies in poorer countries showed that maternal education contributed to the choice of improved fuels and stoves (Lewis and Pattanayak, 2012). In Bangladesh, women with some education were 37% more likely to select an improved cooking stove. Women who had more education than their husbands were 42% more likely to make this choice (Miller and Mobarak, 2013).

Educating mothers helps prevent and treat childhood diarrhoea

Diarrhoea is the fourth biggest child killer, accounting for 9% of child deaths, many of which should be easily preventable (Inter-agency Group for Child Mortality Estimation, 2013). If all women completed secondary education, the reported incidence of diarrhoea would fall by 30% in low and lower middle income countries because better-educated mothers are more likely to take prevention and treatment measures (Infographic: Educated mothers, healthy children).

In terms of prevention, education affects household decisions to purify water through filtering, boiling or other methods. In urban India, the probability of purification increased by 9% when the most educated adult had completed primary education and by 22% when the most educated adult had completed secondary education, even once household wealth is accounted for (Jalan et al., 2009).

In terms of treatment, an educated mother whose child has symptoms of diarrhoea is more likely to seek appropriate health care. In low income countries, mothers who had completed primary school were 12% more likely than mothers with no education to take such action, according to analysis for this Report based on Demographic and Health Surveys. In Niger, 14% of under-5 deaths are due to diarrhoeal diseases (Child Health Epidemiology Reference Group, 2012). About 46% of mothers with primary education sought help when their children had diarrhoea, compared with 33% of mothers with no education.

Educated mothers are also more likely to treat children's diarrhoea by administering oral rehydration solutions, increasing fluids and continuing feeding. In 28 countries in sub-Saharan Africa, the percentage of children under 3 with diarrhoea who received oral rehydration increased by 18 percentage points in rural areas when mothers had at least some secondary education, compared with those without education. In West and Central African countries, the increase was from 26% to 46% (Stallings, 2004).

Education is a key way of saving mothers' lives

A mother's education is just as crucial for her own health as it is for her offspring's. Greater investment in female education, particularly at lower secondary level, would have helped accelerate progress towards the fifth MDG, improving maternal mortality, one of the goals that is most off track.

Maternal mortality is defined as the death of a woman while pregnant, or within 42 days of termination of pregnancy, from any cause related to or aggravated by the pregnancy or its management, though not from accidental or incidental causes. Between 1990 and 2010, the number of such deaths worldwide almost halved. While this is impressive, the maternal mortality ratio – the number of maternal deaths per 100,000 live births – fell by only 3.1% per year on average, well below the annual decline of 5.5% required to achieve the fifth MDG.

Every day, almost 800 women die from preventable causes related to pregnancy and childbirth. Overall, 99% of maternal deaths occur in developing countries. The maternal mortality ratio in these countries is 240 deaths per 100,000 live births, compared with 16 in developed countries. Over half the deaths are in sub-Saharan Africa and over a quarter in South Asia (WHO, 2012b).

Mothers die because of complications during pregnancy, such as pre-eclampsia, bleeding and infections, and because of unsafe abortion. Educated women are more likely to avoid these dangers by adopting simple and low cost practices to maintain hygiene, by reacting to symptoms such as bleeding or high blood pressure, by assessing how and where to have an abortion, by accepting treatment and by making sure a skilled attendant is present at birth.

Policy-makers seldom see education as a way of reducing maternal mortality, however. The World Health Organization's efforts to reduce maternal mortality focus on increasing skilled birth attendance, but education has an equally important role, according to analysis for this Report using data for 108 countries and new estimates of maternal mortality ratios for 1990–2010 (Bhalotra and Clarke, 2013).

In sub-Saharan Africa, young children in rural areas with diarrhoea are more likely to receive oral rehydration when mothers have some secondary education

If all women completed primary education, maternal mortality would fall by 66%

If all women completed primary education, maternal mortality would fall from 210 to 71 deaths per 100,000 births, or by 66%. This would save the lives of 189,000 women every year. If all women in sub-Saharan Africa completed primary education, the maternal mortality ratio would fall from 500 to 150 deaths per 100,000 births, or by 70% (Infographic: A matter of life and death).

At least two-fifths of the effect of education is indirect: educated women are more likely to use public health care services, to have fewer children and not to give birth as teenagers – all factors that reduce maternal mortality. Across the 108 countries studied, 6 out of 100 births were among women aged 15 to 19. If the rate of teenage births were halved, the maternal mortality ratio would fall by more than a third (Bhalotra and Clarke, 2013).

Education's impressive power to reduce maternal mortality can be gauged by looking at generations of young women who have benefited from education progress. In the 1970s, education reforms led to young women receiving 2.2 more years of schooling on average in Nigeria. With these women now approaching the end of their reproductive cycle, analysis for this Report was able to determine that the expansion of education accounted for a 29% decline in the maternal mortality ratio in Nigeria. However, there is a danger that the slowing of education progress in the 2000s – affecting women born in the late 1980s who are now entering their reproductive phase – will lead to a slowdown in the reduction of maternal mortality (Bhalotra and Clarke, 2013).

Education plays a major role in containing disease

Infectious diseases, such as HIV/AIDS, and parasitic diseases, such as malaria, as well as non-communicable conditions, such as heart disease and cancer, pose some of the gravest threats to health – but improving education is a powerful way to help reduce their incidence. It is vital for policy-makers to take this into account. Although there has been progress towards the sixth MDG, which aims to reverse the spread of HIV/AIDS, malaria and other major diseases, large numbers of people are still dying from preventable diseases, and unfinished business will remain to be addressed after 2015.

One broad guide to the prevalence of disease is whether people consider themselves to be in good health. People with more education were consistently more likely to do so, according to the World Health Survey. An additional year of education increased the odds of not reporting poor health by 7.6%, and the globally representative survey showed that education had a significant effect on self-rated health in 48 out of 69 countries (Subramanian et al., 2010). Taking into account the characteristics of each country, completing lower secondary school increased the odds of not reporting poor health by 18%, while completing upper secondary school increased the odds by 59%, compared with having no education or less than primary education (Witvliet et al., 2012).

By looking at how specific health risks affect different populations in different ways, it is possible to see how increasing people's access to quality education can protect them from disease. This section examines in particular the way literacy can help people avoid HIV/AIDS, how education combats malaria by helping people correctly identify its cause, symptoms and treatment, and how education lowers people's risk of dying from non-communicable diseases.

Literacy improves knowledge about HIV/AIDS

Education provides a window of opportunity to increase awareness about HIV prevention among young people and so avert new infections among future generations. Reaching the young is particularly important: while the rate of new infections fell by 27% among those aged 15 to 24 between 2001 and 2011, young people still account for about 40% of new infections. Globally, the incidence of HIV/AIDS is declining, but there were still an estimated 2.5 million new HIV infections and 1.7 million AIDS-related deaths in 2011 (UNAIDS, 2012).

In the early phases of the AIDS epidemic, when knowledge about HIV was scarce, the better educated were more vulnerable to the virus. Since then, however, those with more education have tended to avoid risky behaviour because they understand its consequences better, and

A MATTER OF LIFE AND DEATH

Educated mothers are less likely to die in childbirth

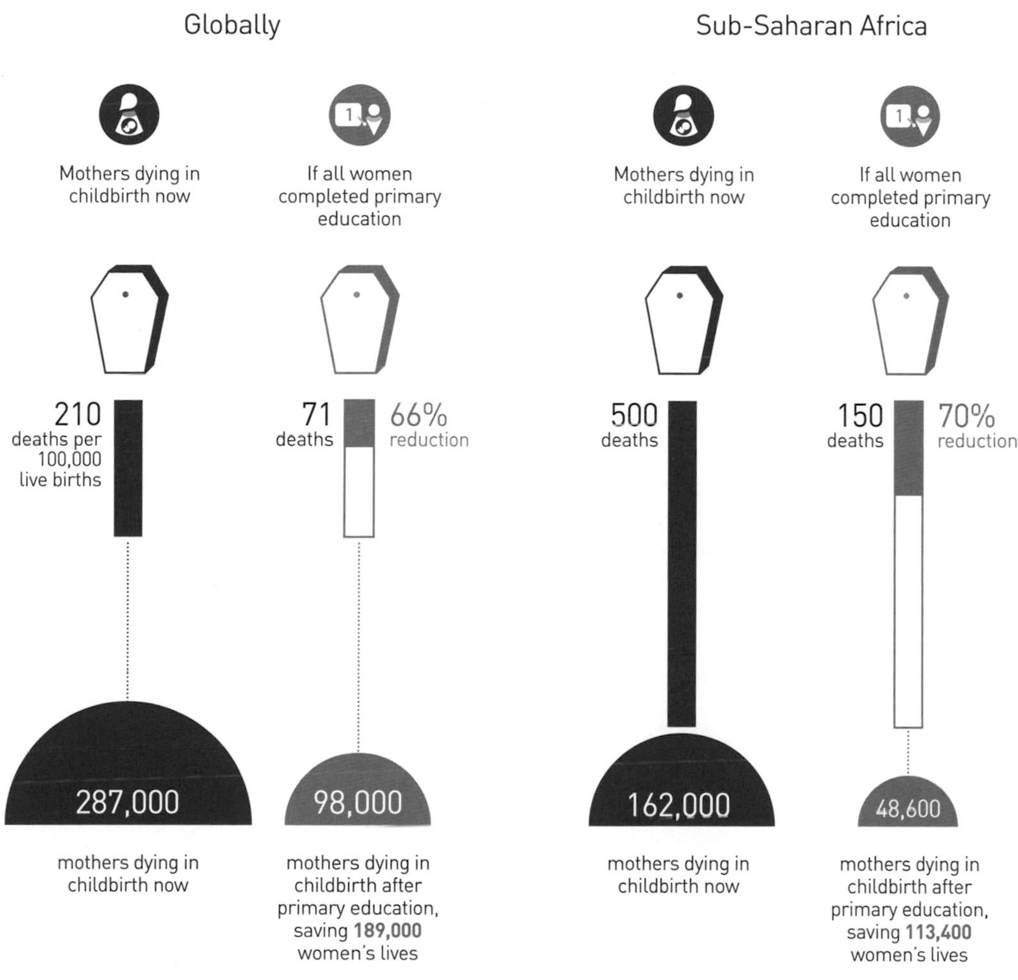

Why does education reduce maternal deaths?

Educated women are more likely to avoid complications during pregnancy, such as pre-eclampsia, bleeding and infections by:

1. adopting simple and low-cost practices to maintain hygiene
2. reacting to symptoms such as bleeding or high blood pressure
3. making sure a skilled attendant is present at birth

Educated women are more likely to:

1. use public health care services
2. not give birth as teenagers
3. have fewer children

Note: Maternal mortality is defined as the death of a woman while pregnant, or within 42 days of termination of pregnancy, from any cause related to or aggravated by the pregnancy or its management, though not from accidental or incidental causes.

Sources: Bhalotra and Clarke (2013); WHO (2012b).

women have been able to exercise more control over their sexual relationships (Hargreaves et al., 2008; Jukes et al., 2008). In the later phases of the epidemic, the better educated have had a lower chance of being infected in 17 sub-Saharan African countries (Iorio and Santaeulàlia-Llopis, 2011).

In South and West Asia, 81% of literate women know that HIV is not spread by sharing food, compared with 57% of those who are not literate

Education's role in HIV prevention is illustrated by an analysis of 26 countries in sub-Saharan Africa and 5 in South and West Asia for this Report. It demonstrates the importance of literacy skills in improving people's knowledge of how HIV is transmitted (Figure 3.4). These countries account for around half of all new infections among adults. In sub-Saharan Africa, 91% of literate women know that HIV is not transmitted through sharing food, compared with 72% of those who are not literate. In South and West Asia, where the infection rate is still increasing in countries such as Bangladesh and Sri Lanka, the gap in knowledge between those who are literate and those who are not is even wider: 81% of literate women know that HIV is not spread by sharing food, compared with 57% of those who are not literate. Misconceptions that HIV can be contracted through mosquito bites are also more widespread among those who are not literate in both South and West Asia and sub-Saharan Africa. Similar patterns hold for young men.

An educated woman is more likely to be aware that she has a right to negotiate safer sex – to refuse sex or request condom use – if she knows that her partner has a sexually transmitted disease. In both South and West Asia and sub-Saharan Africa, literate women are as much as 30 percentage points more likely to be aware of this right, compared with those who are not literate. In sub-Saharan Africa, two-thirds of literate women are aware of it, compared with only a third of illiterate or semi-literate women. In Burundi, Nepal and Senegal, poor women who are literate are more aware of their right to safer sex than richer women who are not literate.

People who are more literate are more likely to be better informed on a wide range of other beliefs and facts about HIV/AIDS. In Niger, 47% of illiterate and semi-literate women believed a healthy-looking person cannot be infected with HIV, compared with 18% of literate women. In Mali, 52% of illiterate and semi-literate women

Figure 3.4: Literacy enhances understanding of how to prevent and respond to HIV/AIDS
Percentage of women aged 15 to 49 agreeing with selected statements, sub-Saharan Africa and South and West Asia, 2005–2011

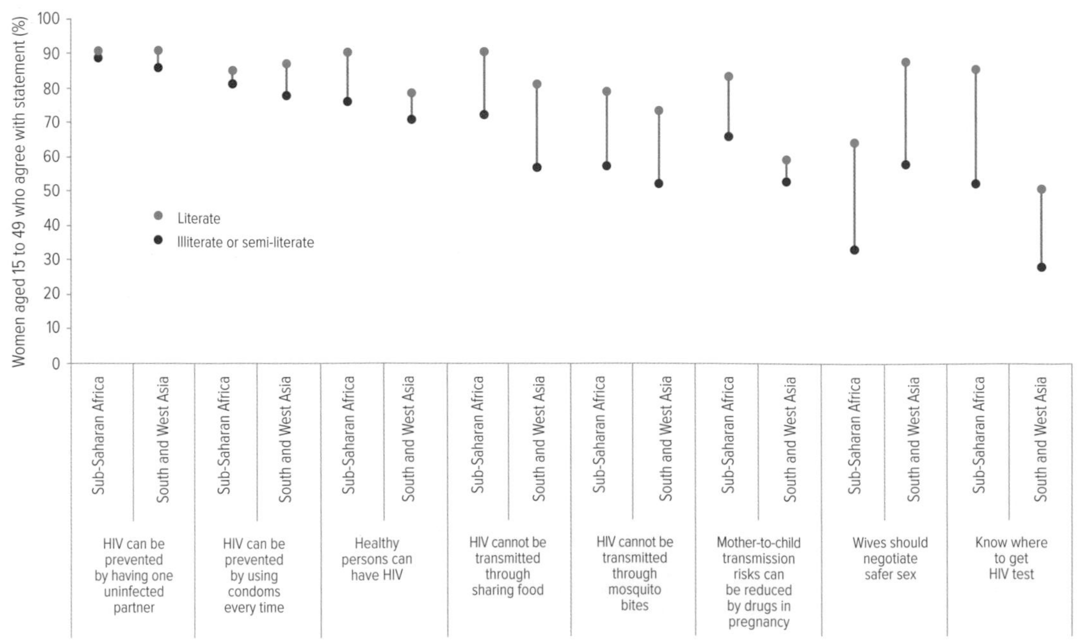

Note: Estimates are based on 26 countries in sub-Saharan Africa and 5 countries in South and West Asia.
Source: EFA Global Monitoring Report team calculations (2013), based on Demographic and Health Surveys.

were not aware that the risk of transmission could be reduced if they took appropriate medication during pregnancy, compared with 20% of literate women.

Knowing where to get tested for HIV is a first step to receiving treatment. Yet only 52% of illiterate or semi-literate women in sub-Saharan Africa, and 28% in South Asia, know where to get tested, compared with 85% and 51% of those who are literate. In Nigeria, 73% of literate young women knew where to get an HIV test, compared with 36% of those who were not literate.

Education's strong contribution to HIV prevention has been put forward as an explanation for the remarkably fast decline in infection rates in Zimbabwe, one of the countries hardest hit by the HIV/AIDS epidemic. By 2010, 75% of women aged 15 to 24 in Zimbabwe had completed lower secondary school, and the HIV prevalence rate had fallen from its peak of 29% in 1997 to under 14%, declining four times faster than in neighbouring Malawi and Zambia where education levels are lower (Halperin et al., 2011). The percentage of women aged 15 to 24 who had completed lower secondary school was 49% in Zambia in 2007 and 42% in Malawi in 2010. In rural parts of South Africa – another country where infection rates are very high – every additional year of education was linked with a 7% lower probability of becoming infected (Bärnighausen et al., 2007).

Education boosts treatment and prevention of malaria

Malaria is one of the world's deadliest but most preventable diseases. Education helps people identify its cause and symptoms and take steps to prevent and treat it. About half the world population is at risk of malaria. Those most at risk are children in Africa, where a child dies of malaria every minute. Concerted efforts have helped save over 1 million lives in the past decade, but there are signs that global funding for malaria prevention and control is stagnating, highlighting the importance of keeping the spotlight on the disease and ways to combat it (WHO, 2012c).

Improved access to quality education cannot replace the need for investment in drugs and in bed nets treated with insecticide – one of the most cost-effective ways to prevent malaria – but it has a crucial role to play in complementing and promoting these measures. In India, literate people with schooling up to lower secondary level were more than twice as likely as illiterate people to know that mosquitoes are the transmitters of malaria. They were also about 45% more likely to know that malaria can be prevented by draining stagnant water (Sharma et al., 2007).

In India, people with schooling up to lower secondary level were more than twice as likely to know that mosquitoes are the transmitters of malaria

The more schooling people have, the more likely they are to use bed nets, as studies have shown in the Democratic Republic of the Congo, where a fifth of the world's malaria-related deaths occur. In a rural study, in a group of which only 44% had spent the previous night under a bed net, if the household head had completed primary education this increased the odds of bed net use by about 75%, even with other possible factors taken into account (Ndjinga and Minakawa, 2010). In an urban study of a group of pregnant women making an antenatal care visit, only a quarter reported having slept under a bed net the previous night. The odds of having used a net among women with at least secondary education were almost three times as high as those with less than secondary education (Pettifor et al., 2008). In rural Kenya, the odds that children whose mothers had at least secondary education had slept under a net were up to three times as high as those whose mothers were not educated (Noor et al., 2006).

Because those with more education are more likely to have taken preventive measures, they are less likely to contract malaria, even after household wealth is taken into account. In Cameroon, where the female secondary gross enrolment ratio was 47% in 2011, if all women had had secondary education, the incidence of malaria would have dropped from 28% to 19% (Gakidou, 2013).

Children of educated mothers are much less likely to contract malaria, as is shown by an analysis of Malaria Indicator Surveys in Angola, Liberia, Madagascar, Nigeria, Rwanda, Senegal, Uganda and the United Republic of Tanzania. For example, the odds of children carrying malaria parasites was 44% lower if the mother had secondary education than if she had no education. Taking into account factors such as whether the child had slept under a bed net the previous night, children of mothers with secondary education in rural areas of these eight countries were 16% less likely than those with uneducated mothers to be infected with the malaria parasite (Siri, 2012).

In 11 sub-Saharan African countries, the odds of malaria parasites in children were 36% lower when mothers had secondary education

Maternal education contributes even more to preventing malaria in areas where the risk of transmission is high. An analysis of 11 sub-Saharan African countries showed that in such areas the odds of malaria parasites in children were 22% lower when mothers had primary education and 36% lower when mothers had secondary education (Infographic: Educated mothers, healthy children). This is after taking into account whether children had slept under a net and whether the household had sprayed indoors with insecticide over the previous year – measures which are both related to education in the first place (Fullman et al., 2013).

Education is needed to fight non-communicable diseases

Education also has a key role to play in preventing early death from non-communicable diseases. While infectious and parasitic diseases take their greatest toll in poorer countries, non-communicable diseases pose a major challenge for all countries. According to the Global Burden of Disease 2010 study, ischaemic heart disease was the first or second cause of death in all regions except sub-Saharan Africa. Lung cancer was the fifth-highest cause for men and tenth for women. Diabetes was the ninth-highest cause for men and sixth for women (Salomon et al., 2012). The global nature of this concern is reflected in the proposal for a universal health goal after 2015 that would be measured using healthy life expectancy, a criterion that covers individuals in all countries regardless of the level of development.

While non-communicable diseases are the leading causes of death in high income countries, the death rate for most of them is actually lower in high income than in low and middle income countries, where early detection and treatment are lacking. Contrary to popular perception, their incidence generally does not increase as countries get richer. If adults in low and middle income countries had the same mortality from cancer, cardiovascular disease, chronic respiratory disease and diabetes as those in high income countries, global mortality from these four diseases would be lower by more than a quarter (Di Cesare et al., 2013).

Education plays an important role in preventing non-communicable diseases by increasing awareness of the long-term consequences of smoking on health. Tobacco use is a key risk factor for cancer, as well as respiratory and cardiovascular disease – and the leading cause of preventable deaths worldwide. Up to half of current users will die of a tobacco-related disease. Nevertheless, consumption of tobacco products is increasing globally, especially in low and middle income countries (WHO, 2013).

In the United States, one of the first countries where smoking was explicitly linked to non-communicable diseases, the gradual arrival of information about the harm caused by smoking led to major behavioural changes – with the more educated responding faster and more emphatically. Before 1957, the more educated were more likely to smoke. By 2000, however, they were less likely to smoke than the less educated by at least 10 percentage points. Completing four years of tertiary education increased the probability of quitting by 18% (de Walque, 2007, 2010).

Similar effects are observed in low and middle income countries. World Health Survey data from 48 low and middle income countries showed that, taking age, income and employment into account, the odds that men with only primary education would smoke were almost 90% higher than of those with higher education (Hosseinpoor et al., 2011). The Global Adult Tobacco Survey showed that in Bangladesh, Egypt and the Philippines, the odds that those with less than secondary education would smoke were over twice as high as of those with tertiary education (Palipudi et al., 2012).

The power of education to improve health by lowering tobacco use is going untapped in many countries. This should be of urgent concern for policy-makers. After taking into account national GDP levels and the diffusion of cigarettes in the population, the gap in smoking between less and more educated young men increases from 16 percentage points in low income countries to 23 percentage points in lower middle income countries and 29 percentage points in upper middle income countries (Pampel et al., 2011).

Hunger will not be eliminated without education

Malnutrition, the underlying cause in 45% of child deaths globally (Inter-agency Group for Child Mortality Estimation, 2013), is not just about the availability of food. To eliminate malnutrition in the long term, education – especially education that empowers women – is vital. Mothers who have been to school are more likely to ensure that their children receive the best nutrients to help them prevent or fight off ill health, even in families that are constrained financially. Educated mothers know more about appropriate health and hygiene practices at home, thereby ensuring their children are healthy enough to benefit fully from their food intake. And they have more power to allocate household resources so that children's nutrition needs are met.

There has been significant global progress in improving nutrition. Eliminating hunger within a generation is feasible – there is enough food in the world to feed everyone (Hoddinott et al., 2012). But in some parts of the world people are finding it harder to get the food they need, partly because of climate change. The first MDG aimed to halve the proportion of people who suffer from hunger by 2015, from a starting point of 23% in 1990–1992. But in 2010–2012 some 15% were still malnourished (FAO et al., 2012). Eliminating hunger deserves to be an even stronger focus of global development efforts after 2015.

The global extent of chronic malnutrition is revealed by the fact that one in four children under the age of 5 suffers from moderate or severe stunting – that is, they are short for their age. Three-quarters of these children live in sub-Saharan Africa and South Asia. The odds that a severely stunted child will die are four times higher than for a well-nourished child, while the odds that children who are severely wasted (underweight for their height) would die are nine times higher (Black et al., 2008). Chronic malnutrition affects children's brain development and their ability to learn. The link between malnutrition and cognitive development is also why early childhood care and education is the first goal in the Education for All framework.

Cross-country comparisons show that increasing the percentage of women who attend secondary school from 50% to 60% would result in a decline in the stunting rate by 1.3% after controlling for wealth, fertility and access to health services (Headey, 2013). The stunting rate in Bangladesh fell from 70% to 48% between 1994 and 2005. Over about the same period, the share of women with at least secondary education doubled. Education could explain more than a fifth of the reduction in stunting. If education's effect on fertility reduction were also taken into account, its influence would be even larger.

Education's power to help reduce malnutrition is apparent in 37 countries where the chance of a child being stunted is lower among those whose mothers have higher levels of education. In seven countries, including Ethiopia, Haiti and Honduras, a child whose mother has reached secondary school is at least half as likely to be stunted as one with a mother who has only primary education. In Honduras, for example, the rate of stunting is 54% for children born to mothers with less than primary education, 33% for those whose mothers have primary education and 10% for children of mothers with at least secondary education.

In low income countries, 46 million children suffer from stunting. If all women completed primary education, 1.7 million fewer children would be in this situation. The number rises to 11.9 million if all women complete secondary education, equivalent to 26% less children affected with stunting (Infographic: Education keeps hunger away). In South Asia, 20 million fewer children would be stunted if all mothers reached secondary education.

Detailed analysis within countries that has tracked children over time provides even stronger evidence that mothers' education improves child nutrition, even after taking into account other factors linked to better nutrition, such as mother's height, breastfeeding practices, water and sanitation, and household wealth. A study commissioned for this Report showed that by age 1 – when adverse effects of malnutrition on life prospects are likely to be irreversible – infants whose mothers had reached lower secondary education were less likely to be stunted by 33% in Ethiopia, 48% in

In Viet Nam, infants whose mothers had reached lower secondary education were 67% less likely to be stunted

EDUCATION KEEPS HUNGER AWAY

Mothers' education improves children's nutrition

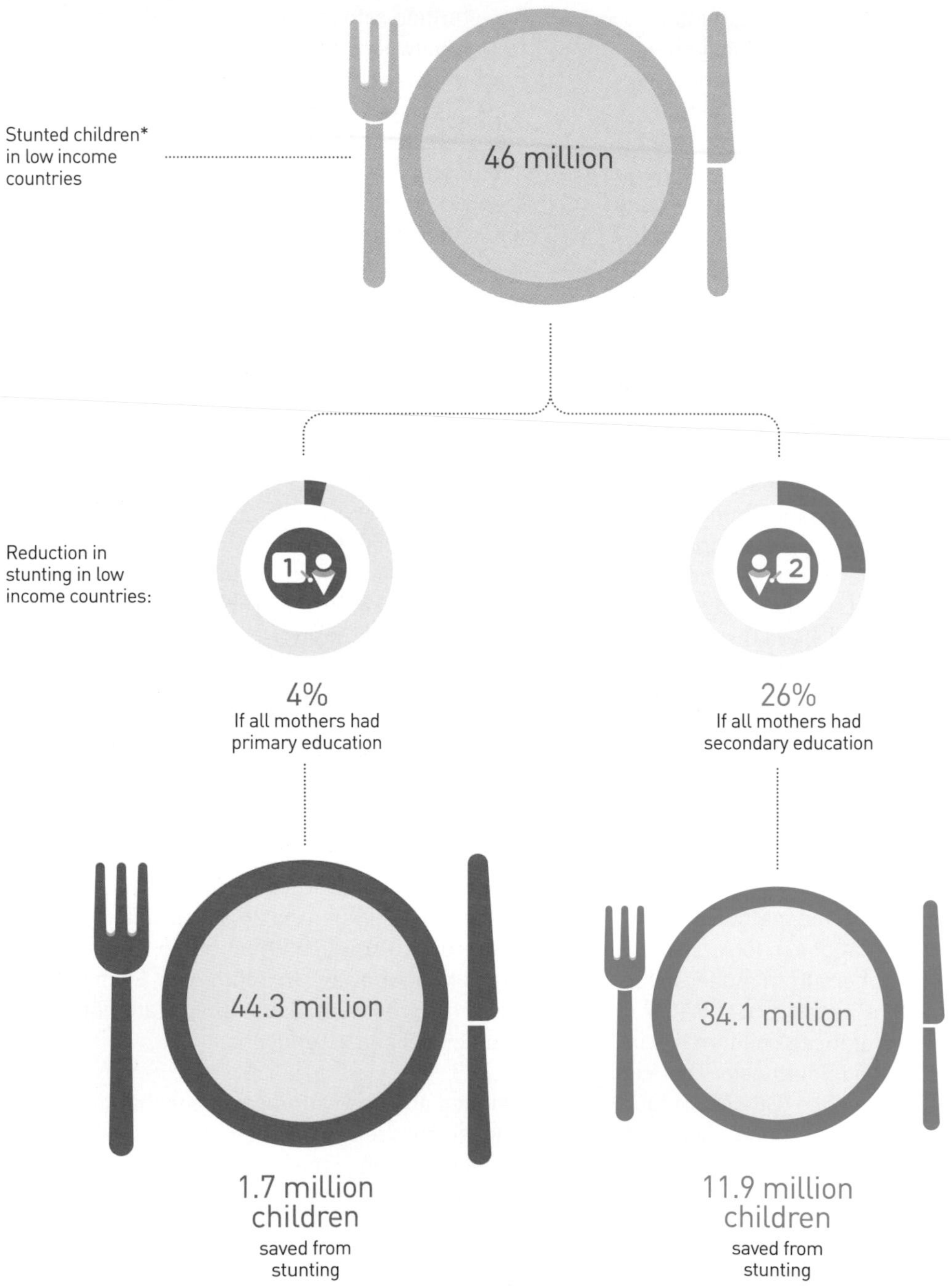

*Stunting is a manifestation of malnutrition in early childhood.

Sources: EFA Global Monitoring Report team analysis (2013), based on Demographic and Health Survey data from 2005-2011; UNICEF et al. (2013).

the state of Andhra Pradesh in India, 60% in Peru and 67% in Viet Nam, compared with those whose mothers had no education.

This new research also highlights the importance of complementing education expansion with reforms in health care to increase the extent to which children benefit from investment in their mothers' education. In Ethiopia, children whose mothers had primary school together with access to antenatal care were 39% less likely to be stunted at age 1 than children whose mothers had primary education but little or no access to antenatal care. For children whose mothers had completed lower secondary school, the difference in likelihood of being stunted at age 1 was 26% between those whose mothers had access to antenatal care and those who had no or limited access to antenatal care (Sabates, 2013).

These impressive findings are supported by evidence from other countries that monitored the nutritional habits of hundreds of thousands of households. In Bangladesh, where 41% of children were stunted in 2011, the odds of a child being stunted were lower by 22% if the mother had primary education, 24% if both parents had primary education and 54% if both parents had secondary education or above. In Indonesia, the odds of stunting fell by 26%, 35% and 59%, respectively, after accounting for maternal height, location and household expenditure (Semba et al., 2008).

A key reason children of educated women are less likely to be stunted is that their mothers have more power to act for the benefit of their children. In rural India, mothers' education has been shown to improve their mobility and their ability to make decisions on seeking care when a child is sick – and infant children of women with such increased autonomy are taller for their age (Shroff et al., 2011).

Malnutrition is caused not only by having too little food to eat, but also by a lack of micronutrients in the diet. Young children lacking vitamin A and iron are more likely to be malnourished and more prone to infections (such as measles and diarrhoeal diseases) and anaemia, which affects their cognitive development. Education helps ensure a varied diet that includes vital micronutrients.

Maternal education is associated with a higher probability of children aged 6 to 23 months consuming food rich in micronutrients in 12 countries analysed for this Report using Demographic and Health Surveys for 2009–2011. In the United Republic of Tanzania, for example, children of this age whose mothers had at least secondary education were almost twice as likely to consume food rich in micronutrients as children whose mothers had less than primary education.

Maternal education is associated with a higher probability of infants consuming food rich in micronutrients

Studies within countries provide further evidence of how education influences diet in ways that can prevent malnutrition, even once other factors are taken into account. In Bangladesh, when both parents had some secondary education, food group diversity in the family diet was 10% greater than when neither parent had any education (Rashid et al., 2011). In Indonesia, only 51% of households where mothers had no education used iodized salt, compared with 95% of households where mothers had completed lower secondary education. Similarly, only 41% of households where mothers had no education provided vitamin A supplements to their children within the past half year, compared with 61% of households where mothers had completed lower secondary education (Semba et al., 2008).

Education promotes healthy societies

Education plays a key role in promoting democratic values

As well as improving individual lives and overall economic prosperity, education has an indispensable role in strengthening the bonds that hold communities and societies together. The need to protect and promote these connections is increasingly being recognized as a vital element of the post-2015 development framework. This section examines three key ways in which education contributes to healthy societies: expanding democratic engagement, protecting the environment and empowering women.

Education helps people understand democracy, promotes the tolerance and trust that underpin it, and motivates people to participate in politics. Education has a vital role in preventing environmental degradation and limiting the causes and effects of climate change. And it can empower vulnerable people to overcome discrimination that prevents them from getting a fair share of the fruits of overall progress when it comes to reducing poverty and improving health.

Education builds the foundations of democracy and good governance

Education's vital role in promoting human rights and the rule of law is enshrined in the Universal Declaration of Human Rights, which states that 'every individual and every organ of society ... shall strive by teaching and education to promote respect for these rights and freedoms'. Good quality education helps people make informed judgements about issues that concern them and engage more actively in national and local political debate.

In many parts of the world, however, human rights and citizens' confidence in government are jeopardized by unfair elections, corrupt officials, weak justice systems and other failures of democracy. When disenfranchized groups feel they have no means to voice their concerns, such failures can lead to conflict.

The critical function of democratic and accountable systems of governance in fulfilling human rights and advancing globally agreed development goals has come to the fore in recent discussions on post-2015 development ambitions. Some observers have argued that a democratic governance goal should have been included in the MDGs and deserves a place in the post-2015 framework (UNDP, 2012).

Education's key role in promoting democratic values is confirmed by analysis over the period from 1960 to 2000 showing that a 10% increase in secondary enrolment is associated with a 1.8-point increase in the Polity IV index, which measures the extent of democracy on a scale ranging from -10 (least democratic) to 10 (most democratic) (Glaeser et al., 2006). Democracy emerges slowly, so a longer period of observation is required to establish education's contribution. Studies of political transitions over more than a century show that universal primary education and literacy have been vital for countries to move from authoritarianism to democracy (Murtin and Wacziarg, 2011).

There is even stronger evidence that education plays a key part in building the social and cultural foundations of democracy, even after taking into account other factors that can have an influence, such as wealth, location and occupation. As this section shows, education helps people understand how democracy functions and what its benefits are. It also promotes values and norms that are crucial ingredients of democracy, notably tolerance and trust. Finally, it spurs individuals to participate actively in politics.

Education improves political knowledge

Education improves knowledge about politics, as evidence from European countries shows: people who have four more years of schooling spend 50% more time, on average, acquiring information by reading newspaper articles on politics and current affairs (Borgonovi et al., 2010).

Education is similarly linked with higher levels of political knowledge in low and middle income countries that are at an earlier stage of the democratic transition. Across 12 sub-Saharan African countries, while 63% of individuals without formal schooling had an understanding of democracy, the share was 71% for those with primary education and 86% for those with secondary education (Bratton et al., 2005). To take one example, five years after Malawi held its first democratic elections, the share of people of voting age who could not provide a definition of democracy was 23% among those who had not received any education but 3% among those with primary schooling (Evans and Rose, 2007).

The degree of political knowledge depends not only on the amount of time a child spends in school, but also on whether education is of sufficient quality to encourage key traits such as critical thinking. Among lower secondary school students in 34 countries, for example, levels of political knowledge were higher where political and social issues were more frequently discussed and where students felt freer to express their opinions, according to the 2009 International Civic and Citizenship Education Study (Schulz et al., 2010).

New analysis for this Report based on the World Values Survey shows that, in all regions, one reason for better knowledge among those with higher levels of education is that they are more interested in politics and so more likely to seek information. In Turkey in 2007, for example, the share of those who said they were interested in politics rose from 41% among those with primary education to 52% among those with secondary education (Chzhen, 2013).

Beyond the formal education system, civic education programmes can help students increase their knowledge. In Kenya, the National Civic Education Programme reached up to 15% of voting age citizens in the run-up to the 2002 elections. An evaluation showed that the programme improved political knowledge, particularly for those with less education (Finkel and Smith, 2011).

Education strengthens support for democracy

Education increases people's support for democracy. Across 18 sub-Saharan African countries, those of voting age with primary education were 1.5 times more likely to express support for democracy than those with no education, and the level doubled among those who had completed secondary education, even once wealth, location and occupation were taken into account (Evans and Rose, 2012).

In the Arab States, notably Egypt and Tunisia, where the Arab Spring originated, a major educational expansion over the last 30 years has given rise to strong democratic aspirations. In Tunisia, while only 22% of those with less than primary education agree that democracy, despite its drawbacks, is the best system of governance, 38% of those with secondary education do so (Figure 3.5).

Education is also found to encourage support for democracy in other predominantly Muslim countries, including Jordan, Lebanon and Pakistan. In urban Pakistan, while only 35% of respondents overall supported democracy, those with secondary education were 15 percentage points more likely to do so than those with less than primary education (Shafiq, 2010). This finding reinforces the urgency of increased investment in education in Pakistan, where current levels remain among the lowest in the world and fully fledged democracy has yet to take hold.

In 17 Latin American countries, many of which have recently gone through democratic transitions, education boosts support for democracy or rejection of authoritarian alternatives, according to evidence from Latinobarómetro surveys. An increase in education level from primary to secondary raised support for democracy by five percentage points among men and eight percentage points among women (Walker and Kehoe, 2013).

In sub-Saharan African countries, those of voting age with primary education were 1.5 times more likely to express support for democracy

Figure 3.5: More education is linked with stronger support for democracy
Percentage of adults who strongly agree that 'A democratic system may have problems, yet it is better than other systems', by education level, Egypt and Tunisia, 2010–2011

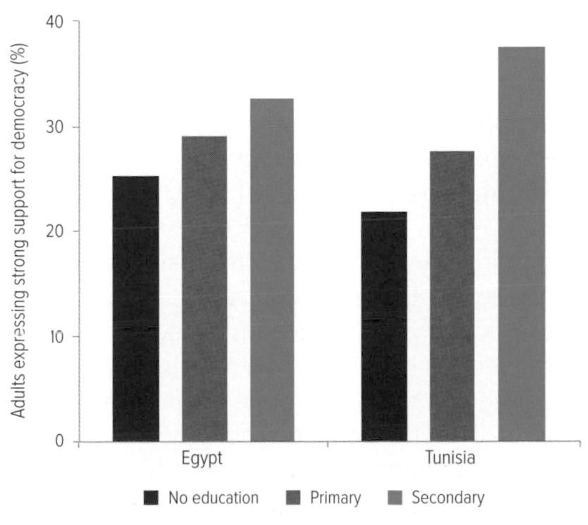

Source: Prepared for *EFA Global Monitoring Report 2013/4* by the Arab Barometer team.

Around the world, educated people tend to be the most critical of their government regimes, as well as the strongest supporters of democracy. For example, in Nicaragua in 2009, support for democracy rose from 54% of young people with less than secondary education to 70% of those who had completed secondary school. At the same time, satisfaction with how democracy functioned fell from 43% of those with less than secondary education to 31% of those who had completed secondary education (Chzhen, 2012).

Education raises political participation

Education not only increases people's political knowledge, but also makes them more likely to participate in political processes such as voting or standing for office, as well as signing petitions or joining demonstrations.

In Africa, Asia and Latin America, education increases the likelihood of turning out to vote

Educated people are more likely to vote. Education leads to a higher rate of voting in democratic elections (Nevitte et al., 2009). This is the case in low and middle income countries in particular. Public opinion surveys in 36 countries in Africa, Asia and Latin America showed that education increased the likelihood of turning out to vote (Bratton et al., 2010). In Yemen, a rise of 20 percentage points in the provincial literacy rate boosted voter registration by 12 points (Pintor and Gratschew, 2002).

In 14 Latin American countries in 2010, the probability of voting was five percentage points higher for those with primary education and nine points higher for individuals with secondary education, compared with those with no education. Education tends to boost voting more in countries where average levels of education are lower, such as El Salvador, Guatemala and Paraguay, than in countries with higher levels of education, such as Argentina and Chile (Carreras and Castañeda-Angarita, 2013).

In high income countries with considerable inequality in election participation, such as the United States, education also increases the likelihood that people will vote (Milligan et al., 2004; Sondheimer and Green, 2010). It also helps young people recognize the importance of voting (Campbell, 2006). According to one study, an additional year of schooling raised voter participation by seven percentage points (Dee, 2004).

Education boosts wider democratic activity. Education contributes to other forms of political participation. In rural areas of the states of Madhya Pradesh and Rajasthan in India, education was positively associated with campaigning, discussing electoral issues, attending rallies and establishing contacts with local government officials (Krishna, 2006). In the state of West Bengal in India, a survey of 85 villages showed that the higher the level of household education, the more likely people were to attend the biannual gram sabha, or village forum, and, especially, to ask questions at the meetings (Bardhan et al., 2009).

Participation also includes joining, and campaigning for, political parties. In Benin, people who had had the chance to attend the first schools that opened in some rural parts of the country were 32% more likely to become party members and 34% more likely to become party campaigners than their peers who did not go to school (Wantchekon et al., 2012).

Education's role in promoting wider forms of participation is also apparent in high income countries. Evidence from the first three rounds of the European Social Survey (2002–2006) shows that each step up the education ladder, from primary to lower secondary, upper secondary and tertiary education, increases the chance of people participating in groups and associations by 10 percentage points (Borgonovi and Miyamoto, 2010).

Education supports alternative forms of political participation. Education increases the likelihood that citizens will make their voices heard in other ways, such as signing petitions, boycotting products or taking part in peaceful demonstrations, according to a new analysis for this Report of 26 low and middle income countries that participated in the 2005–2008 World Values Survey. In Argentina, China and Turkey, for example, citizens were around twice as likely to sign a petition if they had secondary education, compared with those who had only primary schooling. Similarly, in Argentina and Turkey those with secondary education were twice as likely to have taken part in a peaceful demonstration as those with only primary schooling (Figure 3.6).

Figure 3.6: Education leads to more engagement in alternative forms of political participation
Percentage of adults who signed a petition, boycotted a product or took part in a peaceful demonstration, by education level, selected countries, 2005–2008

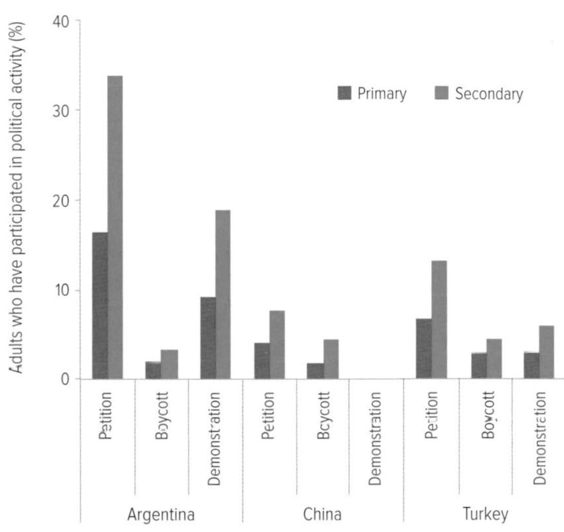

* Respondents in China were not asked the question about involvement in peaceful demonstrations.
Note: The results control for age, sex, labour market status and country GDP per capita.
Source: Chzhen (2013), based on the 2005–2008 World Values Survey.

Education also changes people's attitudes to authority and traditional forms of allegiance. Educated individuals increasingly base their sense of citizenship less on duty and more on their ability and desire to participate directly in decisions that affect their lives (Dalton, 2008). In Kenya, a follow-up to the National Civic Education Programme reached at least 20% of voting-age citizens before the 2007 elections through various forms of public meetings. Interviews with 3,600 people showed that the programme increased their participation in local politics by 10% (Finkel et al., 2012).

Education promotes tolerance and social cohesion

Education is a key mechanism promoting tolerance, as new analysis of the World Values Survey for this Report shows. In Latin America, where levels of tolerance are much higher overall than in the Arab States, people with secondary education were less likely than those with primary education to express intolerance by 47% for people of different race, 39% for people of a different religion, 32% in the case of homosexuals and 45% towards those with HIV/AIDS (Infographic: Love thy neighbour).

Education can play a vital role where intolerance is a particular problem. In the Arab States, for example, people with secondary education were 14% less likely than those with only primary education to express intolerance towards people of a different religion.

In sub-Saharan Africa, those affected by HIV/AIDS often face stigma, which itself can contribute to the spread of the disease by discouraging people from taking preventive measures or seeking treatment. Education can help reduce stigma: compared with those who had not completed primary school, those who had completed primary education were 10% less likely to express intolerance towards people with HIV infection, and those with secondary education were 23% less likely to do so. In Central and Eastern Europe, where intolerance towards immigrants is a cause for concern, those with secondary education were 16% less likely than those who had not completed secondary education to express such intolerance.

In many parts of the world, people remain intransigent in their attitudes towards homosexuality. In the Arab States, as many as 9 out of 10 people express intolerance to homosexuality, regardless of their education. This suggests that education can take time to have an impact on ingrained attitudes, and that specific policy measures are needed to ensure that children learn in school the importance of tolerance. Argentina shows what a difference education can make: those with secondary education were 21% less likely to express intolerant attitudes towards homosexuals than those with only primary education.

In parts of India, animosity among ethnic and linguistic groups can spark violence, so there is an urgent need to increase tolerance through education. Those with secondary education were 19% less likely to express intolerance towards people speaking a different language than those with less than primary education.

By altering attitudes, education also leads eventually to political changes, such as more democratic representation. New research for this Report shows the importance of equitable education on democratic development (Box 3.1).

In the Arab States, people with secondary education were 39% less likely to express intolerance for people of a different religion

LOVE THY NEIGHBOUR?

Education increases tolerance

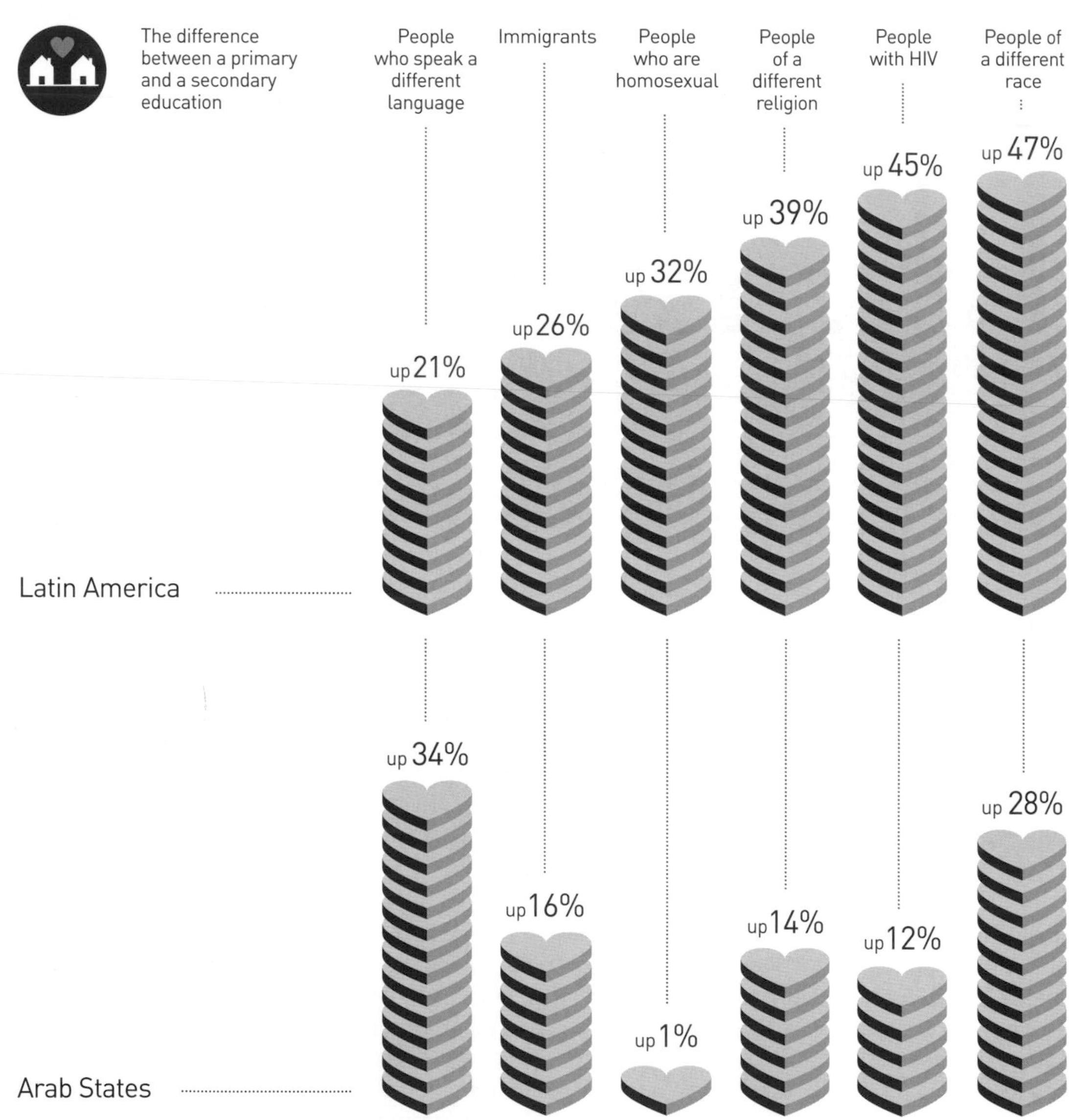

*Answers are in response to the question:

"Who would you prefer not to live next door to?"

Source: Chzhen (2013), based on the 2005–2008 World Values Survey.

Box 3.1: In India, education boosts women's role in politics

India, the world's largest democracy, appears to suffer from voter bias. Over the last three decades, only about 4% of all candidates for state assembly elections were female, and any female candidate received only about 5% of overall votes. New analysis for this Report, which combined information on state assembly elections between 1980 and 2007 with information on literacy rates across 287 districts, shows that narrowing the gender literacy gap raises women's participation and competitiveness in politics. Average literacy over the period was 34% for women and 55% for men. It is estimated that raising the female literacy rate to 42% would increase the share of female candidates by 16%, the share of votes obtained by women candidates by 13% and female voter turnout by 4%.

Improving male literacy also has a positive impact on women's political participation, perhaps because literate men are more likely to vote for women candidates and, as party leaders, to field women candidates.

Raising women's participation in politics is vital not only to achieve gender equality but also because evidence shows that women politicians tend to be both less corrupt and more proactive in representing the interests of children's well-being. Therefore, by stimulating increases in women's political engagement, investing in education improves democratic governance.

Sources: Afridi et al. (2013); Beaman et al. (2009, 2012); Bhalotra et al. (2013a); Brollo and Troiano (2013).

By promoting tolerance, education also builds values, attitudes, norms and beliefs that improve interpersonal trust and increase civic engagement, which are pillars of democracy. A review of estimates from various studies suggested that one year of schooling increases the probability of trusting people by 2.4 percentage points and the probability of civic participation by 2.8 percentage points (Huang et al., 2009).

To be successful in boosting trust, education systems need to ensure equal access to all children and young adults regardless of background, make sure there is no discrimination in the classroom and support those who are failing to learn. Within a group of 15 high income countries, social cohesion – in terms of interpersonal trust, trust in political institutions, attitudes to tax evasion, attitudes to cheating on public transport, and violent crime – was lower in those countries with more unequal distribution of educational outcomes (Green et al., 2003).

Inclusive education policies are just as important in instilling trust in poorer countries. In Kerala state, India, religious fragmentation and caste-based social organization could have been a source of conflict, as they have been in some other parts of the world. The early establishment of universal education helped overcome these challenges (Oommen, 2009). By contrast, in Argentina, which is not only a monolingual society but also richer and less characterized by factors that lead to social rifts, levels of social cohesion have declined, according to World Values Survey results over three decades. A gradual increase in income inequality since the 1970s has gone hand in hand with increased segregation in education and the movement of children from all but the poorest households to private schools between 1992 and 2010. This segregation is confirmed by the 2009 PISA results, which showed that social inclusion rates in schools in Argentina were among the lowest measured (OECD, 2010).

By promoting tolerance, education also builds values and attitudes that improve interpersonal trust and increase civic engagement

Education helps prevent conflict and heal its consequences

If global development goals are to be achieved, it is vital to reduce conflict, which has held back progress towards the MDGs – and education is a key way of doing so. By accelerating growth and promoting employment, education dampens incentives for disaffected young men to engage in armed violence. And tackling educational inequality will help lessen the chances of conflict, because such inequality fosters a sense of injustice that has fuelled many conflicts.

While a low level of education does not automatically lead to conflict, it is an important risk factor. An influential study found that if the male secondary school enrolment ratio were 10 percentage points higher than average, the risk of war would decline by a quarter (Collier and Hoeffler, 2004). The expected risk of conflict is highest in countries that have both a large youth population and low education. For example, in a country with a high ratio of youth to adult population at 38%, doubling the percentage of youth with secondary education, from 30% to 60%, would halve the risk of conflict (Barakat and Urdal, 2009).

An increase in educational expenditure from 2.2% to 6.3% of GDP is estimated to lead to a 54% decrease in the likelihood of civil war

Government commitment to expanding education helps reduce the risk of conflict. Globally, an increase in primary enrolment from 67% to 100% would have resulted in a 35% decrease in the probability of civil war over 1980–1999. Higher spending on education can be a strong signal that the government cares for all citizens. An increase in educational expenditure from 2.2% to 6.3% of GDP is estimated to lead to a 54% decrease in the likelihood of civil war (Thyne, 2006).

Education access and spending need to be increased equally for all population groups, because perceived unfairness can reinforce disillusionment with central authority. A study of 55 low and middle income countries over 1986–2003 showed that if the level of educational inequality doubled, the probability of conflict more than doubled, from 3.8% to 9.5% (Østby, 2008). Similarly, an analysis of the use of force between organized armed groups not involving the government between 1990 and 2008 in sub-Saharan Africa showed that the risk of conflict rose by 83% between a region at the bottom quarter and a region at the top quarter of education inequality (Fjelde and Østby, 2012).

Education not only reduces armed conflict, but also lowers civil strife more broadly. An analysis of violence in 55 major cities in sub-Saharan Africa and Asia between 1960 and 2006 found that an increase in the percentage of the male youth population with secondary education could be expected to lead to a reduction in the number of lethal events (Urdal and Hoelscher, 2009).

Although the frequency of civil conflict has decreased in recent years, new conflicts have emerged or heightened, as in Mali and the Syrian Arab Republic. Urgent action is needed to help heal divisions and resolve the fundamental causes of tension. Expanding educational opportunities and reducing inequality can play a key role in reconstruction efforts, along with changing what is taught and how it is taught (UNESCO, 2011). Such reforms on their own may be insufficient if inequality continues to be a feature of the education system. In addition, separating children according to group identity can perpetuate negative attitudes, as the example of Lebanon shows (Box 3.2).

Box 3.2: Educating to avert conflict in Lebanon

Lebanon is riven by deep sectarian divisions and sharp inequality between its communities, which are further exacerbated by wider tensions across the Middle East. The devastating war between 1976 and 1990 came to an end with the signing of the Taif Agreement, which recognized education as a means of moving towards reconciliation. This prompted large-scale education reform, including changes in curriculum, textbooks and teacher training.

Some materials, such as the teachers' guide for peace and democratic behaviour, were considered models of their kind. But other reforms were thwarted by political considerations; for instance, there is no common history textbook. A key feature of the education system is that most secondary schools are private and segregated along religious lines. In these schools, communities maintain control over the interpretation of events taught in classrooms, which often reflects this segregation.

Even in public schools, the teaching of civic education faces challenges. One study found that most public secondary schools were characterized by a subject-based rather than cross-cutting approach to civic education, and that the classroom and school environment was authoritarian and hierarchical. Some schools even applied admission policies that were not inclusive or restricted what issues teachers could discuss in class. Their students were accordingly found to be less open and trustful of members of other groups. For example, while about 36% of grade 11 students in schools with a passive approach to civic education said they trusted sectarian parties, only 18% did so in schools with an active approach to civic education.

A citizenship education reform is now trying to build on these lessons by emphasizing collaboration, dialogue, student participation, community service and parent councils.

Sources: Frayha (2004); Lebanon Centre for Research and Educational Development (2013); Shuayb (2012); UNDP (2008).

Education helps reduce corruption

A broad-based free schooling system strengthens the foundations of democracy by fostering support for the institutional checks and balances that are necessary to detect and punish abuses of office, and by lowering tolerance towards corruption. An analysis of 78 countries shows that the level of educational attainment is the most powerful factor predicting lower levels of corruption (Rothstein and Uslaner, 2012).

In Brazil, for example, while 53% of voters with no education said they would support a corrupt but competent politician, only 25% of respondents with at least some college education agreed (Pereira et al., 2011).

Better-educated citizens are more likely to stand up to corruption by complaining to government agencies, primarily because they have information about how to complain and defend themselves. In 31 countries that took part in the World Justice Project survey of 2009–2011, those with secondary education were one-sixth more likely than average to complain about deficient government services, and those with tertiary education one-third more likely to do so (Botero et al., 2012).

Education is essential for the justice system to function

Less educated people lack the ability to claim their rights and are often excluded from the legal system (Abregú, 2001). For example, in Sierra Leone, many people cannot use the formal court system because it operates in English, which only people with a higher level of education speak. Translators sometimes interpret into Krio, the lingua franca, but some people only speak local languages, for which interpreters are not available. Accused persons who are less educated can easily be isolated by a system that should support them (Castillejo, 2009).

Even non-formal courts intended to improve less educated people's access to the justice system are burdened by illiteracy. In Eritrea, village courts were set up to help settle cases amicably, as the lowest tier of the court system, but several of the elders appointed as judges were illiterate and lacked basic legal training. The result is that many decisions fell between the two systems, being based neither on customary law nor on national laws (Andemariam, 2011).

Problems can be particularly acute for women when their education levels are lower than men's. In Kenya, lack of knowledge about laws and dependence on male relatives for assistance and resources can prevent women from turning to the formal justice system, for example to resolve disputes such as property conflicts (International Development Law Organization, 2013).

Education needs to be part of the solution to global environmental problems

Education's vital role in preventing environmental degradation and limiting the causes and effects of climate change has not been sufficiently acknowledged or exploited. By improving knowledge, instilling values, fostering beliefs and shifting attitudes, education has considerable power to change lifestyles and behaviours that are harmful for the environment.

There is an urgent need to identify the best ways to tap this potential as it becomes increasingly clear how much human action has led to environmental degradation and climate change, especially through the release of greenhouse gases. As well as altering the balance of nature, consequences such as extreme weather patterns and loss of biodiversity could reverse progress in improving living standards – especially for poorer and more vulnerable populations, even though they are not the ones responsible for environmental degradation.

Education's role in mitigating the effects of climate change needs to be fully acknowledged and exploited

Increased levels of education do not automatically translate into more responsible behaviour towards the environment. But as the influential Stern Review on climate change noted: 'Governments can be a catalyst for dialogue through evidence, education, persuasion and discussion. Educating those currently at school about climate change will help to shape and sustain future policy-making, and a broad public and international debate will support today's policy-makers in taking strong action now' (Stern, 2006, p. xxi).

Education's role in mitigating the effects of climate change has often been played down in discussions on sustainable development. It needs to be fully acknowledged and exploited so that education's benefits are realized. At the same time, education needs to adapt to the challenge of spreading the message of environmental responsibility, as Chapter 6 shows.

Identifying how education can best play this role is urgent. Even though the seventh MDG was intended to ensure environmental sustainability, it is widely acknowledged that it has received insufficient attention. Debates on how to frame global development goals after 2015 have centred on whether the overarching concern should be poverty eradication or sustainable development, while recognizing that the two aims complement each other. One thing is certain: environmental sustainability is a universal issue, affecting people around the world with unprecedented speed. While threats from hunger and poverty need urgent national action, people need to be educated about environmental degradation on a global scale, particularly in rich countries, to make sure those most responsible do not endanger lives in other parts of the world.

Galvanizing the potential of education for tackling climate change

People who are more educated often tend to maintain lifestyles that burden the environment. One reason is that the consequences of climate change are not yet perceptible to the vast majority of people, and many still see it as a distant threat (Weber and Stern, 2011). But experience shows that, when populations are confronted by major challenges, overcoming the inertia of past attitudes is possible – and people with more education respond first. In the case of health threats such as HIV/AIDS, for example, educated people were originally more likely to engage in harmful behaviour such as unprotected sex, but as the dangers became known they were the first to change their behaviour.

Students who scored higher in environmental science also reported being more aware of complex environmental issues

Historically, rich countries that were the first to industrialize are the most responsible for environmental degradation and also have higher education levels, so the relationship would seem to work in the opposite direction. In addition, among the six nations that emit the most carbon dioxide, as education levels increase, emissions also tend to increase. A closer look at the data, however, reveals notable differences and exceptions showing that more education does not necessarily lead to increased emissions. In China in 2008, when the average level of education was seven years, the level of emissions per capita was one-third of what the level in the United States was at a similar average level of education, in 1950 (Box 3.3). And while the average level of education in Germany has increased by five years in the last two decades, emissions per capita have declined by almost 20% (Barro and Lee, 2013; World Resources Institute, 2012).

Box 3.3: Education reform is needed to reduce the United States' impact on the environment

The United States is the world's biggest polluter, accounting for 20% of total and 30% of transport emissions of greenhouse gases in the world. Reducing emissions will depend on changing public attitudes, including through education, as well as on technological progress. Education has been shown to change car use in a country that is highly dependent on private cars: in parts of the country, those with higher levels of education are more likely to drive smaller and more fuel-efficient vehicles. But far more is needed to reduce emissions by up to 65% compared with 2010 levels, the scale of reduction that high income countries need to achieve to limit the average temperature increase to 2°C in this century.

Schools need to strengthen their efforts to influence attitudes to the environment. Experience from US schools that have exemplary environmental education programmes shows that such change is possible: in comparison with a representative sample of US schools, they did significantly better in environmental literacy, in particular due to greater sensitivity towards the environment and improved self-reported environmental behaviour.

Schools with well-developed environmental programmes need to become the norm rather than the exception. And young people need to be taught the science behind climate change and other environmental problems. This can only happen if recent reforms to the science curriculum, aimed at preparing students to make better decisions about scientific and technical issues and to apply science to their daily lives, are not only fully implemented but also become mandatory.

Sources: Choo and Mokhtarian (2004); Flamm (2009); Greene and Plotkin (2011); McBeth et al. (2011); Meinshausen (2007); Pampel and Hunter (2012); World Resources Institute (2012).

Education improves knowledge and understanding of the environment

A key way in which education increases environmental awareness and concern is by improving understanding of the science behind climate change and other environmental issues. Students who scored higher in environmental science across the 57 countries participating in the 2006 PISA also reported being more aware of complex environmental issues. For example, in the 30 OECD countries that took part in the survey, an increase of one unit of the awareness index was associated with an increase of 35 points in the environmental science performance index (OECD, 2009).

The higher the level of education, the more likely it is that people express concern for the environment. In 47 countries covered by the 2005–2008 World Values Survey, 60% of respondents considered global warming a very serious problem. But the positive effect of education was considerable: a person with secondary education was about 10 percentage points more likely to express such concern than a person with primary education (Kvaløy et al., 2012).

Data from the International Social Survey Programme on 29 mostly high income countries similarly showed that the share of those disagreeing that people worry too much about the environment rose from 25% of those with less than secondary education to 37% of people with secondary education and 46% of people with tertiary education, according to a new analysis for this Report (National Centre for Social Research, 2013). In Germany, people with secondary education were twice as likely as those with less than secondary education to express concern, and those with tertiary education three times as likely (Infographic: Schooling can save the planet).

Education promotes political activism that influences policy change

People with more education tend not only to be more concerned about the environment, but also to follow up that concern with activism that promotes and supports political decisions that protect the environment. Such pressure is a vital way of pushing governments towards the type of binding agreement that is needed to control emission levels.

Analysis for this Report of the 2010 round of the International Social Survey Programme showed that in almost all participating countries, respondents with more education were more likely to have signed a petition, given money or taken part in a protest or demonstration, in relation to the environment, over the past five years. The influence of education is apparent in Germany, one of the countries with the highest emissions levels: while 12% of respondents with less than secondary education had taken such political action, the share rose to 26% of those with secondary education and 46% of those with tertiary education (National Centre for Social Research, 2013). These results are corroborated by a household survey in 10 OECD countries, where people with more education – especially those with a university degree – tended strongly to express pro-environment values and to belong to environmental organizations (OECD, 2011). An analysis of the Global Warming Citizen Survey in the United States also showed that the higher the education level of respondents, the greater their activism in terms of policy support, environmental political participation and environment-friendly behaviour (Lubell et al., 2007).

Education can promote more environment-friendly behaviour

By increasing awareness and concern, education can encourage people to reduce their impact on the environment by taking action such as using energy and water more efficiently or recycling household waste. Such behaviour becomes increasingly important as people in high income countries are called upon to modify their consumption and take other measures that limit environmental harm.

People with more education are more likely to have signed a petition or taken part in a demonstration in relation to the environment

In the Netherlands, people with a higher level of education tend to use less energy in the home, even taking account of income (Poortinga et al., 2004). A study of households in 10 OECD countries found that those with more education tended to save water (OECD, 2011), and there have been similar findings in Spain (Aisa and Larramona, 2012). In a group of countries including France, Mexico and the Republic of Korea, people without a high school diploma were found to recycle less glass, plastic, aluminium and paper than people with a post-graduate degree (Ferrara and Missios, 2011).

Education will help the most vulnerable adapt to climate change

As well as encouraging people to take action that reduces greenhouse gas emissions, education can help people adapt to the consequences of climate change. The need for adaptation is becoming increasingly urgent; regardless of the speed with which emissions can be reduced, they have already unleashed forces that are leading to increasing temperatures, rising sea levels and more frequent extreme weather events. Adaptation is especially important for poorer countries, where the capacity of governments to act is most limited and threats to livelihoods will be felt most strongly.

SCHOOLING CAN SAVE THE PLANET

Higher levels of education lead to more concern for the environment

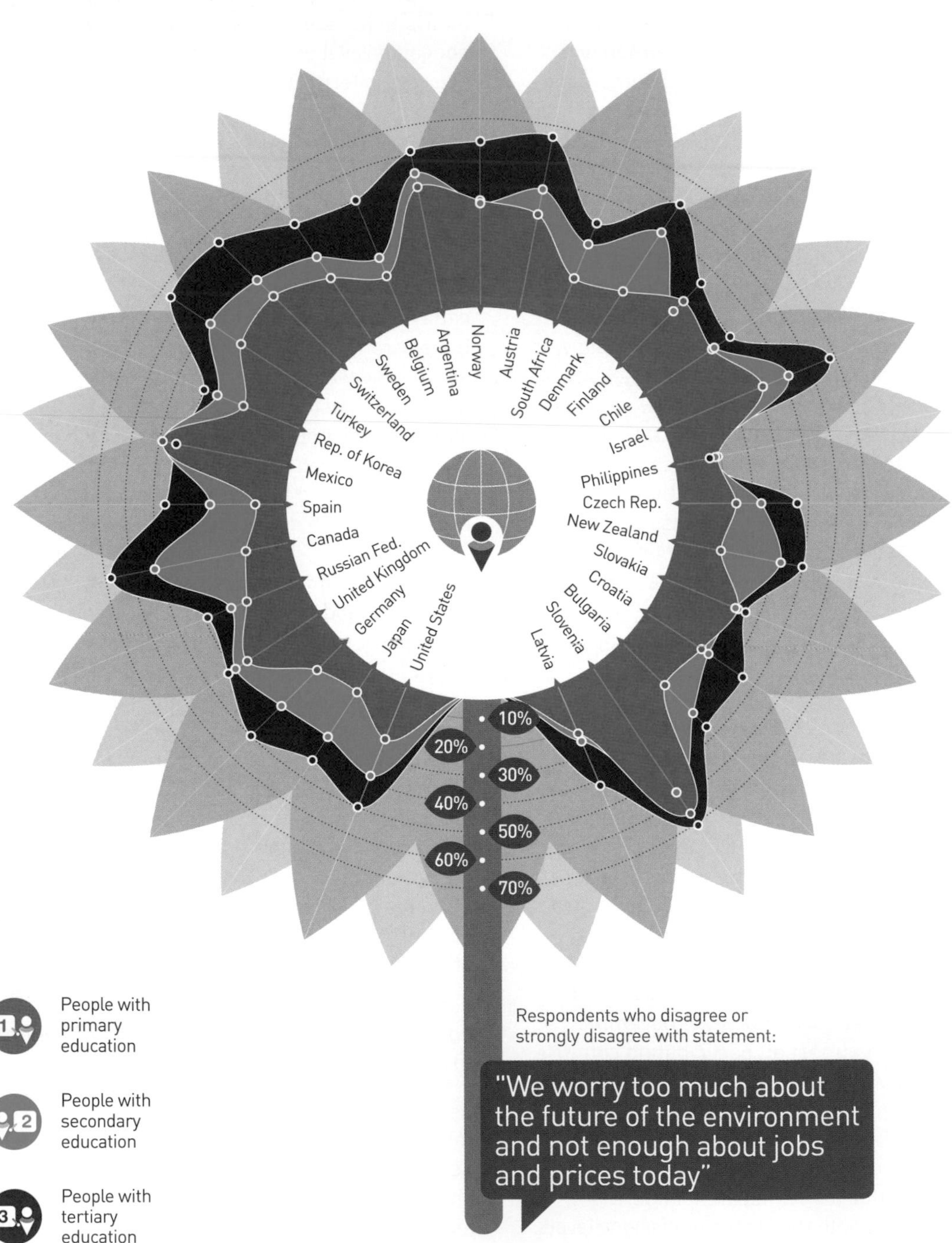

Source: National Centre for Social Research (2013), based on 2010 International Social Survey Programme data.

Education improves people's understanding of the risks posed by climate change, the need to adapt and measures to reduce the impact of climate change on livelihoods. Farmers in low income countries are most vulnerable to climate change, as they depend heavily on rain-fed agriculture (Below et al., 2010). In Ethiopia, six years of education increase by 20% the chance that a farmer will adapt to climate change through techniques such as soil conservation, varying planting dates and changing crop varieties (Deressa et al., 2009). In Uganda, the likelihood that a family will adopt drought-resistant crop varieties increases when the father has basic education (Hisali et al., 2011). And a survey of farmers in Burkina Faso, Cameroon, Egypt, Ethiopia, Ghana, Kenya, Niger, Senegal, South Africa and Zambia showed that those with education were more likely to make at least one adaptation: a year of education reduced the probability of no adaptation by 1.6% (Maddison, 2007).

Education empowers women to make life choices

Discrimination prevents some people from getting a fair share of the fruits of overall progress in terms of reducing poverty or improving health. Education can empower these vulnerable people to overcome such barriers, so improving education access and quality will be an essential way of ensuring that efforts to reach post-2015 development goals benefit everyone, especially those who need support the most.

Education is particularly powerful in helping women overcome unequal and oppressive social limits and expectations so they can make choices about their lives. The third MDG, on promoting gender equality and empowering women, acknowledges the central role of education in its inclusion of gender parity in primary and secondary education as a target. After 2015, it will be vital to build on the progress that has been made towards this target, as tackling gender discrimination in school unleashes education's power to help girls and women overcome broader discrimination.

As this chapter has shown, education empowers women to make choices that improve their own and their children's health and chances of survival and boosts women's work prospects.

This section looks at further ways in which education empowers women to make choices that improve their welfare, including marrying later and having fewer children. When girls spend more years in school, they tend to marry later and have their first child later, but the effect of education goes beyond this to give girls and young women greater awareness of their rights and improve their confidence in their ability to make decisions that affect their lives (Box 3.4).

Education's influence on empowering women is particularly strong in countries where girls are likely to get married or give birth early and have a large number of children. Such empowerment not only benefits women's own choices, but also improves their health and that of their children, and benefits societies by bringing forward the demographic transition to a stable population with lower fertility and lower mortality.

Women's education helps avert child marriage

Around 2.9 million girls are married by the age of 15 in sub-Saharan Africa and South and West Asia, equivalent to one in eight girls in each region, according to new estimates from Demographic and Health Surveys for this Report based on data for 20- to 24-year-olds. These shocking statistics mean millions of girls are robbed of their childhood and denied an education.

While just 8% of literate girls are married by age 15 in South and West Asia, more than one in four of those who are not literate are married by this age

Ensuring that girls stay in school is one of the most effective ways to avert child marriage. If all girls had primary education in sub-Saharan Africa and South and West Asia, child marriage would fall by 14%, from almost 2.9 million to less than 2.5 million, and if they had secondary education it would fall by 64% to just over one million (Infographic: Learning lessens early marriages and births). Education's contribution is evident in the links between literacy and child marriage. While just 4% of literate girls are married by age 15 in sub-Saharan Africa, and 8% in South and West Asia, more than one in five of those who are not literate are married by this age in sub-Saharan Africa, and almost one in four in South and West Asia.

In 13 out of 40 countries, more than 1 girl in 10 marries by the age of 15. And in 28 out of 40 countries this is true for those with less than

Box 3.4: Education gives women the power to claim their rights

Education gives women more power over their own lives in a variety of ways. As well as widening their choices, it can boost their confidence and perception of their freedom. It can also alter the perceptions of men and social barriers to their autonomy. One key aspect of this transformative power is women's freedom to choose a spouse in countries where arranged marriages are common. According to new analysis for this Report, young women with at least secondary education are 30 percentage points more likely to have a say over their choice of spouse than women with no education in India and 15 percentage points more likely in Pakistan.

Education also influences young women's choice of family size. In Pakistan, while only 30% of women with no education believe they can have a say over the number of their children, the share increases to 52% among women with primary education and to 63% among women with lower secondary education.

The education level of a woman's spouse can also have a key role in her fertility choices. In India, the likelihood that the fertility preferences of a woman with primary education were taken into account rose from 65% for those whose husbands had no education to at least 85% for those whose husbands had at least secondary education. Education also helps prevent the abhorrent practice of infanticide in India, where strong preferences over the sex of the child have been linked to millions of killings of children. While 84% of women with no education would prefer to have a boy if they could only have one child, only 50% of women with at least secondary education would have such a preference.

Further evidence of education's power to change attitudes comes from Sierra Leone, where the expansion of schooling opportunities in the aftermath of the civil war led to a steep increase in the amount of education completed by younger women. An additional year of schooling reduced women's tolerance of domestic violence from 36% to 26%.

Adult education can also make a key difference to women's choices. A literacy programme for women in the Indian state of Uttarakhand that provided continuing education and vocational training, covering issues such as alcoholism, village politics and community conflict resolution, led to a significant increase in the percentages of women who felt able to leave their house without permission (from 58% to 75%) and who participated in village council meetings (from 19% to 41%).

Sources: Aslam (2013); Kandpal et al. (2012); Mocan and Cannonier (2012).

In sub-Saharan Africa and South and West Asia, if all women had secondary education, early births would fall by 59%

primary education. In Bangladesh, Mali and Sierra Leone, over one in five young women with primary schooling are married by this age. Girls who make it to secondary school are much less likely to be locked into early marriage. In Ethiopia, while almost one in three young women with no education were married by the age of 15 in 2011, among women with secondary education the share was just 9%.

Women's education reduces the chance of early birth

Empowering women also gives them more control about decisions over when to have their first child. As many as 3.4 million births occur before girls reach age 17 in sub-Saharan Africa and South and West Asia. This corresponds to about one in seven young women in the two regions, according to estimates for this Report using Demographic and Health Survey data for 20- to 24-year-olds. Giving birth so early is a major risk factor for maternal and child deaths.

One reason that girls with more years in school are less likely to give birth early is simply that girls who give birth drop out before they have a chance of more education. But staying in school longer also gives girls more confidence to make choices that prevent them from getting pregnant at a young age. In sub-Saharan Africa and South and West Asia, early births would fall by 10%, from 3.4 to 3.1 million, if all women had primary education. If all women had secondary education, early births would fall by 59%, to 1.4 million (Infographic: Learning lessens early marriages and births).

Average age at first birth differs by more than three years between women without education and women with secondary education. In Nigeria, for example, women with no education gave birth for the first time at age 18, on average, compared with age 25 for those with at least secondary education (ICF International, 2012). Education not only postpones the first birth but also increases the time between births. A period of less than two years between births tends to increase health risks for mothers and their children. In Kenya, the probability that a woman with no education would have another child within two years of the second birth was 27%, compared with 17% among women with secondary education (ICF International, 2012).

LEARNING LESSENS EARLY MARRIAGES AND BIRTHS

Women with higher levels of education are less likely to get married or have children at an early age

Child marriage

14%
fewer marriages if all girls had primary education

64%
fewer marriages if all girls had secondary education

Child marriages for all girls by age 15 in sub-Saharan Africa and South and West Asia

2,867,000

2,459,000

1,044,000

Early births

10%
fewer girls would become pregnant if all girls had primary education

59%
fewer girls would become pregnant if all girls had secondary education

Early births for all girls under 17 in sub-Saharan Africa and South and West Asia

3,397,000

3,071,000

1,393,000

Fertility rate*

No education

Primary education

Secondary education

Average number of births per woman in sub-Saharan Africa

6.7

5.8

3.9

*Fertility rate is the average number of children that would be born to a woman over her lifetime

Sources: EFA Global Monitoring Report team calculations (2013), based on Demographic and Health Surveys; UNPD (2011).

Extending girls' education helps bring the demographic transition forward

Women with more education tend to have fewer children, which benefits them, their families and society more generally. In some parts of the world, education has already been a key factor in bringing forward the transition from high rates of birth and mortality to lower rates. Other parts of the world are lagging, however, particularly sub-Saharan Africa, where women have an average of 5.4 live births, compared with 2.7 in South Asia (UNPD, 2011). Women with no education in sub-Saharan Africa have 6.7 births, on average, while the number falls to 5.8 for those with primary education and to 3.9 for those with secondary education. In Angola, the fertility rate of a woman with no education is 7.8 children, compared with 5.9 children for a woman with primary education and 2.5 children for a woman with secondary education or more.

If all countries expanded their school systems at the same rate as the Republic of Korea, there would be 843 million fewer people in the world by 2050

In seven countries, including Niger, Uganda and Zambia, the fertility rate – the number of live births per woman during her childbearing years – is over six children per woman. If all women in sub-Saharan Africa had primary education, the number of births would fall by 7%, from 31 million to 29 million, while if all women had secondary education, the number would fall by 37%, to 19 million.

Comparing total fertility rates by education level across countries shows that secondary education is of particular importance. For example, in the United Republic of Tanzania in 2010, the fertility rate of a woman with no education was 7 children, compared with 5.6 children for a woman with primary education and 3 children for a woman with secondary education or higher (Figure 3.7).

The potential contribution of education to stabilizing global population growth should not be underestimated: according to recent projections, if all countries expanded their school systems at the same rate as the Republic of Korea and Singapore, there would be 843 million fewer people in the world by 2050, equivalent to the population of sub-Saharan Africa in 2010, than if enrolment ratios had remained at 2000 levels. In Uganda, for example, the population would increase from 24 million in 2000 to 89 million in 2050 if enrolment grew at the fast rate, but to 105 million if it stayed constant, placing considerable stress on resources (Lutz and KC, 2011).

The results of these projections are supported by recent analysis of the determinants of fertility rates in 49 countries, based on Demographic and Health Surveys for 1986–2008, which identified eight countries where declines in fertility stalled in the 2000s. Of these, seven were in sub-Saharan Africa, and six were in the early phase of the demographic transition: Benin, Guinea, Mozambique, Nigeria, the United Republic of Tanzania and Zambia. Mali and Niger had not started their demographic transition. What these countries have in common is slower progress in female education: the share of women with no schooling fell by only 2.5 percentage points, compared to 6 percentage points in countries with declining fertility rates. Taking into account other factors, such as national income and child mortality, a decline in the share of women of child-bearing age with less than primary education in Guinea from 86% to 24% would reduce the fertility rate by 2 children per woman (Shapiro et al., 2011).

In three countries in eastern Africa, Kenya, Uganda and the United Republic of Tanzania, the decline in overall fertility has slowed, held back by persistently high fertility among women with less education. For example, in Kenya, the percentage of women with at least secondary education stagnated at 30% between 1998 and 2003. Over the same period, the fertility rate of women with secondary education fell by 0.3 children per woman, while the fertility rate of women with less than secondary education increased by 0.6 children per woman. The population of Kenya is expected to reach 59 million in 2025; if the lack of progress in education had not slowed the fertility decline, it could have been at least 15 million lower (Ezeh et al., 2009).

Figure 3.7: Maternal education greatly reduces fertility rates
Total fertility rate (number of live births per woman) by level of maternal education, selected countries, 2005–2011

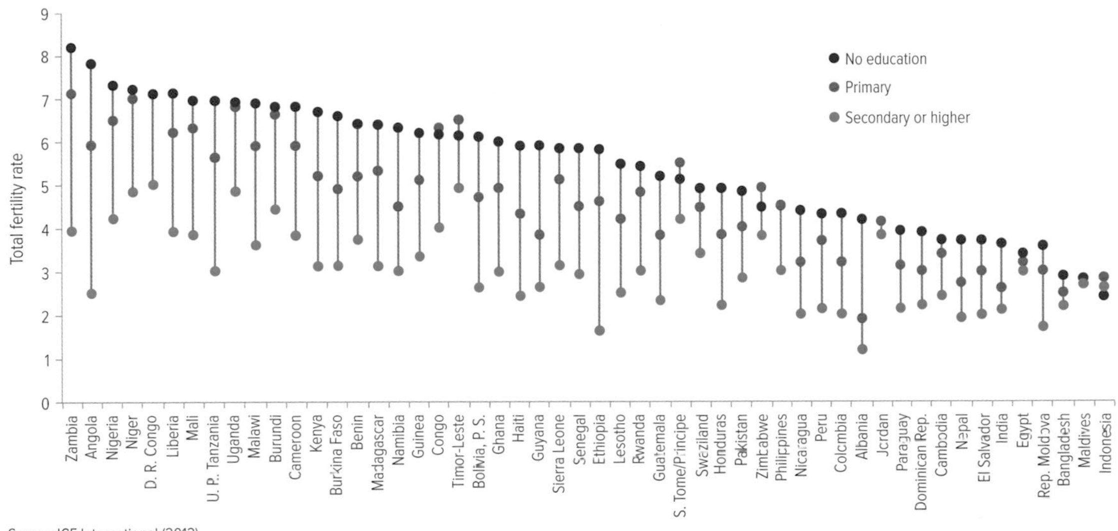

Source: ICF International (2012).

In countries that have undergone the demographic transition, education's contribution is clear. In Brazil, around 70% of the fertility decline during the 1960s and 1970s can be explained by improvements in schooling (Lam and Duryea, 1999).

Education played an important role in reducing fertility in Nigeria. An evaluation of the universal primary education programme implemented in the 1970s showed that four years of schooling reduced fertility by one child per woman by the age of 25 (Osili and Long, 2008). However, the percentage of women with at least secondary education was stagnant between 1999 and 2003. Furthermore, the number of girls out of school increased from 4.1 million in 1999 to 5.5 million in 2010. The total fertility rate stagnated at 5.7 children per woman between 2003 and 2008, which risks shifting Nigeria to a pessimistic scenario in which it would take 20 years longer for total fertility to fall below 3 children per woman. This would push the total population 44 million higher by 2050 and almost 300 million higher by 2100, to more than 1 billion, with potentially disastrous consequences for human development (UNPD, 2011).

Conclusion

The striking evidence laid out in this chapter demonstrates not only education's capacity to accelerate progress towards other development goals, but also how best to tap that potential, most of all by making sure that access to good quality education is available to all, regardless of their circumstances. Education's unique power should secure it a central place in the post-2015 development framework, and in the plans of policy-makers in poor and rich countries alike. This chapter shows why governments and aid donors should renew their political and financial commitment to education not only as a human right and a key goal on its own but also, crucially, as an investment that pays off in every sphere of people's lives and aspirations.

Part 3 Supporting teachers to end the learning crisis

A lack of attention to education quality and a failure to reach the marginalized have contributed to a learning crisis that needs urgent attention. The importance of education quality was recognized when it was established as the sixth Education for All goal in 2000, and again recently when the UN secretary-general made it one of the three priorities of the Global Education First Initiative. But 250 million children – many of them from disadvantaged backgrounds – are not learning even basic literacy and numeracy skills, let alone the further skills they need to get decent work and lead fulfilling lives.

To solve that crisis, all children must have teachers who are trained, motivated and enjoy teaching, who can identify and support weak learners, and who are backed by well-managed education systems. Good teachers close the gap between poor and good quality education by maximizing the benefits of learning in every classroom for every child. But worldwide, children who already face disadvantage and discrimination – because of factors such as poverty, gender, ethnicity, disability and where they live – are much less likely to be taught by good teachers.

As this Report shows, governments can increase access while also making sure that learning improves for all. Adequately funded national education plans that aim explicitly to meet the needs of the disadvantaged and that make equitable access to well-trained teachers must be a policy priority. But few national plans fulfill these requirements. Instead of getting adequate training and teaching conditions, teachers get the blame for poor learning outcomes. While teacher absenteeism and engagement in private tuition are real problems, policy-makers often ignore underlying reasons such as low pay and a lack of career opportunities.

The key to ending the learning crisis is to recruit the best teacher candidates, give them appropriate training, deploy them where they are needed most and give them incentives to make a long-term commitment to teaching (see illustration).

Education quality is undermined by the need for additional teachers, with 1.6 million required to achieve universal primary education by 2015 and 5.1 million to achieve universal lower secondary education by 2030.

Many teachers are untrained or insufficiently trained, and left to teach in overcrowded classrooms with few resources. On low pay, they soon become discontented, contributing to the lowering of education quality.

To ensure that all children are learning, teachers also need the support of an appropriate curriculum and assessment system that pays particular attention to the needs of children in early grades, when the most vulnerable are in danger of dropping out. Well-designed curricula and assessment practices enrich classroom experiences, help teachers identify and support disadvantaged students and promote the values, attitudes and practical skills needed to face future challenges in their lives. Moreover, children who have had to leave school before achieving the basics need a second chance to acquire these skills.

Beyond teaching the basics, teachers must help children gain important transferable skills, and can also help them become responsible global citizens if issues such as environmental sustainability and peace-building are integrated into a curriculum that focuses on practical action.

Four strategies for providing the best teachers

Attracting and retaining the best teachers as a means of ending the learning crisis requires a delicate juggling act on the part of policy-makers:

Recruit the best candidates from a wide range of backgrounds

Teacher recruitment policies and strategies should be designed to make teaching attractive to highly qualified candidates with diverse backgrounds and good subject knowledge. Recruits should be willing to live and work in remote areas or with disadvantaged children. Often this means recruiting teachers from within local communities. Recruiting enough women teachers is essential as well, especially to ensure that disadvantaged girls learn the basics and improve their life chances.

Train all teachers well, both before and during their careers

It is crucial to make sure that all teachers, irrespective of how they enter the profession, receive adequate training that strikes a balance between theory and practice and that makes up for any shortcomings in subject knowledge. Teachers should also be able to help learners with diverse learning needs and backgrounds, and to impart reading skills to children in the early grades. In addition, teachers need training and resources to teach in a language children understand so as to help children start learning early and build strong foundation skills. Ongoing training is essential for all teachers as new learning challenges emerge and new skills are required to meet them.

Allocate teachers effectively by offering incentives to teach in disadvantaged areas

Disadvantaged learners are disproportionately located in poor rural areas or in slums. A mix of incentives, such as good housing, extra allowances or bonuses, is needed to get trained teachers to accept teaching positions in such areas and to maintain their commitment to teaching. Local recruitment can help ensure that there are enough teachers in remote areas while giving disadvantaged children teachers with the cultural sensitivity and language skills to improve learning outcomes.

Retain teachers through improved working conditions and career progression pathways

Low pay, poor working conditions and an unattractive career structure can quickly make teaching unattractive. Performance-related pay may appear to be an appealing solution, but managing it effectively and fairly is challenging, even in well-resourced environments. Improving pay and conditions and providing an attractive career path are the best ways to retain good teachers. Policy-makers should strengthen legislation to address misconduct and gender-based violence, and should tackle the factors underlying teachers' absenteeism and engagement in private tuition.

Chapter 4
The learning crisis hits the disadvantaged hardest

The teacher gap: At this primary school in Shikarpur, Sindh, Pakistan, there is only one teacher for 100 pupils from five grades, so a pupil sometimes stands in for the teacher.

Credit: Amina Sayeed/UNESCO

While many countries have made impressive gains in getting more children into school over the past decade, improvements in quality have not always kept pace. The disadvantaged are most likely to suffer, because of insufficient numbers of trained teachers, overstretched infrastructure and inadequate supply of instructional materials. This chapter shows that unless policy-makers in all countries implement measures designed to improve learning for all, another generation of children and young people will be denied their right to a good quality education.

Introduction

Quality education is at the heart of the Education for All goals, but many countries are not even ensuring that their children achieve the most basic skills in reading and mathematics. In a world of equal learning opportunity, what students could achieve in school would be determined by their ability and effort rather than their circumstances at birth. In reality, factors such as poverty, gender, ethnicity, disability and where a child is born weigh heavily on whether children go to school and, once there, learn.

While many countries have made impressive gains in access to education over the past decade, improvements in quality have not always kept pace. The disadvantaged are most likely to suffer, because of insufficient numbers of trained teachers, overstretched infrastructure and inadequate supply of instructional materials. Yet, as this chapter shows, it is possible for countries to extend access to school while also improving equitable learning. Unless policy-makers implement measures designed to improve learning for all, another generation of children and young people will be denied their right to a good quality education.

The global learning crisis: action is urgent

Millions of primary school age children have not acquired even the most basic literacy and numeracy skills. Unable to read or understand a simple sentence, these children are ill equipped to make the transition to secondary education. Some who do make it into secondary school do not reach even a minimum level of competence. The extreme inequalities in achieving the most basic learning requirements, both between and within countries, add up to a global learning crisis that needs urgent action.

The full severity of the learning crisis is evident when the numbers of those who do not even start or complete primary school are included. Estimates in this Report suggest that of the world's 650 million primary school age children, at least 250 million are not learning the basics in reading and mathematics.[1] Of these, almost 120 million have little or no experience of primary school, having not even reached grade 4. The remaining 130 million stay in primary school for at least four years but do not achieve the minimum benchmarks for learning.

At least 250 million are not learning the basics in reading and mathematics

Wide variations between regions and countries reveal extent of crisis

The global divide between regions in learning achievement is stark. In North America and Western Europe, 96% of children reach grade 4 and achieve the minimum learning benchmark in reading. By contrast, only one-third of children in South and West Asia and two-fifths in sub-Saharan Africa reach grade 4 and achieve the basics (Figure 4.1). These two regions together account for more than three-quarters of those not crossing the minimum learning threshold.

Figure 4.1: 250 million children are failing to learn the basics in reading
Percentage of children of primary school age who reached grade 4 and achieved minimum learning standard in reading, by region

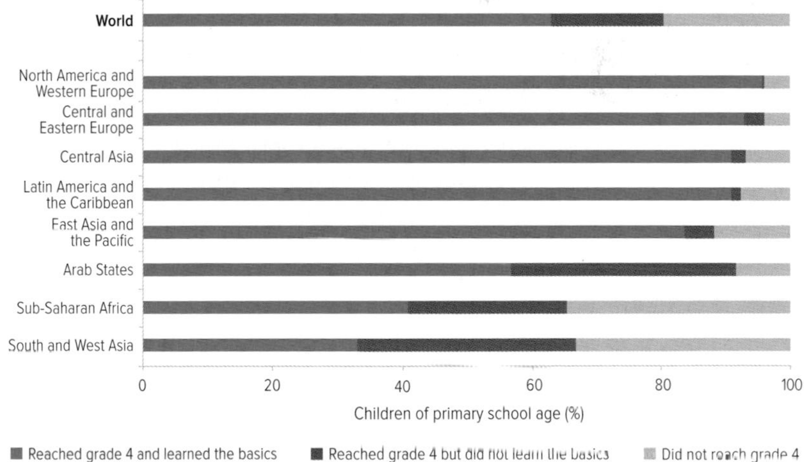

Notes: The definition of children who reached grade 4 is based on the expected cohort completion rate method. The definition of achievement of a minimum learning standard is based on an anchoring process that transforms the results from different surveys to a common scale.
Sources: EFA Global Monitoring Report team calculations (2013) based on (1) expected cohort survival rate to grade 4: UIS database; (2) learning achievement: Altinok (2013b), using data from the 2011 PIRLS, 2007 SACMEQ, 2004–2008 PASEC, 2006 SERCE; and analysis by the 2012 ASER India and 2012 ASER Pakistan survey teams.

1. The figure is an estimate based on information from the following international and regional assessments: Trends in International Mathematics and Science Study (TIMSS), Progress in International Reading Literacy Study (PIRLS), the Southern and Eastern Africa Consortium for Monitoring Educational Quality (SACMEQ), the Programme on the Analysis of Education Systems of the CONFEMEN (PASEC), and the Second Regional Comparative and Explanatory Study (SERCE) of the Latin American Laboratory for Assessment of the Quality of Education. For further information on the methodology, see the technical note on the EFA Global Monitoring Report website.

The cost of 250 million children not learning the basics is equivalent to US$129 billion

International and regional assessments do not cover all countries and cannot measure all aspects of education quality, but they do indicate whether children are learning the most fundamental skills. Analysis for this Report, which uses information on entry into school and progression, and places countries on a common scale of learning achievement, shows that the learning crisis is widespread. In 21 out of the 85 countries for which full data are available, fewer than half of children are learning the basics. Of these 21 countries, 17 are in sub-Saharan Africa; the others are India, Mauritania, Morocco and Pakistan (Figure 4.2).

Glaring disparities between countries show that where children are born determines their opportunity to learn. In Niger, at one end of the scale, 42% of primary school age children either do not make it into school or do not make it as far as grade 4. Half of primary school age children reach grade 4 but are not learning. As a result, in total just 8 out of 100 primary school age children are able to acquire basic reading skills. Students in other western African countries similarly face slim chances of learning. In Benin, Côte d'Ivoire and Mali, fewer than one in five learn the basics. At the other end of the scale, all primary school age children in the Netherlands and Singapore achieve the basics. It is further estimated that a child in eastern or southern Africa achieves the same level of learning after six or seven years in school as a child in an OECD country reaches after two or three years (Global Partnership for Education, 2012).

Comparing countries shows how much difference a country's education system can make in whether children acquire basic skills once they are in school. In both Kenya and Zambia, more than three-quarters of primary school age children make it beyond grade 4, but while in Kenya 70% of these children are able to read, just 44% can in Zambia.

Even in regions with good achievement overall, there are wide disparities between countries. In Latin America and the Caribbean, where on average 90% of primary school age children can read, the share of children who achieve the basics ranges from about 95% in Argentina, Chile, Cuba, Mexico and Uruguay to less than 80% in the Dominican Republic, Guatemala, Honduras, Nicaragua and Paraguay.

Across countries, performance in mathematics is even less encouraging. In Latin America, only around 70 in 100 children are learning the basics in this subject. In Nicaragua, where 60% of children can read, only 37% learn basic mathematics. Even in Chile, where most primary school age children have learned to read, 20% are unable to perform the basics in mathematics.

Some richer countries also perform worse in mathematics. The Netherlands is representative of most rich countries in having ensured basic learning skills in both reading and mathematics for almost all primary school age children. But in Spain, while most have achieved the basics in reading, 8% have not reached the minimum learning benchmark in mathematics by the end of grade 4. Similarly, in Central and Eastern Europe, the Slovenian education system ensures that almost all children in school learn basic mathematics, while 17% of children in Turkey do not.

The learning crisis has costs not only for the future ambitions of children, but also for the current finances of governments. Countries with seemingly low costs per primary pupil can face significantly higher costs if they account only for those who are actually learning. The cost of 250 million children not learning the basics is equivalent to US$129 billion, or 10% of global spending on primary education. Thirty-seven countries are wasting at least half the amount they spend on primary education in this way.

For many countries, low spending is a false economy. Twenty-five countries spend less than US$150 per primary pupil on education – all but two of which (Cambodia and Pakistan) are in sub-Saharan Africa. In 23 of the countries, the cost per learner is more than twice the cost per pupil, and in 13 countries it is over three times. Burundi, for example, spends just US$60 per pupil; only taking into account those pupils who are learning the basics increases its unit cost to US$204, or a total of US$50.3 million, equivalent to 70% of the country's primary education spending.

Figure 4.2: Learning outcomes vary widely between countries

Percentage of children of primary school age who reached grade 4 and achieved minimum learning standard in reading, selected countries

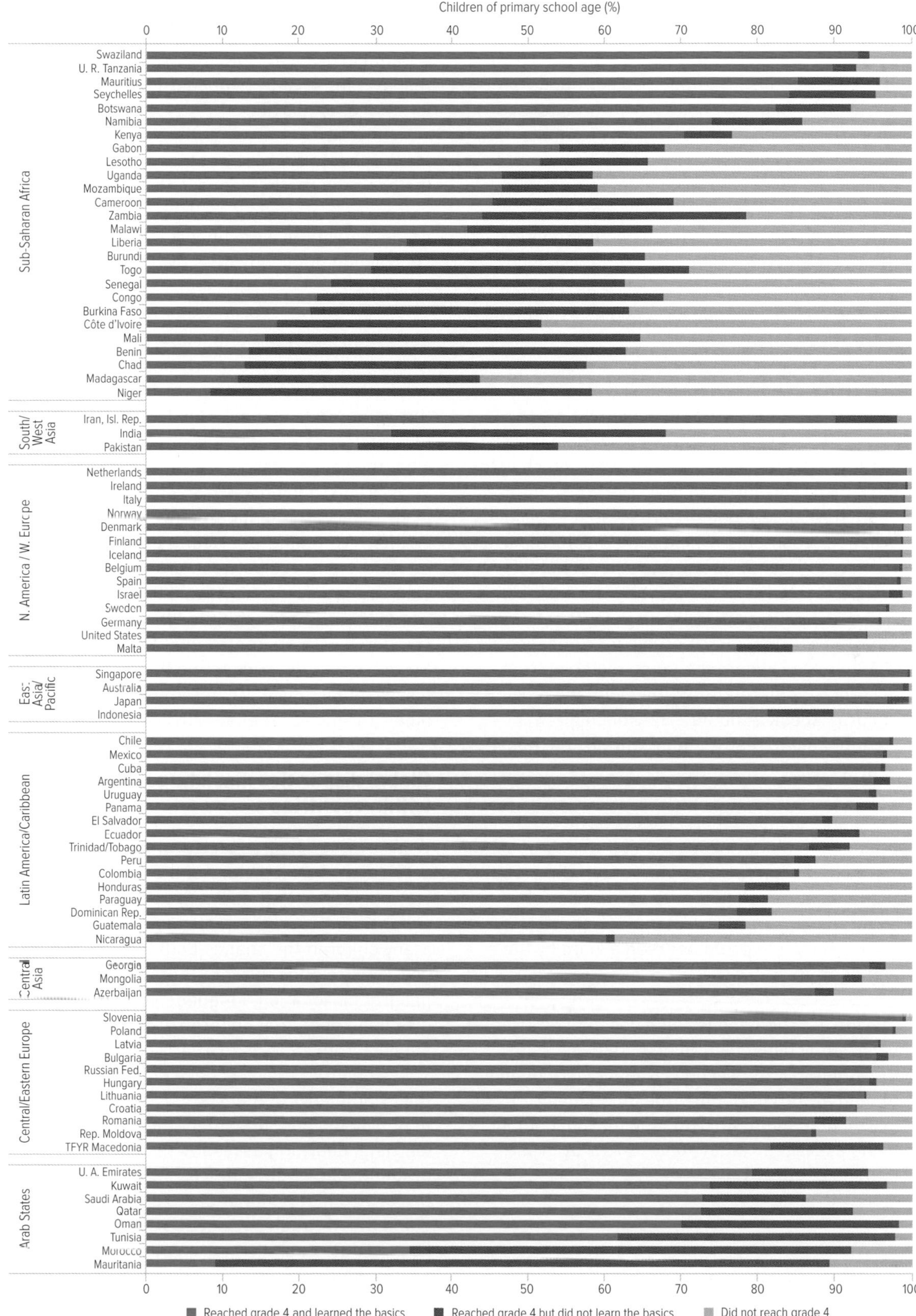

Note: See notes to Figure 4.1.

Sources: EFA Global Monitoring Report team calculations (2013) based on (1) expected cohort survival rate to grade 4: UIS database; (2) learning achievement: Altinok (2013b), using data from the 2011 PIRLS, 2007 SACMEQ, 2004-2008 PASEC, 2006 SERCE; and analysis by the 2012 ASER India and 2012 ASER Pakistan survey teams.

Learning deficits must be tackled early

Learning disparities emerge early in life, before a child even starts school, so children from disadvantaged backgrounds are likely to benefit most from early childhood education opportunities. Evidence from the 2009 PISA assessment found that 15-year-old students who had attended at least a year of pre-primary school outperformed their peers who had not (OECD, 2010). In Argentina, the effect on performance in primary school of attending pre-school was twice as large for students from poor backgrounds as for others (UNESCO, 2012a).

In the poorest countries, millions of children start primary school with little or no experience of pre-school to give them a head start, and suffer from poor nutrition, which holds back their learning potential. The consequences of such weak foundations are evident in early grade assessments, which paint an alarming picture. In 11 of 22 countries, at least half of children tested in grade 2, 3 or 4 were unable to read a single word in the first sentence of a narrative (Global Partnership for Education, 2012). In Mali, where the language of instruction is French – different from the language most children speak at home – 92% of children were unable to read a single word by the end of grade 2.

In Iraq, 61% of grade 2 students were unable to answer a single subtraction question correctly

Language of instruction is not the only problem. In Malawi, 96% of children in grade 2 were unable to read a single word in Chichewa, the language spoken by a large number of children. In parts of Pakistan, 91% of children tested in Pashto could not read a word by the end of grade 2.

Staying in school longer also does not necessarily help children acquire basic skills. In Zambia, 91% of second-graders were unable to read a word in Bemba (the language of instruction and mother tongue for most students being assessed), falling only to 78% by grade 3 (Collins et al., 2012).

There are exceptions, however, suggesting that better quality schools can make a difference. In Rwanda, for example, of those starting in grade 4, only 13% were unable to read a word in Kinyarwanda (Global Partnership for Education, 2012).

Many schools are also not teaching students the basics in mathematics in their early years. In Iraq, 61% of grade 2 students and 41% of grade 3 students were unable to answer a single subtraction question correctly (Brombacher et al., 2012a).

Early grade assessments show that unequal routes in learning start early and the achievement gap widens as children move through primary school. Children need to be able to read accurately and quickly to comprehend what they are reading (Abadzi, 2010). In Jordan, early grade reading assessments conducted in 2012 indicated that differences between children from different wealth groups widened as children moved between grade 2 and 3, with poor students increasing the number of words they read per minute from just 15 to 19, compared with an improvement from 16 to 27 for rich students, suggesting that children's disadvantage has a greater impact as they get older (Brombacher et al., 2012b).

Global disparities mask huge inequalities within countries

While average figures on learning achievement provide an overall picture of the scale of the learning crisis, they can conceal large disparities within countries. Circumstances at birth deny many children the chance both to enter school and to learn once they are there. Poverty, gender, geographic location, language, ethnicity and disability mean that children are likely to get less support from schools to improve their learning. These children may also face difficulties due to their home environment, such as lack of access to nutritious food, that affect their chances of learning. Learning assessments that take into account such circumstances shed light on the disparities that policy-makers should aim to eliminate, through special efforts and measures designed to reach the marginalized.

Poverty denies children the chance to learn

How much a child learns is strongly influenced by the inherited disadvantage that comes with poverty and extreme inequality. In sub-Saharan Africa, being born into the poorest household presents a serious risk of not achieving a strong foundation in learning (Figure 4.3). In all 20 African countries included in this analysis, children from richer households are more likely not only to complete school, but also to achieve a minimum level of learning once in school. In 15 of these countries, no more than one in five poor children reach the last grade and learn the basics.

In Kenya, children have a better chance to learn, on average, but there is a wide gap between rich and poor, mainly because over half of those from poor households drop out early, while only 16% from rich households do so. As a result, around three-quarters of the poor have not achieved the basics, compared with 37% of the rich. Even so, a similar proportion of those from poor households in Kenya are learning as those from rich households in Lesotho, Mozambique and Uganda.

In Namibia, there is vast inequality between rich and poor children. While 40% of those from richer households are in school and learning, only 4% of children from poor backgrounds both complete primary school and achieve the minimum learning level – primarily because they are more likely to leave school before acquiring the basics. Once in school, around half of children are not learning, whether from rich or poor households.

In Malawi, very few children are learning the basics whether rich or poor, but the reasons for this vary. For the poor, the main reason is that only 41% make it to the end of the primary cycle. The rich are more likely to be in school, but the quality of education is so low that 72% are in school but not achieving the minimum learning standards. This leaves only 3% of the poor and 8% of the rich both completing primary education and achieving the basics.

Discrepancies between rich and poor are even more extreme in many west African countries, largely because those from poor households are unable to stay in school. In Burkina Faso, for example, most of those who make it to the end

In African countries, children from richer households are more likely to achieve a minimum level of learning

Figure 4.3. Wealth affects whether primary school age children learn the basics
Percentage of children who completed primary school and achieved minimum learning standard in mathematics, by wealth, Latin America and sub-Saharan Africa

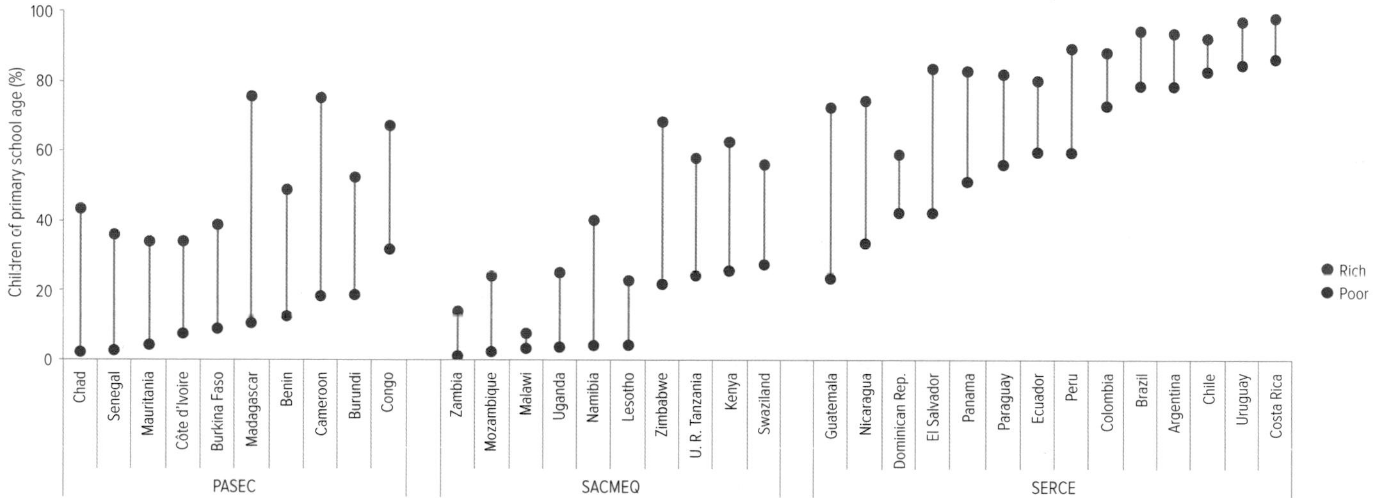

Notes: The definition of primary school completers refers to children aged 14-18 years and is calculated using available household survey data from the year closest to the learning achievement survey. Rich/poor refers to children in the top/bottom quartile in terms of the socio-economic status index in the SERCE, PASEC and SACMEQ surveys. The definition of achievement of a minimum learning standard depends on the benchmark specified in a given survey: level 1 (SERCE); level 1 (PASEC); and level 3 (SACMEQ).
Sources: (1) Primary completion data: for SERCE countries: (2011); for PASEC and SACMEQ countries: EFA Global Monitoring Report team calculations (2013), based on data from Demographic and Health Surveys and Multiple Indicator Cluster Surveys. (2) Learning achievement: Altinok (2013b), based on data from the 2006 SERCE, 2004–2008 PASEC and 2007 SACMEQ surveys.

of the primary cycle are learning the basics. But only a very small number of poor children have this opportunity: around 90% of them do not complete, compared with 54% of the rich.

Even in Latin America, where performance is higher in general, children from disadvantaged backgrounds lag far behind their wealthier peers. Yet patterns of inequality vary among countries. In Chile, Costa Rica and Uruguay, at least 80% of children both complete primary education and achieve the minimum numeracy levels, whether they are rich or poor. However, wealth gaps reach remarkable dimensions in some countries in the region. In El Salvador, 40% of children from the poorest households do not complete primary education compared with 5% of rich children. For those who are still in the education system, wealth gaps in learning outcomes remain large: 42% of children from the poorest households complete primary education and achieve the basics, compared with 84% of those from the richest households. Guatemala not only is one of the poorest performers in the region, but also has the widest gap between rich and poor: almost three-quarters of the rich achieve the basics compared with just one-quarter of the poorest, mainly because the poorest do not make it to the end of the primary cycle.

In Guatemala, almost three-quarters of the rich achieve the basics compared with just one-quarter of the poorest

Being poor and female is a double disadvantage

Wealth-based inequalities are only part of the story. Gender magnifies wealth disparities in learning outcomes for primary school age children. In Benin and Senegal, rich boys perform better than rich girls. Being poor and female also carries a double disadvantage. In Benin, around 60% of rich boys stay in school and attain basic numeracy skills, compared with only 6% of poor girls. Such differences highlight the need to focus policies on eliminating gender gaps (Figure 4.4).

In Kenya and Uganda, gender discrimination for girls occurs among the poorest households. Among the poorest households, 23% of Kenyan girls both complete primary education and achieve the basics, compared with 29% of boys.

Figure 4.4. Poorest girls face the largest barriers to learning
Percentage of children who completed primary school and achieved minimum learning standard in mathematics, by gender and wealth, selected countries, 2005–2007

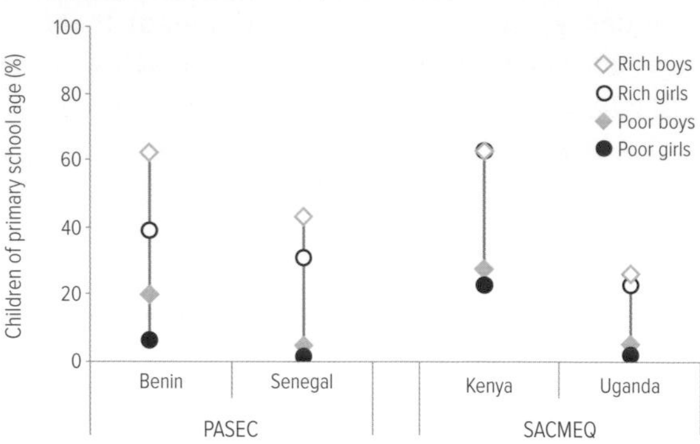

Notes: See notes to Figure 4.3.
Sources: (1) Primary completion: EFA Global Monitoring Report team calculations (2013), based on data from Demographic and Health Surveys. (2) Learning achievement: Altinok (2013b), based on data from PASEC and SACMEQ surveys.

Where children live matters for their learning

Living in rural areas or a disadvantaged part of a country often puts children at a greater risk of not reaching minimum levels of achievement. Living in these areas reinforces disadvantage due to poverty. This in part reflects an unequal distribution of resources to these parts of a country, with schools, teachers and instructional materials often in short supply.

In the United Republic of Tanzania, where average performance in mathematics is better than elsewhere in southern and eastern Africa, only 25% of poor children living in rural areas are in school and learning, compared with 63% of rich children living in urban areas (Altinok, 2013c).

In Ghana, learning disparities associated with geography begin in the early grades and widen through all levels of education. According to national assessment data, the percentage of grade 3 students in urban areas reaching minimum proficiency levels in English in 2011 is twice that of students in rural areas. The difference in learning performance widens by grade 6, with urban students almost three times as likely to achieve minimum reading standards (Ghana Ministry of Education, 2012b).

The rural-urban gap in achievement is also apparent in other parts of the world. In some Latin American countries, including El Salvador, Guatemala, Panama and Peru, the achievement gaps in mathematics and reading between rural and urban students exceed 15 percentage points (Altinok, 2013c).

In addition to the rural-urban divide, regions within countries can have vastly different outcomes. Such geographical disparities within countries often mirror national poverty maps. In South Africa, two of the wealthiest provinces – the Western Cape and Gauteng – registered the highest percentage of students performing above the minimum learning level in mathematics and reading in the 2007 SACMEQ assessment (Spaull, 2011). In these two provinces, almost 60% of students perform above the minimum learning level in mathematics while in the poorest province, Limpopo, only 11% of students are able to do so (Moloi and Chetty, 2010).

Geographical disadvantage is often aggravated by poverty and gender. New analysis for this Report of Annual Status of Education Reports (ASERs) for rural India and Pakistan provides a stark illustration of how disadvantages interact. In rural India, there are wide disparities between richer and poorer states, but even within richer states, the poorest girls perform at much lower levels. In the wealthier states of Maharashtra and Tamil Nadu, most rural children reached grade 5 in 2012. However, only 44% of these children in the grade 5 age group in Maharashtra and 53% in Tamil Nadu could perform a two-digit subtraction (Figure 4.5A). Among rich, rural children in these states, girls performed better than boys, with around two out of three girls able to do the calculations. Yet despite Maharashtra's relative wealth, poor, rural girls there performed only slightly better than their counterparts in the poorer state of Madhya Pradesh.

In the wealthier Indian state of Maharashtra, only 44% of rural children in grade 5 can perform a two-digit subtraction

Widespread poverty in Madhya Pradesh and Uttar Pradesh affects the chance of staying in school until grade 5. In Uttar Pradesh, 70% of

Figure 4.5: In India and Pakistan, poor girls are least likely to be able to do basic calculations
Percentage of all 10- and 11-year-olds able to do a two-digit subtraction, by gender and wealth, selected states/provinces of rural India and rural Pakistan, 2012

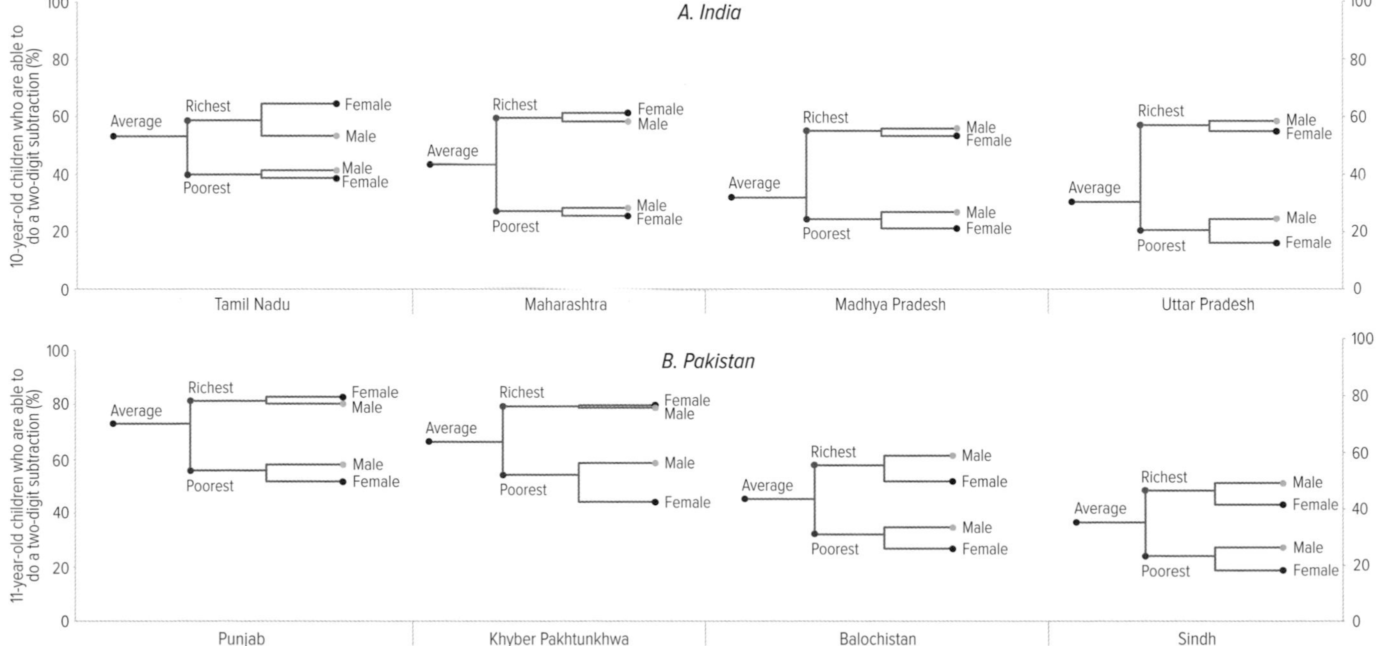

Notes: The analysis includes all children aged 10 (India) and 11 (Pakistan), whether in school or not. Richest/poorest refers to children in the bottom/top quartile of the ASER socio-economic status index.
Sources: Analysis by the 2012 ASER India and ASER Pakistan survey teams.

poor children make it to grade 5 while almost all children from rich households are able to do so. Similarly, in Madhya Pradesh, 85% of poor children reach grade 5, compared with 96% of rich children. Once in school, poor girls have a lower chance of learning the basics: no more than one in five poor girls in Madhya Pradesh and Uttar Pradesh are able to do basic mathematics. The huge disparities within India point to a failure to target support adequately towards those who need it most.

Opportunities to acquire basic skills are also extremely unequal in rural Pakistan, with some provinces doing much better than others (Figure 4.5B). In Balochistan, only 45% of all children of grade 5 age (whether in school or not) could solve a two-digit subtraction, while in the wealthier province of Punjab, 73% could do so.[2] One reason for the difference is the chance of a child getting into school and staying until grade 5: 53% reach grade 5 in Balochistan and 69% in Punjab. Another reason is that the conditions of schooling are considerably better in Punjab: of those in grade 5, 84% knew how to subtract two-digit numbers, compared with 71% in Balochistan.

In Peru, Spanish speakers are more than seven times as likely as indigenous language speakers to reach a satisfactory standard in reading

The interaction between geography, gender and poverty is a potent source of exclusion. Even in the wealthier Punjab province, only around half of poor girls of grade 5 age could do a simple subtraction, compared with more than 80% of rich boys. Girls from poor households in Balochistan face acute learning deficits – only around one-quarter achieved basic numeracy skills, while boys from rich households fared much better, approaching the average in Punjab.

Speaking a minority language can be a source of disadvantage

Being born into a minority ethnic or linguistic group can seriously affect not only children's chance of being in school, but also whether they learn once there. Language and ethnicity are deeply intertwined. While the language a child speaks at home is often a crucial element of personal identity and group attachment, language can be a potent source of disadvantage at school because in many countries children are taught and take tests in languages they do not speak at home. Their parents may also lack literacy skills or familiarity with official languages used in school. Well-designed bilingual programmes taught by qualified teachers can enable children to learn in their mother tongue as well as the official language.

According to the 2011 PIRLS assessment, in seven countries at least 10% of students reported speaking a different language at home from the one they were tested in. In all these countries, their likelihood of achieving minimum learning standards in reading was lower than for students whose home language was the language of assessment. In the Islamic Republic of Iran, around one-fifth of those taking the test in Farsi, the official language of instruction, reported speaking a different language at home. Of these, only about half reached the minimum learning standard, compared with over 80% of Farsi speakers (Altinok, 2013c).

In many parts of western Africa, French continues to be the main language of instruction, so the vast majority of children are taught from the early grades in a language with which they are not familiar, seriously hampering their chance of learning. In Benin, for example, over 80% of grade 5 students who speak the test language at home achieve minimum learning in reading, compared with less than 60% of the 9 out of 10 students who speak another language (Altinok, 2013c).

Indigenous groups often face discrimination in school that is reinforced by the fact that the language used in the classroom may not be one that they speak. In Peru, test score gaps between indigenous and non-indigenous children in grade 2 are sizeable and increasing. In 2011, Spanish speakers were more than seven times as likely as indigenous language speakers to reach a satisfactory standard in reading. The change was mainly due to improvements in learning among Spanish speakers; the proportion of indigenous speakers reaching a satisfactory level remained the same at around 4% (Guadalupe et al., 2013).

Bilingual programmes in Peru aim to ensure that children can learn in their own language together with Spanish. However, children attending these programmes perform badly in both languages. By grade 4, only 1 in 10 Quechua speakers in bilingual programmes, and 1 in

2. Similar differences arise when it comes to literacy skills. In Balochistan, only 24% of all 11-year-olds could read a text in their own language, compared with almost 60% in Punjab.

20 speakers of other indigenous languages, reach a satisfactory level in their own language. Their achievement in Spanish is similarly weak (Guadalupe et al., 2013). This highlights the importance not only of providing instruction in a child's own language, but also of ensuring that schools are of sufficient quality to ensure that learning takes place. One study found that half of teachers in bilingual education schools in southern Peru could not speak the local indigenous language (Cueto et al., 2009).

In mathematics, too, language, culture and poverty often interact to produce an extremely high risk of being left far behind. Poor students speaking a minority language at home are among the lowest performers. In Turkey, for instance, poor grade 4 students speaking a non-Turkish language – predominantly Kurdish – are the lowest performers in the TIMSS assessment. Around 40% of poor non-Turkish speakers achieve minimum learning benchmarks in mathematics, just over half the national average (Altinok, 2013c).

Similarly, of poor rural students in Guatemala speaking a minority language (mostly indigenous) at home, only 47% reach the minimum achievement level in mathematics while 88% reach that level among rich urban students speaking Spanish (Altinok, 2013c). The problem goes beyond schools rarely addressing linguistic diversity: more than half of the achievement gap between indigenous and non-indigenous speakers is attributed to the fact that indigenous children attend schools with fewer instructional materials, lower quality infrastructure and less qualified teachers (McEwan and Trowbridge, 2007). This underscores the importance of redressing such deficits to improve learning outcomes for indigenous children.

Children who learn less are more likely to drop out

Children who fail to develop reading and numeracy skills in their early years are unable to take advantage of further learning opportunities in and out of school. Their commitment to education is likely to diminish and they are more likely to drop out.

In Burundi, Chad and Côte d'Ivoire, for example, those tested at the beginning of grade 5 who did not reach the minimum learning level in French and mathematics were less likely to take part in the follow-up test at the end of the school year. In Côte d'Ivoire, 75% of children who reached the minimum learning level at the beginning of grade 5 were present to take the test at the end of the school year, compared with 25% of those who did not reach it (Altinok, 2013c). This suggests that academic performance at the beginning of the year influences the risk of missing school days or dropping out before the end of the academic year.

In Turkey, only 40% of poor non-Turkish speakers achieve minimum learning benchmarks in mathematics

Research carried out for this Report using a unique data set tracking children over time in Ethiopia, India (Andhra Pradesh), Peru and Viet Nam provides further evidence that weak learning leads to children dropping out. In all four countries, children who achieved lower scores in mathematics at age 12 were more likely to drop out by age 15 than those who performed better. In Viet Nam, for instance, almost half of the poorer performers at age 12 had dropped out by age 15, compared with around one in five of the stronger performers (Figure 4.6). The causes of poor learning and early dropout may be linked. Children from poorer households are more likely to be absent due to ill health or because they have to work for the family, for example – factors that would affect both their performance in school and the likelihood of their dropping out.

Figure 4.6: Weaker learners are more likely to drop out
Percentage of children in school at age 12 in 2006 who had dropped out by age 15 in 2009, by level of achievement in mathematics at age 12, Ethiopia, India, Peru and Viet Nam

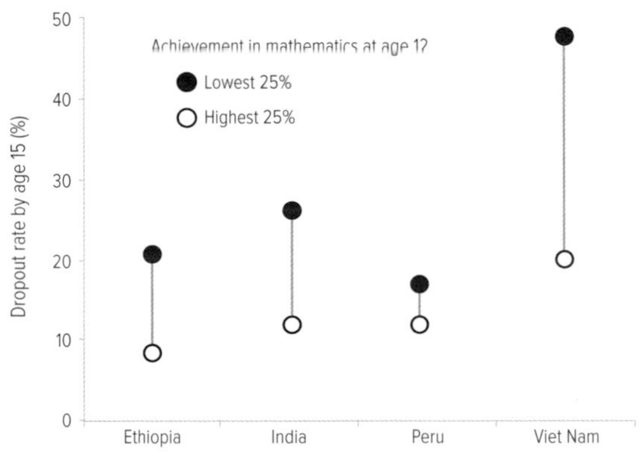

Source: Rolleston et al. (2013), based on Young Lives surveys.

Disadvantage continues into secondary school

In Chile, the learning gap between rich and poor is narrow at grade 4 but widens by grade 8

Many of the most marginalized children do not make it to secondary school. Among those who do, the problems faced in early years in school continue to mark them out for underperformance, even in countries with more resources, according to the latest TIMSS data for grade 8 students. In South Africa, for example, there is a vast gap in learning between rich and poor, with only 14% of poor adolescents achieving the minimum standard in mathematics. This is comparable to the performance of poor students in Ghana, a country that has less than one-fifth of the wealth of South Africa (Figure 4.7).

Such wealth gaps are not inevitable. Botswana has achieved much higher levels of learning, thanks to its much narrower gap between rich and poor. While South Africa's performance is similar to the worst performing, poorer countries participating in the TIMSS assessment, Botswana is at the level of upper middle income countries in other regions. The poorest in Botswana have a similar chance of reaching the minimum benchmark as their counterparts in Chile, Jordan and Turkey, which perform better, on average.

In some countries, the gap between rich and poor becomes more apparent in later grades. In Chile, for example, while the gap is narrow at grade 4, 77% of rich students achieve the minimum standards by grade 8, compared with 44% of poor students. Chile's education reforms in recent years have, if anything, resulted in a widening of inequality, leading students to protest for change. Similarly, in Turkey, the gap widens from grade 4 to grade 8, with rich students being twice as likely as poor students to achieve minimum standards by grade 8.

Adolescents from poor households perform badly in secondary school particularly in rural areas. In several countries, the urban and rural poor face similar disadvantage in learning. In Colombia, for instance, only around 10% of poor urban and rural students reach the minimum standards in mathematics, compared with 55% of the urban and rural rich (Figure 4.8).

Figure 4.7: Poverty holds back learning in lower secondary school
Percentage of grade 8 students scoring above the low international benchmark in mathematics, by wealth, selected countries, 2011 TIMSS

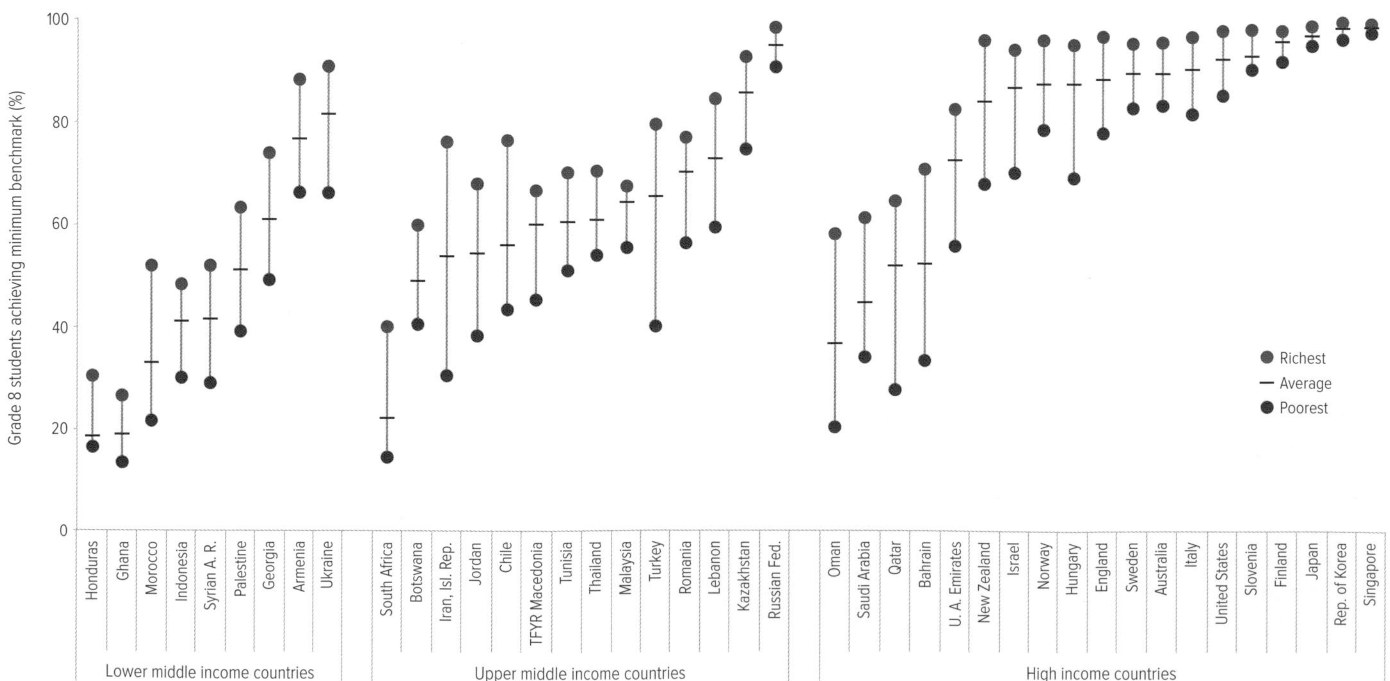

Note: Richest/poorest refers to students in the top/bottom quartile in the TIMSS socio-economic status index.
Source: Altinok (2013c), based on 2011 TIMSS data.

Figure 4.8: In secondary school, the weakest learners are the poor in rural areas
Percentage of 15-year-olds at or above level 2 in mathematics, by wealth and location, selected countries, 2009 PISA

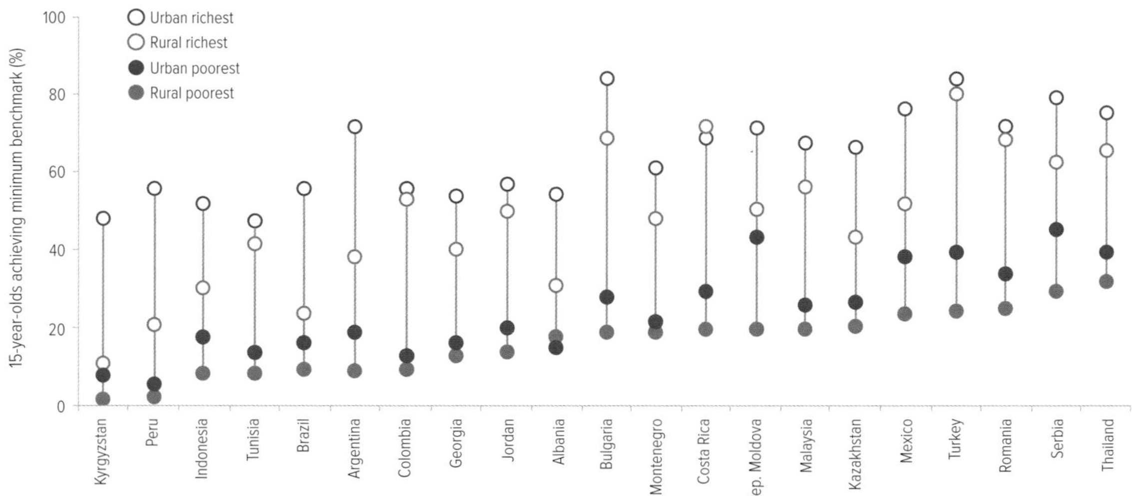

Note: Richest/poorest refers to students in the top/bottom quartile in the PISA economic, social and cultural status index.
Source: Altinok (2012), based on 2009 PISA data.

Inequality is often particularly marked among those within urban areas. In Argentina, more than 70% of all 15-year-olds from rich urban households acquire the basics in mathematics, compared with only 18% of the urban poor.

The gap between rich and poor is wider in urban than in rural areas partly because even the rich in rural areas do not have access to schools of sufficient quality to enable them to reach an adequate standard of learning. In Brazil and Peru, for example, the performance of the rural rich is closer to the very low levels of the rural poor than to the higher levels of the urban rich.

Rich countries are also failing to ensure that the marginalized can learn

While rich countries' achievement levels are generally higher, their education systems also fail significant minorities. For example, over 10% of grade 8 students in England and Norway performed below minimum learning levels in mathematics in 2011. Unless countries tackle inequality by reaching groups marginalized by poverty, immigrant status and other factors associated with wider disadvantage, they will fail to achieve the standards of learning that all their citizens expect and deserve.

Poorer children learn less

In OECD countries, such as England, Italy, New Zealand and Norway, children born into poor households risk learning less than other students.[3] This is also the case for wealthy countries in the Arab States, including Bahrain, Oman, Qatar, Saudi Arabia and the United Arab Emirates (see Figure 4.7). The chance of a poor student in Oman making it over the minimum learning threshold is similar to that of a student in less wealthy countries, such as Ghana or South Africa, on average.

The 2011 TIMSS assessment further shows that the gap between rich and poor widens as children progress through the system in many high income countries. While students from wealthy backgrounds are almost all able to reach the minimum standards in both grade 4 and grade 8, the chances of poor students doing so diminish as they get older. In England, for example, the gap between rich and poor is 8 percentage points at grade 4, but widens to 19 percentage points by grade 8. Evidence from

Over 10% of grade 8 students in England performed below minimum learning levels in mathematics

3. This evidence from 2011 TIMSS is supported by PISA results. An analysis of OECD countries participating in the 2009 PISA reading tests reveals that socio-economically disadvantaged students run a much higher risk of being among the poorest performers (OECD, 2010). On average, a socio-economically advantaged student scores 88 points higher than a socio-economically disadvantaged student, a difference equivalent to more than two years of schooling (OECD, 2013d).

England's national report from the 2009 PISA assessment also shows the problems poor students face in school: reading skills of children from disadvantaged backgrounds were, on average, two and half years behind those from the most affluent backgrounds by the end of compulsory schooling at age 16 (Jerrim, 2012).

In New Zealand, while almost all rich students achieved the minimum standards, only around two-thirds of poor students did so

In Australia and New Zealand, the outlook for poor students is particularly bleak, with wide wealth gaps persisting in both grade 4 and grade 8. In New Zealand, while almost all rich students achieved the minimum standards in both grades, only around two-thirds of poor students did so (Figure 4.9). A poor student in New Zealand has a similar chance of reaching the benchmark as a student in Turkey, on average.

Such gaps in performance between rich and poor pupils are not inevitable. In East Asian countries, including Japan, the Republic of Korea and Singapore, all students make it over the lowest threshold of learning. This is also the case for Finland. What marks these countries out is that they have implemented programmes specifically designed to promote equitable learning, including investing in quality teachers (see Chapter 6).

Figure 4.9: Wide learning disparities exist in developed countries
Percentage of students scoring above the low international benchmark in mathematics, by wealth and grade, selected countries, 2011 TIMSS

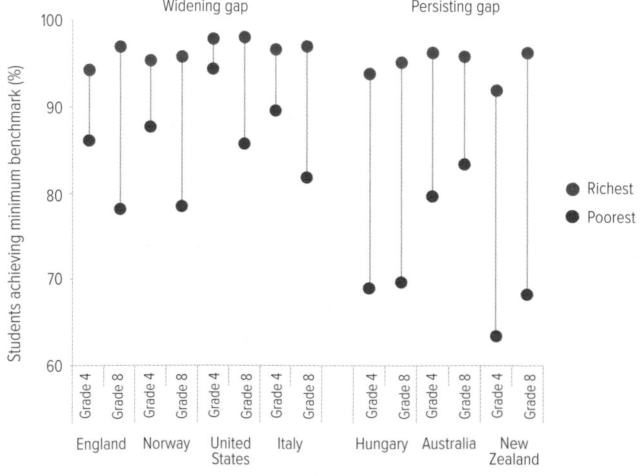

Note: Richest/poorest refers to students in the top/bottom quartile in the TIMSS socio-economic status index.
Source: Altinok (2013c), based on 2011 TIMSS data.

Immigrants and indigenous groups lag behind in developed countries

Even in better performing rich countries, immigrant students face a high risk of marginalization in education, resulting in lower levels of learning achievement. In France, Germany and the United Kingdom, over 80% of 15-year-old students achieve the minimum benchmark in reading, on average. But immigrants perform far worse: in the United Kingdom, the proportion of immigrants making it above the minimum benchmark is no better than the average for Turkey, while Germany's immigrants are on a par with students in Chile (Figure 4.10). Immigrants in France face particular problems, with 60% passing the minimum benchmark – equivalent to the average for students in Mexico.

Broad comparisons of children in immigrant and non-immigrant families may mask differences in the experiences of first-generation immigrants, as well as variations by age at arrival and country of origin. A cross-country analysis of PISA 2009 data found that achievement gaps were wider for young immigrants who had arrived more recently and who did not speak the test language at home (Cobb-Clark et al., 2012).

The difficulty indigenous children face is one reason for the wide gaps in learning between rich and poor students in Australia and New Zealand. Though these gaps are clearly visible in student assessments, they have not received sufficient policy attention, and so have persisted for a decade and a half. In Australia, around two-thirds of indigenous students achieved the minimum benchmark in mathematics in grade 8 between 1994/95 and 2011, compared with almost 90% of their non-indigenous peers (Figure 4.11).

Figure 4.10: Weak learners in rich countries perform as badly as students in some middle income countries
Percentage of 15-year-old students at or above level 2 in reading, immigrants and non-immigrants, selected countries, 2009 PISA

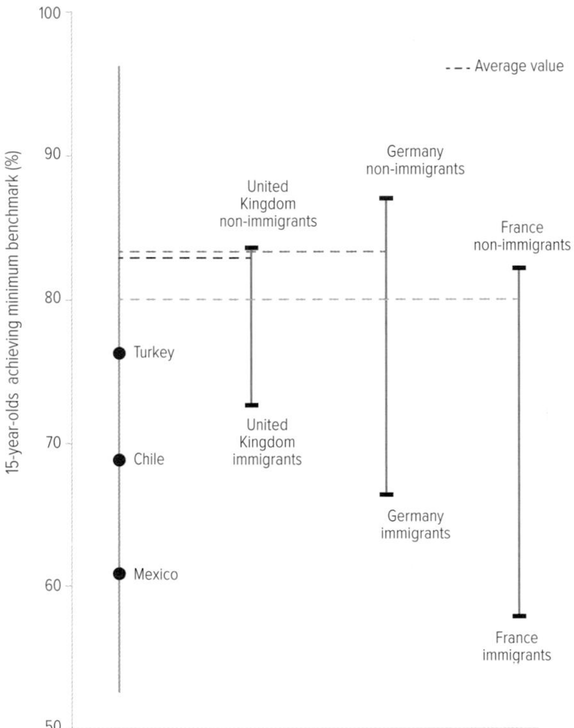

Source: EFA Global Monitoring Report team analysis of Altinok (2012), based on 2009 PISA data.

Figure 4.11: In Australia, learning gaps persist between indigenous and non-indigenous students
Percentage of grade 8 students scoring above the low international benchmark in mathematics, 1994–2011 TIMSS

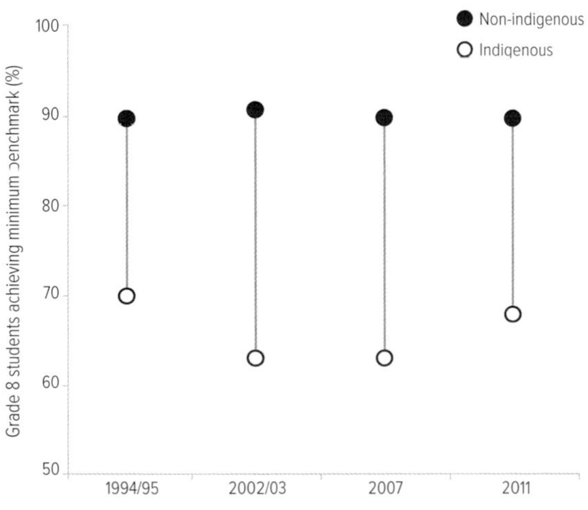

Source: Thomson et al. (2012), based on 1994/95, 2002/03, 2007 and 2011 TIMSS data.

Improving learning while expanding access

With more children entering and completing primary school than ever before, it is often claimed that expanding access inevitably means lowering the quality of education. While vast numbers of children are not learning the basics, some countries have been able to get more children into school while ensuring that they learn once there. This balance is particularly impressive given that new entrants are more likely to come from marginalized households where they tend to have experienced malnutrition and poverty, and where the parents are often illiterate and unable to help them with their studies. Even so, far more needs to be done to bridge the learning gap more quickly, even in richer countries.

Access and learning: a trade-off is not inevitable

Countries have widely varying results in their efforts to provide all students with high quality schooling. Comparing experiences within countries over time can provide a picture of how to increase not only the number of children who get into school, but also the number who learn.

Kenya has made great strides in the numbers reaching the end of primary school and in improving learning

Some countries in southern and eastern Africa have expanded education coverage considerably – especially in primary schooling – while also safeguarding or even improving learning outcomes (Figure 4.12). They have achieved these results even though many children entering school for the first time between the two SACMEQ survey periods (2000 and 2007) came from disadvantaged backgrounds and would be expected to face the greatest challenges in learning. While the quality of education was already low at the beginning of the decade in much of Africa and has not yet reached acceptable levels, this progress calls into question the widespread claim that quality has deteriorated overall as a result of education expansion.

In all eight countries of the subregion with data, the numbers of children entering and completing school rose between 2000 and 2007. Most notably, Kenya and the United Republic of Tanzania made great strides in the numbers reaching the end of primary school, partly

Figure 4.12: Some countries in southern and eastern Africa have both widened access and improved learning
Percentage of children who completed primary school and achieved minimum learning standard in mathematics, selected countries, 2000 and 2007 SACMEQ

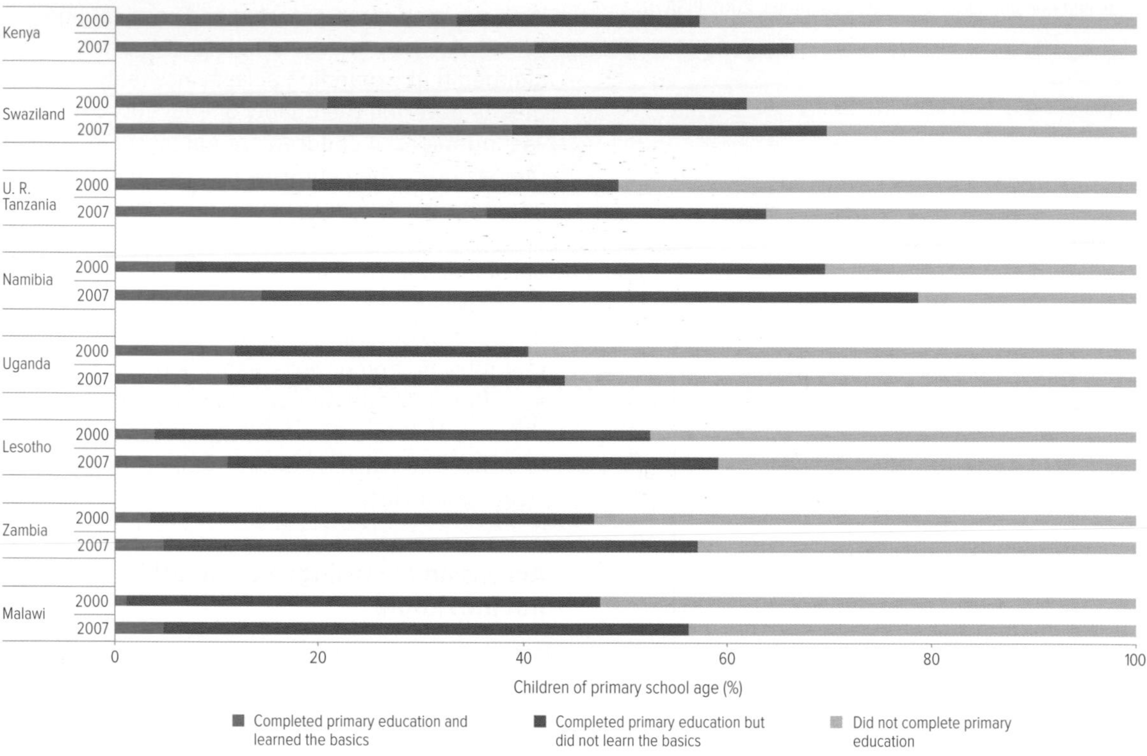

Notes: The definition of primary school completers refers to children aged 14 to 18 and is calculated using a linear interpolation from household survey data around years close to the learning achievement surveys.
Sources: (1) Primary completion: EFA Global Monitoring Report team calculations (2013), based on data from Demographic and Health Surveys. (2) Learning achievement: Altinok (2013c), based on 2007 SACMEQ data, and Hungi et al. (2010), based on 2000 SACMEQ data.

In the United Republic of Tanzania, between 2000 and 2007 around 1.5 million additional children learned the basics

because they abolished primary school fees (the United Republic of Tanzania in 2001 and Kenya in 2003). At the same time, learning outcomes also improved. In the United Republic of Tanzania between 2000 and 2007, the proportion of children who completed primary school rose from half to around two-thirds, while the proportion who were both in school and learning the basics in mathematics increased from 19% to 36%. This is equivalent to around 1.5 million additional children learning the basics. While it is still unacceptable that 27% were in school but not learning the basics, the fact that the problems with quality were already apparent in 2000 suggests that they are more inherent in the education system than directly associated with education expansion.[4]

In Uganda, by contrast, there was a more modest rise in the proportion completing primary school, from 40% in 2000 to 44% in 2007, but learning stagnated, with only around 11% of primary school age children learning the basics. Malawi and Zambia also struggled with both access and quality. Despite having made some progress in the proportion of children completing, around 40% still did not do so in both countries in 2007. Learning improved slightly, but from an extremely low base, so by 2007 only 5% were in school and learning. In these countries, the problem goes beyond quality alone: urgent reform is needed across the education system to ensure children stay in school and learn once they are there.

4. The results of a recent study support this finding, showing that education expansion since 2000 has contributed to higher levels of literacy and numeracy in southern and eastern Africa (Taylor and Spaull, 2013).

Progress in learning needs to reach the poor

Most countries need not only to improve access and quality, but also to ensure that progress is shared equally among various population groups, which often means making a special effort to reach the most disadvantaged.

In the two countries in southern and eastern Africa whose performance improved significantly between 2000 and 2007 – Kenya and the United Republic of Tanzania – children from both poor and rich households benefited from the progress. However, in the United Republic of Tanzania, those from poor households started from an extremely low base: fewer than 1 in 10 achieved the basics in 2000, and by 2007 poor children were still far from reaching the learning levels that the rich had already attained in 2000 (Figure 4.13).

In two countries where access and quality did not improve significantly between 2000 and 2007 – Malawi and Uganda – the gap between rich and poor in learning widened, if anything. In Malawi, learning remained extremely low for both rich and poor. Uganda's experience is of particular concern: learning improved slightly among the richest but the proportion of the poorest learning the basics declined, from an already very low base. These countries face a serious triple challenge, needing to strengthen access, quality and equity.

In Uganda, between 2000 and 2007, the proportion of the poorest learning the basics declined

These findings show that it is vital for countries to make improving access and learning among disadvantaged children a high priority. Support should be targeted at schools serving poor families, addressing the constraints that poor households face in getting children into school and ensuring that poor children learn once they are in school.

Progress in learning trickles down more slowly to disadvantaged areas

Learning deficits are often concentrated in parts of countries with fewer resources, notably rural areas and poorer regions. When little attempt

Figure 4.13: Despite progress, the poor still lag behind in learning
Percentage of children who completed primary school and achieved minimum learning standard in mathematics, by wealth, selected countries, 2000 and 2007 SACMEQ

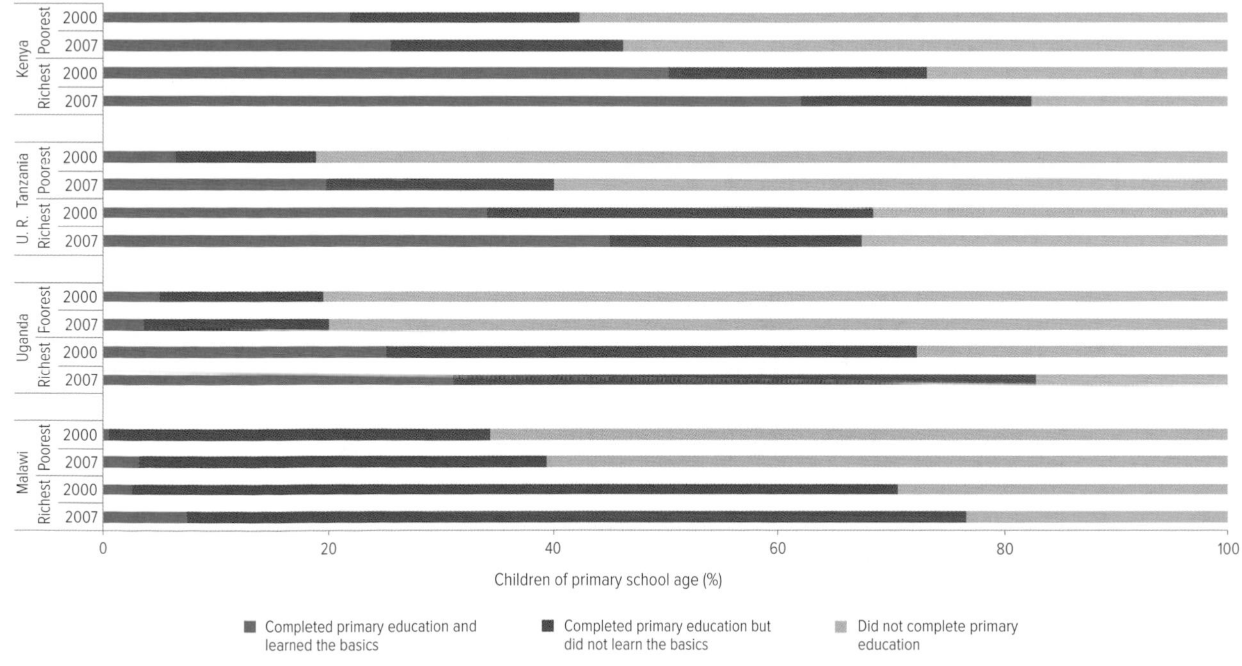

Notes: The definition of primary school completers refers to children aged 14 to 18 and is calculated using a linear interpolation from household survey data around years close to the learning achievement surveys. Richest/poorest refers to pupils in the top/bottom quartile of the SACMEQ socio-economic status index.
Sources: (1) Primary completion: EFA Global Monitoring Report team calculations (2013), based on data from Demographic and Health Surveys. (2) Learning achievement: Altinok (2013c), based on 2007 SACMEQ data, and Hungi et al. (2010), based on 2000 SACMEQ data.

is made to redistribute resources, including teaching and learning resources, to these areas, gaps in learning are likely to persist.

Mexico has improved learning among the disadvantaged through targeted policies

In Peru, for example, learning has improved in recent years on average, but has yet to reach those in disadvantaged areas. Between 2007 and 2011, the proportion of grade 2 students reaching adequate proficiency increased from 16% to 30% in reading and from 7% to 13% in mathematics, according to national assessment data. However, while the proportion of those in urban areas who achieved the benchmark in mathematics increased from 9% to 16%, the proportion achieving this level in rural areas stagnated at just 4%. A similar gap separates those in wealthier areas from those in poorer areas (Guadalupe et al., 2013).

In Kenya, there is a more promising picture of improving learning in some of the most disadvantaged parts of the country, though admittedly from a very low base. According to the national assessment, average achievement at the end of grade 8 remained much the same between the expansion of primary school enrolment in 2003 and the graduation of the first cohort benefiting from free primary education in 2010. However, the picture varies within the country. Arid and semi-arid areas such as Garissa, Mandera, Turkana and Wajir started from a very low base in both access and learning, but showed progress. By contrast, Nairobi's enrolment increased but results in the grade 8 examination did not improve, partly because the quality of education was poor for the large numbers of children living in slums, whether they studied in private or government schools (Oketch and Mutisya, 2013).

In secondary education, access and achievement can increase side by side

While middle income countries achieved near universal primary education some time ago, enrolment continues to increase at the secondary level. Some of these countries have not only expanded secondary schooling, but have also used targeted policies to improve access and quality for disadvantaged groups, showing what can be achieved when governments take direct action.

Mexico illustrates this pattern. The share of students performing at or above the minimum benchmark rose from one-third in 2003 to half in 2009. Both poor and rich registered increases of 15 percentage points (Figure 4.14). Over the same period, enrolment of 15-year-olds increased by nearly eight percentage points. Targeted programmes to improve learning among children who were being left behind contributed to this broad-based progress.

Figure 4.14: In Mexico, progress in access and learning benefitted the poorest

Percentage of students achieving minimum learning standard in mathematics, by gender and wealth, selected countries, 2003 and 2011 TIMSS and 2003 and 2009 PISA

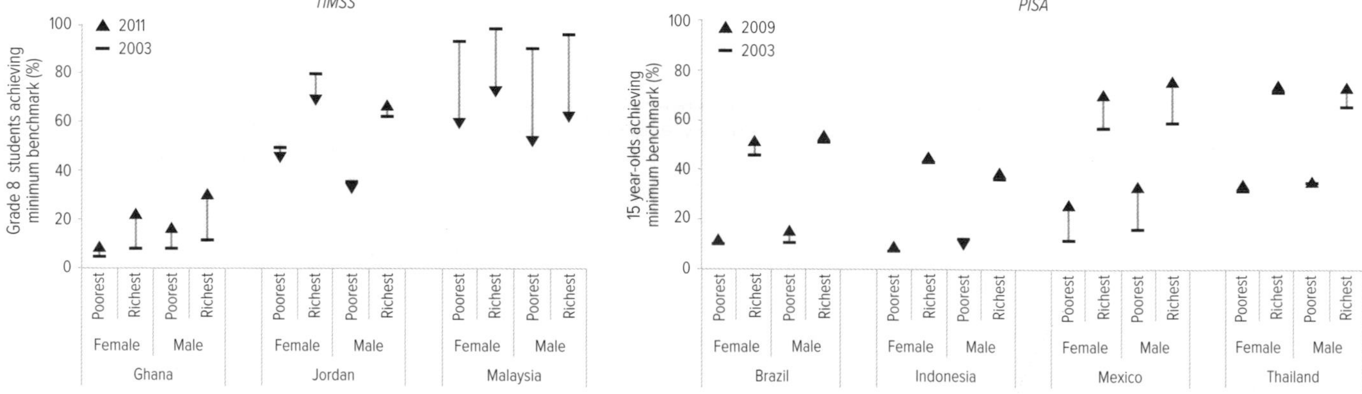

Note: Richest/poorest refers to students in the top/bottom quartile of the TIMSS socio-economic status index and the PISA economic, social and cultural status index.
Sources: Altinok (2013c) for 2011 TIMSS; EFA Global Monitoring Report team analysis (2013) for 2003 TIMSS; Altinok (2012) for 2003 and 2009 PISA.

The Consejo Nacional de Fomento Educativo (National Education Development Council, CONAFE) provides supplemental funds, learning materials – including textbooks in indigenous languages – and teacher support to schools in areas with consistent underperformance and disadvantage. Evaluations indicate that these efforts have narrowed the gap in primary school mathematics scores (Vegas and Petrow, 2008). Despite this impressive progress, the country needs to continue to target policies at disadvantaged groups and areas to ensure not only that progress is evenly spread but also that inequality is narrowed.

While other countries have also made major progress in both expanding access and improving learning outcomes, they have not always been as successful at addressing inequality. In Ghana, the secondary net enrolment ratio rose from 35% in 2003 to 46% in 2009. Over the same period, Ghana recorded a 10 percentage point increase in the proportion making it over the minimum threshold for numeracy at grade 8, admittedly from a very low level of 9% in 2003. This progress was not evenly spread, however; while the richest students benefited, there was less change for the poorest. Gender gaps also more than doubled, with boys continuing to be more likely to reach the minimum benchmark, whether rich or poor.

Inequality also remained wide in countries with longer experience of increasing access, such as Thailand, where the limited progress in improving minimum standards of learning benefited the rich, while only around one-third of the poor made it across the minimum threshold in both 2003 and 2009.

It is clear from this evidence that Ghana, Thailand and countries in a similar situation need urgently to identify policies that not only ensure progress in access and learning, but also guarantee that this progress reaches disadvantaged groups.

Jordan and Malaysia experienced a more worrying trend of worsening learning outcomes coupled with widening inequality, while the number of adolescents out of school also increased. Malaysia witnessed the largest decline in test scores of all countries participating in TIMSS over the decade. In 2003, the vast majority of adolescents passed the minimum benchmark in Malaysia, whether rich or poor. However, standards appear to have declined substantially over the decade, particularly for the poorest boys, only around half of whom reached the minimum benchmark in 2011, compared with over 90% in 2003. Poorest boys moved from being similar to average performers in the United States to similar to those in Botswana.

In Malaysia, learning standards have declined over the decade

Jordan's declining trend was more modest but still a cause for concern. On average, girls had a better chance of achieving the minimum benchmark than boys, with girls from rich households doing particularly well. However, the gap between rich boys and girls narrowed over the decade because girls' performance declined. Meanwhile, the chance of those from poor households reaching the minimum benchmark declined slightly, with around one-third of poor boys and half of poor girls achieving the benchmark. Both Jordan and Malaysia need to implement measures that reverse the downward spiral of worsening access and quality, while ensuring that gaps between rich and poor, and between boys and girls, narrow.

Even when learning outcomes are improving and access is expanding, there is no room for complacency. In Indonesia, the share of 15-year-olds achieving the minimum level of learning in mathematics increased from 20% in 2003 to 34% in 2006, which was particularly impressive given the increased enrolment of more disadvantaged children in the school system. This improvement seems to have been achieved through a combination of better school management and an improved supply of trained teachers (Barrera-Osorio et al., 2011). Between 2006 and 2009, however, Indonesia reverted to its 2003 position for both poor and rich (see Figure 4.14).[5]

5. The declining trend in Indonesia's performance in the late 2000s was echoed in TIMSS results. The share of grade 8 students reaching the low international benchmark in mathematics slipped from 48% in 2007 to 43% in 2011.

Poor quality education leaves a legacy of illiteracy

The quality of education during childhood has a marked bearing on youth and adult literacy. Young people who have never been to school, or who have spent just a few years in school, almost inevitably join the ranks of illiterate adults. But even completing primary school is not a guarantee of becoming literate.

Around 175 million young people living in low and lower middle income countries are unable even to read all or part of a sentence

Data on illiteracy are often based on asking people whether or not they can read or write, rather than actually testing their reading skills. These figures are likely to underestimate the full extent of illiteracy. New analysis for this Report, based on testing young people's reading skills as part of Demographic and Health Surveys, finds that youth illiteracy is more widespread than often suggested: around 175 million young people living in low and lower middle income countries are unable even to read all or part of a sentence.[6] This represents over one-quarter of the youth population in the countries concerned. Youth illiteracy is particularly widespread in sub-Saharan Africa, where 40% of young people are not able to read a sentence (Figure 4.15).

Despite recent advances in girls' education, a generation of young women has been left behind, comprising around 61% of youth who are not literate. The gender gap is particularly wide in South and West Asia, where two out of three of those who cannot read are young women.

Comparisons among countries reveal an even starker picture of the widespread problems of illiteracy. In 9 of the 41 low and lower middle income countries for which data are available for both men and women, more than half of 15- to 24-year-olds are not literate. With the exception of Chad, all these countries are in western Africa. Some countries only tested the literacy of young women.

6. Recent Demographic and Health Surveys ask respondents who have never studied in secondary school to read a short sentence from a card. The interviewer records whether the respondent can read all or part of the sentence. If respondents have reached secondary school, they are assumed to be literate and the question is not asked.

Figure 4.15: Less than three-quarters of young people in low and lower middle income countries are literate

Youth literacy rate, by gender, selected regions and country income groups

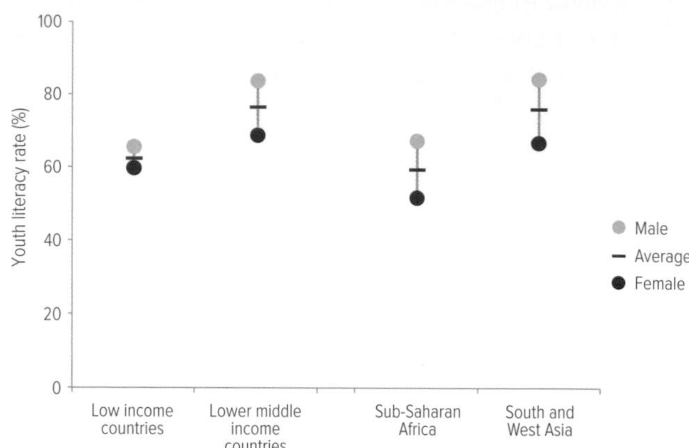

Source: EFA Global Monitoring Report team analysis (2013), based on Demographic and Health Survey data.

Spending no more than four years in school can be a route to illiteracy

It is commonly assumed that children need to spend at least four years in school to become literate, and to retain their literacy into adulthood. This assumption is confirmed by the new analysis: among young people who have spent four years or less in school, around 77% are not able to read all or part of a sentence.

For most regions and countries, spending too little time in school is a key factor in not acquiring basic literacy. In 9 of the 41 countries analysed, more than half of young people have spent no more than four years in school, and almost all of them are not literate. In Niger, for example, almost 75% of young people have spent fewer than four years in school. Of those who have left within this period, only 2% gained literacy skills. Even in the other 32 countries, where fewer leave school before grade 4, those who do so are less likely to have learned the basics. In Uganda in 2011, for example, of the young people who did not make it beyond grade 4, only 17% were able to read (Figure 4.16).

But there are exceptions. Almost half of young people had not spent more than four years in school in Rwanda in 2010, but more than 50%

Figure 4.16: Many young people emerge from several years of primary education without basic literacy skills
Youth literacy rate, by years of schooling, selected countries

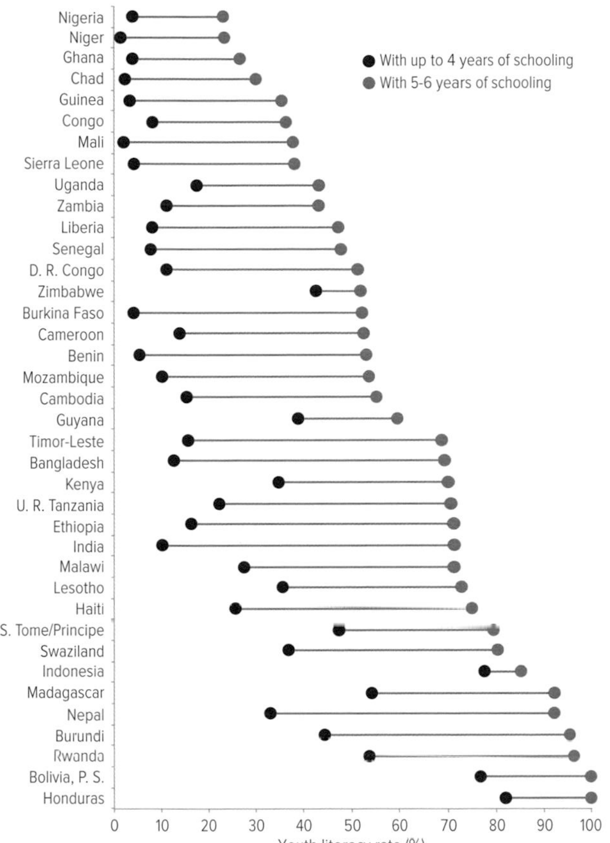

Source: EFA Global Monitoring Report team calculations (2013), based on Demographic and Health Survey data.

of these were able to read a sentence. This suggests that the quality of education in Rwanda in the early grades is helping to ensure that even those spending a limited time in the classroom are learning.

Even a full cycle of primary education does not guarantee literacy

While completing primary school is necessary to become literate in many countries, it is no guarantee. Of those who finished their education after five or six years in school, equivalent in some systems to completing a primary cycle, in the 41 countries analysed around 20 million are still not able to read all or part of a sentence – equivalent to one in three of those who make it to these grades.

In 12 of the 41 countries, half of 15- to 24-year-olds left school after five or six years of primary education without becoming literate. There are substantial cross-country differences in the acquisition of literacy skills. At one end of the spectrum, Ghana, Niger and Nigeria registered the most alarming figures – about 75% of young people who left school after 5 or 6 years have not become literate. At the other end, almost all those who left school after grades 5 or 6 in the Plurinational State of Bolivia, Burundi and Rwanda are literate, suggesting that providing literacy skills to the vast majority of students through a full cycle of primary education is possible (Figure 4.16).

One in three of those who complete primary education are still not able to read all or part of a sentence

Poor youth are more likely to suffer from illiteracy ...

The children with the best prospect of becoming literate tend to come from the wealthiest households; young people from poorer households are far less likely to be able to read in everyday situations. For the 41 countries included in the analysis, more than 80% of those from rich households can read a sentence in 32 countries, but the poor are able to do so in only four. At the other end of the scale, less than half of poor youth can read a sentence in 22 countries, while the rich fall below this threshold only in Niger (Figure 4.17).

In several countries, including Cameroon, Ghana, Nigeria and Sierra Leone, the difference in youth literacy rates between rich and poor is more than 50 percentage points. In Nigeria, only 14% of poor youth are literate, compared with 92% of rich youth. Evidence from Honduras and Indonesia demonstrates that such wide wealth-based gaps are not inevitable, but children from poorer households remain the most likely to be illiterate even in these richer countries that achieve higher levels of literacy overall.

Figure 4.17: In 22 countries, less than half of poor young people are literate
Youth literacy rate, by wealth, selected countries

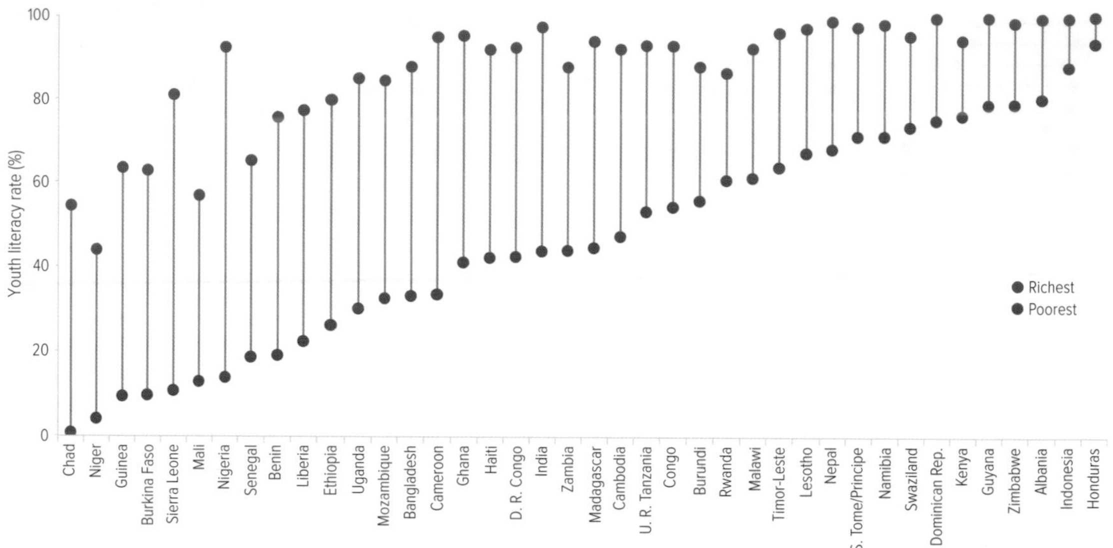

Note: Richest/poorest refers to young people in the top/bottom quintile of the Demographic and Health Survey household wealth index.
Source: EFA Global Monitoring Report team calculations (2013), based on Demographic and Health Survey data.

In Burkina Faso, 72% of rich young men have basic literary skills, compared with 6% of poor young women

... and poor young women are often most at risk

Among the poor, it is almost always young women who are most likely to get left behind, while both young men and women from rich households are likely to achieve basic literacy skills (Figure 4.18). In the Democratic Republic of the Congo, only 23% of poor young women aged 15 to 24 are able to read in everyday situations, compared with 64% of poor young men.

In some countries in western Africa, including Burkina Faso, Mali and Niger, those aged 15 to 24 acquire very low levels of literacy skills, on average, and girls from both rich and poor households tend to be less literate. In Burkina Faso, 72% of rich young men have basic literacy skills, compared with 54% of rich young women, but only 13% of poor men and 6% of poor women.

The gender gap among the poorest can move in the other direction, although this is generally the case among countries that are achieving higher levels of literacy overall and that have narrower gender gaps. In the Philippines, almost all young men and women from rich households have basic literacy skills, compared with 86% of poor young women and 72% of poor young men.

Literacy is lowest for young women in rural areas and for ethnic minorities

Children's level of learning varies widely depending on where they live, and this is mirrored in very poor levels of basic literacy skills among 15- to 24-year olds. In Ethiopia, only 30% of young women in rural areas were literate in 2011, compared with 90% of urban young men. Similarly, in Senegal, the percentage of rural young women able to read in everyday situations was only 20% in 2010, compared with 65% of urban young men. In both countries, the low levels of literacy among rural young women in part reflect the legacy of the education systems. However, these extremely low levels of literacy

Figure 4.18: The poorest young women are the most likely to be illiterate
Youth literacy rate, by gender and wealth, selected countries

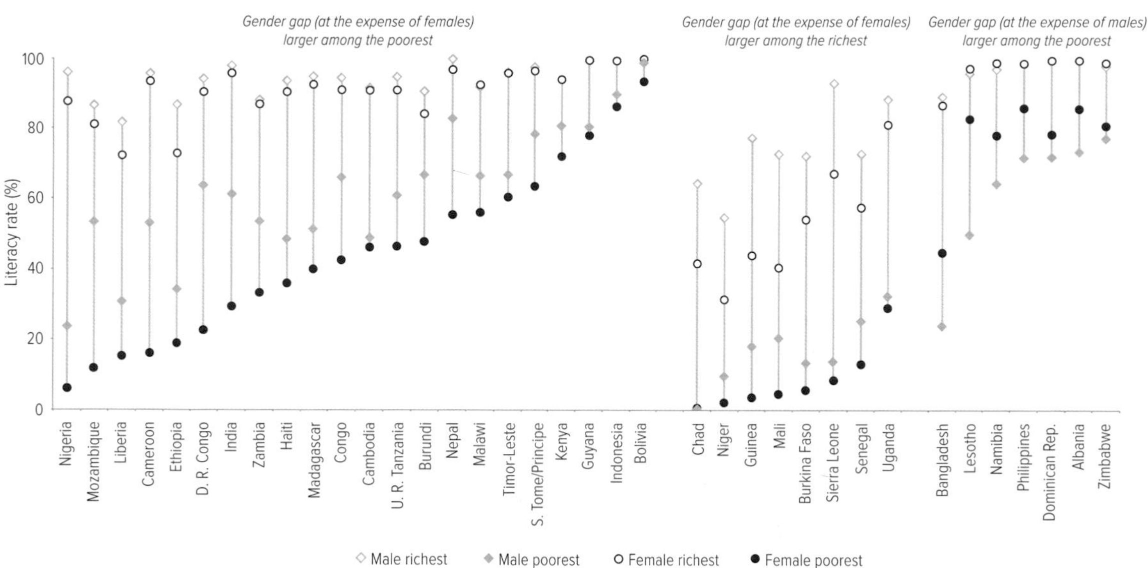

Note: Richest/poorest refers to young people in the top/bottom quintile of the Demographic and Health Survey household wealth index.
Source: EFA Global Monitoring Report team calculations (2013), based on Demographic and Health Survey data.

highlight the importance of ensuring that second-chance education programmes reach young women in underserved parts of the country (UNESCO, 2012).

Disadvantages in acquiring basic skills are further compounded by a combination of poverty, location and ethnicity. In Nigeria, only 2% of poor young women in the north-west can read, compared with 97% of rich young women in the south-east. In Indonesia, rich young women in Bali province have near-universal literacy skills, while just 60% of poor women in Papua province are literate. In Benin, poor young Fula women are among the most disadvantaged in terms of acquiring basic literacy skills. Poor young women living in Tambacounda province of Senegal have the least chance of learning the basics (Figure 4.19).

These outcomes may reflect the combined effects of poverty, isolation, discrimination and cultural practices. However, they also echo failures of education policy to provide learning opportunities for the most disadvantaged populations, and indicate an urgent need to provide these people with a second chance.

Youth literacy is improving, but not always fast enough for most disadvantaged groups

It is clear that a new generation are entering adulthood without basic literacy and numeracy skills, either because they dropped out of school or because they received a poor quality education. Even so, signs of improvement offer hope. Thanks to the expansion of primary schooling over the past decade, the youth literacy rate has improved, suggesting not only that more children are getting into school, but also that more have become literate once there. In Ethiopia, the share of young people who were literate increased from 34% in 2000 to 52% in 2011. Nepal recorded an impressive increase in its youth literacy rate, from 61% in 2001 to 86% in 2011. Youth literacy rates increased more slowly from a higher starting point in Malawi, from 72% in 2000 to 77% in 2010.

In north-west Nigeria, only 2% of poor young women can read

Trends in national averages for youth literacy do not tell the full story. Despite the overall progress, the challenge of inequality remains sizeable. Success in improving literacy among marginalized young people varies widely among countries.

Figure 4.19: Young women's chances of learning depend on wealth, location and ethnicity
Female youth literacy rate, by wealth, location and ethnicity, selected countries

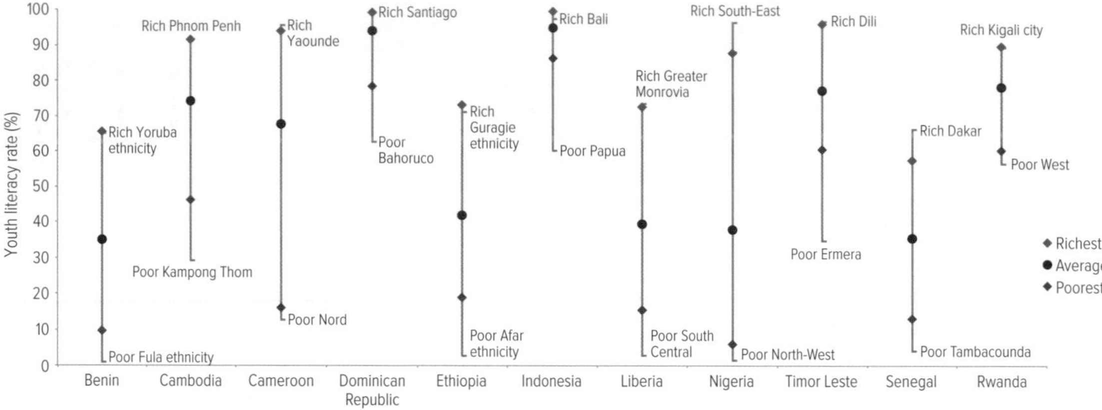

Note: Richest/poorest refers to young people in the top/bottom quintile of the Demographic and Health Survey household wealth index.
Source: EFA Global Monitoring Report team calculations (2013), based on Demographic and Health Survey data.

In Nepal, progress in improving youth literacy has benefited the most disadvantaged groups

In Nepal, progress in improving youth literacy has benefited both young men and women, with most of the gains registered among the most disadvantaged groups, which started with very low levels of literacy. Poor young women and those living in rural areas witnessed by far the largest increase in literacy rates, with literacy among poor young women increasing from 20% in 2001 to 55% in 2011. As a result, the gap between the poorest and richest young women narrowed substantially over the decade, and the same held for men. In Ethiopia, literacy rates also increased substantially for both young men and women in rural areas, but stagnated in urban areas (Figure 4.20).

Progress over the decade was more modest in Malawi. While some gains were made among young women living in rural areas and those from middle income households, there was very little change for young men, whether rural or urban, rich or poor. The expansion in Malawi's education system has yet to improve literacy among young people because of the poor quality of schooling.

Children and young people with disabilities are often the most neglected

Children with disabilities face major challenges in getting into school, but it is difficult to determine the extent of their exclusion because data are incomplete (see Chapter 1). Information on how much children with disabilities are learning is even more scarce, partly because they sometimes do not take part in the tests, and partly because the data are not sufficiently broken down by type of impairment (Evans and Ebersold, 2012). Even where data are disaggregated, as in Demographic and Health Surveys, sample sizes are often too small to allow meaningful analysis.

Uganda provides a rare example where the sample size is sufficient to compare literacy rates of young people according to different types of impairment. In 2011, around 60% of young people with no identified impairment were literate. By contrast, only 47% of young people with physical or hearing impairments were literate. Those with mental impairments were least likely to be literate: only 38% could read or write a simple sentence.

Figure 4.20: Nepal has made big strides toward literacy for disadvantaged youth
Youth literacy rate, by gender, location and wealth, Ethiopia, Malawi and Nepal, 2000/01–2010/11

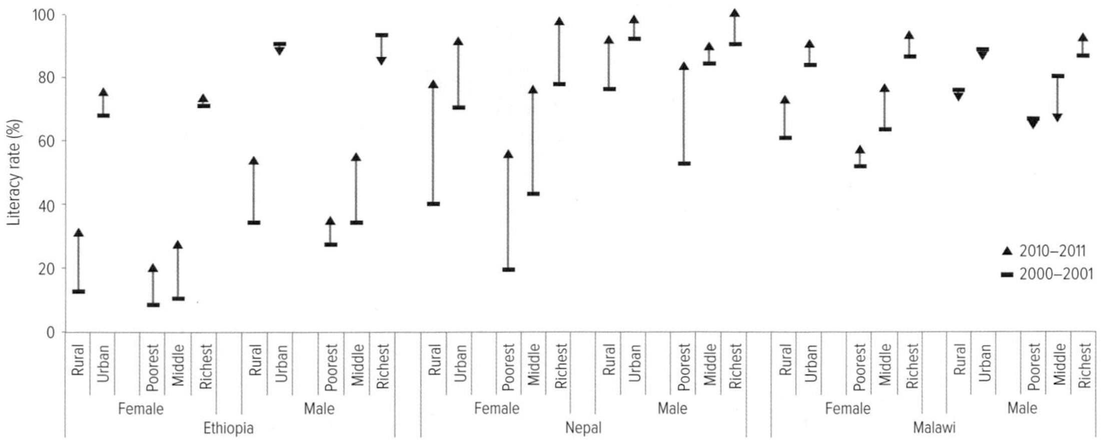

Source: EFA Global Monitoring Report team calculations (2013), based on Demographic and Health Survey data.

Other sources confirm the scale of this disadvantage. In the United Republic of Tanzania, a survey on disability found that the literacy rate for people with a disability was 52%, compared with 75% for people without a disability (U. R. Tanzania National Bureau of Statistics, 2010).

Striving for equal learning, including for children and youth with disabilities, requires the identification of the particular difficulties that children and young people with various types of impairment face, and implementing policies to tackle them. For example, the curriculum may need to be adapted to ensure that all children have the chance to learn. Education systems should aim to develop a system that maximizes the potential of all students.

Conclusion

This chapter has highlighted the extent of the global learning crisis, which afflicts children and young people from poor and vulnerable households in particular. The learning crisis is not inevitable, however. As the following chapters show, if policy-makers take action now to support good quality teaching and ensure a conducive learning environment, it will be possible to make sure that the next generation of children and young people faces better prospects both in getting to school and in learning once they are there.

If policy-makers take action now to support good quality teaching, the next generation of children will face better prospects in learning

New strategies: At a primary school in Johannesburg, South Africa, where teachers are guided by mentors to support them in implementing new teaching methods, students' mathematics and literacy skills have improved.

Credit: Eva-Lotta Jansson/UNESCO

Chapter 5
Making teaching quality a national priority

Strong national policies that make quality teaching and learning a high priority are essential to ensure that all children in school actually obtain the skills and knowledge they are meant to acquire. This chapter lays out the extent to which national education plans aim to improve teaching and learning and make them more equitable. It also reveals the extent of the primary and lower secondary teacher gap to 2015 and beyond, and determines how much governments will need to budget for additional teacher salaries to fill the gap.

Introduction

> *We have a shortage of teachers, with lots of children from nursery to grade 5. With these numbers the teacher cannot give individual attention to every student. If the government collaborates and gives us more teachers, we can ensure a much higher level of students' achievement.*
>
> \- Mubarak, Punjab, Pakistan

Strong national policies that make teaching quality and learning a high priority are essential to ensure that all children in school actually obtain the skills and knowledge they are meant to acquire. Education plans should describe goals and establish benchmarks against which governments can be held to account, as well as ways to achieve the goals. Improving learning, especially among the most disadvantaged children, needs to be made a strategic objective.

Plans should include a range of approaches to improve teacher quality, devised in consultation with teachers and teacher unions. They also need to guarantee that strategies will be backed by sufficient resources to ensure that they can be effectively implemented. One of the features of poor quality education is insufficient numbers of teachers, and in particular insufficient numbers of trained teachers. It is, therefore, vital for education planners to have good information on future teacher needs, and to recruit and train teachers accordingly.

The first section of this chapter examines the extent to which recent national education plans in 40 developing countries aim to improve learning and teaching.[1] The following sections explore in more detail the global need for more teachers and the prospects of recruiting and training enough teachers to meet that need.

1. The 40 countries whose education plans are included in the analysis are Afghanistan, Bangladesh, Belize, Bhutan, Cambodia, Ecuador, Egypt, Ethiopia, the Gambia, Ghana, Guinea-Bissau, Guyana, India, Indonesia, Jamaica, Kenya, the Lao People's Democratic Republic, Lebanon, Lesotho, Liberia, Malawi, Mauritius, Mozambique, Namibia, Nepal, Nigeria, Palestine, Papua New Guinea, Rwanda, Sierra Leone, South Africa, Sri Lanka, Sudan (pre-secession), Swaziland, the United Republic of Tanzania, Timor-Leste, Uganda, the United Arab Emirates, Zambia and Zimbabwe. The references for the plans can be found in Hunt (2013).

Quality must be made a strategic objective in education plans

It is vital that education plans aim explicitly at improving the quality of education and learning outcomes, and set specific targets against which governments can be held to account. Not all do so, however. Of the 40 national education plans reviewed for this Report, 26 list improved learning outcomes as a strategic objective, with varying degrees of detail on how they intend to achieve this aim (Hunt, 2013). Learning outcomes are a clear priority in 15 countries, and are somewhat prioritized in 11 – most often as an intended outcome of increasing the quality of the education system. In an additional 13 countries, improving the quality of the education system is a strategic priority, but with no explicit focus on improving learning outcomes. Increasing quality in this context usually refers to increased teacher education, improved classroom infrastructure, increased learning materials and curriculum reforms.

Education plans must aim to improve learning among the disadvantaged

Clear prioritization of learning outcomes is more typical of the richer economies among the 40 countries, where access to education is already higher. South Africa's plan, for example, includes 13 output goals, 9 of which relate to learning outcomes at various stages of the system. Even so, some poorer countries, such as Bangladesh, Ethiopia, Mozambique and the United Republic of Tanzania, also include improving quality and learning outcomes as an explicit priority alongside expanding access.

Focusing on obstacles to learning among the disadvantaged

Poor quality of education holds back the learning of children from marginalized groups the most, so the global learning crisis cannot be overcome unless policies aim to improve learning among the disadvantaged. While the plans of all 40 countries reviewed address the needs of disadvantaged groups to some extent, they focus mainly on improving their access to education, with learning often left as a by-product of increased access.

All 40 plans include some attention to children with special education needs, a term that is understood in different ways. In Afghanistan and Rwanda, for example, the definition is broad, including reducing the barriers to learning for children who are most vulnerable to exclusion. In others, such as Namibia, it is confined to access to school for children with disabilities.

Less than half the policy documents recognize the importance of teaching children in their home language, particularly in the early grades. Cambodia and the Lao People's Democratic Republic, for example, encourage the recruitment of teachers with specific language skills, and Namibia includes the production of learning materials in minority languages.

Guyana identifies interactive radio instruction as a means of supporting the teaching of mathematics in early grades

Eight countries, including Cambodia, Lesotho, Lebanon, Namibia and Sri Lanka, mention in their education plans that learning achievement data can be used to identify ways to improve student learning. Though the plans usually do not mention this point explicitly, teachers can use assessments to identify and support the weakest learners.

Some plans propose innovative ways to improve learning. Guyana identifies interactive radio instruction as a means of supporting the teaching of mathematics in the early grades; it also proposes catch-up programmes for students who have not reached minimum standards. South Africa proposes involving parents in discussions about their children's learning.

The majority of plans aim to reform the curriculum in some way. Bangladesh's Third Primary Education Development Programme 2011–2016 aims to break up the curriculum in early grades into clearly defined skills and learning outcomes, with teaching geared towards enabling each child to demonstrate that a particular skill has been acquired.

Latin American countries, including Guyana and three whose education plans were not analysed among the 40 countries – Colombia, Paraguay and Peru – go further than some others in identifying reforms to improve the learning of disadvantaged groups, notably ethno-linguistic minorities and the poor. While such reforms mainly focus on extending access, they also include adapting curricula and pedagogical practices to the needs of particular groups. In Paraguay, for example, this involves creating educational materials in various languages (Paraguay Ministry of Education, 2011). In Guyana, the scope of the curriculum is expected to be broadened to include culture-specific skills in Amerindian communities.

Countries' targets for improving learning outcomes should pay attention to raising the standards for children from the most disadvantaged groups, whose learning is often the weakest. However, many countries do not yet have targets and indicators geared to this, or a nationally standardized assessment system in place (see Chapter 1).

National policies should address teacher quality and management

To improve learning, particularly for disadvantaged groups, governments need to develop national education plans that aim to improve teacher quality and management. Strategies designed to achieve this goal are examined in detail in Chapter 6; they include attracting and retaining the best teachers, improving teacher education, deploying teachers more fairly, and providing incentives in the form of better salaries and attractive career paths.

The national education plans reviewed for this Report include a wide range of strategies for increasing teacher quality. All the plans reviewed address teacher education to some extent, but only 17 include strategies for improving teacher education programmes, and only 16 envisage further training of teacher educators.

Some countries' plans aim to improve teaching quality by setting higher qualification standards for teachers; in Bangladesh, for example, a diploma in education is to replace the certification in education by 2014. Other plans emphasize less traditional approaches, such as school cluster-based in-service teacher education in Kenya, Namibia, Sudan and Timor-Leste. Rwanda aims to use mentors in every school to support teacher development. Belize has plans to improve induction and training for newly qualified teachers.

Training for non-formal education teachers is included in 11 of the 40 plans. Uganda emphasizes working with NGO providers to expand primary education to disadvantaged rural and urban areas, including by training teachers in these schools and developing a costed plan to fund their salaries through the government payroll.

It is less common for plans to recognize explicitly that improving teaching quality is a way to enhance learning outcomes. In Kenya, in-service training aims to boost the learning of primary school leavers in poorly performing districts. South Africa's plan goes into more detail than most, highlighting recruitment of new teachers as key in reaching required learning standards. Sri Lanka links demand-driven recruitment to quality and learning outcomes: 'recruitment will be done only if there is a need for that teacher to be hired. This is the only way to mitigate the adverse situation that is causing poor learning in schools and perhaps has also contributed to the growing private coaching culture' (Sri Lanka Ministry of Education, 2006, p. 56). India's plan links decentralization of teacher recruitment to education quality, which is in turn linked to learning outcomes.

Governments need to get incentives right to retain the best teachers. Of the 40 plans reviewed, 10 include reforms to improve teacher pay, and 18 emphasize better career paths. For example, the education sector strategy of the United Republic of Tanzania makes increased pay a high priority, acknowledging that if teachers lack sustained increases in real pay, this may hinder the development of an environment conducive to teaching and learning.

Some plans include strategies that suggest making teachers accountable for delivering better results. Among the 40 plans, 14 focus on teacher accountability for children's learning and 20 include a teacher performance management system or competency framework to monitor and guide teacher practice. Performance-related pay for teachers is proposed in Cambodia, Jamaica, Sri Lanka and Timor-Leste. In Jamaica, for example, performance-based pay is intended to foster a culture in which teachers apply the curriculum and so improve learning outcomes. By contrast, only South Africa and Timor-Leste suggest repercussions for teachers who perform poorly.

Designing teacher reforms to benefit disadvantaged students

While all 40 national education plans reviewed for this Report address issues of teacher quality to varying degrees, only some target teacher reforms at improving learning for disadvantaged students, mainly by getting teachers into disadvantaged areas. Cambodia, Ghana, Liberia and Papua New Guinea provide scholarships for trainees from disadvantaged areas, often people with specific language skills.

Among the 28 plans that aim to send teachers to disadvantaged areas, Cambodia's is notable for including strategies to deploy teachers – especially those from targeted areas and ethnic groups – to the areas where they are most needed. The aim is for 1,500 new trainees (of around 5,000 recruited annually) from disadvantaged areas to be assigned to work in their indigenous areas after completing their education. Overall, about 95% of new graduates from teacher training colleges are to be assigned to understaffed schools and to disadvantaged and remote areas every year. It is even more exceptional that Cambodia has moved beyond proposing this as a priority and is carrying it out (see Chapter 6).

Afghanistan aims to increase the number of female teachers by 50% by 2014

Another way to ensure that teachers are deployed in disadvantaged areas is to provide them with incentives. Of the 28 policy documents that address teacher deployment or redeployment, 22 include incentives, particularly focusing on housing and monetary incentives. In 17 of the 28 policies, housing incentives are mentioned as a way to encourage teacher deployment to difficult areas, and 9 include a monetary allowance. Nigeria proposes a promotion incentive for teachers deployed to disadvantaged areas.

Half of the 28 programmes that mention teacher deployment focus on rural areas, while 8 actively encourage female teachers. Afghanistan aims to increase the number of female teachers by 50% by 2014 under an interim education plan that includes monetary and housing incentives for female teachers, and special teacher training programmes for women in remote areas and women who do not meet current qualification requirements.

In remote areas, where student numbers are often small, teachers may have to teach more than one age group at the same time. In Cambodia, Kenya and Papua New Guinea, there are plans to provide training in multigrade teaching. Cambodia's Education Sector Strategic Plan aims to develop training in multigrade teaching methodology for teachers in remote schools, with priority given to those who already teach multigrade classes. It also aims to develop an annual action plan on multigrade teaching in remote areas and those populated by ethnic minority groups.

Few plans highlight the need for targeted support for students who are falling behind. Guyana is one exception, with key strategies including targeted programmes in mathematics and English for students in grades 6 and 7 who have not reached set standards of literacy and numeracy. Building teachers' capacity to deliver targeted programmes is a priority, along with developing relevant curriculum materials and distance learning using television and DVDs to support remedial programmes.

Resource allocation should support learning and quality objectives

In 10 countries teachers thought it was vital to have influence on the direction of policy, but only 23% felt they had such influence

For plans to be successfully implemented, they need to be backed by sufficient resources. Only 16 of the 40 policy documents reviewed include a budget breakdown detailing teaching and learning costs. These costs are mainly for teacher education, textbooks and learning materials. Bangladesh, Cambodia, Ghana and Palestine specifically categorize projected expenditure items according to objectives to increase education quality. Quality inputs in Papua New Guinea and Malawi amount to over a fifth of the recurrent budget, while in the Lao People's Democratic Republic, Palestine and Sudan, they are 5% or less.[2] Few plans earmark expenditure for the disadvantaged, however.

In Bangladesh, strategies to improve learning are linked to key indicators designed to measure progress, such as children's level of learning according to their grade and the subject, the number of schools that receive new textbooks in the first month of the year, and the percentage of teachers who receive continuous professional development. The plan notably includes financial projections for some actions needed to accomplish these objectives, with detailed expenditure data given for items such as school- and classroom-based assessment, curriculum development, textbook distribution, and teacher education and development. Most of the plans reviewed do not go into this level of detail, however.

While it is commendable that countries are making the financing of education quality a higher priority, in some countries there is a significant gap between the expenditure envisaged and the funds available in the overall education budget. Lesotho's planned expenditure is equivalent to 89% of its available funds, and in Malawi it amounts to 92%. Bangladesh expects 28% of the learning and teaching component to be funded by aid. In Palestine, only 77% of the quality component in the optimal scenario of the education plan is financed from committed funds. Such gaps raise the question of whether these countries' aspirations for improved education quality can be met, and underline the need for significant donor support throughout the periods covered by the plans.

Engaging teachers and teacher unions in reforms to improve education quality

Policies can only be effective if those responsible for implementing them are involved in shaping them. However policy-makers who aim to improve education quality and learning outcomes rarely consult teachers or their unions.

A survey in 10 countries[3] asked teachers how much influence they thought they and their colleagues had over policy and practice in their schools and districts and nationally. In all 10, teachers thought it was vital to have influence on the direction of policy, but only 23% felt they had such influence (Bangs and Frost, 2012). In Jamaica, in a separate study, teachers expressed frustration over being left out of the policy formulation process. Although they said they were willing to play a larger part in developing policies, many felt that policy-makers were not genuinely interested in their opinions, and many said they were anxious about how new policies would affect their day-to-day work (Gulpers, 2013).

2. Comparing countries' expenditures can be difficult for a number of reasons. For example, some quality inputs, such as textbooks, are listed as capital investment in some countries and recurrent expenditure in others. In addition, not all of the plans address the costs of the entire education system, as some only cover primary schooling.

3. Bulgaria, Denmark, Egypt, Greece, Hong Kong (China), the Netherlands, the Former Yugoslav Republic of Macedonia, Turkey, the United Kingdom and the United States.

To ensure that reforms are successfully implemented, it is vital that governments engage more closely with teachers. Given their reach, teacher unions are a key partner for governments. Around 50% of teachers who are members of a union are in countries with poor learning outcomes, such as the Gambia, Liberia and Malawi (Mulkeen, 2010, 2013).

Even when laws require teachers' participation in formulating education policies, however, their voice is often ignored. The 2007 Education Law of Cambodia (Article 29) states that teachers have the right to contribute actively to the development of education standards, from school level to national level, but a study found that teachers felt there was no forum for them to express their views and that there was a lack of transparency (Voluntary Service Overseas, 2011).

Excluding teachers not only is demoralizing but can also lead to inappropriate policies. In a survey in Indonesia, for example, teachers felt that resources that were often lacking or inadequate should be given higher priority. Policy-makers, however, favoured promotion opportunities, which only 20% of teachers considered important, compared with 49% who viewed improving classroom teaching and learning resources as critical (Broekman, 2013).

Failure to consult teachers during the planning phase means they may not become involved in implementing new policy until they are expected to put changes into practice, often at short notice. In Turkey, which introduced a new curriculum in 2004, teachers only became involved at the implementation stage and were highly critical of its design, particularly of the training provided to introduce them to the curriculum. Many teachers were concerned that the substantial reductions in teaching time built into the new curriculum would lower pupils' academic performance (Altinyelken and Verger, 2013).

When teachers are offered opportunities to contribute to policy-making, many are willing to do so. In Peru, a survey revealed that about 40% of teachers were uncertain about the implications of a new teacher evaluation policy and perceived it as too complex. When given a chance to ask questions about it on an online forum, many were highly critical of the policy, which sought to tie sanctions and rewards to teachers' performance as evaluated through written tests which the teachers judged to be inadequate for assessing pedagogical skills (van der Tuin and Verger, 2013).

Teachers and their unions can have a beneficial influence when they are given real chances to reshape policies aimed at improving learning, as Norway's experience shows. In the early 2000s, after results of the OECD Programme for International Student Assessment (PISA) revealed that the country's education system was not as high quality as had been assumed, hearings in Parliament led to new national legislation to raise standards. The legislation included national tests and new forms of teacher professional development and appraisal, but teachers objected to the first national tests, which took place in 2004. The tests were redesigned in 2006 with the cooperation of the Norwegian teacher union. Norway's improved 2009 PISA results have been partly attributed to this effective collaboration (Asia Society Partnership for Global Learning, 2011).

In the Plurinational State of Bolivia, teacher unions were instrumental in improving education quality among indigenous groups

In 2009, Norway took further steps to raise the status of the teaching profession, revamp teacher education, increase the amount of high-quality professional development within a framework of agreed teacher competencies, and improve the quality of school leaders. This process involved the Ministry of Education, teacher unions, and organizations representing teacher education and school leaders at national and regional levels. As a result, teaching received higher ratings as a profession in the media, rising from 14% in 2008 to 59% in 2010. In 2011, the number of applications to teacher education institutions rose by 38% from the previous year. There was, in particular, a significant increase in the number of applications from men, who had been under-represented in the profession (Asia Society Partnership for Global Learning, 2011).

In some countries, the engagement of teacher unions has improved policies aimed at helping disadvantaged groups. In the Plurinational State of Bolivia, for example, the Confederation of Rural Education Teachers was instrumental in improving education quality among indigenous groups by highlighting the need for bilingual, multicultural education. Its promotion of instruction in the indigenous languages

Aymara and Quechua contributed to a decrease in illiteracy. The confederation is the chief advocate of education tailored for indigenous groups and peasants, historically excluded from the education system. Indigenous education rights are now enshrined in the constitution, providing a legal basis on which to advocate for improvements (Gindin and Finger, 2013).

Sometimes teachers' union activities may harm student learning opportunities, however. Teacher strikes, for example, can sometimes lead to significantly fewer teaching days per year, even though they may be held for good reason, such as to protest against low pay or inappropriate policy reform. A review by the South African National Planning Commission found that strike actions, which are sometimes unofficial, lead to a loss of as many as 10 days of teaching a year, equivalent to 5% of school time. Union activity could affect the learning of disadvantaged students in particular, as union meetings in township schools are often held during school time (Irving, 2012).

Between 2011 and 2015, 5.2 million primary school teachers need to be recruited to achieve universal primary education

Teachers campaigning for their rights should ensure that they also tackle issues holding back progress in learning, but do not always do so. In India, teacher unions have a major influence on state legislatures and governments. In Uttar Pradesh, this led to higher pay and security of tenure for civil service teachers, but also to neglect of teacher absenteeism and to low quality of teaching (Kingdon and Muzammil, 2003).

While the interests and activities of unions sometimes harm student learning, there is evidence that teachers and their unions can help ensure that policies are effective. Thus it is important to include them from the early stages in designing new strategies aimed at tackling learning deficits.

Getting enough teachers into classrooms

The quality of education is held back in many of the poorest countries by a lack of teachers, which often results in large class sizes in early grades and in the poorest areas. To address those deficits and meet future demand as enrolment increases, it is vital that countries know how many teachers they require, and that they have the capacity to train them. As most initial teacher education courses last at least two years, it is unlikely that countries with a lack of teachers will be able to fill the gap by the 2015 Education for All deadline. Nevertheless, countries must start planning now to make up the shortfall, not only in primary schools but also at the lower secondary education level.

How many additional primary and lower secondary teachers are needed?

Future teacher recruitment needs are determined by current deficits, demographics, enrolment trends and numbers of children out of school. Analysis by the UNESCO Institute for Statistics (UIS) shows that over the four-year period between 2011 and 2015, 5.2 million primary school teachers need to be recruited – including replacement and additional teachers – to achieve universal primary education (UPE) (Figure 5.1).[4] This amounts to around 1 million teachers per year, equivalent to about 5% of the current primary school teaching force.

UPE may not be achieved by 2015, however, as 57 million children are still out of school, so the analysis has been extended to determine how many teachers would need to be recruited if the goal shifted to 2020 or 2030. To achieve UPE by 2020, recruitment would be spread over more years, but would need to account for projected increases in enrolment, so the number of teachers required would rise to 13.1 million over nine years. Extending the deadline to 2030 would mean recruiting 20.6 million teachers over 19 years.

4. Countries often do not report the numbers of teachers leaving the profession. For the purpose of estimates of teacher needs, UIS assumes an attrition rate of 5% for all countries. This is equivalent to a primary school teacher having a teaching career of around 20 years (UIS, 2012).

Figure 5.1: Globally, 1.6 million additional teachers are needed by 2015

Total number of teachers needed to achieve universal primary education by 2015

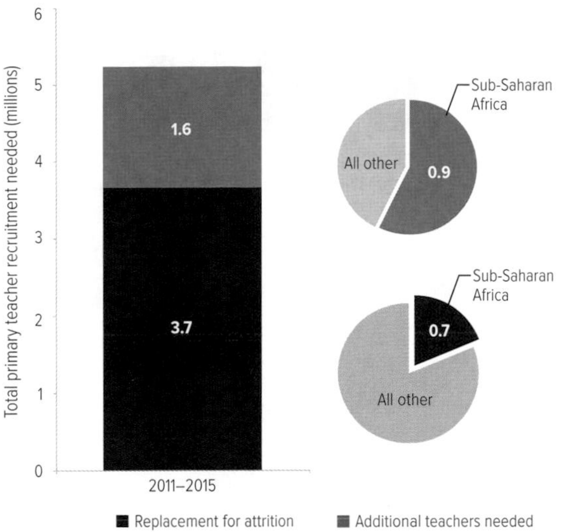

Source: UIS (2013).

Of the teachers required between 2011 and 2015, 3.7 million are needed to replace teachers who retire, change occupations, or leave due to illness or death. The remaining 1.6 million are the additional teachers needed to make up the shortfall, address expanding enrolment and underwrite quality by ensuring that there are no more than 40 students for every teacher. Thus, around 400,000 additional teachers need to be recruited each year if there are to be sufficient teachers by 2015.

Is this feasible? Globally, between 1999 and 2011, the number of primary school teachers grew, on average, by around 330,000 per year. This suggests that, on current trends, the target could be reached with limited additional effort. However, the challenge is unequally distributed across regions. Sub-Saharan Africa requires approximately 225,000 additional teachers per year, but over the past decade the average annual increase has been only 102,000, so the magnitude of the task is significantly greater.

Extending the deadline for UPE would require 2.4 million additional teachers by 2020 and 3.3 million by 2030 (Figure 5.2). This would spread the burden of the annual increase in numbers – from almost 400,000 if the 2015 date is to be achieved to 176,000 if the deadline is extended to 2030 – and hence make the target more feasible for some countries. But it would also delay the time when all children will be in school, with no more than 40 students per teacher, so such an extension is not necessarily desirable.

The challenge of recruiting teachers becomes even greater when the needs of lower secondary education are taken into account. Achieving universal lower secondary enrolment was not a target for the 2015 goals. As a result it has received less attention over the past decade, leaving 69 million adolescents out of school in 2011. To achieve universal lower secondary education by 2015 with 32 students per teacher, an additional 3.5 million teachers would be needed between 2011 and 2015 (Figure 5.2).

Governments need to plan for the 5.1 million additional lower secondary teachers needed between 2011 and 2030

It seems extremely unlikely, however, that recruitment will increase fast enough to reach this level. Between 1999 and 2011, the number of lower secondary school teachers grew by about 240,000 per year, compared with the additional 880,000 per year needed to achieve universal lower secondary education by 2015. It is more plausible that new global education goals will include achieving universal lower secondary education by 2030. To reach this goal, governments need to plan for the 5.1 million additional teachers needed between 2011 and 2030, an average of around 268,000 per year.

Figure 5.2: Around 5.1 million additional lower secondary teachers are needed to achieve universal lower secondary education by 2030

Additional teachers required to achieve universal primary and lower secondary education for target years 2015, 2020, 2025 and 2030

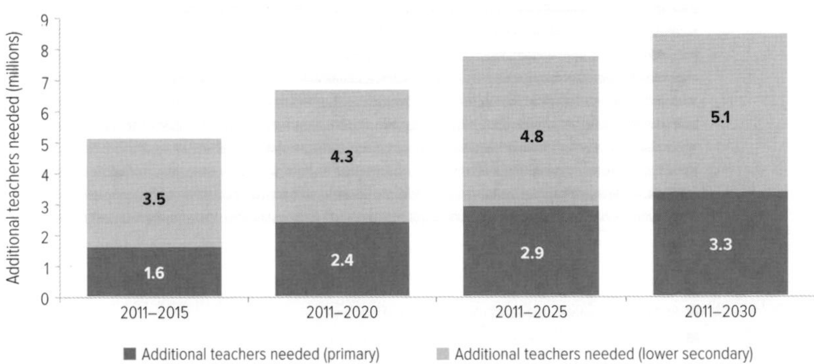

Source: UIS (2013).

Which regions and countries need the most teachers?

Some regions and countries need many more additional teachers in primary and lower secondary schools than others. By far the biggest challenge is in sub-Saharan Africa, which accounts for 57% of the additional primary school teachers needed between 2011 and 2015, or 63% if the deadline is extended to 2030. This is because of the region's lower enrolment, larger class size and continued growth in the school age population.

Sub-Saharan Africa accounts for 57% of the additional primary school teachers needed between 2011 and 2015

Sub-Saharan Africa also accounts for half of the additional lower secondary school teachers needed between 2011 and 2030. An additional 1 million lower secondary school teachers are also required over this period in South and West Asia, where progress has been slower in lower secondary education than in primary schooling.

An assessment of teacher needs by country shows that, whatever the time period, Nigeria has by far the largest gap to fill. Between 2011 and 2015, it needs 212,000 primary school teachers, 13% of the global total (Figure 5.3). Of the 10 countries needing the most additional primary teachers, all but one are in sub-Saharan Africa, the exception being Pakistan.

Figure 5.3: Additional primary teachers are mainly needed in sub-Saharan Africa
Teacher posts that need to be created between 2011 and 2015, percentage of global total

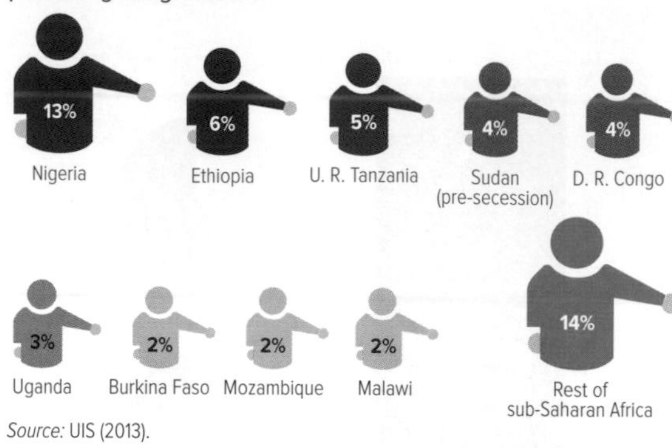

Source: UIS (2013).

The reasons countries need more teachers vary. In some, such as Nigeria, Pakistan and Yemen, enrolment is low so additional teachers are needed to ensure that all children are in school. In those three countries, there are no more than 40 primary school students per teacher, on average. In others, including Ethiopia, Malawi, the United Republic of Tanzania and Zambia, education quality needs to be improved by reducing class size. Malawi, for example, has achieved a net enrolment ratio of 97%, but teacher numbers have not kept pace so the average number of students per teacher rose from 63 in 1999 to 76 in 2011 (Figure 5.4).

Figure 5.4: Some countries need a larger share of additional primary teachers due to low access, others because the number of students per teacher is high
Share of additional teachers needed to reach net enrolment ratio and pupil/teacher ratio targets

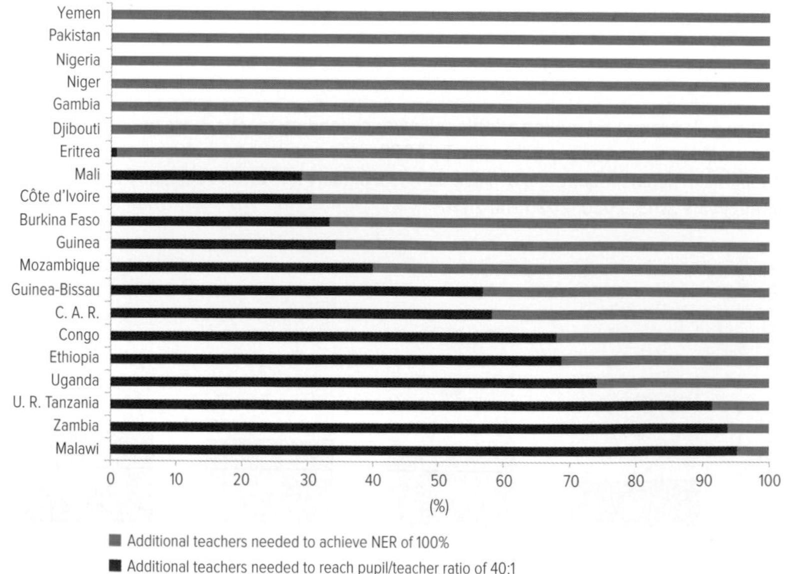

Note: Calculations on the target pupil/teacher ratio of 40:1 are based on enrolment in 2011, which in some countries includes large numbers of children who are over age or under age.
Source: EFA Global Monitoring Report team calculations (2013), based on UIS (2013).

Can countries recruit enough teachers?

It is unlikely that countries with the most severe teacher gaps can recruit the numbers needed by 2015. Analysis by UIS, based on trends in recruiting teachers over the past 10 years and population projections, shows that 93 countries need to find additional primary school teachers. Of these, 32 are in sub-Saharan Africa. Among the 93 countries, 37 will be able to bridge the gap by 2015, but this leaves 56 countries with a shortfall, implying that their hopes of achieving UPE by 2015 will be thwarted due to insufficient teachers.

It is particularly worrying that 29 countries will not even be able to fill the gap until after 2030 if their past trends in recruiting teachers continue. These countries are mainly in sub-Saharan Africa, with

Pakistan a notable exception; they include Côte d'Ivoire, Eritrea, Malawi and Nigeria (Figure 5.5).

The challenge is even greater for lower secondary education. The UIS analysis shows that 148 countries need more teachers at this level by 2015, including almost all countries in sub-Saharan Africa. Twenty-nine countries will not have filled the lower secondary teacher gap by 2030 if their past trends in recruiting teachers continue; almost half are in sub-Saharan Africa.

At the primary level, while some countries are expected to bring the average pupil/teacher ratio down to 40:1 in or before 2015, others need to expand their teacher force much faster than they have previously. Rwanda and Uganda would need to expand recruitment by 6%, on average, compared with a current average increase of 3%. At that pace these countries would not achieve UPE until after 2025.

In the 29 countries not expected to have enough teachers to achieve UPE until after 2030, there is an urgent need for governments to address the teacher shortfall. In Malawi, the teaching force is growing at just 1% per year, far from sufficient to reduce the pupil/teacher ratio from 76:1 to 40:1. For Malawi to meet the UPE goal by 2015, it would need to increase its teaching force by 15% annually between 2011 and 2015. If the UPE target were pushed back to 2020, Malawi would still need to increase the teacher force by 9% annually. The capacity of its teacher education programmes is currently far from sufficient to meet this need (Figure 5.6).

Can countries fill the trained teacher gap?

Teachers need not only to be recruited but also to be trained. Many countries, especially in sub-Saharan Africa, also need to train existing teachers whose skills do not meet minimum standards. This will add further pressure on systems with limited resources.[5]

Many countries have expanded their teacher labour force by engaging untrained teachers on contract, a strategy examined in Chapter 6.

5. Estimating the future need for trained teachers globally is difficult because data are limited. The UIS notes that teacher education programmes are not comparable across countries in terms of their content, duration and qualification levels, so global estimates may be problematic.

Figure 5.5: 29 countries will not fill the primary teacher gap before 2030, on current trends
Number of countries according to the date by which they are expected to fill the teacher gap

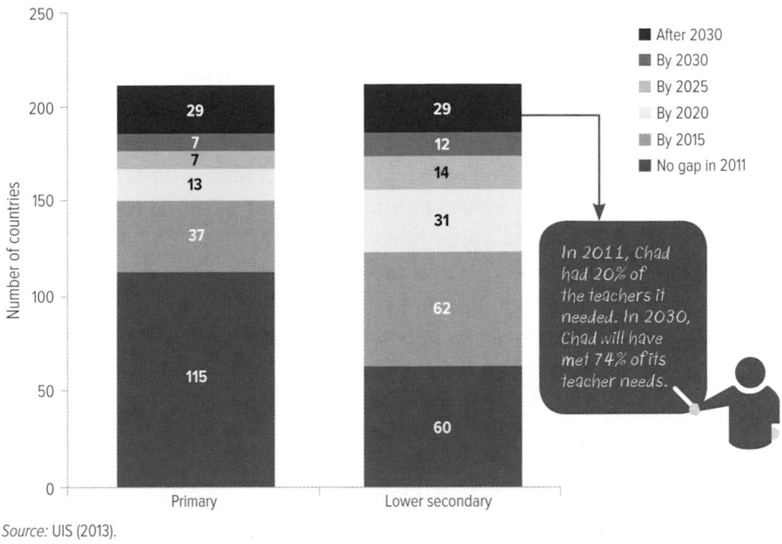

Source: UIS (2013).

At the current rate of recruitment, some of these countries, including Cameroon, Ethiopia, Guinea, Mali and Senegal, appear on course to have sufficient teachers to achieve UPE by 2015 or 2020 – but only by continuing to recruit untrained teachers. Most of these countries are unlikely to both achieve UPE and maintain an acceptable ratio of pupils to teachers trained to national standards.

Figure 5.6: Some countries need to hire teachers at a much faster rate to fill the teacher gap by 2020
Annual compound growth rates in teaching posts needed over 2011–2020 for countries not expected to fill the teacher gap by 2020

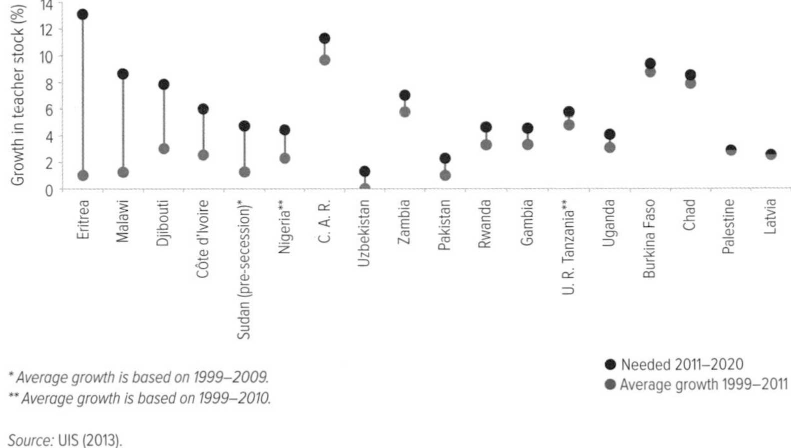

** Average growth is based on 1999–2009.*
*** Average growth is based on 1999–2010.*

Source: UIS (2013).

Mali would need to more than quadruple its annual recruitment to ensure that 6,800 new trained teachers are available by 2020

For example, Mali recruited teachers at a rate of 9% per year over the past decade, which helped lower the number of pupils per teacher from 62 in 1999 to 48 in 2011. If we take account of the fact that one-third of children were out of school, the number of pupils per teacher would be 63. However, many of these teachers are untrained. A study of 804 teachers in Mali found that only 15% have completed upper secondary education, and some have only completed primary education (Pryor et al., 2012). Recruitment of trained teachers was very slow, at about 1,700 per year, between 2008 and 2011. The result is that Mali's ratio of pupils per trained teacher, 92:1, is one of the world's highest. On its past trend of trained teacher recruitment, Mali would not achieve a ratio of 40 pupils per trained teacher until 2030 (Figure 5.7). Meeting that target earlier would require considerable effort. It is projected that Mali would need to more than quadruple its annual recruitment to ensure that 6,800 new trained teachers were available by 2020 to bring its pupil/trained teacher ratio to 40:1.

The efforts of some low income countries to fill the teacher gap are likely to be frustrated because the supply of those who have completed upper secondary school – the minimum qualification for primary teacher trainees – is short and projected to remain so for the immediate future.[6] This constraint is particularly severe in sub-Saharan Africa, especially in West Africa, where even the chances of completing primary school remain low. In 8 out of 14 countries with available data in the region, including Burkina Faso, Mozambique and Rwanda, at least 5% of all upper secondary school graduates in 2020 would need to be drawn into teaching to allow these countries to fill the teacher gap. Niger would need to direct almost a quarter of its expected 20-year-old upper secondary school graduates into primary teacher education programmes to achieve UPE by 2020 (Figure 5.8). By comparison, in middle income countries such as Ecuador,

Figure 5.8: In Niger, 23% of upper secondary school graduates would need to be teachers to achieve universal primary education by 2020

Projected percentage of upper secondary school graduates who would need to become primary teachers to reach universal primary education by 2020, sub-Saharan Africa

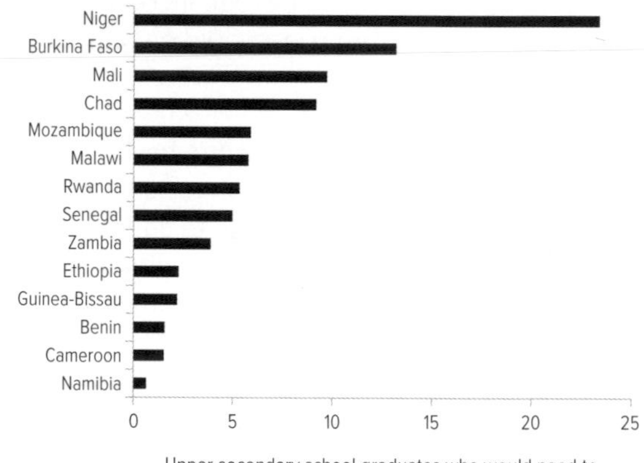

Note: Countries with available data only.

Source: EFA Global Monitoring Report team calculations (2013), based on UIS (2013).

Figure 5.7: Mali faces a huge challenge in recruiting trained teachers

Projected number of teachers and trained teachers, and projected pupil/teacher ratio and pupil/trained teacher ratio, 2011–2030

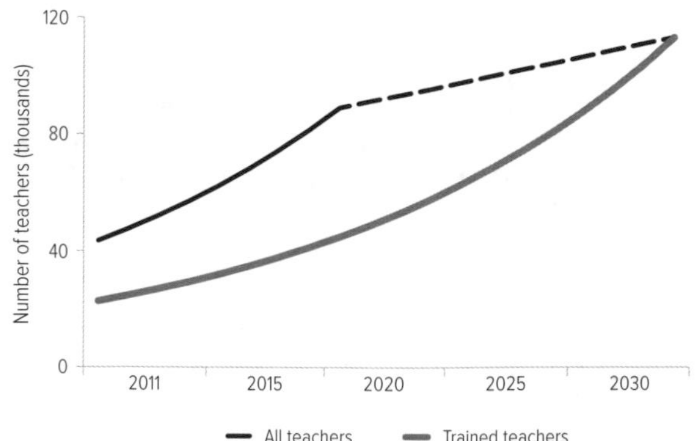

Source: EFA Global Monitoring Report team calculations (2013), based on UIS (2013).

6. This analysis was made by extending projections for this Report on achievement of universal primary and lower secondary education (see Chapter 1) to predict growth in the percentage of the population with upper secondary education.

just over 3% of those in the labour force with at least secondary education are primary school teachers.

Countries where the number of untrained teachers is high need to find ways to train them. In 10 out of 27 countries with available data, including Benin, Guinea-Bissau, Liberia and Sierra Leone, the challenge of training existing teachers is greater than that of recruiting and training new teachers. In Benin, 47% of primary school teachers in 2011 had been trained. The country needs to expand teacher recruitment by just 1.4% per year to achieve UPE by 2020 while also achieving a pupil/teacher ratio of 40:1. This is well below its 8% average annual growth rate since 1999 for all teachers. But the number of existing teachers to be trained needs to grow by almost 9% per year to ensure that there will be 40 pupils per trained teacher in 2020, well above the 6% average annual growth rate since 1999 for trained teachers (Figure 5.9).

The shortage of trained teachers is likely to affect disadvantaged areas in particular. In Nigeria, which needs 70,000 teachers per year to achieve UPE by 2020, only two-thirds of current teachers have the minimum qualifications. In the northern state of Kano, one of the poorer in the country, the pupil/trained teacher ratio exceeded 100 in 2009/10. In more than half of local government authorities the situation was even worse, with at least 150 pupils per trained teacher in the most disadvantaged 25% of schools (Figure 5.10).

Children in the early grades who live in remote areas face a double disadvantage. In Ethiopia, where 48% of teachers are trained, only around 20% of teachers were trained in grades 1 to 4 in 2010, compared with 83% in grades 5 to 8. The percentage of lower primary teachers who were trained was as low as 1% in the Somali region and 4% in Afar, the two most remote rural regions, compared with 43% in Addis Ababa (Nordstrum, 2013).

Figure 5.9: Some countries face a double task: recruiting trained teachers and training untrained teachers

Required annual growth in numbers of new and existing trained teachers to reach universal primary education by 2020

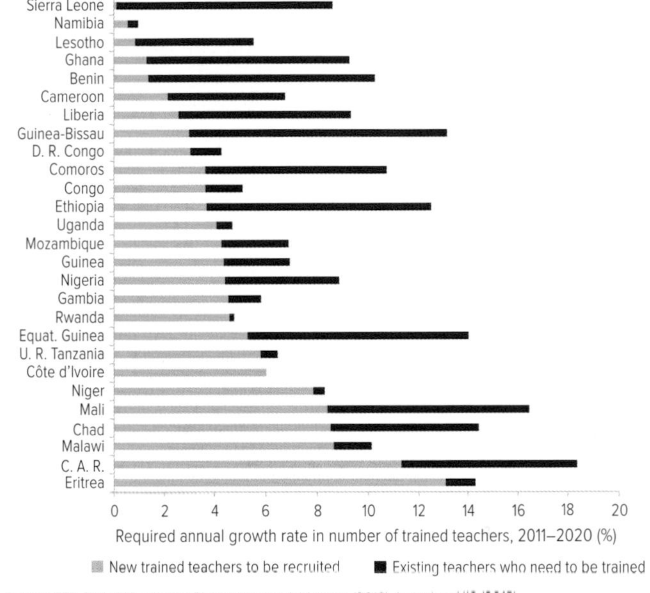

Source: EFA Global Monitoring Report team calculations (2013), based on UIS (2013).

Figure 5.10: In some schools in northern Nigeria, there are more than 200 students per trained teacher

Pupil/teacher and pupil/trained teacher ratio, mean and bottom 25% of government schools, by local government authority, Kano state, Nigeria, 2009/10

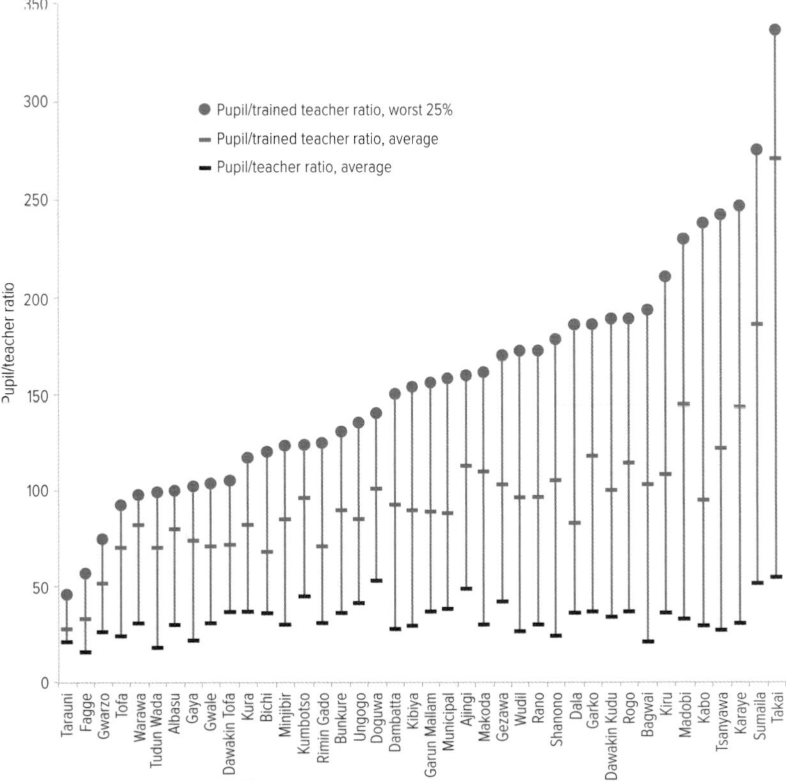

Source: EFA Global Monitoring Report team calculations (2013), based on 2009/10 Kano state annual school census data.

Are the costs of hiring more teachers affordable?

US$4 billion annually is needed in sub-Saharan Africa to pay the salaries of the additional primary school teachers required by 2020

Countries that require additional teachers will have to increase their overall budgets for teacher salaries. In sub-Saharan Africa, where the need for extra teachers is greatest, there are already serious budgetary constraints despite increases in domestic spending in many countries over the past decade. It is therefore essential to identify whether the region can afford to pay for the extra teachers needed so that alternative sources of finance can be found where required.

New analysis by the UIS for this Report finds that US$4 billion annually is needed in sub-Saharan Africa to pay the salaries of the additional primary school teachers required by 2020, after taking into account projected economic growth.[7] This is equivalent to 19% of the region's total education budget in 2011 (Development Finance International and Oxfam, 2013).

The burden is unevenly spread across the continent. Nigeria alone, which requires the most additional teachers, accounts for two-fifths of the gap, while Burkino Faso, Côte d'Ivoire, Mali, the United Republic of Tanzania and Zambia are also responsible for a large share.

Figure 5.11: Some countries need to increase their education budget by at least 20% to cover the cost of additional primary school teachers
Increase in education budget, beyond what is expected from economic growth, required to pay salaries of extra primary teachers needed to achieve universal primary education by 2020

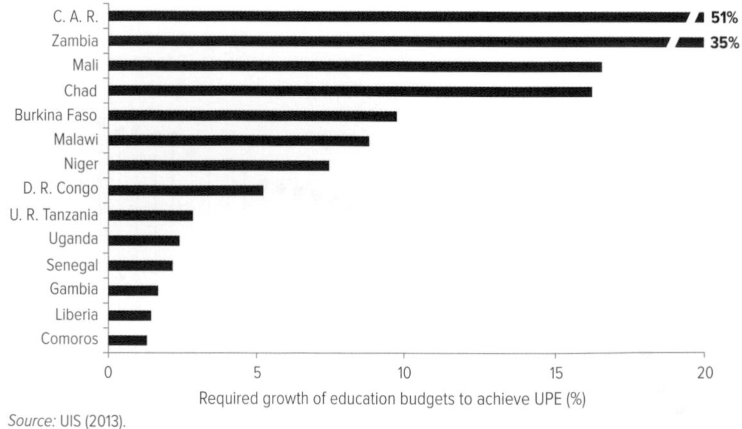

Source: UIS (2013).

7. The estimate is based on the additional annual cost of teacher wages and benefits in the 39 countries in sub-Saharan Africa with data assuming a UPE target date of 2020. It does not include the cost of training, for which data are unavailable. Nor does it include the costs of the additional classrooms and learning materials required. The estimates rely on the assumptions that average annual teacher compensation remains three to five times GDP per capita and that future economic growth is in line with current projections for each country by the International Monetary Fund. See UIS (2013) for further information.

For some countries, bridging the gap would require a considerable increase in the education budget, even after taking economic growth into account. For example, education budgets would have to increase by 51% in the Central African Republic and by 35% in Zambia just to pay the additional teachers' salaries (Figure 5.11).

While the required increases may seem vast, most countries should be able to meet them if their economies grow as projected and if they dedicate a larger share of their GDP to education while staying within the benchmark of 3% allocated to primary education (Figure 5.12). On average, sub-Saharan African countries would have to increase the share of the budget that they allocate to education from 12% to 14% in 2011 to close the teacher gap by 2020 (Development Finance International and Oxfam, 2013).

For the Central African Republic and Zambia, which require large increases in their primary education budgets, the higher spending would still be below the 3% benchmark, as both countries' spending on education is very low. Making the increases would raise their respective spending to only 1.3% and 1.1% of GDP, assuming their economies grow in line with current forecasts. This would leave ample scope to increase spending on classrooms, learning materials and other items needed to ensure that all children are in school and learning.

The only countries that could not afford the additional costs within the 3% benchmark are Comoros and the United Republic of Tanzania. They likely would not be able to expand domestic resources sufficiently and would require donor support, at least initially, to recruit the number of teachers needed. The United Republic of Tanzania, for example, already allocates 3.3% of GDP to primary education. Compensating all the additional teachers required to achieve UPE would add US$335 million per year, equivalent to 26% of the total amount the government allocated to the education sector in its planned 2011 budget (Development Finance International and Oxfam, 2013).

The financing challenge is inevitably greater for lower secondary school. For sub-Saharan Africa, recruiting more lower secondary school teachers to achieve universal education at that level by 2030 would add US$9.5 billion to the education budget annually. In Burkina Faso, for example, the lower secondary education budget would need to grow by 6% by 2030 to achieve this goal.

While many countries should be able to meet the costs of recruiting and paying the required additional primary teachers from their national budgets, they will also need to pay for teacher education programmes, as well as school construction and learning materials, to ensure that children receive an education of a good quality. Expanding the lower secondary teacher workforce will place a further burden on national budgets. Some of the poorest countries are therefore likely to face a substantial financing gap and will require the support of aid donors. This need is likely to be even greater when the costs of expanding the training of teachers are taken into account.

Support by donors for teacher education programmes is, however, limited. Between 2008 and 2011, donors spent only US$189 million per year on pre-service and in-service teacher education programmes on average, equivalent to 2% of the education aid budget. Just over a quarter of aid to teacher training was spent in sub-Saharan Africa, including in Ethiopia, Mozambique, Nigeria and the United Republic of Tanzania. The largest country recipients, however, included richer middle income countries such as Brazil, China and Indonesia. Donors need to both pay more attention to teacher education to support improvements in the quality of education, and also ensure that these funds are directed at the countries most in need.

Figure 5.12: The cost of hiring additional teachers would mostly not exceed the spending benchmark of 3% of GDP on primary education

Additional expenditure in education needed, beyond what is expected from economic growth, required to pay salaries of extra primary teachers needed to achieve universal primary education by 2020

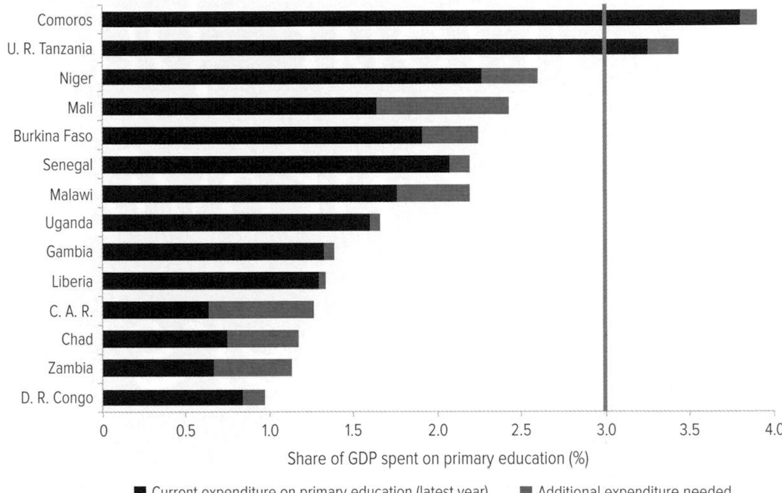

Note: For Comoros, Liberia, the United Republic of Tanzania and Zambia, there is no information for current expenditure on primary education as a share of GDP. For these countries it has been assumed that 50% of total current expenditure on education as a share of GDP is allocated to primary education.
Source: UIS (2013).

Conclusion

Sound education planning, undertaken in consultation with teachers, is an important basis for the successful implementation of strategies aimed at improving the quality of education. Such planning needs to take account of the costs of quality reforms and ensure that resources are available to meet these costs, whether from governments or aid donors. Countries must also ensure that sufficient numbers of teachers are recruited and trained in the coming years so that current and future education goals will be achieved.

Chapter 6
A four-part strategy for providing the best teachers

Credit: Karel Prinsloo/ARETE/UNESCO

A sense of vocation: Bonafice, a teacher in Lodwar, Turkana, Kenya, says 'Teaching is more than just a profession, it's also a calling.'

To end the global learning crisis, policy-makers need to give teachers every chance to put their motivation, energy, knowledge and skills to work in the service of improving learning for all. And they need to provide the best teachers for those who need them most. This chapter describes the strategies governments need to adopt to attract and retain the best teachers, improve teacher education, allocate teachers more fairly and provide incentives in the form of better salaries and attractive career paths. To make sure these strategies are implemented effectively, the chapter also identifies approaches to strengthen teacher governance.

Introduction

To end the global learning crisis, policy-makers need to increase significantly teacher numbers and give them every chance to put their motivation, energy, knowledge and skills acquired through training to work to maximize the learning potential of all children and young people.This chapter describes in detail the four strategies that governments need to adopt to attract and retain the best teachers, improve teacher education, allocate teachers more fairly and provide incentives in the form of appropriate salaries and attractive career paths.

Many teachers enter the profession for the best reasons. But in some countries teaching is seen as second-best; in other cases teachers are not educated well enough themselves. In addition, teaching often does not draw the most appropriate blend of men and women, or enough people who have experience of diversity.

It is crucial, therefore, for governments to ensure that children have the most able and most qualified teachers. That means attracting the right balance of good candidates, preparing them through comprehensive initial teacher education, and supporting them throughout their careers with ongoing training and guidance.

Even when all these criteria are fulfilled, however, learning outcomes remain widely unequal if the best teachers are not deployed to remote or poor areas. Unless governments ensure that teachers are fairly distributed, children who are already disadvantaged will fail to learn because of larger classes, high teacher turnover and a lack of qualified teachers.

Teacher turnover is high when salaries are too low, weakening morale and pushing teachers to take up additional jobs or seek other careers. Governments need to offer teachers a career path with prospects for promotion; where governments face severe budget constraints, salaries need to be at least high enough to ensure that teachers have enough to live on. To reduce disadvantage in learning, policy-makers also need to improve teacher governance by implementing strategies that prevent absenteeism and the encroachment of private tuition on classroom teaching time.

Strategy 1: Attract the best teachers

I chose to be a teacher because I believe that education has the power to transform the society we live in. What motivates me to be a good teacher is to be an active agent in this change that is so necessary for my country, to fight against discrimination, injustice, racism, corruption and poverty. Our responsibility as teachers is enormous, and our commitment to provide quality education must be renewed every day.

– Ana, teacher, Lima, Peru

The quality of an education system is only as good as the quality of its teachers. An analysis for this Report of the 2011 TIMSS results for grade 4 from 45 countries found that, across the countries, the better the teacher quality, the less the incidence of low achievement.[1] In Poland, for example, a student attending a school with low teacher quality was 25% more likely to score below the mathematics benchmark and 34% more likely to score below the science benchmark, compared with a student attending a school with high teacher quality. In Turkey, the effects were 28% in mathematics and 30% in science. Since 42% of schools in Turkey are identified as having teachers of low quality, the effects are felt by a large proportion of students there (Nonoyama-Tarumi and Willms 2013).

Evidence from 45 countries shows that the better the teacher quality, the less the incidence of low achievement

The first step to getting good teachers is to attract the best and most motivated candidates into the profession. Many people who decide to become teachers are driven by the satisfaction of helping students learn, fulfil their potential and develop into confident, responsible citizens. Some have been inspired to emulate their own teachers and pass on their knowledge, skills and love of learning. Many enter teaching because they like working with children and young people.

Teaching does not always draw the best candidates, however. Some have not received enough education themselves. In some countries, teaching is seen as a second-class job for those who do not do well enough academically to enter more prestigious careers, for example as doctors or engineers. In addition, teaching

1. The study used an index of teacher quality, including teachers' job satisfaction, their understanding of the school's curricular goals, their degree of success in using the school's curriculum, their expectations for student achievement, and teacher absenteeism.

often fails to attract the right balance of men and women, or recruit enough people with disabilities or from ethnic minorities, disadvantaged backgrounds or conflict-affected areas. This section examines ways to attract not only the best teachers but also the right mix of teachers.

Getting entry requirements right

It is not enough just to want to teach. People should enter the profession having received a good education themselves. They need to have completed at least secondary schooling of appropriate quality and relevance, so that they have a sound knowledge of the subjects they will be teaching and the ability to acquire the skills needed to teach.

The level of qualification required to enter teaching is a signal of the field's professional status. In some countries, teaching is regarded as a career for those not scoring high enough marks to enter more prestigious professions.

To elevate the status of teaching and attract talented applicants, Egypt has introduced more stringent entry requirements, requiring candidates to have strong performance in secondary school as well as a favourable interview assessment. Once selected, candidates also have to pass an entrance examination to ensure that they match the profile of a good teacher (World Bank, 2010b).

In Singapore, teacher candidates are chosen from the top third of high school graduates

In rich countries where students' level of achievement is high, teaching is a prestigious profession, with future teachers selected from among the best secondary school graduates. In Singapore, candidates are chosen from the top third of high school graduates. In Finland, selection is highly competitive, with only about 10% of applicants gaining entrance to teacher education programmes (OECD, 2011b).

In many poor countries, candidates enter teaching with low levels of academic qualifications. But simply raising the formal educational qualification needed to become a teacher does not necessarily ensure that teachers will be better: the quality of the academic qualification is also important. For example, data for francophone sub-Saharan African countries show no relationship between teachers' academic qualifications and student achievement (Fehrler et al., 2009). This is an indication of the low quality of the education the teachers themselves had received. Raising entry requirements without improving the quality of general education will do little to improve the pool of candidates with the necessary subject knowledge and skills to become better teachers, and risks excluding those from disadvantaged groups with limited access to quality education.

Even having a university degree does not always ensure that those entering teaching have the subject knowledge needed to teach basic school subjects. A study for this Report of the 2007 SACMEQ data found that in most of the countries concerned, teachers with a university education had no better knowledge of basic reading and mathematics than teachers with lower qualifications who might have developed a stronger practical understanding of the subjects (Altinok, 2013a).

Where academic qualifications are not of sufficient quality, and especially where raising them would reduce representation from disadvantaged groups, teacher education policies need to widen recruitment strategies and provide intensive, high quality training to raise subject knowledge.

Recruiting a balance of male and female teachers from a wide range of backgrounds

Teachers in rural areas are usually members of the school communities. We share the same economic and social fortunes with their parents and our children attend the schools we teach in. ... I adapt the syllabus to the day-to-day values of the community and the reality of our lives.

– Fwanshishak, teacher, Kaduna state, Nigeria

Children who feel that their teachers have nothing in common with them or cannot communicate with them are less likely to engage fully in learning. Making sure there are enough female teachers and recruiting teachers from a wide range of backgrounds are important strategies for providing an inclusive, good quality education. Flexible policies for entry qualifications may be required to improve diversity of the teaching force. Recruiting teachers from under-represented groups to work in their own communities ensures that children are taught by teachers familiar with their culture and language. Local recruitment can also help increase the supply of teachers in areas affected by conflict.

The presence of female teachers can improve girls' enrolment and achievement, especially in more conservative settings where the movement and life choices of girls and young women is restricted. In Punjab province, Pakistan, girls' standardized test scores were higher if they had a female teacher (Aslam and Kingdon, 2011). Increasing the proportion of female teachers in a district has been found to improve girls' access to and achievement in education in 30 developing countries, especially in rural areas (Huisman and Smits, 2009a; 2009b).

However, many factors limit the number of women recruited into teaching, particularly in disadvantaged areas. There may simply be not enough women educated enough to become teachers, especially in rural communities and among indigenous and minority populations. In the Lao People's Democratic Republic, for example, few ethnic minority women have become qualified teachers, partly because the number of girls completing school is low (Kirk, 2006).

More stringent qualification requirements can limit the pool of women able to enter teaching, especially those from disadvantaged groups. In Cambodia, for example, policy changes in the late 1990s raised the entry requirement for teachers from 10 to 12 years of basic education, resulting in very low recruitment of women from rural areas, where few have access to upper secondary schools (Geeves and Bredenberg, 2005).

To ensure adequate recruitment of female teachers, affirmative action may be needed. In Mozambique, government action resulted in the numbers of female teachers in grades 1 to 5 almost tripling between 1998 and 2008 and increasing sixfold in grades 6 and 7. The Ministry of Education encouraged the heads of teacher training colleges to take measures aimed at recruiting more women, including allocating more places for female students. As a result, the proportion of women students in these colleges has consistently been at or above 50%. Such affirmative measures have helped increase the number of women teachers quickly (Beutel et al., 2011).

In Afghanistan, women teachers are urgently needed, but the lack of girls' education until recently has meant very few women qualified to become teachers. In 2008, less than 30% of those in initial teacher education were female, even though the numbers had been increasing thanks to programmes enabling women to enter teaching with lower qualifications (Wirak and Lexow, 2008).

In Punjab province, Pakistan, girls' test scores were higher if they had a female teacher

Working with secondary school girls to raise their interest in teaching and offering financial assistance is another strategy that can potentially increase the number of female teachers, as experience from South Sudan illustrates (Box 6.1).

Recruiting teachers from under-represented groups, such as ethnic minorities, to serve in their own communities is one approach to improve the supply of teachers in these areas and ensure that children are taught by teachers familiar with their cultural context. Where access to quality education has been limited, flexible policies on academic requirements can help ensure that greater numbers are recruited. In Cambodia, where teacher trainees normally have to have completed grade 12, this entry requirement is waived for remote areas where upper secondary education is unavailable, increasing the pool of teachers from ethnic minorities. This policy has increased the number of teachers who understand local culture, are motivated to stay in remote areas and can teach in the local language (Benveniste et al., 2008b).

Deploying teachers to conflict zones is difficult because of the dangerous working conditions, particularly as schools and teachers are sometimes attacked. In conflict-affected parts of the Central African Republic and the Democratic Republic of the Congo, teachers have been recruited from local communities to keep education going (UNESCO, 2011).

People with disabilities are likely to face large barriers to achieving the level of education needed to train as a teacher. Flexible policies for entry into teacher education programmes are a possible way to help overcome this. Scholarships and appropriate college facilities and resources for students with disabilities can also support their opportunities for training. In Mozambique, Escolas de Professores do Futuro,

Box 6.1: South Sudan encourages secondary school girls to go into teaching

In South Sudan, where there is an enormous shortage of qualified teachers, less than 1% of girls complete secondary school. Decades of civil war coupled with cultural factors have undermined the role of women in public life and deprived most girls of the opportunity to attend school. Women make up about 65% of the post-war population, yet less than 10% of all teachers are women. Gender equity at all levels of education will be significantly harder to achieve if girls continue to lack female teachers who can support their learning and serve as role models.

To increase the number of female teachers, the Gender Equity through Education Programme provided financial and material incentives to over 4,500 girls to complete secondary school and to train young women graduates to enter the teaching profession. Schools with no female teachers were encouraged to identify a mentor for girls, a local woman who could come to the school regularly to discuss questions, concerns and ideas with girls. Communications materials with positive messages about women teachers and their role in the newly independent country were developed to reach young women. The programme distributed kits containing sanitary pads, developed and distributed learning materials, and supported other government programmes aimed at increasing gender equity in education.

The programme achieved significant success, including greater awareness among teachers and school personnel of girls' needs. The provision of stipends in particular was linked to a substantial increase in the retention of girls in secondary schools. However, about one in five girls said they planned to pursue a career other than teaching, partly because of the low status of the profession. The police, the military and security companies pay three times as much, and teaching is seen as a stepping stone towards other jobs or post-secondary education opportunities. If such initiatives are to encourage more women to go into teaching, salaries and conditions of service need to improve.

Sources: Epstein and Opolot (2012); Globalgiving (2013).

community-based teacher training colleges, run teacher education programmes for primary teachers in rural areas. One of these has been training visually impaired primary school teachers for more than ten years. Each year visually impaired graduates from mainstream schools are identified, with assistance from the local School for the Blind, and encouraged to apply for a scholarship at the college. All teacher educators have been trained in Braille by the school for the blind and the national Union of the Blind, and a number of them read and write Braille fluently. During their training, the visually impaired student teachers teach in practice schools nearby. Communities have become familiar with their children being taught by visually impaired teachers, resulting in a positive change of attitude and helping create a more welcoming environment for teachers and students with disabilities (Lewis and Bagree, 2013).

Teacher education should include classroom experience

Strategy 2: Improve teacher education so all children can learn

Good quality education depends on giving teachers the best possible training, not only before they start teaching but also throughout their careers. Initial teacher education should prepare teachers to help students from a wide range of backgrounds and with different needs, including those with inherited disadvantage, especially in the early grades. It should go beyond the theory of teaching to include classroom experience, and ensure that prospective teachers know enough about the subjects they are going to teach.

Initial teacher education also needs to lay the foundations for ongoing training that reinforces skills and knowledge. In-service training is especially important for teachers who may be untrained or undertrained. In addition, teachers need ongoing training to adapt to new teaching and learning methods, and trainers themselves need ongoing education. For countries with limited capacity to train teachers, technology that enables training from a distance is one way to reach larger numbers of trainees more effectively.

Initial teacher education must promote equitable learning

Initial teacher education should prepare teachers to support the learners who need the most help, especially in early grades when disadvantaged students are at risk of leaving school before they have learned to read a single word. But initial teacher education is not always effective in preparing teachers to deliver good quality, equitable education.

The length and institutional arrangements of initial teacher education vary across countries, as well as within countries depending on the level at which teachers will be teaching (Karras and Wolhuter, 2010). In some programmes, academic subjects are studied concurrently with educational and professional courses; in others, courses in pedagogy are offered to trainees who already have a degree in a specialized subject. A third approach is school-based training, which is more like apprenticeship (Tatto et al., 2012). In addition, flexible distance teacher education is becoming popular for resource-constrained governments wishing to expand their qualified teacher base.

All teacher education programmes aim to ensure that teachers meet proficiency requirements before being certified as 'qualified' or 'trained' – but the quality of teachers graduating from such widely varying programmes can also differ, depending on the quality of the content and how teaching practice is organized. Teacher quality cannot be improved simply by increasing the length of training; the quality of training also needs to be improved. In 14 anglophone African countries, for example, a longer duration of initial teacher education, while positive, was not found to have an impact on the English and mathematics scores of grade 6 pupils, according to an analysis of SACMEQ data (Fehrler et al., 2009).

Initial teacher education should make up for weak subject knowledge

Prospective teachers should ideally enter teacher education programmes knowing enough about the subjects they are going to teach. Teachers' subject knowledge tends to be clearly reflected in student scores or achievement gains (Glewwe et al., 2011).

One way of gauging teachers' knowledge is to see how they perform on tests that their students take. In Peru, as part of the 2004 national assessment of student learning, the teachers of 12,000 grade 6 students from 900 primary schools also took the mathematics and reading comprehension tests. In schools where both subjects were taught by the same teacher, students who scored well in mathematics tended to have teachers who also scored well in that subject – a result which applied for rural and urban locations, and no matter the language spoken at home (Metzler and Woessmann, 2012).

In low income countries, however, teachers often enter the profession lacking core subject knowledge because their own education has been poor. In such circumstances, teacher education programmes need to start by ensuring that all trainees acquire a good understanding of the subjects they will be teaching.

Weak subject knowledge can be found among primary school teachers. In a 2010 survey of primary schools in Kenya, grade 6 teachers scored only 61% on tests of grade 6 mathematics material; none of the teachers had complete mastery of the subject (Ngware et al., 2010). In India, where student learning outcomes remain low, particularly for poor populations, only 9% of primary school teacher candidates passed the Central Teacher Eligibility Test introduced by the government in 2011 with little improvement in subsequent years (Chudgar, 2013).

In Kenya, grade 6 teachers scored only 61% on tests of grade 6 mathematics material

In some countries, teachers are not sufficiently proficient in the language of instruction. In Kano state, northern Nigeria, 78% of 1,200 basic education teachers were found to have 'limited' knowledge of English when tested on their reading comprehension and ability to correct a sentence written by a 10-year-old (Education Sector Support Programme in Nigeria, 2011). In the Gambia, teacher testing undertaken as part of an Early Grade Reading Assessment found that primary teachers, who teach in English, scored poorly on basic English language tests. Only 54% correctly identified which of four words (heavy, hard, huge and rotten) was closest in meaning to 'enormous' (Mulkeen, 2013).

Students being taught by teachers with weak subject knowledge inevitably face difficulties in learning. In southern and eastern Africa, teachers were given similar reading and mathematics tests as their grade 6 students as part of the 2007 SACMEQ. In South Africa, an increase of about 100 points in the teacher score was found to increase the student score by 38 points (Altinok, 2013a). Students with the opportunity to be taught by a teacher from the best 10% instead of a teacher from the worst 10% would see their score improve by 110 points, equivalent to the difference between Mpumalanga province, with the third lowest performance out of nine provinces, and Western Cape, with the highest (Moloi and Chetty, 2010).

Teacher education programmes of the highest scoring countries on the Teacher Education and Development Study in Mathematics in 2007/08, including Singapore and Taiwan Province of China, offer more balance between training in subject knowledge, methods of teaching subject knowledge and general teaching methods than some other countries (Babcock et al., 2010).

In developing countries, teacher education institutions that need to upgrade trainees' weak subject knowledge often do not have time to do so, due partly to competing curriculum demands. For instance, in Uganda the curriculum for initial primary teacher education devotes 262 hours of instructional time to teaching methods and pedagogical theory, and only about 120 hours each to mathematics, language (English) and science. Most of this time is spent learning subject-specific teaching methods, which assume previous solid subject knowledge (World Bank, 2012c). In Kenya, teacher trainees are required to take 10 subjects and go on teaching practice in the first year, with 9 subjects and teaching practice in the second year. This leaves little time to fill gaps in trainees' subject knowledge (Bunyi et al., 2013).

To address such problems in Ghana, teacher education was restructured in the early 2000s. Trainees have to pass an examination on foundation academic subjects at the end of their first year before they can proceed to the second and third years, which focus mainly on pedagogical skills. Trainees who fail can resit the examination, but those who fail a second time are withdrawn from training (Akyeampong, 2003).

In Senegal, only 8% of trainees express any confidence about teaching reading in local languages

Training teachers to teach, particularly in early grades

Teachers need not only sound subject knowledge but also training in how to teach. Knowledge of strategies for teaching subject content varies widely between and within countries. Trainee teachers of lower secondary school mathematics in Taiwan Province of China scored over one and a half times higher in pedagogical knowledge than their counterparts in Chile, for example (Blömeke, 2012). Within Chile, the weakest 5% of trainees scored below 200 points while the strongest 5% scored over 500 points (Tatto et al., 2012). Unless training tackles such divergences, it is bound to perpetuate inequality in student learning.

In sub-Saharan African countries, where learning outcomes are low and often very unequal, pre-service teacher education tends to be based on curricula that place little emphasis on the quality and variety of teaching methods. In Ghana, Kenya, Mali, Senegal, Uganda and the United Republic of Tanzania, for example, trainees are not trained in ways to ensure active participation in the classroom so that students understand the lesson (Akyeampong et al., 2013).

As a result, few primary school teachers demonstrate an adequate level in the methods for teaching their subject. Analysis of videotaped mathematics lessons in Botswana and in North West Province, South Africa, demonstrated that most teachers lacked the ability to help students learn the material. Teachers who did help students learn used a well-planned lesson, with richness and variety in the tasks presented, and had strong communication skills that conveyed mathematical concepts at pupils' level of understanding (Sapire and Sorto, 2012).

Adequate pre-service teacher education is also essential to enable children to acquire good reading skills early. Children should be learning to read, decode and understand text within the first few years of schooling: those that do not risk being left behind. However, teachers are seldom trained to teach these skills. In Mali, a study of pupils' skills using an Early Grade Reading Assessment and teacher observation found that few teachers were able to teach their pupils how to read. Teachers had been inadequately prepared to apply the required teaching methods and did not give sufficient attention to supporting pupils' individual reading. This is no doubt an important reason why nearly half the pupils in Mali cannot read a word in their own language at the end of grade 2 (Varly, 2010).

Teacher education programmes need to support teachers in being able to teach early reading skills in more than one language and to use local language materials effectively. However, teachers are rarely prepared for the reality of multilingual classrooms. A small-scale study of mathematics teaching in Botswana indicated that bilingual teacher education was failing in its aim of preparing teachers for multilingual classrooms where pupils' home language may be different from both the national language and English, the medium of mathematics teaching (Kasule and Mapolelo, 2005). In Senegal, where attempts are being made to use local languages in schools, training is given only in French, and a survey found that only 8% of trainees express any confidence about teaching reading in local languages (Akyeampong et al., 2013).

Preparing teachers to support learners from diverse backgrounds

Teacher education needs to prepare trainees to instruct students from diverse backgrounds, using a wide array of strategies. This is particularly important in poorer countries, where student needs are likely to be especially diverse as large numbers of marginalized children enter school for the first time.

Training in the use of diagnostic and formative assessment tools is crucial, so that teachers can identify weak learners and provide them with targeted support. Yet it is rarely part of initial teacher education in poor countries. For this reason, projects associated with Early Grade Reading Assessments that use diagnostic and continuous assessment to identify and address gaps in early grade reading skills in developing countries include in-service training and mentoring to support teachers in using such approaches (Gove and Cvelich, 2010) (see the section on Improving teacher skills through ongoing education).

Training in diagnostic and formative assessment is also insufficient in rich countries. In a study of EU countries, teachers in half the countries surveyed reported a lack of ability to diagnose student problems swiftly and accurately, and to draw from a wide repertoire of appropriate solutions (European Commission, 2012). Incorporating training in such skills into pre-service curricula, and ensuring that teacher educators know how to teach these skills, is vital so that teachers have a strong foundation for supporting children with diverse learning needs.

As a result of inadequate training, including overemphasis on theory rather than practice, many newly qualified teachers are not confident that they have the skills necessary to support children with more challenging learning needs, including those with severe physical or intellectual disabilities, in mainstream classrooms (Forlin, 2010). In Viet Nam, after the need for adequate human resources to support inclusive education initiatives was recognized, a core national curriculum and guiding framework for inclusive education was developed (Inclusive Education in Action, 2010). It includes learning modules designed to be stand-alone or incorporated into existing programmes at teacher training colleges and universities. In colleges, courses cover creating individual education plans for all learners, designing and adapting activities for children with different learning needs, and assessing learning outcomes of children with special needs or disabilities (Nguyet and Ha, 2010).

Among OECD countries, those where teacher education includes attention to addressing diversity achieve the best outcomes. Finland, which has one of the world's highest PISA scores and very little inequality between students, trains future teachers to identify students with learning difficulties (OECD, 2011b).

Finland trains future teachers to identify students with learning difficulties

Stagnating or declining learning outcomes in high income countries in recent years have prompted policy debate and reforms aimed at training teachers to help weak learners (European Commission, 2012). After scoring below average for OECD countries in the 2000 PISA assessment, Germany introduced teacher education reforms that helped improve student learning, as measured by PISA in 2009. Future teachers are recruited from the top third of high school graduates, and receive extensive preparation at university, with a focus on identifying and addressing problems faced by students with low achievement. They receive an extended period of mentoring by experienced teachers before becoming fully qualified teachers (OECD, 2011b).

A study of pre-service teacher education for lower secondary mathematics teaching in 15 countries[2] found that none of the countries included preparation for student diversity as a key focus of teacher education. In several countries, including Germany and Poland, only a few future teachers indicated they had received professional preparation that included measures to prepare for student diversity. Five countries were classified as having strong preparation for professional challenges: Botswana, Chile, Malaysia, the Philippines and the United States. Student teachers in these countries have more opportunities to learn how to teach students from diverse cultural or socio-economic backgrounds, as well as those with physical disabilities (Blömeke, 2012).

2. Botswana, Chile, Taiwan Province of China, Georgia, Germany, Malaysia, Norway, Oman, the Philippines, Poland, the Russian Federation, Singapore, Switzerland, Thailand and the United States.

In remote or under-resourced schools and classrooms, some teachers need to teach multiple grades and ages in one classroom. In some countries in sub-Saharan Africa, including Burkina Faso, Mali, Niger, Senegal and Togo, at least 10% of students study in multigrade classrooms. In Chad, almost half of students are taught in such classrooms. In some countries, class size is higher in multigrade classrooms: in Mali, for example, there are over 73 students per class, compared with an average of 57 students in single grade classes (UIS, 2012b).

Pre-service education and ongoing training on the needs of the multigrade class are vital. When training in teaching multigrade classes is provided, teacher skills can be raised and learning outcomes improved. For example, a small project in Sri Lanka trained teachers to develop lesson plans and grade-appropriate tasks for classes combining grades 4 and 5. Results found that such methods had a positive impact on pupils' achievement in mathematics (Vithanapathirana, 2006).

In Turkey, a pre-service teacher education course on gender equity had a significant impact on female teachers' gender attitudes

Teachers also need adequate preparation to understand and address gendered dimensions of school and classroom interactions that can negatively affect girls' and boys' learning experiences and outcomes. Teachers, both female and male, need training to understand and recognize their own attitudes, perceptions and expectations, and how these affect their interactions with pupils. In Turkey, a one-term pre-service teacher education course on gender equity had a significant impact on female teachers' gender attitudes and awareness. Those participating in the course, which included topics such as gender socialization, selection of teaching materials and the school environment, showed significant improvement on a scale designed to measure attitudes to gender roles (Erden, 2009).

The Forum for African Women Educationalists has developed a Gender-Responsive Pedagogy model to address the quality of teaching in African schools. The model includes training teachers in the use of gender-equitable teaching and learning materials, classroom arrangements and interaction strategies, along with strategies to eliminate sexual harassment and encourage gender-responsive school management. Since 2005, over 6,600 teachers have been trained using this model (Forum for African Women Educationalists, 2013). Case studies of schools where teachers were trained using this model – as part of a wider package of activities – reported that teachers were more responsive to gender issues and provided greater support to girls; the studies also found improved participation and learning outcomes (Forum for African Women Educationalists, 2006; Haugen et al., 2011).

Initial teacher education needs to provide classroom experience

I think that academic training gave me huge support in learning subject knowledge, but, without a doubt, the training which helped me improve the most was the daily work in the classroom.
– Elena, teacher, Madrid, Spain

Opportunities for teaching practice are essential to ensure that teacher trainees succeed later in improving students' learning. Countries that have achieved high student learning outcomes are also those that ensure sustained periods of learning to teach in classrooms under the supervision of expert teaching staff (OECD, 2011a, 2011b; Schleicher, 2012).

Teacher education programmes in developing countries often fail to ensure that trainees get adequate experience of learning to teach in classrooms, which contributes to the poor quality of teaching. Time spent on teaching practice can be as short as nine weeks out of six months of training in Senegal, or nine weeks out of two years in Kenya. In both countries, teaching in the lowest three grades is supposed to be included as part of teaching practice, but many trainees were not able to experience the breadth of curriculum and grades that they were promised (Akyeampong et al., 2013).

Even where initial teacher education programmes include school-based experience and teaching practice, the timing can be problematic. In some African countries, school-based practice may take place some time after the training programme, severely limiting opportunities for feedback and critical reflection on classroom experiences. A lack of mentoring and erratic support from tutors further compound the problem (Pryor et al., 2012).

To improve teacher quality, Pakistan is committed to replacing traditional training methods such as lectures and seminars with those promoting practical skills and child-centred pedagogy (USAID, 2008). But trainees still spend only around 10% of their course time on practical teaching experience (Nordstrum, 2013).

In poor countries, teachers need to be prepared for the practical challenges of under-resourced and diverse classrooms, particularly in remote, rural areas. Development Aid from People to People, an international non-profit development organization, has established teacher training colleges in Malawi that offer pre-service education designed to equip new teachers with the skills necessary for rural schools. A strong practical orientation and ample time for school-based experience and community work help prepare teachers for the realities of living and teaching in rural areas (Box 6.2).

Box 6.2: Practically oriented pre-service teacher education supports teachers in rural Malawi

Malawi has one of the world's most dramatic teacher shortages, resulting in primary school classes with around 76 students on average. Unless urgent action is taken, the country is unlikely to close the teacher gap by 2030. Shortages are particularly problematic for rural areas, where teachers, especially women, are often unwilling to teach. These circumstances contribute to some of the lowest learning outcomes in the world.

To increase the number of primary teachers equipped to teach and stay in rural areas, Development Aid from People to People Malawi recently established four teacher education colleges in rural districts. Training programmes emphasize the integration of theory and subject content, the practical application of teaching skills, student-led research and reflection, community outreach and social development. Opportunities for teaching experience are provided during initial college-based training and one year of teaching practice. On graduation, the new teachers are expected to work effectively in rural areas, including using teaching and learning materials produced from locally available resources. The training programmes place a strong emphasis on supporting the needs of all learners, including learners at risk, and establishing community-based projects such as school gardens to support vulnerable children.

The training follows a 30-month cycle, divided into eight periods. During the first five periods, trainees are based at the college to build academic, practical and social skills, and are encouraged to carry out research in surrounding communities on strategies for teaching and working in rural areas. They learn about local development issues and partner with nearby schools for experience in classroom teaching, extracurricular activities and community outreach. The sixth period is a full school year in teaching practice, with a pair of trainees taking responsibility for a class, assisted and supervised by a mentor at the primary school and the tutors at the college. The trainees return to the college for the seventh and eighth periods – for reflection, specialization and preparation for final examinations.

In a recent evaluation of the programme, 72% of trainees identified the school practice component as the area of study that most prepared them for teaching in rural areas. The evaluation concluded that the strong practical orientation of the programme provided better preparation than the more theoretical approach in government colleges. The evaluation also found that 80% of the trainees gained experience in providing remedial support to trainees, compared with just 14% in government colleges.

The programme has been particularly beneficial in encouraging young women to train as rural teachers. Of the female students in the programme, 80% found that school practice topics prepared them adequately for teaching in rural areas, compared with 38% of female students in government colleges. Furthermore, 87% of female students in the programme said they would opt for a rural post, compared with 67% of those in government colleges.

The Ministry of Education posted graduates of the programme to rural government schools. By 2011, 564 newly qualified teachers were working in rural primary schools, an additional 750 were training and 1,420 children were receiving remedial lessons. Given the large numbers of rural children needing such support, government colleges need to learn from the programme to ensure that all trainee teachers acquire the skills to teach in areas where they are most needed.

Sources: DeStefano (2011); Development Aid from People to People (2013); Mambo (2011).

months of improved phonics instruction, grade 2 pupils in intervention schools were, on average, correctly reading nearly three times as many syllables as pupils of the same grade in control schools (USAID, 2012).

Another project that has made a substantial impact on pupils' progress by training and supporting teachers in how to teach, monitor and assess early reading is EGRA Plus: Liberia. A two-year pilot programme, subsequently extended, included intensive training and follow-on support, backed by detailed curriculum-based lesson plans and diagnostic and formative assessment tools (Box 6.4).

Box 6.4: Helping teachers track pupils' progress in Liberia

EGRA Plus: Liberia was born out of the poor results in Liberia's Early Grade Reading Assessment, which found that around one-third of grade 2 students were unable to read a word. In 2008, the Ministry of Education, with USAID support, launched the programme to improve reading skills through evidence-based reading instruction and assessment. EGRA Plus: Liberia was designed to investigate the impact of the programme on learning outcomes for grade 2 and 3 pupils. Schools were assigned to one of three groups: full intervention, light intervention or no intervention. All schools participated in an assessment of pupils' reading skills to identify literacy, decoding, and fluency and comprehension levels.

Full intervention consisted of teacher education and support, structured lesson plans, teaching resource materials, and books for children to take home. Teachers participated in an intensive one-week course in early grade reading instruction and how to use formative and diagnostic assessment to identify and support weak learners. This was followed up with classroom-based support from trained mentors for the full programme duration of two years. Parents and community members were regularly informed of learner assessments. In the second year the programme provided sequential, scripted lesson plans that gave teachers and pupils a clear structure. The light intervention was minimal: informing parents and community members of pupils' reading levels through report cards, to examine whether such 'accountability' affected achievement.

The final reading assessments demonstrated that the full intervention had accelerated children's learning. Pupils receiving the full intervention increased their reading comprehension scores by 130%, compared with 33% in light or no intervention schools.

The programme had a higher impact on girls, bringing them up to boys' level from a slightly lower starting position. For example, girls in grade 2 increased their scores by 193% while the boys' increase was 149%. Due to the success of the pilot, the government and USAID have scaled up the programme in 1,300 schools. However, the costs of going to scale are considerable. It is estimated that reading materials alone cost over US$1,000 per school. Teacher education activities, coaches' salaries and transportation add substantially to the costs, requiring measures to ensure the programme's sustainability.

Sources: Davidson and Hobbs (2013); Gove and Cvelich (2010); Piper and Korda (2011).

Mentors offer valuable support to new teachers

Previous to mentoring, the teachers taught according to their own liking. The topics they found perplexing were either left out or taught in a way the students found hard to comprehend. Now, it's not like this because they ask for our advice and, through model lessons, we guide them.

– Arif, teacher mentor, Punjab, Pakistan

Mentoring new teachers once they are in the classroom is vital, particularly in poorer countries where teachers have limited prior practical experience. As part of Ethiopia's second Teacher Development Programme, teacher candidates are expected to work in schools with mentor teachers and supervisors (Nordstrum, 2013). In Ghana, trainees are paired with experienced teachers in early grades (Akyeampong et al., 2013).

The countries that achieve the highest scores in international learning assessments such as PISA and TIMSS emphasize mentoring of all newly qualified teachers, supported by additional resources targeted to their schools (Darling-Hammond et al., 2010). Time is allocated to enable new teachers and their mentors to participate in coaching and other induction activities, and for training of mentors. For example, New Zealand funds 20% release time for new teachers and 10% release time for second-year teachers so that they can meet with mentors, observe other teachers, engage in professional development activities and familiarize themselves with the curriculum (Darling-Hammond et al., 2009; NZEI Te Riu Roa, 2013). Similar models are found in several high performing East Asian countries.

In several countries, including England (United Kingdom), France, Israel, Norway, Singapore and Switzerland, mentor teachers are given formal training. In Norway, principals assign an experienced staff member as a mentor to each new teacher; a teacher education institution then trains the mentor and takes part in in-school guidance (OECD, 2005). Singapore provides government funding for experienced teachers to train for a postgraduate degree to become mentors for other teachers (Darling-Hammond et al., 2009).

Ongoing training to adapt to new teaching and learning approaches

We have started involving students in the classroom. The role of the teacher has changed into a facilitator and a guide. The rest of it is up to the children. They actively take charge of their learning. We have moved to activity-based learning, which is not like we used to teach – writing on the board, giving homework and not being concerned about whether students understood anything or not.
– Mubarak, teacher, Punjab, Pakistan

In many low income countries, teaching relies on traditional approaches such as lecturing, rote learning and repetition, reflecting what teachers experienced themselves at school and how they were taught in teacher education institutions (Hardman, 2012). Many countries have been trying to move from these teacher-dominated approaches towards a learner-centred one in which students are encouraged to 'learn to learn'. Such an approach emphasizes critical thinking, with teachers expected to help students actively construct knowledge through activities, group work and reflection (Vavrus et al., 2011).

Without training, teachers can find the shift to learner-centred pedagogy demanding, particularly in schools with few resources. In rural India, for example, primary school teachers experienced tensions in what they saw as the handing over of greater classroom control to pupils (Sriprakash, 2010). Teachers need ongoing support to help them adapt to new approaches.

A school-based teacher development programme in Kenya shows that such training can be effective in helping teachers adopt learner-centred methods. A teacher development programme for 47,000 primary school teachers in English, mathematics and science combined six months of self-study, based on distance learning materials, and meetings with tutors at cluster resource centres. The programme included 54 hours of self-study in pedagogical practice and 54 hours on the three subjects, and led to certification. It was found to increase teachers' use of their students' mother tongue, of lesson planning and of teaching aids produced with students. Teaching became more interactive, and attitudes towards students, especially girls, became more positive (Hardman et al., 2009).

The Healthy Learning programme, also in Kenya, uses in-service support to primary school teachers to improve pupils' understanding of health and nutrition through active teaching and learning methods. The programme, initiated in 2008 by the Ministry of Education in partnership with the Flemish Association for Development Cooperation and Technical Assistance, includes short training workshops, on-the-job support, exchange visits and practical school projects. Rather than changing the curriculum or introducing new topics, it encourages active teaching and learning approaches within the existing curriculum through practical school-based activities, such as school gardens, agroforestry technology, livestock development and water management, making use of locally available resources at school and district levels. The programme, being implemented in 163 public primary schools in disadvantaged arid and semi-arid areas, has been found to be relevant and effective (Management for Development Foundation, 2013).

Interventions that seek to complement traditional teaching are often organized by NGOs. In a programme in the Philippines, teachers received two days of training to conduct one hour of reading activities every day. After one month, grade 4 students' reading scores had increased significantly (Abeberese et al., 2013). In the Indian state of Bihar, government school teachers received training to use new learning materials adapted to the local context. Combined with other initiatives, including using village volunteers to provide children with support outside school hours, the programme increased achievement (Walton and Banerji, 2011).

In the Philippines, training of teachers to conduct one hour of reading activites every day increased students' reading scores

The benefits of ongoing training can be short-lived if resources are inadequate and the learning environment unsupportive. In 2005/06, Uganda developed a primary school 'thematic curriculum' based on three main principles: rapid development of basic literacy, numeracy and life skills in the early grades; the use of themes relevant to children's lives; and teaching in languages in which children were already proficient. Teachers were asked to use learner-centred methods and to adapt the direction of lessons to take children's reactions into account. Teachers received 10 days of intensive training before the new curriculum was introduced nationwide in early 2007. Teachers interviewed later that year said the training had been too short for them to understand the new curriculum and be prepared to teach it (Altinyelken, 2010).

Traditional pre-service teacher education and school examination practices can prevent teachers from introducing learner-centred approaches. Jordan undertook curriculum reforms and training to promote transferable skills for the 'knowledge economy', including creativity, critical thinking and teamwork. Teachers, however, still relied on rote learning, as this was what the secondary school graduation examination required (Box 6.5).

Box 6.5: In Jordan, rote learning hampers teaching of transferable skills

Jordan has made progress in enrolling its rapidly growing child and youth population, with 91% in primary school and 86% in secondary school, higher than the average rate for middle income countries. Yet while learning outcomes improved in the early 2000s, they have stagnated or even deteriorated in recent years. In 2011, the proportion of students passing the minimum benchmark in mathematics in the TIMSS assessment was lower than in 2007, and national assessment scores in communication and information management in all grades were also well below the targets set by the Ministry of Education.

Progress in the early 2000s might have been facilitated by the first phase of the Education Reform for the Knowledge Economy (2003-2009), which provided in-service training for teachers in using ICT in the classroom and promoting critical thinking and problem-solving by encouraging students' active participation. Implementation of the reform has been limited, however, by the emphasis on rote learning in the Tawjihi, the secondary school graduation examination on which admission to universities depends. In addition, teaching practice is short and most mentors lack the skills needed to train future teachers.

To avoid further deterioration in learning standards and ensure that students acquire the skills needed for Jordan to participate fully in the knowledge economy, the Tawjihi needs to be modernized and teachers need to be trained to adopt strategies that improve learning outcomes.

Responding to training needs, the Queen Rania Teacher Academy, established in 2009, provides subject-based professional development programmes for teachers that focus on using active learning for implementing the national curriculum, and has developed an induction programme for newly appointed teachers. The academy also supports a Schools Network initiative that provides opportunities for teachers, school leaders and supervisors to share ideas regarding instruction and receive support during and after training. The challenge will be for initiatives like this to reach the many teachers who need such support.

Sources: Abu Naba'h et al. (2009); Dakkak (2011); Jordan Ministry of Education (2012); Mullis et al. (2012); Queen Rania Teacher Academy (2011); World Bank (2011a).

Trainers also need training

The key role that teacher educators play in shaping teachers' skills is often the most neglected aspect of teacher preparation systems. Many educators seldom set foot in local schools to learn about the challenges prospective teachers face and how they might address them. Few education policies acknowledge the need for teacher educators to have close contact with schools, or educators' own training needs. There is, therefore, an urgent need to train teacher educators to prepare teachers adequately and effectively.

In most developing countries, teacher educators have very little training. In countries including Kenya, Uganda and the United Republic of Tanzania, teacher educators have no instruction in training teachers for basic education (Pryor et al., 2012).

Analysis of teacher education practices in six sub-Saharan African countries found that educators training teachers in early reading were rarely experts in the field by either experience or training. Trainers' limited knowledge of approaches used in the field impeded their ability to help trainees develop a wider repertoire of effective skills in teaching reading in the early grades. In Mali, teacher educators had no background in teaching how to read. Often educators' understanding of how children could progress in reading was based on the teacher education curriculum, little of which reflected the requirements of the primary education curriculum. For example, a quarter of teacher educators surveyed in Ghana and Uganda thought that comprehension was a skill to be taught only in upper primary, even though it was a stated benchmark for grade 3 in both countries. Significantly, mathematics tutors in all six countries had no special training in teaching primary mathematics at initial teacher education level (Pryor et al., 2012).

One example of supporting teacher educators as a key way of improving teacher training programmes comes from Nicaragua, where a professional development module was designed to address the instructional gaps identified in an Early Grade Reading Assessment in 2008. A first step was a four-day training workshop for about 180 teacher trainers and ministry staff, focusing on using assessment tools to inform and improve instruction. The ministry funded adaptation of the workshop materials – sample lessons, assessment instruments and training materials – and made them into training guides (USAID, 2010).

Curriculum reform requires teacher educators to be adequately prepared to orient teachers in curriculum changes. In Rajasthan state, India, the School and Teacher Education Reform Programme, established in 2010, aims to move schooling away from rote learning and towards teaching based on understanding and grounded in the local context of the child. In an innovative move to build legitmacy and ownership among teacher educators, a group made up of faculty from state, private and NGO teacher training colleges and universities was established to help develop teacher education and school curricula and materials (Saigal and Joshi, 2013).

Reforms aimed at helping weak students need to ensure that teacher educators are trained to give teachers appropriate support. In Viet Nam, where a national core curriculum framework on inclusive education has been developed, many teacher educators had limited awareness of how to deal with diversity. To address this, training was provided for teacher educators from universities and colleges to act as experts on inclusive education in pre-service programmes. In 2008, 47 teacher educators took a five-day intensive training course. All aspects of the new framework were discussed and opportunities were provided to learn, identify and practice the pedagogical skills needed for teaching an inclusive curriculum (Forlin and Dinh, 2010; Inclusive Education in Action, 2010).

With immigrant populations continuing to increase in OECD countries, classrooms are becoming more and more diverse. Teacher educators need to be able to help teachers respond to the learning needs of children from immigrant groups, but this issue is not receiving the attention it deserves. In an online survey about dealing with diversity in classrooms, around half of teacher educators in OECD countries who responded said they felt that teacher education did not sufficiently prepare teachers to handle diversity effectively, with the needs of immigrant children being particularly prominent (Burns and Shadoian-Gersing, 2010).

Distance education can boost countries' capacity to train teachers

What I have learned through online articles and interactive forums is invaluable. I am currently enrolled in an online programme and have discovered great sources of knowledge, inspiration and debate.

– Imza, teacher, Kigali, Rwanda

Not only is the quality of teacher education often lacking, but many teacher education institutions also lack the capacity to train the huge numbers of people that need to be trained, and expansion is costly. Using technology to provide training from a distance is one way to reach larger numbers of trainees more cheaply. Distance learning can be effective if it is complemented by mentoring and face-to-face support at key stages.

Teacher educators in OECD countries feel that teacher education does not sufficiently prepare teachers to handle diversity

Many low and middle income countries in sub-Saharan Africa and South and West Asia are using distance learning to train more teachers, especially those in rural areas who might otherwise be denied the opportunity. Malawi and the United Republic of Tanzania, for example, used distance learning to help expand the number of teachers rapidly after primary enrolment rose when school fees were abolished (Lewin and Stuart, 2003; Mulkeen, 2010). In 2010, Malawi revived distance learning to address severe teacher shortages. The current distance learning programme provides selected trainees with three weeks of orientation, after which they are deployed to schools in the zones where they were recruited. They spend two years at their assigned schools while completing and mailing in self-guided learning modules to a tutor from the local teacher training college. Mentoring is also provided within schools (DeStefano, 2011).

Distance education for teachers increasingly uses new technologies to deliver lessons more flexibly, to provide materials and feedback, and to enhance tutor-student interactions. In China, the Gansu Basic Education Project used a wide range of media to train teachers between 2001 and 2006. The project reached over 103,000 teachers through EU-funded resource centres that provided satellite television, video, Internet access and other computer-based resources. Around 1,600 teachers went on to gain professional diplomas (Robinson and

Wenwu, 2009). China has also built a multilevel network connecting national and provincial institutions with county and school-based training centres, using distance learning to increase the organization, implementation and effectiveness of professional development for rural teachers. A key strategy in this approach is the use of the Internet to establish effective communication and learning support for distance learners through the National Teachers' Web Union and accompanying Continuing Education Website (McQuaide, 2011).

In Zimbabwe, the Virtual and Open Distance Learning programme was recently introduced to alleviate shortages of trained science teachers. The programme combines print-based distance learning modules, online instruction and one-month periods of face-to-face tuition, and support from tutors at seven centres opened across the country in 2010 and 2011. Although the programme is still in its early days, and has faced problems including high attrition rates and inadequate ICT infrastructure, it has gained support from the government for continued expansion. While the number of graduates from the university's conventional programme totalled 1,087 over the previous decade, enrolments in the distance programme reached 1,438 in 2011 alone (Pedzisai et al., 2012).

South Africa targets teachers in rural areas with paper-based distance learning, supplemented by text messaging

Technological advances have supported distance learning even in low income countries. However, the extent to which ICT is used in distance learning for teacher education is dictated by ICT infrastructure and resources, and the needs of target audiences. Low connectivity in countries with less advanced ICT infrastructure can pose difficulties for both institutional hubs and participating teachers in remote areas. In South Africa, the Advanced Certificate in Education, a professional qualification in education management offered as a modular distance learning programme by the University of Pretoria, targets teachers in rural areas. Initial surveys revealed that only 1% of teachers had regular Internet access, but the vast majority had access to mobile phones. The university thus returned to paper-based distance learning, supplemented by text messaging (Aluko, 2009).

The absence of hardware, software and Internet access need not preclude the use of technology to expand teacher education, however. Battery or solar-powered equipment can be used to bring instructional videos and interactive learning modules to teacher trainees, even in remote areas. The USAID-funded Malawi Teacher Training Activity programme provided portable, battery-powered DVD players and projectors together with interactive instructional DVDs to teacher training centres for use during pre-service education (Nordstrum, 2013).

Attrition rates can be high in distance education programmes, as they demand considerable time and teachers may not be able to afford the fees, equipment and materials. For example, a distance learning programme for a certificate course in child guidance and counselling in India resulted in only a 16% completion rate: student teachers were required to put in 480 hours of study with limited tutorial support and had to pay their own fees (Perraton, 2010).

Distance teacher education programmes nevertheless have the potential to reach more future teachers at lower cost than programmes in teacher education institutions. Costs per student graduating from distance programmes have been estimated at between one-third and two-thirds of conventional programmes. For example, Pakistan's Primary Teachers Orientation Course cost between US$128 and US$178 per completing teacher, or between 45% and 70% of the costs for conventional university graduates. Similarly, course costs at the China Television Teachers' College for unqualified primary and secondary teachers were reported to be at most two-thirds of those for conventional colleges (Perraton, 2010). The cost per graduate of Ghana's Untrained Teacher Diploma in Basic Education, which combined distance learning with short residential sessions, was twenty times less than the cost of training a teacher in the full-time three-year residential teacher education programme (Ghana Education Service, 2010).

These examples show that distance learning has the potential to expand the reach of teacher education programmes and enhance flexibility, providing support and training for teacher candidates in more remote areas and those with family responsibilities who cannot spend long periods away from home. Despite its benefits, however, distance education is currently reaching only a small proportion of trainees in some countries that urgently need to expand the teaching force. In Ethiopia, for example, there is still reliance on residential teacher education courses, with only around 3% of graduates in 2010/11 enrolled in distance programmes (Nordstrum, 2013).

To realize the potential of distance education for teachers, substantial investment is necessary to ensure that programmes are of adequate quality, include mentoring and are complemented by face-to-face support for students. The use of ICT for distance education also requires investment in infrastructure, hardware and materials. South Africa is an example of a country that is addressing this need through innovation in Open Education Resources (South African Institute for Distance Education, 2010), which can dramatically reduce costs for participating institutions and learners.

The donor community needs to make a commitment to wider investment in the education sector in countries with severe teacher shortages so that demand for distance education programmes can be met and trained teachers deployed effectively. In Malawi, the introduction of the current distance education programme doubled the government's capacity to supply teachers. However, the number of teacher candidates recruited to the programme is still limited by the budget available to pay them once they become teachers and the capacity of teacher education colleges to support and supervise the trainees (DeStefano, 2011). For the first cohort of recruits in 2010, 22,000 applicants were deemed eligible, but only 3,800 were admitted to the programme (Steiner-Khamsi and Kunje, 2011).

One example of what donor funding can accomplish is the Untrained Teacher Diploma in Basic Education programme in Ghana, which has trained over 16,000 teachers and is being extended to alleviate teacher shortages in remote districts. Currently over half of the untrained teachers in the 57 most disadvantaged districts are being trained using this distance education programme, which will provide an additional 8,000 trained teachers. Financial support from donors will meet many of the costs that student teachers incurred in the past, including tuition, food and accommodation during residential sessions, and self-instruction modules (Ghana Education Sector Mission, 2013).

Strategy 3: Get teachers where they are most needed

In January, we were called by the Department of Education to come and work here. There are no roads, it's underdeveloped. There are so many psychological and emotional problems with the learners, so five of the [teachers] left because of the area.

– Lazola, teacher, Eastern Cape, South Africa

Teachers are understandably reluctant to work in deprived areas, which sometimes lack basic facilities such as electricity, good housing and health care. If the best teachers seldom work in remote, rural, poor or dangerous areas, the learning opportunities of children who are already disadvantaged suffer as a result because of larger class sizes, high rates of teacher turnover and a scarcity of trained teachers. Uneven allocation of trained teachers is a key factor in wide equity gaps in learning. Governments thus need to devise strategies to ensure that teachers are equally allocated, but few have succeeded in doing so effectively.

Unequal distribution of teachers is one reason some children leave school before learning the basics

While in many countries teacher allocation officially depends directly on student enrolment numbers, with minimum and maximum class sizes per school, actual teacher deployment often does not match student numbers. In Yemen, schools with 500 students were found to have between 4 and 27 teachers: in Ryma governorate there were 13 teachers for each average-sized basic school, while in Abyan governorate there were 28 (World Bank, 2010a). In Benin, enrolment in primary schools with four teachers ranged from fewer than 100 to almost 700 students (World Bank, 2009).

Such wide differences in teacher allocation are reflected in the quality of education students receive. South Sudan presents a particularly extreme case. The government stipulates a pupil/teacher ratio of 50:1 for primary schools, but teachers do not seem to be deployed and transferred on this basis. Excluding volunteer teachers, average pupil/teacher ratios vary from 51:1 in Central Equatoria to 145:1 in Jonglei (World Bank, 2012a).

Unequal distribution of teachers is one reason some children leave school before learning the basics. EFA Global Monitoring Report team calculations, based on data from the Bangladesh education management information system, show that the proportion of students reaching the last grade of primary school is 60% in subdistricts where there are 75 students per teacher, compared with three-quarters where there are 30 students per teacher.

Inequality in deployment leads not only to fewer teachers in deprived areas but also to disadvantaged students being taught by teachers with weaker subject knowledge, exacerbating inequality in learning outcomes. According to the SACMEQ survey, in South Africa teachers with better subject knowledge in mathematics and reading were more commonly deployed to urban and better-resourced schools. The average reading score of a teacher at a school serving the wealthiest quartile of students was the highest in southern and eastern Africa, other than Kenya. By contrast, subject knowledge of teachers serving students in the poorest quartile was the worst in the region (Altinok, 2013a).

The unequal allocation of teachers is affected by geography, ethnicity and language, gender, and the subjects taught

The problem of teachers with weaker subject knowledge being assigned to more disadvantaged students is not limited to sub-Saharan Africa. In Mexico and Peru, teachers with the best subject knowledge work in urban areas (Guadalupe et al., 2013; Luschei, 2012b; Metzler and Woessmann, 2012).

The unequal allocation of teachers is affected by four main factors – geography; ethnicity and language; gender; and the subjects taught:

Urban bias: Teachers are often reluctant to be posted in communities that offer poor living conditions due to lack of infrastructure (electricity, telephone, water, health care) and accessibility. This puts rural areas at a disadvantage and creates imbalances within them; for example, a village that is not on a paved road will find it much more difficult to retain teachers than a village with good transport to the nearest town. In Swaziland, teachers are reluctant to be posted in rural areas and receive no bonus for being positioned there. Remote rural schools are mostly staffed with newly recruited, inexperienced teachers, teachers with low qualifications or those with family ties in the area (Steiner-Khamsi and Simelane, 2010). Malawi has one of the world's most severe teacher shortages but also allocates teachers inefficiently, deploying them based on aggregate district enrolment rather than according to individual school requirements. As a result, there are surpluses in urban schools and severe shortages in rural areas, aggravating poor learning outcomes (DeStefano, 2011).

Ethnicity and language: Because ethnic minorities often receive less education than majority groups, fewer minority group members are available for recruitment as teachers. In India, all states have a caste-based reservation of posts to ensure that teachers are available in more disadvantaged areas and schools, but teachers with lower levels of qualifications are hired to fill the reserved positions. There are not enough teachers who speak local languages, and very few bilingual teachers belong to minorities, which compounds the disadvantage children face when their home language is not the medium of instruction. In Mexico, teachers of children whose mother tongue is an indigenous language often have less education and training than other teachers, because fewer teachers entering the profession speak these languages (Chudgar and Luschei, 2013).

Gender: While women teachers provide role models for girls and may make schools safer for them, they are less likely than men to work in disadvantaged areas. Safety is a key concern, especially for unmarried women, who may also find it difficult to find accommodation in some social contexts. Uneven allocation leaves parts of some countries without female teachers. A survey of teachers in 10 districts of Rwanda showed that only 10% of primary school teachers were female in Burera district, compared with 67% in Gisagara district (Bennell and Ntagaramba, 2008). In Sudan, adequate accommodation rarely exists in rural areas, and married women teachers have to be deployed where their husbands live. As 67% of primary school teachers are women, this further reduces the pool of teachers available for rural areas (World Bank, 2012b). In Malawi, a female teacher can request a posting to another district to follow her husband and cannot be denied the opportunity to join him, no matter where he is (World Bank, 2010a).

Subjects: In secondary schools, in particular, there are often shortages of teachers in specific subjects, such as mathematics, sciences and foreign languages. Indonesia, for example, has a surplus of teachers at junior secondary level in Bahasa Indonesia and in religion, but shortages in computer science (Al-Samarrai et al., 2012).

There are no simple solutions to unequal allocation of teachers. Governments attempt to overcome the problem by planning teacher deployment, enabling rural students to study in urban areas, providing incentives for teachers and recruiting teachers from the local community, but all these approaches have met with mixed success.

Planned deployment needs to be well-managed

To achieve a balance of teachers across the country, some governments post teachers, usually newly qualified ones, to disadvantaged areas. Such planned deployment works where the government has control over the assignment of teachers to schools. In Eritrea, the government assigns teachers to one of six regions and to specific schools, strictly depending on student numbers. Young teachers who start their careers as part of national service are sent to the most difficult schools. By 2004/05, the association between teacher and student numbers was strong in all six regions; pupil/teacher ratios ranged from 30:1 to 53:1 (Mulkeen, 2010).

One reason for the Republic of Korea's strong and more equitable learning outcomes is that disadvantaged groups have better access to more qualified and experienced teachers. About 77% of teachers in villages have at least a bachelor's degree, compared with 32% in large cities, and 45% have more than 20 years of experience, compared with 30% in large cities (Luschei et al., 2013). Teacher hiring decisions are made at province or city level, with the highest priority given to disadvantaged areas. The practice of rotating teachers every five years to a different school within the city or province demonstrates commitment to distributing good teachers equitably. Teachers working in disadvantaged schools benefit from incentives such as an additional stipend, smaller class sizes, less teaching time, the chance to choose their next school after teaching in a difficult area and greater promotion opportunities. This helps ensure that disadvantaged groups have highly qualified teachers with strong subject knowledge (Kang and Hong, 2008).

In some countries, planned deployment can leave disadvantaged areas with the least experienced teachers. Oman has large numbers of teachers, resulting in pupil/teacher ratios of 12:1 at primary level and 15:1 at secondary level in 2009. Newly recruited teachers have no choice of school, but are allocated by the Ministry of Education. The distribution of teachers is even across regions, with the average pupil/teacher ratio for primary and secondary education varying in 2009 from 8:1 in Al-Wusta, a remote, sparsely populated region, to 14:1 in Al-Batinah, in the north. However, teachers can request a transfer after one year: in 2009, 5.8% of all teachers were transferred, mostly out of remote regions, which were left with a large proportion of inexperienced teachers. In Al-Wusta in 2009, 59% of teachers had less than five years of experience, compared with 26% nationally (Oman Ministry of Education and World Bank, 2012).

Incentives to rebalance uneven teacher allocation

Teachers should be provided with awards and rewards for serving in challenging schools and deprived areas. Teachers should be provided with required facilities, especially accommodation, child allowance, mobility allowance, heath facilities for serving in such difficult areas.

– Nasreen, teacher, Islamabad, Pakistan

Incentives for teachers to accept difficult postings, such as housing, monetary benefits and accelerated promotion, are usually needed to ensure that all students are taught by good teachers.

In Cambodia, teachers received US$12.50 extra per month for postings in rural areas

Teacher housing is often used to attract teachers, especially female teachers, to rural areas where suitable housing is not available for rent. The Programme to Motivate, Train and Employ Female Teachers in Rural Secondary Schools in Bangladesh (1995–2005) provided women teachers in rural areas with safe housing near schools once they had completed training (Mitchell and Yang, 2012).

Financial incentives such as bonus payments and hardship allowances are another means of promoting deployment to rural areas, but they need to be large to outweigh the difficulties of living in remote areas. In Cambodia, teachers received US$12.50 extra per month for postings in rural areas, or US$15 for districts designated as remote. However, teacher pay was too low for this top-up to be considered sufficient to offset difficulties faced by teachers living in remote areas away from extended family support and with fewer opportunities for additional sources of income, so the policy met with only limited success (Benveniste et al., 2008a). In contrast, in Malawi, the rural hardship allowance introduced in 2010 raises the basic pay of a newly recruited teacher by as much as a quarter (Steiner-Khamsi and Kunje, 2011).

To be attractive, incentives need to be set at an appropriate level. In the Gambia, for instance, teachers used to be allocated randomly by the central government to six regions, and by regional administration to schools. However, qualified teachers were able to refuse positions in rural remote areas; by 2004/05, their share varied by region from 42% to 82%. As a result, the Gambia introduced a hardship allowance of 30% to 40% of base salary for positions in remote regions at schools more than 3 kilometres from a main road. The incentive was large enough to change teachers' attitudes: by 2007, 24% of teachers in the regions where the incentive was offered had requested transfer to hardship schools (Mulkeen, 2010).

A response to the teacher deployment problem is to recruit teachers from within their own communities

An alternative approach adopted by Rwanda is to provide subsidized loans to trained teachers working in hard-to-reach areas. The vast majority of teachers in such areas have participated in the programme, making a minimum monthly contribution of 5% of their salary, with members allowed to borrow up to five times their savings (Bennell and Ntagaramba, 2008).

Recruiting teachers locally

Teachers need to be recruited from the local area to make sure there is continuity in the job.
– Nasreen, teacher, Islamabad, Pakistan

Another response to the teacher deployment problem is to recruit teachers from within their own communities. In Afghanistan, female teachers are vital for girls to be able to enrol in school, but women face cultural barriers in seeking work in areas where they are not chaperoned by family members. As a result there are twice as many female teachers as male teachers in the capital, Kabul, while in Uruzgan province, most of which is remote and unsafe, there are no female teachers who have the minimum qualification (Wirak and Lexow, 2008). Local recruitment of female teachers is one solution to such extreme inequality.

Local recruitment has its benefits, such as teachers' greater acceptance of a rural posting and reduced attrition, but some of the most disadvantaged communities lack competent applicants where access to primary schooling is low, as is the case in Afghanistan. In Lesotho, a system of local recruitment allows school management committees to hire teachers, who apply directly to the schools for vacant posts. This ensures that only teachers willing to work in those schools apply; schools do not have a problem with teachers refusing postings. One major benefit of this system is that most teaching posts are filled, and there is relatively little difference in pupil/teacher ratios between rural and urban areas. Furthermore, almost three-quarters of teachers in the more remote mountainous areas are female. However, many of the rural schools recruit untrained teachers: school census data show that only half of teachers in mountain areas are trained, compared with three-quarters in the more populous lowlands (Mulkeen, 2006).

Teachers may also require incentives to return to their home areas. In China, the government established the Free Teacher Education programme in 2007 to give high performing students at the best universities incentives to teach in rural schools. In addition to having free tuition, graduates have 10 years of job security teaching in their home provinces. In 2007, 90% of participants came from central and western regions that are mostly less developed and economically stagnant. Even if a graduate finds work in an urban area, two years of rural teaching must be completed first (Wang and Gao, 2013).

Local recruitment can bring challenges in deploying teachers effectively over the span of their careers. In Indonesia, locally recruited teachers cannot be easily transferred, which poses a problem as the demographics of the country are changing (Box 6.6). Similarly, in Peru, most teachers are now recruited in the region where they were born and educated, and rarely change positions over their career (Jaramillo, 2012).

Box 6.6: Addressing uneven teacher deployment in Indonesia

Indonesia has no shortage of teachers. Due to massive recruitment since 2001, and a declining child population, by 2010 there were just 16 students per teacher in primary education, 13 in lower secondary and 11 in upper secondary. However, teachers are unequally distributed across regions, urban and rural areas, school levels and academic fields, so teacher shortages exist locally, especially in poor urban or remote rural areas. In 2006, 112 districts had pupil/teacher ratios in primary education below 16:1, yet 53 had ratios between 30:1 and 50:1. Only 20% of primary and lower secondary teachers in remote rural areas have a four-year university degree, compared with more than 50% in urban areas.

Decisions on hiring teachers have largely been decentralized – teachers hired directly by schools now make up 30% of the teaching force at primary level and 36% at lower secondary level. Five ministries issued a joint decree in 2011 providing guidelines to provinces and districts: primary schools with less than 168 students should have at least six teachers, and larger ones should have class sizes between 28 and 32; similar guidelines apply to lower secondary schools.

These standards are compatible with the overall size of the teaching force, but to implement them, 340,000 teachers, 17% of the total, would need to be redeployed. Teachers hired by schools cannot be transferred, however, so the burden would fall on civil service teachers: up to 27% of those teaching in lower secondary school would have to be transferred.

Teacher transfers have not been common in Indonesia, so the adoption of effective transfer systems at district level would be crucial. For instance, the Education Office in the district of Gorontalo identified 634 of its 5,000 teachers who could be redeployed, and implemented measures such as merging small schools, introducing multigrade teaching in schools with fewer than 90 students and providing incentives for teachers to move to remote schools. New teachers were recruited on the condition that they could be transferred. By 2000, some schools in Bantul district had particularly low pupil/teacher ratios, so schools with less than 150 students, not further than 1.5 km apart and not separated by obstacles such as rivers or highways were merged. Teachers supported the changes because they were assured that they would be transferred to schools close to their homes. At the central level, a remote area allowance was introduced in 2007, but it has not been implemented on a large enough scale.

In the near future, a further challenge will be the need for a massive transfer of teachers to urban areas, as two-thirds of Indonesia's population is expected to live in urban areas by 2025, compared with half in 2005.

Sources: Al-Samarrai et al. (2012); World Bank (2010c).

Getting teachers with strong subject knowledge to disadvantaged schools

A very good university degree is crucial. I can say I was fortunate to have this advantage, but a lot of my colleagues were not. The graduates in extreme cases can hardly read and write themselves.
– Daniel, teacher, Kaduma State, Nigeria

Some countries are providing alternative pathways into teaching to attract highly qualified professionals with strong subject knowledge. One approach is exemplified by the Teach for All programmes in a range of countries, including Australia, Chile, China, India, Peru, the United Kingdom and the United States. Such programmes recruit graduates to teach in schools that predominantly serve disadvantaged students and often have trouble attracting trained teachers. Evidence from evaluations of Teach for America suggests that these teachers can help improve students' learning, provided they receive some teacher education (Box 6.7).

Box 6.7: Teach for America – a success, but not a solution

Attracting newly qualified professionals who are committed to supporting children in disadvantaged areas is one way to extend the teaching force to these areas. Teach for America was founded as a non-profit organization in 1989 to reduce inequity in education and redress teacher shortages by recruiting outstanding recent college graduates and sending them to high need schools throughout the United States for a minimum of two years. The programme expanded rapidly, placing 500 teachers in 1990 but sending more than 10,000 in 2012/13 to teach around 750,000 pupils. The presupposition is that a strong academic background compensates for a lack of extensive teacher practice or training. While traditional teacher education programmes typically consist of one to four years of coursework, Teach for America candidates attend a five-week training programme in the summer between graduating from college and beginning their teaching assignments.

After gaining some experience, Teach for America teachers have been found to improve student achievement, particularly in mathematics. Their impact, across different groups of students, has been roughly equivalent to an additional month of instruction.

Teach for America and similar programmes in other countries are playing a key role in getting good teachers to disadvantaged areas, while underlining the need in such areas for the best possible teachers. However, they cannot be seen as the solution to improve learning outcomes for all. Not only is there a high attrition rate among these teachers – sometimes 80% or more by their third or fourth year of teaching – but they make up only about 0.2% of the 3.5 million teachers in the United States. The scale on which they operate is similar in other countries: in the United Kingdom, Teach First has similarly been shown to be successful in improving learning among disadvantaged students but recruits only 1.2% of new entrants into teaching.

Sources: Glazerman et al. (2006); Heilig and Jez (2010); Xu et al. (2009); Sutton Trust (2011).

Strategy 4: Provide incentives to retain the best teachers

Salaries are just one of many factors that motivate teachers, but they are a key consideration in attracting the best candidates and retaining the best teachers. Low salaries are likely to damage morale and can lead teachers to switch to other careers. At the same time, teacher salaries make up the largest share of most education budgets, so they need to be set at a realistic level to ensure that enough teachers can be recruited. In some countries, including Burundi, the Democratic Republic of the Congo and Malawi, at least 80% of the education budget is spent on teacher salaries.

Average teacher salaries are below US$10 per day in eight countries

Governments need to pay competitive salaries to attract the best teachers, but many face a dilemma: higher salaries would raise the public budget unless teachers numbers fell, which would increase class size. In countries where classes are already large, as in much of sub-Saharan Africa, this would reduce education quality.

The level of teacher salaries influences education quality. Six estimates published between 1990 and 2010 found that teacher salaries were directly linked to learning outcomes (Glewwe et al., 2011). And in 39 countries participating in PISA and TIMSS between 1995 and 2005, a 15% increase in teacher pay increased student performance by between 6% and 8% (Dolton and Marcenaro-Gutierrez, 2011).

Paying teachers enough to meet their basic needs

My salary is not enough to cover housing, transport, food and the payments on my student loan. It makes me feel unappreciated, and though my students reassure me every day that I have chosen the right profession, it would be wonderful to receive the same reassurance from administrators.

– Inga, teacher, Rwanda

In some poor countries pay levels do not even cover basic living costs. When salaries are too low, teachers often need to take on additional work – sometimes including private tuition – which can reduce their commitment to their regular teaching jobs and lead to absenteeism.

A comparison of salaries in terms of purchasing power parity, reflecting the money needed to purchase the same goods and services across countries, shows that teachers in high performing countries such as Denmark earn more than 10 times as much as those in countries struggling to ensure that children are learning the basics, such as Chad and Sierra Leone (Figure 6.1).

Teachers in some countries do not even earn enough to lift their households above the poverty line. A teacher who is the only or main breadwinner, and has at least four family members to support, needs to earn at least US$10 per day to keep the family above the poverty line of US$2 per day per person. However, average teacher salaries are below this level in eight countries. This is unacceptable. In the Central African Republic, Guinea-Bissau and Liberia, teachers are paid no more than US$5, on average. Teacher salaries are similarly low in the Democratic Republic of the Congo, where communities have to supplement their low pay. Communities that are too poor to do so suffer from further disadvantage, losing good teachers.

Another common way to measure teacher salaries is to compare them to the average wealth of a country in terms of GDP per capita. This comparison, however, cannot show whether the salary provides enough for teachers to live on or motivates the best teachers to stay in the profession. In a poor country like Niger, for example, teacher salaries are almost seven times GDP per capita, a level which some suggest is a signal that they are not affordable (Bruns et al., 2003). In terms of purchasing power, however, teachers in Niger earn just US$13 per day, barely above the amount needed to keep families above the poverty line.

National data on average teacher pay similarly disguise variations in pay among different types of teachers: salaries are often considerably less than average for teachers at the beginning of their career, unqualified teachers and those on temporary contracts. Averages also mask other differences related to pay scales. In Malawi, for instance, a qualified primary teacher in the lowest category, with two to four years of

Figure 6.1: Teachers in some poor countries are not paid enough to live on
Daily teachers' wages in public primary institutions, latest available year

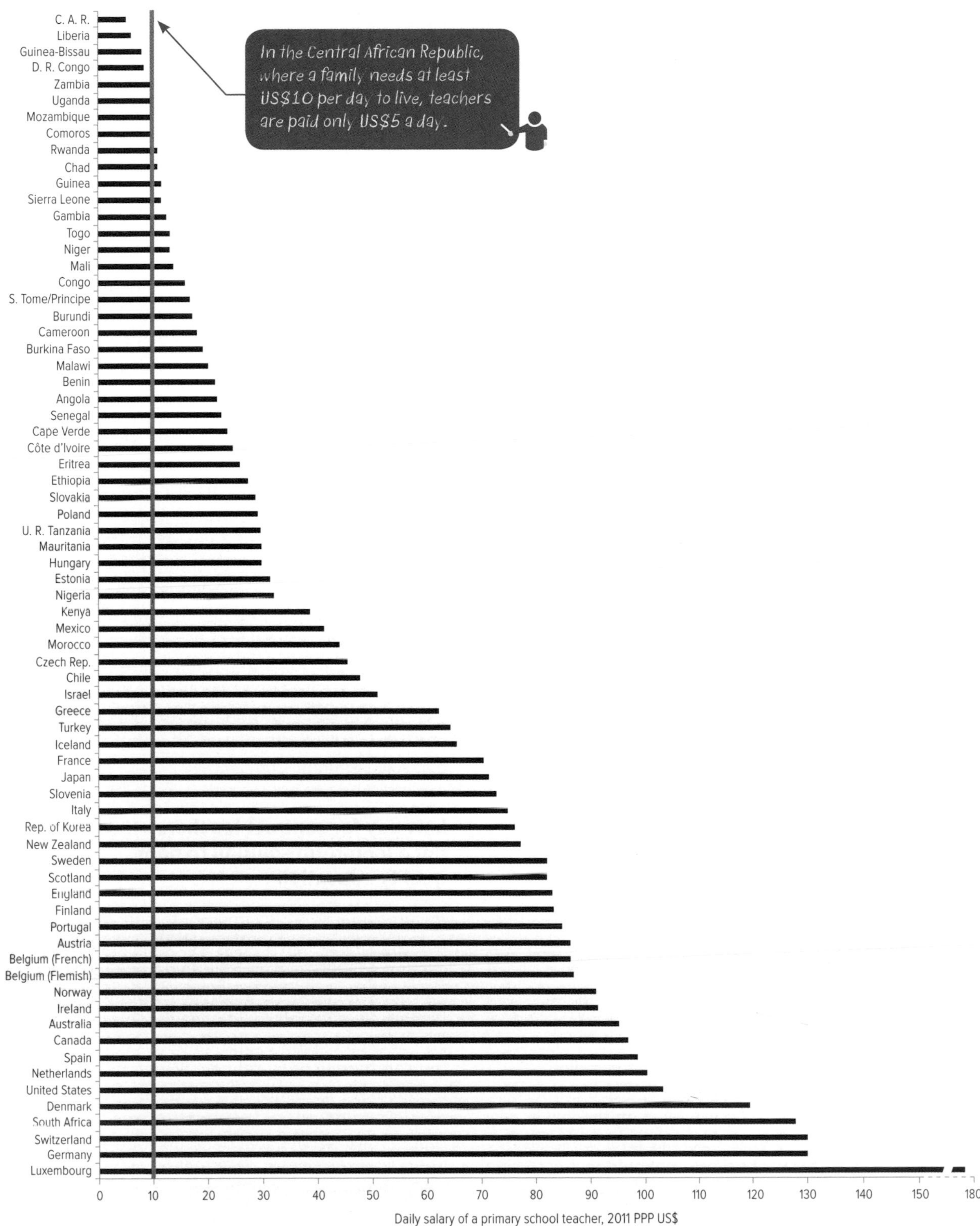

Source: Pôle de Dakar database; OECD (2013b).

secondary education and a teaching diploma, receives less than a third of the salary of a teacher in the highest category, predominantly head teachers (Steiner-Khamsi and Kunje, 2011). Thus those entering the profession, or lacking the academic qualifications needed for promotion, barely have enough to live on: in 2007/08 their salary was equivalent to just US$4 per day (World Bank, 2010a).

Already-low teacher pay has even been falling in some poor countries. In Zimbabwe, teacher pay plummeted, as a result of dire economic conditions and hyperinflation, from around US$500 per month in the 1990s to US$2 per month in early 2009. Although an allowance of US$150 per month was awarded in 2009, teachers were still paid well below the country's poverty line of around US$500 that year.[4] Schools are often expected to supplement low teacher salaries through fees, but parents cannot always afford these costs, especially in rural areas where poverty is high. This has contributed to the wide inequality in teachers' income between urban and rural areas, adding to the difficulty of attracting teachers to rural areas (Zimbabwe Ministries of Education Sport Arts and Culture and Higher and Tertiary Education, 2010).

In rural Zambia, it may cost teachers up to half their wages to collect their pay

In Cambodia, teachers' basic salaries are very low and few teachers can afford basic necessities without taking a second job. In 2007, initial base monthly salaries were around US$44 for primary teachers and US$47 for lower secondary teachers, increasing over a teacher's career by only around 30%. Many teachers expect to receive additional monthly allowances ranging from US$1.50 to US$3.00, depending on location and responsibilities, but these are often delayed or missing because payment procedures are poor (Benveniste et al., 2008a). Salaries have not kept pace with inflation. For example, from 2007 to 2008 the price of rice rose by 94% and the price of fish, the source of some 75% of the protein in an average Cambodian diet, rose by 33%. At 2008 prices, 66% of a primary teacher's base salary would go on these two items alone (Voluntary Service Overseas, 2009). Over two-thirds of primary school teachers in Cambodia have a second job, often as farmers (Benveniste et al., 2008b).

4. Based on a household of five children.

While teacher salaries have tended to decline in real terms in poor countries, they have increased in most rich countries, an indication of the better status teachers enjoy there. Between 2005 and 2011, average teacher salaries in most OECD countries rose by 14% for a primary teacher with 15 years of experience and 11% for a lower secondary teacher. In Luxembourg, primary teachers' salaries increased by a third, and in Poland by almost 50%. There were some exceptions: in the United States salaries fell by 1% at the primary level and 2% at the lower secondary level; in France they fell by 4% at the primary level and 3% at the lower secondary level; in Japan they fell by 7% at both levels and in Greece they fell by 15% at both levels (OECD, 2013b). The decrease in France has become an issue of public policy debate (see Box 6.11).

In poor countries, teachers are often paid not only too little but also too late, which can make it difficult for them to meet basic needs and lead them to look for other career options. In sub-Saharan Africa, late or incorrect payments create considerable difficulties for teachers without access to credit (Mulkeen and Crowe-Taft, 2010). In addition, teachers may have to travel some distance to collect payments, which further reduces their take-home pay. In rural Zambia, for example, it may cost teachers up to half their wages for transport and accommodation to collect their pay from district offices each month (Bennell and Akyeampong, 2007).

Low pay for contract teachers – not a long-term solution to poor quality education

In sub-Saharan Africa and South and West Asia, policy-makers have responded to the need to expand education systems rapidly by recruiting teachers on temporary contracts. Contract teachers are usually paid considerably less than civil service teachers; some are hired directly by the community or by schools. Contract teachers tend to have little formal training and to be employed under less favourable terms than regular civil service teachers, on contracts often limited to one or two years with no guarantee of renewal (Kingdon et al., 2013).

In West Africa, where contract teachers made up half the teaching force by the mid-2000s

(Kingdon et al., 2013), their recruitment has been especially widespread, partly because the salaries of civil service teachers were perceived as high and unaffordable for the state as the need for teachers grew. By the latter part of that decade, there were far more teachers on temporary contracts than on civil service contracts in some countries: the proportion reached almost 80% in Mali and Niger and over 60% in Benin, Cameroon and Chad (Figure 6.2).

There is wide variation both in the amount contract teachers are paid and in the difference between their salaries and those of civil service teachers in West Africa. Senegal was one of the first countries to introduce contract teaching, which was adopted as national policy in 1995 after primary education became free. Teacher salaries then amounted, on average, to over six times GDP per capita and made up 90% of the education budget (Fyfe, 2007). By 2004, 56% of teachers were on temporary contracts that paid one-third of a regular teacher's salary, allowing more teachers to be recruited for the same budget. As a result, the pupil/teacher ratio decreased from 49:1 in 1999 to 33:1 in 2011, while primary enrolment increased by 67%.

In Benin, where contract teachers earn around one-third as much as a civil service teacher, their share doubled between 2006 and 2009 to reach 41% of the teacher workforce (Figure 6.3). In Niger, 79% of teachers are on temporary contracts, earning half the salary of a civil service teacher. Recruiting contract teachers has enabled some countries with the largest teacher shortages, including Benin and Mali, to reduce significantly the numbers of pupils per teacher.

In parts of South and West Asia, too, expansion in enrolment has led to the recruitment of large numbers of contract teachers, who are paid a fraction of what civil service teachers earn. In India, several states no longer recruit civil service teachers, and contract teachers now account for 16% of government primary school teachers. In 2007, contract teachers received 14% of the salary paid to regular teachers in West Bengal state, 23% in Andhra Pradesh and 25% in Rajasthan (Kingdon and Sipahimalani-Rao, 2010). The proportion is also high in some Latin American countries, such as Chile, where 20% of all teachers are contract and community teachers (Kingdon et al., 2013).

Figure 6.2: Many West African countries have a teaching force made up largely of people on short-term contracts

Teacher workforce by type of contract, selected countries in sub-Saharan Africa, latest available year

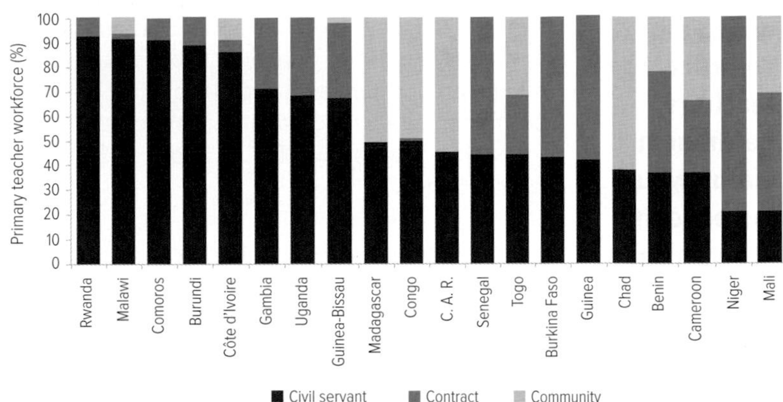

Note: Community teachers are recruited by communities. They differ from other contract teachers, who are recruited directly by the government but get paid less than civil servant teachers.
Source: Pôle de Dakar database.

Figure 6.3: In many African countries, contract teachers earn a fraction of what their civil servant teachers receive

Annual salary of contract and civil servant teachers, selected African countries, latest year available

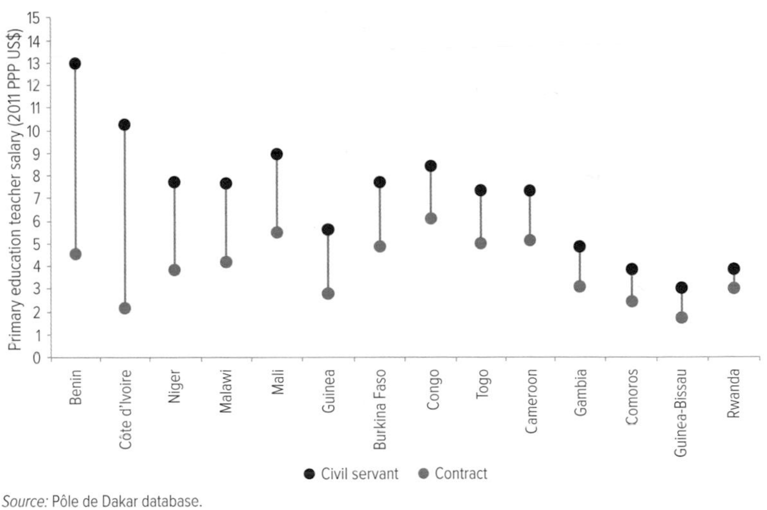

Source: Pôle de Dakar database.

While hiring contract teachers helps alleviate teacher shortages in the short term, it is unlikely to meet the long-term need to extend quality education. Countries that rely heavily on contract teachers, notably those in West Africa, rank at or near the bottom for education access and learning (see Chapter 4).

In Niger, 79% of teachers are on temporary contracts, earning half the salary of a civil service teacher

In some countries, governments eventually hire contract teachers as civil service teachers; in others, the salaries of regular teachers and contract teachers gradually converge. In

In Indonesia, giving all contract teachers permanent status would increase the salary bill for basic education to about US$9 billion

Indonesia, where contract teachers made up 35% of the primary school teaching force in 2010, regular teachers earned up to 40 times their salary but the government guaranteed that contract teachers would eventually attain civil service status. The implications for the education budget are immense: giving all contract teachers permanent status would increase the salary bill for basic education by 35%, to about US$9 billion (World Bank, 2013).

Similarly, in Benin, despite the share of contract teachers having increased, the average teacher salary rose by 45% in real terms between 2006 and 2010 because the salaries of contract and civil service teachers have been converging (Pôle de Dakar database). One reason for the convergence is that, since 2007, these teachers have been absorbed into the civil service and have received training (Pôle de Dakar and République du Bénin, 2011).

In some contexts, contract teachers can be at least as effective as civil service teachers. In India, most studies find that employing contract teachers does not lead to learning outcomes that are lower than those achieved by civil service teachers. However, achievement remains undesirably low in India regardless of the type of teacher a student is taught by (Box 6.8).

In some other countries, students of contract teachers tend to perform less well than those of regular teachers. In Niger, the overall impact of contract teachers on learning achievement in French and mathematics was negative for grade 2 and 5 students. In Togo, contract teachers tended to have a negative effect on pupils in grade 5 (Bourdon et al., 2010).

One reason why there is no clear difference overall in performance between contract teachers and regular teachers in some

Box 6.8: In India, contract teachers have not significantly improved low levels of learning

India's primary school system expanded rapidly in the 1990s and 2000s, necessitating massive recruitment of teachers by state governments at a time of severe fiscal constraints. Many states, especially those whose child populations were still growing rapidly, hired teachers not as civil servants but under contract, with much lower salaries, without tenure and often as employees of local authorities. Recruitment of these contract teachers, often known as para-teachers, was expected to improve the functioning of schools by lowering pupil/teacher ratios – the average national ratio for primary and upper primary education was 50:1 in 2000. Other anticipated benefits included increasing cultural awareness of teachers recruited locally towards their students, and making teachers more accountable to parents and local authorities, who have the power to decide on renewing their contracts.

Contract teachers account for 16% of all government-school teachers at primary level and 10% at lower secondary level. States where child population is stabilizing, such as Kerala and Tamil Nadu, or where average household income is higher, such as Punjab and Gujarat, have recruited few contract teachers, while other states now recruit all new teachers on contracts.

Salary levels differ dramatically. Across nine states, contract teachers were paid between 14% and 68% of regular teachers' salaries in 2007. In some cases, required academic qualifications are lower for contract teachers than for regular teachers but their actual qualifications are higher; nationally, only 29% of contract teachers had not completed upper secondary education, compared with 53% of regular teachers. Furthermore, similar percentages of contract teachers and regular teachers have graduate or post-graduate qualifications. More than three-quarters of contract teachers were aged 18 to 35, while half of regular teachers were 36 or over. Nationwide, 45% of contract teachers had received pre-service training, as opposed to 82% of regular teachers.

Contract teacher programmes have generated much controversy. Contract teachers have mobilized to obtain higher pay and tenure, while government officials have debated whether they were as effective as regular teachers. The available evidence shows that learning outcomes are not systematically different between contract teachers and regular teachers, and sometimes demonstrate a learning advantage for children taught by contract teachers. For example, contract teachers were associated with slightly higher achievement in language and mathematics among grade 2 and 4 students in 62 schools in Uttar Pradesh. Achievement remained poor overall, however, with most pupils scoring very low and showing little improvement between grades.

On balance, contract teacher programmes in India have not worsened the quality of education. Lower levels of training seem to be compensated by higher levels of presence at school, which is likely to be linked to local recruitment rather than their contract type per se. But contract teachers' contribution and impact are minimal, since learning outcomes remain extremely low in most of India regardless of the type of contract a teacher holds, and have been declining in recent years. Given that training for both regular teachers and contract teachers is inadequate, policy-makers need to invest in subject knowledge and pedagogical skills training for all teachers, regardless of their contract type.

Sources: Atherton and Kingdon (2010); Kingdon and Sipahimalani-Rao (2010); Pratham (2013); Pritchett and Murgai (2007).

settings is that ultimately they face similar challenges. Interviews conducted in Lahore, Pakistan, showed that contract teachers experienced the same demotivating factors as civil service teachers – including transport difficulties for female teachers – so their absenteeism was only slightly lower. There was a perception that lower salaries encouraged absenteeism and that contractual employment led to frequent resignation and high teacher turnover (Habib, 2010).

Where contract teachers have been found to be more effective, the reasons for better student achievement is likely to have more to do with factors other than the type of contract that the teacher holds, such as greater parental or community involvement due to the local recruitment of teachers. In one experiment in Kenya, the benefit of halving class size by hiring a contract teacher was observed only in communities where parents had been trained to monitor teachers and relatives of local civil service teachers were not allowed to be hired as contract teachers (Duflo et al., 2012a). Similarly, in Mali, language and mathematics scores of grade 2 and 5 students were consistently higher under contract teachers who were closely monitored by the local community (Bourdon et al., 2010).

Should countries with an acute need for more trained teachers aim to recruit contract teachers on a large scale? Evidence suggests that scaling up will not necessarily address the problem of poor achievement. In 2009, the Kenyan government recruited 18,000 contract teachers, making them equivalent to 12% of the teaching force. The nationwide recruitment generated opposition and mobilization from teacher unions. The government was less effective than NGOs in implementing the programme, as shown by a randomized experiment run during a pilot phase. Of 192 schools, 64 received a contract teacher hired by the government and 64 contract teachers hired by an international NGO while the remaining 64 did not have any contract teacher. Learning outcomes improved in schools where contract teachers had been hired by the NGO, but not where they had been hired by the government. Contract teachers recruited by the government received fewer monitoring visits and experienced long salary delays; nepotism and interference by local political elites were also more common (Bold et al., 2013). This suggests that capacity problems facing government systems exist regardless of the basis on which teachers are hired, and that these problems need to be tackled to ensure that all children learn.

Another factor limiting the possibility of scaling up contract teachers' numbers is that they inevitably start to demand the same rights as civil service teachers, thus increasing government budgets. In Benin, for example, contract teachers, with the support of teacher unions, campaigned to obtain more stable employment conditions as well as payment of 12 months of salary every year instead of 10. In late 2007, a six-week strike led the government to issue a decree absorbing into the civil service contract teachers who had achieved the required qualifications (Imorou, 2010).

Recruiting contract teachers on a large scale cannot be seen as a cost-saving solution to the learning crisis in the long term

Where contract teachers are paid by the community, their sustainability depends on the ability of parents to mobilize funding to help pay their salaries which puts considerable financial pressure on poorer communities. In some cases, this has led to the government taking over some of the responsibility, and so can ultimately add to the budget. In Chad, where community teachers make up over two-thirds of all teachers, subsidies were put in place to relieve parents of some of the financial burden of recruiting teachers. The subsidies were small, however, and often paid several months late. Furthermore, over 8,000 community teachers had yet to receive any subsidies five years after the programme began (World Bank, 2011b). In Madagascar, community teachers, who made up around half of all teachers in 2005/06, were hired directly by parent-teacher associations and generally received less than half of regular teachers' salaries. Since 2006, the government has increasingly taken on the responsibility for paying these community teachers (Glewwe and Maïga, 2011).

Recruiting contract teachers on a large scale cannot be seen, therefore, as a cost-saving solution to the learning crisis in the long term. Ultimately such teachers will need training and better pay, and expect the same conditions as their civil service counterparts, increasing the government's wage bill over time.

Ensuring that teaching is as attractive as similar professions

When teachers are paid less than people in comparable fields, the best students are less likely to become teachers, and teachers are more likely to lose motivation or leave the profession.

In Peru, professionals with similar characteristics to primary school teachers earned 43% more

In Latin America, teachers are generally paid above the poverty threshold, but their salaries do not compare favourably with those working in professions requiring similar qualifications. In 2007, other professionals and technicians with similar characteristics earned 43% more than pre-school and primary school teachers in Brazil and 50% more in Peru. A similar gap is discernible between secondary school teachers and other professionals, who earned 46% more in Paraguay and 50% more in Ecuador. In addition, the gap between teachers and other professionals is wider for those with longer experience, because teachers' salaries do not increase as much as other professionals' pay over time (Mizala and Ñopo, 2012).

Similar problems of a mismatch between the earnings of teachers and those of other professions are apparent in some OECD countries. In 2011, primary school teachers in OECD countries earned 82% of the average for other full-time workers aged 25 to 64 with tertiary education, and upper secondary school teachers earned 89% (OECD, 2013b). In such circumstances, the best students may not choose to become teachers. For example, across 42 of the countries that participated in PISA 2006, the mathematics scores of students who wanted to become teachers were below average in 32, and below the scores of students who wanted to become engineers in all countries except Poland (Bruns et al., 2011a).

In the United States, higher salaries in other occupations were found to have led almost half of teachers with less than six years of experience to leave the profession between 1999/2000 and 2003/04 (Gilpin, 2011). The wage gap is large: after 15 years of experience, US teachers in lower secondary education earn 67% of the average for full-time, full-year workers aged 25 to 64 with tertiary education (OECD, 2013b).

Exceptions do exist. In countries including Canada, Luxembourg, New Zealand and the Republic of Korea, teachers are paid more than the average for full-time workers with tertiary education. In the Republic of Korea, for example, where the status of teaching and student performance are both high, lower secondary school teachers earn 20% more than other professionals with higher education (OECD, 2013b).

Performance-related pay needs to send the right signals

There's a whole host of issues around performance-related pay. How do you judge the performance of a teacher? It's really hard to quantify the impact that we can have on a young person's life and how they perceive themselves, their self-image, their confidence, their aspirations, where they think they're going in the future ... how do you measure that?

– Caroline, teacher, London, UK

Teachers' salaries – and the rates at which they increase – are conventionally determined by formal qualifications, the amount of training and years of experience. But pay structures based on these criteria do not necessarily lead to better learning outcomes. Relating teachers' pay to the performance of their students has intuitive appeal. As a result, some governments advocate performance-related pay as part of a broader agenda of 'accountability' reforms to improve the quality of education (Bruns et al., 2011b; OECD, 2009).

The appeal of performance-related pay is indicated by analysis of 2003 PISA data from 28 OECD countries: those where teachers' salaries are adjusted for student performance have higher scores in reading, mathematics and science (Woessmann, 2011).

However, a closer look at the evidence on performance-related pay from around the world shows that in practice it is not possible to conclude that it has clear-cut benefits. It is also hard to implement well, partly because of the difficulty in evaluating reliably which teachers are the best. It can have unintended side effects that distort or even worsen teaching and learning. If performance-related pay is implemented, it must be designed to avoid these harmful side effects while providing incentives that give the right signals to improve the learning of the weakest and most disadvantaged students.

The introduction of performance-related pay on a large scale in England (United Kingdom) from September 2013 is a recent example of such an approach. It is intended to replace teachers' automatic progression according to length of service with advancement conditional on an annual appraisal (UK Department for Education, 2013). Each school is expected to decide how to implement the new arrangements, using evidence from various sources including teachers' self-assessments, lesson observations and the views of other teachers (UK Department for Education, 2013).

The proposals for England reflect many of the ambitions of performance-based pay worldwide. The aim is to 'raise the status of the profession, support professional development, and reward individuals in line with their contribution to improving pupil outcomes, enabling the most successful teachers to progress faster than at present on the basis of annual appraisal' (UK Department for Education and School Teachers' Review Body, 2012, p. vii). The reform is expected to provide greater flexibility for schools to develop pay policies tailored to their particular needs, support heads in attracting teachers in specific subjects based on their school's needs, and help schools across the country recruit and retain excellent teachers (UK Department for Education, 2013).

Other countries with experience of performance-related pay have encountered a range of problems in evaluating and rewarding teachers' performance, however, often with unintended consequences. Portugal, for example, recently introduced performance-related pay for similar reasons to England's, but found that it reduced cooperation among teachers, which was damaging for student learning (Box 6.9).

Other unintended consequences include encouraging teachers to 'teach to the test' and focus on the best students in order to lift average scores, and rewarding schools and teachers that are already the highest performers rather than those that have helped children improve the most, to the detriment of disadvantaged learners.

Box 6.9: In Portugal, performance-related pay led to lower cooperation among teachers

In Portugal, the government reformed the education system after 2005 in response to the country's poor performance in international assessments such as PISA. The government was particularly concerned that although public spending on education was high, and teacher salaries were comparable to those in other OECD countries, student learning outcomes had not improved.

A key aspect of the reform, which became law in January 2007, was breaking up the single pay scale for teachers into two scales. The gap between the last point in the lower scale and the first point of the higher scale was large, around 25%. Teachers in the higher scale were expected to play a special role in management and pedagogical tasks.

Teachers were no longer assured of virtually automatic progression from the bottom to the top of the pay scale over their careers. Instead, their advancement depended on the academic performance of their students and feedback from parents, along with other criteria including the teacher's attendance record, attendance at training sessions, fulfilment of management and pedagogical duties, and involvement in research projects.

Even if a teacher did well according to these criteria, progression between the two pay scales depended on whether there were upper-scale teacher vacancies, which were determined every two years by the Ministry of Education as a function of the number of students in the school.

Despite the government's best intentions, the new programme led to a decrease in student achievement. Teachers eager for promotion awarded higher internal assessment marks, which carried considerable weight in students' final marks. The policy also inadvertently encouraged competition and reduced cooperation among teachers, which had a detrimental effect on student learning and lowered teachers' job satisfaction.

Source: Martins (2010).

Unintended consequences of performance-related pay include encouraging teachers to focus on the best students

Assessing teachers for performance-related pay relies on sophisticated analysis that is difficult to undertake even in more advanced systems

Evaluating teachers' performance is far from easy

Assessing teachers for performance-related pay relies on sophisticated analysis that is difficult to undertake and interpret even in more advanced systems. In the United States, the ProComp programme was implemented in Denver, Colorado, between 2003 and 2010, providing bonuses to teachers based on their 'value added' – the gains in learning that could be ascribed to teachers by adjusting for students' previous achievement and demographic characteristics. However, test scores increased not just for students whose teachers participated in the programme, but also for other students (Goldhaber and Walch, 2012). A key problem in the United States has been that the 'value added' measures used to determine performance do not accurately reflect differences in actual teacher quality (Hanushek and Rivkin, 2012; Rothstein, 2010).

Using school principals' evaluations and classroom observation is an alternative way of identifying the value that teachers add. In Chicago, such evaluations were found to be an accurate reflection of teacher quality and a good proxy for student performance (Jacob and Walsh, 2011). While there is a risk of principals' views being too subjective, the OECD Teaching and Learning International Survey found that, on average across 23 countries, 83% of teachers who received such appraisal and feedback believed it to be a fair assessment of their work (OECD, 2013b). Principals' objectivity can be enhanced through training in teacher appraisal. Norway introduced a national programme in 2009 intended to ensure that principals were confident that they could make appraisals acceptable to teachers. Principals receive training in setting goals for teaching work, setting and enforcing quality standards, and guiding and giving feedback to teachers (OECD, 2013c).

Using multiple evaluators is another way of producing fair and successful teacher appraisals, but requires considerable time and resources on the part of the evaluators and those being evaluated. In Chile, principals share the responsibility with external accredited evaluators, a local assessment centre and peer evaluators (OECD, 2013c).

Getting the incentives right

Performance-related pay can send the wrong signals. Its use in the United States in relation to the No Child Left Behind Act has been seen as punishing rather than empowering teachers and school administrators, discouraging teachers from working with the lowest-performing students and generating unintended consequences, such as refusal to admit low performing students (Ravitch, 2010). In response to these difficulties, the Obama administration released a Blueprint for Reform on March 2010, giving autonomy to districts and schools in identifying ways to improve student achievement. Teacher evaluation includes classroom observation, peer reviews and professional development, along with test scores (US Department of Education, 2010).

Most performance-related pay programmes aim to provide incentives to individual teachers. Rewarding schools with collective bonuses, as part of a broader set of reforms, may be a more effective way to improve learning outcomes, as a comparison of Brazil and Mexico shows (Box 6.10).

Performance-related pay can have perverse outcomes if it rewards schools that were already performing well, as Chile's experience shows. All public and state-subsidized private primary and secondary schools, which together account for 90% of enrolment, have participated since 1996 in a National System of School Performance Assessment. Schools are divided into homogenous groups based on their region, whether they are in an urban or rural area, and their students' socio-economic status. Within each group, the schools accounting for the 25% of enrolment that has the highest index of student achievement in a national assessment receive a quarterly 'teaching excellence subsidy', 90% of which is shared among all teachers in the school, with 10% allocated by the principal to the best teachers. After the programme was introduced, average achievement increased (Rau and Contreras, 2011). However, the formula used works to the benefit of schools that were already doing well, rather than those that improve the most (Carnoy et al., 2007).

Box 6.10: Performance-related incentives on a large scale – lessons from Mexico and Brazil

A comparison of the incentive structures in Brazil and Mexico's performance-related pay programmes show that such programmes' designs can lead to very different outcomes. Mexico pioneered performance-related incentives for teachers with the nationwide Carrera Magisterial programme, begun in 1993 as part of broader reforms to improve education quality. Teachers who score high enough on a teaching quality index that includes student test scores move to a pay scale that offers much higher salaries. Carrera Magisterial is unlikely to have contributed much to the improvement in learning outcomes in Mexico in recent years, however, partly because there is little incentive to improve on performance once teachers have been promoted, and few teachers have a chance to benefit from the programme.

The salary scale increases that Carrera Magisterial offers to public primary and secondary school teachers are conditional on success in a complex, year-long evaluation process that covers six components: highest degree earned, seniority, pedagogical skills acquired through professional development, peer review of teaching quality, subject knowledge and their students' achievement on standardized tests. A formula combines the six components into a score of up to 100 points, with student achievement contributing a fifth.

For high scoring teachers, the awards are substantial. Teachers who score above 70 are promoted to level A of Carrera Magisterial, with pay 27% higher than the base wage. Teachers can then be promoted successively to levels B, C, D and E, the highest level carrying a 217% premium over the base wage. Participation is voluntary and has been consistently high. In the state of Aguascalientes in central Mexico, 70% to 76% of eligible teachers participated between 1999 and 2004, and in the northern border state of Sonora, 84% to 90% took part.

However, many teachers do not get a chance to participate in the programme: teachers with less than two years' experience, interim teachers and those on part-time contracts are not eligible. This rule probably excludes a number of teachers deployed to rural schools and poorer municipalities with low student achievement. In addition, because it is the level of student achievement, rather than value added by the teacher, used in the formula, some teachers may be inclined to leave schools with lower student scores.

Other adverse effects have been noted. The weighting assigned to achievement in the formula is too low to provide sufficient incentive to improve students' learning, and the fact that promotion is permanent weakens the incentive to perform once it has been granted. Evidence suggests that components of the Carrera Magisterial formula are not strongly correlated to student achievement. In Mexico City, between 1996/97 and 2000/01, while subject and pedagogical knowledge had a small positive impact on student achievement in secondary schools, other components were found to have no impact. Thus, efforts by teachers to be promoted may not necessarily enhance learning.

Reforms in Brazil in recent years have included collective bonuses linked to wider school performance, which have shown encouraging results. In the north-east, Pernambuco state's Educational Performance Bonus, for example, is paid to all employees of a school, depending on how well the school meets student performance targets. Teachers in successful schools may receive a bonus larger than one month's salary. In the first year of the programme, 52% of schools achieved their targets, and the average bonus amounted to 1.8 months of salary.

Between 2008 and 2009, learning levels across Pernambuco improved significantly. Average test scores in Portuguese increased in the grades tested, grades 8 and 11. The programme seems to have had a positive impact on learning achievement, especially for schools setting higher, more ambitious targets. The requirement that schools achieve at least 50% of their targets to receive a school performance bonus is a strong incentive; just missing out on the bonus in the first round had a positive effect on schools' motivation and performance. Teachers in schools that had achieved the school performance bonus spent more time on teaching and were much less likely to be off task or absent from school.

Sources: Bruns et al. (2011a); Luschei (2012a); Santibáñez et al. (2007); Vegas and Petrow (2007).

The risk of teaching to the test

I teach more to what will be tested by the State rather than what I think is most useful for students.
– Glen, teacher, Oregon, United States

Performance-related pay programmes have rarely been implemented on a large scale in poorer countries. Those that exist are fairly recent, often small scale initiatives, frequently run by NGOs. Experience from them suggests that there is a risk of performance-related pay encouraging teachers to teach to the test, rather than promoting wider learning.

In an experiment in Kenyan primary schools, for example, teachers were rewarded for good student test scores and penalized if students did not take end-of-year examinations. Test scores and examination attendance increased, but there is some evidence that teachers focused on preparing students for the tests. For instance, test scores did not increase in subject areas not taken into account in the teacher pay formula. In addition, wider anticipated benefits, such as reducing teacher absenteeism and student dropout, did not materialize (Glewwe et al., 2010).

A politically sensitive path

Implementing performance-related pay programmes on a large scale can be politically difficult. In the United States, teacher unions have opposed incentives based on improved student test scores (West and Mykerezi, 2011). Policy-makers should take into account unions' concerns about a lack of societal consensus on the definition and measurement of a teacher's 'merit', the complexity of programmes – with errors that may result in unfair distribution of bonuses – and distortion in education induced by excessive focus on achievement defined as test scores in a limited number of fields (Levin, 2010). Teacher unions have also argued that individual incentives encourage competition between teachers and discourage collaboration within and between schools, as the case of Portugal illustrates (see Box 6.9).

Most OECD countries use promotion and career progression as incentives rather than directly linking performance appraisals to pay

The mixed success of performance-related pay programmes suggests they need to be implemented with caution. While well-designed programmes can improve achievement, implementation on a large scale is difficult as incentives become weakened or distorted. Problems include identifying the value added by individual teachers, avoiding a reduction in teachers' intrinsic motivation, and preventing teaching to the test and neglect of weaker students.

It should be noted, moreover, that some of the most successful education systems, such as that of the Republic of Korea, have not adopted performance-based pay. This suggests that there are other ways to attract and retain the best teachers, such as improving the status of the teaching profession and offering a path to career progression.

Motivating good teachers by providing a career path

Rather than using teacher evaluations to link pay directly to performance, a more appropriate way of motivating teachers to improve education quality is to offer an attractive career path, with promotion criteria that take into account initiatives by teachers in addressing diversity and supporting weak students. Too often, however, teachers have limited prospects of promotion on this basis. Some countries use teacher evaluations to determine career advancement and reward or censure performance by granting or withholding promotion. In Singapore, the evaluation process is extensive. A planning meeting at the beginning of the school year sets goals for student achievement, professional development and contributions to the school and community. It is followed by a review meeting at mid-year and a final evaluation based on portfolios of work, as well as input from senior teachers and department or subject area heads who have worked with the teacher (OECD, 2009).

Most OECD countries use promotion and career progression as incentives rather than directly linking performance appraisals to pay, although this approach does have an indirect link with salaries. In the Czech Republic, Estonia, Israel, Poland and the Republic of Korea, performance appraisals have a strong influence on promotion (OECD, 2013c).

In some OECD countries, the difference in pay between a more experienced teacher and a new teacher is small and there is little scope for offering chances of promotion. In England, for example, a beginning teacher earns US$32,000 while the most experienced teacher can receive, at most, US$15,000 more. By contrast, the Republic of Korea has a considerably steeper pay structure: a new teacher earns a similar salary to new teachers in England, but an experienced teacher can earn more than twice that (OECD, 2013b). Insufficient career management, together with other inadequate teacher policies, is contributing to a learning crisis in France, particularly for disadvantaged students (Box 6.11).

In many developing countries, teachers' career structures are not sufficiently linked to prospects of promotion that recognize and reward teacher effectiveness. In 2010, Ghana began reviewing its teacher management and development policy to address such concerns. The new policy framework is intended as a mechanism for promoting teachers and ensuring that all teachers, irrespective of their qualifications and location, receive support to improve their teaching (Box 6.12).

Many teachers have limited prospects of promotion, however. Those teaching in remote areas may be especially affected. In Pakistan, teachers have to acquire additional qualifications

Box 6.11: Inadequate teacher policies contribute to declining learning outcomes in France

Learning outcomes in France as measured by international assessments are below average OECD levels and are particularly unequal. They have also been declining continuously over the past decade.

A recent official report found that inadequate teacher management policies had contributed to the decline. For want of adequate information, teaching positions are not allocated to schools on the basis of the needs of their student populations. Meanwhile, teachers are deployed according to a formula that does not take their competencies into account but places a premium on seniority. This is detrimental to young teachers; at secondary level, for example, 45% of teachers assigned to their first position are sent to the two least sought after regional education authorities. Disadvantaged schools receive inexperienced teachers, many of whom request transfer after a few years.

Teachers' pay is 35% lower than that of other French civil servants at the same qualification level and between 15% and 20% lower than that of teachers in other European or OECD countries. Primary teachers are particularly badly paid. Pay depends mostly on seniority and does not reward the best teachers.

Career management is lacking. Teachers are supposed to teach the same way throughout their career, with geographical mobility the only change they can expect. Support for teachers has not evolved in ways that helps them achieve the official objectives of all students acquiring core competencies and 80% of a given cohort graduating from upper secondary education. The hours spent teaching in the classroom were defined for most categories of teachers in 1950 and are the only recognized working hours; other work, including team activities with other teachers and individual guidance to students, are not recognized as part of teachers' working hours, even though a 1989 law states that the responsibilities of a teacher go beyond classroom teaching. Teachers have limited interaction with principals. There are no mentors in schools to support teachers facing difficulties in the classroom.

As a consequence, the French education system is failing to motivate qualified applicants to become teachers (since 2010/11, applicants have to hold a master's degree), despite high unemployment in the country. Between 2009 and 2012, the number of applicants per primary teacher position fell from 6.4 to 3.8, and in 2011 and 2012 more than 20% of positions could not be filled in six fields of secondary education, including mathematics and English.

Source: Cour des Comptes (2013).

Box 6.12: Ghana's new teacher development policy aims to make promotion evidence based

Ghana's teacher development policy replaces promotion on the basis of years of experience with evidence-based promotion under a new career structure that is intended to motivate teachers to improve their instructional practice.

The new structure aims at enhancing the social status of teaching and is based on clearly defined competencies. For example, to become a 'principal teacher', a teacher is expected to be able to mentor other teachers and implement strategies that lead to improvements in teaching and learning. Teachers have to produce evidence through teaching portfolios to support their application for promotion. Participation in in-service training is also linked to career advancement. New career levels provide a basis for mapping salaries to job responsibilities in the classroom and school.

Teachers may choose or be recommended for a career path in education management only after they have demonstrated their capacity for improving education quality, along with management and leadership competence.

The policy took about three years to develop and involved wide-ranging consultations with teacher representatives, teacher unions and NGOs. It was also endorsed by the Ghana Education Service Council, which certifies pre-tertiary education policies.

The policy holds considerable promise for better recognizing teachers' accomplishments and thereby creating new incentives for teacher growth and improvements in quality education. The real challenge is to set up functioning structures that operate transparently to give teachers confidence that their achievements will be duly recognized and rewarded, including for supporting the students who are the most disadvantaged.

Source: Ghana Ministry of Education (2012a).

in order to be promoted, which limits the chances of those working in rural areas, especially women, who have fewer opportunities to study (Bennell and Akyeampong, 2007).

Sometimes mechanisms for promotion are unclear, or teachers believe the system is not sufficiently transparent. A survey of 600 teachers in North West and Northern Cape provinces in South Africa found that 70% felt their career paths and prospects for promotion were unclear. Most had not been promoted within the previous five years and at least 60% did not think they would ever be promoted (Quan-Baffour and Arko-Achemfuor, 2013).

Teacher absenteeism was found to be one reason for poor performance in the United Republic of Tanzania

If promotion criteria are uniform, without recognizing the particular achievements of teachers who help improve learning for disadvantaged groups or weak learners, there is little incentive for good teachers to work in deprived areas or move to more remote schools to help improve education quality. Unfortunately, career structures rarely take this factor into account.

Strengthening teacher governance

Better teacher governance is vital to reduce disadvantage in learning. If days are lost because teachers are absent or devoting more attention to private tuition than classroom teaching, for example, the learning of the poorest children can be harmed. Strong school leadership is required to ensure that teachers are accountable: that they show up on time, work a full week and provide equal support to all. Understanding the reasons behind these problems is crucial for the design of effective strategies to solve them.

Gender-based violence, which is sometimes perpetrated by teachers, damages girls' chances of learning. Strategies to prevent and respond to teacher misconduct, and take action against perpetrators of abuse, require advocacy and support from school leadership, teachers and their unions, as well as parents and their communities, if they are to protect girls and safeguard their learning.

Combating teacher absenteeism

One of the main reasons for [teacher] absenteeism is the weather. With heavy rains, the dirt roads were closed, and teachers could not get to school. Also, the rain made it impossible to teach, as the noise from the metal roof was deafening.

– Zenaida, teacher, Quezon City, Philippines

While many more children are getting to school worldwide, teacher absenteeism sometimes significantly reduces the amount of teaching they receive, undermining their learning. Efforts to reduce absenteeism need to target the reasons teachers fail to turn up to school, which can include low pay and poor teaching conditions.

Teacher absenteeism reinforces disparities in learning

The scale of absenteeism is evident from surveys carried out in a range of poor countries over the past decade. At 100 primary schools each in Bangladesh, Ecuador, Indonesia, Peru and Uganda in the mid-2000s, teacher absenteeism ranged from 11% in Peru to 27% in Uganda (Chaudhury et al., 2006). Similar surveys yielded figures of 15% in Papua New Guinea and 17% in Zambia (Kremer et al., 2005). Teacher absence is often underreported: in the Indian state of Andhra Pradesh, for example, school registers filled in by head teachers showed an absence rate of 18% while direct observation yielded a rate of 25% (Rogers and Vegas, 2009).

In countries where large teacher shortages are already harming children's learning, absenteeism exacerbates the problem. In Kenya, where the typical primary school faces, on average, a shortage of four teachers, 13% of teachers were absent during school visits (Uwezo Kenya, 2011). In February 2013, the United Republic of Tanzania reported poor Form 4 national examination results, with 61% of students failing, compared with 46% in 2011. Teacher absenteeism was found to be one reason for the poor performance. A national survey of 2,000 households reported that 10% of primary and secondary school students said no teacher taught them on the last day they were in school (Twaweza, 2013).

Teacher absenteeism can have particularly adverse effects on poor students and those in remote rural areas. Across Indian states, absenteeism varied from 15% in Maharashtra and 17% in Gujarat – two richer and more urbanized states – to 38% in Bihar and 42% in Jharkhand, two of the poorest states (Kremer et al., 2005). In Peru, the rate was 16% in rural areas and 9% in urban areas. It reached 15% in communities with a poverty rate above 60%, and up to 20% in schools further than 15 km from a paved road (Alcázar et al., 2006). Absenteeism can also reinforce gender disparities. In rural Pakistan, where girls and boys are enrolled in separate schools and taught by a teacher of the same gender, 18% of female primary school teachers were absent in 2004, compared with 9% of male teachers (Ghuman and Lloyd, 2010).

There is much evidence of the harm done to students' learning because of teacher absenteeism (Glewwe et al., 2011). In India, for example, a 10% increase in teacher absence was correlated with 1.8% lower student attendance (Kremer et al., 2005). In Zambia, an increase in teacher absence by 5% reduced the learning gains that grade 5 students made over the year by about 4% in English and mathematics (Das et al., 2007). In Indonesia, a 10 percentage point increase in teacher absenteeism was estimated to lead to a 7 percentage point decrease in mathematics scores, on average, and absenteeism was most likely to harm weaker students: the teacher absence rate was 19% for the quarter of students with the highest mathematics scores, and 22% for the quarter with the lowest scores (Suryadarma et al., 2006).

Although absenteeism is less widespread in high income countries, where substitute teachers are often available in case of longer-term absence, it still has an impact on student learning. In the United States, public school teachers miss 5% to 6% of school days (Miller et al., 2007). In a school district in the northern United States, 10 days of teacher absence resulted in a decrease in mathematics test scores (Miller et al., 2007). In New York City, between 1999/2000 and 2008/09, the availability of substitute teachers did not compensate for the absence of the usual teacher, as the quality of substitute teachers was very low (Herrmann and Rockoff, 2010). Disadvantaged students are most likely to suffer. In North Carolina, teachers in the 25% of schools serving the poorest children were absent one more day per year, on average, than teachers in the 25% of schools serving the richest children (Clotfelter et al., 2009).

Tackling the root causes of teacher absenteeism

I do not get angry with the teachers when they don't come to school as I understand that they may have some problems themselves.

– B. Shravani, student, Andhra Pradesh, India

In some countries, high levels of absenteeism are due to many teachers missing more school days than can be explained by non-teaching duties or illness, rather than extreme absenteeism by a minority of teachers who might be easily identified. In Bangladesh, Ecuador, India, Indonesia, Peru and Uganda, illness accounted for just 10% of absences. In India, official non-teaching duties accounted for only 4% (Chaudhury et al., 2006). In Peru, according to answers given by head teachers, official duties explained 13% of teacher absences, sick leave or authorized leave 23% and unauthorized leave 10%, but no reason was given for 42% (Alcázar et al., 2006).

A wide range of teacher, school and community characteristics affects attendance

Even though teacher absenteeism is widespread in some countries, it is not inevitable, a fact that suggests it is a response to working conditions. In Bangladesh, Ecuador, India, Indonesia, Peru and Uganda, teacher absenteeism was lower when teachers were born in the district where they worked, where the school had better infrastructure and where students' parents were literate (Chaudhury et al., 2006).

Policy-makers need to understand why teachers miss school days. A wide range of teacher, school and community characteristics affects attendance, including their salary, workload, work environment and professional development, as well as school location and various aspects of school management (Guerrero et al., 2012).

Policy-makers need to identify how teachers' motivation can be improved, and how absenteeism can be penalized. They usually have some room for manoeuvre in alleviating non-teaching duties, as well, and providing better health care to teachers to reduce sick leave.

One way of combating absenteeism is for head teachers and the school administration to take action against teachers who take unauthorized leave. In Cambodia, in the areas where head teachers had greater autonomy in taking staff disciplinary action, lower secondary teachers reported fewer absences (Benveniste et al., 2008a). However, penalties often do not exist for civil service teachers, or are not enforced. In Peru, for example, it can take many months to dismiss a teacher who has been absent for long and repeated periods, and it seldom happens (Alcázar et al., 2006).

Head teachers themselves are sometimes absent, impeding effective monitoring of teacher attendance and demonstrating inadequate leadership regarding the problem. A 2011 survey of schools in Uganda found that, on average, 14% of teachers and 21% of head teachers were absent on the day the schools were visited (Uwezo Uganda, 2011).

A good working environment that values teachers' contribution can enhance job satisfaction and reduce absenteeism

Hiring teachers on a contract basis gives head teachers more control over hiring and firing. Such accountability mechanisms do not always improve teacher attendance, however. For instance, contract teachers are more likely to attend school than civil service teachers in Benin and India, but more likely to be absent in Indonesia and Peru (Alcázar et al., 2006; Bhattacharjea et al., 2011; Chaudhury et al., 2006; Senou, 2008). Absenteeism may be lower among contract teachers in countries such as Benin and India partly because they typically live in communities where schools are located and have fewer non-teaching responsibilities than civil service teachers.

Experiments have been undertaken in some countries to identify whether monitoring teachers' attendance can help improve their performance. In 2003–2006, in 120 NGO non-formal education centres in rural Rajasthan, India, photographs were taken of teachers and students every day at the beginning and end of class to monitor attendance and the length of the school day. Teachers' pay depended on the number of days they taught at least eight students for at least six hours. Over the period of the programme, teacher absenteeism fell from 44% to 21% (Duflo et al., 2012b). The key finding of this often-cited experiment – that linking pay with attendance is effective – is important. However, it is less clear whether camera-based monitoring of attendance could be scaled up and extended beyond NGO education programmes. Extending such surveillance on a large scale could undermine the image of the teaching profession and limit its appeal to good candidates.

Combining monitoring with incentives could be more beneficial than penalties. In a study of 178 primary schools in rural Peru, teacher attendance was monitored three times a day by parents trained for the task. In most schools bonuses based on the achievement of individual and group attendance targets were distributed. Average attendance was higher by 17 days a year in these schools than in those with monitoring only: the combination of bonuses and monitoring proved effective. The impact on student achievement in mathematics and reading was limited, however: only grade 5 mathematics scores had increased by the end of the year (Cueto et al., 2008).

Other interventions aimed at enhancing teacher accountability are often expected to reduce teacher absenteeism, but do not necessarily do so. Greater involvement of parents and the community in school management, for example, had limited impact on teacher attendance in El Salvador, India and Madagascar, and no impact on student achievement (Kremer et al., 2009).

The most appropriate way to address teacher absenteeism is to tackle its root causes, which vary according to context. In some countries, teachers are absent because their pay is extremely low, in others because working conditions are poor. A good working environment that values teachers' contribution can enhance job satisfaction and reduce absenteeism. In Malawi, where teachers' pay is low and payment often erratic, 1 in 10 teachers stated that they were frequently absent from school in connection with financial concerns, such as travelling to follow up and collect salaries or securing credit and making loan payments (Moleni and Ndalama, 2004).

In countries struggling with the HIV/AIDS epidemic, high morbidity and mortality rates can take their toll on teacher attendance. In high HIV prevalence districts in Malawi, the three main reasons primary teachers gave for absence from school were personal sickness, attending funerals and caring for sick family members (Moleni and Ndalama, 2004). Malawi and Zambia have introduced strategies to improve living conditions for HIV-positive teachers, including greater access to treatment, provision of nutritional supplements and monthly allowances or loans (Chetty and Khonyongwa, 2008; UNESCO and Education International EFAIDS, 2007). Low pay and poor payment processes may also affect teacher absence, possibly by undermining teachers' motivation. In Cambodia, teachers who did not have to miss school to collect pay reported fewer absences (Benveniste et al., 2008a).

Overall, effective monitoring of teacher attendance, coupled with bonuses or penalties, can only be effective in reducing absenteeism if it tackles root causes such as low or irregular pay and poor working conditions.

Strengthening legislation to address teacher misconduct and gender violence

Gender-based violence, which encompasses sexual and physical violence, intimidation and verbal abuse, is a major barrier to the achievement of quality and equality in education whether it is perpetrated by teachers, community members or pupils. In addition to physical and psychological trauma, gender-based violence has long lasting health consequences such as unwanted pregnancy and the spread of HIV/AIDS, and often prevents students from completing their education.

Gender-based violence in schools is often not reported, so much of it may remain hidden. It is often committed by male pupils, although male teachers may be the main perpetrators of the most extreme forms of abuse and exploitation. A survey of 1,300 students from 123 primary and secondary schools in Sierra Leone found that 27% of incidences of unwanted sexual touching and 22% of incidences of verbal abuse were perpetrated by male pupils at school. A small percentage of cases were attributed to male teachers (4% and 3%, respectively). Almost a third of cases of forced or coerced sex in exchange for money, goods or grades were perpetrated by male teachers (Concern et al., 2010). A survey of gender-based violence in schools in Malawi found that around one-fifth of teachers said they were aware of teachers coercing or forcing girls into sexual relationships. Of those who reported awareness of such incidents, almost three-quarters knew of cases happening at their own school (Burton, 2005).

A survey in schools in Malawi found that one-fifth of teachers said they were aware of teachers coercing or forcing girls into sexual relationships

Programmes and policies addressing gender discrimination and gender-based violence need to protect and empower girls, challenge entrenched practices, bring perpetrators to light and enforce action against them. Legal and policy frameworks that provide general protection for children need to be strengthened and publicized, and teachers need to be made aware of their own roles and responsibilities.

Codes of conduct for teachers need to refer explicitly to violence and abuse, and ensure that penalties are clearly stipulated and consistent with legal frameworks for child rights and protection. In Kenya, for example, a range of penalties is available to discipline teachers in breach of professional conduct, including suspension and interdiction; new Teacher Service Commission regulations state that a teacher convicted of a sexual offence against a pupil is to be deregistered (Kenya Teachers Service Commission, 2013). Conviction rates for sexual violence are notoriously low, however; in Sierra Leone, 1,000 cases of sexual assault were filed in 2009, but no action was taken against perpetrators (Concern et al., 2010).

Advocacy and lobbying through national networks and alliances is an important first step in ensuring that adequate legal and policy frameworks are in place to prevent and respond to gender-based violence in schools:

- In Mozambique, the Stop Violence against Girls in School programme, working with a network of civil society organizations, has published a detailed analysis of laws and policies relating to girls' education and protection. It informed the government's revision of the penal code, which now makes explicit and strengthens laws against sexual violation of minors (Leach et al., 2012).

- In Malawi, the Safe Schools project used national advocacy networks to lobby successfully for revisions to teachers' codes of conduct and call for stronger enforcement of regulations relating to misconduct. Awareness workshops were held for school supervisors and school committee members, who then ran sessions with teachers, pupils, counsellors and parents on the revised code. Manuals developed for training teachers and counsellors included modules on the code as well as support, referral and reporting procedures. An evaluation of the project found that the proportion of teachers who reported having seen the code of conduct rose from about three-quarters to almost all. The number of teachers who said they knew how to report a violation of the code increased by over one-third, and virtually all of those said they had a responsibility to report violations (DevTech Systems, 2008).

Working directly with teacher unions is a way to build support for taking action against teachers who violate codes of conduct

- In Ghana, earlier versions of the teachers' code of conduct were consolidated into a single revised version explicitly addressing gender violence. As in Malawi, a consultative approach was adopted, with a team running workshops for representatives of regional education offices, schools and communities. Once the revised code was approved by a national review committee in 2008 and endorsed by teacher unions, meetings were held with all 428 head teachers and teachers in the 30 project schools to familiarize them with the revised code (DevTech Systems, 2008).

Working directly with teacher unions is a way to build support for taking action against teachers who violate codes of conduct. In Kenya, the Stop Violence against Girls in School advocacy team collaborated with the Teachers' Service Commission, the Ministry of Education, the Kenya National Union of Teachers and the Children's Department to draft a parliamentary bill based on a 2010 Teachers Service Commission circular on sexual abuse. The bill aims to reinforce procedures for reporting incidences of abuse or violence carried out by teachers, and to ensure that convicted teachers are not simply transferred to other schools (Leach et al., 2012). The circular states, moreover, that any failure to report or attempt to cover up an incident would lead to disciplinary action (Kenya Teachers Service Commission, 2010). The union, which previously was often a block to reform, is now reported to be committed to avoid protecting teachers found guilty of an offence, and a centralized database has been established to track teachers convicted of sexual offences (Leach et al., 2012).

Even where existing laws provide adequate legal protection against gender-based violence, enforcing them remains a challenge. A survey in Ghana, Kenya and Mozambique found that reporting mechanisms were generally weak. Of 842 girls who reported experiencing gender-based violence, only a few saw their cases referred through official channels, and a small minority were reported to the school management committee, district education office or police. In Ghana, no more than 7% of cases of various types of sexual violence were reported to the school management committee, 2% to district education offices and 14% to police. In Kenya, a greater proportion of cases, predominantly of forced or coerced sex were reported to the management committee or district education offices. In Mozambique, by contrast, no girls who experienced sexual violence reported the incidents (Parkes and Heslop, 2011).

In order to take action against teachers involved in violence or abuse of pupils, it is critical to ensure that reporting procedures are transparent and child-friendly. A national study in Sierra Leone noted that girls were often fearful of reporting teachers, and schools, parents and community members may be complicit in helping teachers avoid prosecution, especially for serious offences (Concern et al., 2010). Complex bureaucratic processes also tend to dissuade victims and their families from pursuing matters. The establishment of Family Support Units within the Sierra Leone Police, set up to tackle gender-based violence, is a more innovative approach to the problem. 'Mother clubs' in Sierra Leone negotiate difficulties faced by girls wishing to report cases of abuse, and provide moral and sometimes financial support (Concern et al., 2010).

Private tutoring versus classroom teaching: protecting the poorest

Teachers are not paid enough. They have family to care for, and they also need to care for themselves – their health is their wealth. Hence, they go after private tuition, which earns them more income, but also distracts from their main duties in the workplace.

– Emmanuel, teacher, Kano state, Nigeria

Private tuition, if unchecked or uncontrolled, can be a detriment to learning outcomes, especially for the poorest students who are unable to afford it. Whatever perspective policy-makers may have on private tuition, management policies are required to ensure that teachers teach the assigned number of hours and cover the whole curriculum so that private tutoring does not displace classroom teaching.

Some countries where private tutoring is long established, such as Hong Kong (China) and the Republic of Korea, have strong school systems, but elsewhere private tutoring by teachers is often a symptom of badly functioning school systems and low pay that forces teachers to supplement their income. Parents tend to believe that classroom teaching is insufficient for their children to master the curriculum and to perceive private tutoring as an integral part of education (Brehm et al., 2012).

In Cambodia, teacher salaries are very low – they do not cover living expenses, including food, housing and health care – and are often distributed late. As a consequence, a 2004 public expenditure tracking survey found 13% of primary school teachers tutored students, including 42% of those in urban areas and 8% in rural areas. On average, tutoring earnings increased teachers' base salary by two-thirds. Among secondary teachers, 87% reported tutoring after school hours (Benveniste et al., 2008a).

Private tutoring by teachers reinforces disparities between students whose parents can afford to pay the fees and those who cannot. Student achievement in Khmer and mathematics was much higher among those who were privately tutored, especially in urban areas. In rural areas, grade 9 students scored 6.8 points out of 10 in Khmer with tutoring and 3.9 points without. In urban areas the gap was even greater: 8.3 points compared with 3.8 points (Brehm et al., 2012).

Private tuition has also spread in former socialist countries of Central and Eastern Europe and Central Asia since the early 1990s, with teachers forced to earn extra income to escape poverty. By 2010 in Lithuania, 17% of grade 12 students were receiving tutoring from their own teachers, 22% from another teacher at their school and 41% from a teacher from another school (Bray, 2011).

Private tutoring by teachers is also reported to be common in sub-Saharan Africa and South and West Asia. In sub-Saharan Africa, tutoring has become more prominent largely as a means to generate extra income for teachers. SACMEQ II data show that 82% of grade 6 pupils in Uganda received extra tutoring, and that over half of these paid for their tuition (Bray, 2009).

Teacher management policies are required to ensure that private tutoring does not displace classroom teaching

In Bangladesh, about one-third of students in government primary schools and almost two-thirds in secondary schools were privately tutored in 2005, and teachers were reported to expect that students would do most of their learning at home, limiting their classroom responsibility to giving and checking homework (Hossain and Zeitlyn, 2010).

In Egypt, although private tutoring is officially forbidden by the Ministry of Education it continues to occur, displacing teaching in the classroom, to the detriment of the poorest students (Box 6.13).

Some countries have tried to restrict private tuition. Mongolia and Ukraine responded to parental complaints by banning private tuition on school premises and tutoring by teachers of their own students (Bray, 2009). Completely banning private tutoring is likely to be impractical, however. Some countries have tried to do so, but have faced difficulties in implementation. In India, the 2009 Right to Education Act states: 'No teacher shall engage himself or herself in private tuition or private teaching activity'; it covers grades 1 to 7 in government schools and 'aided' private schools, which receive government funding. The law, however, sparked outrage from teachers, who said they needed fees from tutoring to supplement their salaries to reach decent income levels (Iyer, 2012).

Box 6.13: In Egypt, private tutoring damages the educational chances of the poor

In Egypt, children whose families cannot afford private tutoring suffer the consequences of a poor quality formal education system in which teachers are more likely to spend their energy and resources on private tutoring than in the classroom. In urban areas, 44% of students receive private tuition, and in rural areas the share is 35%. In Lower Egypt over half of students receive private tuition. The proportion reaches 60% among secondary school students.

The amount spent annually on private tutoring is reported to be US$2.4 billion, equivalent to 27% of government spending on education in 2011. Private tuition is a significant part of household education spending, averaging 47% in rural areas and 40% in urban areas. The investment is viewed as worth the financial strain for families that can pay. However, not everyone can afford it: children from rich households are almost twice as likely to receive private tuition.

An important reason for widespread private tuition is that the social status of teachers in Egypt has declined in recent decades as the government began hiring less qualified teachers to meet the demand of growing public education. School-leavers often become teachers not by choice but as a last resort. The undervaluing of teachers in Egyptian society has led to teaching being one of the lowest paid government jobs, with a base salary of between US$20 and US$60 per month in 2006. Teachers thus turn to private tutoring to supplement their salaries. If they charge around US$3 per lesson per student, just two lessons per month with four students earn them more than the regular salary of a teacher at the bottom of the salary scale. Private tutoring may actually serve as some teachers' main source of income, even if they keep their low paid government jobs to provide legitimacy and as a means of recruiting customers.

Students complain that, as a result of private tutoring, teachers do not cover the curriculum during the school day, so students need to take private tuition to cover the syllabus to enable them to pass exams. Teachers may also be their students' private tutors, and so are responsible for their grades. Illegal private tutoring is so widespread that, in response, the government has organized study groups after school that are taught by regular teachers for a nominal fee. They are not as popular as other forms of private tuition, however, and are used only by those who can afford nothing else.

Sources: Central Agency for Public Mobilization and Statistics (2013); Elbadawy et al. (2007); Hartmann (2007); UNESCO (2012a).

Strategies should at least be in place to prevent tutoring of pupils by teachers who are responsible for teaching them in their daily classes. This would ensure that full curriculum coverage is available to all students, even those not able to afford supplementary tutoring. Tajikistan's 2004 Law on Education permits tutoring in subjects that are not covered by the state curriculum. In Singapore, teachers need permission to give more than six hours of private tuition per week, and are forbidden to offer it to their own students. However, these regulations need to be rigorously enforced (Bray, 2009).

Are low fee private schools better at ensuring that the disadvantaged learn the basics?

Private schools that charge low fees are seen by some observers as a promising way of expanding access to better quality education for disadvantaged children in areas where government schools are failing. Such schools are also seen as a less expensive way of achieving quality, because they can recruit teachers at lower cost than government schools. Advocates of low fee private schools argue that students in these schools achieve better learning outcomes than students in government schools, but such differences arise partly because teachers in government schools often face more difficult conditions, teaching larger classes and children with a wider diversity of learning needs.

Some evidence for higher learning outcomes in low fee private schools comes from Pakistan, where a child in a private school performed better than the average child in the top one-third of children in government schools, after wealth, age, gender and parental education were taken into account (Andrabi et al., 2008). Even though many low fee private schools perform better than government schools, however, pupils in both systems often barely reach expected levels in key subjects. For example, a study in the Indian state of Andhra Pradesh found that at the age of eight, 72% of private school pupils could not solve a basic two-digit by one-digit multiplication problem, while 79% could not divide – results that were only slightly better than those for government school students (Singh and Sarkar, 2012). According to analysis for this Report by the Annual State of Education Report team in Pakistan, 36% of grade 5 students in private schools could not read a sentence in English, which they should have been able to do by grade 2. Similarly, 45% of children in grade 5 could not do division, which they would be expected to have covered in the curriculum by grade 3.

Teachers in low fee private schools are often recruited on temporary contracts and receive very low wages, sometimes below the minimum wage – conditions similar to those of contract teachers in government schools. In two of the largest Indian states

(Uttar Pradesh and Madya Pradesh), teachers' salaries in low fee private schools are estimated to be one-eighth of government school teachers' salaries in the same district or village (Goyal and Pandey, 2009). In Kenya, across four districts, low fee private school teachers receive around half the basic pay of a government teacher and lack the pension and health insurance arrangements that government teachers are entitled to (Stern and Heyneman, 2013). Teachers in low fee private schools in a slum area of Lagos, Nigeria, receive an average wage of around US$80 per month, compared with the state's minimum wage of US$116 and the starting salary for a government teacher of about US$167 per month (Härmä, 2011).

Low fee private school teachers tend to have less experience than government teachers. In Andhra Pradesh, India, teachers in government schools have more than seven years of experience, on average, while those in private schools have fewer than five years (Singh and Sarkar, 2012). In Punjab, Pakistan, the proportion of teachers who reported having more than 20 years of experience was 43% in government schools but 5% in private schools (Aslam and Kingdon, 2011).

In addition, low fee private schools often have fewer trained teachers. In Ghana, less than 10% of teachers in private schools in economically disadvantaged districts were trained, while nearly half the government teachers in schools serving the same area were trained (Akaguri, 2011). Differences in wages are not, however, due only to the lower experience and training that teachers in low fee private schools often have. In Punjab, Pakistan, private teachers were paid one-third as much as government teachers, even once differences in age, education, training and experience are taken into account (Andrabi et al., 2007).

Low fee private schools often employ young people, especially young women, who are willing to work for wages that are unlikely to be sufficient to support a family. In Pakistan, private schools are more likely to be present in rural areas where there is a government secondary school nearby, with female graduates becoming teachers at local private schools: 76% of private school teachers are women, while they make up only 43% of the government teacher workforce (Andrabi et al., 2007). Similarly, in Andhra Pradesh, India, women make up 69% of the mathematics teacher workforce in private schools but only 34% in government schools (Singh and Sarkar, 2012).

Why do some low fee private schools achieve better learning outcomes? One reason is that lower salaries enable low fee private schools to hire more teachers and keep pupil/teacher ratios low. In 23 private schools across four districts in Nairobi, for example, there are 15 students per teacher, compared with 80 in government schools (Stern and Heyneman, 2013). In Patna in Bihar state, India, there are 22 students for every private school teacher, compared with 42 for every government school teacher (Ramgaraju et al., 2012).

Low fee private schools often employ young women who are willing to work for wages that are unlikely to be sufficient to support a family

Not only is class size smaller in low fee private schools, but the amount of time spent actually teaching in school is greater. In rural India, government school teachers have been found to spend 75% of their time at school teaching, compared with 90% for private school teachers (Kingdon and Banerji, 2009). Another Indian study found that private school pupils received three to four times as much teacher contact time as pupils in government schools (Muralidharan and Kremer, 2009).

Such conditions enable private school teachers to provide more feedback to their pupils. In Andhra Pradesh, around half of teachers in both private and government schools used traditional methods of teacher-directed instruction, but private school teachers offered more feedback to students: 82% of teachers in private schools regularly corrected exercises given to children, compared with 40% of teachers in government schools (Singh and Sarkar, 2012). A survey in Lahore district in Punjab province of Pakistan showed that private school teachers were more likely to try to identify what pupils actually understood, by asking them questions in class, and spent more time planning their lessons. This made a significant impact on pupils' learning (Aslam and Kingdon, 2011).

Teachers in low fee private schools are predominantly hired from within the communities they serve, so they are more likely to understand the challenges children face. In Andhra Pradesh, for example, the proportion of

Chapter 7
Curriculum and assessment strategies that improve learning

Language hurdles: Nguyen Thi Thanh Hoan, a teacher in Muong Khuong county, Viet Nam: 'There are 13 ethnic students in my class. All Hmong girls. Sometimes when you teach in Vietnamese they seem not to understand.'

Credit: Nguyen Thanh Tuan/UNESCO

however, as teachers spent less time focusing on reading, which suggests that teacher support needs to be sustained (Abeberese et al., 2013).

In poor or remote communities where there is little access to print media, providing reading materials and supporting activities to practice reading can improve children's learning. The greatest gains can sometimes be made among low achievers and children whose parents have little education (He and Linden, 2009).

In Malawi, community initiatives and active parental interest helped improve children's reading skills

One example is the Save the Children Literacy Boost programme, first implemented in Malawi, Mozambique, Nepal and Pakistan, and now operating in 13 countries, predominantly in Africa and Asia (Save the Children, 2013). The programme aims to improve early grade reading skills in government schools through teacher- and community-focused interventions. Reading assessments are used to identify gaps and measure improvement in core reading skills. Teachers are trained to teach these skills and monitor pupils' mastery of them. Communities are encouraged to support children's reading and enhance their literate environment. Evaluations in Malawi, Mozambique, Nepal and Pakistan all showed greater learning gains by children in Literacy Boost schools than by their peers, including a reduction in the number of children whose scores were zero, suggesting that the programme benefited low achievers (Dowd et al., 2009; Mithani et al., 2011).

Support outside school hours is one reason for such success. In Pakistan, children who had attended after-school reading camps coordinated by community volunteers showed greater learning gains in reading fluency and accuracy in both Pashto and Urdu than classmates in the same schools (Mithani et al., 2011). In Malawi, community initiatives and active parental interest also helped improve children's reading skills (Box 7.5).

Box 7.5: Schools and communities in partnership to support early literacy in Malawi

In 2009 and 2010, Save the Children implemented the Literacy Boost programme in Zomba district of Malawi. Teachers in government schools received eight training sessions on teaching core reading skills; on using regular, classroom-based assessment to develop these skills; and on supporting second-language acquisition. Sessions were linked to the national curriculum and teachers were given model lessons and other resources. The programme also provided villages with book banks, trained community members to manage these and other resources, and ran workshops for parents on how to support their children's reading. Communities and parents adopted a variety of strategies to support literacy: events to promote reading, reading with children at home, telling folk stories and preparing reading materials from local resources. Literacy Boost communities also increased the frequency and variety of initiatives to support orphaned and other vulnerable children.

An evaluation found that the programme had improved grade 2 pupils' literacy. In 2009, the vast majority of second graders in both Literacy Boost and comparison schools could not read a single word in their local language. After one year, the share unable to read fell to 65% in Literacy Boost schools, but hardly changed in comparison schools, remaining at 91%. Grade 2 pupils whose parents had attended Literacy Boost workshops made greater vocabulary gains than those who had not, and the gains were greatest for children of parents with little or no literacy skills. Grade 2 pupils who borrowed and read books from book banks also demonstrated significantly greater vocabulary gains than peers. For grade 4 pupils, Literacy Boost activities helped mitigate the difficulty of learning in very large classes.

Although the Literacy Boost programme has demonstrated real progress in improving early reading among pupils in rural schools, the numbers of children without basic reading skills remained high: nearly two-thirds of grade 2 pupils were still unable to read a single word in their local language, and many were still struggling to read after grade 2. These results highlight the need for more training to support teachers in developing materials and carrying out continuous assessment; targeted, additional support for weak learners; and support for English oral skills alongside local language literacy.

Sources: Dowd et al. (2009); Gove and Cvelich (2010).

Developing curricula that foster inclusion

When curriculum is standardized to state policies and does not consider the native language, traditions and customs of the people, this creates a barrier that most indigenous people are unable to overcome.
- Natalee, teacher, Bay Islands, Honduras

Curricula that do not acknowledge and address issues of inclusion can alienate disadvantaged groups within the classroom, and so limit their chances to learn effectively. In some countries, curricula reinforce traditional gender stereotypes, placing girls in a subservient role and hindering gender-equitable learning. Analysis of secondary school English-language textbooks published by the Punjab textbook board in Pakistan found that women and girls were seldom represented, or were represented in a discriminatory way. In 20 out of 22 lessons in one English textbook, women were not mentioned at all (Shah, 2012).

Gender-responsive curricula can be used to address issues directly affecting girls and boys and their schooling. The Group Education Activities curriculum developed for the Gender Equity Movement in Schools project in Mumbai, India, included content on gender roles, violence, and sexual and reproductive health for Standard 6 and 7 girls and boys. An evaluation from 2008 to 2010 showed improved scores on tests measuring attitudes regarding a range of gender-related issues, compared with girls and boys in control schools. Participating students tended to oppose early marriage and domestic violence and believed girls should continue to higher education (Achyut et al., 2011).

The Sistema de Aprendizaje Tutorial, a secondary school programme serving girls from the minority Garifuna group in Honduras, aims to empower girls and women. An interdisciplinary curriculum questions dominant power structures and challenges gender stereotypes. Teaching is learner-centred and inquiry-based, and emphasizes dialogue. Graduates displayed greater ability to identify problems and conceive solutions, along with more gender awareness, self-confidence and knowledge (Murphy-Graham, 2008). After two years, adolescents in villages where the programme had been implemented had higher composite test scores than those in other villages (McEwan et al., 2012, cited in Lloyd, 2013).

Education strategies increasingly recognize the importance of accommodating children with disabilities in mainstream schools. However, more needs to be done to implement them effectively by adopting measures such as addressing attitudes of teachers and head teachers through training, and designing curricula that pay attention to the needs of disabled learners. In Canberra, Australia, curriculum reform aims to raise students' awareness of people with disabilities through classroom activities aligned to the new Australian Curriculum. The reform is intended to help teachers improve student attitudes and understanding regarding students with disabilities, improve the quality of interactions and friendships between students with and without disabilities, and enhance the well-being and academic achievement of students with disabilities (Australian Capital Territory Government, 2012).

Identifying and supporting disadvantaged learners

In many developing countries, teachers lack strategies to identify and support low achievers, proceeding with the regular curriculum regardless of their learning needs. This leaves many children at risk of falling behind the curriculum, failing to acquire foundation skills and remaining unable to catch up.

Classroom-based assessment tools can help teachers identify, monitor and support learners at risk of low achievement

Classroom-based assessment tools can help teachers identify, monitor and support learners at risk of low achievement. Assessment innovations designed to provide immediate feedback to pupils and teachers can enhance pupils' learning.

Targeted additional support is key to helping children master the basic literacy and numeracy skills they need for future success. The use of trained teaching assistants to support teachers has been shown to be effective in improving learning outcomes for children with additional learning needs.

Using learning assessments to identify and support weak learners

Assessments allow the responsible teacher to determine the areas in which their students are lacking. As a result they focus on those subjects like maths or English and try to cover the gaps. This is a great help. Because of the assessments we do, our children are less worried before exams. Their course is covered, their preparation is good and the blunders are minimized.

- Ari, teacher, Punjab, Pakistan

Learning assessments help teachers identify students who are struggling to learn, diagnose their learning difficulties and choose strategies to support them. While teachers' ability to use assessments is crucial to students' chances of improving, successful approaches also develop students' ability to assess their own progress.

Uruguay involved teachers directly in assessment activities, improving learning for disadvantaged children

Some countries, particularly in Latin America, have made great strides in using national assessments to identify children with inherited disadvantage who need extra attention (Kellaghan et al., 2009). Uruguay followed up an initial assessment of grade 6 pupils' language and mathematics learning in 1996 with sample assessments every three years. The assessment material and training sessions were also offered to non-sampled schools so that these schools could conduct the tests themselves; about 80% of schools per year volunteered to do so, thus involving teachers directly in assessment activities. This has led to improvement in teachers' experience and use of assessment inside the school system. National assessments in 1996, 1999 and 2002 showed that, while all learners were scoring higher, the improvement was steepest for the most disadvantaged 20%: the percentage of these pupils passing the national assessment test increased from 37% in 1996 to 55% in 2002 (Ravela, 2005).

The use of national assessments for improving learning is less common in sub-Saharan Africa. Uganda, a notable exception, has conducted its survey-based National Assessment of Progress in Education since 1996, and yearly since 2003. The assessment tests literacy and numeracy in grades 3 and 6; in 2008, it was extended to the Senior Two grade of lower secondary level to test mathematics, English and biology. Reporting is disaggregated by age, location (rural or urban), and geographic region and zone (Najjumba and Marshall, 2013). Results are meant to be used for better resource allocation, greater emphasis on classroom-based assessment, and intervention to support struggling pupils, and as a basis for changes to curriculum and teacher education (DFID, 2011; Greaney and Kellaghan, 2008). While the assessment system is fully functional, in practice, assessment results are not used well at the classroom level to improve learning (Najjumba and Marshall, 2013).

Although national assessments can provide useful information to governments and schools to aid them in tackling problems of learning, strategies for effective assessment practices within classrooms are needed that help teachers monitor children's progress and respond to their learning needs. Such classroom-based assessments should lie at the heart of any strategy to improve the quality of education and make it more equitable.

Classroom-based assessments can provide quick results by giving feedback on group progress and on individual pupils to help in diagnosing difficulties. Combined with additional instructional support, assessments can make a real difference to weak learners. Teachers need classroom assessment tools that are clearly linked to instruction, are relevant and simple to use, and can assess performance even among learners with few or no writing skills. Early Grade Reading Assessments (EGRA), for example, are designed to be administered orally in local languages and are sensitive to the lower end of the achievement range, capable of detecting performance on emerging skills (Gove and Cvelich, 2011).

In Liberia, the EGRA Plus project, which trained teachers in the use of classroom-based assessment tools and provided reading resources and scripted lesson plans to guide instruction, made a substantial impact, raising previously low levels of reading achievement among grade 2 and 3 pupils. The project involved several types of continuous assessment. For example, teachers used a simple oral assessment outlined in scripted lesson plans to check pupils' understanding during reading instruction. This allowed teachers to quickly assess responses and identify pupils requiring further assistance. Teachers also applied regular curriculum-based measures to check individual pupils' progress and calculate class averages, reporting both pupil and class progress to parents a minimum of four times a year. Colour-coded report cards allowed parents to visualize their child's progress easily throughout the year. In addition, periodic tests were built into the curriculum to check pupils' mastery of particular skills and determine instructional needs. One challenge was to ensure that teachers understood the importance of the data gathered from assessments and used the tools consistently to inform practice. To address this, trained mentors regularly visited schools to support teachers and ensure the quality of instruction and assessment (Davidson et al., 2011).

To be effective, classroom assessment materials need to be aligned with the curriculum and designed in ways that do not add greatly to teachers' workloads. In situations where teachers have not been trained to develop and use diagnostic tests, prepared assessment packages can be useful. In South Africa, for example, well-designed materials provided an efficient system for recording and reporting learner scores and monitoring progress over time – a crucial element in using assessment to support learning (Kanjee, 2009). Assessment resource banks, with simple-to-use materials designed for teachers with limited teaching experience and pedagogical knowledge, were piloted in 450 rural schools. Workshops were provided to train teachers to use the materials for classroom assessments. Each assessment task was accompanied by instructions, including the learning outcomes to be demonstrated and the level of difficulty of the task. Scoring scales and guidelines on interpreting scores were provided to aid less skilled teachers.

The majority of teachers reported that the materials were clear, simple, and easy to select from and use, though about a third said that due to the language and difficulty level of the materials, they were not helpful in their classrooms. Of the 99 lessons observed as part of an evaluation, the materials were used in 79, with teachers demonstrating varying degrees of understanding of how best to use them; encouragingly, only 10% of teachers were visibly unsure how to use them. In addition, 84% of teachers reported using the materials to help plan their lessons, since they were aligned with the national curriculum.

Students can make considerable gains if they are offered more opportunities to monitor their own learning. An evaluation of the Escuela Nueva programme in rural Colombia, where pupils are guided to assessment tasks through learning materials rather than having the tasks set by the teacher, found that pupils developed the ability to self-diagnose problem areas and learn at their own pace (McEwan, 2008).

Students can make considerable gains if they are offered more opportunities to monitor their own learning

The Activity Based Learning model, which has been mainstreamed in all government and government-aided primary schools in the Indian state of Tamil Nadu, shows that a classroom-based learning process that generates internal feedback to regulate and improve learning can be effective on a large scale. Activity Based Learning builds on innovative multigrade teaching methods developed by Rishi Valley Institute of Educational Resources in Andhra Pradesh (Blum, 2009). For children in the programme, the chance to move at their own pace, without having to compete with classmates doing the same tasks at the same time, builds motivation to keep learning (SchoolScape and Tamil Nadu Government, 2009). There are no examinations and no classroom rankings, lessening possible damage to self-esteem and motivation to drop out. Evaluations show that this approach improves learning outcomes and a range of non-cognitive skills (Box 7.6).

However, in poor learning environments with large classes, as is often the case in developing countries, using assessment to generate frequent feedback and promote active learning can be quite challenging.

Box 7.6: Activity Based Learning boosts pupils' progress in India

The Activity Based Learning model in Tamil Nadu state breaks down learning areas into small, sequenced steps organized into work cards that direct pupils to various learning activities. Sets of activities form 'milestones', arranged in ascending order in 'learning ladders'. The materials are structured to provide feedback at the end of each step through assessment tasks. Self-evaluation cards that are at the heart of assessment can be administered alone or with the help of another child; teachers strategically pair more advanced learners with less advanced ones for certain exercises. These cards are meant to build children's recall ability and reinforce what they have learned. The learning ladder is an important monitoring tool, enabling teachers to keep track of each pupil's progress so as to give remedial support to children who need it.

India's National Council of Educational Research and Training recently evaluated Activity Based Learning's effectiveness, sampling 280 schools in Tamil Nadu. Most teachers viewed the approach positively, especially the adapted curriculum and overall methodology, but underscored the need for continued support in schools after initial training and expressed concern over a reported increase in their workload. Overall achievement in the state was found to be high, above 70%. Children's self-confidence grew and their fear of teachers and assessment diminished, improving pupil-teacher relationships. Pupils also showed greater motivation and cooperation with other children.

In another evaluation of the approach, baseline and post-tests were set for grade 2 and 4 pupils in Tamil Nadu at the start and end of 2008, the first year of implementation. The scores reflected significant increases in average learning levels over the year and, crucially, a reduction in levels of disparity in learning based on gender, urban or rural residence, and social status. In the absence of a control group it is not possible to attribute all learning improvement to the schooling model, but it is likely that the reductions in disparity were due to the new approach.

Evaluations recommend more extensive training for teachers and continuing support. Advocacy with communities is also required, to increase understanding of the benefits of this approach. For the approach to work, schools must have a good supply of learning materials, teacher guidebooks, textbooks and a selection of readers in the classroom. Teacher must also be equipped in the pedagogy and methodology of this approach so they can offer appropriate feedback to help students make the expected progress.

Sources: India National Council of Educational Research and Training (2011); PROBE Team (1999); SchoolScape and Tamil Nadu Government (2009).

Teaching assistants can provide additional support targeted to weak learners

Using trained teaching assistants who work alongside teachers is one way to provide additional support for children identified as being at risk of falling behind. Several programmes using trained teaching assistants to deliver targeted support within mainstream schools have improved learning for disadvantaged groups, including children with disabilities. Community-based assistants working within schools can also promote a more inclusive learning environment and improve learning among marginalized groups.

In high income countries, trained teaching assistants can improve learning outcomes for struggling readers as long as they are assigned clearly defined tasks, working one-to-one with individual children or with small groups. A review of data from 13 interventions, predominantly in the United Kingdom, found that teaching assistants significantly improved the achievement of primary school age children with learning difficulties. The interventions were generally small-scale. In all cases the teaching assistants had received training prior to the intervention and were supported throughout. Where support from teaching assistants was of a more general nature, not directed at pupils with identified difficulties, evidence of any positive effect was less clear-cut and in several instances the impact on outcomes was negligible (Farrell et al., 2010).

Early targeted interventions using trained teaching assistants can result in long-term learning gains for low achievers. An initial early reading intervention delivered by teaching assistants in London schools was found to improve reading skills and have longer-term positive effects for children with poor literacy skills. Trained assistants worked with groups of 6-year-olds, identified as the poorest readers in their year, for nine weeks using rhyming and phonetics-based activities. Results from this initial intervention found that children in the intervention groups made significantly greater average learning gains than pupils who had not received the support (Savage and Carless, 2005). Early gains in certain literacy tasks were maintained over the longer term and the targeted support provided by teaching assistants narrowed the gap between achievement of at-risk children and national norms (Savage and Carless, 2008).

A few studies that have examined the effects of teaching assistants and community volunteers in low income countries indicate that they have an important role in improving learning outcomes for disadvantaged children. In Costa Rica, for example, a tutoring programme using secondary school volunteers to provide structured learning support for pre-school children from low income families was more effective than extra materials for teachers or family support activities in improving reading skills. Children who received tutoring finished the school year with higher scores than those who did not. However, the impact of tutoring was greatest in combination with extra teaching materials and family support, highlighting the importance of integrated approaches (Rolla San Francisco et al., 2006).

Trained teachers in formal schools often come from different cultural or linguistic backgrounds than those of children in marginalized groups. Using teaching assistants who come from pupils' communities can help build a more inclusive learning environment. In Hong Kong, for example, bilingual teaching assistants with a South Asian background took on a dual role of helping South Asian pupils learn Chinese and acting as cultural mediators between the dominant school culture and that of the South Asian community (Gao and Shum, 2010).

Trained and supported community volunteers, working with teachers, can improve learning for marginalized children. One example is the balsakhi programme in India, which provided targeted support for children in government schools lagging behind their peers. Instruction focused on foundation literacy and numeracy skills from a standardized curriculum developed by Pratham, an Indian NGO. A trained female community volunteer (balsakhi or 'child's friend') provided daily support to children identified as low achievers, many of whom were working children who had been unable to attend school regularly. An evaluation conducted in 2001/02 found a significant positive impact on test scores. The greatest learning gains were among previously low scoring children, who were the most likely to have been chosen to receive instruction from the balsakhi. While only 6% of pupils were able to carry out two-digit addition at the start of the study, by the end of the year the proportion had risen to 51% for children in classes with balsakhi, but 39% in other classes (Abdul Latif Jameel Poverty Action Lab, 2006; Banerjee et al., 2005).

Using trained teaching assistants who come from pupils' communities can help build a more inclusive learning environment

Deploying technology to reduce learning disparities

Technology is a medium that, without a doubt, facilitates learning in school, but that will never take the place of the work of a teacher.

- Carlos, teacher, Santiago, Chile

Among technologies that have potential to support classroom teaching, interactive radio and television programmes can lead to improvement in learning outcomes for marginalized and disadvantaged groups. Computers and portable electronic devices can supplement – but not replace – classroom teaching as long as teachers are trained to make the best use of the technology available. If new technology is to have wider benefits for learning among disadvantaged groups, however, learners need better access to information and communication technology (ICT) within and outside of school.

Radio and television can help improve learning outcomes

Radio and television programming can improve learning and narrow achievement gaps for disadvantaged children, particularly those in isolated or underserved settings. The use of radio and television can enrich curriculum delivery and develop familiarity with a second language. Well-designed programmes can improve the flexibility of curriculum delivery, contributing to better learning in a variety of contexts.

Interactive radio programming is an enduring and successful example of the use of technology to deliver basic education to underserved groups. Popular since the 1970s as a means of expanding access, radio broadcasting has had a resurgence, with several well-funded projects using interactive radio instruction to counteract poor resources, inadequate teacher training and low levels of learner achievement

(Ho and Thukral, 2009). Interactive learning activities such as song, movement and role-playing are introduced and guided by classroom teachers or, in non-formal contexts, trained community teachers, who follow broadcast instructions. Several such programmes aim to benefit not just learners but also teachers, who can learn new methods of teaching (International Research Foundation for Open Learning, 2004).

Interactive radio instruction is associated with higher achievement, particularly for early-grade pupils in hard-to-reach communities

A review of 15 projects showed that interactive radio instruction was associated with higher achievement of learners in English and mathematics in a range of developing countries, particularly for early grade pupils in hard-to-reach communities and schools in fragile states. The review identified encouraging trends in narrowing of urban-rural disparities in learning outcomes, which were particularly pronounced for children in very remote areas. In Pakistan, for example, the positive effects of interactive radio programming on the learning outcomes of grade 1 pupils were greatest in schools categorized as isolated. In such remote contexts, radio addresses barriers to learning raised by distance, poor access to resources, and an insufficient supply of quality teachers and of teacher supervision and support (Ho and Thukral, 2009).

Interactive radio instruction also holds promise as a strategy to support second-language acquisition. In Guinea, the Fundamental Quality and Equity Levels project builds on traditions of storytelling and song to encourage children to read and speak French; in contrast, standard French literacy education in Guinea focuses on recitation and memorization (Education Development Center, 2006). The programme has helped to narrow achievement gaps. Rural pupils who participated in the programme scored as high or almost as high as their urban counterparts on French tests (World Bank, 2005).

Radio broadcasts can be successfully incorporated into both formal and non-formal settings, increasing access to quality education, as an early childhood project in Zanzibar (United Republic of Tanzania) demonstrates. The Radio Instruction to Strengthen Education project was established in 2006 to develop and pilot models for extending early childhood education to underserved communities. By 2010 it was reaching over 20,000 children on the islands of Pemba and Unguja. The project uses interactive radio instruction to build children's foundation skills and prepare them for primary school, using games, song, stories and problem-solving activities linked to the Zanzibar curriculum. An evaluation in 2008 found that children who had received interactive radio instruction, whether in non-formal or formal settings, had greater overall learning gains than children in formal classrooms who had not received radio instruction. Overall, learning gains, relative to the control group, were 12% higher for the non-formal group and 15% higher for the formal group. Results also show greater learning gains for children from Pemba communities, which have lower incomes, lower adult literacy, and poorer access to health and social services than those in Unguja (USAID and Education Development Center, 2009).

Radio can also support education in fragile states, including those emerging from conflict, by allowing education systems with shortages of infrastructure, qualified teachers and learning materials to reach large numbers of children and provide second-chance education to returning refugees and out-of-school youth. For example, between 2006 and 2011, the South Sudan Interactive Radio Instruction project enrolled over 473,000 pupils through Learning Village audio lessons targeting grades 1 to 4. The half-hour lessons were linked to the national curriculum and included instruction in English, local language literacy, mathematics, and life skills elements such as HIV/AIDS and landmine risk awareness. In addition, the project has reached 55,000 out-of-school youth with 180 audio lessons offering the primary school curriculum, together with civics, health and English-language content, via a non-formal accelerated learning programme. In locations that are out of range of any radio signal, the project distributed digital MP3 players to be used by trained teachers (Leigh and Epstein, 2012).

Television-assisted instruction, similar in approach to interactive radio instruction, is popular in parts of Latin America, where there have been several long-running, large-scale programmes. Telesecundaria in Mexico, for example, was launched in 1968 to extend access to lower secondary education; by 2010, 1.26 million students were enrolled in the programme (UNESCO, 2012b).

Digital classrooms can enhance learning and bridge knowledge and skills gaps among less qualified teachers. Digital Study Hall is a small, innovative project that uses ICT to improve the accessibility and quality of education for disadvantaged children in India and, more recently, in Pakistan and Nepal. It provides digital video recordings of classes taught by expert teachers in Indian schools that correspond to state curricula. The recordings are distributed on DVDs to rural and slum schools, along with a TV, a DVD player and a means of providing electricity, such as a car battery or inverter (Digital Study Hall, 2013). Teachers are expected to mediate the recorded lessons and facilitate interactive learning, while the video provides a structured framework, content and a model of teaching for less qualified teachers. An evaluation of four schools in Uttar Pradesh state in India found that, after eight months, 72% of pupils had improved test scores; of these, 44% had an increase greater than 150% and almost a third improved by more than 200% (Sahni et al., 2008).

New technology can be used to supplement children's learning, but disadvantaged groups need support

We are studying with mobile phones. You get questions sent and you answer them and then you get the correct answer. It has helped me to improve my grades in my examinations. I enjoy studying with the phone; it's given me more enthusiasm to like reading.

- Joshua, aged 14, Mathare North, Kenya

Innovation in the use of technology can help improve learning by enriching teachers' curriculum delivery and encouraging flexibility in pupil learning. Greater access to computers in schools helps reduce the digital divide between low and high income groups. However, new technology is not a substitute for good teaching. Opportunities for computer-assisted learning need teachers' support. They must also be targeted at children who are denied the greater access to ICT enjoyed by those from higher income backgrounds and urban dwellers.

Rapid advances in ICT and availability of computers and mobile devices have made it possible for these new technologies to be used as teaching tools in many countries. However, simply introducing computers in schools is not enough to improve learning, nor can they replace teachers as the primary source of classroom instruction: several studies in Europe and the United States have found little or no correlation between greater general ICT availability in schools and increased pupil achievement (Sprietsma, 2007). A recent experimental study of 1,123 grade 6 to grade 10 students in 15 schools in California found no effect on grades or test scores (Fairlie and Robinson, 2013).

Introducing computers in schools cannot replace teachers as the primary source of classroom instruction

In poorer countries, the availability of ICT infrastructure remains a crucial consideration. Many countries cannot yet support widespread computer-assisted learning because schools lack internet access or, in some cases, even electricity supply. But, given the investment required by poorer countries to ensure that all schools have electricity supply or internet access, the use of ICT is unlikely to be as cost-effective as spending more on teachers to reduce class sizes. Teachers remain central to curriculum delivery, particularly for low achievers needing additional support.

ICT can be more effective as a means to improve learning and address learning disparities if it plays a complementary role, serving as an additional resource for teachers and students. A study in India evaluated computer-assisted mathematics programmes, implemented both as a stand-alone substitute for regular teaching in an in-school programme and as an after-school programme to reinforce teachers' curriculum delivery. The results showed that the in-school programme, far from leading to improved scores, actually caused pupils to learn significantly less than they otherwise would have done. By contrast, using the after-school programme to supplement regular teaching brought increased learning gains, particularly for low achievers (Linden, 2008).

Teachers' ability to use ICT as an educational resource plays a critical role in improving learning. A study in Brazil found that the introduction of computer laboratories in schools had a negative impact on pupils' performance in and of itself, but that teachers' use of the internet as a pedagogical resource to support innovative classroom teaching and learning resulted in improved test scores, especially in mathematics (Sprietsma, 2007).

A programme in rural India showed higher achievers are better able to take advantage of the benefits of learner-led mobile learning

Children from low income backgrounds can benefit from access to computer-aided learning that includes well-designed interactive software supporting skills development, alongside curriculum-based competencies. A small-scale study in schools in low income areas of Tel Aviv found that grade 5 pupils using a computer-aided programme of interactive learning activities, delivered via individual laptops, had significantly higher learning gains than pupils taught in a traditional learning environment. The specifically designed software, aligned to the national curriculum, allowed teachers to provide different materials to pupils with different levels of achievement and let pupils work according to their own ability (Rosen and Manny-Ikan, 2011).

Effective use of ICT for learning requires careful consideration of how pupils' overall access to technology affects learning outcomes. Children from low income groups are less likely to have experience of ICT outside school, and may thus take longer to adapt to it. In low income countries, the digital divide is often extreme and strategies are needed to ensure that ICT exposure outside school does not exacerbate disparities for disadvantaged groups. In Rwanda, a study found that 79% of students who used computers in secondary schools had previously used ICT and the internet outside school (primarily in internet cafés) for various activities and that this additional exposure supported their learning in school. However, girls and rural children were at a disadvantage because they were less likely to have access to internet cafés or other ICT resources in their communities (Rubagiza et al., 2011; Were et al., 2009).

One promising way of increasing the accessibility of ICT for teaching and learning is 'mobile learning' – the use of mobile phones and other portable electronic devices, such as MP3 players. Mobile phones have perhaps the greatest potential for ICT-based learning, particularly in low income countries, where they are often the only widely available technology. Mobile phones do not require the same level of infrastructure as computers, networks are more widely available and phones increasingly have internet access and video capabilities. However, while they can increase learning opportunities, these new technologies need to tailor content and delivery to the varying needs of learners, especially weaker students.

In rural India, an after-school programme for children from low income families used mobile phone games to support English language learning. Two-hour sessions were conducted for a total of 38 days. This resulted in significant learning gains on tests of the spelling of common English nouns. However, the learning gains were greatest for children in more advanced grades who had stronger foundation skills. As higher achievers are better able to take advantage of the benefits of learner-led mobile learning, more attention is needed to develop software and other support mechanisms to include weaker learners (Kam et al., 2009).

Beyond the basics: transferable skills for global citizenship

While it is vital that all children and young people acquire foundation skills, to thrive they also need to learn to become responsible global citizens – and schools need to be able to help them achieve this goal. Global citizenship education includes issues such as environmental sustainability and peace-building – which require core transferable skills such as critical thinking, communication, cooperation, problem-solving, conflict resolution, leadership and advocacy – and the promotion of core values such as tolerance, appreciation of diversity and civic responsibility. It is essential for curricula to address these themes in a manner that is relevant to children's situation and motivates them, particularly those in difficult circumstances. Global themes and skills can be made more relevant by adapting them to national and local contexts and real-life situations, with core values being taught across the curriculum.

A study commissioned for this Report highlights the extent to which countries are emphasizing the need for such transferable skills in their national curricula. Communication and social competence were the most evident: among 88 countries, 71 include these qualities in their curricula. Emphasis is also placed on problem-solving (in 55 countries), creativity (52) and ICT use (51). About half the countries incorporate civic competence, collaboration, critical thinking and entrepreneurship in their curriculum frameworks and policy documents (Amadio, 2013).

Promoting responsible attitudes and behaviour towards the environment

Curricula that aim to increase understanding of the science behind climate change and other environmental concerns can improve knowledge, raise awareness, and shape attitudes and behaviour that mitigate environmental damage. Students in OECD countries with higher science performance also demonstrated a stronger sense of responsibility for sustainable development (Bybee, 2008).

Environmental knowledge and its practical applications are most effective when integrated into existing subject areas across the curriculum. An integrated approach also contributes to the development of transferable skills important for sustainable development, such as critical thinking, problem-solving, and respect for people and the environment. The study of national curricula commissioned for this Report shows that 57 out of the 88 countries take a cross-cutting approach to teaching sustainability and environmental issues (Amadio, 2013).

Global citizenship education requires transferable skills such as critical thinking, communication, problem-solving and conflict resolution

An interdisciplinary approach that involves hands-on, locally relevant educational activities can develop students' understanding of the environment and build skills for promoting sustainable development. Between 1999 and 2004, Germany introduced an interdisciplinary programme known as BLK-21 in around 200 secondary schools; it fostered participatory learning and provided opportunities for students to work together on innovative projects for sustainable living. An evaluation found that students in the programme had a greater understanding of sustainable development than their peers, and 75% to 80% of the students said they had gained transferable skills, such as foresight and teamwork, that helped them evaluate and solve problems in sustainable development (de Haan, 2006).

Educational activities that connect the curriculum to local, tangible problem-solving are more likely to be successful in supporting positive environmental attitudes and behaviours. Whole-school approaches that reinforce learning through practical demonstrations of sustainable living offer a promising model (Choi et al., 2013). The Eco-School initiative in South Africa, for example, provides certification for schools that link environmental learning and action. Hands-on teaching and learning approaches and school-wide projects are used to link the curriculum to practical actions such as adopting recycling systems and water harvesting in schools, using alternative energy sources for cooking, cleaning up public spaces, creating indigenous gardens, and planting trees (Wildlife and Environment Society of South Africa, 2013). Participating

A citizenship programme in Burundi improved relationships among pupils and between teachers and pupils

schools have reported increased environmental awareness and improved sustainability practices at school and in homes (Rosenburg, 2008).

Strategies to empower children through communication and advocacy can also lead to practical actions that reduce their vulnerability to risk. In the Philippines, which is prone to environmental disasters, a strong commitment from government and non-state providers to integrate disaster risk reduction into the education sector has led children to take an active role in making their communities safer (Box 7.7).

Box 7.7: Supporting child-led disaster risk reduction in the Philippines

The Philippines suffers from typhoons, floods, droughts, cyclones, earthquakes, landslides, volcanic eruptions and other natural hazards. In 2007, the Department of Education prioritized programmes and projects to reduce risk from environmental disaster. This initiative, which involves international partners, includes integrating disaster risk reduction into the school curriculum.

Children learn about climate change adaptation and how to reduce their vulnerability to disaster while studying existing subjects, including science and social studies. Teaching and learning materials include workbooks with practical information on what to do before, during and after a disaster, using techniques such as disaster simulation, drills and family disaster plans. Child-centred activities such as songs, poems, role play, quizzes, puppetry and pantomime support learning and raise awareness.

Local theatre is an important cultural activity in the Philippines. A Plan International programme has encouraged children to use this medium to express what they have learned and share information on potential hazards and practical solutions in their communities. Theatre also provides psychosocial therapy for child survivors of disasters. Children are empowered to take an active role in their schools and communities and to become advocates for change. In Santa Paz in Southern Leyte province, for example, children lobbied for the transfer of their school from an unsafe location to a safer one, organized school safety campaigns and participated in meetings of local disaster coordinating councils.

Sources: Plan International (2008); Selby and Kagawa (2012).

Education for peace-building

I go to school and I love it because it creates relationships and builds a community. You might meet a Kikuyu or a Turkana and you can relate. There's no tribalism involved here.

– Diansu, 13 years, Turkana county, Kenya

Citizenship and peace-building programmes that emphasize inclusion and conflict resolution can promote positive learning environments and support individuals' rights. An example is the Responsible Citizenship programme in Burundi, designed to support integration of returning refugees into secondary schools. It began in 2009, developed through community-based workshops, and focused on core skills such as communicating effectively, including others and mediating conflicts. Curriculum delivery through participatory learning and interactive teaching, including radio programmes and student-led theatre, encouraged those involved to learn from personal experiences and draw solutions from them. The focus was on developing personal and civic responsibility. An evaluation conducted almost two years into the programme highlighted several improvements in relationships among pupils and between teachers and pupils. Trained teachers abandoned corporal punishment, pupils were consulted over school rules, the use of participatory teaching methods increased, issues such as sexual violence and corruption were more freely discussed, and pupils acted as mediators in the resolution of minor conflicts at school and in the community (Servas, 2012).

The development and implementation of curricula to build greater understanding and lasting peace require government commitment and political support and advocacy, particularly within traditionally divided societies. Legislation is important for meaningful and long-term implementation, as are processes of wider curriculum reform. Biased curricula and teaching methods can reinforce tensions and exclusion and become key drivers of conflict (UNICEF, 2011). Critical curriculum review is a necessary first step in redressing historical biases and teaching about past conflicts in a manner respectful of multiple perspectives (Cole, 2012). Curriculum development in consultation with pupils, families and community leaders can enable more effective engagement with the needs of teachers and pupils, and make the introduction of the new curriculum less vulnerable to accusations of political manipulation.

Such an approach was used in Northern Ireland's Local and Global Citizenship programme, which aimed at facilitating the inclusion of citizenship education in the curriculum. The approach met with broad success in terms of its acceptance and integration into school settings and its impact on pupils' awareness, attitudes and behaviour in relation to citizenship issues. It was introduced as a whole-school agenda delivered through a combination of discrete, scheduled learning areas integrated across the curriculum, and extracurricular activities. The emphasis was on providing young people with the knowledge and skills to think critically about contemporary issues and make informed decisions on how to behave. In 2007, legislation established Local and Global Citizenship as part of the statutory curriculum, giving the government responsibility for including it in teacher education programmes (Arlow, 2012). As a result of this approach, students became more interested in local and international politics and had greater expectations of democratic environments in schools. Perceptions of community relations were also more positive (O'Connor et al., 2008).

Conclusion

Together the chapters in this Report offer the ingredients for a global push towards a world where all children are not only in school, but are actually acquiring the skills and knowledge they need to fulfil their potential. Chapter 4 shows that many children across the world are failing to learn – especially those who start with disadvantage and discrimination because of poverty, location, gender, ethnicity or the language they speak. Chapters 5 and 6 explore ways to improve the quality of teaching to give all students a better chance.

To succeed, good teachers need curricula designed to meet the needs of all students

To succeed, however, good teachers need the right tools. This chapter has laid out ways to redress learning failures by giving teachers those tools: curricula designed to meet the needs of all students for foundation skills and transferable skills, and assessment strategies that can be used to target additional support at those who need it most.

© Karel Prinsloo/ARETE/UNESCO

Recommendations

An outdoor class in Turkana County, northwestern Kenya. Teacher education needs to prepare teachers for such remote schools.

MULTIPLICATION
5X1=5
5X2=

Unlocking teachers' potential to solve the learning crisis

Children's educational opportunities should never be determined by where they grow up, their parents' income, their ethnicity, their gender or whether they have a disability. Yet, in a quarter of the world's countries, less than half of children are learning basic literacy and numeracy skills, and about 80% of those not learning these basic skills live in sub-Saharan Africa. In total, 250 million children are not learning the basics. Urgent action is needed to ensure that these children do not become a lost generation.

How governments and donor agencies respond to this crisis will determine whether good quality education for all can be achieved. Learning disparities emerge early in life, even before children start school, so it is vital to see that all children benefit from early childhood education and go on to receive primary schooling of good quality in the early grades. If children learn to read with comprehension and understand basic mathematics by the time they complete primary school, they acquire the foundations for making further progress in education and gaining the skills they will need to get good jobs.

To acquire these foundation skills, children need trained and motivated teachers. This Report identifies the 10 most important teacher reforms that policy-makers should adopt to achieve equitable learning for all.

1 Fill teacher gaps

Many countries, especially the poorest, suffer from chronic teacher shortages. It is vital that policy-makers introduce strategies to recruit new teachers and to train, deploy and retain them. It is particularly crucial that in the 29 countries not expected to have enough teachers to achieve universal primary education until after 2030, governments, supported by donor agencies, redouble efforts to make up teacher shortages. The need for additional teachers becomes even more acute when teacher shortages in lower secondary school are included. To achieve universal lower secondary education by 2030 – a likely target date in the next set of global goals – with 32 students per teacher, an additional 5.1 million teachers will be needed, half of them in sub-Saharan Africa. South and West Asia requires an additional 1 million lower secondary school teachers. Thus, countries in these regions need to activate policies that begin to address the vast shortfall.

2 Attract the best candidates to teaching

Children need the best teachers to optimize their learning opportunities. These teachers should be drawn from a wide range of backgrounds, reflecting learners' diversity. It is vital that they have at least a good secondary education.

Affirmative action should be considered to attract more women into teaching. To increase the pool of better-educated female teachers, policy-makers should also aim to improve girls' access to secondary education, especially in disadvantaged areas.

In addition, recruitment efforts should focus on hiring and training teachers from under-represented groups, such as ethnic minorities, to serve in their communities. Such teachers, familiar with the cultural context and local language, can increase the number of disadvantaged children who are learning.

3 Train teachers to meet the needs of all children

Every teacher should receive training to equip them to meet the learning needs of all children, especially those from disadvantaged backgrounds. Many teacher candidates are recruited with weak subject knowledge because they have also suffered from a poor quality education. Rather than leave this problem to be addressed through ongoing training, policy-makers should remedy it through good quality pre-service teacher education programmes.

Pre-service training should equip teachers with the skills to teach children to read and to understand basic mathematics in the early grades. Trained teachers will not have the set of skills needed to improve learning for all children if they do not have sufficient time learning to teach in real classrooms. Policy-makers should therefore ensure that adequate classroom teaching experience is an essential part of training to become a qualified teacher.

In ethnically diverse societies, where local language instruction plays a crucial role in securing foundation skills, teachers should learn to teach in more than one language. Teacher education programmes should also prepare teachers to teach multiple grades and ages in one classroom, and to understand how teachers' attitudes to gender differences can affect learning outcomes.

More broadly, every teacher should have access to regular ongoing training to develop and strengthen teaching skills. Such training should enhance teachers' practical skills, especially in methods of teaching and assessment to support disadvantaged learners, and keep them up to date with innovation in the curriculum.

The capacity of many teacher education programmes is far from sufficient to meet the needs of the numbers of teachers to be trained. Innovative approaches such as distance teacher education, combined with face-to-face training and mentoring, should be encouraged to extend both pre-service and ongoing teacher education to reach more teachers and accelerate progress towards good quality education for all.

4 Prepare teacher educators and mentors to support teachers

Globally, the training of teacher educators has largely been ignored, with the result that most teacher educators have little knowledge and experience of real classroom teaching challenges. Policy-makers should give training of teacher educators high priority, ensuring that educators have adequate exposure to the classroom learning requirements facing those teaching in difficult circumstances.

Once teachers qualify to teach, the professional support they receive in the early stages of their career is vital to their effectiveness. Policy-makers should ensure that trained mentors are available to help newly qualified teachers translate teaching knowledge into activities that improve learning for all children.

5 Get teachers to where they are needed most

Recruiting the best teachers and giving them the best training will amount to little if they do not teach in the areas where they are most needed. Often poor, remote areas do not attract the best teachers because of inadequate infrastructure and harsh working conditions. Adequate compensation, bonus pay, good housing and support in the form of professional development opportunities should be used to encourage trained teachers to accept positions in disadvantaged areas. In remote or rural areas with acute teacher shortages, governments should recruit teachers locally and provide them with ongoing training to ensure that all children, irrespective of their location, have teachers with the capacity to improve their learning.

6 Use competitive career and pay structures to retain the best teachers

Many low income countries find it difficult to raise teacher salaries substantially because of budget constraints. Governments should nonetheless do all they can to make teachers' pay more competitive. Paying teachers low salaries sends a negative signal to society about the value of teachers' contribution to education quality. In some poor countries, teachers barely earn enough to lift their families above the poverty line. To recruit the best teachers and retain them, teacher pay must be similar to that of professionals in comparable fields to avoid the risk of teachers losing motivation or leaving the profession.

Performance-related pay programmes should be considered with caution. They often tend to reward teachers who are already in good schools teaching high achieving students. Ultimately, these programmes can be a disincentive to teach students who face difficulties in learning, including those living in poor communities.

Attractive career and pay structures should be used as incentives for all teachers. Career and pay structures should recognize and reward teachers in remote areas and those who teach disadvantaged children.

Governments should also invest in strengthening school leadership. Strong school leadership is required to provide teachers with professional support, and also to make sure that teachers give equal guidance to all students.

7 Improve teacher governance to maximize impact

Teacher governance policies that recognize and reward good teacher behaviour should be given top priority, but it is also necessary to tackle unprofessional behaviour such as absenteeism, private tutoring and gender-based violence.

Governments should work more closely with teacher unions to formulate policies. This should include seeking their advice on strategies to support weak learners, as well as the adoption of effective codes of conduct. Such codes should refer explicitly to violence against pupils, ensuring that penalties are consistent with legal frameworks for child rights and protection. A range of penalties, such as suspension and interdiction, should be used to tackle serious cases of teacher misconduct.

Teacher absences often signal low morale and poor job satisfaction. To raise morale and reduce absenteeism, it is vital to improve teachers' working conditions, make sure they are not overburdened with non-teaching duties and offer them access to good health care.

When teachers engage in private tutoring of their own students, the poorest students suffer most because their families cannot afford tutoring and their teacher is often spending less time covering the curriculum in the classroom. In some instances, the root cause is low teacher pay, so improving teachers' salaries is one way to help address this problem. Banning private tutoring outright is likely to be difficult to enforce, but at a minimum teachers should not be permitted to tutor students privately whom they are also supposed to be teaching in the classroom. Providing clear guidelines should ensure that teachers do not sacrifice classroom time to teach the school curriculum privately.

8 Equip teachers with innovative curricula to improve learning

Teachers need the support of inclusive and flexible curriculum strategies designed to meet the learning needs of children from disadvantaged groups, including those who have had their schooling interrupted. Teachers and teaching assistants should be supported with curriculum content and delivery methods that not only improve learning, but also reduce learning disparities, allowing low achievers to catch up.

Policy-makers should ensure that the early grade curriculum focuses on securing strong foundation skills for all, is delivered in a language children understand and is backed with appropriate resources. It is important that curriculum expectations match learners' abilities, as overambitious curricula limit what teachers can achieve in helping children progress.

In countries with a large population of out-of-school children and youth, governments and donors should give priority to investment in second-chance and accelerated learning programmes and recruit and equip teachers with the skills to run them.

In many countries, technology is being used to supplement and improve children's learning. To maximize the use of technology tools, teachers in both formal and non-formal settings need to be taught to use these resources innovatively and effectively while making sure the technology is accessible to all.

It is not sufficient for children only to learn foundation skills in school. A curriculum that encourages interdisciplinary and participatory learning is vital to foster transferable skills that promote global citizenship.

9 Develop classroom assessments to help teachers identify and support students at risk of not learning

Teachers need strong skills in classroom-based assessment practices to identify and help learners who are struggling. Pre-service and ongoing teacher education should train teachers how to use assessment tools to detect learning difficulties early, and how to devise appropriate strategies to tackle these difficulties.

Students can make considerable gains if they are offered more opportunities to monitor their own learning. Teachers should be provided with skills to help students use learning materials to evaluate and monitor their progress.

Targeted additional support via trained teaching assistants or community volunteers is another key way of improving learning for students at risk of falling behind.

10 Provide better data on trained teachers

To achieve good quality education for all, it is crucial to know how many trained teachers each country has and how many additional teachers are needed, but in many poor countries reliable information is often lacking.

Countries should invest in collecting and analysing annual data on the number of trained teachers available in different parts of the country, and by gender, language, ethnicity and disability, at all levels of education. These data should be complemented by information on the capacity of teacher education programmes, with an assessment of the competencies teachers are expected to acquire through the programmes. Just as internationally agreed standards are available for primary and secondary schooling, similar standards need to be developed for teacher education programmes. Such information will enable national governments and the international community to monitor the quality of teachers and to plan more effectively to meet demand for trained teachers.

More and better quality data on teacher salaries in low and middle income countries are also needed to enable national governments and the international community to monitor how well teachers are paid, and to raise global awareness of the need to pay them sufficiently. Teacher salary data from OECD countries, for example, enable analysis of differences between beginning salaries and what teachers earn 15 years later. This provides useful information on the relationship between pay structure and career progression, as well as comparability with other professions.

Conclusion

To end the learning crisis, all countries, rich or poor, have to make sure every child has access to a well-trained and motivated teacher. The 10 strategies outlined here are based on the evidence of successful policies, programmes and strategies from a wide range of countries and educational environments. By implementing such teaching reforms, countries can ensure that all children and young people, especially the disadvantaged, receive the education they need to realize their potential and lead fulfilling lives.

Improving the scores: A mathematics class in one of the poorest areas of London. Thanks to strong teaching policies, the school records outstanding results.

The Education for All Development Index

The EFA Development Index (EDI) is a composite index that provides a snapshot of overall progress towards Education for All.[1] Due to data constraints, the standard index captures only four of the six goals. The value of the standard EDI for a given country is the arithmetic mean of four components:

- universal primary education (goal 2), measured by the primary adjusted net enrolment ratio;
- adult literacy (goal 4), measured by the literacy rate for those aged 15 and above;
- gender parity and equality (goal 5), measured by the gender-specific EFA index (GEI), an average of the gender parity indices (GPIs) of the primary and secondary gross enrolment ratios and the adult literacy rate;[2]
- quality of education (goal 6), measured by the survival rate to grade 5.[3]

The EDI value falls between 0 and 1, with 1 representing full achievement of EFA across the four goals.

The EDI in 2011

Out of 205 countries, 115 had the data on all four indicators required to calculate the standard EDI for the school year ending in 2011. By region, the country coverage ranged from 30% in East Asia and the Pacific to over 80% in Central and Eastern Europe and North America and Western Europe. This low coverage, combined with the fact that the index excludes goals 1 and 3, means it provides only a partial overview of progress towards EFA as a whole.

In 2011, Kazakhstan and the United Kingdom had the highest EDI score (0.995) while, as in 2010, Niger had the lowest (0.563). Countries are grouped in three categories according to the value of the EDI:

- Fifty-five countries, mostly high and upper middle income countries in Central and Eastern Europe and in North America and Western Europe, had achieved EFA or were close (EDI>0.95). No country in sub-Saharan Africa or South and West Asia belonged to this category.
- Thirty-six countries, mostly lower and upper middle income countries in the Arab States and in Latin America and the Caribbean, were at mid-distance to overall EFA achievement (EDI between 0.80 and 0.95). In many of these countries, progress across the EDI components has been unbalanced, with more progress on universal primary enrolment than on other goals. For example, in most of the Arab States countries in this category, the level of adult literacy was low (below 80% in Algeria, Egypt and Tunisia). In Latin American and Caribbean countries in this category, many children did not reach the last primary school grade. For example, in Guatemala the survival rate to grade 5 was 72%.
- Twenty-four countries, mostly low income countries in sub-Saharan Africa, were still further from EFA (EDI<0.80). This category also includes Mauritania and Yemen (Arab States) as well as Bangladesh, Nepal and Pakistan (South and West Asia). While most of these countries had a poor record across the four EFA goals, a few, such as Bangladesh and Rwanda, had achieved or were close to universal primary enrolment.

1. Additional information on the EDI, including the methodology and data on its components, is available on the Report's website.

2. When expressed as the ratio of female to male enrolment ratio or literacy rate, the GPI can exceed unity when more females than males are enrolled or literate. In such cases, and for the purpose of the EDI where all values should range from 0 to 1, the GEI is calculated inverting the standard formula of GPI (F/M) to male over female (M/F). This ensures that the GEI remains below 1 while maintaining its ability to show gender disparity. Once all necessary adjustments are made, the GEI is obtained by calculating a simple average of the three GPIs.

3. In the absence of comparable indicators on quality, notably on learning outcomes for a large number of countries, the survival rate to grade 5 is used as a proxy because of its positive correlation with average international learning assessment scores.

In most countries in the low EDI category, the GEI is also below 0.80, while some of the medium EDI countries also suffer from gender disparities, such as upper middle income countries in Latin America and the Caribbean where gender disparities are at the expense of boys notably at upper secondary education.

The inclusion of the ECCE index[4] in an extended EDI tends to pull down its value in many countries. For example, Tajikistan has a high EDI score (0.977), but falls to the middle category with an extended EDI score of 0.908 because it has a high stunting rate (30%) and a very low pre-primary education adjusted net enrolment ratio (26%).

Changes between 1999 and 2011

For the 37 countries for which the EDI could be tracked between 1999 and 2011, the value increased by 5% on average (Figure EDI.1). The goal 2 component increased the most (8.7%), followed by the components for goal 6 (5.6%), goal 4 (4.2%) and goal 5 (3.4%).

The value of the EDI increased by more than 20% in Ghana, Mauritania and Nepal. Ghana was also one of three countries (with Guatemala and the Lao People's Democratic Republic) that moved from the low to the middle EDI category over the period. In Mauritania, the EDI increased mainly as a result of improvement in the probability of children reaching the fifth grade of primary school (from 55% in 2001 to 82% in 2008). In Nepal, the EDI rose as a result of both an improvement in the education participation rate of primary school age children and a reduction in gender disparity.

How many countries are likely to achieve EFA by 2015?

Building on the analysis in Chapter 1 of prospects for achieving each EFA goal by 2015, it is possible to assess to what extent countries are likely to achieve EFA as a whole in 2015, in terms of the value of the EDI index. In 2011, 39 of the 77 countries for which the analysis was possible had already achieved EFA, while nine were close. Two more countries, Chile and Turkey, are likely to achieve the overall goal by 2015. Nine countries are expected to be in the low category, the same group as in 2011: Burkina Faso, Eritrea, Ethiopia, Lesotho, Mali, Malawi, Mozambique, Niger and Senegal.

Bhutan, Burkina Faso, Ethiopia, Mali, Mozambique and Niger are expected to increase their EDI scores by 6% or more between 2011 and 2015, although all except Bhutan are still likely to be very far from achieving EFA as a whole. It is projected that, by 2015, Senegal will have made the largest improvement since 1999, increasing its EDI value by more than 25%.

Figure EDI.1: Some countries have made strong progress towards EFA goals
Change in EDI scores, 1999-2011

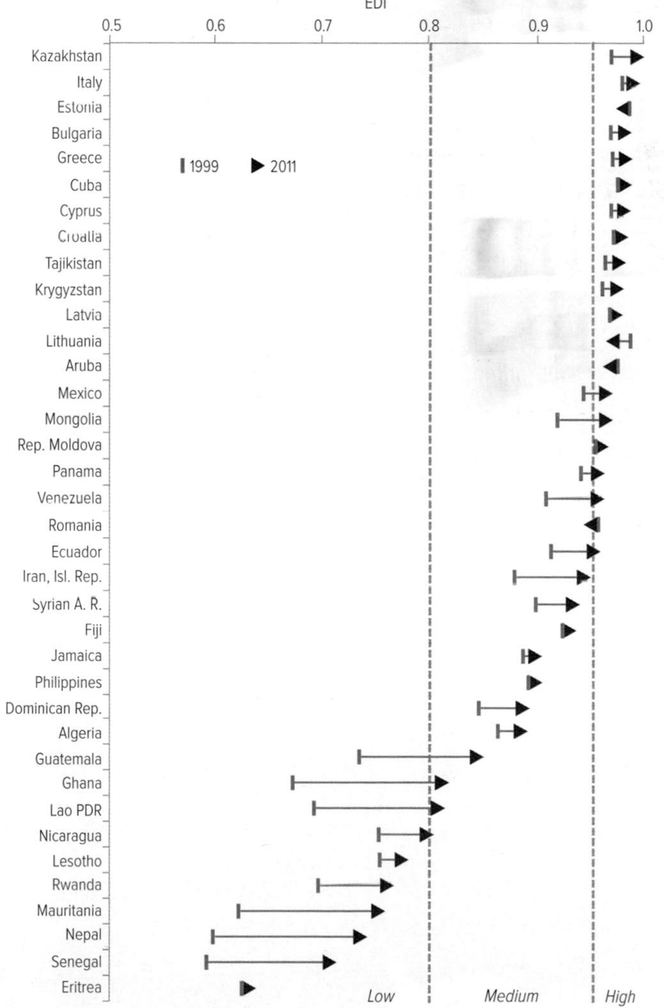

Source: EFA Global Monitoring Report team calculations (2013).

4. The ECCE index summarizes the results of early childhood development policies on (i) health, measured by the percentage of children who survive beyond their fifth birthday; (ii) nutrition, measured by the percentage of children under 5 who do not suffer from moderate or severe stunting; and (iii) education, measured by the percentage of children aged 3 to 7 who are enrolled in either pre-primary or primary school. The value of the ECCE index is the mean of these three indicators.

Learning conditions: At a primary school in a poor area of Antofagasta, Chile, learning has improved since the city and private foundations joined forces to improve infrastructure

Credit: Hugo Infante/UNESCO

Statistical tables[1]

Introduction

The most recent data on pupils, students, teachers and education expenditure presented in these statistical tables are for the school and financial years ending in 2011.[2] They are based on survey results reported to and processed by the UNESCO Institute for Statistics (UIS) before the end of March 2013. Data received and processed after that date are published on the UIS website and will be used in the next EFA Global Monitoring Report. A small number of countries submitted data for the school year ending in 2012, presented in bold in the statistical tables.[3]

These statistics refer to all formal schools, both public and private, by level of education. They are supplemented by demographic and economic statistics collected or produced by other international organizations, including the Joint United Nations Programme on HIV/AIDS (UNAIDS), the Organisation for Economic Co-operation and Development (OECD), the United Nations Children's Fund (UNICEF), the United Nations Population Division (UNPD), the World Bank and the World Health Organization.

The statistical tables list a total of 205 countries and territories. Most of them report their data to the UIS using standard questionnaires issued by the Institute. For some countries, however, education data are collected by the UIS via surveys carried out under the auspices of the World Education Indicators programme, or jointly by the UIS, OECD and the Statistical Office of the European Union (Eurostat) through the UIS/OECD/Eurostat (UOE) questionnaires. These countries are indicated with symbols at the end of the introduction.

Population

The indicators on school access and participation in the statistical tables are based on the 2010 revision of population estimates produced by the UNPD. Because of possible differences between national population estimates and those of the United Nations, these indicators may differ from those published by individual countries or by other organizations.[4] The UNPD does not provide data by single year of age for countries with a total population of fewer than 50,000. Where no UNPD estimates exist, national population figures (when available) or UIS estimates were used to calculate enrolment ratios.

ISCED classification

Education data reported to the UIS since 1998 are in conformity with the 1997 revision of the International Standard Classification of Education (ISCED97). Data for the school year ending in 1991, presented in Statistical Tables 12 and 13 (website), were collected according to the previous version of the classification, ISCED76. Where possible, the UIS has adjusted these data to comply with ISCED97 and to minimize any inconsistencies with data for years after 1997.[5] ISCED is used to harmonize data and introduce more international comparability across national education systems. Countries may have their own definitions of education levels that do not correspond to ISCED. Some differences between nationally and internationally reported education statistics may be due, therefore, to the use of these nationally defined education levels rather than the ISCED standard, in addition to the population issue raised above.

1. A full set of statistics and indicators related to this introduction is posted in the form of Excel tables on the *EFA Global Monitoring Report* website at www.efareport.unesco.org.

2. This means 2010/2011 for countries with a school year that overlaps two calendar years and 2011 for those with a calendar school year. The most recent reference year for education finance for the WEI/UOE countries is the year ending in 2010.

3. Bhutan, Burkina Faso, Djibouti, Ghana, Guinea, Kazakhstan, Montenegro, Morocco, Mozambique, Nepal, Niger, Sao Tome and Principe, Thailand (except primary education and education expenditure), Togo and the United Republic of Tanzania.

4. Where obvious inconsistencies exist between enrolment reported by countries and the United Nations population data, the UIS may decide not to calculate or publish the enrolment ratios. This is the case with Bahrain, Brazil, Kuwait and Singapore, where enrolment ratios at all levels of education are not published for one or both of the reference school years, and with Albania, Andorra, Armenia, Belize, Benin, British Virgin Islands, Macao (China), Malaysia and the United Arab Emirates, where enrolment ratios at some levels of education are not published.

5. To improve comparisons over time, the UIS has harmonized time-series data, adjusting data from before 1997 so that they comply with the ISCED97 classification.

Adult participation in education

ISCED does not classify education programmes by participants' age. For example, any programme with a content equivalent to primary education, or ISCED 1, may be classed as ISCED 1 even if provided to adults. The guidance the UIS provides for respondents to its regular annual education survey asks countries to exclude 'data on programmes designed for people beyond regular school age'. As for the guidance for the UOE and WEI questionnaires, until 2005 it stated that 'activities classified as "continuing", "adult" or "non-formal" education should be included' if they 'involve studies with subject content similar to regular educational programmes' or if 'the underlying programmes lead to similar potential qualifications' as the regular programmes. Since 2005, however, the countries involved in the UOE/WEI survey have been requested to report data for such programmes separately so that the UIS can exclude them when calculating internationally comparable indicators. Despite the UIS instructions, data from some countries in the annual survey may still include students (or participants) who are substantially above the official age for basic education.

Literacy data

UNESCO has long defined literacy as the ability to read and write, with understanding, a short simple statement related to one's daily life. However, a parallel definition arose with the introduction in 1978 of the notion of functional literacy, which emphasizes the use of literacy skills. That year the UNESCO General Conference approved defining as functionally literate those who can engage in all activities in which literacy is required for the effective functioning of their group and community and also for enabling them to continue to use reading, writing and calculation for their own and the community's development.

In many cases, the literacy statistics in the corresponding table rely on the first definition and are largely based on data sources that use self or third party declaration methods, in which respondents are asked whether they and the members of their household are literate, as opposed to being asked a more comprehensive question or to demonstrate the skill.[6] Some countries assume that persons who complete a certain level of education are literate.[7] As definitions and methodologies used for data collection differ by country, data need to be used with caution.

Literacy data in this report cover adults aged 15 years and over as well as youth aged 15 to 24 years old. They refer to two periods, 1985–1994 and 2005–2011, and include both national observed data from censuses and household surveys, indicated with an asterisk (*) and UIS estimates. The latter are for 1994 and 2011 and are based on the most recent national observed data. They were produced using the Global Age-specific Literacy Projections Model.[8] The reference years and literacy definitions for each country are presented in the table of metadata for literacy statistics posted on the EFA Global Monitoring Report website.

In many countries, interest in assessing the literacy skills of the population is growing. In response to this interest, the UIS has developed a methodology and data collection instrument called the Literacy Assessment and Monitoring Programme (LAMP). Following the example of the OECD's International Adult Literacy Survey (IALS), LAMP is based on the assessment of actual and functional literacy skills. It aims to provide better quality literacy data based on the concept of a continuum of literacy skills rather than the common literate/illiterate dichotomy.

Estimates and missing data

Both observed and estimated education data are presented throughout the statistical tables. When data are not reported to the UIS using the standard questionnaires, estimates are often necessary. Wherever possible, the UIS encourages countries to make their own

6. In the latest data released by the UIS, some literacy rates are based on direct assessments rather than individuals' declarations. This is the case for Benin, the Democratic Republic of the Congo, Ethiopia, Guyana, Haiti, Kenya, Lesotho, Liberia, Madagascar, Malawi, Namibia, Nepal, Nigeria, Rwanda, Sao Tome and Principe, the United Republic of Tanzania, Zambia and Zimbabwe. The use of the assessment measure largely explains the observed decline in literacy rates for some years in many of these countries. Care should therefore be taken when analysing trends over time and in interpreting these results.

7. For reliability and consistency reasons, the UIS does not publish literacy data based on educational attainment proxies. Only data reported by countries based on self-declaration or household declaration are included in the statistical tables. However, in the absence of such data, educational attainment proxies for some countries, particularly developed ones, are used to compute regional weighted averages and the EFA Development Index.

8. For a description of the methodology, see UNESCO (2005, p. 261) and UIS (2006).

estimates, which are presented as national estimates and marked with one asterisk (*). Where this does not happen, the UIS may make its own estimates if sufficient supplementary information is available. These estimates are marked with two asterisks (**). In addition, gaps in the tables may also arise where data submitted by a country are found to be inconsistent. The UIS makes every attempt to resolve such problems with the countries concerned, but reserves the final decision to omit data it regards as problematic.

To fill the gaps in the statistical tables, data for the most recent school years are included when information for the school years ending in 1999 and 2011 is not available. Such cases are indicated by a footnote.

Regional and other country grouping averages

Regional figures for literacy rates, gross and adjusted net intake rates, gross, net and adjusted net enrolment ratios, school life expectancy and pupil/teacher ratios are weighted averages, taking into account the relative size of the relevant population of each country in each region. The figures for countries with larger populations thus have a proportionately greater influence on the regional aggregates. The averages are derived from both published data and imputed values for countries for which no recent data or reliable publishable data are available. Weighted averages marked with two asterisks (**) in the tables are UIS partial imputations due to incomplete country coverage (between 33% and 60% of the population of a given region or country grouping). Where insufficient reliable data are available to produce an overall weighted mean, a median figure is calculated based only on countries with available data.

Capped figures

There are cases where an indicator theoretically should not exceed 100% (the net intake rates and net enrolment ratio, for example), but data inconsistencies may have resulted nonetheless in the indicator exceeding the theoretical limit. In these cases, the total male and female values of the given indicator are recalculated and lowered using a capping factor so that the gender parity index of the new set of values remains the same as for the uncapped values. The theoretical maximum value is determined on the basis of the raw data used to calculate the family of related indicators to which a given indicator belongs.

For instance, net enrolment ratios in primary education are capped using a factor that takes into account the male and female primary school age populations and enrolment of primary school age boys and girls in pre-primary, primary and secondary education. If the total enrolment of primary school age children (whether male or female) is higher than the corresponding population, all net enrolment indicators (net enrolment ratio, adjusted net enrolment ratio, etc.) and their derivative indicators (out-of-school rate, etc.) are capped based on the same capping factor. In this case, the capping factor is calculated by taking the maximum of the male and female enrolments and dividing by the population of primary school age.

Symbols used in the statistical tables (printed and web versions)

*	National estimate
**	UIS partial estimate
...	No data available
-	Magnitude nil or negligible
.	Category not applicable or does not exist

Footnotes to the tables, along with the glossary following the statistical tables, provide additional help in interpreting the data and information.

Composition of regions and other country groups

World classification[9]

- Countries in transition (18): 12 countries of the Commonwealth of Independent States, including 4 in Central and Eastern Europe (Belarus, Republic of Moldova, Russian Federation° and Ukraine) and the countries of Central Asia minus Mongolia; and 6 countries in Central and Eastern Europe formerly in the developed countries group: Albania, Bosnia and Herzegovina, Croatia, Montenegro, Serbia and the former Yugoslav Republic of Macedonia.

9. This is a United Nations Statistical Division world classification, in three main country groupings, as revised in September 2011.

- Developed countries (39):
  North America and Western Europe (minus Cyprus°); Central and Eastern Europe (minus Albania, Belarus, Bosnia and Herzegovina, Croatia, Montenegro, Republic of Moldova, Russian Federation°, Serbia, the former Yugoslav Republic of Macedonia, Turkey° and Ukraine); Australia°, Bermuda, Japan° and New Zealand°.

- Developing countries (148):
  Arab States; East Asia and the Pacific (minus Australia°, Japan° and New Zealand°); Latin America and the Caribbean (minus Bermuda); South and West Asia; sub-Saharan Africa; Cyprus°, Mongolia and Turkey°.

EFA regions[10]

- Arab States (20 countries/territories)
  Algeria, Bahrain, Djibouti, Egypt^w, Iraq, Jordan°, Kuwait, Lebanon, Libya, Mauritania, Morocco, Oman, Palestine, Qatar, Saudi Arabia, Sudan[11], Syrian Arab Republic, Tunisia^w, United Arab Emirates and Yemen.

- Central and Eastern Europe (21 countries)
  Albania, Belarus, Bosnia and Herzegovina, Bulgaria°, Croatia, Czech Republic°, Estonia°, Hungary°, Latvia°, Lithuania°, Montenegro, Poland°, Republic of Moldova, Romania°, Russian Federation°, Serbia, Slovakia°, Slovenia°, the former Yugoslav Republic of Macedonia°, Turkey° and Ukraine.

- Central Asia (9 countries)
  Armenia, Azerbaijan, Georgia, Kazakhstan, Kyrgyzstan, Mongolia, Tajikistan, Turkmenistan and Uzbekistan.

- East Asia and the Pacific (33 countries/ territories)
  Australia°, Brunei Darussalam, Cambodia, China^w, Cook Islands, Democratic People's Republic of Korea, Fiji, Indonesia^w, Japan°, Kiribati, Lao People's Democratic Republic, Macao (China), Malaysia^w, Marshall Islands, Micronesia (Federated States of), Myanmar, Nauru, New Zealand°, Niue, Palau, Papua New Guinea, Philippines^w, Republic of Korea°, Samoa, Singapore, Solomon Islands, Thailand^w, Timor-Leste, Tokelau, Tonga, Tuvalu, Vanuatu and Viet Nam.

  - East Asia (16 countries/territories)
    Brunei Darussalam, Cambodia, China^w, Democratic People's Republic of Korea, Indonesia^w, Japan°, Lao People's Democratic Republic, Macao (China), Malaysia^w, Myanmar, Philippines^w, Republic of Korea°, Singapore, Thailand^w, Timor-Leste and Viet Nam.

  - Pacific (17 countries/territories)
    Australia°, Cook Islands, Fiji, Kiribati, Marshall Islands, Micronesia (Federated States of), Nauru, New Zealand°, Niue, Palau, Papua New Guinea, Samoa, Solomon Islands, Tokelau, Tonga, Tuvalu and Vanuatu.

- Latin America and the Caribbean (41 countries/territories)
  Anguilla, Antigua and Barbuda, Argentina^w, Aruba, Bahamas, Barbados, Belize, Bermuda, Plurinational State of Bolivia, Brazil°, British Virgin Islands, Cayman Islands, Chile°, Colombia, Costa Rica, Cuba, Dominica, Dominican Republic, Ecuador, El Salvador, Grenada, Guatemala, Guyana, Haiti, Honduras, Jamaica^w, Mexico°, Montserrat, Netherlands Antilles, Nicaragua, Panama, Paraguay^w, Peru^w, Saint Kitts and Nevis, Saint Lucia, Saint Vincent and the Grenadines, Suriname, Trinidad and Tobago, Turks and Caicos Islands, Uruguay° and Bolivarian Republic of Venezuela.

  - Caribbean (22 countries/territories)
    Anguilla, Antigua and Barbuda, Aruba, Bahamas, Barbados, Belize, Bermuda, British Virgin Islands, Cayman Islands, Dominica, Grenada, Guyana, Haiti, Jamaica^w, Montserrat, Netherlands Antilles, Saint Kitts and Nevis, Saint Lucia, Saint Vincent and the Grenadines, Suriname, Trinidad and Tobago, and Turks and Caicos Islands.

  - Latin America (19 countries)
    Argentina^w, Plurinational State of Bolivia, Brazil°, Chile°, Colombia, Costa Rica, Cuba, Dominican Republic, Ecuador, El Salvador, Guatemala, Honduras, Mexico°, Nicaragua, Panama, Paraguay^w, Peru^w, Uruguay° and Bolivarian Republic of Venezuela.

10. These are region classifications as defined in 1998 for the Education for All (EFA) 2000 assessment.

11. Sudan pre-secession is presented in the statistical tables only for indication since all weighted averages for the Arab States' region prior to the secession still include data for this former entity.

- North America and Western Europe (26 countries/territories)
  Andorra, Austria[o], Belgium[o], Canada[o], Cyprus[o], Denmark[o], Finland[o], France[o], Germany[o], Greece[o], Iceland[o], Ireland[o], Israel[o], Italy[o], Luxembourg[o], Malta[o], Monaco, Netherlands[o], Norway[o], Portugal[o], San Marino, Spain[o], Sweden[o], Switzerland[o], United Kingdom[o] and United States[o].

- South and West Asia (9 countries)
  Afghanistan, Bangladesh, Bhutan, India[w], Islamic Republic of Iran, Maldives, Nepal, Pakistan and Sri Lanka[w].

- Sub-Saharan Africa (46 countries)
  Angola, Benin, Botswana, Burkina Faso, Burundi, Cameroon, Cape Verde, Central African Republic, Chad, Comoros, Congo, Côte d'Ivoire, Democratic Republic of the Congo, Equatorial Guinea, Eritrea, Ethiopia, Gabon, Gambia, Ghana, Guinea, Guinea-Bissau, Kenya, Lesotho, Liberia, Madagascar, Malawi, Mali, Mauritius, Mozambique, Namibia, Niger, Nigeria, Rwanda, Sao Tome and Principe, Senegal, Seychelles, Sierra Leone, Somalia, South Africa, South Sudan, Swaziland, Togo, Uganda, United Republic of Tanzania, Zambia and Zimbabwe.

o Countries whose education data are collected through UOE questionnaires
w WEI programme countries

Income groups[12]

- Low income (37 countries)
  Afghanistan, Bangladesh, Benin, Burkina Faso, Burundi, Cambodia, Central African Republic, Chad, Comoros, Democratic People's Republic of Korea, Democratic Republic of the Congo, Eritrea, Ethiopia, Gambia, Guinea, Guinea Bissau, Haiti, Kenya, Kyrgyzstan, Liberia, Madagascar, Malawi, Mali, Mauritania, Mozambique, Myanmar, Nepal, Niger, Rwanda, Sierra Leone, Somalia, Tajikistan, Togo, Tokelau, Uganda, United Republic of Tanzania and Zimbabwe.

- Lower middle income (52 countries)
  Armenia, Belize, Bhutan, Plurinational State of Bolivia, Cameroon, Cape Verde, Congo, Côte d'Ivoire, Djibouti, Egypt, El Salvador, Fiji, Georgia, Ghana, Guatemala, Guyana, Honduras, India, Indonesia, Iraq, Kiribati, Lao People's Democratic Republic, Lesotho, Marshall Islands, Micronesia (Federated States of), Mongolia, Morocco, Nicaragua, Nigeria, Pakistan, Palestine, Papua New Guinea, Paraguay, Philippines, Republic of Moldova, Samoa, Sao Tome and Principe, Senegal, Solomon Islands, South Sudan, Sri Lanka, Sudan, Swaziland, Syrian Arab Republic, Timor-Leste, Tonga, Ukraine, Uzbekistan, Vanuatu, Viet Nam, Yemen and Zambia.

- Upper middle income (58 countries)
  Albania, Algeria, Angola, Antigua and Barbuda, Argentina, Azerbaijan, Belarus, Bosnia and Herzegovina, Botswana, Brazil, Bulgaria, Chile, China, Colombia, Cook Islands, Costa Rica, Cuba, Dominica, Dominican Republic, Ecuador, Gabon, Grenada, Iran (Islamic Republic of), Jamaica, Jordan, Kazakhstan, Latvia, Lebanon, Libya, Lithuania, Malaysia, Maldives, Mauritius, Mexico, Montenegro, Montserrat, Namibia, Nauru, Niue, Palau, Panama, Peru, Romania, Russian Federation, Saint Lucia, Saint Vincent and the Grenadines, Serbia, Seychelles, South Africa, Suriname, Thailand, the former Yugoslav Republic of Macedonia, Tunisia, Turkey, Turkmenistan, Tuvalu, Uruguay and Venezuela (Bolivarian Republic of).

- High income (58 countries)
  Andorra, Anguilla, Aruba, Australia, Austria, Bahamas, Bahrain, Barbados, Belgium, Bermuda, British Virgin Islands, Brunei Darussalam, Canada, Caymans Islands, Croatia, Cyprus, Czech Republic, Denmark, Equatorial Guinea, Estonia, Finland, France, Germany, Greece, Hungary, Iceland, Ireland, Israel, Italy, Japan, Kuwait, Luxembourg, Macao (China), Malta, Monaco, Netherlands, Netherlands Antilles, New Zealand, Norway, Oman, Poland, Portugal, Qatar, Republic of Korea, Saint Kitts and Nevis, San Marino, Saudi Arabia, Singapore, Slovakia, Slovenia, Spain, Sweden, Switzerland, Trinidad and Tobago, Turks and Caicos Islands, United Arab Emirates, United Kingdom, United States.

12. Country groupings by level of income presented in the statistical tables are as defined by the World Bank but include EFA countries only. The present list of countries by income group is that of the July 2012 revision.

Table 1
Background statistics

	DEMOGRAPHY[1]			GNP, AID AND POVERTY						
				GNP per capita[2]				Net official development assistance received (% of GDP)[3]	Population below income poverty line	
	Total population (000)	Average annual growth rate (%) total population	Average annual growth rate (%) age 0–4 population	Current US$		PPP US$			PPP US$1.25 a day[3] (%)	National poverty line[3] (%)
Country or territory	2013	2010–2015	2010–2015	1998	2011	1998	2011	2011	2002–2011[4]	2002–2011[4]
Arab States										
Algeria	36 984	1.4	-0.1	1 570	4 470	4 870	8 310	0.1	...	...
Bahrain	1 377	2.1	4.6	10 110	...	18 800	...	...	...	...
Djibouti	940	1.9	1.4	730	...	1 590	...	11.4	19	...
Egypt	85 378	1.7	0.5	1 220	2 600	3 330	6 120	0.2	2	22
Iraq	34 776	3.1	1.7	...	2 640	...	3 750	1.1	3	23
Jordan	6 573	1.9	-1.8	1 590	4 380	2 920	5 930	3.4	0.1	13
Kuwait	2 959	2.4	-2.1	20 430	...	43 080	...	...	...	...
Lebanon	4 324	0.7	-0.5	4 250	9 140	7 580	14 470	1.2	...	...
Libya	6 506	0.8	-0.6	...	...	...	...	...	...	...
Mauritania	3 704	2.2	1.3	570	1 000	1 520	2 400	8.9	23	42
Morocco	32 926	1.0	-0.4	1 280	2 970	2 440	4 880	1.4	2	9
Oman	2 957	1.9	-1.2	6 460	...	14 770	...	...	...	...
Palestine	4 394	2.8	2.1	...	...	...	...	...	0.0	22
Qatar	1 977	2.9	4.3	...	80 440	...	86 440	...	...	...
Saudi Arabia	29 319	2.1	-0.7	8 300	17 820	17 720	24 700	...	...	...
Sudan	...			...	...	...	...	2	...	...
Syrian Arab Republic	21 469	1.7	-1.7	950	...	3 300	...	...	2	...
Tunisia	10 814	1.0	0.1	2 190	4 070	4 630	9 030	2	1	4
United Arab Emirates	8 208	2.2	3.0	...	40 760	...	47 890	...	...	...
Yemen	26 358	3.0	2.6	370	1 070	1 650	2 170	2	18	35
Sudan (pre-secession)	46 823	2.4	1.4	330	1 310	1 020	2 120	...	...	...
Central and Eastern Europe										
Albania	3 238	0.3	-0.5	890	3 980	3 550	8 820	3	0.6	12
Belarus	9 498	-0.3	0.4	1 550	5 830	4 490	14 460	0.2	0.1	5
Bosnia and Herzegovina	3 736	-0.2	-1.7	1 430	4 780	4 790	9 190	3	0.0	14
Bulgaria	7 349	-0.7	-0.6	1 240	6 530	5 350	14 160	...	...	...
Croatia	4 379	-0.2	0.4	5 360	13 530	10 020	18 760	...	0.1	11
Czech Republic	10 590	0.3	1.2	...	18 620	14 260	24 370	...	...	...
Estonia	1 339	-0.1	0.5	...	15 260	8 360	20 850	...	0.5	...
Hungary	9 934	-0.2	0.5	4 380	12 730	10 050	20 310	...	0.2	...
Latvia	2 226	-0.4	1.0	2 650	12 350	6 980	17 700	...	0.1	6
Lithuania	3 278	-0.4	1.1	2 860	12 280	7 820	19 640	...	...	...
Montenegro	633	0.1	-0.9	...	7 140	...	13 700	3	0.1	7
Poland	38 332	0.04	1.4	4 310	12 480	9 310	20 430	...	...	...
Republic of Moldova	3 496	-0.7	-0.9	460	1 980	1 460	3 640	7	0.4	22
Romania	21 339	-0.2	0.1	1 520	7 910	5 280	15 120	...	...	...
Russian Federation	142 558	-0.1	0.6	2 140	10 730	5 250	20 560	...	0.0	11
Serbia	9 835	-0.1	-1.1	...	5 690	5 910	11 540	3	0.3	9
Slovakia	5 489	0.2	1.2	5 290	16 070	10 330	22 130	...	0.1	...
Slovenia	2 045	0.2	0.5	10 870	23 610	15 730	26 510	...	0.1	...
The former Yugoslav Rep. of Macedonia	2 069	0.1	-0.9	1 930	4 730	5 220	11 090	2	0.0	19
Turkey	75 359	1.1	-0.6	3 390	10 410	8 570	16 940	0.4	0.0	18
Ukraine	44 697	-0.5	0.3	850	3 130	2 880	7 040	0.5	0.1	3
Central Asia										
Armenia	3 118	0.3	-0.04	590	3 360	1 830	6 100	4	1	36
Azerbaijan	9 533	1.2	2.2	510	5 290	1 810	8 960	0.5	0.4	16
Georgia	4 278	-0.6	-1.6	820	2 860	2 120	5 350	4	15	25
Kazakhstan	16 551	1.0	0.1	1 390	8 260	4 000	11 250	0.1	0.1	8
Kyrgyzstan	5 503	1.1	1.1	360	880	1 150	2 180	8	6	34
Mongolia	2 888	1.5	1.1	520	2 310	1 850	4 290	4	...	35
Tajikistan	7 184	1.5	1.2	180	870	740	2 300	5	7	47
Turkmenistan	5 235	1.2	0.5	560	4 800	2 830	8 690	0.1	...	...
Uzbekistan	28 398	1.1	0.3	620	1 510	1 310	3 420	0.5	...	...
East Asia and the Pacific										
Australia	27 722	1.3	1.7	21 810	49 130	23 480	38 110	...	...	...
Brunei Darussalam	420	1.7	-0.2	14 740	...	41 000	...	...	...	...
Cambodia	14 656	1.2	-0.1	280	820	740	2 230	6	23	30
China	1 359 368	0.4	-0.6	790	4 940	1 960	8 390	-0.0	13	3
Cook Islands	21	0.5	...	...	...	...	...	...	...	...
Democratic People's Republic of Korea	24 654	0.4	-0.05	...	...	...	...	...	...	...
Fiji	883	0.8	-0.3	2 300	3 720	3 050	4 610	2	...	...
Indonesia	247 188	1.0	-0.8	650	2 940	2 060	4 500	0.0	18	12
Japan	126 345	-0.1	-0.3	33 510	44 900	24 690	35 330	...	...	...
Kiribati	104	1.5	...	1 530	2 030	3 300	3 300	38	...	...
Lao People's Democratic Republic	6 459	1.3	-0.4	310	1 130	1 030	2 580	5	34	28
Macao, China	579	2.0	4.4	15 520	...	21 560	...	...	...	...
Malaysia	29 787	1.6	0.5	3 610	8 770	7 810	15 650	0.0	...	...
Marshall Islands	57	1.6	...	2 530	3 910	...	...	47	...	...
Micronesia (Federated States of)	555	0.5	-0.4	2 020	2 860	2 510	3 580	43	...	...
Myanmar	49 120	0.8	-0.4	...	...	...	...	...	...	...
Nauru	10	0.6	...	...	...	...	...	...	...	...
New Zealand	4 508	1.0	0.6	15 450	...	18 080	...	...	...	...
Niue	1	-2.8	...	...	...	...	...	...	...	...
Palau	21	0.8	...	6 110	6 510	11 750	11 080	13	...	...

Table 1 (continued)

	DEMOGRAPHY[1]			GNP, AID AND POVERTY						
				GNP per capita[2]				Net official development assistance received (% of GDP)[3]	Population below income poverty line	
	Total population (000)	Average annual growth rate (%) total population	Average annual growth rate (%) age 0–4 population	Current US$		PPP US$			PPP US$1.25 a day[3] (%)	National poverty line[3] (%)
Country or territory	2013	2010–2015	2010–2015	1998	2011	1998	2011	2011	2002–2011[4]	2002–2011[4]
Papua New Guinea	7 327	2.2	0.8	780	1 480	1 650	2 570	5	...	...
Philippines	98 113	1.7	0.6	1 150	2 210	2 430	4 140	-0.1	18	26
Republic of Korea	48 775	0.4	0.2	9 200	20 870	13 290	30 370	...	...	...
Samoa	186	0.5	-1.1	1 380	3 160	2 440	4 270	16	...	...
Singapore	5 301	1.1	2.1	25 190	42 930	29 260	59 380	...	...	...
Solomon Islands	581	2.5	1.0	1 330	1 110	2 360	2 350	39	...	...
Thailand	70 243	0.5	-1.6	2 040	4 440	4 250	8 360	-0.0	0.4	8.1
Timor-Leste	1 224	2.9	2.0	...	...	...	...	26	37	50
Tokelau	1	0.3	...	...	...	...	...	...	...	...
Tonga	105	0.4	-1.3	2 210	3 820	3 220	5 000	22	...	...
Tuvalu	10	0.2	...	...	4 950	...	...	119	...	...
Vanuatu	258	2.4	1.5	1 420	2 750	3 080	4 330	12	...	...
Viet Nam	90 657	1.0	-0.5	360	1 270	1 230	3 250	3	40	29
Latin America and the Caribbean										
Anguilla	16	1.6	...	...	...	...	...	...	...	...
Antigua and Barbuda	91	1.0	...	7 730	11 940	13 370	17 900	1	...	...
Argentina	41 474	0.9	0.1	8 010	9 740	9 150	17 130	0.0	0.9	...
Aruba	109	0.3	-0.7	...	...	...	...	...	...	...
Bahamas	355	1.1	0.6	15 770	...	24 130	...	...	...	...
Barbados	275	0.2	0.2	8 200	...	14 560	...	...	...	...
Belize	331	2.0	1.0	2 700	3 710	3 920	6 090	2	...	34
Bermuda	65	0.2	...	...	...	...	...	...	...	...
Bolivia, Plurinational State of	10 410	1.6	0.5	1 000	2 020	3 030	4 890	3	16	60
Brazil	200 050	0.8	-0.8	4 870	10 720	6 520	11 420	0.0	6	21
British Virgin Islands	24	0.9	...	...	...	...	...	...	...	...
Cayman Islands	58	0.8	...	...	...	...	...	...	...	...
Chile	17 574	0.9	-0.03	5 260	12 280	8 600	16 330	0.1	...	...
Colombia	48 165	1.3	-0.3	2 560	6 070	5 750	9 560	0.3	8	37
Costa Rica	4 860	1.4	0.2	3 510	7 640	6 400	11 860	0.1	...	...
Cuba	11 244	-0.0	-1.7	2 240	...	...	...	...	...	...
Dominica	68	0.0	...	3 360	7 030	7 270	13 000	5	...	...
Dominican Republic	10 309	1.2	-0.2	2 370	5 240	4 340	9 420	0.4	2	34
Ecuador	15 061	1.3	-0.3	1 820	4 200	4 690	8 510	0.2	5	33
El Salvador	6 303	0.6	-0.1	1 900	3 480	4 170	6 640	1	...	...
Grenada	106	0.4	0.4	2 990	7 350	5 750	10 350	2	...	...
Guatemala	15 528	2.5	1.6	1 670	2 870	3 270	4 760	0.8	14	51
Guyana	759	0.2	-1.1	880	...	1 900	...	6	...	...
Haiti	10 388	1.3	0.04	...	700	...	1 180	23	...	...
Honduras	8 072	2.0	0.7	750	1 980	2 380	3 820	4	18	60
Jamaica	2 771	0.4	-0.9	2 700	...	...	...	0.3	...	...
Mexico	117 478	1.1	-0.9	3 950	9 420	7 740	15 390	0.1	1	51
Montserrat	6	0.9	...	...	...	...	...	...	...	...
Netherlands Antilles	206	0.7	-0.7	...	...	...	...	...	...	...
Nicaragua	6 042	1.4	-0.3	880	1 510	2 110	3 730	7	12	46
Panama	3 678	1.5	-0.2	3 540	7 470	6 450	14 510	0.4	...	...
Paraguay	6 798	1.7	0.9	1 650	3 020	3 640	5 390	0.4	7	35
Peru	30 075	1.1	-0.4	2 230	5 150	4 610	9 440	0.3	5	31
Saint Kitts and Nevis	54	1.2	...	6 160	12 610	10 950	16 470	2	...	...
Saint Lucia	180	1.0	-0.4	3 830	6 820	7 090	11 220	3	...	...
Saint Vincent and the Grenadines	109	0.0	-1.5	2 790	6 070	5 680	10 440	3	...	...
Suriname	539	0.9	-0.5	2 360	...	5 140	...	2	...	...
Trinidad and Tobago	1 355	0.3	-0.4	4 470	...	10 220	...	...	...	...
Turks and Caicos Islands	40	1.2	...	...	...	...	...	...	...	...
Uruguay	3 403	0.3	-0.4	7 280	11 860	8 550	14 640	0.0	0.2	19
Venezuela, Bolivarian Republic of	30 341	1.5	0.1	3 360	11 820	8 480	12 430	0.0	...	...
North America and Western Europe										
Andorra	89	1.5	...	19 310	...	...	...	...	...	...
Austria	8 441	0.2	-1.0	27 280	48 190	25 860	42 050	...	...	...
Belgium	10 816	0.3	0.02	26 030	45 990	24 800	39 190	...	...	...
Canada	34 994	0.9	1.1	20 310	45 560	24 630	39 660	...	...	...
Cyprus	1 141	1.1	0.6	14 770	...	18 220	...	...	...	...
Denmark	5 611	0.3	-0.5	32 940	60 120	25 830	41 900	...	...	...
Finland	5 419	0.3	0.5	24 850	47 770	22 040	37 670	...	...	...
France	63 783	0.5	-0.04	25 070	42 420	22 840	35 910	...	...	...
Germany	81 804	-0.2	0.4	27 060	44 270	23 890	40 230	...	...	...
Greece	11 446	0.2	-0.2	13 010	24 480	16 720	25 100	...	...	...
Iceland	332	1.2	0.8	28 400	34 820	27 190	31 020	...	...	...
Ireland	4 631	1.1	0.1	20 640	39 930	21 310	34 180	...	...	...
Israel	7 819	1.7	1.5	16 850	28 930	19 150	27 110	...	...	...
Italy	61 087	0.2	-0.4	21 310	35 290	23 650	32 400	...	...	...
Luxembourg	530	1.4	1.9	43 810	77 580	39 770	64 260	...	...	...
Malta	421	0.3	-0.02	9 940	...	15 990	...	...	...	...
Monaco	35	0.0	...	86 960	...	...	...	...	...	...
Netherlands	16 762	0.3	-0.7	25 810	49 650	25 200	43 140	...	...	...
Norway	4 992	0.7	0.7	35 410	88 890	27 100	61 460	...	...	...

Table 1 (continued)

	DEMOGRAPHY[1]			GNP, AID AND POVERTY						
				GNP per capita[2]				Net official development assistance received (% of GDP)[3]	Population below income poverty line	
	Total population (000)	Average annual growth rate (%) total population	Average annual growth rate (%) age 0–4 population	Current US$		PPP US$			PPP US$1.25 a day[3] (%)	National poverty line[3] (%)
Country or territory	2013	2010–2015	2010–2015	1998	2011	1998	2011	2011	2002–2011[4]	2002–2011[4]
Portugal	10 705	0.0	-2.0	12 070	21 210	15 600	24 440	...	...	...
San Marino	32	0.6	...	...	...	...	...	...	...	...
Spain	47 043	0.6	-0.1	15 220	30 890	18 700	31 400	...	...	...
Sweden	9 546	0.6	0.6	29 520	53 150	24 050	42 200	...	...	...
Switzerland	7 762	0.4	0.5	42 630	76 400	31 860	52 570	...	...	...
United Kingdom	63 177	0.6	0.5	23 480	37 840	23 570	36 010	...	...	...
United States	318 498	0.9	0.1	30 930	48 620	32 060	48 820	...	...	...
South and West Asia										
Afghanistan	34 500	3.1	2.2	...	470	...	1 140	37	...	...
Bangladesh	154 394	1.3	-0.5	360	780	800	1 940	1	43	32
Bhutan	762	1.5	-0.02	570	2 130	1 830	5 570	8	10	23
India	1 275 138	1.3	-0.1	420	1 410	1 340	3 590	0.2	33	30
Iran, Islamic Republic of	76 407	1.0	-0.6	1 700	...	6 210	...	0.0	...	...
Maldives	329	1.3	0.5	1 930	5 720	3 320	7 430	2	...	...
Nepal	31 536	1.7	-0.05	210	540	730	1 260	5	25	25
Pakistan	183 189	1.8	0.6	450	1 120	1 520	2 870	2	21	22
Sri Lanka	21 394	0.8	-1.2	810	2 580	2 330	5 520	1	7	9
Sub-Saharan Africa										
Angola	20 714	2.7	1.3	130	3 830	1 710	5 230	0.2	...	...
Benin	9 607	2.7	1.8	370	780	1 060	1 620	9	47	39
Botswana	2 075	1.1	0.1	3 300	7 470	7 780	14 550	0.8	...	...
Burkina Faso	18 012	3.0	2.7	230	570	710	1 300	10	45	0
Burundi	8 911	1.9	1.8	150	250	440	610	25	81	67
Cameroon	20 914	2.1	1.2	640	1 210	1 450	2 330	2	10	40
Cape Verde	510	0.9	-1.1	1 260	3 540	1 600	3 980	13	...	...
Central African Republic	4 667	2.0	1.6	290	480	660	810	13	...	...
Chad	12 142	2.6	1.8	220	690	700	1 360	4	62	55
Comoros	793	2.5	1.1	410	770	910	1 110	8	...	...
Congo	4 324	2.2	1.7	570	2 250	2 040	3 240	2	54	50
Côte d'Ivoire	21 057	2.2	1.2	740	1 090	1 560	1 710	6	24	43
Democratic Rep. of the Congo	71 420	2.6	1.6	110	190	250	340	35	88	71
Equatorial Guinea	761	2.7	2.3	940	15 670	4 380	25 620	0.1	...	...
Eritrea	5 748	2.9	1.4	210	430	610	580	5	...	...
Ethiopia	88 356	2.1	0.3	130	370	420	1 110	11	39	39
Gabon	1 594	1.9	1.9	3 920	8 080	11 780	13 740	0.4	...	...
Gambia	1 874	2.7	1.7	670	500	1 230	1 750	15	34	48
Ghana	26 131	2.3	1.0	390	1 410	870	1 810	5	29	28
Guinea	10 754	2.5	1.6	450	430	720	1 020	4	43	53
Guinea-Bissau	1 613	2.1	1.4	150	600	820	1 240	12	...	...
Kenya	43 924	2.7	2.3	440	820	1 110	1 710	7	43	46
Lesotho	2 240	1.0	0.5	580	1 220	1 220	2 050	10	43	57
Liberia	4 349	2.6	1.5	130	330	190	540	50	84	64
Madagascar	22 555	2.8	2.1	260	430	740	950	4	81	69
Malawi	16 407	3.2	3.7	200	360	570	870	14	74	52
Mali	16 808	3.0	2.2	250	610	610	1 040	12	50	47
Mauritius	1 321	0.5	-0.8	3 780	8 040	7 120	14 330	2	...	...
Mozambique	25 028	2.2	1.0	220	470	390	970	16	60	55
Namibia	2 404	1.7	0.3	2 030	4 700	3 870	6 560	2	32	38
Niger	17 240	3.5	3.1	200	360	550	720	11	44	60
Nigeria	170 901	2.5	2.2	270	1 280	1 130	2 290	1	68	55
Rwanda	11 608	2.9	3.1	260	570	560	1 270	20	63	45
Sao Tome and Principe	175	2.0	0.7	...	1 350	...	2 080	30	...	66
Senegal	13 454	2.6	1.4	550	1 070	1 240	1 940	7	34	51
Seychelles	87	0.3	...	7 320	11 130	15 150	25 140	2	...	...
Sierra Leone	6 255	2.1	0.3	180	340	380	840	14	53	66
Somalia	10 053	2.6	2.2	...	...	...	...	...	...	...
South Africa	50 981	0.5	-0.4	3 290	6 960	6 290	10 710	0.3	14	23
South Sudan	...	...	...	...	...	...	...	6	...	...
Swaziland	1 237	1.4	0.7	1 690	3 300	3 770	5 930	3	41	69
Togo	6 413	2.0	0.9	330	570	810	1 040	15	39	62
Uganda	36 759	3.1	2.3	280	510	630	1 310	9	52	31
United Republic of Tanzania	49 153	3.1	3.0	250	540	700	1 500	10	68	33
Zambia	14 315	3.0	4.2	320	1 160	820	1 490	5	68	59
Zimbabwe	13 328	2.2	1.3	590	660	...	...	7	...	72

Table 1 (continued)

	DEMOGRAPHY[1]			GNP, AID AND POVERTY						
				GNP per capita[2]				Net official development assistance received (% of GDP)[3]	Population below income poverty line	
	Total population (000)	Average annual growth rate (%) total population	Average annual growth rate (%) age 0–4 population	Current US$		PPP US$			PPP US$1.25 a day[3] (%)	National poverty line[3] (%)
Country or territory	2013	2010–2015	2010–2015	1998	2011	1998	2011	2011	2002–2011[4]	2002–2011[4]
	Sum	Weighted average		Median				Median	Median	
World	7 096 421	1.1	0.3	1 900	4 290	4 295	8 310	3	...	...
Countries in transition	303 939	0.1	0.4	835	4 755	2 880	8 890	3	0.3	14
Developed countries	1 036 335	0.5	0.2	21 310	37 840	22 040	34 180	...	...	...
Developing countries	5 756 146	1.3	0.3	1 355	2 640	2 975	4 310	3	24	38
Arab States	368 767	1.9	0.7	1 580	4 225	3 980	7 215	2	2	...
Central and Eastern Europe	401 419	0.1	0.2	2 140	10 410	6 445	16 940	...	0.1	11
Central Asia	82 688	1.0	0.6	560	2 860	1 830	5 350	4	4	34
East Asia and the Pacific	2 215 239	0.6	-0.5	2 040	3 720	3 150	4 500	12	...	...
East Asia	2 172 889	0.6	-0.5	2 040	4 440	4 250	8 360	0.05	21	27
Pacific	42 351	1.4	1.2	2 115	3 440	3 080	4 300	22	...	...
Latin America and the Caribbean	604 772	1.1	-0.4	2 890	6 445	6 075	10 395	0.8	...	...
Caribbean	17 906	1.0	-0.1	3 360	...	7 180	...	2	...	...
Latin America	586 866	1.1	-0.4	2 370	5 655	5 220	9 500	0.3	6	36
North America and Western Europe	776 915	0.6	0.1	25 070	45 560	23 890	39 190	...	...	...
South and West Asia	1 777 648	1.4	-0.0	450	1 410	1 710	3 590	2	23	24
Sub-Saharan Africa	868 973	2.4	1.8	350	690	820	1 495	7	47	52
Countries with low income	849 416	2.1	1.4	250	540	705	1 160	10	46	47
Countries with middle income	5 134 216	1.0	0.1	1 580	4 025	3 440	6 840	2	7	26
Lower middle	2 606 856	1.5	0.4	815	2 210	2 060	3 785	4	18	35
Upper middle	2 527 360	0.6	-0.5	2 605	6 960	5 750	11 480	0.4	...	...
Countries with high income	1 112 788	0.5	0.2	18 080	39 930	21 435	35 330	...	...	...

Note A: The statistical tables still include data for Sudan (pre-secession) for reference purposes as those for the two new entities since July 2011, Sudan and South Sudan, are just becoming available. The country groupings by level of income are as defined by the World Bank but include EFA countries only. They are based on the list of countries by income group as revised in July 2012.

Note B: The median values for 1998 and 2011 are not comparable since they are not necessarily based on the same number of countries.

1. The demographic indicators are from the United Nations Population Division estimates, revision 2010 (United Nations, 2011). They are based on the median variant.

2. World Bank database, December 2012 update.

3. OECD-DAC database; World Bank (2013); UNDP (2013).

4. Data are for the most recent year available during the period specified. For more details see UNDP (2013).

(. . .) No data available.

Table 2 (continued)

Country or territory	ADULT LITERACY RATE (15 and over) (%)									ADULT ILLITERATES (15 and over)					
	1985–1994[1]			2005–2011[1]			Projected 2015			1985–1994[1]		2005–2011[1]		Projected 2015	
	Total	Male	Female	Total	Male	Female	Total	Male	Female	Total (000)	% Female	Total (000)	% Female	Total (000)	% Female
Papua New Guinea	…	…	…	62	65	59	64	66	63	…	…	1 614	53	1 719	51
Philippines	94 *	94 *	93 *	95 *	95 *	96 *	96	96	97	2 328	53 *	2 635	46 *	2 495	44
Republic of Korea	…	…	…	…	…	…	…	…	…	…	…	…	…	…	…
Samoa	98 *	98 *	97 *	99	99	99	99	99	99	2	59 *	1	58	1	56
Singapore	89 *	95 *	83 *	96 *	98 *	94 *	97	98	95	260	78 *	172	76 *	147	75
Solomon Islands	…	…	…	…	…	…	…	…	…	…	…	…	…	…	…
Thailand	…	…	…	94 *	96 *	92 *	95	97	94	…	…	3 361	67 *	2 768	66
Timor-Leste	…	…	…	58 *	64 *	53 *	67	71	63	…	…	252	56 *	241	56
Tokelau	…	…	…	…	…	…	…	…	…	…	…	…	…	…	…
Tonga	…	…	…	99 *	99 *	99 *	99	99	99	…	…	0.6	48 *	0.5	46
Tuvalu	…	…	…	…	…	…	…	…	…	…	…	…	…	…	…
Vanuatu	…	…	…	…	…	…	…	…	…	…	…	…	…	…	…
Viet Nam	88 *	93 *	83 *	93	95	91	94	96	92	5 002	73 *	4 528	66	4 294	65
Latin America and the Caribbean															
Anguilla	…	…	…	…	…	…	…	…	…	…	…	…	…	…	…
Antigua and Barbuda	…	…	…	99	98	99	…	…	…	…	…	0.7	29	…	…
Argentina	96 *	96 *	96 *	98	98	98	98	98	98	890	53 *	658	51	615	50
Aruba	…	…	…	97 *	97 *	97 *	98	98	98	…	…	3	55 *	2	53
Bahamas	…	…	…	…	…	…	…	…	…	…	…	…	…	…	…
Barbados	…	…	…	…	…	…	…	…	…	…	…	…	…	…	…
Belize	70 *	70 *	70 *	…	…	…	…	…	…	33	51 *	…	…	40	49
Bermuda	…	…	…	…	…	…	…	…	…	…	…	…	…	…	…
Bolivia, Plurinational State of	80 *	88 *	72 *	91 *	96 *	87 *	94	93	94	823	71 *	543	76 *	439	48
Brazil	…	…	…	90 *	90 *	91 *	92	91	92	…	…	13 984	50 *	12 890	49
British Virgin Islands	…	…	…	…	…	…	…	…	…	…	…	…	…	…	…
Cayman Islands	…	…	…	99 *	99 *	99 *	…	…	…	…	…	0.5	44 *	…	…
Chile	94 *	95 *	94 *	99 *	99 *	98 *	99	99	99	548	54 *	191	53 *	195	53
Colombia	81 *	81 *	81 *	94 *	93 *	94 *	95	95	95	4 222	52 *	2 157	51 *	1 920	51
Costa Rica	…	…	…	96	96	96	97	96	97	…	…	134	46	130	46
Cuba	…	…	…	100	100	100	100	100	100	…	…	16	52	15	52
Dominica	…	…	…	…	…	…	…	…	…	…	…	…	…	…	…
Dominican Republic	…	…	…	90 *	90 *	90 *	92	91	92	…	…	690	50 *	631	48
Ecuador	88 *	90 *	86 *	92 *	93 *	90 *	95	95	94	732	59 *	818	59 *	601	58
El Salvador	74 *	77 *	71 *	84 *	87 *	82 *	88	90	86	845	59 *	653	62 *	565	62
Grenada	…	…	…	…	…	…	…	…	…	…	…	…	…	…	…
Guatemala	64 *	72 *	57 *	76	81	71	78	83	74	1 921	61 *	2 098	63	2 127	63
Guyana	…	…	…	85	82	87	88	87	89	…	…	75	43	66	44
Haiti	…	…	…	49	53	45	61	64	58	…	…	3 028	55	2 748	55
Honduras	…	…	…	85 *	85 *	85 *	88	88	89	…	…	735	51 *	636	50
Jamaica	…	…	…	87	82	92	89	84	93	…	…	254	33	234	31
Mexico	88 *	90 *	85 *	94 *	95 *	92 *	94	95	93	6 437	62 *	5 300	61 *	5 011	61
Montserrat	…	…	…	…	…	…	…	…	…	…	…	…	…	…	…
Netherlands Antilles	95 *	95 *	95 *	97	97	97	97	97	97	7	53 *	6	55	5	54
Nicaragua	…	…	…	78 *	78 *	78 *	83	82	83	…	…	743	51 *	728	50
Panama	89 *	89 *	88 *	94 *	95 *	93 *	95	96	94	176	52 *	147	55 *	135	56
Paraguay	90 *	92 *	89 *	94 *	95 *	93 *	96	96	96	255	59 *	263	57 *	209	51
Peru	87 *	93 *	82 *	90 *	95 *	85 *	93	96	89	1 850	72 *	1 991	75 *	1 573	75
Saint Kitts and Nevis	…	…	…	…	…	…	…	…	…	…	…	…	…	…	…
Saint Lucia	…	…	…	…	…	…	…	…	…	…	…	…	…	…	…
Saint Vincent and the Grenadines	…	…	…	…	…	…	…	…	…	…	…	…	…	…	…
Suriname	…	…	…	95 *	95 *	94 *	96	96	95	…	…	20	57 *	18	57
Trinidad and Tobago	97 *	98 *	96 *	99	99	98	99	99	99	26	70 *	12	68	11	65
Turks and Caicos Islands	…	…	…	…	…	…	…	…	…	…	…	…	…	…	…
Uruguay	95 *	95 *	96 *	98 *	98 *	98 *	98	98	99	102	46 *	50	41 *	46	40
Venezuela, Bolivarian Republic of	90 *	91 *	89 *	96 *	96 *	95 *	96	96	96	1 240	54 *	898	52 *	828	52
North America and Western Europe															
Andorra	…	…	…	…	…	…	…	…	…	…	…	…	…	…	…
Austria	…	…	…	…	…	…	…	…	…	…	…	…	…	…	…
Belgium	…	…	…	…	…	…	…	…	…	…	…	…	…	…	…
Canada	…	…	…	…	…	…	…	…	…	…	…	…	…	…	…
Cyprus	94 *	98 *	91 *	99 *	99 *	98 *	99	99	99	33	80 *	12	72 *	9	71
Denmark	…	…	…	…	…	…	…	…	…	…	…	…	…	…	…
Finland	…	…	…	…	…	…	…	…	…	…	…	…	…	…	…
France	…	…	…	…	…	…	…	…	…	…	…	…	…	…	…
Germany	…	…	…	…	…	…	…	…	…	…	…	…	…	…	…
Greece	93 *	96 *	89 *	97	98	96	98	99	97	615	74 *	262	70	221	68
Iceland	…	…	…	…	…	…	…	…	…	…	…	…	…	…	…
Ireland	…	…	…	…	…	…	…	…	…	…	…	…	…	…	…
Israel	…	…	…	…	…	…	…	…	…	…	…	…	…	…	…
Italy	…	…	…	99	99	99	99	99	99	…	…	533	64	444	63
Luxembourg	…	…	…	…	…	…	…	…	…	…	…	…	…	…	…
Malta	88 *	88 *	88 *	92 *	91 *	94 *	94	93	96	32	50 *	26	43 *	20	39
Monaco	…	…	…	…	…	…	…	…	…	…	…	…	…	…	…
Netherlands	…	…	…	…	…	…	…	…	…	…	…	…	…	…	…
Norway	…	…	…	…	…	…	…	…	…	…	…	…	…	…	…

Table 2

YOUTH LITERACY RATE (15–24) (%)									YOUTH ILLITERATES (15–24)						
1985–1994[1]			2005–2011[1]			Projected 2015			1985–1994[1]		2005–2011[1]		Projected 2015		
Total	Male	Female	Total	Male	Female	Total	Male	Female	Total (000)	% Female	Total (000)	% Female	Total (000)	% Female	Country or territory
…	…	…	71	67	75	72	66	79	…	…	391	42	418	37	Papua New Guinea
97 *	96 *	97 *	98 *	97 *	98 *	98	97	99	425	45 *	406	33 *	412	25	Philippines
…	…	…	…	…	…	…	…	…	…	…	…	…	…	…	Republic of Korea
99 *	99 *	99 *	100	99	100	100	99	100	0.4	49 *	0.2	38	0.2	36	Samoa
99 *	99 *	99 *	100 *	100 *	100 *	…	…	…	6	44 *	2	45 *	2	41	Singapore
…	…	…	…	…	…	…	…	…	…	…	…	…	…	…	Solomon Islands
…	…	…	98 *	98 *	98 *	99	99	99	…	…	208	53 *	135	50	Thailand
…	…	…	80 *	80 *	79 *	82	82	83	…	…	47	51 *	52	48	Timor-Leste
…	…	…	…	…	…	…	…	…	…	…	…	…	…	…	Tokelau
…	…	…	99 *	99 *	100 *	100	99	100	…	…	0.1	38 *	0.1	36	Tonga
…	…	…	…	…	…	…	…	…	…	…	…	…	…	…	Tuvalu
…	…	…	…	…	…	…	…	…	…	…	…	…	…	…	Vanuatu
94 *	94 *	93 *	97	97	97	98	98	97	842	53 *	517	56	384	56	Viet Nam
															Latin America and the Caribbean
…	…	…	…	…	…	…	…	…	…	…	…	…	…	…	Anguilla
…	…	…	…	…	…	…	…	…	…	…	…	…	…	…	Antigua and Barbuda
98 *	98 *	99 *	99	99	99	99	99	99	92	43 *	53	37	47	37	Argentina
…	…	…	99 *	99 *	99 *	99	99	99	…	…	0.1	40 *	0.1	54	Aruba
…	…	…	…	…	…	…	…	…	…	…	…	…	…	…	Bahamas
…	…	…	…	…	…	…	…	…	…	…	…	…	…	…	Barbados
76 *	76 *	77 *	…	…	…	89	87	90	10	50 *	…	…	8	46	Belize
…	…	…	…	…	…	…	…	…	…	…	…	…	…	…	Bermuda
94 *	96 *	92 *	99 *	100 *	99 *	99	98	99	83	70 *	12	74 *	25	30	Bolivia, P. S.
…	…	…	98 *	97 *	98 *	98	97	99	…	…	836	33 *	635	32	Brazil
…	…	…	…	…	…	…	…	…	…	…	…	…	…	…	British Virgin Islands
…	…	…	99 *	99 *	99 *	…	…	…	…	…	0.1	62 *	…	…	Cayman Islands
98 *	98 *	99 *	99 *	99 *	99 *	99	99	99	38	41 *	33	49 *	37	50	Chile
91 *	89 *	92 *	98 *	98 *	99 *	99	98	99	655	43 *	150	36 *	116	33	Colombia
…	…	…	98	98	99	98	98	99	…	…	15	36	13	35	Costa Rica
…	…	…	100	100	100	100	100	100	…	…	0.2	55	0.2	59	Cuba
…	…	…	…	…	…	…	…	…	…	…	…	…	…	…	Dominica
…	…	…	97 *	96 *	98 *	98	97	99	…	…	55	33 *	41	34	Dominican Republic
96 *	97 *	96 *	99 *	98 *	99 *	99	99	99	79	54 *	36	42 *	22	39	Ecuador
85 *	85 *	85 *	96 *	96 *	96 *	97	97	98	167	51 *	53	46 *	36	43	El Salvador
…	…	…	…	…	…	…	…	…	…	…	…	…	…	…	Grenada
76 *	82 *	71 *	87	89	86	89	90	88	461	62 *	377	58	361	56	Guatemala
…	…	…	93	92	94	94	94	95	…	…	9	45	9	45	Guyana
…	…	…	72	74	70	82	83	82	…	…	570	54	391	52	Haiti
…	…	…	96 *	95 *	97 *	97	96	98	…	…	67	37 *	49	32	Honduras
…	…	…	96	93	98	97	94	99	…	…	22	17	19	16	Jamaica
95 *	96 *	95 *	98 *	98 *	99 *	99	99	99	832	56 *	322	49 *	254	45	Mexico
…	…	…	…	…	…	…	…	…	…	…	…	…	…	…	Montserrat
97 *	97 *	97 *	98	98	98	99	99	99	0.9	44 *	0.3	50	0.2	50	Netherlands Antilles
…	…	…	87 *	85 *	89 *	92	90	94	…	…	153	43 *	107	38	Nicaragua
95 *	95 *	95 *	98 *	98 *	97 *	98	98	98	25	52 *	14	55 *	12	52	Panama
96 *	96 *	95 *	99 *	99 *	99 *	99	98	100	37	52 *	18	45 *	17	12	Paraguay
95 *	97 *	94 *	97 *	98 *	97 *	98	98	98	215	67 *	143	62 *	107	54	Peru
…	…	…	…	…	…	…	…	…	…	…	…	…	…	…	Saint Kitts and Nevis
…	…	…	…	…	…	…	…	…	…	…	…	…	…	…	Saint Lucia
…	…	…	…	…	…	…	…	…	…	…	…	…	…	…	Saint Vincent/Grenadines
…	…	…	98 *	98 *	99 *	99	98	100	…	…	1	37 *	0.9	17	Suriname
99 *	99 *	99 *	100	100	100	100	100	100	2	50 *	1.0	49	0.7	48	Trinidad and Tobago
…	…	…	…	…	…	…	…	…	…	…	…	…	…	…	Turks and Caicos Islands
99 *	98 *	99 *	99 *	98 *	99 *	99	98	99	6	37 *	6	31 *	7	30	Uruguay
95 *	95 *	96 *	99 *	98 *	99 *	99	99	99	175	39 *	79	40 *	60	43	Venezuela, B. R.
															North America and Western Europe
…	…	…	…	…	…	…	…	…	…	…	…	…	…	…	Andorra
…	…	…	…	…	…	…	…	…	…	…	…	…	…	…	Austria
…	…	…	…	…	…	…	…	…	…	…	…	…	…	…	Belgium
…	…	…	…	…	…	…	…	…	…	…	…	…	…	…	Canada
100 *	100 *	100 *	100 *	100 *	100 *	100	100	100	0.5	42 *	0.3	43 *	0.2	41	Cyprus
…	…	…	…	…	…	…	…	…	…	…	…	…	…	…	Denmark
…	…	…	…	…	…	…	…	…	…	…	…	…	…	…	Finland
…	…	…	…	…	…	…	…	…	…	…	…	…	…	…	France
…	…	…	…	…	…	…	…	…	…	…	…	…	…	…	Germany
99 *	99 *	99 *	99	99	99	99	100	99	16	49 *	8	54	6	56	Greece
…	…	…	…	…	…	…	…	…	…	…	…	…	…	…	Iceland
…	…	…	…	…	…	…	…	…	…	…	…	…	…	…	Ireland
…	…	…	…	…	…	…	…	…	…	…	…	…	…	…	Israel
…	…	…	100	100	100	100	100	100	…	…	5	47	4	46	Italy
…	…	…	…	…	…	…	…	…	…	…	…	…	…	…	Luxembourg
98 *	97 *	99 *	98 *	97 *	99 *	99	99	99	1	26 *	1	25 *	1	26	Malta
…	…	…	…	…	…	…	…	…	…	…	…	…	…	…	Monaco
…	…	…	…	…	…	…	…	…	…	…	…	…	…	…	Netherlands
…	…	…	…	…	…	…	…	…	…	…	…	…	…	…	Norway

Table 2 (continued)

Country or territory	ADULT LITERACY RATE (15 and over) (%)									ADULT ILLITERATES (15 and over)					
	1985–1994[1]			2005–2011[1]			Projected 2015			1985–1994[1]		2005–2011[1]		Projected 2015	
	Total	Male	Female	Total	Male	Female	Total	Male	Female	Total (000)	% Female	Total (000)	% Female	Total (000)	% Female
Portugal	88 *	92 *	85 *	95	97	94	96	98	95	960	67 *	415	69	328	69
San Marino	...	...	...	...	...	...	...	...	...	...	...	...	...	...	...
Spain	96 *	98 *	95 *	98 *	99 *	97 *	98	99	98	1 104	73 *	882	68 *	755	67
Sweden	...	...	...	...	...	...	...	...	...	...	...	...	...	...	...
Switzerland	...	...	...	...	...	...	...	...	...	...	...	...	...	...	...
United Kingdom	...	...	...	...	...	...	...	...	...	...	...	...	...	...	...
United States	...	...	...	...	...	...	...	...	...	...	...	...	...	...	...
South and West Asia															
Afghanistan	...	...	...	...	...	...	...	...	...	...	...	...	...	...	...
Bangladesh	35 *	44 *	26 *	58	62	53	61	65	58	40 252	55 *	44 137	55	43 876	54
Bhutan	...	...	...	53 *	65 *	39 *	64	73	54	...	...	206	60 *	205	60
India[2]	48 *	62 *	34 *	63 *	75 *	51 *	71	81	61	287 272	61 *	287 355	65 *	266 367	67
Iran, Islamic Republic of	66 *	74 *	56 *	85 *	89 *	81 *	91	94	88	10 687	63 *	8 256	64 *	5 680	66
Maldives	96 *	96 *	96 *	98 *	98 *	98 *	99	100	99	5	46 *	3	49 *	2	84
Nepal	33 *	49 *	17 *	57	71	47	66	79	53	7 531	62 *	8 150	66	7 524	70
Pakistan	...	...	...	55 *	69 *	40 *	60	72	47	...	...	49 507	65 *	51 037	65
Sri Lanka[2]	...	...	...	91 *	93 *	90 *	93	94	92	...	...	1 373	59 *	1 221	58
Sub-Saharan Africa															
Angola	...	...	...	70	83	59	71	82	61	...	...	3 126	71	3 491	69
Benin	27 *	40 *	17 *	29	41	18	38	50	27	1 998	61 *	3 097	60	3 578	60
Botswana	69 *	65 *	71 *	85	85	86	87	87	88	251	47 *	205	48	183	47
Burkina Faso	14 *	20 *	8 *	29 *	37 *	22 *	36	43	29	4 326	56 *	5 806	57 *	6 752	57
Burundi	37 *	48 *	28 *	87 *	89 *	85 *	85	88	82	1 944	61 *	646	60 *	856	61
Cameroon	...	...	...	71 *	78 *	65 *	75	81	68	...	...	3 317	62 *	3 343	63
Cape Verde	63 *	75 *	53 *	85	90	80	87	91	83	70	69 *	52	66	48	66
Central African Republic	34 *	48 *	20 *	57	70	44	59	71	48	1 059	62 *	1 166	66	1 213	65
Chad	11 *	18 *	5 *	35	46	25	39	48	31	3 155	55 *	4 069	58	4 313	58
Comoros	...	...	...	76	81	71	78	82	74	...	...	106	60	106	59
Congo	...	...	...	...	...	...	...	...	...	...	...	...	...	...	...
Côte d'Ivoire	34 *	44 *	23 *	57	66	48	60	67	51	4 149	54 *	5 160	59	5 399	59
Democratic Rep. of the Congo	...	...	...	61	77	46	64	78	50	...	...	12 418	71	14 948	70
Equatorial Guinea	...	...	...	94	97	91	95	97	93	...	...	25	74	23	71
Eritrea	...	...	...	69	79	59	73	82	65	...	...	983	68	954	68
Ethiopia	27 *	36 *	19 *	39 *	49 *	29 *	49	57	40	21 815	57 *	26 847	59 *	29 280	59
Gabon	72 *	79 *	65 *	89	92	86	91	94	88	165	64 *	110	65	97	66
Gambia	...	...	...	51	61	42	56	64	48	...	...	489	61	504	61
Ghana	...	...	...	71 *	78 *	65 *	76	81	71	...	...	4 208	61 *	4 038	60
Guinea	...	...	...	25 *	37 *	12 *	30	38	23	...	...	4 300	58 *	4 569	55
Guinea-Bissau	...	...	...	55	69	42	60	72	48	...	...	407	66	406	65
Kenya	...	...	...	72	78	67	78	81	75	...	...	5 934	61	5 872	57
Lesotho	...	...	...	76	66	85	79	70	88	...	...	326	32	306	29
Liberia	43	55	32	43	61	27	48	62	33	639	61	1 105	65	1 360	64
Madagascar	...	...	...	64	67	62	65	67	63	...	...	4 039	55	4 945	53
Malawi	49 *	65 *	34 *	61	72	51	66	73	59	2 212	68 *	3 100	64	3 235	61
Mali	...	...	...	33 *	43 *	25 *	39	49	29	...	...	5 550	58 *	5 814	59
Mauritius	80 *	85 *	75 *	89	91	87	90	92	88	150	63 *	115	61	106	60
Mozambique	...	...	...	51 *	67 *	36 *	59	73	45	...	...	6 235	68 *	6 173	69
Namibia	76 *	78 *	74 *	76	74	78	81	79	84	201	56 *	316	47	303	43
Niger	...	...	...	29 *	43 *	15 *	36	49	23	...	...	4 731	61 *	6 072	61
Nigeria	55 *	68 *	44 *	51	61	41	59	69	49	24 489	64 *	41 845	60	42 127	62
Rwanda	58 *	...	...	66	71	62	70	73	67	1 511	61 *	2 060	59	2 096	56
Sao Tome and Principe	73 *	85 *	62 *	70	80	60	75	82	69	17	73 *	28	68	28	64
Senegal	27 *	37 *	18 *	50 *	62 *	39 *	58	69	47	2 600	57 *	3 400	63 *	3 426	64
Seychelles	88 *	87 *	89 *	92	91	92	...	...	...	6	47 *	5	46	...	...
Sierra Leone	...	...	...	43	55	33	48	59	38	...	...	1 941	61	1 963	62
Somalia	...	...	...	...	...	...	...	...	...	...	...	...	...	...	...
South Africa	...	...	...	93 *	94 *	92 *	94	95	93	...	...	2 474	57 *	2 133	59
South Sudan	...	...	...	...	...	...	...	...	...	...	...	...	...	...	...
Swaziland	67 *	70 *	65 *	88	88	87	89	89	89	123	59 *	91	54	131	42
Togo	...	...	...	60 *	74 *	48 *	66	78	55	...	...	1 464	67 *	1 414	68
Uganda	56 *	68 *	45 *	73 *	83 *	65 *	78	85	71	4 140	64 *	4 560	67 *	4 444	66
United Republic of Tanzania	59 *	71 *	48 *	68	75	61	71	76	65	5 205	65 *	7 920	62	8 453	59
Zambia	65 *	73 *	57 *	61	72	52	63	71	56	1 487	62 *	2 478	63	2 953	60
Zimbabwe	84 *	89 *	79 *	84	88	80	86	89	84	979	66 *	1 275	63	1 214	58

Table 2

YOUTH LITERACY RATE (15–24) (%)									YOUTH ILLITERATES (15–24)						
1985–1994[1]			2005–2011[1]			Projected 2015			1985–1994[1]		2005–2011[1]		Projected 2015		
Total	Male	Female	Total	Male	Female	Total	Male	Female	Total (000)	% Female	Total (000)	% Female	Total (000)	% Female	Country or territory
99 *	99 *	99 *	100	100	100	100	100	100	13	46 *	3	43	2	42	Portugal
...	...	...	...	...	...	...	...	...	...	...	...	...	...	...	San Marino
100 *	100 *	100 *	100 *	100 *	100 *	100	100	100	29	47 *	19	38 *	11	37	Spain
...	...	...	...	...	...	...	...	...	...	...	...	...	...	...	Sweden
...	...	...	...	...	...	...	...	...	...	...	...	...	...	...	Switzerland
...	...	...	...	...	...	...	...	...	...	...	...	...	...	...	United Kingdom
...	...	...	...	...	...	...	...	...	...	...	...	...	...	...	United States
															South and West Asia
...	...	...	...	...	...	...	...	...	...	...	...	...	...	...	Afghanistan
45 *	52 *	38 *	79	77	80	83	81	86	12 116	55 *	6 469	45	5 254	41	Bangladesh
...	...	...	74 *	80 *	68 *	89	90	87	...	...	38	59 *	17	55	Bhutan
62 *	74 *	49 *	81 *	88 *	74 *	90	93	87	65 244	64 *	41 275	67 *	23 738	62	India[2]
87 *	92 *	81 *	99 *	99 *	99 *	99	99	99	1 392	71 *	235	54 *	114	45	Iran, Islamic Republic of
98 *	98 *	98 *	99 *	99 *	99 *	100	100	100	0.7	46 *	0.5	45 *	0.2	100	Maldives
50 *	68 *	33 *	82	89	77	87	91	83	1 862	67 *	1 049	67	885	64	Nepal
...	...	...	71 *	79 *	61 *	77	82	72			10 820	64 *	9 038	59	Pakistan
...	...	...	98 *	98 *	99 *	99	98	99			61	37 *	39	33	Sri Lanka[2]
															Sub-Saharan Africa
...	...	...	73	80	66	73	79	67	...	...	1 052	63	1 212	61	Angola
40 *	55 *	27 *	42	55	31	52	63	42	580	63 *	882	61	954	61	Benin
89 *	86 *	92 *	95	93	97	98	96	99	31	35 *	21	31	10	12	Botswana
20 *	27 *	14 *	39 *	47 *	33 *	45	48	43	1 518	54 *	1 838	55 *	2 076	51	Burkina Faso
54 *	59 *	48 *	89 *	90 *	88 *	88	87	88	494	56 *	204	54 *	236	49	Burundi
...	...	...	81 *	85 *	76 *	84	87	80	...	...	773	62 *	705	60	Cameroon
88 *	90 *	86 *	98	98	99	99	98	100	8	57 *	2	23	1	19	Cape Verde
48 *	63 *	35 *	66	72	59	67	72	63	265	64 *	318	60	323	58	Central African Republic
17 *	26 *	9 *	48	54	42	53	55	50	1 013	56 *	1 186	55	1 208	53	Chad
...	...	...	86	86	86	88	87	88	...	...	19	50	19	46	Comoros
...	...	...	...	...	...	...	...	...	...	...	...	...	...	...	Congo
49 *	60 *	38 *	68	72	63	69	73	66	1 059	60 *	1 330	57	1 372	55	Côte d'Ivoire
...	...	...	66	79	53	69	80	57	...	...	4 072	69	4 848	68	Democratic Rep. of the Congo
...	...	...	98	98	98	98	98	99	...	...	3	41	3	34	Equatorial Guinea
...	...	...	90	93	88	93	95	92	...	...	106	62	77	60	Eritrea
34 *	39 *	28 *	55 *	63 *	47 *	69	71	68	6 808	54 *	7 090	59 *	6 222	53	Ethiopia
93 *	94 *	92 *	98	99	97	98	99	98	12	59 *	7	71	6	73	Gabon
...	...	...	68	73	64	73	76	71	...	...	110	58	110	55	Gambia
...	...	...	86 *	88 *	83 *	91	91	90	...	...	689	58 *	495	53	Ghana
...	...	...	31 *	38 *	22 *	45	43	47	...	...	1 391	55 *	1 229	47	Guinea
...	...	...	73	79	67	77	81	74	...	...	83	61	76	58	Guinea-Bissau
...	...	...	82	83	82	86	85	87	...	...	1 436	52	1 268	47	Kenya
...	...	...	83	74	92	85	77	93	...	...	85	23	77	22	Lesotho
60	66	54	49	63	37	54	65	44	164	57	345	63	399	61	Liberia
...	...	...	65	66	64	65	65	65	...	...	1 384	51	1 703	50	Madagascar
59 *	70 *	49 *	72	74	70	75	75	75	621	64 *	846	54	883	49	Malawi
...	...	...	47 *	56 *	39 *	54	61	46	...	...	1 631	57 *	1 631	57	Mali
91 *	91 *	92 *	97	96	98	97	96	98	19	47 *	7	34	6	31	Mauritius
...	...	...	67 *	80 *	57 *	77	84	70	...	...	1 426	68 *	1 237	65	Mozambique
88 *	86 *	90 *	87	83	91	90	86	93	36	40 *	59	36	53	33	Namibia
...	...	...	37 *	52 *	23 *	46	56	36	...	...	1 440	64 *	1 880	60	Niger
71 *	81 *	62 *	66	76	58	73	80	65	5 256	66 *	9 815	62	9 434	62	Nigeria
75 *	76 *	71 *	77	77	78	80	78	82	334	56 *	501	49	450	46	Rwanda
94 *	96 *	92 *	80	83	77	83	84	82	1	65 *	7	57	7	52	Sao Tome and Principe
38 *	49 *	28 *	65 *	74 *	56 *	75	82	68	817	59 *	874	63 *	730	64	Senegal
99 *	98 *	99 *	99	99	99	...	...	...	0.2	36 *	0.1	30	...	...	Seychelles
...	...	...	61	70	52	67	76	59	...	...	453	63	424	64	Sierra Leone
...	...	...	...	...	...	...	...	...	...	...	...	...	...	...	Somalia
...	...	...	99 *	98 *	99 *	99	99	99	...	...	122	34 *	73	36	South Africa
...	...	...	...	...	...	...	...	...	...	...	...	...	...	...	South Sudan
84 *	83 *	84 *	94	92	95	94	93	96	23	51 *	19	37	36	24	Swaziland
...	...	...	80 *	87 *	73 *	85	89	81	...	...	258	68	205	63	Togo
70 *	77 *	63 *	87 *	90 *	85 *	91	90	91	1 051	62 *	837	59 *	733	49	Uganda
82 *	86 *	78 *	75	76	73	76	77	76	827	62 *	2 251	54	2 378	51	United Republic of Tanzania
66 *	67 *	66 *	64	70	58	66	69	62	524	51 *	864	58	1 029	55	Zambia
95 *	97 *	94 *	91	90	92	92	90	93	101	62 *	287	43	268	40	Zimbabwe

Table 2 (continued)

Country or territory	ADULT LITERACY RATE (15 and over) (%)								
	1985–1994[1]			2005–2011[1]			Projected 2015		
	Total	Male	Female	Total	Male	Female	Total	Male	Female
	Weighted average								
World	76	82	69	84	89	80	86	90	82
Countries in transition	98	99	97	100	100	99	100	100	100
Developed countries	...	...	...	...	...	...	...	...	...
Developing countries	67	76	58	80	86	74	83	88	78
Arab States	55	68	42	77	85	68	79	87	71
Central and Eastern Europe	96	98	94	99	99	98	98	99	97
Central Asia	98 **	99 **	97 **	100	100	99	100	100	100
East Asia and the Pacific	82	89	75	95	97	93	96	98	94
East Asia	82	89	74	95	97	93	96	98	94
Pacific	...	...	...	...	...	...	...	...	...
Latin America and the Caribbean	86 **	87 **	84 **	92	92	91	93	93	92
Caribbean	...	...	...	69	71	68	73	74	72
Latin America	86 **	88 **	85 **	92	93	92	93	94	93
North America and Western Europe	...	...	...	...	...	...	...	...	...
South and West Asia	47	59	34	63	74	52	70	80	61
Sub-Saharan Africa	53 **	64 **	43 **	59	68	51	64	72	56
Countries with low income	51 **	60 **	41 **	61	69	54	66	72	59
Countries with middle income	72	80	64	83	89	79	86	90	81
Lower middle	59	69	48	71	80	62	76	83	68
Upper middle	82	88	75	94	96	92	95	97	94
Countries with high income	...	...	...	...	...	...	...	...	...

Country or territory	ADULT ILLITERATES (15 and over)					
	1985–1994[1]		2005–2011[1]		Projected 2015	
	Total (000)	% Female	Total (000)	% Female	Total (000)	% Female
	Sum	% F	Sum	% F	Sum	% F
World	880 504	63	773 549	64	742 799	64
Countries in transition	4 698	85	1 190	69	649	60
Developed countries	...	...	...	...	...	...
Developing countries	865 961	63	763 987	64	733 847	64
Arab States	51 697	63	47 603	66	47 629	67
Central and Eastern Europe	12 077	79	4 919	78	6 506	80
Central Asia	937	77 **	290	63	247	58
East Asia and the Pacific	231 557	69	89 478	71	76 014	71
East Asia	230 154	69	87 652	71	74 173	71
Pacific	...	...	...	...	...	...
Latin America and the Caribbean	42 204	55 **	35 614	55	32 681	54
Caribbean	...	...	3 503	54	3 388	53
Latin America	39 300	56 **	32 112	55	29 293	54
North America and Western Europe	...	...	...	...	...	...
South and West Asia	400 974	60	407 021	64	381 909	65
Sub-Saharan Africa	133 172	62 **	181 950	61	191 376	61
Countries with low income	149 510	60 **	183 552	60	189 550	60
Countries with middle income	722 271	64	582 835	65	544 545	66
Lower middle	458 704	61	470 164	65	450 953	65
Upper middle	263 567	67	112 671	67	93 592	67
Countries with high income	...	...	...	...	...	...

Source: UNESCO Institute for Statistics database (UIS) database.

Note A: The statistical tables still include data for Sudan (pre-secession) for reference purposes as those for the two new entities since July 2011, Sudan and South Sudan, are just becoming available. The country groupings by income level are as defined by the World Bank. They are based on the list of countries by income group as revised in July 2012.

Note B: For countries indicated with (*), national observed literacy data are used. For all others, UIS literacy estimates are used. The estimates were generated using the UIS Global Age-specific Literacy Projections model. Those in the most recent period are for 2011 and are based on the most recent observed data available for each country.

Note C: The population used to generate the number of illiterates is from the United Nations Population Division estimates, revision 2010 (United Nations, 2011). It is based on the median variant. For countries with national observed literacy data, the population corresponding to the year of the census or survey was used. For countries with UIS estimates, populations used are for 1994 and 2011.

1. Data are for the most recent year available during the period specified. See the introduction to the statistical tables and the table of metadata on literacy statistics for a broader explanation of national literacy definitions, assessment methods, and sources and years of data.

(**) For country level data: UIS partial estimate; for regional and other country-grouping sums and weighted averages: partial imputation due to incomplete country coverage (between 33% and 60% of population for the region or other country grouping).

(. . .) No data available.

YOUTH LITERACY RATE (15–24) (%)									YOUTH ILLITERATES (15–24)						
1985–1994[1]			2005–2011[1]			Projected 2015			1985–1994[1]		2005–2011[1]		Projected 2015		
Total	Male	Female	Total	Male	Female	Total	Male	Female	Total (000)	% Female	Total (000)	% Female	Total (000)	% Female	Country or territory
Weighted average									Sum	% F	Sum	% F	Sum	% F	
83	88	79	89	92	87	92	93	90	167 781	62	123 198	61	98 431	57	World
100	100	100	100	100	100	100	100	100	116	46	120	41	74	39	Countries in transition
...	...	...	...	...	...	...	...	...	...	...	...	...	...	...	Developed countries
80	85	75	88	91	85	90	92	89	167 157	62	122 578	61	97 870	57	Developing countries
74	83	65	90	93	87	91	94	89	10 177	67	6 037	65	5 170	63	Arab States
98	99	98	99	99	99	99	99	99	968	72	386	59	507	65	Central and Eastern Europe
100 **	100 **	100 **	100	100	100	100	100	100	30	47 **	45	33	42	31	Central Asia
95	97	93	99	99	99	99	99	99	19 840	69	4 081	51	3 314	45	East Asia and the Pacific
95	97	93	99	99	99	99	99	99	19 458	69	3 650	52	2 873	46	East Asia
...	...	...	...	...	...	...	...	...	...	...	...	...	...	...	Pacific
93 **	93 **	93 **	97	97	97	98	97	98	6 166	48 **	3 043	45	2 403	42	Latin America and the Caribbean
...	...	...	81	82	81	87	87	87	...	...	621	52	457	50	Caribbean
93 **	93 **	94 **	98	97	98	98	98	98	5 649	47 **	2 422	43	1 946	41	Latin America
...	...	...	...	...	...	...	...	...	...	...	...	...	...	...	North America and Western Europe
60	70	49	81	87	75	88	91	86	96 043	61	61 778	64	39 993	59	South and West Asia
66 **	73 **	59 **	70	76	64	74	78	70	34 282	60 **	47 558	60	46 751	57	Sub-Saharan Africa
60 **	67 **	53 **	73	77	69	77	79	59	41 631	59 **	42 586	57	40 395	54	Countries with low income
84	88	79	91	94	88	93	95	82	126 765	63	81 145	64	59 137	60	Countries with middle income
71	78	63	84	89	79	89	92	68	102 323	62	75 739	65	54 948	60	Lower middle
94	96	92	99	99	99	99	99	94	24 442	66	5 406	52	4 190	48	Upper middle
...	...	...	...	...	...	...	...	...	...	...	...	...	...	...	Countries with high income

Table 3A

Early childhood care and education (ECCE): care

	CHILD SURVIVAL[1]		CHILD WELL-BEING[2]						
					% of 1-year-old children immunized against				
	Infant mortality rate (‰)	Under-5 mortality rate (‰)	Infants with low birth weight (%)	% of children under age 5 suffering from moderate or severe stunting	Tuberculosis	Diphtheria, Pertussis, Tetanus	Polio	Measles	Hepatitis B
					Corresponding vaccines:				
					BCG	DPT3	Polio3	Measles	HepB3
Country or territory	2010–2015	2010–2015	2007–2011[3]	2005–2012[3]	2011	2011	2011	2011	2011
Arab States									
Algeria	21	27	6	16	99	95	95	95	95
Bahrain	7	9	...	...	...	99	99	99	99
Djibouti	75	104	...	34	89	87	87	84	87
Egypt	22	25	13	29	98	96	96	96	96
Iraq	33	41	15	28	92	77	78	76	76
Jordan	19	22	13	8	95	98	98	98	98
Kuwait	8	10	...	4	99	99	99	99	99
Lebanon	20	24	12	...	...	81	75	79	81
Libya	13	15	...	21	99	98	98	98	98
Mauritania	70	106	34	23	86	75	73	67	75
Morocco	29	31	15	15	99	99	98	95	98
Oman	8	11	12	10	99	99	99	99	99
Palestine	20	22	7	12	98	99	99	99	98
Qatar	8	10	...	...	97	93	93	99	93
Saudi Arabia	16	19	...	...	98	98	98	98	98
Sudan		...	...	35	92	93	93	87	93
Syrian Arab Republic	14	16	10	28	90	72	75	80	66
Tunisia	18	23	5	9	98	98	98	96	98
United Arab Emirates	7	8	...	...	98	94	94	94	94
Yemen	44	57	...	...	59	81	81	71	81
Sudan (pre-secession)	57	87	...	38	...	...	...	...	...
Central and Eastern Europe									
Albania	17	19	7	19	99	99	99	99	99
Belarus	6	9	4	4	99	98	98	99	98
Bosnia and Herzegovina	13	16	4	12	94	88	89	89	88
Bulgaria	9	11	9	...	98	95	95	95	96
Croatia	6	7	5	...	99	96	96	96	97
Czech Republic	3	4	7	...	...	99	99	98	99
Estonia	4	7	4	...	99	93	93	94	94
Hungary	5	7	8	...	99	99	99	99	...
Latvia	7	8	5	...	95	94	94	99	91
Lithuania	6	9	4	...	98	92	92	94	95
Montenegro	8	9	4	8	97	95	95	91	91
Poland	6	7	6	...	93	99	96	98	98
Republic of Moldova	14	19	6	11	98	93	96	91	96
Romania	12	15	8	...	99	89	89	93	96
Russian Federation	11	16	6	...	95	97	97	98	97
Serbia	11	13	5	7	99	91	91	95	89
Slovakia	6	7	7	...	97	99	99	98	99
Slovenia	3	4	...	...	...	96	96	95	...
The former Yugoslav Rep. of Macedonia	13	15	6	5	98	95	95	98	90
Turkey	20	23	11	12	97	97	97	97	96
Ukraine	12	15	4	...	90	50	58	67	21
Central Asia									
Armenia	24	27	7	19	96	95	96	97	95
Azerbaijan	38	43	10	27	82	74	80	67	48
Georgia	26	27	5	11	96	94	90	94	92
Kazakhstan	24	29	6	18	96	99	99	99	99
Kyrgyzstan	33	42	5	18	98	96	94	97	96
Mongolia	31	37	5	16	99	99	99	98	99
Tajikistan	51	65	10	30	97	96	97	98	96
Turkmenistan	49	62	4	...	98	97	97	99	97
Uzbekistan	44	53	5	20	99	99	99	99	99
East Asia and the Pacific									
Australia	4	5	7	...	...	92	92	94	92
Brunei Darussalam	5	6	...	...	96	97	99	91	93
Cambodia	53	69	11	40	94	94	94	93	94
China	20	24	3	9	99	99	99	99	99
Cook Islands	...	...	3	...	98	93	93	89	93
Democratic People's Republic of Korea	25	32	6	32	98	94	99	99	94
Fiji	17	22	10	...	99	99	99	94	99
Indonesia	25	31	9	36	82	63	70	89	63
Japan	3	3	8	...	94	98	96	94	...
Kiribati	...	...	...	...	86	99	95	90	95
Lao People's Democratic Republic	37	46	11	48	77	78	79	69	78
Macao, China	4	5	...	...	...	...	...	...	...
Malaysia	7	9	10	17	99	99	99	95	97
Marshall Islands	...	...	18	...	99	94	95	97	97
Micronesia (Federated States of)	31	38	18	...	75	84	83	92	83
Myanmar	45	57	9	35	93	99	99	99	52
Nauru	...	...	27	24	99	99	99	99	99
New Zealand	5	6	6	...	...	95	95	93	95
Niue	...	...	0	...	99	98	98	99	98
Palau	...	...	...	...	...	84	98	85	91

Table 3A (continued)

	CHILD SURVIVAL[1]		CHILD WELL-BEING[2]						
					% of 1-year-old children immunized against				
	Infant mortality rate (‰)	Under-5 mortality rate (‰)	Infants with low birth weight (%)	% of children under age 5 suffering from moderate or severe stunting	Tuberculosis	Diphtheria, Pertussis, Tetanus	Polio	Measles	Hepatitis B
					Corresponding vaccines:				
					BCG	DPT3	Polio3	Measles	HepB3
Country or territory	**2010–2015**	**2010–2015**	**2007–2011[3]**	**2005–2012[3]**	**2011**	**2011**	**2011**	**2011**	**2011**
Papua New Guinea	44	58	11	44	83	61	58	60	62
Philippines	21	27	21	32	84	80	80	79	76
Republic of Korea	4	5	4	...	99	99	98	99	99
Samoa	20	24	10	...	99	91	91	67	91
Singapore	2	2	8	...	99	96	96	95	96
Solomon Islands	35	43	12	33	89	88	93	73	88
Thailand	11	13	7	16	99	99	99	98	98
Timor-Leste	56	76	12	58	68	67	66	62	67
Tokelau	...	...	...	...	...	...	...	...	...
Tonga	21	25	3	...	99	99	99	99	99
Tuvalu	...	...	6	10	99	96	96	98	96
Vanuatu	24	29	10	26	81	68	67	52	59
Viet Nam	18	23	5	23	98	95	96	96	95
Latin America and the Caribbean									
Anguilla	...	...	...	...	...	...	...	...	...
Antigua and Barbuda	...	...	5	...	...	99	99	99	99
Argentina	12	14	7	...	99	93	95	93	93
Aruba	15	17	...	...	...	...	...	...	...
Bahamas	14	18	10	...	...	98	97	90	95
Barbados	12	14	12	...	...	91	91	93	91
Belize	16	21	14	22	98	95	95	98	95
Bermuda	...	...	...	...	...	...	...	...	...
Bolivia, Plurinational State of	41	54	6	27	90	82	82	84	82
Brazil	19	24	8	7	99	96	97	97	96
British Virgin Islands	...	...	...	...	...	...	...	...	...
Cayman Islands	...	...	...	...	...	...	...	...	...
Chile	7	8	6	2.0	91	94	93	91	94
Colombia	17	23	6	13	83	85	85	88	85
Costa Rica	9	11	7	6	78	85	82	83	84
Cuba	5	6	5	...	99	96	99	99	96
Dominica	...	...	10	...	99	98	99	99	98
Dominican Republic	22	28	11	10	98	84	84	79	80
Ecuador	19	23	8	...	99	99	99	98	98
El Salvador	19	23	9	21	91	89	89	89	90
Grenada	13	15	9	...	...	94	95	95	94
Guatemala	26	34	11	48	89	85	86	87	85
Guyana	37	46	14	18	97	93	93	98	93
Haiti	58	76	25	30	75	59	59	59	...
Honduras	24	33	10	30	99	98	98	99	98
Jamaica	22	26	12	4	99	99	99	88	99
Mexico	14	17	7	14	99	97	97	98	98
Montserrat	...	...	...	...	...	...	...	...	...
Netherlands Antilles	12	14	...	...	...	...	...	...	...
Nicaragua	18	22	9	22	98	98	99	99	98
Panama	16	21	10	19	97	87	91	97	87
Paraguay	27	33	6	18	94	90	87	93	90
Peru	18	28	8	20	91	91	91	96	91
Saint Kitts and Nevis	...	...	8	...	99	97	98	99	98
Saint Lucia	12	16	11	...	97	97	97	95	97
Saint Vincent and the Grenadines	21	25	8	...	99	95	95	99	96
Suriname	20	27	11	11	...	86	86	85	86
Trinidad and Tobago	24	31	19	...	...	90	91	92	90
Turks and Caicos Islands	...	...	...	...	...	...	...	...	...
Uruguay	12	15	9	8	99	95	95	95	95
Venezuela, Bolivarian Republic of	15	20	8	13	95	78	78	86	78
North America and Western Europe									
Andorra	...	...	...	...	...	99	99	99	99
Austria	4	5	7	...	...	83	83	76	83
Belgium	4	5	...	...	...	98	98	95	97
Canada	5	6	6	...	...	95	99	98	70
Cyprus	4	5	...	...	...	99	99	87	96
Denmark	4	5	4	...	...	91	91	87	...
Finland	3	3	4	...	...	99	99	97	...
France	3	4	...	...	...	99	99	89	65
Germany	3	4	...	...	...	99	95	99	93
Greece	4	5	...	...	91	99	99	99	95
Iceland	2	3	4	...	...	96	96	93	...
Ireland	4	4	...	...	41	95	95	92	95
Israel	3	4	8	...	...	94	94	98	99
Italy	3	4	...	...	...	96	96	90	96
Luxembourg	2	3	8	...	...	99	99	96	95
Malta	5	7	6	...	...	96	96	84	82
Monaco	...	...	...	...	89	99	99	99	99
Netherlands	4	5	...	...	...	97	97	96	...
Norway	3	4	5	...	...	94	94	93	...

Table 3B

Early childhood care and education (ECCE): education

		Age Group	ENROLMENT IN PRE-PRIMARY EDUCATION				Enrolment in private institutions as % of total enrolment		GROSS ENROLMENT RATIO (GER) IN PRE-PRIMARY EDUCATION (%)							
			School year ending in				School year ending in		School year ending in							
			1999		2011		1999	2011	1999				2011			
	Country or territory	2011	Total (000)	% F	Total (000)	% F			Total	Male	Female	GPI (F/M)	Total	Male	Female	GPI (F/M)
	Arab States															
1	Algeria	5-5	36	49	490	49	.	14	2	2	2	1.01	75	74	75	1.02
2	Bahrain[1]	3-5	14	48	27	50	100	100	38	39	37	0.96	...	...	...	...
3	Djibouti	4-5	0.2	60	**2**	**50**	100	**57**	0.4	0.3	0.5	1.50	**4**	**4**	**4**	**1.01**
4	Egypt	4-5	328	48	912	48	54	...	10	11	10	0.95	26	27	25	0.95
5	Iraq	4-5	68	48	...	...	.	...	5	5	5	1,00	...	...	...	...
6	Jordan	4-5	74	46	99[z]	47[z]	100	83[z]	29	31	28	0.91	32[z]	33[z]	31[z]	0.94[z]
7	Kuwait[1]	4-5	57	49	78	49	24	43	85	84	87	1.03	...	...	...	...
8	Lebanon	3-5	143[**]	48	154	49	78[**]	82	61[**]	62[**]	60[**]	0.97[**]	83	83	82	0.98
9	Libya	4-5	10	48	...	...	.	...	5	5[**]	5[**]	0.98[**]	...	...	...	...
10	Mauritania	3-5	...	...	...	...	...	...	...	...	...	...	...	...	...	...
11	Morocco	4-5	805	34	**683**	**43**	100	**90**	62	81	42	0.53	**58**	**65**	**50**	**0.77**
12	Oman	4-5	...	...	56	49	...	66	...	...	...	...	53	54	53	0.98
13	Palestine	4-5	77	48	96	48	100	100	35	36	35	0.96	41	41	41	0.98
14	Qatar	3-5	8	48	30	49	100	81	25	26	25	0.96	57	56	58	1.03
15	Saudi Arabia	3-5	...	...	210	...	...	50	...	...	...	...	12	...	...	...
16	Sudan	4-5	...	...	659[z]	50[z]	...	25[z]	...	...	...	...	...	...	...	...
17	Syrian Arab Republic	3-5	108	46	172	47	67	71	8	9	8	0.90	11	11	11	0.97
18	Tunisia	3-5	78	47	...	...	88	...	14	14	13	0.93	...	...	...	...
19	United Arab Emirates[1]	4-5	64	48	131	49	68	80	64	64	64	0.99	...	...	...	...
20	Yemen	3-5	12	45	30	46	37	45	0.7	0.7	0.6	0.86	1	1	1	0.88
21	Sudan (pre-secession)	4-5	366	...	632[y]	50[y]	90[**]	23[y]	19	...	...	...	27[y]	26[y]	27[y]	1.04[y]
	Central and Eastern Europe															
22	Albania	3-5	82	50	76	47	...	5	43	42	45	1.06	57	58	57	0.98
23	Belarus	3-5	278	47	297	48	-	...	83	86	79	0.92	103	104	101	0.98
24	Bosnia and Herzegovina	3-5	...	...	17	47	...	15	...	...	...	...	17	18	17	0.96
25	Bulgaria	3-6	219	48	218[z]	48[z]	0.1	0.8[z]	68	69	68	0.99	79[z]	80[z]	79[z]	0.99[z]
26	Croatia	3-6	81	48	99[z]	48[z]	5	14[z]	39	40	39	0.98	61[z]	62[z]	61[z]	0.98[z]
27	Czech Republic	3-5	312	50	332	48	2	2	89	86	91	1.07	111	112	109	0.98
28	Estonia	3-6	55	48	48[z]	48[z]	0.7	3[z]	93	94	92	0.99	88[z]	88[z]	87[z]	0.98[z]
29	Hungary	3-6	376	48	338	48	3	6	80	81	79	0.98	87	88	87	0.99
30	Latvia	3-6	58	48	75	48	1.0	3	56	58	55	0.95	86	87	84	0.97
31	Lithuania	3-6	94	48	87	49	0.3	0.6	50	51	50	0.97	73	74	72	0.98
32	Montenegro	3-5	***11***	***48***	**14**	**47**	.	**2**	***34***	***34***	***33***	***0.98***	**60**	**61**	**59**	**0.96**
33	Poland	3-6	958	49	994[z]	49[z]	3	13[z]	49	49	49	1,00	71[z]	71[z]	72[z]	1.01[z]
34	Republic of Moldova[2,3]	3-6	103	48	116	48	...	0.1	48	49	48	0.96	77	77	77	0.99
35	Romania	3-6	625	49	666[z]	49[z]	0.6	2[z]	68	67	69	1.03	79[z]	79[z]	79[z]	1.01[z]
36	Russian Federation	3-6	4 379	...	5 105[y]	48[y]	...	0.8[y]	71	...	...	...	90[y]	91[y]	89[y]	0.98[y]
37	Serbia[2]	3-6	175	46	153	49	...	0.8	54	57	51	0.90	53	53	53	1,00
38	Slovakia	3-5	169	...	144	48	0.4	4	79	...	...	...	91	92	89	0.98
39	Slovenia	3-5	59	46	52	48	1	3	75	79	72	0.91	93	95	91	0.96
40	The former Yugoslav Rep. of Macedonia	3-5	33	49	17[z]	49[z]	.	.[z]	27	27	27	1.01	25[z]	25[z]	26[z]	1.05[z]
41	Turkey	3-5	261	47	981[z]	48[z]	6	9[z]	7	7	6	0.94	26[z]	27[z]	26[z]	0.96[z]
42	Ukraine	3-5	1 103	48	1 273	48	0.04	1.0	50	51	50	0.98	99	100	97	0.97
	Central Asia															
43	Armenia	3-5	57	...	58	49	-	2	26	...	...	...	43	41	47	1.14
44	Azerbaijan[2,4]	3-5	88	46	98	46	-	0.8	18	19	17	0.89	27	27	26	0.97
45	Georgia	3-5	74	48	...	...	0.1	...	35	36	35	0.98	...	...	...	...
46	Kazakhstan	3-6	165	48	**618**	**49**	10	**6**	15	15	15	0.96	**53**	**53**	**52**	**0.99**
47	Kyrgyzstan	3-6	48	43	85	49	1	3	10	11	9	0.80	21	21	21	1,00
48	Mongolia	3-5	74	54	122	50	4	7	26	24	29	1.18	82	80	84	1.04
49	Tajikistan	3-6	56	42	62	44	.	-	8	9	7	0.77	9	10	8	0.82
50	Turkmenistan	3-6	...	...	...	...	...	...	...	...	...	...	...	...	...	...
51	Uzbekistan	3-6	616	47	523	49	...	0.6	24	24	23	0.93	26	26	26	1,00
	East Asia and the Pacific															
52	Australia	4-4	***273***	***49***	218[z]	48[z]	***63***	75[z]	***103***	***103***	***104***	***1,00***	78[z]	79[z]	78[z]	0.98[z]
53	Brunei Darussalam	4-5	11	49	13	49	66	74	81	79	82	1.04	88	87	89	1.03
54	Cambodia	3-5	58[**]	50	115	50	22[**]	...	5[**]	5[**]	5[**]	1.03[**]	13	13	14	1.05
55	China	4-6	24 030	46	29 767	45	...	47	37	37	37	1,00	61	61	62	1.02
56	Cook Islands[2]	4-4	0.4	47	0.5	49	25	34	86	87	85	0.98	181	180	181	1.01
57	Democratic People's Republic of Korea	5-6	...	...	...	...	...	...	...	...	...	...	...	...	...	...
58	Fiji	3-5	9	49	9[y]	50[y]	...	...	15	15	15	1.01	18[y]	17[y]	19[y]	1.07[y]
59	Indonesia	5-6	1 981[**]	49	4 055	50	99[**]	97	23[**]	22[**]	23[**]	1.01[**]	46	45	46	1.04
60	Japan	3-5	2 962	49	2 904[z]	...	65	70[z]	83	83[**]	84[**]	1.02[**]	88[z]	...	...	...
61	Kiribati	3-5	...	...	...	...	...	...	...	...	...	...	...	...	...	...
62	Lao People's Democratic Republic	3-5	37	52	97	50	18	24	8	7	8	1.11	24	23	24	1.06
63	Macao, China	3-5	17	47	11	49	94	97	91	93	88	0.95	85	87	83	0.95
64	Malaysia	4-5	572	50	805[z]	51[z]	49	46[z]	54	53	55	1.04	69[z]	66[z]	71[z]	1.08[z]
65	Marshall Islands	4-5	2	50	1	50	19	18	57	56	59	1.05	46	45	47	1.05
66	Micronesia (Federated States of)	3-5	3	...	...	...	...	...	37	...	...	...	...	...	...	...
67	Myanmar	3-4	41	...	159[z]	51[z]	90	61[z]	2	...	...	...	10[z]	10[z]	10[z]	1.06[z]
68	Nauru[2]	3-5	*0.6*	*45*	...	...	...	...	*74*	*79*	*69*	*0.88*	...	...	...	...
69	New Zealand	3-4	101	49	111[z]	50[z]	...	98[z]	85	85	85	1.01	93[z]	91[z]	95[z]	1.04[z]
70	Niue[2]	4-4	0.1	44	...	...	.	...	154	159	147	0.93	...	...	...	...
71	Palau[2]	3-5	0.7	54	...	...	24	...	63	56	69	1.23	...	...	...	...

Table 3B

GROSS ENROLMENT RATIO (GER) IN PRE-PRIMARY AND OTHER ECCE PROGRAMMES (%)				NET ENROLMENT RATIO (NER) IN PRE-PRIMARY EDUCATION (%)				NEW ENTRANTS TO THE FIRST GRADE OF PRIMARY EDUCATION WITH ECCE EXPERIENCE (%)			
School year ending in 2011				School year ending in 2011				School year ending in 2011			
Total	Male	Female	GPI (F/M)	Total	Male	Female	GPI (F/M)	Total	Male	Female	
										Arab States	
…	…	…	…	68	67	69	1.03	33 [y]	34 [y]	32 [y]	1
…	…	…	…	…	…	…	…	85	86	85	2
4	**4**	**4**	**1.01**	**3**	**3**	**3**	**1,00**	**12**	**11**	**12**	3
26	27	25	0.95	21 [**, y]	22 [**, y]	20 [**, y]	0.95 [**, y]	…	…	…	4
…	…	…	…	…	…	…	…	…	…	…	5
32 [z]	33 [z]	31 [z]	0.94 [z]	32 [z]	33 [z]	31 [z]	0.94 [z]	52 [z]	53 [z]	51 [z]	6
…	…	…	…	…	…	…	…	…	…	…	7
83	83	82	0.98	80	80	79	0.99	100	100	100	8
…	…	…	…	…	…	…	…	…	…	…	9
…	…	…	…	…	…	…	…	…	…	…	10
58	**65**	**50**	**0.77**	**52**	**59**	**46**	**0.78**	**48**	**49**	**47**	11
…	…	…	…	44	44	44	0.99	…	…	…	12
41	41	41	0.98	36	37	36	0.98	…	…	…	13
57	56	58	1.03	46	44	47	1.06	…	…	…	14
12	…	…	…	…	…	…	…	…	…	…	15
…	…	…	…	…	…	…	…	…	…	…	16
11	11	11	0.97	11	11	11	0.97	…	…	…	17
…	…	…	…	…	…	…	…	…	…	…	18
…	…	…	…	…	…	…	…	85	80	91	19
1	1	1	0.88	1.0	1.0	0.9	0.89	2 [z]	2 [z]	2 [z]	20
27 [y]	26 [y]	27 [y]	1.04 [y]	…	…	…	…	65 [y]	61 [**, y]	70 [**, y]	21
										Central and Eastern Europe	
57	58	57	0.98	54	54	54	0.98	…	…	…	22
123	125	121	0.97	92	92	92	0.99	…	…	…	23
…	…	…	…	12	13	12	0.98	…	…	…	24
79 [z]	80 [z]	79 [z]	0.99 [z]	76 [z]	76 [z]	76 [z]	0.99 [z]	…	…	…	25
61 [z]	62 [z]	61 [z]	0.98 [z]	61 [z]	61 [z]	61 [z]	0.99 [z]	…	…	…	26
111	112	109	0.98	…	…	…	…	…	…	…	27
88 [z]	88 [z]	87 [z]	0.98 [z]	87 [z]	88 [z]	87 [z]	0.99 [z]	…	…	…	28
87	88	87	0.99	85	85	84	0.99	…	…	…	29
86	87	84	0.97	84	85	83	0.98	…	…	…	30
73	74	72	0.98	72	73	72	0.98	…	…	…	31
60	**61**	**59**	**0.96**	**44**	**45**	**43**	**0.96**	…	…	…	32
71 [z]	71 [z]	72 [z]	1.01 [z]	69 [z]	69 [z]	70 [z]	1.01 [z]	…	…	…	33
77	77	77	0.99	76	76	76	1,00	98	97	98	34
79 [z]	79 [z]	79 [z]	1.01 [z]	78 [z]	77 [z]	78 [z]	1.01 [z]	…	…	…	35
90 [y]	91 [y]	89 [y]	0.98 [y]	73 [y]	73 [y]	72 [y]	0.99 [y]	…	…	…	36
…	…	…	…	53	53	53	1,00	91	92	91	37
91	92	89	0.98	…	…	…	…	…	…	…	38
93	95	91	0.96	91	93	90	0.97	…	…	…	39
25 [z]	25 [z]	26 [z]	1.05 [z]	24 [z]	24 [z]	25 [z]	1.03 [z]	…	…	…	40
…	…	…	…	26 [**, z]	27 [**, z]	26 [**, z]	0.96 [**, z]	…	…	…	41
99	100	97	0.97	…	…	…	…	…	…	…	42
										Central Asia	
43	41	47	1.14	…	…	…	…	…	…	…	43
31	31	30	0.97	23	23	22	0.97	10	10	11	44
…	…	…	…	…	…	…	…	…	…	…	45
53	**53**	**52**	**0.99**	**52**	**53**	**52**	**0.99**	…	…	…	46
21	21	21	1,00	17	17	17	1.01	20	20	20	47
106	103	108	1.05	61	60	62	1.04	69	68	70	48
9	10	8	0.82	7	8	7	0.82	2	2	2	49
…	…	…	…	…	…	…	…	…	…	…	50
26	26	26	1,00	20	20	20	1.01	…	…	…	51
										East Asia and the Pacific	
78 [z]	79 [z]	78 [z]	0.99 [z]	51 [z]	52 [z]	51 [z]	[illegible]	…	…	…	52
…	…	…	…	64	64	65	1.01	…	…	…	53
26	25	27	1.06	13	12	13	1.05	23 [z]	23 [z]	24 [z]	54
61	61	62	1.02	…	…	…	…	92	…	…	55
181	180	181	1.01	…	…	…	…	…	…	…	56
…	…	…	…	…	…	…	…	…	…	…	57
18 [y]	17 [y]	19 [y]	1.07 [y]	…	…	…	…	…	…	…	58
46	45	46	1.04	31 [z]	31 [z]	31 [z]	1.02 [z]	61	61	61	59
106 [z]	…	…	…	88 [z]	…	…	…	…	…	…	60
…	…	…	…	…	…	…	…	…	…	…	61
25	25	26	1.06	24	23	24	1.06	32	31	32	62
85	87	83	0.95	83	85	81	0.95	…	…	…	63
69 [z]	66 [z]	71 [z]	1.08 [z]	59 [z]	57 [z]	62 [z]	1.07 [z]	100 [z]	100 [z]	100 [z]	64
46	45	47	1.05	…	…	…	…	…	…	…	65
…	…	…	…	…	…	…	…	…	…	…	66
…	…	…	…	10 [z]	10 [z]	10 [z]	1.06 [z]	20 [z]	19 [z]	21 [z]	67
…	…	…	…	…	…	…	…	…	…	…	68
…	…	…	…	92 [z]	90 [z]	94 [z]	1.04 [z]	…	…	…	69
…	…	…	…	…	…	…	…	…	…	…	70
…	…	…	…	…	…	…	…	…	…	…	71

Table 3B (continued)

	Country or territory	Age Group 2011	ENROLMENT IN PRE-PRIMARY EDUCATION – School year ending in 1999 – Total (000)	1999 – % F	2011 – Total (000)	2011 – % F	Enrolment in private institutions as % of total enrolment – School year ending in 1999	2011	GROSS ENROLMENT RATIO (GER) IN PRE-PRIMARY EDUCATION (%) – School year ending in 1999 – Total	1999 – Male	1999 – Female	1999 – GPI (F/M)	2011 – Total	2011 – Male	2011 – Female	2011 – GPI (F/M)
145	Portugal	3-5	220	49	274 [z]	48 [z]	52	49 [z]	67	67	66	1,00	83 [z]	83 [z]	83 [z]	0.99 [z]
146	San Marino[2,5]	3-5	*1,0*	*47*	1	48	.	.	...	...	...	...	108	104	113	1.09
147	Spain	3-5	1 131	49	1 875	49	32	36	99	99	99	1,00	127	127	127	1,00
148	Sweden	3-6	360	49	409	49	10	17	76	75	76	1.01	95	95	95	1,00
149	Switzerland	5-6	158	48	149	49	6	4	92	93	92	1,00	101	100	101	1.01
150	United Kingdom	3-4	1 155	49	1 175 [z]	50 [z]	6	21 [z]	77	77	77	1,00	83 [z]	82 [z]	85 [z]	1.04 [z]
151	United States	3-5	7 183	48	8 840 [z]	50 [z]	34	45 [z]	59	60	58	0.97	69 [z]	68 [z]	70 [z]	1.04 [z]
	South and West Asia															
152	Afghanistan	3-6	...	...	...	...	...	...	...	...	...	...	...	...	...	...
153	Bangladesh[7]	3-5	1 825	50	2 376	48	...	49	18	18	19	1.04	26	26	25	0.98
154	Bhutan	4-5	0.3	48	**3**	**48**	100	**40**	1	1	1	0.92	**9**	**9**	**9**	**0.96**
155	India	3-5	13 869	48	41 301 [z]	49 [z]	...	...	19	18	19	1.02	55 [z]	54 [z]	56 [z]	1.04 [z]
156	Iran, Islamic Republic of	5-5	220	50	475	51	16	25	14	14	15	1.03	43	41	45	1.10
157	Maldives	3-5	12	48	18	50	...	97	56	56	57	1.01	115	113	117	1.04
158	Nepal[7]	3-4	216 [*]	42	**1 056**	**48**	...	**17**	11 [*]	13 [*]	10 [*]	0.77 [*]	**82**	**83**	**81**	**0.98**
159	Pakistan	3-4	*5 160* [*]	*40* [*]	...	...	...	...	*63* [*]	*74* [*]	*51* [*]	*0.70* [*]	...	...	...	...
160	Sri Lanka	4-4	...	...	318	49	...	80	...	...	...	...	84	84	85	1.01
	Sub-Saharan Africa															
161	Angola	5-5	389 [**]	40	668 [*,z]	50 [*,z]	...	1 [*,z]	27 [**]	33 [**]	22 [**]	0.66 [**]	104 [*,z]	103 [*,z]	105 [*,z]	1.02 [*,z]
162	Benin	4-5	18	48	109	50	20	26	4	5	4	0.93	20	20	20	1.03
163	Botswana	3-5	...	...	24 [y]	50 [y]	...	...	...	...	...	...	19 [y]	19 [y]	19 [y]	1.02 [y]
164	Burkina Faso	3-5	20	50	**60**	**49**	34	76 [z]	2	2	2	1.03	**4**	**4**	**4**	**1.01**
165	Burundi	4-6	5	50	43	50	49	34	0.8	0.8	0.8	1.01	7	7	7	1.02
166	Cameroon	4-5	104	48	340	50	57	61	11	11	11	0.95	30	30	30	1.03
167	Cape Verde	3-5	*20* [**]	*50*	23	50	...	54	*53* [**]	*53* [**]	*54* [**]	*1.02* [**]	74	75	74	1,00
168	Central African Republic	3-5	...	...	21	51	...	55	...	...	...	...	6	6	6	1.02
169	Chad	3-5	...	...	22	46	...	59	...	...	...	...	2	2	2	0.87
170	Comoros	3-5	1	51	...	...	100	...	3	3	3	1.07	...	...	...	...
171	Congo	3-5	6	61	45	49	85	73	2	2	3	1.61	13	13	13	0.99
172	Côte d'Ivoire	3-5	36	49	75	50	46	40	2	3	2	0.96	4	4	4	1,00
173	Democratic Rep. of the Congo	3-5	***40***	***49***	245	51	***93***	91 [y]	***0.8***	***0.8***	***0.8***	***0.99***	4	4	4	1.05
174	Equatorial Guinea	4-6	17	51	42	50	37	53	27	27	28	1.04	74	74	74	1,00
175	Eritrea	5-6	12	47	46	49	97	52	5	6	5	0.89	15	15	15	0.97
176	Ethiopia	4-6	90	49	383	48	100	98	1	1	1	0.97	5	6	5	0.95
177	Gabon	3-5	***16***	***50***	45	50	***68***	74	***14***	***14*** [**]	***14*** [**]	***1.02*** [**]	42	41	43	1.04
178	Gambia	3-6	29	47	65 [z]	51 [z]	...	77 [z]	18	19	17	0.91	30 [z]	30 [z]	31 [z]	1.04 [z]
179	Ghana	4-5	506	49	**1 543**	**50**	26 [**]	**22**	47	46	48	1.03	**114**	**112**	**116**	**1.04**
180	Guinea	4-6	...	...	152	49	...	72 [z]	...	...	...	...	17	17	17	0.98
181	Guinea-Bissau	4-6	4 [**]	51	9 [z]	51 [z]	62 [**]	84 [z]	4 [**]	4 [**]	4 [**]	1.06 [**]	7 [z]	7 [z]	7 [z]	1.06 [z]
182	Kenya	3-5	1 188	50	1 914 [y]	49 [y]	10	38 [y]	43	43	43	1,00	52 [y]	52 [y]	52 [y]	0.99 [y]
183	Lesotho	3-5	33 [**]	52	53 [z]	...	100 [**]	...	20 [**]	19 [**]	21 [**]	1.08 [**]	33 [z]	...	...	...
184	Liberia	3-5	112	42	...	...	39	...	47	54	40	0.75	...	...	...	...
185	Madagascar	3-5	50 [**]	51	164 [z]	50 [z]	...	91 [z]	3 [**]	3 [**]	3 [**]	1.02 [**]	9 [z]	9 [z]	9 [z]	1.03 [z]
186	Malawi	3-5	...	...	...	...	...	...	...	...	...	...	...	...	...	...
187	Mali	3-6	21	51	71	50	...	73	1	1	2	1.10	3	3	3	1.05
188	Mauritius[1,7]	3-4	42	50	36	49	85	81	...	...	...	...	113	115	112	0.98
189	Mozambique	3-5	...	...	...	...	...	...	...	...	...	...	...	...	...	...
190	Namibia	5-6	35	53	...	...	100	...	33	31	35	1.15	...	...	...	...
191	Niger	4-6	12	50	**110**	**50**	33	**13**	1	1	1	1.05	**7**	**6**	**7**	**1.06**
192	Nigeria	3-5	***939***	***48***	2 021 [z]	49 [z]	...	27 [z]	***8***	***8***	***8***	***0.94***	14 [z]	14 [z]	14 [z]	0.99 [z]
193	Rwanda	4-6	***18***	***50***	112	51	...	100	***3***	***3***	***3***	***0.98***	11	11	12	1.05
194	Sao Tome and Principe	3-5	4	52	**9**	**51**	-	**14**	24	23	26	1.13	**61**	**60**	**62**	**1.04**
195	Senegal	4-6	24	50	161	53	68	45	3	3	3	1,00	14	13	15	1.14
196	Seychelles	4-5	3	49	3	48	5	10	110	110	111	1.01	99	103	94	0.92
197	Sierra Leone	3-5	*17*	...	37	51	...	41	*4*	...	...	...	7	7	7	1.03
198	Somalia	3-5	...	...	...	...	...	...	...	...	...	...	...	...	...	...
199	South Africa	6-6	207	50	667 [y]	50 [y]	26	5 [y]	21	21	21	1.01	65 [y]	65 [y]	65 [y]	1,00 [y]
200	South Sudan	3-5	...	...	56	48	...	70	...	...	...	...	...	...	...	...
201	Swaziland	3-5	...	...	24	50	...	100	...	...	...	...	26	26	26	1.02
202	Togo	3-5	11	50	**66**	**51**	53	**30**	3	3	3	0.99	**13**	**13**	**13**	**1.03**
203	Uganda	3-5	...	...	499 [z]	51 [z]	...	100 [z]	...	...	...	...	14 [z]	14 [z]	14 [z]	1.05 [z]
204	United Republic of Tanzania	5-6	...	...	**1 035**	**49**	...	**5**	...	...	...	...	**35**	**35**	**34**	**0.97**
205	Zambia	3-6	...	...	...	...	...	...	...	...	...	...	...	...	...	...
206	Zimbabwe	3-5	...	...	...	...	...	...	...	...	...	...	...	...	...	...

Table 3B

GROSS ENROLMENT RATIO (GER) IN PRE-PRIMARY AND OTHER ECCE PROGRAMMES (%)				NET ENROLMENT RATIO (NER) IN PRE-PRIMARY EDUCATION (%)				NEW ENTRANTS TO THE FIRST GRADE OF PRIMARY EDUCATION WITH ECCE EXPERIENCE (%)			
School year ending in 2011				School year ending in 2011				School year ending in 2011			
Total	Male	Female	GPI (F/M)	Total	Male	Female	GPI (F/M)	Total	Male	Female	
83[z]	83[z]	83[z]	0.99[z]	82[z]	82[z]	82[z]	1,00[z]	...	...	...	145
108	104	113	1.09	76	68	85	1.25	.	.	.	146
127	127	127	1,00	97	97	98	1.01	...	...	...	147
95	95	95	1,00	95	95	94	1,00	...	...	...	148
101	100	101	1.01	76	76	76	1,00	...	...	...	149
...	...	...	...	78[z]	76[z]	79[z]	1.04[z]	...	...	...	150
...	...	...	...	64[z]	62[z]	65[z]	1.05[z]	...	...	...	151
										South and West Asia	
...	...	...	...	...	...	...	...	...	...	...	152
26	26	25	0.98	24[*]	24[*]	23[*]	0.98[*]	...	...	...	153
9	**9**	**9**	**0.96**	...	...	...	...	...	...	...	154
55[z]	54[z]	56[z]	1.04[z]	...	...	...	...	...	...	...	155
43	41	45	1.10	...	...	...	...	39	37	41	156
115	113	117	1.04	92	90	94	1.04	91	89	92	157
...	...	...	...	**56**	**55**	**56**	**1.02**	**54**	**53**	**55**	158
...	...	...	...	...	...	...	...	100	100	100	159
...	...	...	...	...	...	...	...	98	97	99	160
										Sub-Saharan Africa	
...	...	...	...	66[*,z]	65[*,z]	67[*,z]	1.04[*,z]	...	...	...	161
20	20	20	1.03	10	10	10	0.99	...	...	...	162
...	...	...	...	15[y]	15[y]	16[y]	1.04[y]	...	...	...	163
...	...	...	...	**3**	**3**	**3**	**1.01**	**7**	**6**	**7**	164
7	7	7	1.02	5	5	6	1.02	7	8	7	165
30	30	30	1.03	21	21	22	1.04	...	...	...	166
74	75	74	1,00	69	69	69	1,00	...	...	...	167
6	6	6	1.02	6	6	6	1.02	...	...	...	168
2	2	2	0.87	2	2	2	0.87	4	4	4	169
...	...	...	...	...	...	...	...	...	...	...	170
13	13	13	0.99	12	12	12	0.98	9[z]	9[z]	10[z]	171
4	4	4	1,00	4[y]	4[y]	4[y]	0.98[y]	...	...	...	172
4	4	4	1.05	4	4	4	1.05	...	...	...	173
74	74	74	1,00	53	53	53	1,00	89	90	89	174
...	...	...	...	10	10	10	0.97	...	...	...	175
5	6	5	0.95	4	5	4	0.95	...	...	...	176
42	41	43	1.04	42	41	43	1.04	...	...	...	177
...	...	...	...	27[z]	27[z]	28[z]	1.04[z]	...	...	...	178
...	...	...	...	**73**[**]	**72**[**]	**75**[**]	**1.04**[**]	**88**	**88**	**88**	179
17	17	17	0.98	12	12	11	0.98	...	...	...	180
...	...	...	...	5[z]	5[z]	5[z]	1.05[z]	...	...	...	181
52[y]	52[y]	52[y]	0.99[y]	29[y]	27[y]	30[y]	1.12[y]	...	...	...	182
...	...	...	...	...	...	...	...	...	...	...	183
...	...	...	...	...	...	...	...	...	...	...	184
10[z]	10[z]	10[z]	1.03[z]	8[z]	8[z]	8[z]	1.03[z]	...	...	...	185
...	...	...	...	...	...	...	...	...	...	...	186
3	3	3	1.05	3[**]	3[**]	3[**]	1.04[**]	16[z]	15[z]	16[z]	187
...	...	...	...	99	100	98	0.98	96	96	97	188
...	...	...	...	...	...	...	...	...	...	...	189
...	...	...	...	...	...	...	...	51[z]	52[z]	51[z]	190
7	**6**	**7**	**1.06**	**5**	**5**	**5**	**1.05**	13[y]	12[y]	14[y]	191
...	...	...	...	...	...	...	...	...	...	...	192
11	11	12	1.05	10[**]	10[**]	11[**]	1.05[**]	...	...	...	193
...	...	...	...	**57**	**55**	**58**	**1.04**	42	38	45	194
14	13	15	1.14	9	9	10	1.15	...	...	...	195
...	...	...	...	88	91	84	0.93	100	100	100	196
...	...	...	...	...	...	...	...	...	...	...	197
...	...	...	...	...	...	...	...	...	...	...	198
88[y]	88[y]	88[y]	1,00[y]	...	...	...	...	...	...	...	199
...	...	...	...	...	...	...	...	...	...	...	200
26	26	26	1.02	19[**]	18[**]	19[**]	1.01[**]	...	...	...	201
13	**13**	**13**	**1.03**	11	11	11	1.02	...	...	...	202
...	...	...	...	14[z]	14[z]	14[z]	1.05[z]	...	...	...	203
35	**35**	**34**	**0.97**	33[z]	33[z]	34[z]	1.02[z]	...	...	...	204
...	...	...	...	...	...	...	...	15	15	15	205
...	...	...	...	...	...	...	...	...	...	...	206

Table 3B (continued)

	Country or territory	Age Group	ENROLMENT IN PRE-PRIMARY EDUCATION				Enrolment in private institutions as % of total enrolment		GROSS ENROLMENT RATIO (GER) IN PRE-PRIMARY EDUCATION (%)							
			School year ending in				School year ending in		School year ending in							
			1999		2011		1999	2011	1999				2011			
		2011	Total (000)	% F	Total (000)	% F			Total	Male	Female	GPI (F/M)	Total	Male	Female	GPI (F/M)
			Sum	% F	Sum	% F	Median		Weighted Average				Weighted Average			
I	World	...	111 980	48	170 008 **	48 **	28	33	33	33	32	0.97	50 **	50 **	50 **	1,00 **
II	Countries in transition	...	7 456	47 **	9 089 **	48 **	.	0.8	46	47 **	45 **	0.94 **	66 **	66 **	65 **	0.98 **
III	Developed countries	...	25 310	49	28 513 **	49 **	8	13	75	76	75	0.99	85 **	84 **	85 **	1.01 **
IV	Developing countries	...	79 214	47	132 406 **	48 **	47	49	27	27	26	0.96	45 **	45 **	45 **	1,00 **
V	Arab States	...	2 408	42	4 142	47 **	88	71	15	17	13	0.77	23	24 **	23 **	0.94 **
VI	Central and Eastern Europe	...	9 443	48	11 448 **	48 **	0.7	2.6	51	52	50	0.96	72 **	72 **	71 **	0.98 **
VII	Central Asia	...	1 272	48	1 713	49	0.6	2.4	19	20	19	0.96	32	32	32	1,00
VIII	East Asia and the Pacific	...	36 812	47	47 603	47	49	54	39	39	39	1,00	62	61	62	1.01
IX	East Asia	...	36 360	47	47 020	47	49	54	39	39	39	1,00	62	61	62	1.01
X	Pacific	...	453 **	49 **	583 **	48 **	...	...	67 **	67 **	67 **	1,00 **	78 **	78 **	78 **	1,00 **
XI	Latin America and the Caribbean	...	16 009	49	20 999	49	34	30	54	54	55	1.02	73	73	73	1.01
XII	Caribbean	...	...	...	...	...	83	80	...	...	...	...	...	...	...	...
XIII	Latin America	...	15 712	49	20 682	49	23	23	55	55	56	1.01	75	74	75	1.01
XIV	North America and Western Europe	...	19 098	48	22 341 **	49 **	27	21	76	77	76	0.98	85 **	85 **	86 **	1.01 **
XV	South and West Asia	...	21 533	46	49 539 **	49 **	...	45	22	22	21	0.93	50 **	49 **	50 **	1.02 **
XVI	Sub-Saharan Africa	...	5 405 **	48 **	12 222 **	50 **	53	55	10 **	10 **	10 **	0.95 **	18 **	18 **	18 **	1,00 **
XVII	Countries with low income	...	5 725 **	49 **	10 743 **	49 **	...	55	11 **	11 **	10 **	0.98 **	17 **	17 **	17 **	0.99 **
XVIII	Countries with middle income	...	80 723	47	129 359 **	48 **	24	27	32	32	31	0.97	54 **	54 **	54 **	1.01 **
XIX	Lower middle	...	30 817	47	65 195 **	49 **	42	32	22	23	21	0.93	46 **	45 **	46 **	1.01 **
XX	Upper middle	...	49 905	48	64 164	47	19	23	43	43	43	1,00	67	66	67	1.02
XXI	Countries with high income	...	25 532	48	29 906 **	49 **	33	34	72	73	72	0.99	82 **	82 **	83 **	1.01 **

Source: UNESCO Institute for Statistics database (UIS) database. Enrolment ratios are based on the United Nations Population Division estimates, revision 2010 (United Nations, 2011), median variant.

Note A: The statistical tables still include data for Sudan (pre-secession) for reference purposes as those for the two new entities since July 2011, Sudan and South Sudan, are just becoming available. The country groupings by income level are as defined by the World Bank. They are based on the list of countries by income group as revised in July 2012.

Note B: The median values for 1999 and 2011 are not comparable since they are not necessarily based on the same number of countries.

1. GER or NER, or both, for one or both of the two school years were not calculated due to inconsistencies in the population data.

2. National population data were used to calculate enrolment ratios.

3. Enrolment and population data exclude Transnistria.

4. Enrolment and population data exclude the Nagorno-Karabakh region.

5. GER or NER, or both, for one or both of the two school years were not calculated due to lack of United Nations population data by age.

6. Data include French overseas departments and territories.

7. Enrolment ratios are based on the United Nations Population Division estimates, revision 2012 (United Nations, 2013), median variant.

Data in bold are for the school year ending in 2012, those in italics are for 2000 and those in bold italic are for 2001.

(z) Data are for the school year ending in 2010.

(y) Data are for the school year ending in 2009.

(*) National estimate.

(**) For country level data: UIS partial estimate; for regional and other country-grouping sums and weighted averages: partial imputation due to incomplete country coverage (between 33% and 60% of population for the region or other country grouping).

- Magnitude nil or negligible.

(.) The category is not applicable or does not exist.

(. . .) No data available.

Table 3B

GROSS ENROLMENT RATIO (GER) IN PRE-PRIMARY AND OTHER ECCE PROGRAMMES (%)				NET ENROLMENT RATIO (NER) IN PRE-PRIMARY EDUCATION (%)				NEW ENTRANTS TO THE FIRST GRADE OF PRIMARY EDUCATION WITH ECCE EXPERIENCE (%)			
School year ending in 2011				School year ending in 2011				School year ending in 2011			
Total	Male	Female	GPI (F/M)	Total	Male	Female	GPI (F/M)	Total	Male	Female	
Weighted Average				Weighted Average				Median			
...	...	...	...	...	...	...	...	...	...	...	I
...	...	...	...	...	...	...	...	...	...	...	II
...	...	...	...	...	...	...	...	...	...	...	III
...	...	...	...	...	...	...	...	...	...	...	IV
...	...	...	...	...	...	...	...	...	...	...	V
...	...	...	...	...	...	...	...	...	...	...	VI
...	...	...	...	...	...	...	...	...	...	...	VII
...	...	...	...	...	...	...	...	...	...	...	VIII
...	...	...	...	...	...	...	...	...	...	...	IX
...	...	...	...	...	...	...	...	...	...	...	X
...	...	...	...	...	...	...	...	88	87	88	XI
...	...	...	...	...	...	...	...	100	100	100	XII
...	...	...	...	...	...	...	...	...	...	...	XIII
...	...	...	...	...	...	...	...	...	...	...	XIV
...	...	...	...	...	...	...	...	91	89	92	XV
...	...	...	...	...	...	...	...	...	...	...	XVI
...	...	...	...	...	...	...	...	...	...	...	XVII
...	...	...	...	...	...	...	...	...	...	...	XVIII
...	...	...	...	...	...	...	...	...	...	...	XIX
...	...	...	...	...	...	...	...	...	...	...	XX
...	...	...	...	...	...	...	...	...	...	...	XXI

Table 4
Access to primary education

Country or territory	Compulsory education (age group)[1]	Official primary school entry age	New entrants (000)		GROSS INTAKE RATE (GIR) IN PRIMARY EDUCATION (%)							
			School year ending in		School year ending in							
		2011	1999	2011	1999				2011			
					Total	Male	Female	GPI (F/M)	Total	Male	Female	GPI (F/M)
Arab States												
Algeria	6-16	6	745	664	101	102	100	0.98	103	104	102	0.98
Bahrain[2]	6-15	6	13	16	108	106	110	1.03	...	...	...	...
Djibouti	6-16	6	6	**12**	29	33	24	0.74	**58**	**61**	**55**	**0.90**
Egypt	6-14	6	1 451[**]	1 799	90[**]	92[**]	88[**]	0.96[**]	105	106	104	0.98
Iraq	6-12	6	709[**]	...	107[**]	113[**]	101[**]	0.89[**]	...	...	...	...
Jordan	6-16	6	126	146[z]	100	100	101	1,00	96[z]	97[z]	96[z]	0.99[z]
Kuwait[2]	6-14	6	35	49	104	103	105	1.01	...	...	...	...
Lebanon	6-12	6	75[**]	72	99[**]	102[**]	95[**]	0.93[**]	112	113	111	0.98
Libya	6-15	6	...	...	...	...	...	...	...	...	...	...
Mauritania	6-14	6	***73***	102	***96***	***96***	***95***	***0.99***	109	106	112	1.05
Morocco	6-15	6	731	**626**	112	115	108	0.94	**108**	**108**	**107**	**0.99**
Oman	.	6	52	53	88	87	88	1.02	104	106	101	0.95
Palestine	6-16	6	95	108	95	95	95	1,00	95	96	95	0.98
Qatar	6-18	6	11[**]	18	108[**]	107[**]	109[**]	1.02[**]	110	110	109	0.99
Saudi Arabia	6-11	6	...	570	...	...	...	...	101	100	101	1.01
Sudan	6-13	6	...	728[z]	...	...	...	...	...	...	...	...
Syrian Arab Republic	6-12	6	466	633	109	113	106	0.94	122	121	123	1.02
Tunisia	6-16	6	204	169	102	103	101	0.98	107	107	106	0.99
United Arab Emirates[3]	6-14	6	47	77	95	96	94	0.99	110	110	110	1,00
Yemen	6-15	6	440	747	76	89	63	0.71	105	111	98	0.88
Sudan (pre-secession)	6-14	6	*447*	915[y]	*47*	*51*	*42*	*0.81*	79[y]	83[**,y]	75[**,y]	0.91[**,y]
Central and Eastern Europe												
Albania[2]	6-14	6	*66*	39	*105*	*106*	*104*	*0.98*	...	...	...	...
Belarus[2]	6-15	6	173	88	130	131	130	0.99	96	96	96	1,00
Bosnia and Herzegovina	6-14	6	...	34	...	...	...	...	97	97	97	1,00
Bulgaria	7-16	7	93	63[z]	101	102	100	0.98	98[z]	98[z]	98[z]	0.99[z]
Croatia	6-15	7	50	39[z]	94	95	93	0.98	92[z]	92[z]	92[z]	1,00[z]
Czech Republic	6-15	6	124	96	100	101	99	0.98	104	103	104	1.01
Estonia	7-17	7	18	12[z]	97	98	97	0.99	98[z]	98[z]	99[z]	1.01[z]
Hungary	6-18	7	127	94	104	106	102	0.97	99	99	98	0.99
Latvia	7-16	7	32	19	96	96[**]	95[**]	0.99[**]	97	98	95	0.98
Lithuania	6-16	7	54	28	104	104	103	0.99	94	95	93	0.98
Montenegro	6-15	6	***9***	***7***	***104***	***106***	***103***	***0.97***	**92**	**93**	**91**	**0.98**
Poland	6-18	7	535	356[y]	101	...	...	...	99[y]	99[y]	99[y]	1,00[y]
Republic of Moldova[4,5]	7-16	7	62	35	105	105[**]	104[**]	1,00[**]	97	97	97	1,00
Romania	6-16	7	269	202[z]	89	90	89	0.99	94[z]	94[z]	94[z]	0.99[z]
Russian Federation	6-18	7	1 866	1 322[y]	93	...	...	...	102[y]	...	...	...
Serbia[4]	7-15	7	...	74	...	...	...	...	94	94	94	1,00
Slovakia	6-16	6	75	51	98	98	97	0.99	99	99	99	1,00
Slovenia	6-15	6	21	18	97	97	96	0.99	100	99	101	1.02
The former Yugoslav Rep. of Macedonia	6-19	6	32	23[z]	103	103	103	1,00	98[z]	97[z]	100[z]	1.03[z]
Turkey	6-14	6	...	1 332[z]	...	...	...	...	107[z]	107[z]	106[z]	0.99[z]
Ukraine	6-17	6	...	411	...	...	...	...	103	102	103	1.01
Central Asia												
Armenia[2]	7-16	6	...	37	...	...	...	...	...	...	...	...
Azerbaijan[4,6]	6-16	6	175	120	100	99	101	1.02	99	100	98	0.99
Georgia	6-12	6	74	51	96	96	96	1,00	111	110	112	1.02
Kazakhstan	7-18	7	*303*[**]	**273**	*101*[**]	*100*[**]	*103*[**]	*1.02*[**]	**111**	**111**	**111**	**0.99**
Kyrgyzstan	7-16	7	120[*]	102	99[*]	98[*]	99[*]	1.02[*]	107	108	105	0.98
Mongolia	6-15	6	70	47	108	110	107	0.97	104	106	103	0.97
Tajikistan	7-18	7	177	161	98	100	95	0.95	97	99	95	0.96
Turkmenistan	7-17	7	...	...	...	...	...	...	...	...	...	...
Uzbekistan	7-19	7	677	482	102	101[**]	103[**]	1.01[**]	96	97	94	0.96
East Asia and the Pacific												
Australia	6-17	5	...	...	...	...	...	...	...	...	...	...
Brunei Darussalam	6-15	6	8	7	112	113	111	0.99	97	97	97	1,00
Cambodia	6-15	6	397	395	110	113	107	0.95	137	140	134	0.95
China[7]	6-15	7	***19 598***	16 966	***93***	...	...	...	101	99	104	1.06
Cook Islands[4]	5-16	5	0.6	0.3	131[*]	...	...	...	121	116	127	1.09
Democratic People's Republic of Korea	5-16	7	...	...	...	...	...	...	...	...	...	...
Fiji	6-15	6	21	17	108	108	107	0.99	103	103	103	1,00
Indonesia	7-15	7	*4 755*[**]	5 406	*108*[**]	*112*[**]	*104*[**]	*0.93*[**]	122	121	124	1.02
Japan	6-15	6	1 222	1 149[z]	101	101	101	1,00	102[z]	102[z]	102[z]	1,00[z]
Kiribati	6-14	6	3	...	117	114	120	1.05	...	...	...	...
Lao People's Democratic Republic	6-10	6	180	178	116	122	109	0.89	128	130	125	0.97
Macao, China	5-15	6	6	...	89	87	90	1.04	...	...	...	...
Malaysia[2]	6-11	6	509	461[z]	97	98	97	0.99	...	...	...	...
Marshall Islands	6-14	6	1	2	100	96	103	1.07	100	102	99	0.97
Micronesia (Federated States of)	6-14	6	...	...	...	...	...	...	...	...	...	...
Myanmar	5-9	5	1 226	1 196[z]	133	132	135	1.02	152[z]	152[z]	151[z]	0.99[z]
Nauru[4]	6-16	6	***0.3***	...	***118***	***124***	***111***	***0.89***	...	...	...	...
New Zealand	6-16	5	...	...	...	...	...	...	...	...	...	...
Niue[4]	5-16	5	0.05	...	105	79	137	1.73	...	...	...	...
Palau[4]	6-17	6	*0.4*	...	*117*	*116*	*118*	*1.01*	...	...	...	...

Table 4

NET INTAKE RATE (NIR) IN PRIMARY EDUCATION (%)								SCHOOL LIFE EXPECTANCY (expected number of years of formal schooling from primary to tertiary education)						
School year ending in								School year ending in						
1999				2011				1999			2011			
Total	Male	Female	GPI (F/M)	Total	Male	Female	GPI (F/M)	Total	Male	Female	Total	Male	Female	Country or territory
														Arab States
77	78	76	0.97	88	89	87	0.98	11.0 **	...	...	14.1	13.8	14.3	Algeria
86	84	88	1.05	...	...	...	...	13.2	12.7 **	13.9 **	...	...	...	Bahrain[2]
21	24	18	0.75	**45**	**47**	**42**	**0.89**	3.0	3.5	2.5	5.7	6.2	5.3	Djibouti
...	...	...	...	89 **, z	90 **, z	88 **, z	0.98 **, z	11.3 **	...	...	12.4 **, z	12.7 **, z	12.1 **, z	Egypt
83 **	86 **	79 **	0.91 **	...	...	...	...	8.5 **	9.7 **	7.3 **	...	...	...	Iraq
67 **	66 **	68 **	1.02 **	...	...	...	...	...	...	...	12.7 z	12.4 z	12.9 z	Jordan
66	67	65	0.97	...	...	...	...	14.6 **	14.1 **	15.3 **	...	...	...	Kuwait[2]
73 **	74 **	71 **	0.96 **	71	73	70	0.96	12.7 **	12.6 **	12.8 **	14.4	14.0	14.8	Lebanon
...	...	...	...	...	...	...	...	...	...	...	...	...	...	Libya
29	***29***	***29***	***0.99***	37	37	38	1.04	6.7 **	...	...	8.2 **	8.3 **	8.1 **	Mauritania
50	52	48	0.93	**73**	**74**	**73**	**0.99**	8.0 **	8.9 **	7.1 **	11.2 **, z	11.7 **, z	10.6 **, z	Morocco
71	70	72	1.03	76	77	74	0.95	...	...	...	13.8	13.6	14.1	Oman
...	...	...	...	78	80	76	0.95	11.6	11.6	11.5	13.4	12.6	14.1	Palestine
...	...	...	...	66	65	67	1.03	12.9 **	11.9 **	14.0 **	12.9	12.3	14.2	Qatar
...	...	...	...	80	80	80	1.01	...	...	...	14.9 **	15.2 **	14.6 **	Saudi Arabia
...	...	...	...	...	...	...	...	...	...	...	...	...	...	Sudan
62	62	61	0.98	...	...	...	...	...	...	...	...	...	...	Syrian Arab Republic
...	...	...	...	91	92	91	0.98	13.0 **	13.3 **	12.7 **	14.9	14.5	15.3	Tunisia
49	49	50	1.01	51	51	50	0.98	...	...	...	10.8	...	...	United Arab Emirates[3]
25	30	20	0.68	45	49	42	0.87	7.5 **	10.2 **	4.7 **	...	...	...	Yemen
...	...	...	...	...	...	...	...	4.5 **	...	...	...	...	...	Sudan (pre-secession)
														Central and Eastern Europe
...	...	...	...	...	...	...	...	10.9 **	11.0 **	10.9 **	...	...	...	Albania[2]
76	76	76	0.99	...	...	...	...	...	...	...	15.3	14.7 *	15.8 *	Belarus[2]
...	...	...	...	84	83	84	1.02	...	...	...	13.6 **	13.2 **	14.0 **	Bosnia and Herzegovina
...	...	...	...	...	...	...	...	13.0	12.6	13.4	14.0 z	13.8 z	14.2 z	Bulgaria
68	69	67	0.96	...	...	...	...	12.0	11.9	12.2	14.1 z	13.5 z	14.8 z	Croatia
...	...	...	...	...	...	...	...	13.2	13.1 **	13.2 **	16.0 **	15.5 **	16.5 **	Czech Republic
...	...	...	...	...	...	...	...	14.3	13.8	14.9	16.0 z	15.1 z	16.9 z	Estonia
...	...	...	...	...	...	...	...	13.9	13.7	14.1	15.4	15.1	15.6	Hungary
...	...	...	...	...	...	...	...	13.6 **	12.9 **	14.3 **	14.5	13.9	15.2	Latvia
...	...	...	...	...	...	...	...	13.9	13.5	14.4	15.5	14.8	16.1	Lithuania
...	...	...	...	...	...	...	...	...	...	...	15.0 **, z	14.7 z	15.2 z	Montenegro
...	...	...	...	...	...	...	...	14.7	14.3	15.1	15.4 z	14.7 z	16.1 z	Poland
...	...	...	...	76	77	75	0.97	11.4	11.3	11.6	11.9	11.5	12.2	Republic of Moldova[4,5]
...	...	...	...	69 y	70 y	68 y	0.97 y	11.7	11.6	11.8	14.5 z	14.0 z	15.0 z	Romania
...	...	...	...	...	...	...	...	12.1 **	...	...	14.3 y	13.8 y	14.8 y	Russian Federation
...	...	...	...	89	89	89	1,00	...	...	...	13.6	13.2	14.0	Serbia[4]
...	...	...	...	...	...	...	...	12.9	12.7	13.0	14.7 **	14.2 **	15.3 **	Slovakia
...	...	...	...	...	...	...	...	14.6	14.1	15.1	16.9	16.0	17.9	Slovenia
...	...	...	...	85 y	85 y	86 y	1.01 y	11.8	11.8	11.8	13.4 z	13.2 z	13.6 z	The former Yugoslav Rep. of Macedonia
...	...	...	...	...	...	...	...	10.6 **	11.8 **	9.3 **	13.8 **, z	14.3 **, z	13.2 **, z	Turkey
...	...	...	...	...	...	...	...	12.8 **	12.6 **	13.0 **	14.8	14.6 *	15.0 *	Ukraine
														Central Asia
...	...	...	...	...	...	...	...	11.1	...	...	12.2 **, z	11.7 **, z	12.6 **, z	Armenia[2]
...	...	...	...	76	77	75	0.97	...	...	...	11.8	11.9	11.6	Azerbaijan[4,6]
...	...	...	...	88	88	89	1.02	11.4 **	11.4 **	11.4 **	13.2 y	...	...	Georgia
66 **	*66* **	*66* **	*1,00* **	...	...	...	...	12.1	11.9	12.3	**15.4**	**15.1**	**15.8**	Kazakhstan
58 *	58 *	58 *	0.99 *	61 *	63 *	60 *	0.95 *	11.4 **	11.3 **	11.6 **	12.5 *	12.3 *	12.7 *	Kyrgyzstan
81	82	79	0.97	87	87	86	0.99	8.9 **	8.0 **	9.7 **	14.5	13.8	15.1	Mongolia
84	87	82	0.95	...	...	...	...	9.7	10.5	8.9	11.5	12.4	10.6	Tajikistan
...	...	...	...	...	...	...	...	...	...	...	...	...	...	Turkmenistan
...	...	...	...	77 y	79 y	76 y	0.96 y	10.6	10.7	10.5	11.6 **	11.8 **	11.4 **	Uzbekistan
														East Asia and the Pacific
...	...	...	...	...	...	...	...	20.3 **	20.0 **	20.6 **	19.6 z	19.2 z	20.0 z	Australia
...	...	...	...	67 z	66 z	68 z	1.03 z	13.7	13.5	14.0	15.1	14.8	15.5	Brunei Darussalam
65	66	64	0.97	90 z	90 z	91 z	1.01 z	...	...	...	...	...	...	Cambodia
...	...	...	...	...	...	...	...	***10.1*** **	...	...	11.9	11.6	12.2	China[7]
...	...	...	...	80 z	82 z	77 z	0.94 z	10.6	10.5	10.6	12.5	11.9	13.1	Cook Islands[4]
...	...	...	...	...	...	...	...	...	...	...	...	...	...	Democratic People's Republic of Korea
72	72	73	1.02	77	76	77	1.02	...	...	...	15.7	...	...	Fiji
...	...	...	...	45 y	43 y	46 y	1.07 y	*10.3* **	*10.5* **	*10.1* **	13.2	13.2	13.1	Indonesia
...	...	...	...	...	...	...	...	14.5 **	14.7 **	14.3 **	15.3 z	15.5 z	15.1 z	Japan
...	...	...	...	...	...	...	...	10.0 **	9.6 **	10.4 **	...	...	...	Kiribati
52	53	51	0.96	91	91	91	0.99	8.2	9.2	7.2	10.5	11.1	9.9	Lao People's Democratic Republic
63	60	66	1.10	...	...	...	...	12.4	12.7	12.2	...	...	...	Macao, China
...	...	...	...	...	...	...	...	11.6	11.5	11.8	...	...	...	Malaysia[2]
...	...	...	...	99	100	97	0.97	...	...	...	...	...	...	Marshall Islands
...	...	...	...	...	...	...	...	...	...	...	...	...	...	Micronesia (Federated States of)
...	...	...	...	...	...	...	...	...	...	...	...	...	...	Myanmar
...	...	...	...	...	...	...	...	*8.8*	*7.8*	*9.9*	...	...	...	Nauru[4]
...	...	...	...	...	...	...	...	17.2 **	16.6 **	17.9 **	19.7 z	18.8 z	20.5 z	New Zealand
...	...	...	...	...	...	...	...	11.9	11.5	12.4	...	...	...	Niue[4]
...	...	...	...	...	...	...	...	*13.7* **	*12.9* **	*14.6* **	...	...	...	Palau[4]

Table 4 (continued)

Country or territory	Compulsory education (age group)[1]	Official primary school entry age	New entrants (000)		GROSS INTAKE RATE (GIR) IN PRIMARY EDUCATION (%)							
			School year ending in		School year ending in							
		2011	1999	2011	1999				2011			
					Total	Male	Female	GPI (F/M)	Total	Male	Female	GPI (F/M)
Portugal	6-18	6	...	112 [z]	...	...	...	...	101 [z]	100 [z]	102 [z]	1.01 [z]
San Marino[4,8]	6-16	6	*0.3*	0.3	...	...	...	...	90	91	89	0.99
Spain	6-16	6	411	473	107	107	107	1,00	100	100	100	1,00
Sweden	7-16	7	127	102	105	106	104	0.98	101	101	101	1,00
Switzerland	6-16	7	82	72	97	95	99	1.04	96	95	98	1.04
United Kingdom	5-16	5	...	...	...	...	...	...	...	...	...	...
United States	5-18	6	4 322	4 138 [z]	107	110	104	0.95	100 [z]	101 [z]	98 [z]	0.97 [z]
South and West Asia												
Afghanistan	7-16	7	...	1 126	...	...	...	...	116	133	98	0.74
Bangladesh[3]	6-10	6	...	4 120 [*]	...	...	...	...	130 [*]	130 [*]	130 [*]	1,00 [*]
Bhutan	.	6	12	**13**	79	83	74	0.89	**89**	**90**	**87**	**0.97**
India	6-14	6	29 639	29 951 [z]	121	130	111	0.86	120 [z]	121 [z]	120 [z]	0.99 [z]
Iran, Islamic Republic of	6-14	6	1 563	1 177	98	99	97	0.98	108	109	108	0.99
Maldives	...	6	8	5	103	102	104	1.02	102	105	100	0.95
Nepal[3]	.	5	879	**1 034**	144	163	123	0.75	**154**	**150**	**159**	**1.06**
Pakistan	5-16	5	...	4 315	...	...	...	...	111	120	102	0.85
Sri Lanka	5-14	5	***330***	347	***103***	***103***	***103***	***1,00***	93	94	93	0.99
Sub-Saharan Africa												
Angola	6-14	6	...	1 029 [*,z]	...	...	...	...	165 [*,z]	182 [*,z]	148 [*,z]	0.82 [*,z]
Benin[2]	6-11	6	*205* [**]	399	*104* [**]	*119* [**]	*89* [**]	*0.75* [**]	153	161	145	0.90
Botswana	6-15	6	50	47 [**,y]	113	114	112	0.99	111 [**,y]	114 [**,y]	108 [**,y]	0.95 [**,y]
Burkina Faso	6-16	6	154	**470**	44	51	36	0.72	**91**	**94**	**88**	**0.94**
Burundi	...	7	138	339	70	78	63	0.81	167	169	165	0.98
Cameroon	6-11	6	335 [**]	727	75 [**]	83 [**]	67 [**]	0.81 [**]	135	143	126	0.88
Cape Verde	6-11	6	13 [**]	10	105 [**]	107 [**]	104 [**]	0.97 [**]	97	98	96	0.98
Central African Republic	6-15	6	...	116	...	...	...	...	96	108	85	0.79
Chad	6-16	6	175	468	73	86	61	0.71	135	151	119	0.79
Comoros	6-14	6	13	25	93	102	85	0.84	117	117	116	0.99
Congo	6-16	6	32	119 [z]	39	38	39	1.03	109 [z]	109 [z]	108 [z]	0.99 [z]
Côte d'Ivoire	6-15	6	309	458	68	75	60	0.80	83	88	78	0.88
Democratic Rep. of the Congo	6-15	6	767	2 526	49	48	51	1.08	121	127	115	0.90
Equatorial Guinea	7-12	7	...	17	...	...	...	...	94	96	92	0.96
Eritrea	6--10	7	57	77	54	60	49	0.81	53	57	48	0.85
Ethiopia	.	7	1 537	3 645	81	96	66	0.69	157	168	146	0.87
Gabon	6-16	6	***33***	...	***92***	***93***	***92***	***0.99***	...	...	...	...
Gambia	...	7	36 [**]	47	98 [**]	103 [**]	93 [**]	0.91 [**]	93	92	94	1.02
Ghana	4-15	6	469	**721**	90	91	88	0.97	**110**	**110**	**111**	**1.01**
Guinea	7-16	7	119	**314**	50	56	44	0.80	**109**	**116**	**102**	**0.88**
Guinea-Bissau	7-13	7	35 [**]	67 [z]	105 [**]	120 [**]	90 [**]	0.75 [**]	166 [z]	169 [z]	164 [z]	0.97 [z]
Kenya	...	6	892	...	99	101	98	0.97	...	...	...	...
Lesotho	.	6	51	53 [**]	95	95	96	1.01	99 [**]	103 [**]	95 [**]	0.93 [**]
Liberia	6-16	6	...	152	...	...	...	...	127	132	123	0.93
Madagascar	6-10	6	495	1 111	110	111	109	0.98	184	185	184	1,00
Malawi	6-13	6	616	716	178	177	180	1.02	158	155	161	1.04
Mali	6-15	7	171 [**]	374	53 [**]	60 [**]	46 [**]	0.77 [**]	79	82	76	0.92
Mauritius[3]	5-16	5	22	18	...	...	...	...	107	108	107	1,00
Mozambique	6-12	6	536	**1 227**	102	111	94	0.84	**164**	**168**	**160**	**0.95**
Namibia	7-16	7	54	53 [z]	106	105	108	1.03	95 [z]	95 [z]	96 [z]	1.01 [z]
Niger	4-16	7	133	**475**	42	49	35	0.71	**93**	**97**	**88**	**0.91**
Nigeria	6-15	6	3 606 [**]	3 974 [z]	105 [**]	116 [**]	94 [**]	0.81 [**]	88 [z]	93 [z]	83 [z]	0.89 [z]
Rwanda	7-12	7	295	574	137	138	135	0.98	192	194	191	0.98
Sao Tome and Principe	6-11	6	4	**5**	108	109	106	0.97	**117**	**117**	**117**	**1.01**
Senegal	6-16	7	190	373	70	...	...	...	104	100	109	1.09
Seychelles	6-16	6	2	1	115	116	115	0.99	106	105	106	1.01
Sierra Leone	6-15	6	*99*	218	*87*	*90*	*84*	*0.93*	127	133	121	0.91
Somalia	...	6	...	...	...	...	...	...	...	...	...	...
South Africa	7-15	7	1 157	926 [y]	115	117	114	0.97	91 [y]	94 [y]	88 [y]	0.94 [y]
South Sudan	...	6	...	348	...	...	...	...	...	...	...	...
Swaziland	.	6	31	31	94	96	93	0.97	104	109	99	0.91
Togo	6-15	6	139	238	104	111	97	0.88	147	151	143	0.95
Uganda[10]	6-12	6	*1 437*	1 636	*180*	*182*	*177*	*0.98*	143	142	144	1.02
United Republic of Tanzania	7-13	7	714	**1 312**	73	74	73	0.99	**93**	**93**	**94**	**1.01**
Zambia	7-13	7	252	494	87	87	87	1.01	122	121	124	1.03
Zimbabwe	6-12	6	...	...	...	...	...	...	...	...	...	...

Table 4

NET INTAKE RATE (NIR) IN PRIMARY EDUCATION (%)								SCHOOL LIFE EXPECTANCY (expected number of years of formal schooling from primary to tertiary education)						
School year ending in								School year ending in						
1999				2011				1999			2011			
Total	Male	Female	GPI (F/M)	Total	Male	Female	GPI (F/M)	Total	Male	Female	Total	Male	Female	Country or territory
…	…	…	…	96 z	95 z	97 z	1.02 z	15.4	15.0	15.7	16.2 z	16.0 z	16.4 z	Portugal
…	…	…	…	86 **,z	87 **,z	84 **,z	0.96 **,z	…	…	…	15.4 **	14.8 **	16.1 **	San Marino[4,8]
…	…	…	…	98	98	98	1.01	15.9	15.5	16.2	17.1	16.8	17.5	Spain
…	…	…	…	98	98	98	1,00	18.9	17.3	20.5	15.9	15.1	16.6	Sweden
…	…	…	…	…	…	…	…	15.1	15.5	14.6	15.8	15.9	15.7	Switzerland
…	…	…	…	…	…	…	…	15.9 **	15.7 **	16.1 **	16.7 z	16.3 z	17.2 z	United Kingdom
…	…	…	…	75 z	75 z	75 z	1,00 z	15.7	…	…	16.8 z	15.9 z	17.6 z	United States
														South and West Asia
…	…	…	…	…	…	…	…	***1.9*** **	…	…	8.1 y	10.1 y	6.1 y	Afghanistan
…	…	…	…	92 *,z	92 *,z	93 *,z	1.01 *,z	…	…	…	10.0 **	9.7 **	10.3 **	Bangladesh[3]
20 **	21 **	19 **	0.90 **	…	…	…	…	7.2 **	8.0 **	6.5 **	12.4	12.3	12.4	Bhutan
…	…	…	…	…	…	…	…	…	…	…	10.9 z	11.2 **,z	10.5 **,z	India
…	…	…	…	82	87	76	0.87	11.9 **	12.5 **	11.2 **	13.8 **	13.9 **	13.7 **	Iran, Islamic Republic of
…	…	…	…	72 z	74 z	70 z	0.95 z	11.6 **	11.6 **	11.7 **	…	…	…	Maldives
…	…	…	…	…	…	…	…	*9.3* **	*10.8* **	*7.9* **	12.4 **	12.2 **	12.5 **	Nepal[3]
…	…	…	…	…	…	…	…	…	…	…	7.5 *	8.3 *	6.6 *	Pakistan
95 **	***95*** **	***95*** **	***1,00*** **	…	…	…	…	…	…	…	13.8	13.5	14.2	Sri Lanka
														Sub-Saharan Africa
…	…	…	…	64 *,z	71 *,z	57 *,z	0.81 *,z	…	…	…	10.2 **,z	11.5 **,z	9.0 **,z	Angola
…	…	…	…	56	61	52	0.85	6.8 **	8.7 **	4.9 **	…	…	…	Benin[2]
22	20	24	1.20	…	…	…	…	11.5 **	11.5 **	11.6 **	…	…	…	Botswana
19	22	15	0.71	**27**	**28**	**27**	**0.96**	3.2	3.8	2.6	6.9	7.4	6.4	Burkina Faso
…	…	…	…	68 y	68 y	67 y	0.99 y	…	…	…	11.3 **,z	11.8 **,z	10.9 **,z	Burundi
…	…	…	…	59 y	63 y	55 y	0.88 y	7.2 **	…	…	11.5	12.4	10.6	Cameroon
68 **	67 **	69 **	1.02 **	95	95	94	0.98	…	…	…	13.0 **	12.6 **	13.4 **	Cape Verde
…	…	…	…	41 z	45 z	37 z	0.84 z	***5.6*** **	…	…	7.2 **	…	…	Central African Republic
22	26	19	0.72	57	63	51	0.81	…	…	…	8.2 **	9.9 **	6.4 **	Chad
21	24 **	17 **	0.70 **	…	…	…	…	8.1	8.9	7.4	…	…	…	Comoros
…				51 *,z	52 *,z	51 *,z	1,00 *,z	…	…	…	…	…	…	Congo
28	31	25	0.79	…	…	…	…	6.5 **	7.8 **	5.2 **	…	…	…	Côte d'Ivoire
22	21	23	1.10	58	61	55	0.90	…	…	…	8.5	9.7	7.3	Democratic Rep. of the Congo
…	…	…	…	31	33	30	0.90	*8.5* **	*9.6* **	*7.4* **	…	…	…	Equatorial Guinea
17	18	16	0.89	20 **	22 **	18 **	0.84 **	4.1 **	4.7 **	3.5 **	4.6 z	5.2 z	4.1 z	Eritrea
21	23	19	0.80	82	85	79	0.92	4.1 **	5.1 **	3.1 **	9.1 **	9.7 **	8.4 **	Ethiopia
…	…	…	…	…	…	…	…	12.1	12.4	11.7	…	…	…	Gabon
…	…	…	…	…	…	…	…	…	…	…	…	…	…	Gambia
30 **	30 **	31 **	1.01 **	39 **,y	38 **,y	39 **,y	1.04 **,y	7.6 **	8.2 **	7.0 **	**11.6** **	**12.2** **	**11.0** **	Ghana
19	20	18	0.87	**54**	**57**	**51**	**0.89**	…	…	…	9.5 **	10.8 **	8.1 **	Guinea
…	…	…	…	42 z	43 z	41 z	0.96 z	…	…	…	…	…	…	Guinea-Bissau
28 **	27 **	29 **	1.08 **	…	…	…	…	…	…	…	11.1 **,y	11.4 **,y	10.7 **,y	Kenya
25	24	26	1.06	58 **	59 **	57 **	0.97 **	9.0 **	8.5 **	9.5 **	…	…	…	Lesotho
…	…	…	…	7	7	7	0.96	8.6 **	10.2 **	7.0 **	…	…	…	Liberia
…	…	…	…	…	…	…	…	…	…	…	10.4 **,y	10.7 **,y	10.2 **,y	Madagascar
…	…	…	…	78	76	81	1.06	11.2 **	11.9 **	10.5 **	10.8 **	10.8 **	10.9 **	Malawi
…	…	…	…	20	21	19	0.90	4.2 **	5.0 **	3.4 **	7.5	8.3	6.7	Mali
…	…	…	…	87	87	86	1,00	…	…	…	…	…	…	Mauritius[3]
18	18	17	0.93	**68**	**69**	**68**	**0.99**	5.4 **	6.3 **	4.5 **	9.7	10.3	9.1	Mozambique
60	59	62	1.06	51 **,z	49 **,z	54 **,z	1.09 **,z	11.6 **	11.4 **	11.7 **	…	…	…	Namibia
27	31	21	0.68	**64**	**68**	**60**	**0.89**	…	…	…	5.3	5.9	4.6	Niger
…	…	…	…	…	…	…	…	7.5 **	8.2 **	6.8 **	…	…	…	Nigeria
…	…	…	…	…	…	…	…	6.7	…	…	11.1 **	11.0 **	11.2 **	Rwanda
…	…	…	…	…	…	…	…	…	…	…	10.8 z	10.8 z	10.8 z	Sao Tome and Principe
39	…	…	…	…	…	…	…	5.4	…	…	8.2 *,z	8.3 **,z	8.0 **,z	Senegal
…	…	…	…	75	75	76	1.01	13.4	13.2	13.6	13.2	12.7	13.6	Seychelles
…	…	…	…	…	…	…	…	…	…	…	…	…	…	Sierra Leone
…	…	…	…	…	…	…	…	…	…	…	…	…	…	Somalia
43	44	42	0.95	…	…	…	…	…	…	…	…	…	…	South Africa
…	…	…	…	…	…	…	…	…	…	…	…	…	…	South Sudan
40	38	41	1.07	40	40	41	1.04	9.4	9.7	9.2	11.3 **	11.8 **	10.9 **	Swaziland
42	45	39	0.87	…	…	…	…	…	…	…	12.9 **	…	…	Togo
…	…	…	…	66	65	66	1.03	*10.7* **	*11.3* **	*10.2* **	11.1 **,y	11.3 **,y	10.8 **,y	Uganda[10]
14	13	15	1.16	…	…	…	…	…	…	…	**9.2** **	**9.4** **	**9.1** **	United Republic of Tanzania
39	37	40	1.07	53 **	52 **	55 **	1.06 **	…	…	…	…	…	…	Zambia
…	…	…	…	…	…	…	…	…	…	…	…	…	…	Zimbabwe

Table 5
Participation in primary education

		Age Group	School-age population (000)	ENROLMENT IN PRIMARY EDUCATION				Enrolment in private institutions as % of total enrolment		GROSS ENROLMENT RATIO (GER) IN PRIMARY EDUCATION (%)			
				School year ending in				School year ending in		School year ending in			
				1999		2011		1999	2011	1999			
	Country or territory	2011	2011[1]	Total (000)	% F	Total (000)	% F			Total	Male	Female	GPI (F/M)
	Arab States												
1	Algeria	6-10	3 086	4 779	47	3 363	47	.	0.5	106	110	101	0.91
2	Bahrain[3]	6-11	...	76	49	93	49	19	32	107	107	107	1,00
3	Djibouti	6-10	103	38	41	**64**	**47**	9	**11**	33	39	27	0.71
4	Egypt	6-11	10 033	8 086 **	47 **	10 266	47	...	...	98 **	102 **	93 **	0.91 **
5	Iraq	6-11	5 237	3 604	44	...	...	.	...	97	105	88	0.83
6	Jordan	6-11	914	706	49	820 [z]	49 [z]	29	33 [z]	96	95	96	1.01
7	Kuwait[3]	6-10	...	140	49	224	49	32	41	106	105	107	1.02
8	Lebanon	6-11	424	414 **	48 **	457	48	67 **	74	112 **	115 **	110 **	0.96 **
9	Libya	6-11	750	822	48	...	...	.	...	122	123	121	0.99
10	Mauritania	6-11	531	346	48	536	51	2	11	84	85	83	0.97
11	Morocco	6-11	3 518	3 462	44	**4 017**	**48**	4	**13**	87	95	78	0.82
12	Oman	6-11	285	316	48	296	49	5	17	89	89	88	0.99
13	Palestine	6-9	447	368	49	411	49	9	12	100	100	100	1,00
14	Qatar	6-11	91	61	48	95	49	37	57	104	102	107	1.05
15	Saudi Arabia	6-11	3 158	...	...	3 348	49	...	10	...	...	...	...
16	Sudan	6-11	...	...	...	4 024 [z]	47 [z]	...	5 [z]	...	...	...	...
17	Syrian Arab Republic	6-9	2 064	2 738	47	2 507	48	4	4	108	113	104	0.92
18	Tunisia	6-11	936	1 443	47	1 028	48	1	2	115	119	111	0.93
19	United Arab Emirates[4]	6-10	302	270	48	335	49	44	72	94	95	94	0.99
20	Yemen	6-11	4 019	2 303	35	3 641	44	1	5	72	92	51	0.56
21	Sudan (pre-secession)	6-11	6 794	2 513 **	45 **	4 744 [y]	46 [y]	2 **	4 [y]	48 **	52 **	44 **	0.85 **
	Central and Eastern Europe												
22	Albania[3]	6-10	...	292	48	216	47	...	5	109	110	108	0.98
23	Belarus	6-9	360	***561***	***48***	354	49	***0.1***	0.1	***111***	***112***	***111***	***0.99***
24	Bosnia and Herzegovina	6-10	189	...	...	171	49	...	2	...	...	...	...
25	Bulgaria	7-10	257	412	48	260 [z]	48 [z]	0.3	0.8 [z]	104	106	103	0.97
26	Croatia	7-10	173	203	49	167 [z]	49 [z]	0.1	0.3 [z]	93	94	92	0.98
27	Czech Republic	6-10	447	655	49	468	49	0.8	2	103	103	102	0.99
28	Estonia	7-12	75	127	48	73 [z]	48 [z]	1.3	4 [z]	99	101	97	0.97
29	Hungary	7-10	383	503	48	387	48	5	9	102	103	101	0.98
30	Latvia	7-12	114	141	48	114	49	1.0	1	95	97	94	0.97
31	Lithuania	7-10	123	220	48	116	48	0.4	1	101	102	100	0.98
32	Montenegro	6-10	41	...	...	**38**	**48**	...	**.**	...	...	...	...
33	Poland	7-12	2 189	3 434	48	2 235 [z]	49 [z]	...	3 [z]	100	101	98	0.97
34	Republic of Moldova[5,6]	7-10	148 *	*252*	*49*	138	48	...	0.9	*101*	*102*	*101*	*0.99*
35	Romania	7-10	860	1 285	49	842 [z]	48 [z]	-	0.3 [z]	96	97	95	0.98
36	Russian Federation[7]	7-10	5 306	6 743	49	5 015 [y]	49 [y]	...	0.6 [y]	103	104	103	0.99
37	Serbia[5]	7-10	304 *	387 **	49 **	289	49	...	0.1	112 **	112 **	111 **	0.99 **
38	Slovakia	6-9	209	317	49	209	49	4	6	99	99	98	0.98
39	Slovenia	6-11	108	92	48	107	49	0.1	0.4	98	99	98	0.99
40	The former Yugoslav Rep. of Macedonia	6-10	120	130	48	111 [z]	48 [z]	.	. [z]	102	103	101	0.98
41	Turkey	6-10	6 288	6 583	47	6 635 [z]	49 [z]	...	...	103	107	98	0.91
42	Ukraine	6-9	1 566	2 200	49	1 563	49	0.3	0.5	108	108	107	0.99
	Central Asia												
43	Armenia[3]	6-9	...	255	...	137	47	...	2	98	...	...	...
44	Azerbaijan[5,8]	6-9	505 *	707	49	483	46	-	0.3	98	98	98	1,00
45	Georgia	6-11	268	302	49	286	47	0.5	10	94	94	94	0.99
46	Kazakhstan	7-10	890	*1 208*	*49*	**1 008**	**49**	*0.5*	**0.9**	*96*	*96*	*97*	*1.01*
47	Kyrgyzstan	7-10	387	470	49	391	49	0.2	0.7	96	97	96	0.99
48	Mongolia	6-10	222	251	50	266	49	0.5	5	96	95	96	1.01
49	Tajikistan	7-10	666	*692*	*47*	669	48	.	0.9	*97*	*100*	*93*	*0.93*
50	Turkmenistan	7-9	293	...	...	...	...	...	...	...	...	...	...
51	Uzbekistan	7-10	2 059	2 570	49	1 948	48	...	.	98	98	98	1,00
	East Asia and the Pacific												
52	Australia	5-11	1 941	1 885	49	2 015 [z]	49 [z]	27	31 [z]	101	101	101	1,00
53	Brunei Darussalam[3]	6-11	42	46	47	44	48	36	37	116	118	113	0.95
54	Cambodia	6-11	1 770	2 127	46	2 224	48	2	1	101	108	94	0.87
55	China[9]	7-11	88 187	***130 133***	***48***	99 708	46	...	5	***114***	***112***	***116***	***1.03***
56	Cook Islands[5]	5-10	2 *	3	46	2	49	15	23	96	99	94	0.95
57	Democratic People's Republic of Korea	7-10	1 513	...	...	...	...	...	...	...	...	...	...
58	Fiji	6-11	97	116	48	101	48	...	...	104	104	103	0.99
59	Indonesia	7-12	25 908	*28 202* **	*48* **	30 662	50	*16* **	17	*106* **	*108* **	*105* **	*0.97* **
60	Japan	6-11	6 830	7 692	49	7 099 [z]	49 [z]	0.9	1 [z]	101	101	101	1,00
61	Kiribati	6-11	13	14	49	16 [y]	50 [y]	...	...	108	108	109	1.01
62	Lao People's Democratic Republic	6-10	714	828	45	900	47	2	4	112	121	103	0.85
63	Macao, China[3]	6-11	...	47	47	24	48	95 **	97	100	101	100	0.99
64	Malaysia[3]	6-11	...	2 912	48	2 948 [z]	48 [z]	2	1.0 [z]	95	96	95	0.98
65	Marshall Islands	6-11	8	8	48	9	48	25	18	90	90	89	0.99
66	Micronesia (Federated States of)	6-11	16	...	...	...	...	...	...	...	...	...	...
67	Myanmar	5-9	4 004	4 733	49	5 126 [z]	50 [z]	.	. [z]	101	102	100	0.98
68	Nauru[5]	6-11	1 *	*2*	*53*	...	...	...	...	*99*	*86*	*115*	*1.33*
69	New Zealand	5-10	347	361	49	348 [z]	49 [z]	...	2 [z]	100	101	100	1,00
70	Niue[5]	5-10	0.2 *	0.3	46	...	...	.	...	99	99	98	1,00
71	Palau[5]	6-10	1 *	2	47	...	...	18	...	114	118	109	0.93

Table 5

GROSS ENROLMENT RATIO (GER) IN PRIMARY EDUCATION (%)				PRIMARY EDUCATION ADJUSTED NET ENROLMENT RATIO (ANER) (%)								OUT-OF-SCHOOL CHILDREN (000)[2]				
School year ending in				School year ending in								School year ending in				
2011				1999				2011				1999		2011		
Total	Male	Female	GPI (F/M)	Total	Male	Female	GPI (F/M)	Total	Male	Female	GPI (F/M)	Total	% F	Total	% F	
															Arab States	
109	112	106	0.94	92	94	91	0.96	98	98	97	0.99	340	61	71	64	1
...	...	...	...	99	98	100	1.02	...	...	...	...	0.7	9	...	...	2
61	**64**	**58**	**0.89**	27	32	23	0.73	**54**	**57**	**51**	**0.89**	84	53	**48**	**53**	3
102	105	99	0.94	92**	95**	88**	0.93**	98**	...	...	...	674**	70**	222**	...	4
...	...	...	...	89	95	82	0.87	...	...	...	...	423	76	...	...	5
92[z]	92[z]	92[z]	1,00[z]	92**	92**	93**	1.01**	91[z]	91[z]	91[z]	1,00[z]	57**	45**	83[z]	49[z]	6
...	...	...	...	98	97	99	1.01	...	...	...	...	2.5	30	...	...	7
108	109	106	0.97	94**	95**	93**	0.97**	97	97	97	0.99	22**	60**	12	54	8
...	...	...	...	...	...	...	...	...	...	...	...	...	...	...	...	9
101	98	104	1.06	61**	62**	60**	0.97**	75	73	77	1.06	161**	50**	131	45	10
115	**118**	**112**	**0.95**	71**	76**	66**	0.86**	**96**	**97**	**96**	**0.99**	1 157**	58**	**123**	**55**	11
104	105	103	0.98	80	79	81	1.03	98	98	97	0.98	70	45	7	66	12
92	92	92	0.99	94	94	94	1,00	90	90	90	1,00	23	48	46	50	13
105	106	104	0.98	95	92	100	1.09	95	95	95	0.99	2.7	2	4.6	53	14
106	106	106	1,00	...	...	...	...	97**	97**	97**	1,00**	...	...	108**	50**	15
...	...	...	...	...	...	...	...	...	...	...	...	...	...	...	...	16
121	122	121	0.99	97	...	...	...	100	99	100	1,00	87	...	8.2	32	17
110	112	108	0.96	95**	97**	93**	0.96**	99	...	...	...	64**	68**	5	...	18
111	...	...	...	85	85	85	1,00	96	...	...	...	42	48	12	...	19
91	100	81	0.82	57	71	42	0.58	76	83	70	0.84	1 386	66	949	63	20
73[y]	76[y]	69[y]	0.90[y]	43**	47**	39**	0.83**	...	...	...	...	2 989**	53**	...	...	21
															Central and Eastern Europe	
...	...	...	...	99**	...	...	...	...	...	...	...	2**	...	...	...	22
98	98	98	1,00	***94*** **	...	...	...	92	...	...	...	***28*** **	...	30	...	23
90	90	91	1.01	...	...	...	...	90	89	91	1.02	...	...	19	45	24
103[z]	103[z]	102[z]	1,00[z]	98	99	98	0.98	100[z]	99[z]	100[z]	1,00[z]	6.3	74	1.3[z]	26[z]	25
93[z]	93[z]	93[z]	1,00[z]	93	93	92	0.99	96[z]	95[z]	97[z]	1.02[z]	16	53	7[z]	36[z]	26
105	105	105	1,00	...	...	...	...	...	...	...	...	...	...	...	...	27
99[z]	99[z]	98[z]	0.99[z]	98	98	98	1,00	97[z]	98[z]	97[z]	0.99[z]	2	51	2[z]	55[z]	28
101	101	101	0.99	97	97	97	1,00	98	97	98	1,00	15	48	9	44	29
100	100	100	0.99	94**	94**	93**	0.99**	96	95	96	1.02	9**	53**	5	40	30
94	95	93	0.98	97	97	97	1,00	94	94	93	1,00	7	47	8	49	31
95	**95**	**95**	**1,00**	...	...	...	...	**94**	**93**	**94**	**1.01**	...	...	**2.6**	**46**	32
99[z]	99[z]	98[z]	0.99[z]	97	98	97	0.99	97[z]	97[z]	97[z]	1,00[z]	91	55	73[z]	50[z]	33
94	94	93	0.99	*93*	*93* **	*92* **	*0.99* **	91	91	90	0.99	*19*	*52* **	14	50	34
96[z]	96[z]	95[z]	0.99[z]	93	93	92	1,00	88[z]	88[z]	87[z]	0.99[z]	99	50	109[z]	50[z]	35
99[y]	99[y]	99[y]	1,00[y]	...	...	...	...	96[y]	95[y]	96[y]	1.01[y]	...	...	221[y]	42[y]	36
95	95	95	1,00	...	...	...	...	94	95	94	1,00	...	...	17	50	37
100	101	100	0.99	...	...	...	...	...	...	...	...	...	...	...	...	38
99	99	99	1,00	96	97	96	1,00	98	98	98	1,00	3.4	51	2	48	39
90[z]	89[z]	91[z]	1.01[z]	95	96	94	0.98	98[z]	97[z]	99[z]	1.02[z]	6	59	2.2[z]	22[z]	40
104[z]	105[z]	104[z]	0.99[z]	94	98	90	0.92	99[z]	100[z]	98[z]	0.99[z]	374	82	68[z]	77[z]	41
100	99	100	1.01	...	...	...	...	92	92*	93*	1.01*	...	...	124	45*	42
															Central Asia	
...	...	...	...	...	...	...	...	...	...	...	...	...	...	...	...	43
96	96	95	0.98	89**	88**	89**	1.01**	87	88	86	0.97	82**	46**	64	51	44
106	105	108	1.03	...	...	...	...	98	...	...	...	...	...	4	...	45
110	**110**	**110**	**1,00**	*94* **	*93* **	*95* **	*1.03* **	**100**	**100**	**100**	**1,00**	*75* **	*39* **	**4**	**49**	46
101	102	100	0.99	93**	93**	93**	1,00**	96	96	96	0.99	34**	50**	15	53	47
120	121	118	0.98	90	89	91	1.02	99	99	98	0.99	27	46	2.7	73	48
100	102	98	0.96	*96*	*99*	*93*	*0.93*	98	100	96	0.96	*28*	*91*	16	90	49
...	...	...	...	...	...	...	...	...	...	...	...	...	...	...	...	50
95	96	93	0.97	...	...	...	...	93**	94**	91**	0.97**	...	...	148**	58**	51
															East Asia and the Pacific	
105[z]	105[z]	105[z]	0.99[z]	95**	94**	95**	1.01**	97[z]	97[z]	98[z]	1.01[z]	103**	45**	54[z]	43[z]	52
105	104	106	1.01	...	...	...	...	...	...	...	...	...	...	...	...	53
126	129	122	0.95	87	92	81	0.88	98	...	...	...	274	70	31	...	54
113	111	115	1.04	...	...	...	...	...	...	...	...	...	...	...	...	55
111	110	113	1.03	86	88	85	0.96	98[z]	...	...	...	0.4	54	0,0[z]	...	56
...	...	...	...	...	...	...	...	...	...	...	...	...	...	...	...	57
105	105	105	1,00	94	94	95	1.01	99	...	...	...	6	46	1,0	...	58
118	117	119	1.02	*94* **	*96* **	*92* **	*0.97* **	99	98	100	1.02	*1 599* **	*63* **	262	-	59
103[z]	103[z]	103[z]	1,00[z]	100	...	...	...	100[z]	...	...	...	0.5	...	2[z]	...	60
113[y]	111[y]	115[y]	1.04[y]	99**	...	...	...	...	...	...	...	0.1**	...	...	...	61
126	130	122	0.94	77	81	74	0.92	97	98	96	0.98	168	57	19	66	62
...	...	...	...	86	84	88	1.05	...	...	...	...	7	41	...	...	63
...	...	...	...	95	96	94	0.99	...	...	...	...	148	56	...	...	64
102	102	101	0.99	...	...	...	...	99	...	...	...	...	...	0	...	65
...	...	...	...	...	...	...	...	...	...	...	...	...	...	...	...	66
126[z]	126[z]	126[z]	1,00[z]	...	...	...	...	...	...	...	...	...	...	...	...	67
...	...	...	...	...	...	...	...	...	...	...	...	...	...	...	...	68
101[z]	101[z]	101[z]	1,00[z]	100**	100**	100**	1,00**	99[z]	99[z]	100[z]	1,00[z]	1.7**	48**	1.8[z]	33[z]	69
...	...	...	...	99	...	...	...	...	...	...	...	0,0	...	...	...	70
...	...	...	...	...	...	...	...	...	...	...	...	...	...	...	...	71

Table 5 (continued)

		Age Group	School-age population (000)	ENROLMENT IN PRIMARY EDUCATION				Enrolment in private institutions as % of total enrolment		GROSS ENROLMENT RATIO (GER) IN PRIMARY EDUCATION (%)			
				School year ending in				School year ending in		School year ending in			
				1999		2011		1999	2011	1999			
	Country or territory	2011	2011[1]	Total (000)	% F	Total (000)	% F			Total	Male	Female	GPI (F/M)
72	Papua New Guinea	7-12	1 049	*560*	*45*	...	...	...	...	*71*	*76*	*66*	*0.86*
73	Philippines	6-11	13 312	12 503	49	13 687 y	48 y	8	8 y	110	110	110	1,00
74	Republic of Korea	6-11	2 946	3 946	47	3 306 z	48 z	1	1 z	103	103	104	1.01
75	Samoa	5-10	29	27	48	30	49	16	17	98	98	97	0.98
76	Singapore[3]	6-11	...	...	...	295 y	48 y	...	8 y	...	...	...	...
77	Solomon Islands	6-11	84	58	46	119 z	48 z	...	25 z	90	93	88	0.94
78	Thailand	6-11	5 854	6 120	48	5 371 y	48 y	13	18 y	97	98	95	0.97
79	Timor-Leste	6-11	195	***185***	...	242	48	...	13	***123***	...	...	...
80	Tokelau[5]	5-10	0.1 *	*0.2*	*48*	...	...	.	...	*105*	*98*	*113*	*1.15*
81	Tonga	5-10	16	17	46	...	...	7	...	112	115	109	0.95
82	Tuvalu[5]	6-11	1 *	1	48	...	...	...	...	98	97	99	1.02
83	Vanuatu	6-11	36	34	48	42 z	47 z	...	28 y	118	119	117	0.98
84	Viet Nam	6-10	6 629	10 250	47	7 048	47	0.3	0.5	111	115	106	0.93
	Latin America and the Caribbean												
85	Anguilla[10]	5-11	...	***1***	***49***	2	49	***7***	12	***104*** **	***105*** **	***104*** **	***0.98*** **
86	Antigua and Barbuda	5-11	11	*13*	...	11	48	*38*	52	*124*	...	...	...
87	Argentina	6-11	3 947	4 664	49	4 698 z	49 z	20	25 z	113	113	112	0.99
88	Aruba	6-11	8	9	49	9	48	83	76	113	114	112	0.98
89	Bahamas	5-10	29	34	49	34 z	50 z	...	30 z	97	99	95	0.97
90	Barbados	5-10	18	25	49	23 *	49 *	...	11 *	103	101	105	1.04
91	Belize	5-10	43	44	48	52	49	...	82	110	115	105	0.91
92	Bermuda	5-10	5	***5***	***50***	4	49	***34***	37	***101***	***101***	***102***	***1.01***
93	Bolivia, Plurinational State of	6-11	1 440	1 445	49	1 429 z	49 z	...	8 z	114	115	113	0.98
94	Brazil[3]	7-10	...	20 939	48	16 487	47	8	15	155	159	150	0.94
95	British Virgin Islands[5,10]	5-11	...	3	49	3	48	13	26	112	113	110	0.97
96	Cayman Islands	5-10	4	3	47	4	50	36	37	112	115	108	0.93
97	Chile	6-11	1 493	1 805	48	1 520	48	...	59	101	102	99	0.97
98	Colombia	6-10	4 411	5 162	49	4 924	48	20	19	119	119	119	1,00
99	Costa Rica	6-11	472	570	48	507	48	7	8	112	113	112	0.99
100	Cuba	6-11	820	1 074	48	828	48	.	.	102	104	100	0.97
101	Dominica	5-11	7	*12*	*48*	8	49	*26*	35	*120*	*119*	*121*	*1.02*
102	Dominican Republic	6-11	1 225	1 315	49	1 310	47	14	23	111	112	110	0.98
103	Ecuador	6-11	1 760	1 899	49	2 121	49	21	26	114	114	114	1,00
104	El Salvador	7-12	787	***968***	***48***	901	48	***11***	10	***106***	***108***	***104***	***0.97***
105	Grenada	5-11	13	*16*	*49*	14 z	48 z	...	77 z	*91*	*93*	*90*	*0.97*
106	Guatemala	7-12	2 330	1 824	46	2 653 z	48 z	15	10 z	102	109	94	0.87
107	Guyana	6-11	114	107	49	99	49	1.0	6	107	107	107	1.01
108	Haiti	6-11	1 420	...	...	...	...	...	...	...	...	...	...
109	Honduras	6-11	1 104	*1 095*	*50*	1 259	49	...	10	*107*	*107*	*108*	*1.01*
110	Jamaica	6-11	321	320 **	49 **	299 z	49 z	6 **	11 z	96 **	96 **	96 **	1,00 **
111	Mexico	6-11	13 227	14 698	49	14 935	49	7	8	110	112	109	0.98
112	Montserrat[10]	5-11	...	***0.4***	***45***	0.5 y	49 y	***35***	33 y	***105***	***105***	***104***	***0.99***
113	Netherlands Antilles	6-11	17	25	48	...	...	74	...	135	138	131	0.95
114	Nicaragua	6-11	779	830	49	924 z	48 z	16	16 z	102	102	102	1.01
115	Panama	6-11	410	393	48	440	48	10	12	107	109	105	0.97
116	Paraguay	6-11	864	951	48	839 z	48 z	...	18 z	119	121	117	0.96
117	Peru	6-11	3 471	4 350	49	3 671	49	13	24	124	125	123	0.99
118	Saint Kitts and Nevis	5-11	7	***7***	***50***	6	50	***18***	21	***109***	***108***	***110***	***1.02***
119	Saint Lucia	5-11	20	26	49	19	49	2 **	5	104	106	101	0.95
120	Saint Vincent and the Grenadines	5-11	13	*19*	*48*	14 z	48 z	*4*	5 z	*118*	*121*	*115*	*0.95*
121	Suriname	6-11	62	***65***	***49***	72	48	***48***	44	***118***	***118***	***118***	***0.99***
122	Trinidad and Tobago	5-11	126	172	49	131 z	48 z	72 **	72 z	97	97	96	0.99
123	Turks and Caicos Islands[10]	6-11	...	2	49	3 y	49 y	18	...	...	...	...	...
124	Uruguay	6-11	302	366	49	342 z	48 z	...	16 z	111	112	111	0.99
125	Venezuela, Bolivarian Republic of	6-11	3 384	3 261	49	3 466	48	15	18	99	100	99	0.98
	North America and Western Europe												
126	Andorra[3]	6-11	...	...	...	4	48	...	2	...	...	...	...
127	Austria	6-9	331	389	48	326	49	4	6	104	105	104	0.99
128	Belgium	6-11	714	763	49	732 z	49 z	55	54 z	108	108	107	0.99
129	Canada	6-11	2 158	2 429	49	2 193 y	49 y	6	6 y	100	100	100	1,00
130	Cyprus[5]	6-11	54 *	64	48	55 z	49 z	4	8 z	97	98	97	1,00
131	Denmark	7-12	403	372	49	403 z	49 z	11	14 z	101	101	101	1,00
132	Finland	7-12	349	383	49	346	49	1	2	101	101	100	1,00
133	France[11]	6-10	3 814	3 944	49	4 172	49	15	15	105	106	104	0.99
134	Germany	6-9	2 910	3 767	49	3 068 z	49 z	2	4 z	103	103	103	0.99
135	Greece	6-11	638	646	48	643 z	49 z	7	7 z	95	95	95	1,00
136	Iceland	6-12	30	30	48	30 z	49 z	1	2 z	100	101	99	0.98
137	Ireland	5-12	476	457	49	511	49	0.9	0.8	102	102	102	0.99
138	Israel	6-11	783	662	49	807 z	49 z	.	22 z	105	105	104	0.99
139	Italy	6-10	2 811	2 876	48	2 822 z	48 z	7	7 z	105	105	104	0.99
140	Luxembourg	6-11	36	31	49	35 z	49 z	7	9 z	99	99	100	1.01
141	Malta	5-10	24	35	49	25 z	49 z	36	41 z	100	100	101	1,00
142	Monaco[10]	6-10	...	2	50	2	50	31	22	...	...	...	...
143	Netherlands	6-11	1 210	1 268	48	1 294 z	49 z	68	...	109	110	108	0.98
144	Norway	6-12	424	412	49	424 z	49 z	1	2 z	101	101	101	1,00

GROSS ENROLMENT RATIO (GER) IN PRIMARY EDUCATION (%)				PRIMARY EDUCATION ADJUSTED NET ENROLMENT RATIO (ANER) (%)								OUT-OF-SCHOOL CHILDREN (000)[2]				
School year ending in				School year ending in								School year ending in				
2011				1999				2011				1999		2011		
Total	Male	Female	GPI (F/M)	Total	Male	Female	GPI (F/M)	Total	Male	Female	GPI (F/M)	Total	% F	Total	% F	
...	...	...	...	...	...	...	...	...	...	...	...	...	...	...	...	72
106[y]	107[y]	105[y]	0.98[y]	90	90	90	1.01	89[y]	88[y]	90[y]	1.02[y]	1 156	47	1 460[y]	45[y]	73
106[z]	106[z]	105[z]	0.99[z]	99	99	100	1.01	99[**,z]	99[**,z]	98[**,z]	0.99[**,z]	26	0	35[**,z]	70[**,z]	74
105	103	107	1.04	94	94	94	0.99	93	91	96	1.06	1.6	51	1.9	28	75
...	...	...	...	...	...	...	...	...	...	...	...	...	...	...	...	76
145[z]	146[z]	144[z]	0.99[z]	...	...	...	...	88[z]	88[z]	87[z]	1,00[z]	...	...	10[z]	49[z]	77
91[y]	91[y]	90[y]	0.99[y]	...	...	...	...	90[y]	90[y]	89[y]	0.99[y]	...	...	611[y]	50[y]	78
124	126	122	0.96	...	...	...	...	91	91	91	0.99	...	...	18	51	79
...	...	...	...	...	...	...	...	...	...	...	...	...	...	...	...	80
...	...	...	...	91	94	89	0.94	...	...	...	...	1.3	63	...	...	81
...	...	...	...	...	...	...	...	...	...	...	...	...	...	...	...	82
117[z]	120[z]	114[z]	0.95[z]	98[**]	98[**]	97[**]	0.99[**]	...	...	...	...	0.7[**]	62[**]	...	...	83
106	109	103	0.94	98	...	...	...	99	...	...	...	195	...	39	...	84
Latin America and the Caribbean																
...	...	...	...	***99***[**]	...	...	...	...	...	...	...	***0,0***[**]	...	...	...	85
99	102	95	0.93	...	...	...	...	86[**]	87[**]	85[**]	0.97[**]	...	...	1.5[**]	54[**]	86
118[z]	119[z]	117[z]	0.98[z]	99	100	99	0.99	...	...	...	...	24	80	...	...	87
109	112	106	0.95	98	98	99	1.01	100[z]	...	...	...	0.1	29	0,0[z]	...	88
114[z]	113[z]	115[z]	1.02[z]	91	92	91	0.98	98[z]	...	...	...	3	54	0.7[z]	...	89
126[*]	126[*]	125[*]	0.98[*]	95[**]	93[**]	98[**]	1.05[**]	...	...	...	...	1.1[**]	21[**]	...	...	90
121	126	116	0.92	92[**]	94[**]	89[**]	0.94[**]	97	...	...	...	3[**]	68[**]	1	...	91
90	91	89	0.98	...	...	...	...	91[**,z]	91[**,z]	91[**,z]	0.99[**,z]	...	...	0.4[**,z]	51[**,z]	92
100[z]	101[z]	99[z]	0.99[z]	96[**]	96[**]	96[**]	1,00[**]	91[**,z]	91[**,z]	91[**,z]	1,00[**,z]	52[**]	51[**]	123[**,z]	48[**,z]	93
...	...	...	...	92[**]	...	...	...	...	...	...	...	1 039[**]	...	...	...	94
...	...	...	...	98[**]	98[**]	99[**]	1.01[**]	...	...	...	...	0,0[**]	42[**]	...	...	95
95	92	99	1.07	96[*]	...	...	...	90	86	94	1.09	0.1[*]	...	0.4	30	96
102	103	100	0.97	...	...	...	...	93	93	93	1,00	...	...	99	49	97
112	114	110	0.96	96	95[**]	96[**]	1.01[**]	90	90	90	1,00	182	42[**]	435	50	98
107	108	107	0.99	...	...	...	...	...	...	...	...	...	...	...	...	99
101	102	100	0.98	99	99	98	0.99	98	98	98	1,00	13	59	13	50	100
119	119	118	0.99	*98*	...	...	...	98[y]	...	...	...	*0.2*	...	0.1[y]	...	101
107	112	102	0.91	84	83	84	1.01	92	93	91	0.98	191	47	96	56	102
121	121	120	1,00	99	99	100	1.01	99[y]	...	...	...	14	8	24[y]	...	103
114	117	112	0.95	***86***	***85***	***87***	***1.01***	96	96	96	1,00	***128***	***47***	33	48	104
103[z]	105[z]	102[z]	0.97[z]	*83*[**]	*87*[**]	*80*[**]	*0.92*[**]	97[y]	96[y]	99[y]	1.04[y]	*3*[**]	*60*[**]	0.3[y]	14[y]	105
116[z]	118[z]	114[z]	0.96[z]	84	88	80	0.91	98[z]	99[z]	97[z]	0.99[z]	289	61	45[z]	63[z]	106
87	85	89	1.04	...	...	...	...	83	81	85	1.04	...	...	20	43	107
...	...	...	...	...	...	...	...	...	...	...	...	...	...	...	...	108
114	114	114	1,00	*89*	*88*	*89*	*1.01*	97	97	98	1.02	*115*	*48*	30	35	109
89[z]	91[z]	87[z]	0.95[z]	93[**]	93[**]	93[**]	1,00[**]	82[z]	83[z]	81[z]	0.98[z]	24[**]	50[**]	59[z]	53[z]	110
113	113	112	0.99	100[**]	99[**]	100[**]	1.01[**]	99	99	100	1.01	59[**]	16[**]	70	10	111
...	...	...	...	***100***	...	...	...	...	...	...	...	-	...	...	...	112
...	...	...	...	...	...	...	...	...	...	...	...	...	...	...	...	113
118[z]	119[z]	116[z]	0.98[z]	81[**]	81[**]	82[**]	1.02[**]	94[z]	93[z]	95[z]	1.01[z]	153[**]	47[**]	48[z]	44[z]	114
107	109	106	0.97	96[**]	96[**]	96[**]	1,00[**]	98	98	97	1,00	14[**]	52[**]	10	52	115
98[z]	100[z]	96[z]	0.96[z]	97	97	97	1,00	84[z]	84[z]	84[z]	0.99[z]	26	46	136[z]	50[z]	116
106	106	105	0.99	100[**]	...	...	...	97	97	97	1,00	4[**]	...	100	48	117
90	89	91	1.02	***98***	...	...	...	87	86	89	1.03	***0.1***	...	0.8	44	118
93	94	92	0.98	93[**]	94[**]	91[**]	0.96[**]	88	88	88	1,00	1.8[**]	61[**]	2	49	119
105[z]	109[z]	101[z]	0.93[z]	*98*[**]	...	...	...	98[z]	...	...	...	*0.3*[**]	...	0.2[z]	...	120
115	118	112	0.96	***91***[**]	***90***[**]	***93***[**]	***1.03***[**]	93	92	93	1.01	***5***[**]	***41***[**]	4	46	121
105[z]	107[z]	103[z]	0.97[z]	92	92	93	1.01	97[z]	98[z]	97[z]	0.99[z]	14	47	3[z]	56[z]	122
...	...	...	...	...	...	...	...	...	...	...	...	...	...	...	...	123
112[z]	114[z]	110[z]	0.97[z]	...	...	...	...	100[z]	...	...	...	...	...	0.5[z]	...	124
102	104	101	0.97	87	86	87	1.01	95	95	95	1,00	439	47	176	47	125
North America and Western Europe																
...	...	...	...	...	...	...	...	...	...	...	...	...	...	...	...	126
99	99	98	0.99	...	...	...	...	...	...	...	...	...	...	...	...	127
104[z]	104[z]	104[z]	1,00[z]	99	99	99	1,00	99[z]	99[z]	99[z]	1,00[z]	6	43	7[z]	41[z]	128
100[y]	100[y]	100[y]	1,00[y]	100	100	100	1,00	...	...	...	...	6	16	...	...	129
102[z]	102[z]	102[z]	1,00[z]	98	98	98	1,00	99[z]	99[z]	99[z]	1,00[z]	1.3	49	0.4[z]	36[z]	130
99[z]	99[z]	99[z]	1,00[z]	98	98	98	1,00	96[z]	95[z]	97[z]	1.02[z]	8	46	17[z]	36[z]	131
99	99	99	0.99	100	...	...	...	98	98	98	1,00	0.7	...	7	48	132
109	110	109	0.99	100	100	100	1,00	99	...	...	...	10	36	33	...	133
102[z]	103[z]	102[z]	1,00[z]	100[**]	100[**]	100[**]	1,00[**]	100[**,z]	...	...	...	14[**]	51[**]	7[**,z]	...	134
101[z]	101[z]	101[z]	1,00[z]	96	96	97	1.01	99[z]	99[z]	99[z]	1,00[z]	25	45	6[z]	38[z]	135
99[z]	99[z]	99[z]	1,00[z]	99	...	...	...	99[z]	99[z]	99[z]	1,00[z]	0.3	...	0.3[z]	39[z]	136
107	108	107	1,00	100	...	...	...	100	...	...	...	0.3	...	1	...	137
104[z]	104[z]	105[z]	1,00[z]	98	98	97	1,00	97[z]	97[z]	98[z]	1.01[z]	15	53	20[z]	42[z]	138
102[z]	102[z]	101[z]	0.99[z]	100	...	...	...	99[z]	100[z]	99[z]	0.99[z]	3	...	25[z]	80[z]	139
97[z]	96[z]	98[z]	1.01[z]	97	96	98	1.02	95[z]	94[z]	96[z]	1.02[z]	1,0	34	2[z]	39[z]	140
101[z]	101[z]	101[z]	1.01[z]	94	93	94	1.01	94[z]	93[z]	94[z]	1.01[z]	2	43	2[z]	45[z]	141
...	...	...	...	...	...	...	...	...	...	...	...	...	...	...	...	142
108[z]	108[z]	107[z]	0.99[z]	99	100	99	0.99	100[z]	...	...	...	7.4	99	0.3[z]	...	143
99[z]	99[z]	99[z]	1,00[z]	*100*	100	100	1,00	99[z]	99[z]	99[z]	1,00[z]	0.9	72	4[z]	43[z]	144

Table 5 (continued)

	Country or territory	Age Group 2011	School-age population (000) 2011[1]	ENROLMENT IN PRIMARY EDUCATION, School year ending in 1999: Total (000)	1999: % F	2011: Total (000)	2011: % F	Enrolment in private institutions as % of total enrolment, School year ending in 1999	2011	GROSS ENROLMENT RATIO (GER) IN PRIMARY EDUCATION (%), School year ending in 1999: Total	Male	Female	GPI (F/M)
145	Portugal	6-11	662	*811*	*48*	734 [z]	48 [z]	*10*	12 [z]	*122*	*125*	*119*	*0.96*
146	San Marino[5,10]	6-10	2 [*]	*1*	*48*	2	47	.	.	...	...	...	...
147	Spain	6-11	2 657	2 580	48	2 773	48	33	33	106	107	105	0.99
148	Sweden	7-12	577	763	49	578	49	3	10	110	108	112	1.03
149	Switzerland	7-12	472	530	49	487	48	3	5	106	106	105	0.99
150	United Kingdom	5-10	4 134	4 661	49	4 422 [z]	49 [z]	5	5 [z]	101	101	101	1,00
151	United States	6-11	24 472	24 938	49	24 393 [z]	49 [z]	12	9 [z]	103	102	104	1.03
	South and West Asia												
152	Afghanistan	7-12	5 542	957	7	5 440	40	...	2	26	46	4	0.08
153	Bangladesh[4]	6-10	16 140	...	...	18 432 [*]	50 [*]	...	42 [*]	...	...	...	...
154	Bhutan	6-12	100	81	46	**111**	**50**	2	**3**	75	81	68	0.85
155	India	6-10	123 616	*113 613*	*44*	138 414 [z]	48 [**, z]	*17*	...	*94*	*102*	*85*	*0.84*
156	Iran, Islamic Republic of	6-10	5 282	8 667	47	5 678	48	...	7	101	105	98	0.94
157	Maldives	6-12	39	74	49	40	48	3	4 [z]	131	130	131	1.01
158	Nepal[4]	5-9	3 465	3 588	42	**4 783**	**50**	...	**14**	122	138	104	0.76
159	Pakistan	5-9	19 515	***14 205*** [*]	***39*** [*]	18 051	44	...	32	***71*** [*]	***85*** [*]	***57*** [*]	***0.67*** [*]
160	Sri Lanka	5-9	1 782	***1 768***	***49***	1 735	49	**-**	3	***108***	***109***	***107***	***0.99***
	Sub-Saharan Africa												
161	Angola	6-11	3 541	...	...	4 273 [z]	45 [z]	...	2 [z]	...	...	...	...
162	Benin[3]	6-11	1 452	872	39	1 869	47	7	16	83	102	65	0.64
163	Botswana	6-12	298	322	50	331 [y]	49 [y]	5	6 [y]	103	103	103	1,00
164	Burkina Faso	6-11	2 776	816	40	**2 344**	**48**	11	**16**	42	49	34	0.70
165	Burundi	7-12	1 183	557	45	1 946	50	-	1	51	56	45	0.81
166	Cameroon	6-11	3 003	2 134	45	3 585	46	28	21	85	93	77	0.82
167	Cape Verde	6-11	63	92	49	69	48	-	0.5	125	129	122	0.95
168	Central African Republic	6-11	689	***459*** [*]	***41*** [*]	648	42	...	14	***78*** [*]	***93*** [*]	***64*** [*]	***0.68*** [*]
169	Chad	6-11	1 914	840	37	1 929	43	...	9	64	81	47	0.58
170	Comoros	6-11	119	83	45	117	45	12	14	100	108	92	0.85
171	Congo	6-11	626	276	49	727	48	10	36	59	60	58	0.97
172	Côte d'Ivoire	6-11	3 135	1 911	43	2 758	45	12	14	74	85	63	0.74
173	Democratic Rep. of the Congo	6-11	11 547	4 022	47	11 083	46	...	83 [y]	48	50	46	0.91
174	Equatorial Guinea	7-12	100	*73*	*49* [**]	87	49	...	53	*108*	*110* [**]	*105* [**]	*0.96* [**]
175	Eritrea	7-11	669	262	45	312	45	11	7	52	57	47	0.83
176	Ethiopia	7-12	13 542	5 168	38	14 298	47	...	10 [**]	50	63	38	0.61
177	Gabon	6-10	175	265	50	318	49	17	44	140	140	140	1,00
178	Gambia	7-12	284	170	46	228	51	14	27	84	91	77	0.84
179	Ghana	6-11	3 598	2 377	47	**4 062**	**47**	13	**22**	81	83	77	0.93
180	Guinea	7-12	1 568	727	38	**1 600**	**45**	15	**28**	56	68	43	0.64
181	Guinea-Bissau	7-12	230	145 [**]	40 [**]	279 [z]	48 [z]	19 [**]	28 [z]	78 [**]	93 [**]	63 [**]	0.67 [**]
182	Kenya	6-11	6 721	4 782	49	7 150 [y]	49 [y]	...	11 [y]	90	92	89	0.97
183	Lesotho	6-12	374	365	52	385	49	...	0.7	100	96	103	1.08
184	Liberia	6-11	655	396	42	675	47	38	33	94	107	80	0.75
185	Madagascar	6-10	2 902	2 012	49	4 305	49	22	18	97	98	95	0.97
186	Malawi	6-11	2 523	2 582	49	3 564	51	...	...	138	141	135	0.96
187	Mali	7-12	2 590	959	41	2 115	46	22	39	53	62	45	0.72
188	Mauritius[4]	5-10	108	133	49	116	49	24	28	...	...	...	...
189	Mozambique	6-12	4 739	2 302	43	**5 359**	**47**	...	**2**	69	79	59	0.74
190	Namibia	7-13	382	383	50	407 [z]	49 [z]	4	5 [z]	116	115	116	1.01
191	Niger	7-12	2 698	530	39	**2 051**	**45**	4	**3**	31	37	25	0.68
192	Nigeria[12]	6-11	25 476	17 907	44	20 682 [z]	47 [z]	...	8 [**, z]	93	102	83	0.81
193	Rwanda	7-12	1 652	1 289	50	2 341	51	...	2	98	99	97	0.98
194	Sao Tome and Principe	6-11	26	24	49	**34**	**49**	-	**0.5**	110	112	108	0.97
195	Senegal	7-12	2 002	1 034	45	1 726	51	12	14	68	74	61	0.83
196	Seychelles	6-11	8	***10***	***49***	9	50	***4***	9	***112***	***112***	***112***	***1,00***
197	Sierra Leone	6-11	958	*443*	*48*	1 195	49	...	3	*70*	*75*	*66*	*0.89*
198	Somalia	6-11	1 568	...	...	...	...	...	...	...	...	...	...
199	South Africa	7-13	7 053	7 935	49	7 128 [y]	49 [y]	2	3 [y]	113	114	111	0.97
200	South Sudan	6-11	...	...	...	1 451	39	...	...	...	...	...	...
201	Swaziland	6-12	208	213	49	240	47	-	1	94	96	92	0.96
202	Togo	6-11	932	954	43	**1 368**	**48**	36	**28**	126	144	108	0.75
203	Uganda	6-12	7 153	6 288	47	8 098	50	...	13	130	137	123	0.90
204	United Republic of Tanzania	7-13	8 509	4 190	50	**8 247**	**50**	0.2	**3**	67	67	67	1,00
205	Zambia	7-13	2 582	1 556	48	3 030	50	...	3	84	87	80	0.92
206	Zimbabwe	6-12	2 207	...	...	...	...	...	...	...	...	...	...

GROSS ENROLMENT RATIO (GER) IN PRIMARY EDUCATION (%)				PRIMARY EDUCATION ADJUSTED NET ENROLMENT RATIO (ANER) (%)								OUT-OF-SCHOOL CHILDREN (000)[2]				
School year ending in				School year ending in								School year ending in				
2011				1999				2011				1999		2011		
Total	Male	Female	GPI (F/M)	Total	Male	Female	GPI (F/M)	Total	Male	Female	GPI (F/M)	Total	% F	Total	% F	
112[z]	113[z]	110[z]	0.97[z]	*97*	…	…	…	99[z]	99[z]	100[z]	1.01[z]	*20*	…	4[z]	27[z]	145
92	92	91	0.99	…	…	…	…	…	…	…	…	…	…	…	…	146
104	105	104	0.99	100	100	100	1,00	100	100	100	1,00	8	76	8	27	147
100	101	100	1,00	100	…	…	…	99	100	99	0.99	2	…	3	72	148
103	104	103	1,00	99	99	100	1,00	100	99	100	1.01	2.6	29	2.2	13	149
107[z]	107[z]	107[z]	0.99[z]	100	100	100	1,00	100[z]	100[z]	100[z]	1,00[z]	1.7	30	12[z]	59[z]	150
102[z]	102[z]	101[z]	0.99[z]	97	97[**]	97[**]	1,00[**]	96[z]	95[z]	96[z]	1.01[z]	743	47[**]	1 023[z]	45[z]	151
														South and West Asia		
98	114	81	0.71	…	…	…	…	…	…	…	…	…	…	…	…	152
114[*]	111[*]	118[*]	1.06[*]	…	…	…	…	96[*,z]	94[*,z]	98[*,z]	1.05[*,z]	…	…	621[*,z]	20[*,z]	153
110	**110**	**111**	**1.01**	56	59	52	0.88	**90**	**89**	**92**	**1.03**	48	54	**10**	**43**	154
112[z]	112[**,z]	112[**,z]	1,00[**,z]	*83*[**]	*90*[**]	*76*[**]	*0.84*[**]	99[z]	99[z]	99[z]	1,00[z]	*20 008*[**]	*70*[**]	1 674[z]	52[z]	155
108	108	107	0.99	86[**]	88[**]	85[**]	0.96[**]	100	…	…	…	1 157[**]	55[**]	8	…	156
104	105	103	0.98	98	97	98	1.01	95	94	95	1.01	1.3	42	2.1	44	157
139	**134**	**145**	**1.08**	69[*]	78[*]	60[*]	0.77[*]	**90**[**]	**91**[**]	**90**[**]	**0.99**[**]	906[*]	63[*]	**334**[**]	**50**[**]	158
92	101	83	0.82	***58***[**]	***69***[**]	***46***[**]	***0.67***[**]	72[*]	79[*]	65[*]	0.82[*]	***8 399***[**]	***62***[**]	5 436[*]	62[*]	159
97	98	97	0.99	***100***	…	…	…	93	93	93	1.01	***3***	…	125	47	160
														Sub-Saharan Africa		
124[z]	137[z]	112[z]	0.81[z]	…	…	…	…	86[*,z]	93[*,z]	78[*,z]	0.84[*,z]	…	…	493[*,z]	76[*,z]	161
129	137	120	0.87	…	…	…	…	…	…	…	…	…	…	…	…	162
110[y]	112[y]	108[y]	0.96[y]	80	78	81	1.04	87[**,y]	87[**,y]	88[**,y]	1.01[**,y]	64	46	38[**,y]	47[**,y]	163
82	**84**	**80**	**0.95**	33	39	27	0.70	**64**	**66**	**63**	**0.95**	1 310	54	**1 015**	**51**	164
165	164	165	1,00	38[**]	41[**]	34[**]	0.84[**]	…	…	…	…	687[**]	53[**]	…	…	165
119	128	111	0.87	…	…	…	…	94[**,z]	100[**,z]	87[**,z]	0.88[**,z]	…	…	189[**,z]	97[**,z]	166
109	114	105	0.92	99[**]	…	…	…	94[**]	95[**]	92[**]	0.97[**]	1,0[**]	…	4[**]	61[**]	167
94	109	79	0.73	…	…	…	…	69	78	60	0.76	…	…	214	66	168
101	115	86	0.75	52	65	40	0.62	…	…	…	…	623	63	…	…	169
98	106	90	0.85	66	71	60	0.85	…	…	…	…	28	57	…	…	170
116	119	113	0.95	…	…	…	…	93	95	90	0.95	…	…	47	64	171
88	96	80	0.83	57	65	49	0.76	61[y]	67[y]	56[y]	0.83[y]	1 099	59	1 161[y]	57[y]	172
96	103	89	0.87	33	34	32	0.95	…	…	…	…	5 614	50	…	…	173
87	88	86	0.98	*72*[**]	…	…	…	59	59	59	1,00	*19*[**]	…	41	50	174
47	51	42	0.83	33	36	31	0.87	37	40	34	0.86	338	52	422	52	175
106	111	101	0.91	37	43	30	0.69	87[**]	90[**]	84[**]	0.93[**]	6 509	55	1 703[**]	62[**]	176
182	184	179	0.97	…	…	…	…	…	…	…	…	…	…	…	…	177
81	79	82	1.03	70	75	65	0.87	70	68	71	1.05	61	58	86	47	178
110	**113**	**107**	**0.95**	61[**]	62[**]	60[**]	0.97[**]	**83**[**]	**83**[**]	**82**[**]	**0.98**[**]	1 138[**]	50[**]	**641**[**]	**51**[**]	179
100	**108**	**92**	**0.85**	43	51	35	0.69	**83**	**90**	**76**	**0.84**	739	56	**273**	**70**	180
123[z]	127[z]	119[z]	0.94[z]	50[**]	59[**]	42[**]	0.71[**]	75[z]	77[z]	73[z]	0.96[z]	93[**]	59[**]	57[z]	53[z]	181
113[y]	115[y]	112[y]	0.98[y]	63[**]	62[**]	63[**]	1.02[**]	84[**,y]	84[**,y]	85[**,y]	1.01[**,y]	1 980[**]	49[**]	1 010[**,y]	48[**,y]	182
103	105	101	0.97	56	53	60	1.13	75[**]	74[**]	76[**]	1.04[**]	160	46	93[**]	47[**]	183
103	108	98	0.91	46[**]	52[**]	41[**]	0.78[**]	41	42	40	0.94	226[**]	55[**]	386	50	184
148	150	147	0.98	66	65	66	1.01	…	…	…	…	715	50	…	…	185
141	139	144	1.04	99	…	…	…	97[y]	…	…	…	17	…	62[y]	…	186
82	87	76	0.88	42[**]	49[**]	36[**]	0.73[**]	67	72	63	0.87	1 038[**]	55[**]	850	56	187
108	108	107	0.99	…	…	…	…	98	97	98	1.01	…	…	3	44	188
110	**115**	**105**	**0.91**	52[**]	58[**]	46[**]	0.79[**]	**91**	**93**	**88**	**0.95**	1 598[**]	56[**]	**459**	**62**	189
107[z]	108[z]	106[z]	0.99[z]	88	85	92	1.08	86[z]	84[z]	88[z]	1.06[z]	39	36	53[z]	41[z]	190
73	**79**	**67**	**0.85**	26	31	21	0.68	**66**	**71**	**60**	**0.84**	1 254	52	**957**	**57**	191
83[z]	87[z]	79[z]	0.91[z]	61[**]	67[**]	56[**]	0.84[**]	58[**,z]	60[**,z]	55[**,z]	0.91[**,z]	7 444[**]	56[**]	10 542[**,z]	52[**,z]	192
142	140	143	1.03	78	78	78	1.01	99[z]	…	…	…	289	49	20[z]	…	193
127	**129**	**125**	**0.97**	88	88	87	0.99	99[z]	…	…	…	2.6	52	0.4[z]	…	194
86	83	89	1.07	57	62	52	0.84	79	77	81	1.06	660	55	423	44	195
113	113	113	1,00	***92***	***91***	***92***	***1.01***	…	…	…	…	***0.7***	***46***	…	…	196
125	129	120	0.93	…	…	…	…	…	…	…	…	…	…	…	…	197
…	…	…	…	…	…	…	…	…	…	…	…	…	…	…	…	198
102[y]	104[y]	100[y]	0.96[y]	96[**]	95[**]	97[**]	1.03[**]	90[**,y]	90[**,y]	91[**,y]	1.01[**,y]	269[**]	33[**]	679[**,y]	47[**,y]	199
…	…	…	…	…	…	…	…	…	…	…	…	…	…	…	…	200
115	121	109	0.90	71	69	72	1.04	…	…	…	…	67	47	…	…	201
145	**151**	**139**	**0.92**	89	…	…	…	…	…	…	…	86	…	…	…	202
113	112	114	1.02	…	…	…	…	94	93	95	1.03	…	…	439	39	203
94	**92**	**95**	**1.03**	49	48	50	1.03	…	…	…	…	3 190	49	…	…	204
117	118	117	0.99	71[**]	72[**]	70[**]	0.96[**]	97	96	98	1.02	541[**]	52[**]	71	29	205
…	…	…	…	…	…	…	…	…	…	…	…	…	…	…	…	206

Table 5 (continued)

				ENROLMENT IN PRIMARY EDUCATION				Enrolment in private institutions as % of total enrolment		GROSS ENROLMENT RATIO (GER) IN PRIMARY EDUCATION (%)			
		Age Group	School-age population (000)	School year ending in				School year ending in		School year ending in			
				1999		2011		1999	2011	1999			
	Country or territory	2011	2011[1]	Total (000)	% F	Total (000)	% F			Total	Male	Female	GPI (F/M)
			Sum	Sum	% F	Sum	% F	Median		Weighted average			
I	World	...	651 974	651 203	47	698 693 **	48 **	7	9	99	103	95	0.92
II	Countries in transition	...	13 689	17 705	49	13 475 **	49 **	0.2	0.7	102	102	101	0.99
III	Developed countries	...	63 976	69 885	49	65 771 **	49 **	4	5	103	102	103	1,00
IV	Developing countries	...	574 308	563 614	46	619 447 **	48 **	11	13	98	103	94	0.91
V	Arab States	...	43 145	35 024	45	42 771	47	9	12	89	96	83	0.87
VI	Central and Eastern Europe	...	19 511	24 885	48	19 552 **	49 **	0.4	0.9	103	104	101	0.97
VII	Central Asia	...	5 452	6 838	49	5 468	48	0.5	0.9	97	97	97	0.99
VIII	East Asia and the Pacific	...	165 462	224 524 **	48 **	184 257	47	13	13	111 **	111 **	110 **	0.99 **
IX	East Asia	...	161 820	221 402 **	48 **	180 875	47	2	6	111 **	111 **	111 **	0.99 **
X	Pacific	...	3 642	3 122	48	3 382 **	48 **	...	...	95	96	93	0.97
XI	Latin America and the Caribbean	...	58 327	69 982	48	65 686	48	15	19	121	123	119	0.97
XII	Caribbean	...	2 246	2 413 **	49 **	2 396 **	49 **	26	33	108 **	109 **	107 **	0.98 **
XIII	Latin America	...	56 081	67 569	48	63 290	48	14	16	122	123	120	0.97
XIV	North America and Western Europe	...	50 144	52 822	49	51 686 **	49 **	6	7	103	103	104	1.01
XV	South and West Asia	...	175 386	155 075	44	192 850 **	48 **	...	6	89	97	81	0.83
XVI	Sub-Saharan Africa	...	134 547	82 053	46	136 423 **	48 **	11	12	80	87	74	0.85
XVII	Countries with low income	...	117 123	74 823	46	126 870	48	9	11	78	83	72	0.86
XVIII	Countries with middle income	...	464 027	500 117	46	498 872 **	47 **	6	8	102	106	98	0.92
XIX	Lower middle	...	278 568	244 078	45	293 937 **	48 **	7	10	93	100	86	0.86
XX	Upper middle	...	185 460	256 039 **	48 **	204 934	47	6	7	114 **	114 **	113 **	0.99 **
XXI	Countries with high income	...	70 823	76 263	49	72 951 **	49 **	7	10	102	102	102	1,00

Sources: UNESCO Institute for Statistics database (UIS) database. Enrolment ratios are based on the United Nations Population Division estimates, revision 2010 (United Nations, 2011), median variant.

Note A: The statistical tables still include data for Sudan (pre-secession) for reference purposes as those for the two new entities since July 2011, Sudan and South Sudan, are just becoming available. The country groupings by income level are as defined by the World Bank. They are based on the list of countries by income group as revised in July 2012.

Note B: The median values for 1999 and 2011 are not comparable since they are not necessary based on the same and number of countries.

1. Data are for 2011 except for countries with a split calendar school year, in which case data are for 2010.

2. Data reflect the actual number of children not enrolled at all, derived from the age-specific or adjusted net enrolment ratio (ANER) of primary school age children, which measures the proportion of those who are enrolled either in primary or in secondary schools.

3. GER or NER, or both, for one or both of the two school years were not calculated due to population data inconsistencies.

4. Enrolment ratios are based on the United Nations Population Division estimates, revision 2012 (United Nations, 2013), median variant.

5. National population data were used to calculate enrolment ratios.

6. Enrolment and population data exclude Transnistria.

7. Two education structures formerly existed, both starting at age 7. The most widespread one, lasting three years, was used to calculate indicators; the other, accounting for about one-third of primary pupils, had four grades. In 2004, the four-grade structure was extended over the whole country.

8. Enrolment and population data exclude the Nagorno-Karabakh region.

9. Children enter primary school at age 6 or 7. Since 7 is the most common entrance age, enrolment ratios were calculated using the 7–11 age group for population.

10. GER or NER, or both, for one or both of the two school years were not calculated due to lack of United Nations population data by age.

11. Data include French overseas departments and territories (DOM-TOM).

12. Due to the continuing discrepancy in enrolment by single age, the NER is estimated using the age distribution from the 2007 MICS as from the school year ending in 2007.

Data in bold are for the school year ending in 2012, those in italics are for 2000 and those in bold italic are for 2001.

(z) Data are for the school year ending in 2010.

(y) Data are for the school year ending in 2009.

(*) National estimate.

(**) For country level data: UIS partial estimate; for regional and other country grouping sums and weighted averages: partial imputation due to incomplete country coverage (between 33 to 60% of population the region or other country grouping).

- Magnitude nil or negligeable

(.) The category is not applicable or does not exist.

(. . .) No data available.

Table 5

GROSS ENROLMENT RATIO (GER) IN PRIMARY EDUCATION (%)				PRIMARY EDUCATION ADJUSTED NET ENROLMENT RATIO (ANER) (%)								OUT-OF-SCHOOL CHILDREN (000)[2]				
School year ending in				School year ending in								School year ending in				
2011				1999				2011				1999		2011		
Total	Male	Female	GPI (F/M)	Total	Male	Female	GPI (F/M)	Total	Male	Female	GPI (F/M)	Total	% F	Total	% F	
Weighted average				Weighted average				Weighted average				Sum	% F	Sum	% F	
107 **	108 **	106 **	0.97 **	84 **	87 **	80 **	0.93 **	91 **	92 **	90 **	0.98 **	107 434 **	58 **	57 186 **	54 **	I
98 **	99 **	98 **	1,00 **	92 **	92 **	91 **	1,00 **	95 **	95 **	95 **	1,00 **	1 450 **	50 **	742 **	48 **	II
103 **	103 **	102 **	0.99 **	98	98	98	1,00	98 **	97 **	98 **	1,00 **	1 297	49	1 517 **	46 **	III
108 **	109 **	106 **	0.97 **	82 **	85 **	78 **	0.92 **	90 **	91 **	89 **	0.98 **	104 686 **	58 **	54 927 **	54 **	IV
99	103	95	0.92	79	83	74	0.90	89	91 **	86 **	0.95 **	8 371	59	4 823	60 **	V
100 **	100 **	100 **	1,00 **	93 **	94 **	92 **	0.98 **	96 **	96 **	96 **	1,00 **	1 705 **	57 **	732 **	49 **	VI
100	101	99	0.98	94 **	94 **	93 **	0.99 **	95	95	94	0.99	438 **	52 **	290	55	VII
111	110	112	1.02	95 **	95 **	95 **	0.99 **	97 **	97 **	97 **	1,00 **	10 212 **	51 **	5 118 **	44 **	VIII
112	111	113	1.02	95 **	95 **	95 **	0.99 **	97 **	97 **	97 **	1,00 **	9 873 **	51 **	4 627 **	43 **	IX
93 **	94 **	92 **	0.98 **	90	90	89	0.98	87 **	88 **	85 **	0.97 **	339	52	491 **	54 **	X
113	114	111	0.97	94	94	93	0.99	95 **	95 **	96 **	1.01 **	3 609	55	2 726 **	45 **	XI
107 **	108 **	105 **	0.98 **	73 **	73 **	73 **	1,00 **	70 **	70 **	70 **	1,00 **	612 **	49 **	677 **	49 **	XII
113	115	111	0.97	95	95	94	0.98	96 **	96 **	97 **	1.01 **	2 996	56	2 049 **	44 **	XIII
103 **	103 **	103 **	0.99 **	98	98	98	1,00	98 **	97 **	98 **	1,00 **	902	48	1 249 **	45 **	XIV
110 **	111 **	109 **	0.98 **	77 **	84 **	69 **	0.83 **	93 **	94 **	92 **	0.97 **	40 081 **	64 **	12 450 **	57 **	XV
101 **	105 **	98 **	0.93 **	59	63	55	0.87	78 **	80 **	76 **	0.95 **	42 115	55	29 798 **	54 **	XVI
108	111	106	0.95	59 **	63 **	56 **	0.88 **	82 **	84 **	80 **	0.96 **	39 259 **	54 **	21 370 **	54 **	XVII
108 **	109 **	106 **	0.98 **	86 **	90 **	83 **	0.92 **	93 **	93 **	92 **	0.98 **	65 992 **	61 **	34 163 **	53 **	XVIII
106 **	107 **	104 **	0.96 **	79 **	85 **	73 **	0.86 **	90 **	91 **	89 **	0.97 **	54 653 **	63 **	27 826 **	55 **	XIX
111	111	110	1,00	95 **	95 **	95 **	0.99 **	97 **	97 **	96 **	1,00 **	11 339 **	52 **	6 337 **	49 **	XX
103 **	103 **	103 **	0.99 **	97	97	97	1,00	98 **	98 **	98 **	1,00 **	2 183	50	1 653 **	46 **	XXI

Table 6

Internal efficiency in primary education: repetition, dropouts and completion

			INTERNAL EFFICIENCY											
			REPETITION IN PRIMARY EDUCATION											
			REPEATERS, ALL GRADES (%)						NUMBER OF REPEATERS, ALL GRADES (000)					
		Duration[1] of primary education	School year ending in						School year ending in					
			1999			2011			1999			2011		
	Country or territory	2011	Total	Male	Female	Total	Male	Female	Total	Male	Female	Total	Male	Female
	Arab States													
1	Algeria	5	12.0	15.0	9.0	7.0	9.0	5.0	568	373	195	250	163	87
2	Bahrain	6	4.0	5.0	3.0	1.0	1.0	1.0	3	2	1	1.1	0.6	0.5
3	Djibouti	5	17.0	17.0 **	16.0 **	**9.0**	**9.0**	**9.0**	6	4 **	3 **	**6**	**3**	**3**
4	Egypt	6	6.0 **	7.0 **	5.0 **	3.0	4.0	3.0	483 **	308 **	176 **	358	234	124
5	Iraq	6	10.0	11.0	9.0	...	...	...	362	216	146	...	...	...
6	Jordan	6	1.0	1.0	1.0	...	...	...	5	2	3	...	...	...
7	Kuwait	5	3.0	3.0	3.0	1.0	1.0	1.0	5	2	2	1.7	1,0	0.7
8	Lebanon	6	9.0 **	10.0 **	8.0 **	9.0	11.0	8.0	38 **	22 **	15 **	42	25	17
9	Libya	6	...	...	...	...	...	...	...	...	...	...	...	...
10	Mauritania	6	*15.0* **	*15.0* **	*15.0* **	3.0[z]	3.0[z]	4.0[z]	*54* **	*28* **	*27* **	18[z]	9[z]	10[z]
11	Morocco	6	12.0	14.0	10.0	**7.0**	**9.0**	**6.0**	429	274	155	**292**	**184**	**108**
12	Oman	6	8.0	9.0	6.0	1.0	1.0	1.0	25	16	10	2.8	1.3	1.5
13	Palestine	4	2.0	2.0	2.0	1.0	1.0	1.0	8	4	4	2	1	1
14	Qatar	6	3.0 **	3.0 **	2.0 **	0.0	0.0	0.0	1.7 **	1.1 **	0.6 **	0.2	0.1	0.1
15	Saudi Arabia	6	...	...	...	2.0	2.0	2.0	...	...	...	66	33	34
16	Sudan	6	...	...	...	4.0[z]	4.0[z]	4.0[z]	...	...	...	171[z]	95[z]	76[z]
17	Syrian Arab Republic	4	6.0	7.0	6.0	7.0	9.0	6.0	178	106	72	188	111	77
18	Tunisia	6	18.0	20.0	16.0	7.0[y]	8.0[y]	5.0[y]	264	152	112	70[y]	45[y]	25[y]
19	United Arab Emirates	5	3.0	4.0	2.0	-	-	-	9	6	3	-	-	-
20	Yemen	6	11.0	12.0 *	9.0 *	9.0	10.0	8.0	244	175 *	70 *	323	201	122
21	Sudan (pre-secession)	6	11.0 **	11.0 **	12.0 **	4.0[y]	4.0[y]	4.0[y]	284 **	150 **	133 **	174[y]	97[y]	78[y]
	Central and Eastern Europe													
22	Albania	5	*4.0*	*5.0*	*3.0*	1.0	1.0	1.0	*11*	*7*	*4*	1.9	1.1	0.7
23	Belarus	4	1.0	1.0	1.0	0.1	0.1 *	0.1 *	3	2	2	0.2	0.1 *	0.1 *
24	Bosnia and Herzegovina	5	...	...	...	0.1	0.1	0.0	...	...	...	0.1	0.1	0,0
25	Bulgaria	4	3.0	4.0	3.0	1.0[z]	1.0[z]	1.0[z]	13	8	5	1.6[z]	1,0[z]	0.6[z]
26	Croatia	4	0.0	1.0	0.0	0.0[z]	0.0[z]	0.0[z]	0.9	0.6	0.3	0.5[z]	0.3[z]	0.2[z]
27	Czech Republic	5	1.0	1.0	1.0	1.0	1.0	0.0	8	5	3	3	2	1
28	Estonia	6	2.0	4.0	1.0	1.0[z]	1.0[z]	0.0[z]	3	2	1	0.4[z]	0.3[z]	0.1[z]
29	Hungary	4	2.0	2.0	2.0	2.0	2.0	1.0	11	6	5	7	4	3
30	Latvia	6	2.0	3.0 **	1.0 **	2.0	3.0	2.0	2.9	2,0 **	0.9 **	3	2	1
31	Lithuania	4	1.0	1.0	1.0	1.0	1.0	0.0	2,0	1.4	0.5	0.6	0.4	0.2
32	Montenegro	5	...	...	...	**0.1**	**0.0**	**0.1**	...	...	...	**0.03**	**0.02**	**0.01**
33	Poland	6	1.0	...	...	1.0[z]	1.0[z]	0.0[z]	40	...	...	18[z]	13[z]	5[z]
34	Republic of Moldova	4	1.0	...	...	-	-	-	2	...	...	-	-	-
35	Romania	4	3.0	4.0	3.0	2.0[z]	2.0[z]	2.0[z]	43	27	16	15[z]	9[z]	6[z]
36	Russian Federation	4	1.0	...	...	0.0[y]	...	...	93	...	...	19[y]	...	...
37	Serbia	4	...	...	...	0.0	0.0	0.0	...	...	...	1.1	0.7	0.4
38	Slovakia	4	2.0	3.0	2.0	3.0	3.0	3.0	7	4	3	6	3	3
39	Slovenia	6	1.0	1.0	1.0	1.0	1.0	1.0	0.9	0.6	0.3	0.8	0.5	0.3
40	The former Yugoslav Rep. of Macedonia	5	0.05	0.05	0.04	0.0[z]	0.0[z]	0.0[z]	0.1	0,0	0,0	0.2[z]	0.1[z]	0.1[z]
41	Turkey	5	...	...	...	2.0[z]	2.0[z]	2.0[z]	...	...	...	112[z]	53[z]	59[z]
42	Ukraine	4	1.0	1.0 *	1.0 *	0.06	0.06	0.06	17	9 *	8 *	1,0	0.5	0.5
	Central Asia													
43	Armenia	4	...	...	...	0.0	0.0	0.0	...	...	...	0.2	0.1	0.1
44	Azerbaijan	4	0.0	0.0	0.0	0.0	0.0	0.0	3	2	1	1.4	0.7	0.6
45	Georgia	6	0.0	...	...	0.1[z]	0.0[z]	0.1[z]	1	...	...	0.3[z]	0.2[z]	0.1[z]
46	Kazakhstan	4	0.0	...	...	**0.1**	**0.1**	**0.0**	4	...	...	**0.5**	**0.4**	**0.2**
47	Kyrgyzstan	4	0.0	0.0	0.0	0.1	0.1	0.1	1.5	1,0	0.5	0.3	0.2	0.1
48	Mongolia	5	1.0	1.0	1.0	0.0	0.0	0.08	2	1	1	0.3	0.2	0.1
49	Tajikistan	4	1.0	...	...	0.1	0.1	0.1	4	...	...	0.6	0.3	0.3
50	Turkmenistan	3	...	...	...	...	...	...	...	...	...	...	...	...
51	Uzbekistan	4	0.07	...	...	0,00	0.01	0,00	2	...	...	0.08	0.07	0.02
	East Asia and the Pacific													
52	Australia	7	...	...	...	...	...	...	...	...	...	...	...	...
53	Brunei Darussalam	6	.	.	.	0.0	0.0	0.09	.	.	.	0.06	0.04	0.02
54	Cambodia	6	24.0	25.0	23.0	7.0	8.0	6.0	515	290	225	159	92	67
55	China	5	...	...	...	0.0	0.0	0.0	...	...	...	257	150	107
56	Cook Islands	6	3.0	...	...	-	-	-	0.1	...	...	-	-	-
57	Democratic People's Republic of Korea	4	...	...	...	...	...	...	...	...	...	...	...	...
58	Fiji	6	.	.	.	1.0	1.0	0.0	.	.	.	0.6	0.4	0.2
59	Indonesia	6	***6.0***	***6.0***	***6.0***	3.0	3.0	3.0	***1 769***	***910***	***859***	878	435	443
60	Japan	6	...	...	...	-[z]	-[z]	-[z]	...	...	...	-[z]	-[z]	-[z]
61	Kiribati	6	.	.	.	...	...	...	.	.	.	...	...	...
62	Lao People's Democratic Republic	5	21.0	22.0	19.0	12.0	13.0	11.0	173	102	71	112	64	48
63	Macao, China	6	6.0	7.0	5.0	5.0	7.0	4.0	3	2	1	1.3	0.8	0.5
64	Malaysia	6	.	.	.	.[z]	.[z]	.[z]	.	.	.	.[z]	.[z]	.[z]
65	Marshall Islands	6	.	.	.	.	.	.	.	.	.	.	.	.
66	Micronesia (Federated States of)	6	...	...	...	...	...	...	...	...	...	...	...	...
67	Myanmar	5	2.0	2.0 **	2.0 **	0.0[z]	0.0[z]	0.0[z]	81	41 **	40 **	15[z]	7[z]	9[z]
68	Nauru	6	-	-	-	...	...	...	-	-	-	...	...	...
69	New Zealand	6	...	...	...	...	...	...	...	...	...	...	...	...
70	Niue	6	.	.	.	...	...	...	.	.	.	...	...	...
71	Palau	5	-	0.07	-	...	...	...	-	-	-	...	...	...

INTERNAL EFFICIENCY															
PRIMARY EDUCATION COMPLETION															
SURVIVAL RATE TO LAST GRADE (%)						NUMBER OF EARLY SCHOOL LEAVERS, ALL GRADES (000)						PRIMARY COHORT COMPLETION RATE (%)			
School year ending in						School year ending in						School year ending in			
1999			2010			1999			2011			2010			
Total	Male	Female	Total	Male	Female	Total	Male	Female	Total	Male	Female	Total	Male	Female	
														Arab States	
91	90	93	95	94	95	*61*	*38*	*24*	36	21	16	...	...	...	1
90	89	91	98	97	98	1,0	0.5	0.5	0.4	0.2	0.1	...	...	...	2
...	...	...	64 **,x	64 **,x	64 **,x	...	...	...	4 **,y	2 **,y	2 **,y	...	...	...	3
...	...	...	99	99	99	...	...	...	21	10	10	...	...	...	4
49 **	51 **	47 **	...	...	...	*358* **	*186* **	*172* **	...	...	...	...	...	...	5
96	97	96	...	...	...	*5*	*2*	*2*	...	...	...	...	...	...	6
94	93	95	96 y	96 y	96 y	3	2	1	1.8 z	0.9 z	0.9 z	...	...	...	7
90 **	87 **	94 **	90	88	94	*7* **	*5* **	*2* **	7	5	2	86.4 **,x	81.3 **,x	91.8 **,x	8
...	...	...	...	...	...	...	...	...	...	...	...	...	...	...	9
40	***39***	***42***	81 x	80 x	82 x	...	...	...	19 y	10 y	9 y	...	...	...	10
75	75	76	**88**	**89**	**88**	220	118	102	**74**	**36**	**37**	**82.5**	**82.7**	**82.3**	11
92	92	92	...	...	...	4	2	2	...	...	...	...	...	...	12
99	99	98	96	...	...	*1.4*	*0.4*	*1,0*	4	...	...	...	...	...	13
...	...	...	...	...	...	...	...	...	...	...	...	...	...	...	14
...	...	...	...	...	...	...	...	...	...	...	...	...	...	...	15
...	...	...	...	...	...							...	...	...	16
87	87	87	96	95	96	59	...	...	28	16	12	93.6	93.1	94.1	17
87	86	88	95 x	94 x	95 x	*26*	*14*	*11*	9 y	5 y	4 y	89.4 x	87.8 x	91.0 x	18
89	90	89	84	85	84	1.7	0.9	0.8	12	6	6	...	...	...	19
69 **	***72*** **	***64*** **	76	82	68	...	...	...	181	72	109	...	...	...	20
77 **	74 **	81 **	...	...	...	*102* **	*66* **	*36* **	...	...	...	...	...	...	21
														Central and Eastern Europe	
90	*86*	*93*	98	98	98	***7***	***5***	***2***	0.8	0.5	0.4	93.9	93.5	94.3	22
99	99	99	98 *	97 *	100 *	11	10	1	1.6 *	1.4 *	0.2 *	99.7 *	...	...	23
...	...	...	81	81	80	...	...	...	7	3	3	...	...	...	24
93	93	93	97 y	98 y	97 y	9	5	4	1.7 z	0.8 z	0.9 z	...	...	...	25
99	99	100	99 y	99 y	100 y	0.3	0.2	0.1	0.4 z	0.3 z	0.1 z	...	...	...	26
98	98	99	99	99	99	*2.1*	*1.2*	*0.8*	0.8	0.4	0.4	...	...	...	27
98	98	99	98 y	97 y	98 y	0.4	0.1	0.3	0.3 z	0.2 z	0.1 z	...	...	...	28
96	95	98	98 x	98 x	98 x	5	3	2	2 y	1 y	1 y	...	...	...	29
97	97	97	93	93	93	*0.9*	*0.5*	*0.4*	1.3	0.7	0.7	...	...	...	30
99	99	100	96	96	97	0.6	0.2	0.4	1,0	0.6	0.4	...	...	...	31
...	...	...	**80**	**80**	**81**	...	...	...	**1.4**	**0.8**	**0.7**	**...**	**...**	**...**	32
98	...	...	99 y	99 y	100 y	-	...	...	9 y	5 y	4 y	...	...	...	33
95	...	...	95	96	95	*3*	...	...	1.6	0.8	0.8	93.4	93.6	93.3	34
96	95	96	97 y	97 y	97 y	12	7	5	6 z	3 z	3 z	...	...	...	35
95	...	...	96 x	...	...	*87*	...	...	51 y	...	...	...	...	...	36
...	...	...	98	98	98	...	...	...	1.4	0.9	0.6	97.6	96.5	98.7	37
97	96	98	98	98	98	1.9	0.8	1,0	1,0	0.6	0.4	...	...	...	38
100	100	100	99	99	98	0.2	0.1	0.1	0.3	0.1	0.2	...	...	...	39
97	96	99	...	...	...	0.5	0.3	0.2	...	...	...	...	...	...	40
...	...	...	99 y	98 y	100 y	...	...	...	10 z	...	...	...	...	...	41
97 *	96 *	97 *	98	98	99	...	...	...	8	5	3	...	...	...	42
														Central Asia	
...	...	...	96	96	96	...	...	...	1.5	0.8	0.7	...	...	...	43
96	95	97	97	99	96	12	8	4	3.4	0.9	2.4	93.8	90.6	97.5	44
99	99	100	96 y	94 y	99 y	*0.6*	*0.5*	*0.1*	1.7 z	1.4 z	0.3 z	94.5 y	94.7 y	94.3 y	45
95 **	*97* **	*92* **	**100**	**99**	**100**	***15*** **	***4*** **	***11*** **	**1.2**	**0.9**	**0.3**	**93.1**	**92.8**	**93.4**	46
95 *	95 *	94 *	95	95	96	*6* *	*3* *	*3* *	5	3	2	97.6	97.8	97.3	47
87	85	90	93	92	94	9	5	3	3	2	1	92.8	91.9	93.7	48
97	...	...	99	99	99	6	...	...	1.7	0.8	1,0	95.9	96.6	95.1	49
...	...	...	...	...	...	...	...	...	...	...	...	...	...	...	50
100 **	...	...	98	98	98	*3* **	...	...	9	5	4	99.6	99.5	99.8	51
														East Asia and the Pacific	
...	...	...	...	...	...	...	...	...	...	...	...	...	...	...	52
...	...	...	97	...	...	0.5	...	...	0.2	...	...	86.7	...	...	53
55	*56*	*53*	61	61	62	222	114	108	153	81	72	48.8 x	46.3 x	51.7 x	54
...	...	...	...	...	...	...	...	...	...	...	...	...	...	...	55
...	...	...	...	...	...	0.3 **	...	...	...	...	...	...	...	...	56
...	...	...	...	...	...	...	...	...	...	...	...	...	...	...	57
82	82	82	91 x	93 x	88 x	3	2	1	1.5 y	0.6 y	0.9 y	91.0 x	...	...	58
86	***83***	***89***	88	...	...	...	...	...	649	...	...	86.6	...	...	59
...	...	...	100 y	100 y	100 y	...	...	...	0.6 z	0.2 z	0.4 z	...	...	...	60
69	***72***	***67***	...	...	...	...	...	...	...	...	...	...	...	...	61
55	55	54	68	67	69	82	46	37	57	30	26	67.2	66.4	68.0	62
...	...	...	98 y	...	...	...	...	...	...	...	...	94.8 y	...	...	63
...	...	...	99 y	99 y	100 y	...	...	...	3.5 z	3.2 z	0.3 z	88.1 y	...	...	64
...	...	...	83 x	87 x	80 x	...	...	...	0.2 y	0.1 y	0.1 y	...	...	...	65
...	...	...	...	...	...	...	...	...	...	...	...	...	...	...	66
55	*55*	*55*	75 y	72 y	77 y	***563***	***285*** 8	***278*** 8	302 z	169 z	133 z	68.5 y	68.6 y	68.5 y	67
...	...	...	...	...	...	...	...	...	...	...	...	...	...	...	68
...	...	...	...	...	...	...	...	...	...	...	...	...	...	...	69
...	...	...	...	...	...	...	...	...	...	...	...	...	...	...	70
...	...	...	...	...	...	...	...	...	...	...	...	...	...	...	71

Table 6 (continued)

		Duration[1] of primary education	INTERNAL EFFICIENCY											
			REPETITION IN PRIMARY EDUCATION											
			REPEATERS, ALL GRADES (%)						NUMBER OF REPEATERS, ALL GRADES (000)					
			School year ending in						School year ending in					
			1999			2011			1999			2011		
	Country or territory	2011	Total	Male	Female	Total	Male	Female	Total	Male	Female	Total	Male	Female
72	Papua New Guinea	6	-	-	-	...	...	...	-	-	-	...	...	...
73	Philippines	6	2.0	2.0	1.0	3.0 y	3.0 y	2.0 y	237	153	83	346 y	228 y	118 y
74	Republic of Korea	6	-	-	-	0.0 z	0.0 z	0.0 z	-	-	-	0.08 z	0.07 z	0.01 z
75	Samoa	6	1.0	1.0	1.0	2.0	1.0	2.0	0.3	0.2	0.1	0.5	0.2	0.3
76	Singapore	6	...	...	...	0.0 y	0.0 y	0.0 y	...	...	...	1.2 y	0.6 y	0.5 y
77	Solomon Islands	6	...	...	...	...	...	...	...	...	...	...	...	...
78	Thailand	6	3.0	3.0	4.0	...	...	...	213	109	104	...	...	...
79	Timor-Leste	6	...	...	...	18.0	20.0	16.0	...	...	...	44	25	19
80	Tokelau	6	.	.	.	...	...	...	.	.	.	...	...	...
81	Tonga	6	9.0	8.0	9.0	...	...	...	1.5	0.8	0.7	...	...	...
82	Tuvalu	6	.	.	.	...	...	...	.	.	.	...	...	...
83	Vanuatu	6	11.0 **	11.0 **	10.0 **	13.0 z	15.0 z	12.0 z	4 **	2 **	2 **	6 z	3 z	2 z
84	Viet Nam	5	4.0	4.0	3.0	2.0	...	...	385	229	157	106	...	...
	Latin America and the Caribbean													
85	Anguilla	7	0.0	0.0	0.0	-	-	-	0,0	0,0	0,0	-	-	-
86	Antigua and Barbuda	7	...	...	...	5.0	5.0	4.0	...	...	...	0.5	0.3	0.2
87	Argentina	6	6.0	7.0	5.0	5.0 z	6.0 z	4.0 z	277	165	112	219 z	133 z	86 z
88	Aruba	6	8.0	9.0	6.0	7.0 z	8.0 z	6.0 z	0.7	0.4	0.3	0.7 z	0.4 z	0.3 z
89	Bahamas	6	.	.	.	4.0 z	4.0 z	3.0 z	.	.	.	1.2 z	0.7 z	0.4 z
90	Barbados	6	.	.	.	. *	. *	. *	.	.	.	.	.	.
91	Belize	6	10.0	11.0	8.0	8.0	10.0	7.0	4	2	2	4	3	2
92	Bermuda	6	.	.	.	.	.	.	.	.	.	.	.	.
93	Bolivia, Plurinational State of	6	2.0	3.0	2.0	6.0 z	6.0 z	5.0 z	35	19	16	82 z	47 z	36 z
94	Brazil	4	24.0	24.0	24.0	...	...	...	5 035	2 632	2 403	...	...	...
95	British Virgin Islands	7	4.0 **	4.0 **	4.0 **	7.0	10.0	4.0	0.1 **	0.1 **	0,0 **	0.2	0.2	0.1
96	Cayman Islands	6	0.0	0.0	0.0	-	-	-	0,0	0,0	0,0	-	-	-
97	Chile	6	2.0	3.0	2.0	5.0	6.0	4.0	44	27	17	75	48	27
98	Colombia	5	5.0	6.0	5.0	3.0	3.0	2.0	269	151	117	125	76	49
99	Costa Rica	6	9.0	10.0	8.0	5.0	6.0	5.0	51	30	21	28	17	11
100	Cuba	6	2.0	3.0	1.0	1.0	1.0	0.0	20	15	6	5	4	1
101	Dominica	7	4.0	4.0	3.0	7.0	9.0	5.0	0.4	0.2	0.2	0.6	0.4	0.2
102	Dominican Republic	6	4.0	4.0	4.0	8.0	10.0	5.0	54	30	24	103	71	32
103	Ecuador	6	3.0	3.0	2.0	1.0	2.0	1.0	51	29	23	30	17	13
104	El Salvador	6	7.0 **	8.0 **	6.0 **	6.0	7.0	5.0	67 **	38 **	29 **	52	32	19
105	Grenada	7	6.0 **	8.0 **	5.0 **	3.0 z	4.0 z	2.0 z	1,0 **	0.6 **	0.4 **	0.5 z	0.3 z	0.2 z
106	Guatemala	6	15.0	16.0	14.0	12.0 z	13.0 z	11.0 z	271	155	116	317 z	174 z	143 z
107	Guyana	6	3.0	4.0	3.0	.	.	.	3	2	1	.	.	.
108	Haiti	6	...	...	...	...	...	...	...	...	...	...	...	...
109	Honduras	6	...	...	...	5.0	5.0	4.0	...	...	...	58	34	24
110	Jamaica	6	5.0	7.0	4.0	2.0 z	3.0 z	2.0 z	17	11	6	7 z	4 z	3 z
111	Mexico	6	7.0	8.0	6.0	3.0	4.0	2.0	970	577	393	467	293	175
112	Montserrat	7	1.0	1.0	-	2.0 y	2.0 y	2.0 y	0,0	0,0	-	0,0 y	0,0 y	0,0 y
113	Netherlands Antilles	6	...	...	...	...	...	...	...	...	...	...	...	...
114	Nicaragua	6	5.0	5.0	4.0	8.0 z	9.0 z	7.0 z	39	22	17	73 z	44 z	30 z
115	Panama	6	6.0	7.0	5.0	6.0	7.0	5.0	25	15	10	25	15	10
116	Paraguay	6	8.0	9.0	7.0	5.0 z	6.0 z	4.0 z	74	43	31	40 z	25 z	15 z
117	Peru	6	10.0	10.0	10.0	5.0	6.0	5.0	444	232	212	201	108	92
118	Saint Kitts and Nevis	7	.	.	.	2.0	3.0	2.0	.	.	.	0.14	0.09	0.05
119	Saint Lucia	7	3.0 **	4.0 **	2.0 **	2.0	3.0	2.0	0.8 **	0.5 **	0.3 **	0.4	0.3	0.2
120	Saint Vincent and the Grenadines	7	...	...	...	5.0 z	6.0 z	3.0 z	...	...	...	0.7 z	0.4 z	0.2 z
121	Suriname	6	11.0 **	9.0 **	14.0 **	16.0	19.0	13.0	7 **	3 **	4 **	11	7	4
122	Trinidad and Tobago	7	5.0	5.0	4.0	6.0 z	7.0 z	5.0 z	8	4	4	8 z	5 z	3 z
123	Turks and Caicos Islands	6	8.0	9.0	8.0	2.0 y	3.0 y	1.0 y	0.2	0.1	0.1	0.05 y	0.04 y	0.01 y
124	Uruguay	6	8.0	9.0	6.0	6.0 z	7.0 z	4.0 z	29	18	12	19 z	12 z	7 z
125	Venezuela, Bolivarian Republic of	6	7.0 **	8.0 **	5.0 **	4.0	4.0	3.0	229 **	142 **	86 **	122	80	42
	North America and Western Europe													
126	Andorra	6	...	...	...	2.0	2.0	2.0	...	...	...	0.09	0.05	0.04
127	Austria	4	2.0	2.0	1.0	2.0	3.0	2.0	6	4	2	8	5	3
128	Belgium	6	...	...	...	3.0 z	3.0 z	3.0 z	...	...	...	24 z	13 z	11 z
129	Canada	6	-	-	-	- y	- y	- y	-	-	-	- y	- y	- y
130	Cyprus	6	0.0	1.0	0.0	0.0 z	0.0 z	0.0 z	0.3	0.2	0.1	0.1 z	0.1 z	0,0 z
131	Denmark	6	-	-	-	0.0 z	0.0 z	0.0 z	-	-	-	0.8 z	0.5 z	0.3 z
132	Finland	6	0.0	1.0	0.0	0.0	0.0	0.0	1.7	1.1	0.5	1.3	0.9	0.5
133	France	5	4.0	...	...	...	...	...	165	...	...	...	...	...
134	Germany	4	2.0	2.0	2.0	1.0 z	1.0 z	0.0 z	65	37	28	16 z	9 z	7 z
135	Greece	6	-	-	-	1.0 z	1.0 z	1.0 z	-	-	-	5 z	3 z	2 z
136	Iceland	7	-	-	-	- z	- z	- z	-	-	-	- z	- z	- z
137	Ireland	8	2.0	2.0	2.0	1.0	1.0	1.0	8	5	4	3	2	1
138	Israel	6	...	...	...	1.0 z	2.0 z	1.0 z	...	...	...	10 z	7 z	3 z
139	Italy	5	0.0	0.0	0.0	0.0 z	0.0 z	0.0 z	11	7	4	9 z	6 z	3 z
140	Luxembourg	6	5.0	...	...	- z	- z	- z	2	...	...	- z	- z	- z
141	Malta	6	2.0	2.0	2.0	1.0 z	1.0 z	1.0 z	0.7	0.4	0.3	0.2 z	0.1 z	0.1 z
142	Monaco	5	-	-	-	- y	- y	- y	-	-	-	- y	- y	- y
143	Netherlands	6	.	.	.	. z	. z	. z	.	.	.	. z	. z	. z
144	Norway	7	.	.	.	. z	. z	. z	.	.	.	. z	. z	. z

Table 6

INTERNAL EFFICIENCY															
PRIMARY EDUCATION COMPLETION															
SURVIVAL RATE TO LAST GRADE (%)						NUMBER OF EARLY SCHOOL LEAVERS, ALL GRADES (000)						PRIMARY COHORT COMPLETION RATE (%)			
School year ending in						School year ending in						School year ending in			
1999			2010			1999			2011			2010			
Total	Male	Female	Total	Male	Female	Total	Male	Female	Total	Male	Female	Total	Male	Female	
...	...	...	...	...	...	...	...	...	...	...	...	...	...	...	72
75	***71***	***80***	76[x]	72[x]	80[x]	758	465	293	679[y]	416[y]	263[y]	...	...	...	73
99	99	99	99[y]	99[y]	99[y]	5	2	3	3.4[z]	1.9[z]	1.5[z]	...	...	...	74
90[*]	88[*]	92[*]	77	74	79	*0.5*[*]	*0.3*[*]	*0.2*[*]	1.2	0.7	0.5	...	...	...	75
...	...	...	99[x]	99[x]	99[x]	...	...	...	0.6[y]	0.3[y]	0.3[y]	...	...	...	76
...	...	...	...	...	...	...	...	...	...	...	...	...	...	...	77
...	...	...	...	...	...	...	...	...	...	...	...	...	...	...	78
...	...	...	84	82	85	...	...	...	6	4	3	65.6	63.3	68.0	79
...	...	...	...	...	...	...	...	...	...	...	...	...	...	...	80
91	...	...	...	...	...	***0.3***	...	...	...	...	...	...	...	...	81
...	...	...	...	...	...	...	...	...	...	...	...	...	...	...	82
69	67	71	71[x]	74[x]	69[x]	*1.9*	*1.1*	*0.9*	1.8[y]	0.9[y]	0.9[y]	...	...	...	83
83	80	86	94	...	...	*342*	*209*	*133*	90	...	...	...	...	...	84
Latin America and the Caribbean															
...	...	...	86[x]	...	...	...	...	...	0.03[y]	...	...	...	...	...	85
...	...	...	...	...	...	...	...	...	...	...	...	...	...	...	86
89	86	91	95[y]	95[y]	96[y]	60	29	31	35[z]	20[z]	15[z]	...	...	...	87
96	97	94	93[y]	...	...	*0.1*	*0,0*	*0,0*	0.1[z]	...	...	88.3[y]	...	...	88
...	...	...	89[y]	91[y]	88[y]	...	...	...	0.6[z]	0.2[z]	0.3[z]	...	...	...	89
91	92	90	...	...	...	*0.3*	*0.1*	*0.2*	0.2[*]	...	...	90.2[*,x]	...	...	90
74	74	73	91	93	89	*2*	*1*	*1*	0.7	0.3	0.4	87.6	83.9	91.4	91
87	...	...	...	...	...	...	...	...	...	...	...	...	...	...	92
80	82	77	85[y]	85[y]	85[y]	64	29	35	32[z]	16[z]	16[z]	78.0[y]	78.4[y]	77.6[y]	93
80	...	...	...	...	...	***812***	...	...	...	...	...	...	...	...	94
...	...	...	...	...	...	...	...	...	...	...	...	...	...	...	95
92	...	...				**0,0**	...	...	...	...	...	...	...	...	96
98	97	98	98	98	98	4	3	1	5	2	3	...	...	...	97
67	64	69	87	88	87	463	295	169	122	63	59	81.2	81.0	81.5	98
89	87	90	91	90	93	*10*	*6*	*4*	4[y]	3[y]	2[y]	83.8[*]	82.0[*]	85.7[*]	99
95	94	96	95	94	96	*8*	*5*	*3*	6	4	2	95.4	96.2	94.6	100
79	...	...	91	85	96	***0.3***	...	...	0.1	0.1	0,0	86.8	83.5	90.4	101
71	66	75	75[y]	...	...	88	55	33	56[z]		...	...	...	...	102
75	74	75	92	91	93	94[**]	50[**]	44[**]	28	16	12	...	...	...	103
62[**]	63[**]	62[**]	84	82	86	78[**]	41[**]	37[**]	21	12	9	83.5	82.8	84.2	104
...	...	...	...	...	...	...	...	...	...	...	...	...	...	...	105
52	50	54	68[y]	68[y]	68[y]	*204*	*110*	*94*	144[z]	73[z]	71[z]	75.5[y]	75.4[y]	75.7[y]	106
65	*62*	*69*	83[x]	85[x]	82[x]	***8***	***5***	***4***	2[y]	1[y]	1[y]	...	...	...	107
...	...	...	...	...	...	...	...	...	...	...	...	...	...	...	108
...	...	...	75	72	78	...	...	...	56	33	23	76.5	72.9	80.5	109
85	**...**	**...**	95[y]	94[y]	96[y]	***8***	...	...	1.9[z]	1.2[z]	0.7[z]	...	...	...	110
87	86	88	95	94	96	333	183	149	119	71	48	...	...	...	111
...	...	...	...	...	...	...	...	...	...	...	...	...	...	...	112
...	...	...	...	...	...	...	...	...	...	...	...	...	...	...	113
46	42	50	...	...	...	*111*	*62*	*48*	...	...	...	...	...	...	114
90	90	91	94	92	96	*7*	*4*	*3*	4	3	1	93.4	93.0	93.7	115
73[**]	71[**]	76[**]	83[y]	81[y]	84[y]	46[**]	24[**]	22[**]	24[z]	13[z]	11[z]	...	...	...	116
83	84	82	82	82	81	108	54	54	113	55	58	...	...	...	117
74	...	...	74[y]	78[y]	70[y]	***0.3***	...	...	0.2[z]	0.1[z]	0.1[z]	...	...	...	118
...	...	...	92	90	94	...	...	...	0.2	0.1	0.1	90.0	93.5	86.4	119
...	...	...	...	...	...	...	...	...	...	...	...	...	...	...	120
...	...	...	90[x]	82[x]	100[x]	...	...	...	1,0[y]	1,0[y]	0,0[y]	...	...	...	121
89	...	...	89[*,y]	87[*,y]	92[*,y]	***2***	...	...	2,0[*,z]	1.3[*,z]	0.7[*,z]	92.2[*,y]	91.6[*,y]	92.7[*,y]	122
...	...	...	...	...	...	...	...	...	...	...	...	...	...	...	123
87	*85*	*88*	95[y]	94[y]	96[y]	9	6	3	2.6[z]	1.6[z]	1,0[z]	...	...	...	124
88	84	92	95	92	98	*68*	*46*	*22*	30	24	6	91.0	88.7	93.4	125
North America and Western Europe															
...	...	...	...	...	...	...	...	...	...	...	...	...	...	...	126
...	...	...	99	99	100	2.9	1.9	1,0	0.5	...	...	...	...	...	127
...	...	...	97[y]	95[y]	98[y]	...	...	...	3.6[z]	2.7[z]	0.9[z]	...	...	...	128
99	98	99	...	...	...	11	9	2	...	...	...	...	...	...	129
95	94	96	...	...	...	*0.5*	*0.4*	*0.2*	...	...	...	...	...	...	130
100	100	100	99[y]	99[y]	99[y]	0.1	0.1	0.1	0.7[z]	0.5[z]	0.3[z]	...	...	...	131
99	100	99	100	100	99	0.3	0.2	0.2	0.2	0,0	0.2	...	...	...	132
98	...	...	...	...	...	*14*	...	...	...	...	...	...	...	...	133
99	99	99	96[y]	96[y]	97[y]	*8*	*5*	*2*	28[z]	16[z]	11[z]	...	...	...	134
...	...	...	...	...	...	...	...	...	...	...	...	...	...	...	135
98	**...**	**...**	98[y]	97[y]	99[y]	0.08	0.05	0.04	0.1[z]	0.1[z]	0,0[z]	...	...	...	136
...	...	...	...	...	...	...	...	...	...	...	...	...	...	...	137
99	***100***	***98***	99[y]	...	...	...	...	...	2[z]	...	...	...	...	...	138
94	**...**	**...**	100[y]	99[y]	100[y]	*34*	...	...	2,0[z]	1.5[z]	0.5[z]	...	...	...	139
...	...	...	...	...	...	...	...	...	...	...	...	...	...	...	140
98	...	...	80[x]	83[x]	76[x]	0.2	0.1	0.1	0.8[y]	0.3[y]	0.5[y]	...	...	...	141
...	...	...	...	...	...	...	...	...	...	...	...	...	...	...	142
98	99	98	...	...	...	*3*	*1*	*2*	...	...	...	...	...	...	143
100	100	99	99[y]	99[y]	99[y]	0.7	0.2	0.5	0.5[z]	0.2[z]	0.3[z]	...	...	...	144

Table 6 (continued)

			INTERNAL EFFICIENCY											
			REPETITION IN PRIMARY EDUCATION											
			REPEATERS, ALL GRADES (%)						NUMBER OF REPEATERS, ALL GRADES (000)					
		Duration[1] of primary education	School year ending in						School year ending in					
			1999			2011			1999			2011		
	Country or territory	2011	Total	Male	Female	Total	Male	Female	Total	Male	Female	Total	Male	Female
145	Portugal	6	...	...	...	...	...	...	...	...	...	...	...	...
146	San Marino	5	-	-	-	-	-	-	-	-	-	-	-	-
147	Spain	6	...	...	...	3.0	3.0	2.0	...	...	...	70	41	29
148	Sweden	6	-	-	-	-	-	-	-	-	-	-	-	-
149	Switzerland	6	2.0	2.0	2.0	1.0[z]	2.0[z]	1.0[z]	9	5	4	7[z]	4[z]	3[z]
150	United Kingdom	6	-	-	-	-[z]	-[z]	-[z]	-	-	-	-[z]	-[z]	-[z]
151	United States	6	-[**]	-[**]	-[**]	-[**,z]	-[**,z]	-[**,z]	-[**]	-[**]	-[**]	-[**,z]	-[**,z]	-[**,z]
	South and West Asia													
152	Afghanistan	6	...	...	...	...	...	...	...	...	...	...	...	...
153	Bangladesh	5	...	...	...	9.0[*]	10.0[*]	9.0[*]	...	...	...	1 727[*]	882[*]	845[*]
154	Bhutan	7	12.0	12.0	12.0	**5.0**	**6.0**	**5.0**	10	6	4	**6**	**3**	**2**
155	India	5	4.0	4.0	4.0	...	...	...	4 453	2 486	1 967	...	...	...
156	Iran, Islamic Republic of	5	*5.0*	*7.0*	*4.0*	2.0	2.0	1.0	*447*	*287*	*160*	88	53	34
157	Maldives	7	...	...	...	4.0	4.0	3.0	...	...	...	1.5	0.9	0.7
158	Nepal	5	23.0	22.0	24.0	**12.0**	**12.0**	**12.0**	821	463	358	**568**	**282**	**285**
159	Pakistan	5	...	...	...	4.0	4.0	4.0	...	...	...	758	438	320
160	Sri Lanka	5	***1.0***	***2.0***	***1.0***	1.0	1.0	1.0	***25***	***15***	***10***	12	7	5
	Sub-Saharan Africa													
161	Angola	6	...	...	...	11.0[z]	10.0[z]	12.0[z]	...	...	...	463[z]	240[z]	223[z]
162	Benin	6	*20.0*[**]	*20.0*[**]	*20.0*[**]	11.0	11.0	11.0	*186*[**]	*111*[**]	*74*[**]	202	109	94
163	Botswana	7	3.0	4.0	3.0	5.0[**,y]	5.0[**,y]	4.0[**,y]	11	6	4	15[**,y]	9[**,y]	6[**,y]
164	Burkina Faso	6	18.0	18.0	18.0	**8.0**	**8.0**	**8.0**	145	85	59	**192**	**100**	**92**
165	Burundi	6	25.0	26.0	25.0	36.0	36.0	36.0	142	78	63	705	349	356
166	Cameroon	6	27.0[**]	27.0[**]	26.0[**]	12.0	13.0	12.0	569[**]	315[**]	253[**]	448	249	199
167	Cape Verde	6	12.0[**]	13.0[**]	10.0[**]	11.0	13.0	8.0	11[**]	6[**]	5[**]	7	5	3
168	Central African Republic	6	...	...	...	23.0	22.0	23.0	...	...	...	147	82	64
169	Chad	6	26.0	26.0	26.0	22.0	21.0	22.0	218	137	81	417	235	182
170	Comoros	6	26.0	26.0	25.0	24.0	...	...	22	12	10	28	...	...
171	Congo	6	39.0	40.0	38.0	18.0	19.0	18.0	108	57	51	134	72	62
172	Côte d'Ivoire	6	24.0	23.0[**]	25.0[**]	17.0	...	...	452	250[**]	202[**]	457	...	...
173	Democratic Rep. of the Congo	6	16.0	19.0	12.0	12.0	12.0	13.0	625	398	227	1 368	723	645
174	Equatorial Guinea	6	12.0	9.0	15.0	19.0	20.0	18.0	9	4	5	17	9	8
175	Eritrea	5	19.0	18.0	21.0	11.0	12.0	10.0	51	26	25	35	21	14
176	Ethiopia	6	11.0	10.0	12.0	8.0	7.0	10.0	546	316	231	1 215	534	681
177	Gabon	5	***36.0***	***37.0***	***36.0***	...	...	...	***97***	***50***	***47***	...	...	...
178	Gambia	6	9.0	9.0	9.0	3.0	3.0	3.0	16	9	7	7	3	3
179	Ghana	6	4.0	4.0	4.0	**3.0**	**3.0**	**3.0**	100	54	46	**112**	**58**	**54**
180	Guinea	6	26.0	25.0	27.0	**14.0**	**14.0**	**14.0**	190	115	76	**227**	**123**	**105**
181	Guinea-Bissau	6	24.0[**]	24.0[**]	24.0[**]	14.0[z]	14.0[z]	14.0[z]	35[**]	20[**]	14[**]	39[z]	20[z]	19[z]
182	Kenya	6	...	...	...	...	...	...	...	...	...	...	...	...
183	Lesotho	7	20.0	23.0	18.0	20.0[**]	23.0[**]	17.0[**]	74	41	34	77[**]	46[**]	31[**]
184	Liberia	6	...	...	...	7.0	6.0	7.0	...	...	...	44	22	22
185	Madagascar	5	28.0[**]	28.0[**]	29.0[**]	19.0	21.0	18.0	570[**]	284[**]	286[**]	836	448	389
186	Malawi	6	14.0	14.0	14.0	20.0	20.0	19.0	372	191	181	699	351	348
187	Mali	6	17.0	17.0	18.0	13.0	13.0	13.0	167	97	70	272	147	125
188	Mauritius	6	4.0	4.0	3.0	4.0	4.0	3.0	5	3	2	4	3	2
189	Mozambique	7	24.0	23.0	25.0	**8.0**	**8.0**	**7.0**	548	307	242	**404**	**221**	**183**
190	Namibia	7	12.0	14.0	11.0	16.0	18.0[z]	13.0[z]	47	27	20	63[z]	37[z]	26[z]
191	Niger	6	12.0	12.0	12.0	**4.0**	**3.0**	**4.0**	64	40	24	**72**	**40**	**32**
192	Nigeria	6	3.0[**]	3.0[**]	3.0[**]	.[z]	.[z]	.[z]	550[**]	306[**]	244[**]	.[z]	.[z]	.[z]
193	Rwanda	6	29.0	29.0	29.0	14.0[z]	14.0[z]	14.0[z]	375	189	187	317[z]	159[z]	158[z]
194	Sao Tome and Principe	6	31.0	33.0	29.0	**11.0**	**13.0**	**10.0**	7	4	3	**4**	**2**	**2**
195	Senegal	6	14.0	14.0	15.0	3.0	3.0	3.0	149	81	67	52	26	26
196	Seychelles	6	.	.	.	.	.	.	.	.	.	.	.	.
197	Sierra Leone	6	...	...	...	16.0	15.0	16.0	...	...	...	187	93	94
198	Somalia	6	...	...	...	...	...	...	...	...	...	...	...	...
199	South Africa	7	10.0	12.0	9.0	...	...	...	824	468	357	...	...	...
200	South Sudan	6	...	...	...	10.0	9.0	11.0	...	...	...	146	81	64
201	Swaziland	7	17.0	20.0	14.0	15.0	18.0	13.0	36	21	15	37	22	15
202	Togo	6	31.0	31.0	32.0	22.0	21.0	22.0	297	168	130	280	146	134
203	Uganda	7	***10.0***	***10.0***	***9.0***	10.0	10.0	10.0	***656***	***342***	***314***	830	423	407
204	United Republic of Tanzania	7	3.0	3.0	3.0	**3.0**	**3.0**	**3.0**	133	66	66	**218**	**113**	**105**
205	Zambia	7	6.0	6.0	6.0	6.0	6.0	6.0	95	52	43	179	94	85
206	Zimbabwe	7	...	...	...	...	...	...	...	...	...	...	...	...

Table 6

INTERNAL EFFICIENCY															
PRIMARY EDUCATION COMPLETION															
SURVIVAL RATE TO LAST GRADE (%)						NUMBER OF EARLY SCHOOL LEAVERS, ALL GRADES (000)						PRIMARY COHORT COMPLETION RATE (%)			
School year ending in						School year ending in						School year ending in			
1999			2010			1999			2011			2010			
Total	Male	Female	Total	Male	Female	Total	Male	Female	Total	Male	Female	Total	Male	Female	
…	…	…	…	…	…	…	…	…	…	…	…	…	…	…	145
…	…	…	94[x]	…	…	…	…	…	0,0[y]	…	…	…	…	…	146
…	…	…	98	98	97	…	…	…	11	5	6	…	…	…	147
98	99	98	96	96	96	*2.1*	*0.9*	*1.1*	5	2	2	…	…	…	148
…	…	…	…	…	…	…	…	…	…	…	…	…	…	…	149
…	…	…	…	…	…	…	…	…	…	…	…	…	…	…	150
…	…	…	…	…	…	…	…	…	…	…	…	…	…	…	151
South and West Asia															
…	…	…	…	…	…	…	…	…	…	…	…	…	…	…	152
…	…	…	66[*,y]	62[*,y]	71[*,y]	…	…	…	1 246[*,z]	709[*,z]	537[*,z]	60.3[*,y]	60.5[*,y]	60.0[*,y]	153
82	78	86	**95**	**91**	**99**	3	2	1	**0.6**	**0.6**	**0.1**	**87.7**	**82.1**	**93.4**	154
62	63	60	…	…	…	*11 336*	*6 142*	*5 194*	…	…	…	…	…	…	155
97	*98*	*97*	98	98	98	***35***	***13***	***22***	22	10	12	94.5[y]	96.6[y]	92.3[y]	156
…	…	…	…	…	…	…	…	…	…	…	…	…	…	…	157
59	57	63	…	…	…	*360*	*217*	*143*	…	…	…	…	…	…	158
…	…	…	52	53	51	…	…	…	2 062	1 111	951	44.1	45.9	42.0	159
98	***98***	***98***	97	100	95	…	…	…	9.3	0.1	9.1	…	…	…	160
Sub-Saharan Africa															
…	…	…	32[*,y]	37[*,y]	27[*,y]	…	…	…	701[*,z]	364[*,z]	337[*,z]	24.0[y]	26.0[y]	21.8[y]	161
76	*82*	*66*	56	58	53	***52***	***21***	***31***	177	88	89	…	…	…	162
82	79	86	93[**,x]	91[**,x]	95[**,x]	9	6	3	3[**,y]	2[**,y]	1[**,y]	…	…	…	163
61	60	63	**69**	**66**	**73**	**63**	39	24	**146**	**85**	**61**	50.4[x]	…	…	164
54	*54*	*54*	51	47	54	***70***[**]	***38***[**]	***32***[**]	167	91	76	30.7	…	…	165
76[**]	…	…	57	57	57	*84*[**]	…	…	312	168	144	45.7[**]	45.3[**]	46.1[**]	166
89[**]	***87***[**]	***91***[**]	89	90	89	…	…	…	1.1	0.5	0.5	81.4	…	…	167
…	…	…	46	49	41	…	…	…	62	33	29	…	…	…	168
48	51	42	49	51	47	98	55	43	237	128	109	20.8	21.9	19.0	169
…	…	…	…	…	…	…	…	…	…	…	…	…	…	…	170
…	…	…	…	…	…	…	…	…	…	…	…	…	…	…	171
63	67	56	61[x]	62[x]	59[x]	*117*	*57*	*60*	161[y]	84[y]	77[y]	…	…	…	172
…	…	…	54	60	49	…	…	…	1 150	534	616		…	…	173
…	…	…	55	53	58	…	…	…	7	4	3	…	…	…	174
94	96	91	69[y]	71[y]	67[y]	*4*	*2*	*3*	18[z]	9[z]	9[z]	72.9[y]	73.8[y]	72.0[y]	175
51	49	54	41	40	42	857	521	336	2 163	1 182	982	…	…	…	176
…	…	…	…	…	…	…	…	…	…	…	…	…	…	…	177
66[**]	65[**]	66[**]	63	60	66	*13*[**]	*7*[**]	*6*[**]	17	9	8	…	…	…	178
59	*61*	*58*	72[x]	76[x]	69[x]	***187***	***93***	***94***	191[y]	85[y]	106[y]	…	…	…	179
…	…	…	**59**	**65**	**52**	…	…	…	**130**	**61**	**69**	40.5[y]	42.8[y]	37.9[y]	180
…	…	…	…	…	…	…	…	…	…	…	…	…	…	…	181
…	…	…	…	…	…	…	…	…	…	…	…	…	…	…	182
59	52	67	66[**]	58[**]	76[**]	23	14	10	18[**]	12[**]	6[**]	66.9[**]	…	…	183
…	…	…	68[x]	73[x]	62[x]	…	…	…	48[y]	21[y]	26[y]	…	…	…	184
52	52	53	40	39	40	321[**]	171[**]	149[**]	672	342	330	30.5	30.1	30.8	185
36	39	34	51	50	52	386[**]	185[**]	201[**]	351	176	175	…	…	…	186
65[**]	66[**]	62[**]	75	77	74	*64*[**]	*34*[**]	*30*[**]	92	45	47	45.5	47.9	42.6	187
98	99	98	97	97	98	0.4	0.3	0.1	0.5	0.3	0.2	78.9	75.4	82.5	188
29	32	27	**31**	**32**	**29**	*418*	*216*	*202*	**852**	**431**	**420**	**21.9**	**22.3**	**21.4**	189
82	80	84	84[y]	82[y]	87[y]	15	9	7	8[z]	5[z]	3[z]	…	…	…	190
69	*70*	*67*	69	71	67	***49***	***28***	***21***	144	73	71	32.6	34.0	30.7	191
…	…	…	80[y]	77[y]	83[y]	…	…	…	798[z]	487[z]	311[z]	65.4[y]	66.4[y]	64.3[y]	192
31	*31*	*31*	37[y]	35[y]	39[y]	***186***	***91***	***95***	336[z]	174[z]	161[z]	25.2[y]	25.3[y]	25.2[y]	193
59[**]	***53***[**]	***65***[**]	66[y]	…	…	…	…	…	2[z]	…	…	…	…	…	194
63	*67*	*59*	59	59	60	***84***	***38***	***46***	152	74	78	34.6	…	…	195
96	96	97	94	95	93	*0.1*	*0,0*	*0,0*	0.1	0,0	0.1	…	…	…	196
…	…	…	…	…	…	…	…	…	…	…		…	…	…	197
…	…	…	…	…	…	…	…	…	…	…	…	…	…	…	198
57	59	56	…	…	…	348	192	156	…	…	…	…	…	…	199
…	…	…	…	…	…	…	…	…	…	…	…	…	…	…	200
65	63	66	67	…	…	12	8	4	10	…	…	…	…	…	201
46	49	42	52	55	48	*74*	*37*	*37*	115	54	61	50.8	47.1	57.0	202
38	*38*	*38*	25	25	25	***929***	***462***	***467***	1 229	613	617	27.0	27.5	26.4	203
74	*71*	*77*	81[y]	76[y]	87[y]	191	106	84	235[z]	151[z]	84[z]	…	…	…	204
66	70	62	53[x]	55[x]	52[x]	91	36	55	216[y]	104[y]	113[y]	…	…	…	205
…	…	…	…	…	…	…	…	…	…	…	…	…	…	…	206

Table 6 (continued)

			INTERNAL EFFICIENCY											
			REPETITION IN PRIMARY EDUCATION											
			REPEATERS, ALL GRADES (%)						NUMBER OF REPEATERS, ALL GRADES (000)					
		Duration[1] of primary education	School year ending in						School year ending in					
			1999			2011			1999			2011		
	Country or territory	2011	Total	Male	Female	Total	Male	Female	Total	Male	Female	Total	Male	Female
			Weighted average			Weighted average			Sum			Sum		
I	World	...	5.3	5.5 **	5.0 **	4.6 **	4.7 **	4.5 **	34 314	19 116 **	15 199 **	32 359 **	17 293 **	15 065 **
II	Countries in transition	...	0.8	0.7 **	1.0 **	0.2 **	...	...	146	61 **	85 **	29 **	...	...
III	Developed countries	...	1.0	0.8	1.3	0.8 **	0.5 **	1.2 **	731	300	432	555 **	177 **	378 **
IV	Developing countries	...	5.9 **	6.2 **	5.6 **	5.1 **	5.3 **	5.0 **	33 437 **	18 755 **	14 682 **	31 775 **	17 140 **	14 635 **
V	Arab States	...	9.2	10.4	7.7	6.7	7.8	5.4	3 222	1 991	1 232	2 852	1 762	1 091
VI	Central and Eastern Europe	...	2.1	2.1 **	2.2 **	1.0 **	0.6 **	1.4 **	525	266 **	258 **	190 **	61 **	129 **
VII	Central Asia	...	0.3	0.4 **	0.2 **	0.1	0.1	0.1	20	12 **	7 **	4	2	2
VIII	East Asia and the Pacific	...	2.2 **	2.3 **	2.1 **	1.4	1.5	1.3	4 995 **	2 749 **	2 246 **	2 571	1 465	1 106
IX	East Asia	...	2.2 **	2.3 **	2.1 **	1.4	1.5	1.3	4 903 **	2 696 **	2 207 **	2 484	1 412	1 072
X	Pacific	...	...	...	...	...	...	...	...	...	...	...	...	...
XI	Latin America and the Caribbean	...	12.0	12.6	11.3	8.3 **	8.6 **	7.9 **	8 397	4 564	3 833	5 430 **	2 918 **	2 512 **
XII	Caribbean	...	12.5 **	13.0 **	12.1 **	12.7 **, z	13.2 **, z	12.3 **, z	302 **	160 **	142 **	308 **, z	163 **, z	145 **, z
XIII	Latin America	...	12.0	12.6	11.3	8.1 **	8.4 **	7.8 **	8 095	4 404	3 691	5 124 **	2 756 **	2 368 **
XIV	North America and Western Europe	...	1.0	0.6	1.4	0.8 **	0.4 **	1.3 **	519	162	357	433 **	101 **	332 **
XV	South and West Asia	...	4.7	4.7	4.7	5.0 **, y	5.1 **, y	4.8 **, y	7 296	4 115	3 181	9 511 **, y	5 140 **, y	4 371 **, y
XVI	Sub-Saharan Africa	...	11.4	11.8	10.9	8.7 **	8.6 **	8.9 **	9 340	5 256	4 084	11 911 **	6 143 **	5 768 **
XVII	Countries with low income	...	11.8 **	12.0 **	11.5 **	10.2	10.2	10.1	8 793 **	4 846 **	3 947 **	12 889	6 733	6 156
XVIII	Countries with middle income	...	4.9 **	5.2 **	4.6 **	3.8 **	3.9 **	3.6 **	24 602 **	13 860 **	10 741 **	18 829 **	10 341 **	8 488 **
XIX	Lower middle	...	5.0	5.2	4.8	4.0 **	4.2 **	3.7 **	12 279	6 976	5 303	11 633 **	6 423 **	5 210 **
XX	Upper middle	...	4.8 **	5.2 **	4.4 **	3.5	3.6	3.4	12 322 **	6 884 **	5 438 **	7 196	3 919	3 278
XXI	Countries with high income	...	1.2	1.0	1.4	0.9 **	0.6 **	1.2 **	920	409	511	641 **	219 **	421 **

Source: UNESCO Institute for Statistics database (UIS) database.

Note: The statistical tables still include data for Sudan (pre-secession) for reference purposes as those for the two new entities since July 2011, Sudan and South Sudan, are just becoming available. The country groupings by level of income are as defined by the World Bank but include EFA countries only. They are based on the list of countries by income group as revised in July 2012.

1. Duration in this table is defined according to ISCED97 and may differ from that reported nationally.

Data in bold are for the school year ending in 2011 for survival and primary cohort completion rates, and the school year ending in 2012 for percentage and number of repeaters (all grades) and number of early school leavers (all grades). Those in italic are for 2000 and those in bold italic are for 2001.

(z) Data are for the school year ending in 2010.

(y) Data are for the school year ending in 2009.

(x) Data are for the school year ending in 2008.

(*) National estimate.

(**) UIS partial estimate.

(-) Magnitude nil or negligible.

(.) The category is not applicable or does not exist.

(. . .) No data available.

Table 6

INTERNAL EFFICIENCY															
PRIMARY EDUCATION COMPLETION															
SURVIVAL RATE TO LAST GRADE (%)						NUMBER OF EARLY SCHOOL LEAVERS, ALL GRADES (000)						PRIMARY COHORT COMPLETION RATE (%)			
School year ending in						School year ending in						School year ending in			
1999			2010			1999			2011			2010			
Total	Male	Female	Total	Male	Female	Total	Male	Female	Total	Male	Female	Total	Male	Female	
Weighted average			Weighted average			Sum			Sum			Median			
74	74	74	75 **	74 **	76 **	35 679	19 195 **	16 484 **	34 348 **	18 444 **	15 904 **	...	...	...	I
96	96 **	97 **	97 **	96 **	98 **	221	131 **	90 **	103 **	66 **	37 **	...	...	...	II
93	92	93	94 **	96 **	92 **	902	508	394	635 **	220 **	414 **	...	...	...	III
71	71 **	71 **	73 **	72 **	73 **	34 556 **	18 556 **	16 000 **	33 611 **	18 158 **	15 453 **	...	...	...	IV
79 **	80 **	78 **	87	87	86	1 386	709	677	1 055	535	520	...	...	...	V
96	95 **	97 **	98 **	97 **	98 **	250	150 **	99 **	103 **	71 **	33 **	...	...	...	VI
97	97	97	98	98	98	73	35	38	30	16	13	95	95	95	VII
84 **	84 **	83 **	89 **	89 **	89 **	7 018 **	3 603 **	3 415 **	3 503	1 892	1 611	...	...	...	VIII
84 **	84 **	84 **	89 **	89 **	90 **	6 856 **	3 518 **	3 338 **	3 367	1 823	1 544	78	...	...	IX
67 **	67 **	67 **	...	...	...	162 **	84 **	77 **	...	...	...	...	...	...	X
77	75	80	84 **	82 **	86 **	3 222	1 867	1 355	2 002 **	1 172 **	830 **	...	...	...	XI
44 **	43 **	45 **	43 **	42 **	44 **	286 **	152 **	133 **	282 **	150 **	132 **	...	...	...	XII
78	76	81	86 **	83 **	88 **	2 936	1 714	1 222	1 720 **	1 022 **	698 **	...	...	...	XIII
92	92	93	94 **	96 **	92 **	738	423	315	523 **	164 **	359 **	...	...	...	XIV
62	63	61	64 **	62 **	66 **	15 817	8 637	7 180	15 124 **	8 340 **	6 784 **	...	...	...	XV
58	59	56	56 **	56 **	56 **	7 176	3 771	3 404	12 009 **	6 254 **	5 754 **	...	...	...	XVI
55	56	54	59	58	59	8 412	4 369	4 043	11 358	5 969	5 389	...	...	...	XVII
75	75 **	75 **	77 **	76 **	78 **	26 247 **	14 260 **	11 987 **	22 293 **	12 232 **	10 061 **	...	...	...	XVIII
68	68	68	69 **	68 **	71 **	18 805	10 334	8 471	18 421 **	10 153 **	8 268 **	...	...	...	XIX
85 **	85 **	85 **	90 **	89 **	90 **	7 442 **	3 926 **	3 516 **	3 872	2 079	1 793	...	...	...	XX
92	92	93	94 **	96 **	92 **	1 020	566	454	697 **	243 **	454 **	...	...	...	XXI

Table 7

Participation in secondary education[1]

	Country or territory	TRANSITION FROM PRIMARY TO SECONDARY GENERAL EDUCATION (%) School year ending in 2010			ENROLMENT IN SECONDARY EDUCATION Age group 2011	School-age population (000) 2011[3]	Total enrolment, School year ending in 1999		Total enrolment, School year ending in 2011		Enrolment in private institutions as % of total enrolment Median, School year ending in 2011	Enrolment in technical and vocational education, School year ending in 2011		Lower Secondary, School year ending in 2011			
		Total	Male	Female			Total (000)	% F	Total (000)	% F		Total (000)	% F	Total	Male	Female	GPI (F/M)
	Arab States																
1	Algeria	92	92	92	11-17	4 500	2 985	49	4 573	50	0.3	381	34	135	140	130	0.93
2	Bahrain[4]	99	99	99	12-17	...	59	51	84	49	22	6	12	...	...	...	...
3	Djibouti	**66**	**70**	**62**	11-17	141	16	42	**55**	**43**	**10**	**2**	**39**	**44**	**50**	**39**	**0.79**
4	Egypt	...	...	...	12-17	9 483	7 671[**]	47[**]	6 846[z]	48[z]	...	1 202[z]	45[z]	94[z]	95[z]	93[z]	0.98[z]
5	Iraq	...	...	...	12-17	4 345	1 105	38	...	...	...	...	...	...	...	...	...
6	Jordan	...	...	...	12-17	842	579	49	710[z]	50[z]	19[z]	24[z]	39[z]	94[z]	93[z]	95[z]	1.02[z]
7	Kuwait[4]	99[y]	99[y]	99[y]	11-17	...	235[**]	49[**]	262	50	33	-	-	...	...	...	...
8	Lebanon	86	84	89	12-17	474	389[**]	52[**]	394	52	61	68	43	90	86	95	1.10
9	Libya	...	...	...	12-17	653	...	...	...	...	...	...	...	...	...	...	...
10	Mauritania	34[x]	38[x]	31[x]	12-17	465	63[**]	42[**]	126[**]	45[**]	25[**]	...	...	29[**]	31[**]	27[**]	0.87[**]
11	Morocco	**83**	**85**	**81**	12-17	3 713	1 470	43	**2 554**	**45**	...	**155**	**38**	**85**	**93**	**76**	**0.81**
12	Oman	...	...	...	12-17	289	229	49	301	49	7	.	.	107	107	107	1,00
13	Palestine	95	93	98	10-17	838	444	50	706	51	6	3	10	87	85	90	1.06
14	Qatar	100	100	100	12-17	72	44	49	73	49	40	1	-	99	98	100	1.02
15	Saudi Arabia	96[y]	...	...	12-17	2 939	...	...	3 153[**]	46[**]	...	...	...	115[**]	121[**]	108[**]	0.90[**]
16	Sudan	...	...	...	12-16	...	...	...	1 687[z]	46[z]	13[z]	31[z]	22[z]	...	...	...	...
17	Syrian Arab Republic	96	95	96	10-17	3 842	1 030	47	2 821	49	4	123	40	92	94	91	0.97
18	Tunisia	93[y]	92[y]	94[y]	12-18	1 244	1 059	49	1 152	50	5	161	32	117	123	112	0.91
19	United Arab Emirates[4]	96[*]	92[*]	100[*]	11-17	...	202	50	348	51	58	3	11	...	...	...	...
20	Yemen	84	84	83	12-17	3 590	1 042	26	1 643	38	4	12	5	56	67	43	0.65
21	Sudan (pre-secession)	94[**, x]	96[**, x]	92[**, x]	12-16	4 966	966[**]	...	1 837[y]	46[y]	12[y]	28[y]	24[y]	54[y]	59[y]	49[y]	0.83[y]
	Central and Eastern Europe																
22	Albania[4]	98	98	98	11-17	...	364	48	355	47	7	19	26	...	...	...	...
23	Belarus	98	100[*]	97[*]	10-16	691	...	...	723	48	0.5	114	37	97	97	97	1,00
24	Bosnia and Herzegovina	84[y]	84[y]	83[y]	11-18	354	...	...	316	49	1	113	45	92	92	93	1.01
25	Bulgaria	98[y]	98[y]	98[y]	11-18	572	700	48	532[z]	48[z]	1[z]	160[z]	39[z]	83[z]	86[z]	80[z]	0.94[z]
26	Croatia	100[y]	100[y]	99[y]	11-18	401	416	49	389[z]	50[z]	1[z]	144[z]	49[z]	105[z]	103[z]	106[z]	1.03[z]
27	Czech Republic	99	98	100	11-18	887	928	50	805	49	8	319	45	97	97	97	1,00
28	Estonia	99[y]	99[y]	99[y]	13-18	84	116	50	95[z]	49[z]	3[z]	19[z]	34[z]	104[z]	106[z]	102[z]	0.96[z]
29	Hungary	98[y]	98[y]	99[y]	11-18	877	1 007	49	883	48	13	139	38	100	101	98	0.97
30	Latvia	96	95	97	13-18	142	255	50	136	48	1	34	39	95	98	92	0.94
31	Lithuania	99	98	99	11-18	329	407	49	325	48	1	37	33	96	97	94	0.97
32	Montenegro	...	...	...	11-18	66	...	...	**63**	**48**	**0.2**	**21**	**45**	**93**	**94**	**93**	**0.99**
33	Poland	98[y]	99[y]	98[y]	13-18	2 806	3 984	49	2 842[z]	49[z]	4[z]	814[z]	37[z]	97[z]	98[z]	96[z]	0.98[z]
34	Republic of Moldova[5,6]	98	98	98	11-17	330[*]	415	50	289	49	1	33	40	88	88	88	0.99
35	Romania	98[y]	98[y]	97[y]	11-18	1 821	2 218	49	1 822[z]	48[z]	2[z]	608[z]	43[z]	96[z]	97[z]	96[z]	0.99[z]
36	Russian Federation	100[x]	...	...	11-17	9 630	15 863	...	9 614[y]	48[y]	0.7[y]	1 557[y]	37[y]	90[y]	89[y]	91[y]	1.01[y]
37	Serbia[5]	99	99	100	11-18	630[*]	737[**]	49[**]	576	49	0.8	217	47	98	98	98	0.99
38	Slovakia	97	97	97	10-18	581	674	50	530	49	10	185	45	95	95	94	0.98
39	Slovenia	99	99	99	12-18	138	220	49	135	48	1	48	41	95	96	95	1,00
40	The former Yugoslav Rep. of Macedonia	99[y]	98[y]	99[y]	11-18	230	219	48	197[z]	48[z]	1[z]	58[z]	44[z]	90[z]	90[z]	90[z]	1,00[z]
41	Turkey	97[x]	97[x]	97[x]	11-17	9 172	5 523	40	7 531[z]	47[z]	...	1 640[z]	42[z]	99[z]	101[z]	97[z]	0.96[z]
42	Ukraine	100	100[*]	100[*]	10-16	3 113	5 214	50[*]	2 926	48[*]	0.4	258	35	100	100[*]	100[*]	1,00[*]
	Central Asia																
43	Armenia	...	...	...	10-16	289	347	...	281[z]	48[z]	1[z]	6[z]	25[z]	96[z]	95[z]	97[z]	1.02[z]
44	Azerbaijan[5,7]	98	99	98	10-16	1 027[*]	...	...	1 023	47	14	178	50	92	93	90	0.97
45	Georgia	100[y]	100[y]	100[y]	12-17	343	442	49	342[y]	...	6[y]	5[y]	...	93[y]	95[y]	90[y]	0.95[y]
46	Kazakhstan	**100**	**100**	**100**	11-17	1 686	1 966	49	**1 643**	**48**	**0.8**	**110**	**30**	**109**	**109**	**109**	**1,00**
47	Kyrgyzstan	98	98	98	11-17	775	633	50	683[*]	49[*]	2[*]	61[*]	42[*]	93	93	92	1,00
48	Mongolia	99	98	99	11-16	301	205	55	279	51	9	32	45	88	87	90	1.04
49	Tajikistan	99	99	98	11-17	1 181	769	46	1 045	46	1	23	22	98	102	94	0.93
50	Turkmenistan	...	...	...	10-16	688	...	...	...	...	...	...	...	...	...	...	...
51	Uzbekistan	99	100	98	11-17	4 136	3 411	49	4 370	49	.	...	...	95	96	94	0.98
	East Asia and the Pacific																
52	Australia[8]	...	...	...	12-17	1 745	2 491	49	2 282[z]	47[z]	33[z]	749[z]	42[z]	113[z]	115[z]	111[z]	0.97[z]
53	Brunei Darussalam	100	100	100	12-18	45	34	51	50	48	14[z]	4	44	118	118	119	1.01
54	Cambodia	80	79	81	12-17	2 010	316	34	...	...	...	...	...	59	60	58	0.97
55	China	...	...	...	12-17	119 773	77 436	...	97 452	47	11	20 300	45	90	88	93	1.06
56	Cook Islands[5]	99	99	100	11-17	2[*]	2	50	2	52	14	.	.	98	93	103	1.11
57	Democratic People's Republic of Korea	...	...	...	11-16	2 496	...	...	...	...	...	...	...	...	...	...	...
58	Fiji	96[x]	95[x]	97[x]	12-18	112	98	51	101	50	...	2	24	102	100	104	1.05
59	Indonesia	89	84	96	13-18	25 732	*14 264*[**]	*48*[**]	20 778	49	41	3 737	42	94	93	95	1.02
60	Japan	...	...	...	12-17	7 106	8 959	49	7 296[z]	49[z]	19[z]	859[z]	43[z]	103[z]	103[z]	103[z]	1,00[z]
61	Kiribati	...	...	...	12-17	14	7	54	...	...	...	...	...	95[y]	95[y]	95[y]	0.99[y]
62	Lao People's Democratic Republic	81	83	80	11-17	1 071	240	40	490	45	3	2	46	57	61	53	0.86
63	Macao, China	93	92	94	12-17	39	32	51	37	48	95	2	41	112	116	109	0.94
64	Malaysia	99[y]	100[y]	98[y]	12-18	3 852	2 177	51	2 616[z]	51[z]	4[z]	162[z]	43[z]	90[z]	89[z]	91[z]	1.02[z]
65	Marshall Islands	91[x]	92[x]	90[x]	12-17	6	6	50	5[y]	50[y]	21[y]	...	...	110[y]	109[y]	112[y]	1.03[y]
66	Micronesia (Federated States of)	...	...	...	12-17	16	...	...	...	...	...	...	...	...	...	...	...
67	Myanmar	77[y]	77[y]	77[y]	10-15	5 217	2 059	50	2 852[z]	51[z]	.[z]	-[z]	-[z]	62[z]	61[z]	64[z]	1.05[z]
68	Nauru[5]	...	...	...	12-17	1[*]	*0.7*	*54*	...	...	...	...	...	...	...	...	...
69	New Zealand	...	...	...	11-17	424	437	50	512[z]	50[z]	19[z]	79[z]	49[z]	104[z]	105[z]	104[z]	0.99[z]
70	Niue[5]	...	...	...	11-16	0.1[*]	0.3	54	...	...	...	...	...	...	...	...	...
71	Palau[5]	...	...	...	11-17	2[*]	2	49	...	...	...	...	...	...	...	...	...

GROSS ENROLMENT RATIO (GER) IN SECONDARY EDUCATION (%)												OUT-OF-SCHOOL ADOLESCENTS (000)[2]						
Upper secondary				Total Secondary														
School year ending in				School year ending in								School year ending in Sum			School year ending in			
2011				1999				2011				1999			2011			
Total	Male	Female	GPI (F/M)	Total	Male	Female	GPI (F/M)	Total	Male	Female	GPI (F/M)	Total	Male	Female	Total	Male	Female	
																	Arab States	
64	53	74	1.39	66	66	67	1.01	102	100	104	1.04	...	...	...	...	...	...	1
...	...	...	...	96	91	101	1.10	...	...	...	...	0.4	...	...	...	...	...	2
32	**37**	**27**	**0.72**	14	16	12	0.72	**39**	**44**	**34**	**0.76**	***55***	***26***	***29***	...	...	...	3
51 [z]	53 [z]	49 [z]	0.92 [z]	80 [**]	84 [**]	76 [**]	0.91 [**]	72 [z]	74 [z]	71 [z]	0.96 [z]	...	...	...	...	...	...	4
...	...	...	...	35	42	27	0.64	...	...	...	...	840	349	491	...	...	...	5
73 [z]	68 [z]	79 [z]	1.16 [z]	85	83	87	1.04	87 [z]	85 [z]	89 [z]	1.06 [z]	63 [**]	37 [**]	26 [**]	101 [z]	85 [z]	17 [z]	6
...	...	...	...	109 [**]	107 [**]	111	1.03 [**]	...	...	...	...	1 [**]	...	...	...	...	...	7
76	72	81	1.13	77 [**]	73 [**]	80 [**]	1.09 [**]	83	79	88	1.11	...	...	...	34	18	16	8
...	...	...	...	...	...	...	...	...	...	...	...	...	...	...	...	...	...	9
23 [**]	26 [**]	20 [**]	0.76 [**]	18 [**]	21 [**]	15 [**]	0.75 [**]	27 [**]	29 [**]	25 [**]	0.84 [**]	***104*** [**]	***51*** [**]	***53*** [**]	...	...	...	10
55	**58**	**53**	**0.91**	37	41	32	0.78	**70**	**75**	**64**	**0.85**	968 [**]	410 [**]	558 [**]	...	...	...	11
101	103	100	0.97	71	71	72	1.01	104	105	103	0.98	35	17	17	0.6	...	...	12
74	66	83	1.27	78	77	79	1.02	84	80	88	1.10	69	37	32	95	56	39	13
...	...	...	...	88	83	92	1.11	102	98	106	1.09	3	2	1,0	0.6	0.3	0.3	14
100 [**]	107 [**]	93 [**]	0.87 [**]	...	...	...	...	107 [**]	114 [**]	101 [**]	0.88 [**]	...	...	...	0.7 [**]	...	...	15
...	...	...	...	...	...	...	...	...	...	...	...	...	...	...	...	...	...	16
40	38	42	1.11	44	46	42	0.92	73	73	73	1,00	448	202	245	261	114	147	17
76	70	83	1.18	74	74	74	0.99	93	91	94	1.03	...	...	...	...	...	...	18
...	...	...	...	83	80	87	1.09	...	...	...	...	9	4	5	...	...	...	19
36	44	27	0.62	40	58	21	0.37	46	56	35	0.63	568	134	434	619 [**]	203 [**]	416 [**]	20
28 [y]	29 [y]	28 [y]	0.95 [y]	26 [**]	...	...	...	39 [y]	41 [y]	36 [y]	0.88 [y]	...	...	...	...	...	...	21
																	Central and Eastern Europe	
89	94	85	0.91	73	74	71	0.95	...	...	...	...	*9*	*1*	*6*	...	...	...	22
121	127	116	0.91	...	...	...	...	105	106	103	0.97	***43*** [**]	...	...	16	...	...	23
86	84	89	1.05	...	...	...	...	89	88	91	1.03	...	...	...	...	...	...	24
94 [z]	95 [z]	92 [z]	0.97 [z]	92	93	91	0.98	89 [z]	91 [z]	87 [z]	0.95 [z]	17	8	10	34 [z]	17 [z]	18 [z]	25
87 [z]	82 [z]	92 [z]	1.12 [z]	84	84	85	1.02	96 [z]	93 [z]	99 [z]	1.07 [z]	16	8	9	2 [z]	...	...	26
86	86	86	1,00	82	80	84	1.04	91	91	91	1,00	...	...	...	...	...	...	27
109 [z]	107 [z]	110 [z]	1.03 [z]	94	92	96	1.04	107 [z]	107 [z]	107 [z]	1,00 [z]	1	...	...	2 [z]	1 [z]	1 [z]	28
102	103	101	0.98	93	92	94	1.01	101	102	100	0.98	15	7	8	7	3	4	29
97	98	95	0.98	89	87	90	1.04	96	98	94	0.96	...	...	...	8	4	4	30
106	106	105	0.99	96	95	96	1,00	99	100	97	0.97	1	...	...	19	10	9	31
98	**96**	**99**	**1.03**	...	...	...	...	**95**	**95**	**96**	**1.01**	...	...	...	...	...	...	32
97 [z]	97 [z]	97 [z]	1,00 [z]	100	100	99	0.99	97 [z]	98 [z]	96 [z]	0.99 [z]	15	5	11	88 [y]	46 [y]	42 [y]	33
87	84	90	1.08	83	84	82	0.98	88	87	89	1.02	*19*	*13*	*6* [**]	30	15	15	34
98 [z]	99 [z]	97 [z]	0.99 [z]	81	81	82	1.01	97 [z]	98 [z]	97 [z]	0.99 [z]	43	21	22	52 [y]	27 [y]	24 [y]	35
86 [y]	90 [y]	82 [y]	0.91 [y]	92	...	...	...	89 [y]	90 [y]	87 [y]	0.98 [y]	...	...	...	671 [y]	380 [y]	291 [y]	36
86	84	87	1.04	93 [**]	93 [**]	94 [**]	1.01 [**]	91	91	92	1.02	...	...	...	10	5	5	37
88	87	89	1.03	84	83	85	1.02	91	91	91	1.01	...	...	...	...	...	...	38
99	100	98	0.98	100	98	101	1.03	97	98	97	0.99	5	3	2	1.4	0.6	0.7	39
78 [z]	78 [z]	77 [z]	0.99 [z]	82	83	81	0.98	84 [z]	84 [z]	83 [z]	0.99 [z]	...	...	...	...	...	...	40
70 [z]	74 [z]	65 [z]	0.88 [z]	69	82	56	0.69	82 [z]	86 [z]	79 [z]	0.92 [z]	899 [**]	275 [**]	625 [**]	102 [**,z]	23 [**,z]	79 [**,z]	41
81	85 [*]	77 [*]	0.90 [*]	98	97 [*]	100 [*]	1.03 [*]	94	95 [*]	93 [*]	0.97 [*]	...	...	...	83	44 [*]	38 [*]	42
																	Central Asia	
85 [z]	83 [z]	86 [z]	1.04 [z]	92	...	...	...	92 [z]	91 [z]	93 [z]	1.02 [z]	...	...	...	...	...	...	43
115	115	115	1,00	...	...	...	...	100	100	98	0.98	119 [**]	59 [**]	60 [**]	88	43	45	44
81 [y]	...	...	...	79	80	78	0.98	86 [y]	...	...	...	...	...	...	14 [y]	...	...	45
87	**91**	**82**	**0.90**	93	93	93	1,00	**102**	**103**	**100**	**0.97**	*32* [**]	...	...	**1**	...	...	46
78 [*]	78 [*]	78 [*]	1,00 [*]	83	82	84	1.02	88 [*]	88 [*]	88 [*]	1,00 [*]	...	...	...	47 [*]	24 [*]	23 [*]	47
101	96	105	1.09	61	54	68	1.26	93	90	95	1.06	57 [**]	36 [**]	20 [**]	12	7	5	48
65	76	53	0.70	75	80	69	0.86	89	94	82	0.87	195	91	104	31	...	...	49
...	...	...	...	...	...	...	...	...	...	...	...	...	...	...	...	...	...	50
129	131	128	0.97	86	87	86	0.98	106	107	104	0.98	...	...	...	...	...	...	51
																	East Asia and the Pacific	
167 [z]	172 [z]	161 [z]	0.93 [z]	157	157	157	1,00	131 [z]	135 [z]	128 [z]	0.95 [z]	...	...	...	20 [z]	11 [z]	10 [z]	52
109	108	110	1.02	88	85	92	1.09	112	111	113	1.02	...	...	...	0,0	...	...	53
...	...	...	... [**]	16	20	11	0.53	...	...	...	...	947	463	484	...	...	...	54
73	72	74	1.04	61	...	...	...	81	80	83	1.05	...	...	...	...	...	...	55
62	52	73	1.40	60	58	63	1.08	82	75	89	1.20	0,0	...	...	0.1	...	...	56
...	...	...	...	...	...	...	...	...	...	...	...	...	...	...	...	...	...	57
76	71	81	1.15	78	74	83	1.11	90	87	94	1.08	3	...	...	1	...	...	58
68	69	67	0.97	*53* [**]	*54* [**]	*51* [**]	*0.95* [**]	81	81	81	1,00	*4 795* [**]	*2 377* [**]	*2 418* [**]	1 339	651	688	59
102 [z]	102 [z]	102 [z]	1,00 [z]	101	101	102	1.01	102 [z]	102 [z]	102 [z]	1,00 [z]	-	...	...	0.1 [z]	...	...	60
...	...	...	...	59	53	65	1.23	...	...	...	...	...	...	...	...	...	...	61
31	34	28	0.83	33	39	27	0.70	46	49	42	0.85	97	36	62	169	76	93	62
83	86	80	0.93	80	78	82	1.05	96	99	92	0.92	2	1	1	2	1	1	63
52 [z]	49 [z]	56 [z]	1.16 [z]	66	64	69	1.08	69 [z]	67 [z]	72 [z]	1.07 [z]	98	57	40	179 [z]	101 [z]	78 [z]	64
92 [y]	90 [y]	93 [y]	1.03 [y]	68	66	70	1.06	99 [y]	97 [y]	100 [y]	1.03 [y]	...	...	...	...	...	...	65
...	...	...	...	...	...	...	...	...	...	...	...	...	...	...	...	...	...	66
38 [z]	36 [z]	41 [z]	1.13 [z]	36	36	36	1,00	54 [z]	53 [z]	56 [z]	1.06 [z]	...	...	...	...	...	...	67
...	...	...	...	*47*	*43*	*51*	*1.17*	...	...	...	...	...	...	...	...	...	...	68
137 [z]	131 [z]	145 [z]	1.11 [z]	111	108	114	1.05	119 [z]	116 [z]	122 [z]	1.05 [z]	...	...	...	0.8 [z]	...	...	69
...	...	...	...	98	93	103	1.10	...	...	...	...	0,0	...	...	...	...	...	70
...	...	...	...	101	98	105	1.07	...	...	...	...	...	...	...	...	...	...	71

Table 7 (continued)

		TRANSITION FROM PRIMARY TO SECONDARY GENERAL EDUCATION (%)			ENROLMENT IN SECONDARY EDUCATION												
						School-age population (000)	Total enrolment				Enrolment in private institutions as % of total enrolment Median	Enrolment in technical and vocational education		Lower Secondary			
		School year ending in			Age group		School year ending in				School year ending in	School year ending in		School year ending in			
		2010			2011	2011[3]	1999		2011		2011	2011		2011			
	Country or territory	Total	Male	Female			Total (000)	% F	Total (000)	% F		Total (000)	% F	Total	Male	Female	GPI (F/M)
72	Papua New Guinea	...	...	...	13-18	913	...	...	...	...	...	...	...	...	...	...	...
73	Philippines	98[x]	99[x]	97[x]	12-15	8 197	5 117	51	6 767[y]	51[y]	20[y]	.[y]	.[y]	88[y]	85[y]	90[y]	1.05[y]
74	Republic of Korea	100[x]	100[x]	100[x]	12-17	3 974	4 177	48	3 951[z]	47[z]	32[z]	466[z]	45[z]	100[z]	100[z]	99[z]	0.99[z]
75	Samoa	94	94	93	11-17	31	22	50	26	51	33	.	.	99	99	99	1,00
76	Singapore[4]	89[x]	86[x]	92[x]	12-15	...	...	...	232[y]	48[y]	6[y]	27[y]	35[y]	...	...	...	...
77	Solomon Islands	...	...	...	12-18	84	17	41	40[z]	45[z]	34[z]	.[z]	.[z]	70[z]	71[z]	69[z]	0.96[z]
78	Thailand	...	...	...	12-17	6 177	***4 072***	***49*** **	**4 786**	**51**	**16**	**739**	**42**	**88**	**88**	**89**	**1.02**
79	Timor-Leste	91	90	92	12-17	186	***44***	...	108	50	26	7	46	64	63	65	1.03
80	Tokelau[5]	...	...	...	11-15	0.1 *	*0.2*	*49*	...	...	...	...	...	...	...	...	...
81	Tonga	...	...	...	11-16	14	15	50	...	...	...	...	...	...	...	...	...
82	Tuvalu[5]	...	...	...	12-17	1 *	***0.9***	***46***	...	...	...	...	...	...	...	...	...
83	Vanuatu	79[y]	79[y]	79[y]	12-18	38	9	45	20[z]	49[z]	...	2[z]	39[z]	65[z]	63[z]	66[z]	1.05[z]
84	Viet Nam	100	...	...	11-17	10 787	...	...	...	...	...	...	...	90	91	89	0.98
	Latin America and the Caribbean																
85	Anguilla[9]	97	93	100	12-16	...	1	53	1	51	.	0.01	9	...	...	...	...
86	Antigua and Barbuda	77[y]	...	...	12-16	8	*5*	*50* **	8	50	20	0.5	44	119	126	112	0.89
87	Argentina	97[y]	97[y]	96[y]	12-17	4 076	3 344	50	3 694[z]	52[z]	28[z]	286[z]	37[z]	112[z]	110[z]	114[z]	1.04[z]
88	Aruba	97[x]	99[x]	96[x]	12-16	8	6	51	7	50	92	1	39	107	110	104	0.94
89	Bahamas	98[y]	99[y]	98[y]	11-16	35	27	49	34[z]	51[z]	30[z]	.[z]	.[z]	101[z]	100[z]	103[z]	1.03[z]
90	Barbados	...	...	...	11-15	19	22	51	20	50	5 *	.	.	105	101	109	1.08
91	Belize[4]	91	89	93	11-16	...	22	51	34	51	63	2	50	...	...	...	...
92	Bermuda	86	78 **	95 **	11-17	6	***5***	***51***	4	53	44	.	.	85	78	91	1.16
93	Bolivia, Plurinational State of	89[y]	89[y]	90[y]	12-17	1 338	830	48	...	...	...	...	...	93[z]	95[z]	92[z]	0.97[z]
94	Brazil[4]	...	...	...	11-17	...	...	...	23 399	51	14	1 417	57	...	...	...	...
95	British Virgin Islands[5,9]	...	...	...	12-16	...	2	47	2	50	16	0.1 *	19 *	...	...	...	...
96	Cayman Islands	...	...	...	11-16	4	2	48	3	49	28	.	.	85	87	82	0.94
97	Chile	91	88	93	12-17	1 657	1 305	50	1 493	50	59	354	47	98	98	98	1,00
98	Colombia	96	97	95	11-16	5 264	3 589	52	5 131	51	20	288	54	106	103	108	1.05
99	Costa Rica	92	94	90	12-16	413	255	51	419	50	10	64	50	119	119	119	1,00
100	Cuba	98	98	99	12-17	885	740	50	798	48	.	215	38	96	98	95	0.97
101	Dominica	96	96	95	12-16	7	7	57	7	50	29	0.3	69	108	107	108	1.01
102	Dominican Republic	89	84	94	12-17	1 181	611	55	899	52	21	39	62	86	84	87	1.04
103	Ecuador	96	99	93	12-17	1 699	904	50	1 488	49	30	324	49	97	99	96	0.97
104	El Salvador	93	92	93	13-18	884	406	49	598	49	16	93	51	89	89	88	0.99
105	Grenada	80[x]	76[x]	85[x]	12-16	10	...	...	12[z]	50[z]	62[z]	0.5[z]	32[z]	121[z]	125[z]	117[z]	0.94[z]
106	Guatemala	94[y]	97[y]	92[y]	13-17	1 713	435	45	1 082[z]	48[z]	62[z]	299[z]	51[z]	71[z]	75[z]	67[z]	0.89[z]
107	Guyana	95[y]	93[y]	97[y]	12-16	93	62	50 **	87	50	9	5	48	98	96	102	1.06
108	Haiti	...	...	...	12-18	1 580	...	...	...	...	...	...	...	...	...	...	...
109	Honduras	...	...	...	12-16	896	...	...	663	54	27	...	...	75	70	80	1.13
110	Jamaica	91[y]	92[y]	91[y]	12-16	294	231 **	50 **	265[z]	50[z]	6[z]	.[z]	.[z]	91[z]	92[z]	91[z]	0.98[z]
111	Mexico	96	96	95	12-17	13 049	8 722	50	11 836	51	13	1 885	56	119	115	124	1.08
112	Montserrat[9]	...	...	...	12-16	...	0.3	47	0.4[y]	48[y]	.[y]	.[y]	.[y]	...	...	...	...
113	Netherlands Antilles	...	...	...	12-17	15	15	54	...	...	...	...	...	...	...	...	...
114	Nicaragua	...	...	...	12-16	662	321 **	54 **	465[z]	52[z]	22[z]	7[z]	60[z]	80[z]	78[z]	81[z]	1.04[z]
115	Panama	97	98	96	12-17	389	230	51	286	51	16	46	49	92	91	93	1.03
116	Paraguay	91[y]	90[y]	92[y]	12-17	832	425	50	561[z]	50[z]	22[z]	57[z]	50[z]	79[z]	78[z]	81[z]	1.03[z]
117	Peru	92	93	91	12-16	2 894	2 278	48	2 640	49	26	-	-	100	102	98	0.97
118	Saint Kitts and Nevis	95 *,[y]	...	...	12-16	5	*5*	*50*	4	50	4	.	.	99	100	99	0.99
119	Saint Lucia	95	93	97	12-16	16	12	56	16	49	3	0.2	18	94	95	93	0.98
120	Saint Vincent and the Grenadines	...	...	...	12-16	11	*10* **	*57* **	11[z]	50[z]	24[z]	.[z]	.[z]	119[z]	123[z]	114[z]	0.93[z]
121	Suriname	47[x]	40[x]	53[x]	12-18	65	***42***	***53***	55	56	18	24	50	90	85	94	1.10
122	Trinidad and Tobago	88 *,[y]	87 *,[y]	89 *,[y]	12-16	94	117	52	...	...	...	...	...	89 *,[z]	88 *,[z]	90 *,[z]	1.02 *,[z]
123	Turks and Caicos Islands[9]	...	...	...	12-16	...	1	51	2[y]	52[y]	...	.[y]	.[y]	...	...	...	...
124	Uruguay	80[y]	74[y]	86[y]	12-17	315	284	53	287[z]	52[z]	15[z]	44[z]	46[z]	111[z]	107[z]	114[z]	1.07[z]
125	Venezuela, Bolivarian Republic of	99	98	99	12-16	2 740	1 439	54	2 287	51	28	120	50	90	88	92	1.05
	North America and Western Europe																
126	Andorra	...	...	...	12-17	5	...	...	4	48	2[z]	0.4	48	87	88	85	0.97
127	Austria	99	99	99	10-17	736	748	48	724	48	9	285	44	102	102	102	1,00
128	Belgium	98[x]	...	...	12-17	723	1 033	51	806[z]	48[z]	69[z]	322[z]	44[z]	117[z]	120[z]	114[z]	0.95[z]
129	Canada	...	...	...	12-17	2 523	2 512	49	2 658[y]	48[y]	7[y]	...	...	100[y]	101[y]	100[y]	0.99[y]
130	Cyprus[5]	100[y]	100[y]	100[y]	12-17	68 *	63	49	64[z]	49[z]	17[z]	4[z]	16[z]	97[z]	97[z]	97[z]	1,00[z]
131	Denmark	99[y]	99[y]	99[y]	13-18	426	422	50	504[z]	49[z]	14[z]	132[z]	43[z]	117[z]	116[z]	117[z]	1.02[z]
132	Finland	100	100	100	13-18	392	480	51	423	50	9	134	47	100	100	100	1,00
133	France[10]	...	...	...	11-17	5 184	5 955	49	5 888	49	26	1 178	43	110	111	110	0.99
134	Germany	...	...	...	10-18	7 302	8 185	48	7 664[z]	47[z]	8[z]	1 557[z]	39[z]	101[z]	102[z]	100[z]	0.99[z]
135	Greece	...	...	...	12-17	651	771	49	717[z]	47[z]	5[z]	112[z]	35[z]	109[z]	112[z]	106[z]	0.95[z]
136	Iceland	100[y]	100[y]	100[y]	13-19	33	32	50	36[z]	49[z]	12[z]	8[z]	42[z]	96[z]	97[z]	95[z]	0.98[z]
137	Ireland	...	...	...	13-17	279	346	50	331	49	0.7	53	51	111	110	111	1.01
138	Israel	99[y]	98[y]	99[y]	12-17	708	629	49	708[z]	49[z]	11[z]	133[z]	45[z]	103[z]	101[z]	104[z]	1.03[z]
139	Italy	100[y]	100[y]	100[y]	11-18	4 589	4 450	49	4 626[z]	48[z]	8[z]	1 709[z]	40[z]	107[z]	107[z]	106[z]	0.99[z]
140	Luxembourg	...	...	...	12-18	43	33	50	43[z]	50[z]	18[z]	13[z]	47[z]	115[z]	114[z]	116[z]	1.02[z]
141	Malta	...	...	...	11-17	36	38	45	37[z]	46[z]	29[z]	6[z]	34[z]	103[z]	105[z]	100[z]	0.95[z]
142	Monaco[9]	...	...	...	11-17	...	3	51	3	49	22	0.5	44	...	...	...	...
143	Netherlands	...	...	...	12-17	1 207	1 365	48	1 475[z]	48[z]	...	698[z]	46[z]	127[z]	130[z]	124[z]	0.95[z]
144	Norway	100[y]	100[y]	100[y]	13-18	395	378	49	435[z]	48[z]	8[z]	131[z]	41[z]	98[z]	98[z]	98[z]	1,00[z]

Table 7

GROSS ENROLMENT RATIO (GER) IN SECONDARY EDUCATION (%)												OUT-OF-SCHOOL ADOLESCENTS (000)[2]						
Upper secondary				Total Secondary														
School year ending in				School year ending in								School year ending in Sum			School year ending in			
2011				1999				2011				1999			2011			
Total	Male	Female	GPI (F/M)	Total	Male	Female	GPI (F/M)	Total	Male	Female	GPI (F/M)	Total	Male	Female	Total	Male	Female	
...	...	...	...	...	...	...	...	...	...	...	...	...	...	...	...	...	...	72
76[y]	69[y]	83[y]	1.20[y]	74	71	78	1.10	85[y]	82[y]	88[y]	1.08[y]	1 262	675	587	332[y]	202[y]	130[y]	73
94[z]	95[z]	94[z]	0.98[z]	100	100	99	1,00	97[z]	98[z]	96[z]	0.99[z]	77	44	33	9[**,z]	...	...	74
75	68	84	1.24	80	76	84	1.11	82	77	88	1.15	0.8	0.5	0.3	0.1	0.1	0,0	75
...	...	...	...	...	...	...	...	...	...	...	...	...	...	...	...	...	...	76
31[z]	35[z]	26[z]	0.74[z]	26	29	22	0.76	48[z]	51[z]	45[z]	0.88[z]	...	...	...	1.2[z]	0.5[z]	0.6[z]	77
68	**64**	**73**	**1.15**	***62***	***63***[**]	***62***[**]	***0.98***[**]	**78**	**75**	**81**	**1.08**	...	...	...	286[y]	157[y]	128[y]	78
51	51	52	1.02	***38***	...	...	...	58	57	59	1.03	...	...	...	31	16	15	79
...	...	...	...	*92*	*92*	*93*	*1.01*	...	...	...	...	...	...	...	...	...	...	80
...	...	...	...	105	99	113	1.14	...	...	...	...	0.3	...	...	...	...	...	81
...	...	...	...	***80***	***76***	***84***	***1.10***	...	...	...	...	...	...	...	...	...	...	82
41[z]	42[z]	39[z]	0.93[z]	30	32	28	0.88	55[z]	54[z]	55[z]	1.02[z]	5[**]	2[**]	3[**]	...	...	...	83
...	...	...	...	...	...	...	...	...	...	...	...	*1 204*[**]	...	...	...	...	...	84
Latin America and the Caribbean																		
...	...	...	...	...	...	...	...	...	...	...	...	*0.03*[**]	...	...	...	...	...	85
84	76	91	1.21	*79*	*82*[**]	*76*[**]	*0.92*[**]	105	106	104	0.98	...	...	...	0.1[z]	...	...	86
68[z]	61[z]	76[z]	1.24[z]	85	83	87	1.05	90[z]	85[z]	95[z]	1.11[z]	...	...	...	23[z]	...	...	87
80	77	84	1.09	99	96	102	1.06	91	90	91	1.02	0,0	...	...	0.4[y]	0.2[y]	0.2[y]	88
90[z]	87[z]	94[z]	1.08[z]	78	78	77	0.99	96[z]	93[z]	98[z]	1.05[z]	1.4	0.6	0.8	1.1[z]	0.7[z]	0.4[z]	89
102	94	111	1.18	108	103	115	1.12	104	98	110	1.12	0.4[**]	...	...	0.7[*]	...	...	90
51	49	53	1.08	62	60	64	1.07	...	...	...	...	3[**]	2[**]	2[**]	...	...	...	91
72	65	78	1.19	***79***	***77***	***82***	***1.07***	77	71	83	1.18	...	...	...	0.4[**,z]	0.1[**,z]	0.3[**,z]	92
...	...	...	...	77	80	74	0.93	...	...	...	...	19[**]	4[**]	15[**]	30[**,z]	15[**,z]	15[**,z]	93
...	...	...	...	...	...	...	...	...	...						...	...	...	94
...	...	...	...	99	103	94	0.91	...	...	...	...	0,0[**]	...	...	...	...	...	95
77	74	80	1.07	99	101	97	0.96	81	81	81	1,00	0.1[**]	0.1[**]	0.1[**]	0.3	0.1	0.2	96
86	85	88	1.05	79	78	81	1.04	90	89	91	1.03	...	...	...	13	6	7	97
81	74	89	1.20	73	69	77	1.11	97	93	102	1.09	*475*[**]	*287*[**]	*188*[**]	166	88	77	98
76	69	82	1.18	62	59	65	1.10	101	99	104	1.05	...	...	...	...	...	...	99
84	84	85	1,00	80	77	82	1.06	90	91	90	0.99	18	11	7	14	6	8	100
85	78	92	1.18	100	86	115	1.33	98	95	102	1.07	0.4[**]	...	...	0.2[**]	...	...	101
71	65	78	1.19	56	50	62	1.24	76	72	81	1.13	69	37	32	30	14	17	102
78	75	81	1.08	57	56	57	1.03	88	87	88	1.02	229	113	115	65	31	34	103
46	45	47	1.04	53	53	52	0.98	68	68	68	1,00	***87***	***42***	***46***	38	18	20	104
89[z]	80[z]	99[z]	1.25[z]	...	...	...	...	108[z]	106[z]	109[z]	1.03[z]	...	...	...	...	...	...	105
54[z]	55[z]	54[z]	0.99[z]	33	36	30	0.84	64[z]	67[z]	62[z]	0.92[z]	352[**]	143[**]	209[**]	165[z]	57[z]	108[z]	106
84	78	91	1.16	83	83[**]	83[**]	1.01[**]	93	89	98	1.10	...	...	...	10[z]	6[z]	4[z]	107
...	...	...	...	...	...	...	...	...	...	...	...	...	...	...	...	...	...	108
72	61	84	1.38	...	...	...	...	74	67	82	1.22	...	...	...	...	...	...	109
95[z]	90[z]	100[z]	1.11[z]	88[**]	88[**]	88[**]	1.01[**]	93[z]	91[z]	94[z]	1.03[z]	9[**]	4[**]	4[**]	23[z]	11[z]	12[z]	110
63	62	65	1.05	70	70	70	1.01	91	88	94	1.07	903[**]	385[**]	518[**]	216	113	103	111
...	...	...	...	183	212	158	0.75	...	...	...	...	0,0	...	...	...	...	...	112
...	...	...	...	91	84	97	1.15	...	...	...	...	0.1	...	...	...	...	...	113
54[z]	49[z]	60[z]	1.23[z]	52[**]	47[**]	56[**]	1.18[**]	69[z]	66[z]	73[z]	1.10[z]	*126*	*71*	*55*	69[z]	36[z]	33[z]	114
54	50	59	1.19	67	65	69	1.07	74	71	77	1.08	35[**]	18[**]	18[**]	19	10	8	115
56[z]	54[z]	58[z]	1.07[z]	58	57	59	1.04	68[z]	66[z]	70[z]	1.05[z]	71	33	38	52[z]	26[z]	26[z]	116
78	77	79	1.03	83	86	81	0.94	91	92	91	0.99	62[**]	20[**]	42[**]	94	48	46	117
87	81	93	1.14	*97*	*95*	*99*	*1.04*	94	93	96	1.04	*0,0*[**]	...	...	0.2	0.1	0.1	118
97	99	96	0.97	71	62	79	1.26	95	97	94	0.97	3[**]	2[**]	1[**]	0.7[**,z]	0.3[**,z]	0.4[**,z]	119
91[z]	81[z]	101[z]	1.24[z]	*82*[**]	*71*[**]	*95*[**]	*1.34*[**]	107[z]	106[z]	109[z]	1.02[z]	*1.2*[**]	*0.9*[**]	*0.3*[**]	0.4[z]	0.1[z]	0.2[z]	120
79	57	102	1.80	***73***	***67***	***80***	***1.19***	85	74	97	1.31	...	...	...	6	3	3	121
...	...	...	...	78	74	81	1.09	...	...	...	...	11[**]	6[**]	5[**]	7[z]	4[z]	3[z]	122
...	...	...	...	...	...	...	...	...	...	...	...	...	...	...	...	...	...	123
71[z]	63[z]	79[z]	1.26[z]	92	85	100	1.17	90[z]	85[z]	96[z]	1.14[z]	...	...	...	35[z]	17[z]	19[z]	124
73	67	79	1.18	57	51	63	1.22	83	80	87	1.09	397	218	179	158	92	66	125
North America and Western Europe																		
88	81	96	1.19	...	...	...	...	87	86	88	1.03	...	...	...	0.6	0.3	0.3	126
95	98	92	0.93	98	100	95	0.95	98	100	96	0.96	...	...	...	...	...	...	127
107[z]	109[z]	106[z]	0.98[z]	141	136	146	1.07	111[z]	112[z]	109[z]	0.97[z]	...	...	...	...	...	...	128
102[y]	103[y]	101[y]	0.97[y]	103	102	104	1.02	102[y]	103[y]	100[y]	0.98[y]	...	...	...	...	...	...	129
87[z]	86[z]	88[z]	1.02[z]	93	92	95	1.03	91[z]	91[z]	92[z]	1.01[z]	1.1	0.5	0.6	1.3[z]	0.7[z]	0.6[z]	130
121[z]	121[z]	121[z]	1,00[z]	125	122	128	1.05	119[z]	118[z]	119[z]	1.01[z]	*1.4*	*1.0*	*0.5*	1[z]	1[z]	0[z]	131
116	111	120	1.08	121	116	126	1.09	108	106	110	1.05	0.2	...	...	4	2	2	132
118	117	119	1.03	109	109	109	1,00	114	113	114	1.01	95	54	40	4	...	...	133
107[z]	114[z]	100[z]	0.88[z]	98	99	97	0.98	103[z]	106[z]	100[z]	0.95[z]	...	...	...	...	...	...	134
110[z]	112[z]	108[z]	0.96[z]	91	89	93	1.04	109[z]	112[z]	107[z]	0.96[z]	40	23	17	1,0[z]	...	...	135
117[z]	115[z]	119[z]	1.03[z]	109	106	112	1.05	108[z]	107[z]	109[z]	1.02[z]	0.7	0.5	0.3	0.5[z]	0.2[z]	0.3[z]	136
131	127	135	1.07	106	102	109	1.06	119	117	121	1.03	2.6	2.3	0.2	3	...	...	137
102[z]	100[z]	103[z]	1.02[z]	100	101	100	0.99	102[z]	101[z]	103[z]	1.02[z]	4	...	...	0.1[z]	...	...	138
97[z]	98[z]	96[z]	0.99[z]	92	93	92	0.99	100[z]	101[z]	100[z]	0.99[z]	14	...	...	9[z]	...	...	139
90[z]	89[z]	92[z]	1.04[z]	98	95	100	1.05	101[z]	100[z]	103[z]	1.03[z]	1,0	0.6	0.4	0.4[z]	0.3[z]	0.1[z]	140
97[z]	110[z]	84[z]	0.76[z]	89	95	81	0.85	101[z]	107[z]	95[z]	0.89[z]	...	...	...	1.2[z]	0.5[z]	0.7[z]	141
...	...	...	...	...	...	...	...	...	...	...	...	...	...	...	...	...	...	142
116[z]	114[z]	118[z]	1.03[z]	123	126	121	0.96	121[z]	122[z]	121[z]	0.99[z]	1	...	...	15[z]	9[z]	6[z]	143
124[z]	126[z]	122[z]	0.97[z]	119	118	121	1.02	111[z]	112[z]	110[z]	0.98[z]	3	2	2	4[z]	2[z]	2[z]	144

Table 7 (continued)

	Country or territory	TRANSITION FROM PRIMARY TO SECONDARY GENERAL EDUCATION (%)			ENROLMENT IN SECONDARY EDUCATION												
		School year ending in 2010			Age group	School-age population (000)	Total enrolment				Enrolment in private institutions as % of total enrolment Median	Enrolment in technical and vocational education		Lower Secondary			
					2011	2011[3]	School year ending in 1999		School year ending in 2011		School year ending in 2011	School year ending in 2011		School year ending in 2011			
		Total	Male	Female			Total (000)	% F	Total (000)	% F		Total (000)	% F	Total	Male	Female	GPI (F/M)
145	Portugal	...	...	...	12-17	656	847	51	721[z]	50[z]	16[z]	183[z]	42[z]	116[z]	118[z]	115[z]	0.97[z]
146	San Marino[5,9]	99	100	98	11-18	2[*]	*1.0*	*49*	2	48	.	0.5	29	95[*]	95[*]	95[*]	1,00[*]
147	Spain	94[y]	93[y]	95[y]	12-17	2 527	3 299	50	3 248	49	27	567	46	122	123	121	0.99
148	Sweden	100	100	100	13-18	711	946	54	699	48	19	227	44	98	98	97	0.98
149	Switzerland	99[y]	...	...	13-19	634	544	47	605	48	10	207	42	109	108	111	1.02
150	United Kingdom	...	...	...	11-17	5 176	5 202	49	5 538[z]	49[z]	29[z]	733[z]	47[z]	113[z]	115[z]	111[z]	0.97[z]
151	United States	...	...	...	12-17	24 784	22 445	...	24 193[z]	49[z]	8[z]	.[z]	.[z]	103[z]	102[z]	103[z]	1.01[z]
	South and West Asia																
152	Afghanistan	...	...	...	13-18	4 663	***362***	-	2 265	34	...	...	...	60	76	43	0.57
153	Bangladesh	90[*]	84[*]	95[*]	11-17	22 241	9 912	49	11 543	53	95	364	33	68	60	77	1.28
154	Bhutan	**95**	**94**	**97**	13-18	90	20	44	**66**	**51**	**10**	**-**	**-**	**89**	**85**	**93**	**1.10**
155	India	...	...	...	11-17	170 732	67 090	39	107 687[z]	46[z]	...	...	...	81[z]	83	79[z]	0.95[z]
156	Iran, Islamic Republic of	97	97	97	11-17	8 448	9 727	47	7 237	48	12	801	33	102	104	99	0.95
157	Maldives	86[x]	84[x]	89[x]	13-17	34	15	51	...	...	...	...	...	118	118	118	1,00
158	Nepal[11]	...	...	...	10-16	4 512	1 265	40	**3 015**	**50**	...	...	...	**88**	**85**	**92**	**1.08**
159	Pakistan	73	72	73	10-16	28 413	...	...	9 939	41	31	390	42	46	51	40	0.78
160	Sri Lanka	98	99	97	10-17	2 515	...	...	2 574	50	7	151	44	103	103	102	0.99
	Sub-Saharan Africa																
161	Angola	34[x]	26[x]	45[x]	12-17	2 817	300	43	850[z]	41[z]	11[z]	363[z]	33[z]	39[z]	45[z]	34[z]	0.76[z]
162	Benin	67	68	66	12-18	1 408	213	31	724	38	19	25	38	64	76	51	0.67
163	Botswana	...	...	...	13-17	218	158	51	...	...	...	...	...	91[y]	89[y]	93[y]	1.05[y]
164	Burkina Faso	**51**	**53**	**48**	12-18	2 673	173	38	**676**	**44**	**41**	**27**	**46**	**34**	**37**	**31**	**0.85**
165	Burundi	37	42	32	13-19	1 363	***113***	...	381	42	9	19	39	38	43	33	0.77
166	Cameroon	52	49	56	12-18	3 069	643[**]	45[**]	1 574	46	25	322	37	64	68	59	0.86
167	Cape Verde	90	87	93	12-17	69	*45*[**]	...	62	54	14	2	49	113	109	118	1.09
168	Central African Republic	45[x]	45[x]	45[x]	12-18	699	***70***[**]	...	126	36	10[y]	5	38	24	32	17	0.53
169	Chad	72	76	65	12-18	1 798	123	21	457	30	15	7	37	29	40	19	0.47
170	Comoros	...	...	...	12-18	105	29	44	...	...	...	...	...	53	53	54	1.01
171	Congo	71	...	...	12-18	612	*173*	*41*	...	...	...	...	...	...	...	...	...
172	Côte d'Ivoire	46[x]	47[x]	45[x]	12-18	3 159	592[**]	35[**]	...	...	...	...	...	...	...	...	...
173	Democratic Rep. of the Congo	...	...	...	12-17	9 509	...	...	3 783	37	16[z]	...	...	...	...	...	...
174	Equatorial Guinea	85	86	84	13-18	89	20	27	...	...	...	...	...	45	46	44	0.96
175	Eritrea	90	91	89	12-18	787	115	41	257	44	5	2	37	45	49	40	0.81
176	Ethiopia	82	84	80	13-18	12 087	1 060	40	4 542	46	11	371	46	47	50	44	0.88
177	Gabon	...	...	...	11-17	243	87	46	...	...	...	...	...	...	...	...	...
178	Gambia	85	84	85	13-18	237	...	...	124[**,z]	49[**,z]	...	...	...	63[z]	62[z]	63[z]	1.02[z]
179	Ghana	**91**	**90**	**91**	12-18	3 695	1 024	44	**2 216**	**46**	**16**	**80**	**37**	**83**	**85**	**80**	**0.94**
180	Guinea	59	62	54	13-19	1 535	168[**]	26[**]	**669**	**38**	**34**	**33**	**47**	**49**[**]	**59**[**]	**38**[**]	**0.65**[**]
181	Guinea-Bissau	...	...	...	13-17	170	*26*	*36*	...	...	...	...	...	...	...	...	...
182	Kenya	...	...	...	12-17	5 537	1 822	49	3 204[y]	47[y]	13[y]	16[y]	58[y]	91[y]	94[y]	88[y]	0.93[y]
183	Lesotho	74[**]	72[**]	76[**]	13-17	267	74	57	131[**]	58[**]	1[**]	...	...	60[**]	50[**]	69[**]	1.39[**]
184	Liberia	78[x]	81[x]	74[x]	12-17	530	114	39	238	44	...	18	50	50	54	45	0.83
185	Madagascar	70	70	69	11-17	3 508	...	...	1 022[**,y]	49[**,y]	40[**,y]	...	...	42[y]	43[y]	41[y]	0.96[y]
186	Malawi	76	76	75	12-17	2 155	556	41	736	47	...	-	-	42	43	41	0.94
187	Mali	79	80	78	13-18	2 080	218	34	821	41	31	94	41	53	61	45	0.75
188	Mauritius	71	66	76	11-17	146	104	49	...	...	54[**,z]	...	...	96	96	96	1,00
189	Mozambique	**49**	**47**	**51**	13-17	2 715	103	39	**728**	**47**	**13**	**32**	**34**	**34**	**36**	**32**	**0.90**
190	Namibia	82[y]	81[y]	84[y]	14-18	263	116	53	...	...	...	...	...	...	...	...	...
191	Niger	**54**	**56**	**52**	13-19	2 371	105	38	**373**	**39**	20[**,y]	**7**	**54**	**21**	**25**	**17**	**0.69**
192	Nigeria	...	...	...	12-17	21 088	3 845	47	9 057[z]	46[z]	22[z]	...	...	47[z]	49[z]	44[z]	0.89[z]
193	Rwanda	...	...	...	13-18	1 358	105	51	486	52	21	59	50	47	45	49	1.09
194	Sao Tome and Principe	68	65	70	12-16	20	...	...	**14**	**53**	**3**	**0.5**	**27**	**97**	**91**	**104**	**1.14**
195	Senegal	92	93	91	13-19	1 982	234	39	834[*]	47[*]	19[*]	38[*]	51[*]	...	...	...	...
196	Seychelles	97	95	98	12-16	6	8	50	7	50	8	-	-	131	129	133	1.03
197	Sierra Leone	...	...	...	12-17	798	***156***	***42***[**]	...	...	...	...	...	58	65	52	0.79
198	Somalia	...	...	...	12-17	1 240	...	...	...	...	...	...	...	...	...	...	...
199	South Africa	...	...	...	14-18	4 950	4 239	53	4 688[y]	51[y]	3[y]	269[y]	43[y]	96[y]	96[y]	97[y]	1.01[y]
200	South Sudan	...	...	...	12-17	...	...	...	...	...	...	...	...	...	...	...	...
201	Swaziland	90	90	90	13-17	151	62	50	91	49	3	-	-	69	70	67	0.96
202	Togo	**75**	**78**	**71**	12-18	966	232	29	546	...	23	28	...	70	...	...	...
203	Uganda	58	60	57	13-18	4 793	*547*	*43*	1 278[**,y]	45[**,y]	...	83[**,y]	38[**,y]	34[y]	37[y]	31[y]	0.84[y]
204	United Republic of Tanzania	41[**,y]	45[**,y]	37[**,y]	14-19	5 890	...	...	**2 118**	**46**	...	**234**	**47**	**47**	**49**	**44**	**0.89**
205	Zambia	56	61	51	14-18	1 500	...	...	...	...	...	...	...	70	75	64	0.86
206	Zimbabwe	...	...	...	13-18	1 930	...	...	...	...	...	...	...	...	...	...	...

Table 7

GROSS ENROLMENT RATIO (GER) IN SECONDARY EDUCATION (%)												OUT-OF-SCHOOL ADOLESCENTS (000)[2]						
Upper secondary				Total Secondary														
School year ending in				School year ending in								School year ending in Sum			School year ending in			
2011				1999				2011				1999			2011			
Total	Male	Female	GPI (F/M)	Total	Male	Female	GPI (F/M)	Total	Male	Female	GPI (F/M)	Total	Male	Female	Total	Male	Female	
102[z]	98[z]	106[z]	1.08[z]	103	99	107	1.08	109[z]	108[z]	110[z]	1.02[z]	0.3	…	…	…	…	…	145
95	94	96	1.02	…	…	…	…	95	94	96	1.01	…	…	…	…	…	…	146
141	137	144	1.05	109	106	112	1.06	129	128	129	1.01	38	21	17	1	…	…	147
99	99	98	0.99	156	139	175	1.26	98	99	98	0.99	3	2	1	26	14	12	148
86	89	82	0.93	96	99	92	0.93	95	97	94	0.97	7	4	3	10	5	4	149
100[z]	97[z]	102[z]	1.05[z]	101	100	101	1.01	105[z]	105[z]	106[z]	1.01[z]	20	8	12	4[z]	…	…	150
90[z]	89[z]	91[z]	1.01[z]	94	…	…	…	96[z]	96[z]	97[z]	1.01[z]	462	…	…	122[z]	…	…	151
															South and West Asia			
35	46	24	0.52	11	22	-	-	49	62	34	0.55	…	…	…	…	…	…	152
40	39	40	1.03	47	47	47	0.99	52	48	56	1.17	…	…	…	2 645[*]	1 849[*]	795[*]	153
50	52	47	0.92	37	41	33	0.80	75	73	77	1.05	13	6	7	6	4	2	154
50[z]	53[z]	47[z]	0.88[z]	43	51	36	0.70	63[z]	66[z]	60[z]	0.92[z]	…	…	…	20 277[z]	10 006[z]	10 271[z]	155
76	77	74	0.96	79	82	76	0.93	86	87	84	0.96	…	…	…	89	31	57	156
…	…	…	…	41	40	43	1.08	…	…	…	…	2,0	1.1	0.9	…	…	…	157
47	47	48	1.01	36	43	28	0.66	66	65	67	1.04	…	…	…	…	…	…	158
27	32	21	0.67	…	…	…	…	35	40	30	0.73	…	…	…	6 964	3 234	3 731	159
102	98	107	1.09	…	…	…	…	102	100	104	1.04	…	…	…	46	30	15	160
															Sub-Saharan Africa			
22[z]	28[z]	16[z]	0.56[z]	13	15	11	0.75	31[z]	37[z]	25[z]	0.69[z]	…	…	…	166[**,z]	…	…	161
33	46	21	0.45	22	31	14	0.44	51	64	39	0.60	…	…	…	…	…	…	162
…	…	…	…	73	71	76	1.07	…	…	…	…	11[**]	7[**]	4[**]	5[**,y]	3[**,y]	2[**,y]	163
11	13	8	0.62	9	11	7	0.62	25	27	22	0.81	918	443	475	854	414	440	164
15	18	11	0.62	11	…	…	…	28	32	24	0.74	…	…	…	…	…	…	165
34	38	31	0.80	26[**]	28[**]	24[**]	0.84[**]	51	56	47	0.84	…	…	…	579	247	332	166
67	58	77	1.33	68[**]	…	…	…	90	83	97	1.17	…	…	…	3[**,z]	…	…	167
9	11	7	0.63	12[**]	…	…	…	18	23	13	0.55	…	…	…	224[**]	88[**]	136[**]	168
19	28	10	0.36	10	16	4	0.26	25	35	15	0.44	549	235	314	…	…	…	169
…	…	…	…	30	33	27	0.81	…	…	…	…	…	…	…	…	…	…	170
…	…	…	…	36	42	29	0.70	…	…	…	…	…	…	…	…	…	…	171
…	…	…	…	23[**]	30[**]	16[**]	0.54[**]	…	…	…	…	1 175[**]	539[**]	636[**]	…	…	…	172
…	…	…	…	…	…	…	…	40	50	29	0.59	…	…	…	…	…	…	173
…	…	…	…	33	48	18	0.37	…	…	…	…	13[**]	…	…	…	…	…	174
23	27	20	0.74	22	26	18	0.68	33	37	29	0.78	113	52	61	206	96	110	175
17	19	15	0.78	13	16	11	0.67	38	40	35	0.87	3 599	1 521	2 078	3 194[**]	1 469[**]	1 725[**]	176
…	…	…	…	48	52	44	0.86	…	…	…	…	…	…	…	…	…	…	177
45[**,z]	48[**,z]	41[**,z]	0.85[**,z]	…	…	…	…	54[**,z]	56[**,z]	53[**,z]	0.95[**,z]	…	…	…	32[**,z]	16[**,z]	15[**,z]	178
41	44	37	0.84	40	44	36	0.81	59	62	56	0.90	507[**]	234[**]	273[**]	275[y]	138[y]	137[y]	179
34[**]	42[**]	26[**]	0.61[**]	14[**]	20[**]	7[**]	0.37[**]	43	52	33	0.64	507	215	292	424	181	243	180
…	…	…	…	19	24	13	0.55	…	…	…	…	42	16	27	…	…	…	181
44[y]	47[y]	41[y]	0.87[y]	38	39	38	0.96	60[y]	63[y]	57[y]	0.90[y]	225[**]	124[**]	101[**]	30[**,y]	…	…	182
33[**]	27[**]	39[**]	1.42[**]	30	26	35	1.36	49[**]	41[**]	57[**]	1.40[**]	31[**]	22[**]	9[**]	40[**]	24[**]	16[**]	183
39	44	35	0.80	31	38	24	0.65	45	49	40	0.81	…	…	…	…	…	…	184
15[**,y]	16[**,y]	14[y]	0.87[**,y]	…	…	…	…	31[**,y]	32[**,y]	30[y]	0.94[**,y]	626[**]	299[**]	327[**]	…	…	…	185
17	19	15	0.79	38	45	32	0.70	34	36	33	0.91	68	…	…	319[y]	160[y]	159[y]	186
24	30	18	0.62	14	19	10	0.54	39	46	33	0.71	…	…	…	563	247	317	187
…	…	…	…	76	76	75	0.98	…	…	…	…	14[**]	7[**]	7[**]	…	…	…	188
12	13	12	0.88	5	6	4	0.63	26	27	25	0.89	730[**]	310[**]	420[**]	656	283	373	189
…	…	…	…	57	54	61	1.12	…	…	…	…	18	11	7	…	…	…	190
5	7	4	0.53	7	9	5	0.59	15	18	12	0.66	787	375	412	1 170	564	606	191
41[z]	44[z]	38[z]	0.87[z]	23	24	22	0.91	44[z]	47[z]	41[z]	0.88[z]	…	…	…	…	…	…	192
23	23	22	0.96	10	10	10	1.01	36	35	37	1.05	…	…	…	…	…	…	193
25	24	26	1.08	…	…	…	…	69	65	74	1.13	…	…	…	1.7[z]	0.8[z]	0.9[z]	194
…	…	…	…	16	19	12	0.65	42[*]	44[*]	40[*]	0.92[*]	…	…	…	…	…	…	195
115	102	129	1.26	105	103	107	1.04	124	117	131	1.12	0,0	…	…	0.1	…	…	196
…	…	…	…	28	33[**]	22[**]	0.68[**]	…	…	…	…	…	…	…	…	…	…	197
…	…	…	…	…	…	…	…	…	…	…	…	…	…	…	…	…	…	198
92[y]	89[y]	95[y]	1.08[y]	88	83	94	1.13	94[y]	92[y]	96[y]	1.05[y]	161[**]	89[**]	72[**]	…	…	…	199
…	…	…	…	…	…	…	…	…	…	…	…	…	…	…	…	…	…	200
47	47	47	0.99	44	44	44	1,00	60	61	59	0.97	20	10	10	…	…	…	201
37	…	…	…	31	45	18	0.40	56	…	…	…	135	27	107	…	…	…	202
15[**,y]	18[**,y]	13[**,y]	0.72[**,y]	16	19	14	0.76	28[**,y]	31[**,y]	26[**,y]	0.82[**,y]	…	…	…	650[**,z]	305[**,z]	344[**,z]	203
10	12	8	0.70	…	…	…	…	35	37	33	0.87	…	…	…	…	…	…	204
…	…	…	…	…	…	…	…	…	…	…	…	…	…	…	…	…	…	205
…	…	…	…	…	…	…	…	…	…	…	…	…	…	…	…	…	…	206

Table 8

Teaching staff in pre-primary, primary and secondary education

	PRE-PRIMARY EDUCATION									PRIMARY EDUCATION						
	Teaching staff				Trained teachers (%)[1]			Pupil/teacher ratio[2]		Teaching staff				Trained teachers (%)[1]		
	School year ending in				School year ending in			School year ending in		School year ending in				School year ending in		
	1999		2011		2011			1999	2011	1999		2011		2011		
Country or territory	Total (000)	% F	Total (000)	% F	Total	Male	Female			Total (000)	% F	Total (000)	% F	Total	Male	Female
Arab States																
Algeria	1	93	19	74	...	...	...	28	25	170	46	145	55	...	...	...
Bahrain	0.7	100	2	100	46	-	46	21	16	*4* [**]	*72* [**]	...	...	...	...	...
Djibouti	0.0	100	0.08 [y]	75 [y]	100 [y]	100 [y]	100 [y]	28	16 [y]	1.0	28	**2**	**25**	100	100	100
Egypt	***17*** [**]	***99*** [**]	33 [z]	98 [z]	...	...	...	**22** [**]	30 [z]	***353*** [**]	***53*** [**]	380 [z]	53 [z]	...	...	...
Iraq	*5*	*100*	...	...	...	...	...	*15*	...	*170*	*72*	...	...	...	...	...
Jordan	3	100	5 [z]	100 [z]	100 [z]	100 [z]	100 [z]	22	18 [z]	...	...	...	...	...	...	...
Kuwait	4	100	7	100	72	-	73	15	11	10	73	26	90	78	55	80
Lebanon	11 [**]	95 [**]	10	99	...	...	...	13 [**]	15	29 [**]	83 [**]	32	87	...	...	...
Libya	1	100	...	...	...	...	...	8	...	...	...	...	...	...	...	...
Mauritania	...	...	...	...	...	...	...	...	...	7	26	14	36	100	100	100
Morocco	40	40	**38**	**69**	**100**	**100**	**100**	20	**18**	123	39	**155**	**52**	**100**	**100**	**100**
Oman	...	...	2 [y]	99 [y]	100	.	100	...	19 [y]	12	52	...	...	...	...	...
Palestine	3	100	5	100	100 [y]	100 [y]	100 [y]	29	19	10	54	16	70	100	100	100
Qatar	0.4 [**]	96 [**]	2	97	29	69	28	21 [**]	15	5	75	8	92	43 [**,z]	80 [**,z]	38 [**,z]
Saudi Arabia	...	...	20 [*]	100 [*]	...	...	...	...	10 [*]	...	...	304 [*]	50 [*]	...	...	...
Sudan	...	...	...	...	...	...	...	...	...	...	...	...	...	...	...	...
Syrian Arab Republic	5	96	9	95	...	...	...	24	19	110	65 [**]	...	...	...	...	...
Tunisia	4	95	...	...	...	...	...	20	...	60	50	59	56	...	...	...
United Arab Emirates	3	100	7	98	100	100	100	19	18	17	73	20	87	...	...	...
Yemen	0.8	93	2	97	...	...	...	17	15	103 [**]	20 [**]	120	27	...	...	...
Sudan (pre-secession)	***13***	***84***	[y]	100 [y]	71 [y]	. [y]	71 [y]	***27***	30 [y]	***117*** [**]	***52*** [**]	124 [**,y]	61 [**,y]	60 [**,y]	64 [**,y]	57 [**,y]
Central and Eastern Europe																
Albania	4	100	4	100	...	...	...	20	19	*13*	*75*	11	83	...	...	...
Belarus	54	...	45	99	61	41	62	5	7	32	99	24	...	100	...	...
Bosnia and Herzegovina	...	...	1	98	...	...	...	...	14	...	...	...	...	...	...	...
Bulgaria	19	...	18 [z]	100 [z]	...	...	...	11	12 [z]	23	...	15 [z]	94 [z]	...	...	...
Croatia	6	100	8 [z]	99 [z]	...	...	...	13	13 [z]	11	89	12 [z]	92 [z]	...	...	...
Czech Republic	17	100 [**]	24	100	...	...	...	18	14	36	85	25	97	...	...	...
Estonia	7	100	8 [z]	100 [z]	...	...	...	8	6 [z]	8	86 [**]	6 [z]	93 [z]	...	...	...
Hungary	32	100	30	100	...	...	...	12	11	47	85	37	96	...	...	...
Latvia	7	99	7	100	...	...	...	9	11	9	97	10	93	...	...	...
Lithuania	13	99	12	99	...	...	...	7	7	13	98	9	96	...	...	...
Montenegro	***0.6***	...	**1**	**94**	...	...	...	***20***	**9**	...	...	**5**	**74**	...	...	...
Poland	*74*	...	59 [z]	98 [z]	...	...	...	*12*	17 [z]	***289***	***83***	240 [z]	84 [z]	...	...	...
Republic of Moldova	*10*	*100*	12	100	...	.	91	*9*	10	12	96	9	98	...	...	...
Romania	37	100	38 [z]	100 [z]	...	...	...	17	17 [z]	69	86	52 [z]	86 [z]	...	...	...
Russian Federation	642	100 [*]	607 [y]	96 [y]	...	...	...	7	8 [y]	367	98	278 [y]	98 [y]	...	...	...
Serbia	8	98 [**]	12	99	76	75	76	21	13	...	...	19	84	70	46	75
Slovakia	16	100	12	100	...	...	...	10	12	17	93	14	89	...	...	...
Slovenia	5	99 [*]	6	98	...	...	...	11	9	6	96	6	97	...	...	...
The former Yugoslav Rep. of Macedonia	3	99	2 [z]	99 [z]	...	...	...	10	7 [z]	6	66	7 [z]	79 [z]	...	...	...
Turkey	17	...	43 [z]	95 [z]	...	...	...	15	23 [z]	...	...	...	...	...	...	...
Ukraine	143	100	141	99	...	...	...	8	9	107	98	99	99	100	...	...
Central Asia																
Armenia	8	...	6	100	79	100	79	7	9	...	...	...	...	...	...	...
Azerbaijan	12	100	11	99	92	85	92	7	9	37	83	43	89	100	100	100
Georgia	*7*	*100*	...	...	...	...	...	*11*	...	*18*	*95*	35 [*,z]	86 [*,z]	95 [*,y]	92 [*,y]	95 [*,y]
Kazakhstan	19	...	**64**	**98**	...	...	...	9	**10**	*65* [**]	*97* [**]	**62**	**98**	...	...	...
Kyrgyzstan	3	100	3	99	46	48	46	18	27	19	95	16	98	70	70	70
Mongolia	3	100	5	98	93	84	93	25	26	8	93	9	96	99	98	99
Tajikistan	***5***	***100***	5	100	87	.	87	***11***	13	***31***	***60***	29	75	94	94	94
Turkmenistan	...	...	...	...	...	...	...	...	...	...	...	...	...	...	...	...
Uzbekistan	66	96	56	96	100	100	100	9	9	123	84	125	87	100	100	100
East Asia and the Pacific																
Australia	...	...	...	...	...	...	...	...	...	105 [**]	...	...	...	...	...	...
Brunei Darussalam	0.6 [*]	83 [*]	0.7 [z]	97 [z]	73 [z]	95 [z]	72 [z]	20 [*]	20 [z]	3 [*]	66 [*]	4	76	88	94	87
Cambodia	***3***	***98***	4	95	97	...	...	***24***	27	***46***	***39***	47	48	99	...	...
China	875	94	1 286	97	...	...	...	27	23	***5 860***	***51***	5 939	58	...	...	...
Cook Islands	0.03	100	0.03	97	70	100	69	14	16	0.1	86	0.1	...	97	...	...
Democratic People's Republic of Korea	...	...	...	...	...	...	...	...	...	...	...	...	...	...	...	...
Fiji	*0.3*	*99*	...	...	...	...	...	*21*	...	*4*	*56*	3	61	100	100	100
Indonesia	118 [**]	98 [**]	387	98	...	...	...	17 [**]	10	*1 256* [**]	*54* [**]	1 923	64	...	...	...
Japan	96	...	109 [z]	...	...	...	...	31	27 [z]	367	...	399 [z]	...	...	...	...
Kiribati	...	...	...	...	...	...	...	...	...	0.6	62	...	...	...	...	...
Lao People's Democratic Republic	2	100	5	97	97	90	98	18	18	27	43	34	52	94	98	90
Macao, China	0.5	100	0.6	98	92	82	92	31	17	2	87	2	87	86	72	88
Malaysia	21	100	45 [z]	97 [z]	...	...	...	27	18 [z]	143	66	232 [z]	69 [z]	...	...	...
Marshall Islands	0.1	...	...	...	...	...	...	11	...	0.6	...	...	...	...	...	...
Micronesia (Federated States of)	...	...	...	...	...	...	...	...	...	...	...	...	...	...	...	...
Myanmar	2	...	9 [z]	97 [z]	59 [z]	56 [z]	59 [z]	22	17 [z]	155	73	182 [z]	84 [z]	100 [z]	100 [z]	100 [z]
Nauru	*0.1*	*98*	...	...	...	...	...	*13*	...	*0.07*	*92*	...	...	...	...	...
New Zealand	7	98	10 [z]	98 [z]	...	...	...	15	11 [z]	20	82	24 [z]	84 [z]	...	...	...
Niue	0.01	100	...	...	...	...	...	10	...	0.02	100	...	...	...	...	...
Palau	*0.1*	*98*	...	...	...	...	...	*10*	...	0.1	82	...	...	...	...	...

PRIMARY EDUCATION			SECONDARY EDUCATION														
Pupil/teacher ratio[2]		Pupil/trained teacher ratio[2]	Teaching staff, total secondary				Trained teachers (%)[1]			Pupil/teacher ratio[2]							
										Lower secondary		Upper secondary		Total secondary			
School year ending in		School year ending in	School year ending in				School year ending in			School year ending in		School year ending in		School year ending in			
1999	2011	2011	1999		2011		2011			1999	2011	1999	2011	1999	2011		
			Total (000)	% F	Total (000)	% F	Total	Male	Female							Country or territory	
																Arab States	
28	23	...	...	...	...	...	...	...	...	...	...	...	...	...	...	Algeria	
18[**]	...	...	*4*[**]	*52*[**]	...	...	...	...	...	*15*[**]	...	*13*[**]	...	*14*[**]	...	Bahrain	
40	**35**	35	1	22	**2**	**24**	100	...	...	26	**32**	16	**20**	23	**27**	Djibouti	
22[**]	28[z]	...	***491***[**]	***40***[**]	549[y]	44[y]	...	...	...	***21***[**]	16[y]	***13***[**]	8[y]	***17***[**]	12[y]	Egypt	
21	...	...	*62*	*69*	...	...	...	...	...	*22*	...	*16*	...	*20*	...	Iraq	
...	...	...	...	...	...	...	...	...	...	...	...	17	...	...	...	Jordan	
13	9	11	22[**]	56[**]	34	54	75	70	79	12[**]	8	9[**]	7	11[**]	8	Kuwait	
14[**]	14	...	43[**]	52[**]	42	58	...	...	...	9[**]	11	8[**]	8	9[**]	9	Lebanon	
...	...	...	...	...	...	...	...	...	...	...	...	...	...	...	...	Libya	
47	39	39	2	10	...	...	...	...	...	...	38[**,y]	...	...	26[**]	...	Mauritania	
28	**26**	**26**[8]	88[**]	33[**]	...	...	...	...	...	19[**]	...	14[**]	18[**,y]	17[**]	...	Morocco	
25	...	...	13	50	...	...	...	...	...	19	...	16	20[y]	18	...	Oman	
38	26	26	18	47	34	51	100	100	100	26	21	19	18	25	20	Palestine	
13	11	28[**,z]	4[**]	57[**]	7	55	67	72	62	13[**]	9	8[**]	12	10[**]	10	Qatar	
...	11[*]	...	...	...	264[**,y]	52[**,y]	...	...	...	...	11[**,y]	...	12[**,y]	...	11[**,y]	Saudi Arabia	
...	...	...	...	...	...	...	...	...	...	...	...	...	...	...	...	Sudan	
25	...	...	54	...	...	...	...	...	...	...	...	...	8	19	...	Syrian Arab Republic	
24	17	...	56[**]	40[**]	85	51	...	...	...	23[**]	...	15[**]	...	19[**]	14	Tunisia	
16	17	...	16	55	29	58	100	100	100	14	16	10	9	12	12	United Arab Emirates	
22[**]	30	...	48[**]	19[**]	102	29	...	...	...	22[**]	11	21	59	22[**]	16	Yemen	
24[**]	38[**,y]	64[**,y]	***52***[**]	***49***[**]	83[**,y]	55[**,y]	61[**,y]	63[**,y]	59[**,y]	***24***[**]	28[**,y]	***20***	17[y]	***22***[**]	22[**,y]	Sudan (pre-secession)	
																Central and Eastern Europe	
23	20	...	*22*	*54*	23	63	...	...	...	*16*	14	*18*	18	*16*	15	Albania	
20	15	15	...	...	...	...	...	...	...	...	...	...	...	...	...	Belarus	
...	...	...	...	...	...	...	...	...	...	...	...	...	12	...	...	Bosnia and Herzegovina	
18	17[z]	...	56	...	44[z]	79[z]	...	...	...	13	12[z]	12	12[z]	13	12[z]	Bulgaria	
19	14[z]	...	33	64	48[z]	69[z]	...	...	...	14	9[z]	11	7[z]	12	8[z]	Croatia	
18	19	...	***93***	***66***	71	66	...	...	...	***13***	11	***9***	12	***11***	11	Czech Republic	
16	12[z]	...	11	81[**]	11[z]	77[z]	...	...	...	11	8[z]	10	9[z]	10	9[z]	Estonia	
11	11	...	100	71	88	71	...	...	...	11	10	9	10	10	10	Hungary	
15	11	...	25	80	16	82	...	...	...	10	8	10	9	10	8	Latvia	
17	12	...	*38*	...	38	81	...	...	...	...	9	...	8	*11*	9	Lithuania	
...	**8**	...	...	...	...	...	...	...	...	...	...	...	**13**	...	...	Montenegro	
11	9[z]	...	***301***	***66***	273[z]	70[z]	...	...	...	***11***	12[z]	***15***	9[z]	***13***	10[z]	Poland	
21	15	...	33	72	29	77	...	...	...	13	9	12	11	13	10	Republic of Moldova	
19	16[z]	...	177	64	146[z]	68[z]	...	...	...	12	10[z]	13	15[z]	13	12[z]	Romania	
18	18[y]	...	...	...	1 136[y]	81[y]	...	...	...	...	...	...	...	...	8[y]	Russian Federation	
...	15	22	...	...	62	64	44	34	50	...	9	14	10	...	9	Serbia	
19	15	...	54[**]	72[**]	45	74	...	...	...	13	11	12[**]	12	13[**]	12	Slovakia	
14	17	...	17	69	15	73	...	...	...	14	7	13	11	13	9	Slovenia	
22	16[z]	...	13	49	17[z]	56[z]	...	...	...	16	11[z]	16	14[z]	16	12[z]	The former Yugoslav Rep. of Macedonia	
...	...	...	...	...	...	...	...	...	...	...	...	*16*	18[z]	...	...	Turkey	
20	16	16	400	76	...	...	...	...	...	...	...	...	...	13	...	Ukraine	
																Central Asia	
...	...	...	...	...	42[z]	84[z]	99[z]	98[z]	99[z]	...	...	...	...	...	7[z]	Armenia	
19	11	11	...	...	...	...	...	...	...	...	...	...	...	...	...	Azerbaijan	
17	8[*,z]	9[*,y]	*59*	*76*	45[*,y]	86[*,y]	95[*,y]	92[*,y]	95[*,y]	*9*	8[*,y]	*5*	8[*,y]	*7*	8[*,y]	Georgia	
19[**]	**16**	...	*177*[**]	*83*[**]	**191**	**85**	...	...	...	...	...		...	*11*[**]	**9**	Kazakhstan	
24	25	36	48	68	44[z]	83[z]	85[z]	77[z]	86[z]	...	...	...	...	13	15[*,z]	Kyrgyzstan	
32	29	30	11	69	19[z]	73[z]	98[z]	96[z]	98[z]	19	...	17	...	19	14[z]	Mongolia	
22	23	25	47	43	68	46	...	...	...	...	...	...	...	16	15	Tajikistan	
...	...	...	...	...	...	...	...	...	...	...	...	...	...	...	...	Turkmenistan	
21	16	16	307	57	329	62	100	100	100	...	...	...	...	11	13	Uzbekistan	
																Central Asia	
18[**]	...	...	...	...	...	...	...	...	...	...	...	...	...	...	...	Australia	
14[*]	11	13	3	48	5	65	91	90	91	12[*]	...	10[*]	...	11	10	Brunei Darussalam	
53	47	48	***20***	***29***	...	...	...	...	...	***18***	24[z]	***24***	...	***20***	...	Cambodia	
22	17	...	*4 763*	*41*[**]	6 431	49	...	...	...	*18*	14	*16*	16	*17*	15	China	
18	16	16	*0.1*	...	0.1	57	88	80	95	...	...	...	...	*14*	14	Cook Islands	
...	...	...	...	...	...	...	...	...	...	...	...	...	...	...	...	Democratic People's Republic of Korea	
28	31	31	5	47	4	50	100	100	100	...	...	...	...	21	26	Fiji	
22[**]	16	...	***1 040***	***40***	1 407	54	...	...	...	***15***	14	***13***	16	***14***	15	Indonesia	
21	18[z]	...	630	...	614[z]	...	...	...	...	16	14[z]	13	11[z]	14	12[z]	Japan	
25	...	...	***0.4***	***47***	...	...	...	...	...	...	...	...	...	***21***	...	Kiribati	
31	27	29	12	40	25	48	...	...	...	20	19	22	21	20	20	Lao People's Democratic Republic	
31	15	17	1	56	3	59	72	63	78	24	16	21	14	23	15	Macao, China	
20	13[z]	...	*120*[**]	*62*[**]	191[z]	67[z]	...	...	...	*18*[**]	...	*18*[**]	...	*18*[**]	14[z]	Malaysia	
15	...	...	0.3	...	...	...	...	...	...	28	...	18	12[y]	22	...	Marshall Islands	
...	...	...	...	...	...	...	...	...	...	...	...	...	...	...	...	Micronesia (Federated States of)	
31	28[z]	28[z]	68	76	84[z]	85[z]	99[z]	99[z]	99[z]	28	36[z]	38	28[z]	30	34[z]	Myanmar	
21	...	...	*0.04*	*39*	...	...	...	...	...	...	...	...	...	*17*	...	Nauru	
18	14[z]	...	28	58	35[z]	62[z]	...	...	...	18	15[z]	13	14[z]	15	15[z]	New Zealand	
16	...	...	0.02	44	...	...	...	...	...	6	...	20	...	11	...	Niue	
15	...	...	0.2	51	...	...	...	...	...	14	...	12	...	13	...	Palau	

Table 8 (continued)

	PRE-PRIMARY EDUCATION									PRIMARY EDUCATION						
	Teaching staff				Trained teachers (%)[1]			Pupil/teacher ratio[2]		Teaching staff				Trained teachers (%)[1]		
	School year ending in				School year ending in			School year ending in		School year ending in				School year ending in		
	1999		2011		2011			1999	2011	1999		2011		2011		
Country or territory	Total (000)	% F	Total (000)	% F	Total	Male	Female			Total (000)	% F	Total (000)	% F	Total	Male	Female
Papua New Guinea	...	...	...	...	...	...	...	...	...	16 **	39 **	...	...	...	...	...
Philippines	18	92 **	...	...	...	...	...	33	...	360	87	435 y	90 y	...	...	...
Republic of Korea	...	...	...	...	...	...	...	...	...	122	67	158 z	78 z	...	...	...
Samoa	0.1 **	94 **	0.3	96	...	...	...	42 **	12	1 **	71 **	1.0 z	77 z	...	...	...
Singapore	...	...	...	...	...	...	...	...	...	...	...	17 y	81 y	94 y	93 y	95 y
Solomon Islands	...	...	1 z	87 z	31 z	20 z	33 z	...	19 z	3	41	5 z	45 z	58 z	59 z	57 z
Thailand	111	79	95	78	...	...	...	25	29	298	63	...	...	...	...	...
Timor-Leste	...	...	...	...	...	...	...	...	...	3	30 **	8	40	...	...	...
Tokelau	0.01	100	...	...	...	...	...	11	...	0.03	76	...	...	...	...	...
Tonga	0.1	100	...	...	...	...	...	18	...	0.8	67	...	...	...	...	...
Tuvalu	0.04	100	...	...	...	...	...	18	...	0.07	...	...	...	...	...	...
Vanuatu	0.8	99	0.8 z	94 z	...	...	...	10	14 z	1	49	2 z	54 z	...	...	...
Viet Nam	94	100	159	...	99	...	...	23	19	337	78	359	77	99	99	99
Latin America and the Caribbean																
Anguilla	0.03	100	0.03	100	74	.	74	18	14	0.07	87	0.1	75	71	14	90
Antigua and Barbuda	0.3	100	0.3	100	58	.	58	6	9	0.7	79	0.7	91	65	55	66
Argentina	50	96	...	...	...	...	...	24	...	221	88	...	...	...	...	...
Aruba	0.1	100	0.1	98	99	100	99	26	19	0.5	78	0.6	85	100	99	100
Bahamas	0.2	97	...	...	...	...	...	9	...	2	63	2 z	92 z	92 z	...	...
Barbados	0.3 **	93 **	0.3	96	47 *	21 *	48 *	18 **	16 *	1 **	76 **	2	78	55 *	51 *	57 *
Belize	0.2	98	0.4	98	16	70	14	19	16	2	64	2	73	48	45	48
Bermuda	0.06	100	0.06	100	100	.	100	7	6	0.5	89	0.5	91	100	100	100
Bolivia, Plurinational State of	5	93	...	...	...	...	...	42	...	60 **	61 **	...	...	...	...	...
Brazil	304	98	409	97	...	...	...	19	17	807	93	775	90	...	...	...
British Virgin Islands	0.03 **	100 **	0.1	100	...	...	...	13 **	11	0.2	86	0.3	93	...	...	...
Cayman Islands	0.05	96	...	...	...	...	...	9	...	0.2	89	0.3	85	95	98	94
Chile	19	99	57	99	...	...	...	24	9	56	77	69	78	...	...	...
Colombia	59	94	51	96	100	100	100	18	26	215	77	179	79	100	100	100
Costa Rica	4	97	8	94	81	66	82	21	14	21	81	29	80	91	92	91
Cuba	26	98	30	100	100	.	100	19	13	91	79	91	78	100	100	100
Dominica	0.1	100	0.2	100	...	...	...	18	11	0.6	75	0.5	86	58	38	61
Dominican Republic	8	95	10	94	95	90	96	24	24	42	75	51	78	85	70	89
Ecuador	13	88	37	84	78	69	80	15	12	83	68	117	71	84	81	85
El Salvador	...	...	9	89	92	73	95	...	24	...	...	31	73	96	93	97
Grenada	0.2	96	0.2 z	100 z	45 z	. z	45 z	18	14 z	0.8	76	0.9 z	79 z	65 z	...	...
Guatemala	12	...	26 z	91 z	...	...	...	26	21 z	48	...	99 z	66 z	...	...	...
Guyana	2	99	2	100	63	62	63	18	15	4	86	4	88	68	60	69
Haiti	...	...	...	...	...	...	...	...	...	...	...	...	...	...	...	...
Honduras	6	...	9 y	94 y	...	...	...	19	27 y	32	...	37 y	73 y	...	...	...
Jamaica	6	...	6 z	97 z	...	...	...	24	25 z	10 **	...	15 z	91 z	...	...	...
Mexico	150	94	185	96	82 z	...	...	22	25	540	62	531	67	96 z	...	...
Montserrat	0.01	100	0.01 y	100 y	79 y	. y	79 y	12	9 y	0.02	84	0.04 y	97 y	59 y	- y	61 y
Netherlands Antilles	0.3	99	...	...	...	...	...	21	...	1	86	...	...	...	...	...
Nicaragua	6	97	10 z	96 z	33 z	32 z	33 z	26	21 z	24	83	31 z	77 z	75 z	61 z	79 z
Panama	3	98	5	94	48	6	50	19	19	15	75	19	76	92	93	91
Paraguay	...	...	...	...	...	...	...	...	...	...	...	...	...	...	...	...
Peru	26	98	76	95	...	...	...	39	18	151	62	188	66	...	...	...
Saint Kitts and Nevis	...	...	0.09	100	...	...	...	...	20	0.4	83	0.5	88	64	56	65
Saint Lucia	0.3 **	100 **	0.3	100	...	...	...	13 **	10	1	83	1	87	87	76	88
Saint Vincent and the Grenadines	...	...	0.4 y	100 y	...	...	...	...	8 y	1 **	71 **	0.9 z	78 z	84 z	76 z	87 z
Suriname	0.7	99 **	0.7	90	...	...	...	22	25	3 **	82 **	5	94	100 y	100 y	100 y
Trinidad and Tobago	2 **	100 **	...	...	...	...	...	13 **	...	8	76	7 *, z	79 *, z	88 *, z	59 *, z	96 *, z
Turks and Caicos Islands	0.06 **	92 **	...	...	...	...	...	13 **	...	0.1 **	92 **	...	...	...	...	...
Uruguay	3	98 **	5 z	...	...	...	...	31	26 z	18	92 **	25 z	...	...	...	...
Venezuela, Bolivarian Republic of	...	...	...	...	...	...	...	...	...	...	...	...	...	...	...	...
North America and Western Europe																
Andorra	...	...	0.2	92	100	100	100	...	13	...	...	0.4	79	100	100	100
Austria	14	99	20	99	...	...	...	16	12	29	89	30	90	...	...	...
Belgium	27	92	31 z	98 z	...	...	...	15	14 z	65 **	78 **	66 z	81 z	...	...	...
Canada	30	68 **	...	...	...	...	...	17	...	141	68 **	...	...	...	...	...
Cyprus	1.0	99	1 z	100 z	...	...	...	19	17 z	4	67	4 z	83 z	...	...	...
Denmark	45	92	...	...	...	...	...	6	...	37	63	...	...	...	...	...
Finland	10	96	15	97	...	...	...	12	11	22	71	25	79	...	...	...
France	128	78	128	83	...	...	...	19	20	209	78	238	83	...	...	...
Germany	...	...	230 z	98 z	...	...	...	...	10 z	221	82	242 z	86 z	...	...	...
Greece	9	100 **	...	...	...	...	...	16	...	48	57 **	...	...	...	...	...
Iceland	3	98	2 z	96 z	...	...	...	4	6 z	...	...	...	...	...	...	...
Ireland	...	...	...	...	...	...	...	...	...	21	85	33	85	...	...	...
Israel	...	...	...	...	...	...	...	...	...	50 **	85 **	62 z	85 z	...	...	...
Italy	119	99	...	...	...	...	...	13	...	254	95	...	...	...	...	...
Luxembourg	0.9 **	97 **	1 z	98 z	...	...	...	15 **	11 z	3	67	4 z	74 z	...	...	...
Malta	0.9	99	0.6 z	100 z	...	...	...	12	14 z	2	87	2 z	85 z	...	...	...
Monaco	0.04	100	...	...	...	...	...	25	...	0.09	87	...	...	...	...	...
Netherlands	...	...	...	...	...	...	...	...	...	...	...	...	...	...	...	...
Norway	...	...	...	...	...	...	...	...	...	...	...	...	...	...	...	...

PRIMARY EDUCATION			SECONDARY EDUCATION														
Pupil/teacher ratio[2]		Pupil/trained teacher ratio[2]	Teaching staff, total secondary				Trained teachers (%)[1]			Pupil/teacher ratio[2]							
										Lower secondary		Upper secondary		Total secondary			
School year ending in		School year ending in	School year ending in				School year ending in			School year ending in		School year ending in		School year ending in			
1999	2011	2011	1999		2011		2011			1999	2011	1999	2011	1999	2011		
			Total (000)	% F	Total (000)	% F	Total	Male	Female							Country or territory	
35 [**]	...	...	...	...	...	...	...	...	...	...	...	...	...	...	...	Papua New Guinea	
35	31 [y]	...	150	76	194 [y]	76 [y]	...	...	...	41	39 [y]	21	25 [y]	34	35 [y]	Philippines	
32	21 [z]	...	189	41	225 [z]	55 [z]	...	...	...	22	19 [z]	22	16 [z]	22	18 [z]	Republic of Korea	
24 [**]	30 [z]	...	1 [**]	57 [**]	1 [z]	58 [z]	...	...	...	26 [**]	24 [z]	17	20 [z]	20 [**]	21 [z]	Samoa	
...	17 [y]	18 [y]	...	...	16 [y]	66 [y]	92 [y]	90 [y]	93 [y]	...	15 [y]	...	15 [y]	...	15 [y]	Singapore	
19	25 [z]	43 [z]	1	33	1 [z]	29 [z]	71 [z]	71 [z]	71 [z]	...	33 [z]	...	22 [z]	13	28 [z]	Solomon Islands	
21	...	...	***169*** [**]	***53*** [**]	246	51	...	...	...	***23*** [**]	22	***25*** [**]	18	***24*** [**]	20	Thailand	
62	31	...	***2***	...	4	29	...	...	...	***30***	25	***25***	23	***28***	24	Timor-Leste	
10	...	...	*0.01*	*64*	...	...	...	...	...	...	...	...	...	*16*	...	Tokelau	
21	...	...	1.0 [**]	48 [**]	...	...	...	...	...	15 [**]	...	13 [**]	...	15 [**]	...	Tonga	
19	...	...	...	...	...	...	...	...	...	***25***	...	...	...	...	...	Tuvalu	
24	22 [z]	...	0.4	47	...	...	...	...	...	...	...	...	...	23	...	Vanuatu	
30	20	20	...	...	...	...	...	...	...	29	16	...	...	...	...	Viet Nam	
																Latin America and the Caribbean	
22	15	21	0.1 [**]	63 [**]	0.1	68	57	50	61	...	...	...	...	15 [**]	9	Anguilla	
19	15	22	*0.4*	*71* [**]	0.7	71	47	55	44	*12*	...	*16*	...	*13*	12	Antigua and Barbuda	
21	...	...	*311*	*69*	...	...	...	...	...	*11*	...	*12*	...	*11*	...	Argentina	
19	15	15	0.4	49	0.5 [z]	59 [z]	96 [z]	96 [z]	96 [z]	...	...	...	...	16	14 [z]	Aruba	
14	14 [z]	15 [z]	2 [**]	...	3 [z]	76 [z]	89 [z]	...	...	16 [**]	12 [z]	16 [**]	12 [z]	16 [**]	12 [z]	Bahamas	
18 [**]	13 [*]	24 [*]	1 [**]	58 [**]	...	...	...	...	...	...	...	...	...	18 [**]	...	Barbados	
23	22	46	*1.0*	*64*	2	60 [**]	36	30	40	*23*	17 [**]	*23*	14 [**]	*23*	16	Belize	
9	9	9	***0.6***	***67***	0.7	67	100	100	100	***8***	6	***7***	6	***7***	6	Bermuda	
25 [**]	...	...	39 [**]	52 [**]	...	...	...	...	...	24 [**]	...	20	...	21 [**]	...	Bolivia, Plurinational State of	
26	21	...	...	...	1 431	66	...	...	...	23	18	...	15	...	16	Brazil	
18	12	...	0.2	63	0.2	64	...	...	...	6	9	10	7	7	8	British Virgin Islands	
15	12	13	0.2	46	0.4	48	100	100	99	11	9	7	9	9	9	Cayman Islands	
32	22	...	45	62	71	62	...	...	...	32	22	27	21	29	21	Chile	
24	28	28	200	49	201	51	97	97	98	...	27	...	23	18	26	Colombia	
27	17	19	13	53	28	60	90	90	89	20	15	19	14	20	15	Costa Rica	
12	9	9	65	60	88	55	100	100	100	12	10	10	8	11	9	Cuba	
20	16	28	0.4 [**]	68 [**]	0.5	72	41	30	42	21 [**]	15	15 [**]	9	19 [**]	12	Dominica	
31	25	30	...	...	31	67	79	74	82	...	29	28	29	...	29	Dominican Republic	
23	18	22	*68* [**]	*49* [**]	136	54	75	69	79	*13* [**]	12	*14* [**]	10	*14* [**]	11	Ecuador	
...	29	31	...	...	25	53	91	89	94	...	25	...	23	...	24	El Salvador	
20	16 [z]	25 [z]	...	...	0.7 [z]	62 [z]	25 [z]	49 [z]	11 [z]	...	...	...	...	...	15 [z]	Grenada	
38	27 [z]		33	...	77 [?]	45 [?]	...	...	...	15	15 [z]	11	12 [z]	13	14 [z]	Guatemala	
27	25	36	...	...	4	69	57 [z]	49 [z]	61 [z]	...	21	...	20	...	21	Guyana	
...	...	...	...	...	...	...	...	...	...	...	...	...	...	...	...	Haiti	
34	34 [y]	...	...	...	...	...	...	...	...	...	...	...	...	...	...	Honduras	
34 [**]	21 [z]	...	*12* [**]	...	18 [z]	73 [z]	...	...	...	*18* [**]	...	*20* [**]	...	*19* [**]	15 [z]	Jamaica	
27	28	29 [z]	519	44	670	49	91 [z]	...	...	18	19	14	16	17	18	Mexico	
21	13 [y]	22 [y]	0.03	62 [**]	0.03 [y]	74 [y]	44 [y]	29 [y]	50 [y]	10 [**]	15 [**, y]	10 [**]	11 [**, y]	10	13 [y]	Montserrat	
20	...	...	1	53	...	...	...	...	...	12	...	21	...	15	...	Netherlands Antilles	
34	30 [z]	40 [z]	10 [*]	56 [*]	15 [z]	55 [z]	53 [z]	45 [z]	59 [z]	31 [*]	...	31 [**]	...	31 [**]	31 [z]	Nicaragua	
26	23	25	14	55	19	60	87	87	88	17	16	15	13	16	15	Panama	
...	...	...	39	62	...	...	...	...	...	...	...	...	...	11	...	Paraguay	
29	20	...	105	89	160	44	...	...	...	22	...	22	...	22	16	Peru	
19	13	21	*0.3*	*56*	0.5	64	56	55	56	...	11	...	7	*14*	9	Saint Kitts and Nevis	
24	18	20	***0.7***	***65***	1.0 [*]	70 [*]	65 [*]	60 [*]	67 [*]	...	15 [*]	...	16 [*]	***17***	15 [*]	Saint Lucia	
19 [**]	16 [z]	19 [z]	*0.4*	*57*	0.7 [z]	64 [z]	63 [z]	63 [z]	63 [z]	*24* [**]	18 [z]	*24* [**]	15 [z]	*24* [**]	17 [z]	Saint Vincent and the Grenadines	
20 [**]	15	15 [y]	***3*** [**]	***63*** [**]	4	72	100 [y]	100 [y]	100 [y]	***17*** [**]	14	***13*** [**]	11	***15*** [**]	13	Suriname	
21	18 [*, z]	20 [*, z]	6 [**]	59 [**]	...	...	...	...	...	22 [**]	12 [*, z]	19 [**]	...	21 [**]	...	Trinidad and Tobago	
18 [**]	...	...	0.1 [**]	62 [**]	...	...	...	...	...	9 [**]	...	9 [**]	...	9 [**]	...	Turks and Caicos Islands	
20	14 [z]	...	19	72	25 [z]	...	...	...	...	12	10 [z]	23	14 [z]	15	11 [z]	Uruguay	
...	...	...	...	...	...	...	...	...	...	...	...	...	...	...	...	Venezuela, Bolivarian Republic of	
																North America and Western Europe	
...	10	10	...	...	...	...	...	...	...	...	7	...	...	...	...	Andorra	
13	11	...	73	57	75	63	...	...	...	9	8	12	11	10	10	Austria	
12 [**]	11 [z]	...	*105*	*57*	...	...	...	...	...	...	7 [z]	...	...	*10*	...	Belgium	
17	...	...	...	...	...	...	...	...	...	...	...	...	13 [y]	...	...	Canada	
18	14 [z]	...	5	51	7 [z]	64 [z]	...	...	...	...	10 [z]	...	10 [z]	13	10 [z]	Cyprus	
10	...	...	44	45	...	...	...	...	...	10	...	9	...	10	...	Denmark	
17	14	...	39	64	44	65	...	...	...	10	9	14	10	12	10	Finland	
19	18	...	495	57	464	59	...	...	...	13	14	11	11	12	13	France	
17	13 [z]	...	533	51	594 [z]	59 [z]	...	...	...	15	12 [z]	16	15 [z]	15	13 [z]	Germany	
14	...	...	75	56 [**]	...	...	...	...	...	10	...	10	...	10	...	Greece	
...	...	...	...	...	...	...	...	...	...	...	...	14	12 [z]	...	...	Iceland	
22	16	...	...	...	...	...	...	...	...	...	...	...	...	...	...	Ireland	
13 [**]	13 [z]	...	61 [**]	70 [**]	71 [**, y]	73 [**, y]	...	...	...	12 [**]	11 [**, y]	9	9 [y]	10 [**]	10 [**, y]	Israel	
11	...	...	422	65	...	...	...	...	...	10	...	11	...	11	...	Italy	
12	9 [z]	...	3	38	5 [z]	52 [z]	...	...	...	...	11 [z]	...	7 [z]	12	8 [z]	Luxembourg	
20	14 [z]	...	4	48	4 [z]	60 [z]	...	...	...	9	8 [z]	38	15 [z]	11	9 [z]	Malta	
22	...	...	0.3	59	...	...	...	...	...	15	...	8	...	10	...	Monaco	
...	...	...	...	...	107 [z]	49 [z]	...	...	...	...	...	...	...	...	14 [z]	Netherlands	
...	...	...	...	...	...	...	...	...	...	...	...	8	...	...	...	Norway	

Table 8 (continued)

Country or territory	PRE-PRIMARY EDUCATION: Teaching staff, School year ending in 1999, Total (000)	1999, % F	2011, Total (000)	2011, % F	Trained teachers (%)[1], School year ending in 2011, Total	Male	Female	Pupil/teacher ratio[2], School year ending in 1999	2011	PRIMARY EDUCATION: Teaching staff, School year ending in 1999, Total (000)	1999, % F	2011, Total (000)	2011, % F	Trained teachers (%)[1], School year ending in 2011, Total	Male	Female
Portugal	*14*	...	18[z]	97[z]	...	...	...	*16*	16[z]	*61*	*82*	68[z]	80[z]	...	...	...
San Marino	*0.1*	*99*	0.1	96	...	...	...	*8*	8	*0.2*	*91*	0.2	92	...	...	...
Spain	68	93	156	95	...	...	...	17	12	172	68	224	75	...	...	...
Sweden	***36***	***97***	...	...	...	...	...	***9***	...	62	80	62	82	...	...	...
Switzerland	...	...	...	...	...	...	...	...	...	...	...	...	...	...	...	...
United Kingdom	*51*	*95*	64[z]	95[z]	...	...	...	*23*	18[z]	249	81	252[z]	87[z]	...	...	...
United States	327	95	541[z]	94[z]	...	...	...	22	16[z]	1 618	86	1 795[z]	87[z]	...	...	...
South and West Asia																
Afghanistan	...	...	...	...	...	...	...	...	...	...	...	122	31	...	...	...
Bangladesh	68	33	...	...	...	...	...	27	...	...	...	458	54	58	60	56
Bhutan	0.01	31	**0.2**	**93**	...	...	...	22	**11**	2	32	**5**	**40**	...	...	...
India	*504*	...	...	...	...	...	...	*35*	...	3 135[*]	33[*]	...	...	...	...	...
Iran, Islamic Republic of[3]	9	98	...	...	...	...	...	23	...	***315***	***54***	278[y]	57[y]	...	...	...
Maldives	0.4	90	0.7	88	50	3	56	31	25	3	60	3	72	81	84	80
Nepal	*11*[**]	*32*[**]	**45**	**90**	**85**	**51**	**89**	*24*[**]	**23**	92	23	**174**	**42**	**93**	**93**	**92**
Pakistan	...	...	...	...	...	...	...	...	...	*424*[**]	*45*[**]	453	48	83	91	74
Sri Lanka	...	...	...	...	...	...	...	...	...	***67***	...	72	85	82	...	...
Sub-Saharan Africa																
Angola	...	...	18[z]	40[z]	45[z]	43[z]	48[z]	...	37[*,z]	...	...	94[z]	...	...	...	...
Benin	0.6	61	4	...	51[z]	63[z]	46[z]	28	27	16	23	42	20	47	47	47
Botswana	...	...	2[y]	98[y]	50[y]	46[y]	50[y]	...	13[y]	12	81	13[y]	76[y]	100[y]	100[y]	100[y]
Burkina Faso	*0.7*[**]	*66*[**]	**3**	**83**	22	76	9	*29*[**]	**24**	***19***	***23***	**49**	**38**	**95**	**93**	**98**
Burundi	0.2[**]	99[**]	1	82	55	19	63	28[**]	35	12	54	40	53	94	...	...
Cameroon	4	97	15	96	48	41	48	23	22	41	36	79	50	67	63	72
Cape Verde	***0.8***	***100***	1	100	32	.	32	***25***	20	3[**]	62[**]	3	67	92	90	93
Central African Republic	...	...	0.5	88	...	...	...	...	44	...	...	8	18	57	55	69
Chad	...	...	0.7	79	73	77	72	...	34	12	9	31	15	62	59	81
Comoros	0.05[**]	94[**]	...	...	...	...	...	26[**]	...	2	26	4	28	55	...	...
Congo	0.6	100	2[z]	96[z]	94[z]	90[z]	94[z]	10	23[z]	*7*	*37*	14[z]	53[z]	87[z]	82[z]	91[z]
Côte d'Ivoire	*2*	*83*	4	92	100	100	100	*22*	19	*43*	*20*	56	27	100	100	100
Democratic Rep. of the Congo	***2***	***88***	10	95	23	...	...	***25***	25	155	21	297	27	90	...	...
Equatorial Guinea	0.4	36	...	...	...	...	...	43	...	1	28	3	40	49	47	52
Eritrea	0.3	97	1	98	53	55	53	36	38	6	35	8	41	91	91	91
Ethiopia	2	93	14	70	86[z]	28[z]	100[z]	36	27	*87*	*29*	260	37	48	49	46
Gabon	***0.5***	***98***	...	...	...	...	...	***30***	...	***5***	***48***	13	53	...	...	...
Gambia	0.8	55	...	...	...	...	...	37	...	*5*	*32*	6	29	90	90	89
Ghana	18[**]	92[**]	**42**	**83**	**35**	**31**	**36**	28[**]	**36**	80	32	**123**	**37**	**52**	**44**	**66**
Guinea	...	...	4[z]	53[z]	...	...	...	...	34[z]	16	25	**37**	**30**	**75**	**72**	**81**
Guinea-Bissau	*0.2*	*73*	0.3[z]	69[z]	26[z]	28[z]	25[z]	*21*	29[z]	*3*	*20*	5[z]	22[z]	39[z]	33[z]	59[z]
Kenya	*47*[**]	*64*[**]	93[y]	83[y]	77[y]	92[y]	74[y]	*26*[**]	21[y]	148	42	153[**,y]	44[**,y]	97[**,y]	96[**,y]	98[**,y]
Lesotho	*2*	*99*	2[z]	...	...	...	...	*19*	24[z]	8	80	11	...	66	...	...
Liberia	6	19	...	...	...	...	...	18	...	10	19	25	14	56	55	63
Madagascar	...	...	7[z]	97[z]	51[z]	83[z]	50[z]	...	23[z]	43	58	100	56	95	96	94
Malawi	...	...	...	...	...	...	...	...	...	41[**]	40[**]	47[**]	40[**]	88[**]	88[**]	90[**]
Mali	***1***[**]	***73***[**]	2	94	59	83	57	***21***[**]	44	15[*]	23[*]	44	28	52	51	57
Mauritius	3	100	3	99	99	92	99	16	14	5	54	6	71	100	100	100
Mozambique	...	...	...	...	...	...	...	...	...	37	25	**98**	**41**	**84**	**81**	**87**
Namibia	1	88	...	...	...	...	...	27	...	***13***	***66***	14[z]	68[z]	96[z]	95[z]	97[z]
Niger	0.6	98	**3**	**88**	**90**	**81**	**91**	21	**32**	13	31	**53**	**46**	**97**	**97**	**98**
Nigeria	...	...	...	...	...	...	...	...	...	432	48	574[z]	48[z]	66[z]	61[z]	72[z]
Rwanda	***0.5***	***86***	3	80	38	33	39	***35***	38	24	55	40	52	98	98	99
Sao Tome and Principe	0.1	95	0.3[z]	94[z]	47[y]	77[y]	45[y]	28	19[z]	1	...	**1**	**56**	48[y]	47[y]	49[y]
Senegal	1	78	6	78	15[z]	22[z]	13[z]	19	25	21	22	52	31	48[z]	51[z]	40[z]
Seychelles	0.2	100	0.2	100	99[y]	...	...	16	17	0.7	85	1	88	99[y]	...	...
Sierra Leone	***0.9***	***83***	2	82	42	32	45	***19***	17	***15***	***38***	38	25	48	43	64
Somalia	...	...	...	...	...	...	...	...	...	...	...	...	...	...	...	...
South Africa	...	...	...	...	...	...	...	...	...	227	78	232[y]	77[y]	87[y]	93[y]	86[y]
South Sudan	...	...	2	57	39	32	44	...	36	...	...	29[**]	12[**]	44[**]	...	...
Swaziland	...	...	2	98	51	56	51	...	12	6	75	8	71	78	75	80
Togo	*1*	*97*	**2**	**94**	54	42	54	*17*	**33**	23	13	**33**	**14**	71	71	67
Uganda	...	...	20[z]	83[z]	...	...	...	...	25[z]	110	33	170	...	95	...	...
United Republic of Tanzania	...	...	16[z]	54[z]	18[z]	7[z]	28[z]	...	57[z]	***106***	***45***	**181**	**52**	**97**	**96**	**97**
Zambia	...	...	...	...	...	...	...	...	...	26[**]	49[**]	48[**]	51[**]	...	...	...
Zimbabwe	...	...	...	...	...	...	...	...	...	...	...	...	...	...	...	...

PRIMARY EDUCATION			SECONDARY EDUCATION													
Pupil/teacher ratio[2]		Pupil/trained teacher ratio[2]	Teaching staff, total secondary				Trained teachers (%)[1]			Pupil/teacher ratio[2] Lower secondary		Upper secondary		Total secondary		
School year ending in		School year ending in	School year ending in				School year ending in			School year ending in		School year ending in		School year ending in		
1999	2011	2011	1999		2011		2011			1999	2011	1999	2011	1999	2011	
			Total (000)	% F	Total (000)	% F	Total	Male	Female							Country or territory
13	11[z]	…	*85*	*68*	98[z]	69[z]	…	…	…	*11*	8[z]	*9*	7[z]	*10*	7[z]	Portugal
5	6	…	…	…	0.1	76	…	…	…	*5*	…	…	…	…	16	San Marino
15	12	…	277	52	294	55	…	…	…	…	11	…	11	12	11	Spain
12	9	…	63	56	73	59	…	…	…	12	9	17	10	15	10	Sweden
…	…	…	…	…	…	…	…	…	…	…	…	…	…	…	…	Switzerland
19	18[z]	…	355	56	…	…	…	…	…	16	…	14	…	15	…	United Kingdom
15	14[z]	…	1 504	56	1 758[z]	61[z]	…	…	…	16	13[z]	14	14[z]	15	14[z]	United States
																South and West Asia
…	45	…	…	…	…	…	…	…	…	…	44	…	…	…	…	Afghanistan
…	40[*]	70[*]	265	13	377	22	54	53	57	43	33	32	28	37	31	Bangladesh
42	**24**	…	0.6	32	**3**	**39**	…	…	…	35	*23*	27	*14*	32	*20*	Bhutan
35[*]	…	…	1 995[**]	34[**]	4 252[z]	40[z]	…	…	…	…	31[z]	…	21[z]	34[**]	25[z]	India
25	20[y]	…	…	…	…	…	…	…	…	…	…	…	…	…	…	Iran, Islamic Republic of[3]
24	12	15	0.9	25	…	…	…	…	…	18	8	9	…	17	…	Maldives
39	**28**	**30**	40	9	**102**	**22**	…	…	…	38	**37**	24	**23**	32	**30**	Nepal
33[**]	40	48	…	…	…	…	…	…	…	…	…	…	…	…	…	Pakistan
26	24	29	…	…	149	…	82	…	…	**21**	17	…	18	…	17	Sri Lanka
																Sub-Saharan Africa
…	46[z]	…	16[**]	33[**]	22[z]	…	…	…	…	…	37[z]	…	43[z]	18[**]	39[z]	Angola
53	44	94	*10*	*12*	…	…	…	…	…	*27*	…	*15*	…	*23*	…	Benin
27	25[y]	26[y]	9	45	…	…	…	…	…	…	…	…	…	18	…	Botswana
47	**48**	**51**	6[**]	…	**26**	**17**	**48**	**48**	**52**	29[**]	…	23[**]	…	28[**]	**26**	Burkina Faso
46	48	51	…	…	13	20	72	77	53	…	…	…	…	…	29	Burundi
52	45	68	28[**]	22[**]	65	28	29	26	36	…	…	…	…	23[**]	24	Cameroon
29[**]	23	25	*3*	*11*	*1*	*11*	*81[z]*	*79[z]*	*85[z]*	…	18	…	16	*24*	17	Cape Verde
…	81	141	…	…	2	12	…	…	…	…	…	…	…	…	67	Central African Republic
68	63	101	4	5	14	7	…	…	…	41	44	23	20	34	32	Chad
35	28	50	…	…	…	…	…	…	…	…	15	…	…	…	…	Comoros
60	49[z]	57[z]	…	…	…	…	…	…	…	…	…	…	…	…	…	Congo
45	49	49	20[**]	…	…	…	…	…	…	34[**]	…	21[**]	…	29[**]	…	Côte d'Ivoire
26	37	42	…	…	249	…	33[z]	33[z]	32[z]	…	…	…	…	…	15	Democratic Rep. of the Congo
57	28	57	0.9	5	…	…	…	…	…	25	…	15	…	23	…	Equatorial Guinea
47	40	44	2	12	6	15	71	70	77	55	42	45	37	51	39	Eritrea
67	55	115	…	…	113	26	…	…	…	*28*	44	…	27	…	40	Ethiopia
49	25	…	3[**]	16[**]	…	…	…	…	…	28[**]	…	28[**]	…	28[**]	…	Gabon
37	38	42	…	…	…	…	…	…	…	24	38	…	…	…	…	Gambia
30	**33**	**63**	52	22	**124**	**25**	**72**	**68**	**82**	20	**16**	19	**22**	20	**18**	Ghana
47	**44**	**58**	…	…	**22**	**6**	…	…	…	31	**34[**]**	…	**27[**]**	…	**31**	Guinea
44	52[z]	133[z]	*2[**]*	*6[**]*	…	…	…	…	…	*17*	…	*11[**]*	…	*15[**]*	…	Guinea-Bissau
32	47[**,y]	48[**,y]	**68[**]**	**39[**]**	108[**,y]	41[**,y]	93[**,y]	94[**,y]	91[**,y]	…	33[**,y]	…	27[y]	**29[**]**	30[**,y]	Kenya
44	34	51	3	51	5[**,z]	56[**,z]	…	…	…	…	…	…	…	22	24[**,z]	Lesotho
39	27	48	7	16	…	…	…	…	…	17	14	18	…	17	…	Liberia
47	43	45	…	…	44[y]	45[y]	…	…	…	…	25[y]	…	18[**,y]	…	23[**,y]	Madagascar
63[**]	76[**]	86[**]	9[**]	32[**]	17[**]	28[**]	59[**]	54[**]	73[**]	…	…	…	…	60[**]	42[**]	Malawi
62[*]	48	92	8[*]	14[*]	33	11	…	…	…	31[*]	38	24	13	28[*]	25	Mali
26	20	20	5	47	8[z]	58[z]	…	…	…	…	…	…	…	20	…	Mauritius
61	**55**	**66**	…	…	**22[**]**	**19[**]**	**84[**]**	**83[**]**	**87[**]**	…	…	…	…	…	**33[**]**	Mozambique
32	30[z]	31[z]	5	46	…	…	…	…	…	25	…	21	…	24	…	Namibia
41	**39**	**40**	*4*	18	**9**	**21**	17[z]	17[z]	17[z]	34	**42**	12	**30**	24	**40**	Niger
41	36[z]	54[z]	129	36	274[z]	46[z]	66[z]	63[z]	69[z]	…	31[z]	…	36[z]	30	33[z]	Nigeria
54	58	59	*6*	*21*	21	28	…	…	…	…	…	…	…	*23*	24	Rwanda
36	**29**	54[y]	…	…	0.6	20[**]	45	43[**]	49[**]	…	19	…	21	…	20	Sao Tome and Principe
49	33	70[z]	*9*	*15*	30[*]	18[*]	…	…	…	*31*	…	*20*	…	*27*	27[*]	Senegal
15	13	14[y]	0.6	54	0.6	58	91	…	…	14[**]	…	14[**]	…	14	12	Seychelles
37	31	65	**6**	**27**	…	…	…	…	…	**23**	19	**34**	…	**27**	…	Sierra Leone
…	…	…	…	…	…	…	…	…	…	…	…	…	…	…	…	Somalia
35	31[y]	35[y]	145	50	187[y]	55[y]	…	…	…	…	…	…	…	29	25[y]	South Africa
…	50[**]	113[**]	…	…	…	…	…	…	…	…	48[**]	…	…	…	…	South Sudan
33	29	37	*3*	…	6	48	75	76	73	…	…	…	…	*17*	16	Swaziland
41	**42**	58	7	13	21	…	…	…	…	44	34	20	16	35	26	Togo
57	48	50	*31*	*21*	…	…	…	…	…	…	…	…	…	*18*	…	Uganda
46	**46**	**47**	…	…	**80**	**28**	…	…	…	…	…	…	…	…	**26**	United Republic of Tanzania
61[**]	63[**]	…	…	…	…	…	…	…	…	18[**]	32[**]	…	…	…	…	Zambia
…	…	…	…	…	…	…	…	…	…	…	…	…	…	…	…	Zimbabwe

Table 9

Financial commitment to education: public spending

Country or territory	Total public expenditure on education as % of GNP		Total public expenditure on education as % of total government expenditure		Public current expenditure on primary education as % of public current expenditure on education		Public current expenditure on primary education per pupil (unit cost) at PPP in constant 2010 US$		Public current expenditure on secondary education as % of public current expenditure on education		Public current expenditure on secondary education per pupil (unit cost) at PPP in constant 2010 US$		Primary education textbooks and other teaching material as % of public current expenditure on primary education		Primary education teachers' compensation as % of public current expenditure on primary education	
	1999	2011	1999	2011	1999	2011	1999	2011	1999	2011	1999	2011	1999	2011	1999	2011
Arab States																
Algeria	...	4.4[x]	...	20.3[x]	...	...	...	...	...	...	...	...	...	...	...	...
Bahrain	...	3.1[x]	...	11.7[x]	...	...	...	...	...	...	...	...	4.2	...	...	...
Djibouti	7.5	...	...	...	...	...	...	...	...	...	...	...	...	0.7[x]	...	81.6[x]
Egypt	...	3.7[x]	...	11.9[x]	...	...	...	...	...	...	...	...	...	...	...	...
Iraq	...	...	...	...	...	...	...	...	...	...	...	...	...	...	...	...
Jordan	5.0	...	20.6	...	...	...	483	599[x]	...	...	559	732[x]	...	...	77.8	97.2[y]
Kuwait	***5.6***[**]	...	...	...	...	...	...	5 200[x]	...	...	...	7 042[x]	...	7.1[x]	...	80.7[x]
Lebanon	2.0	1.7	10.4	7.1	...	...	...	...	...	...	...	...	...	...	69.1	...
Libya	...	...	...	...	...	...	...	...	...	...	...	...	...	...	...	...
Mauritania	2.4[**]	4.1	...	14.7	...	48.8	...	288	...	22.9	...	574[**]	...	...	...	...
Morocco	5.5	5.5[y]	25.7	25.7[x]	39.1	...	511	683[x]	43.5	...	1 339	...	...	1.8[y]	...	75.9[y]
Oman	4.2	4.6[y]	21.3	...	***37.3***	32.8[y]	1 909	3 376	***51.7***	40.0[y]	3 711	3 801	1.5	1.4	74.9	61.7
Palestine	...	...	...	...	...	...	...	...	...	...	...	...	...	...	...	...
Qatar	...	2.4[x]	...	7.1[x]	...	...	...	4 785[y]	...	...	...	5 082[y]	...	...	...	...
Saudi Arabia	7.0	5.5[x]	26.0	19.3[x]	...	...	...	...	...	...	...	...	...	...	...	...
Sudan	...	...	...	...	...	...	...	...	...	...	...	...	...	...	...	...
Syrian Arab Republic	***4.5***	5.2[y]	***13.8***[**]	18.9[y]	...	...	388	693[y]	...	...	670	598[y]	*1.9*	...	...	...
Tunisia	6.5	6.6[z]	*17.4*[**]	21.5[z]	*38.3*[**]	...	*925*[**]	...	*42.9*[**]	...	*1 328*[**]	...	...	...	...	...
United Arab Emirates	***1.3***[**]	...	*22.2*[*]	...	...	...	3 660	...	...	...	4 775	...	...	2.7[y]	...	72.5[y]
Yemen	*10.5*	5.5[x]	*32.8*	16.0[x]	...	...	...	347	...	...	...	233	...	...	...	...
Sudan (pre-secession)	...	...	...	...	...	...	...	...	...	...	...	...	...	...	...	...
Central and Eastern Europe																
Albania	3.3	...	9.6	...	...	...	...	...	...	...	...	...	...	...	...	...
Belarus	6.0	5.4	...	18.1	...	...	...	...	...	...	...	...	...	...	...	...
Bosnia and Herzegovina	...	...	...	...	...	...	...	...	...	...	...	...	...	...	...	...
Bulgaria	***3.5***	4.2[z]	***8.8***	10.8[z]	***20.8***	19.8[z]	***1 391***	3 128[z]	***46.6***	43.5[z]	***1 677***	3 366[z]	...	...	***53.3***	58.5[z]
Croatia	...	4.4[z]	...	...	...	...	...	...	...	...	...	...	...	...	...	...
Czech Republic	3.9	4.6[z]	9.7	9.7[z]	17.8[**]	16.1[z]	1 743[**]	3 500[z]	49.8[**]	46.5[z]	3 435[**]	5 618[z]	...	...	45.0	46.8[z]
Estonia	6.8	6.0[z]	15.4	14.0[z]	...	25.5[z]	...	4 975[z]	...	39.0[z]	...	5 826[z]	...	...	...	...
Hungary	4.9	5.1[z]	12.8	9.8[z]	19.5[**]	18.1[z]	2 694[**]	4 224[z]	40.6[**]	41.6[z]	2 804[**]	4 160[z]	...	...	...	...
Latvia	5.8	4.9[z]	*14.4*	11.3[z]	...	...	...	...	...	...	...	...	...	...	...	...
Lithuania	***6.0***	5.5[z]	***16.0***	13.2[z]	...	17.2[z]	...	4 299[z]	...	45.9[z]	...	4 088[z]	...	...	...	68.2[z]
Montenegro	...	...	...	...	...	...	...	...	...	...	...	...	...	...	...	...
Poland	4.7	5.4[z]	11.4	11.4[z]	...	30.3[z]	...	5 056[z]	...	35.6[z]	...	4 677[z]	...	...	...	...
Republic of Moldova	4.6	7.9	16.4	22.0	...	19.2	...	1 298	...	36.7	...	1 189	...	0.4	...	50.7
Romania	*2.9*	4.2[y]	*7.5*	10.3[y]	...	20.0[y]	...	2 717[y]	...	38.1[y]	...	2 377[y]	...	...	...	...
Russian Federation	*3.0*	4.2[x]	*10.6*	11.9[x]	...	...	...	...	...	...	...	...	...	...	...	...
Serbia	...	4.8[z]	...	9.5[y]	...	46.2[z]	...	6 243[z]	...	23.3[z]	...	1 510[z]	...	...	...	...
Slovakia	4.2	4.5[z]	13.8	10.6[z]	14.5	20.7[z]	1 425	4 530[z]	55.7	49.6[z]	2 571	4 195[z]	...	...	62.1	49.4[z]
Slovenia	***5.9***	5.8[z]	***12.4***	11.4[z]	...	28.0[z]	...	7 581[z]	...	37.8[z]	...	7 904[z]	...	...	...	...
The former Yugoslav Rep. of Macedonia	...	...	...	...	...	...	...	...	...	...	...	...	...	...	...	...
Turkey	3.0	...	...	...	...	...	...	...	...	...	...	...	...	...	...	89.8[z]
Ukraine	3.7	...	13.6	...	...	...	...	...	...	...	...	...	...	...	...	...
Central Asia																
Armenia	2.2	3.0	*9.5*	11.7	...	...	...	893[z]	...	...	...	1 015[y]	...	...	...	...
Azerbaijan	4.3	3.0[z]	24.4	10.0[z]	...	...	...	...	...	...	...	...	...	...	...	...
Georgia	2.0	2.8	10.3	7.7[*,y]	...	38.3	...	554	...	38.2	...	...	...	...	...	...
Kazakhstan	4.0	3.4[y]	14.4	...	...	...	...	...	...	...	...	...	...	...	...	...
Kyrgyzstan	4.3	6.3[z]	21.4	18.6[z]	...	...	...	...	...	...	...	...	...	...	...	...
Mongolia	5.1	6.1	15.2	11.9	...	35.2	...	783	...	32.6	...	692	0.2	2.3	...	40.9
Tajikistan	2.1	4.0	11.8	13.8	...	...	...	...	...	...	...	...	...	...	...	...
Turkmenistan	...	...	...	...	...	...	...	...	...	...	...	...	...	...	...	...
Uzbekistan	...	...	...	...	...	...	...	...	...	...	...	...	...	...	...	...
East Asia and the Pacific																
Australia	*5.0*	5.3[y]	*14.3*	13.5[x]	*33.7*	34.5[y]	*5 178*	6 654[y]	*38.4*	37.3[y]	*4 337*	6 365[y]	...	...	*64.2*	62.1[y]
Brunei Darussalam	4.9	2.0[z]	9.3	**16.9**	...	28.7[z]	...	2 544[z]	...	46.8[z]	...	3 849[z]	...	...	...	...
Cambodia	1.0	2.7[z]	8.7	...	*61.7*	...	*59*	...	***11.8***	...	***75***	...	...	...	...	...
China	1.9	...	13.0	...	34.3[**]	...	...	...	38.4[**]	...	303[**]	...	...	...	...	...
Cook Islands	...	3.2	13.1[**]	...	53.0	...	...	...	40.0	...	...	...	...	...	...	...
Democratic People's Republic of Korea	...	...	...	...	...	...	...	...	...	...	...	...	...	...	...	...
Fiji	5.3	4.3	18.3	14.4	...	44.8	...	728	...	15.2	...	249	...	...	...	...
Indonesia	***2.8***[**]	2.8	***11.5***[**]	15.2	...	39.9	...	344	...	24.9	...	316	...	...	...	...
Japan	3.5	3.7[z]	9.3	9.4[x]	...	...	...	...	...	...	...	...	...	...	...	...
Kiribati	6.7	...	...	...	...	...	...	...	...	...	...	...	...	...	...	...
Lao People's Democratic Republic	1.0	3.4[z]	*7.4*	13.2[z]	...	...	...	...	...	...	...	...	...	...	...	...
Macao, China	3.6	2.9[z]	13.5	15.3[z]	...	...	...	...	...	...	...	...	...	...	...	...
Malaysia	6.1	5.3[z]	25.2	21.3[z]	*30.9*[**]	35.4[y]	*1 108*[**]	2 049[y]	*34.7*[**]	42.4[y]	*1 708*[**]	2 895[y]	...	...	69.6	62.3[z]
Marshall Islands	11.0	...	...	...	...	...	...	...	...	...	...	...	...	...	...	...
Micronesia (Federated States of)	6.2	...	...	...	...	...	...	...	...	...	...	...	...	...	...	...
Myanmar	0.6	0.8	8.0	...	...	56.1	...	...	***33.4***	25.9	...	...	...	0.1	...	59.3
Nauru	...	...	...	...	...	...	...	...	...	...	...	...	...	...	...	...
New Zealand	7.1	7.6[z]	***16.1***	16.1[x]	26.7[**]	23.3[z]	4 534[**]	5 839[z]	39.8[**]	38.0[z]	5 569[**]	6 464[z]	...	...	...	...
Niue	...	...	...	...	...	...	...	...	...	...	...	...	...	...	...	...
Palau	*9.4*[**]	...	...	...	...	...	...	...	...	...	...	...	...	...	...	...

Table 9 (continued)

	Total public expenditure on education as % of GNP		Total public expenditure on education as % of total government expenditure		Public current expenditure on primary education as % of public current expenditure on education		Public current expenditure on primary education per pupil (unit cost) at PPP in constant 2010 US$		Public current expenditure on secondary education as % of public current expenditure on education		Public current expenditure on secondary education per pupil (unit cost) at PPP in constant 2010 US$		Primary education textbooks and other teaching material as % of public current expenditure on primary education		Primary education teachers' compensation as % of public current expenditure on primary education	
Country or territory	1999	2011	1999	2011	1999	2011	1999	2011	1999	2011	1999	2011	1999	2011	1999	2011
Papua New Guinea	...	...	...	...	...	...	...	...	...	...	...	...	...	...	...	...
Philippines	*3.3*	2.7[y]	*13.9*	15.0[y]	*59.5*[**]	56.0[y]	*325*[**]	303[x]	*22.0*[**]	29.1[y]	*285*[**]	301[x]	...	...	...	82.4[x]
Republic of Korea	3.8	5.0[y]	13.1	15.8[x]	43.5[**]	32.2[y]	2 912[**]	5 246[y]	38.3[**]	36.6[y]	2 419[**]	5 214[y]	...	...	77.6	59.1[y]
Samoa	4.5	6.3[x]	13.3	13.4[x]	32.4[**]	...	285[**]	...	26.9[**]	...	302[**]	...	...	...	...	...
Singapore	*3.3*	**3.4**	...	**22.7**	*25.2*	**19.0**	...	5 494[z]	*29.8*	**22.5**	...	8 378[z]	...	...	...	...
Solomon Islands	2.3[**]	8.9[z]	...	34.0[z]	...	...	...	...	...	...	...	...	...	...	...	...
Thailand	5.1	6.0	28.1	29.5	***33.6***[**]	47.8[y]	***1 024***[**]	1 892[y]	***19.1***[**]	15.9[y]	***860***[**]	710[y]	...	...	...	...
Timor-Leste	...	3.1[z]	...	8.1	...	...	...	...	...	...	...	...	...	...	...	...
Tokelau	...	...	*11.2*	...	...	...	...	...	...	...	...	...	...	...	...	...
Tonga	5.2[**]	...	*16.5*	...	...	...	...	...	...	...	...	...	...	...	...	...
Tuvalu	...	...	...	...	...	...	...	...	...	...	...	...	...	...	...	...
Vanuatu	6.3	5.4[y]	17.4	23.7[y]	38.9	55.3[y]	429	733[y]	51.9	30.4[y]	2 185	...	3.9	...	94.3	90.9[y]
Viet Nam	...	6.8[z]	...	19.8[x]	...	32.8[z]	...	701[z]	...	40.8[z]	...	...	...	...	...	...
Latin America and the Caribbean																
Anguilla	...	3.4[x]	...	10.7[x]	...	...	...	...	...	...	...	...	...	...	...	89.2[x]
Antigua and Barbuda	3.4	2.6[y]	...	9.8[y]	...	49.4[y]	...	1 736[y]	...	47.3[y]	...	2 191[y]	6.8	...	66.4	...
Argentina	4.6	5.9[z]	13.3	14.0[y]	36.7	32.8[z]	1 418	2 499[z]	35.4	39.4[z]	1 906	3 826[z]	...	...	***52.7***	69.6[z]
Aruba	...	7.2[z]	13.8	21.8[z]	29.9	24.3[z]	...	...	32.3	25.8[z]	...	...	...	...	...	...
Bahamas	*2.9*[**]	...	*19.7*[**]	...	...	...	...	...	...	...	...	...	...	...	...	...
Barbados	5.3	7.7[z]	15.4	13.5[z]	21.5[**]	...	2 092[**]	...	31.3	28.2[z]	3 463	5 383[z]	0.1	...	...	...
Belize	5.7[**]	7.1[z]	17.1[**]	18.7[x]	*61.7*	...	*908*	...	*32.0*	...	*909*	...	*0.5*	...	...	...
Bermuda	...	2.2[z]	...	13.1[z]	...	30.9[z]	...	...	...	45.3[z]	...	...	...	...	...	...
Bolivia, Plurinational State of	5.8	7.9[z]	15.8	24.6[z]	41.0[**]	39.7[z]	433[**]	915[z]	22.2[**]	26.1[z]	409[**]	658[x]	...	...	...	...
Brazil	4.0	5.9[z]	10.5	18.1[z]	33.3[**]	31.5[z]	861[**]	2 218[z]	36.1[**]	44.8[z]	...	2 266[z]	...	...	...	...
British Virgin Islands	...	4.2[z]	***9.0***	13.6[z]	***29.5***	28.1[z]	...	...	***33.6***	38.1[z]	...	...	...	2.1[z]	***84.6***	75.5[z]
Cayman Islands	...	...	...	...	...	...	...	...	...	...	...	...	...	...	...	...
Chile	4.0	4.4	17.0	17.8[z]	44.5	32.7	1 499	2 473	36.5	32.2	1 699	2 480	...	...	...	...
Colombia	4.5	4.7	16.9	14.9[x]	...	35.6	...	1 043	...	36.3	...	1 020	...	4.7	91.0[*]	81.4
Costa Rica	5.5	6.5[y]	***21.1***	23.1[y]	47.2	28.0[y]	1 395	1 633[y]	29.1	21.1[y]	1 926	1 612[y]	...	...	...	68.6[y]
Cuba	6.9	13.0[z]	13.7	18.3[z]	*35.5*[*]	29.2[z]	...	...	*37.9*[*]	28.9[z]	...	...	**1.2**	0.8[z]	...	...
Dominica	5.5[**]	3.6[z]	...	9.3[z]	...	...	...	1 783	...	...	...	1 745[z]	...	...	...	...
Dominican Republic	*2.0*[**]	...	***13.1***	...	***54.7***	...	...	624	...	...	...	583	***1.7***	2.0	***81.8***	67.4
Ecuador	2.0	5.3	9.7	15.5	...	27.4	...	763[y]	...	42.0	...	1 288[z]	...	...	...	...
El Salvador	2.4[**]	3.5	17.1[**]	...	...	40.1[x]	...	561[x]	...	21.4[x]	...	556[x]			...	50.0[x]
Grenada	...	...	...	...	...	...	...	...	...	...	...	...	...	...	...	...
Guatemala	...	2.9[z]	...	18.5[z]	...	55.6[z]	...	401[z]	...	14.8[z]	...	262[z]	1.8	3.0[x]	...	...
Guyana	9.3[**]	3.6	18.4[**]	13.5	...	30.1	...	260[z]	...	32.1	...	371[z]	...	...	...	81.1
Haiti	...	...	...	...	...	...	...	...	...	...	...	...	...	...	...	...
Honduras	...	...	...	...	...	...	...	...	...	...	...	...	...	0.1[*, z]	...	98.9[*, z]
Jamaica	*5.2*	6.7[z]	*10.8*	11.5[z]	***30.2***[**]	31.3[y]	...	...	***34.5***[**]	37.1[y]	...	...	...	...	...	79.5[y]
Mexico	4.5	5.3[z]	22.6	...	40.8	36.7[z]	1 508	2 058[z]	...	30.6[z]	...	2 188[z]	...	...	86.3	87.2[z]
Montserrat	...	6.3[y]	10.7[**]	8.4[y]	***20.3***	...	...	...	***29.3***	...	...	...	*4.0*	...	*84.0*[**]	...
Netherlands Antilles	...	...	14.0	...	...	...	...	...	...	...	...	...	...	...	...	...
Nicaragua	3.0	4.8[z]	17.8	26.4[z]	...	43.3[z]	...	404[z]	...	13.8[z]	...	255[z]	...	...	...	78.7[z]
Panama	5.1	4.4	***7.3***	14.8	...	29.0	1 151	1 174	...	24.1	1 641	1 504	...	...	**...**	...
Paraguay	5.1	4.2[z]	8.8	10.6[z]	*47.9*[**]	39.6[z]	*554*[**]	602[z]	29.7	35.7[z]	748	812[z]	...	...	...	74.2[z]
Peru	3.4	2.8	21.1	18.1	40.4	38.4	422	636	28.4	31.4	566	725	...	...	87.8	65.2
Saint Kitts and Nevis	4.9	...	14.0	...	...	...	...	...	...	...	...	...	...	...	...	...
Saint Lucia	7.7	4.6	21.3	11.9	52.7[**]	41.6	1 790[**]	1 810	32.6[**]	45.2	2 394[**]	2 380	...	...	87.6	72.0[x]
Saint Vincent and the Grenadines	7.2[**]	5.3[z]	*13.4*[**]	10.2[z]	*49.0*	...	*1 224*	...	*25.8*	...	*1 281*[**]	...	*1.6*	6.6[z]	*94.0*	87.0[z]
Suriname	...	...	...	...	...	...	...	...	...	...	...	...	...	...	...	...
Trinidad and Tobago	3.9	...	*12.5*[**]	...	39.8	...	1 535	3 265[y]	31.1	...	1 764	2 958[**, x]	...	...	77.5	...
Turks and Caicos Islands	...	...	17.4	...	29.7	...	...	...	39.6	...	...	...	3.7[**]	...	63.5[**]	...
Uruguay	2.4	...	*11.8*	...	32.4	...	709	...	36.9	...	1 042	...	...	...	71.3	...
Venezuela, Bolivarian Republic of	...	...	...	...	...	...	...	...	...	...	...	...	...	...	...	...
North America and Western Europe																
Andorra	...	2.9[z]	...	16.5	...	28.7	...	...	...	21.3	...	...	...	...	...	...
Austria	6.4	6.0[y]	12.4	11.4[y]	19.0	17.6[y]	8 083	10 153[y]	45.1	47.7[y]	9 965	11 941[y]	...	...	71.5	62.2[y]
Belgium	***5.9***	6.4[z]	***12.2***	12.5[z]	...	23.2[z]	...	8 359[z]	...	42.7[z]	...	13 939[z]	...	...	***73.7***	66.9[z]
Canada	5.9	5.6[z]	***12.5***	...	...	...	...	...	...	...	...	...	...	...	...	...
Cyprus	5.3	7.5[z]	*14.5*	15.8[z]	33.9	30.3[z]	4 284	9 222[z]	52.5	44.3[z]	6 762	11 607[z]	...	...	*73.6*	79.8[z]
Denmark	8.2	8.6[y]	14.9	15.1[y]	***21.4***[**]	23.4[y]	8 959	10 538[y]	***34.6***[**]	33.8[y]	14 121	12 558[y]	...	...	48.9	50.5[y]
Finland	6.2	6.7[z]	12.5	12.3[z]	21.1	19.6[z]	4 866	7 020[z]	39.3	41.5[z]	7 230	12 083[z]	...	...	59.0	55.9[z]
France	5.7	5.8[y]	11.5	10.4[y]	20.2[**]	20.2[y]	5 231	5 719[y]	49.8[**]	44.4[y]	8 551	8 908[y]	...	...	...	57.0[y]
Germany	...	4.9[y]	...	10.5[y]	...	13.9[y]	...	6 428[y]	...	47.4[y]	...	8 912[y]	...	...	...	...
Greece	3.2	...	7.0	...	...	...	...	...	***38.1***	...	2 990	...	...	...	...	...
Iceland	6.7	9.7[y]	17.1	15.3[y]	34.2	31.6[y]	5 545	8 983[y]	34.1	32.2[y]	5 159	7 787[y]	...	...	...	...
Ireland	4.9	7.8[y]	13.2	13.3[y]	32.2	35.4[y]	3 607	7 744[y]	36.8	34.6[y]	5 430	11 578[y]	...	...	83.3	76.2[y]
Israel	7.5	6.1[z]	13.9	13.6[y]	33.9	40.0[z]	4 478	5 623[z]	30.0	25.7[z]	4 166	4 120[z]	...	...	...	...
Italy	4.7	4.5[z]	9.6	9.1[y]	26.1[**]	25.3[z]	7 202[**]	7 396[z]	46.5[**]	43.7[z]	8 291[**]	7 796[z]	...	...	*66.4*	63.8[z]
Luxembourg	***4.2***	...	***9.8***	...	...	...	...	11 323[x]	...	...	...	16 754[x]	...	...	***70.2***	80.4[y]
Malta	...	5.9[y]	...	12.6[y]	...	22.6[y]	...	5 127[y]	...	46.1[y]	...	6 497[y]	...	...	...	46.2[y]
Monaco	1.2	1.2[y]	5.1	8.1	17.7	14.5	...	...	50.9	38.5	...	...	...	...	...	...
Netherlands	4.8	6.1[z]	11.1	11.6[z]	...	24.3[z]	...	7 752[z]	...	40.7[z]	...	11 381[z]	...	...	...	...
Norway	7.2	6.8[z]	15.6	15.2[z]	...	25.7[z]	...	10 663[z]	...	34.6[z]	...	14 002[z]	...	...	...	...

Crowded classrooms: At a school in Eastern Cape, South Africa, classes can have as many as 172 pupils.

Credit: Eva-Lotta Jansson/UNESCO

Aid tables

Introduction[1]

The data on aid used in this Report are derived from the OECD International Development Statistics (IDS) databases, which record information provided annually by all member countries of the OECD Development Assistance Committee (DAC), as well as a growing number of donors that are not members of the committee. The IDS databases are the DAC databases, which provided project- and activity-level data. In this Report, total figures for net official development assistance (ODA) comes from the DAC database while those for gross ODA, sector-allocable aid and aid to education come from the Creditor Reporter System (CRS). Both are available at www.oecd.org/dac/stats/idsonline.

Official development assistance is public funds provided to developing countries to promote their economic and social development. It is concessional; that is, it takes the form either of a grant or a loan carrying a lower rate of interest than is available on the market and, usually, a longer repayment period.

A more extensive version of the aid tables including ODA per recipient is available on the Report's website, www.efareport.unesco.org.

Aid recipients and donors

Developing countries are those in Part 1 of the DAC List of Aid Recipients: all low and middle income countries except twelve Central and Eastern European countries and a few more advanced developing countries.

Bilateral donors are countries that provide development assistance directly to recipient countries. Most are members of the DAC, a forum of major bilateral donors established to promote aid and its effectiveness. Bilateral donors also contribute substantially to the financing of multilateral donors through contributions recorded as multilateral ODA.

Multilateral donors are international institutions with government membership that conduct all or a significant part of their activities in favour of developing countries. They include multilateral development banks (e.g. the World Bank and Inter-American Development Bank), United Nations agencies and regional groupings (e.g. the European Commission). The development banks also make non-concessional loans to several middle and higher income countries; these are not counted as part of ODA.

Types of aid

Total ODA: bilateral and multilateral aid for all sectors, as well as aid that is not allocable by sector, such as general budget support and debt relief. In Table 1, total ODA from bilateral donors is bilateral aid only, while aid as a percentage of gross national income (GNI) is bilateral and multilateral ODA.

Sector-allocable ODA: aid allocated to a specific sector, such as education or health. It does not include aid for general development purposes (e.g. general budget support), balance-of-payments support, debt relief or emergency assistance.

Debt relief: includes debt forgiveness, i.e. the extinction of a loan by agreement between the creditor (donor) and debtor (aid recipient), and other action on debt, including debt swaps, buy-backs and refinancing. In the DAC database, debt forgiveness is reported as a grant and therefore counts as ODA.

Country programmable aid: defined by subtracting from total gross ODA aid that:

- is unpredictable by nature (humanitarian aid and debt relief);
- entails no cross-border flows (administrative costs, imputed student costs, and costs related to promotion of development awareness, research in donor countries);

1. A full set of statistics and indicators related to the introduction is posted in Excel format on the *EFA Global Monitoring Report* website at www.efareport.unesco.org.

Table 3 (continued)

Country or territory	TOTAL AID TO EDUCATION Constant 2011 US$ millions 2002–2003 annual average	2010	2011	TOTAL AID TO BASIC EDUCATION Constant 2011 US$ millions 2002–2003 annual average	2010	2011	TOTAL AID TO BASIC EDUCATION PER PRIMARY SCHOOL-AGE CHILD Constant 2011 US$ millions 2002–2003 annual average	2010	2011	DIRECT AID TO EDUCATION Constant 2011 US$ millions 2002–2003 annual average	2010	2011	DIRECT AID TO BASIC EDUCATION Constant 2011 US$ millions 2002–2003 annual average	2010	2011
Brazil	41	116	105	4	23	23	0	2	2	41	116	105	2	5	5
Chile	15	34	33	1	8	7	1	5	5	15	34	33	0	3	2
Colombia	34	70	68	5	18	18	1	4	4	34	70	68	2	10	11
Costa Rica	3	10	9	0	3	2	1	6	5	3	10	9	0	1	1
Cuba	12	9	10	3	2	3	3	3	4	12	9	10	3	2	2
Dominica	1	3	2	0	1	1	35	177	107	1	0	1	-	0	-
Dominican Republic	21	58	14	14	30	9	12	25	7	21	51	14	13	9	7
Ecuador	18	39	35	3	14	11	2	8	6	18	39	35	3	5	6
El Salvador	9	50	32	3	17	15	4	21	19	9	50	32	3	10	7
Grenada	0	5	1	-	2	0	-	141	19	0	1	0	-	0	-
Guatemala	31	46	38	16	28	24	8	12	10	31	46	38	13	20	17
Guyana	17	1	2	6	0	1	54	4	6	15	1	2	3	0	0
Haiti	24	175	143	13	104	89	9	73	63	24	127	133	10	74	62
Honduras	38	35	53	29	17	35	27	15	32	37	31	51	24	12	31
Jamaica	12	13	10	9	9	3	27	25	10	9	5	10	6	4	3
Mexico	33	60	61	2	10	10	0	1	1	33	60	61	1	3	2
Nicaragua	63	66	42	35	24	20	42	31	25	53	61	38	24	15	13
Panama	5	5	5	0	1	1	1	3	3	5	5	5	0	1	0
Paraguay	8	42	38	4	22	30	5	26	34	8	41	38	3	6	26
Peru	35	57	59	10	20	21	3	6	6	35	57	53	7	13	10
Saint Kitts and Nevis	0	1	3	0	1	2	2	91	240	0	0	0	-	-	-
Saint Lucia	1	3	4	0	2	2	12	99	79	1	3	3	0	1	0
Saint Vincent and the Grenadines	0	5	6	0	2	3	5	161	228	0	5	5	0	0	-
Suriname	3	3	2	1	1	0	22	10	2	3	3	2	1	0	-
Trinidad and Tobago	1	1	-	0	-	-	0	-	-	1	1	-	-	-	-
Uruguay	4	9	6	1	3	2	2	11	6	4	9	6	0	1	0
Venezuela, B.R.	9	15	16	1	3	3	0	1	1	9	15	16	1	1	1
South and West Asia	**967**	**2 267**	**2 417**	**597**	**1 309**	**1 445**	**4**	**8**	**8**	**775**	**2 238**	**2 412**	**463**	**996**	**1 014**
Unallocated within the region	*-*	*8*	*3*	*-*	*7*	*0*	...	...	...	*-*	*8*	*3*	*-*	*6*	*0*
Afghanistan	42	420	381	27	288	217	6	53	39	34	413	377	17	239	158
Bangladesh	153	368	365	98	254	249	6	16	16	144	368	365	90	232	226
Bhutan	9	12	9	5	3	2	45	29	18	9	10	8	4	1	1
India	379	580	792	280	387	578	2	3	5	361	580	792	261	336	497
Iran, Islamic Republic of	40	66	72	1	1	2	0	0	0	40	66	72	1	1	0
Maldives	9	5	4	3	1	1	66	31	21	9	5	4	3	1	0
Nepal	54	152	171	35	75	78	21	20	21	52	142	171	27	47	27
Pakistan	225	574	554	130	271	288	6	14	15	80	564	553	49	126	90
Sri Lanka	54	82	66	18	22	29	11	13	16	46	82	66	13	6	14
Sub-Saharan Africa	**2 816**	**3 959**	**3 647**	**1 490**	**1 891**	**1 757**	**13**	**13**	**13**	**2 231**	**3 187**	**2 831**	**933**	**930**	**782**
Unallocated within the region	*92*	*233*	*159*	*65*	*152*	*74*	...	...	...	*91*	*212*	*140*	*50*	*123*	*47*
Angola	44	28	27	26	10	12	14	3	3	44	28	27	19	6	8
Benin	45	74	81	17	35	43	14	24	30	39	56	74	11	18	28
Botswana	3	37	21	0	18	9	2	61	32	3	37	21	0	0	0
Burkina Faso	93	143	146	56	79	80	26	29	29	65	97	105	36	45	38
Burundi	14	49	44	6	23	24	5	19	20	10	31	34	2	10	14
Cameroon	103	117	117	21	14	17	44	7	5	90	113	117	13	5	5
Cape Verde	39	43	24	5	4	1	64	63	23	36	36	22	2	0	0
Central African Republic	10	19	19	1	7	9	2	11	13	9	11	19	1	2	2
Chad	29	17	16	14	9	8	9	5	4	19	17	16	5	7	5
Comoros	14	16	14	4	4	3	49	37	27	13	13	14	4	0	0
Congo	27	23	28	2	4	7	5	6	12	27	22	27	1	3	3
Côte d'Ivoire	96	77	189	34	28	85	12	9	27	56	63	33	9	18	5
D. R. Congo	127	154	134	57	94	76	6	8	7	32	114	99	5	64	48
Equatorial Guinea	10	11	10	5	5	5	68	53	47	10	11	10	3	2	4
Eritrea	19	19	57	9	10	29	16	15	44	19	19	57	5	4	10
Ethiopia	106	320	315	59	162	165	5	12	12	81	284	293	31	40	40
Gabon	32	32	33	6	1	4	27	5	25	31	32	33	4	1	2
Gambia	10	8	7	6	3	3	28	11	11	8	7	6	5	2	1
Ghana	127	177	193	80	96	102	26	27	28	79	99	111	46	35	35
Guinea	46	41	50	27	7	12	20	5	8	42	41	46	24	4	4
Guinea-Bissau	10	23	12	4	10	5	21	46	24	10	20	10	4	1	2
Kenya	89	51	131	56	25	68	10	4	10	84	51	68	50	19	29
Lesotho	25	22	24	13	12	12	33	33	32	21	8	20	8	3	1
Liberia	3	53	45	2	39	33	5	62	51	3	48	37	2	29	27
Madagascar	86	56	51	38	25	24	16	9	8	68	56	51	21	21	19
Malawi	75	162	70	44	106	56	21	43	22	71	104	70	30	59	47
Mali	105	167	155	57	96	86	29	38	33	81	141	120	32	68	44
Mauritius	18	29	30	0	8	11	3	69	90	18	15	15	0	1	3
Mozambique	158	277	254	88	149	141	24	32	30	115	188	165	48	55	53
Namibia	27	22	32	14	9	14	39	24	37	27	22	32	12	2	1
Niger	58	52	42	30	15	20	15	6	8	36	49	23	8	9	8
Nigeria	34	176	140	17	77	56	1	3	2	33	176	140	12	26	24
Rwanda	64	111	145	28	41	64	21	25	39	45	84	111	5	14	13
Sao Tome and Principe	6	7	9	1	0	2	49	12	72	6	7	9	1	0	1
Senegal	122	183	177	39	66	67	24	34	33	117	168	161	21	31	30

DIRECT AID TO SECONDARY EDUCATION Constant 2011 US$ millions			DIRECT AID TO POST-SECONDARY EDUCATION Constant 2011 US$ millions			DIRECT AID TO EDUCATION, LEVEL UNSPECIFIED Constant 2011 US$ millions			SHARE OF EDUCATION IN TOTAL ODA (%)			SHARE OF DIRECT AID TO EDUCATION IN TOTAL SECTOR-ALLOCABLE ODA (%)			SHARE OF BASIC EDUCATION IN TOTAL AID TO EDUCATION (%)		
2002–2003 annual average	2010	2011	2002–2003 annual average	2010	2011	2002–2003 annual average	2010	2011	2002–2003 annual average	2010	2011	2002–2003 annual average	2010	2011	2002–2003 annual average	2010	2011
4	6	3	30	71	61	5	34	36	9	18	12	16	19	13	11	19	22
1	2	2	11	19	19	2	9	10	19	15	31	21	19	34	9	24	22
4	7	6	22	36	37	6	16	14	4	7	7	5	8	7	16	26	26
0	0	1	3	4	5	0	5	3	5	6	12	7	7	13	11	31	27
2	1	1	7	6	5	1	1	1	15	7	11	18	8	12	26	24	31
0	-	-	0	0	0	-	0	0	7	7	7	4	1	4	29	50	37
4	3	3	2	2	1	2	36	3	10	22	5	16	24	5	68	53	62
5	5	6	9	11	12	2	18	12	6	15	14	8	15	15	18	36	33
2	22	6	2	4	4	2	14	15	4	12	9	7	13	10	37	35	46
0	1	0	0	0	0	-	0	0	2	14	6	2	7	3	0	40	28
6	6	3	7	4	3	5	16	15	9	10	9	12	12	11	51	61	63
7	-	-	1	0	1	4	1	1	19	1	1	26	1	1	35	48	42
1	9	16	7	33	10	6	11	45	12	4	8	17	11	12	52	59	62
2	9	11	2	4	2	9	6	7	8	6	8	15	5	8	76	49	67
0	0	6	0	0	1	2	0	1	11	7	11	12	4	11	74	63	30
7	4	4	23	38	40	2	15	15	14	9	6	15	9	6	6	17	16
3	15	12	13	18	4	12	13	9	9	10	7	14	10	7	56	37	47
3	0	0	1	3	2	0	1	2	11	3	4	14	3	4	9	27	28
1	2	3	2	1	2	2	31	6	8	23	24	14	23	25	49	53	78
7	10	7	16	20	21	5	15	16	5	7	7	8	7	8	27	35	35
-	0	0	0	0	0	0	0	0	1	12	17	1	1	2	28	48	49
0	1	1	0	0	0	0	1	2	4	8	10	4	9	9	34	61	37
0	1	0	0	0	0	0	4	5	5	35	28	7	35	32	25	41	49
0	-	-	1	2	2	0	1	0	7	3	3	7	3	3	42	18	5
0	0	-	1	1	-	0	-	-	15	13	-	15	14	-	1	0	-
0	1	1	2	2	2	1	5	3	19	13	15	22	13	15	17	40	29
1	1	2	7	9	10	1	3	5	11	28	34	15	31	39	10	18	18
57	**209**	**226**	**179**	**436**	**316**	**76**	**596**	**856**	**8**	**11**	**12**	**11**	**13**	**14**	**62**	**58**	**60**
-	*0*	*1*	-	*2*	*1*	-	*0*	*0*	-	8	3	-	15	4	-	79	19
1	29	57	4	54	47	12	91	115	3	6	6	5	7	7	63	69	57
25	62	64	21	29	29	8	44	47	10	17	16	12	19	18	64	69	68
2	4	1	1	4	5	3	1	1	14	8	6	16	8	6	53	24	20
14	50	49	67	92	83	19	101	162	10	12	12	13	12	15	74	67	73
1	2	2	38	62	68	0	1	3	26	52	60	39	67	68	2	2	2
3	1	1	3	2	2	1	1	1	40	4	8	57	5	8	36	23	20
3	20	19	9	29	23	13	46	102	11	15	17	12	16	18	64	50	46
2	19	20	12	139	48	17	280	395	6	15	13	7	25	25	58	47	52
7	21	11	23	24	11	3	31	30	7	7	6	10	9	7	34	27	44
139	**380**	**257**	**629**	**728**	**659**	**530**	**1 149**	**1 134**	**9**	**8**	**7**	**15**	**10**	**9**	**53**	**48**	**48**
3	*10*	*10*	*9*	*42*	*48*	*28*	*37*	*34*	*5*	*5*	*4*	*8*	*6*	*4*	*71*	*65*	*46*
1	8	8	12	5	4	13	8	8	8	9	11	19	9	12	58	36	44
4	4	6	20	19	17	5	16	23	12	10	12	16	9	12	37	47	53
1	0	0	1	0	2	1	36	18	6	21	15	8	22	15	15	49	46
7	5	10	10	24	15	11	23	43	13	13	14	15	12	14	60	56	55
0	7	4	3	5	6	5	9	5	5	7	8	7	6	8	44	47	55
2	4	3	72	89	86	3	15	23	9	17	17	25	23	22	20	12	14
3	14	9	29	21	11	2	0	1	27	12	9	31	13	12	12	9	6
1	1	1	7	5	3	1	2	13	13	6	7	18	8	10	12	40	46
1	1	1	6	5	4	7	4	6	8	3	3	7	7	6	48	54	51
1	0	0	9	8	8	0	5	5	36	21	24	40	24	30	31	27	22
0	3	3	23	15	13	3	1	7	24	1	8	43	18	22	9	17	26
2	16	4	35	22	20	10	7	4	8	8	12	17	10	7	35	37	45
4	14	14	14	16	16	9	21	21	3	2	2	4	8	6	45	61	57
2	1	0	1	1	5	4	6	1	28	11	35	35	32	38	49	49	46
3	1	6	3	1	2	8	13	39	6	12	44	11	15	54	45	52	52
5	18	10	16	17	16	30	209	227	6	9	9	8	11	11	55	51	52
2	4	1	23	26	25	1	0	4	20	23	30	39	26	33	17	3	13
1	3	1	2	0	0	2	2	3	13	7	5	14	7	5	63	40	49
3	8	6	10	13	18	21	43	52	11	10	10	12	7	8	63	54	53
4	2	1	11	29	29	4	7	12	13	16	14	18	18	16	59	17	24
1	1	1	5	2	2	0	15	5	7	7	3	17	18	10	41	45	48
5	5	10	21	15	14	7	12	14	13	3	5	16	3	4	63	48	52
5	1	1	2	0	0	6	3	18	21	8	8	23	4	8	50	55	51
0	3	4	0	1	2	1	15	4	3	3	5	15	11	9	71	73	73
2	5	3	31	22	19	14	8	10	12	11	12	15	13	14	44	45	47
16	4	2	2	5	2	23	35	19	12	15	9	17	15	10	58	65	80
6	21	9	18	20	18	25	32	49	14	14	12	16	15	12	54	58	56
-	3	1	17	11	10	0	0	1	35	18	14	36	17	11	2	29	35
4	15	10	26	19	15	36	99	88	6	13	12	10	13	12	56	54	55
8	4	3	4	2	3	4	14	25	18	8	11	20	8	11	51	42	43
3	2	3	4	28	6	21	9	6	11	7	6	13	10	6	51	30	48
2	17	15	10	32	38	9	101	62	8	7	7	9	8	7	51	44	40
5	7	20	8	36	10	27	27	68	13	10	11	16	9	11	44	37	44
1	2	2	4	5	4	0	0	2	14	15	13	19	24	18	18	4	21
3	19	17	61	64	57	31	54	57	17	18	16	21	20	17	32	36	38

Learning Metrics Task Force. 2013. *Towards Universal Learning: A Global Framework for Measuring Learning*. Montreal, Canada/Washington, DC, UNESCO Institute for Statistics/ Brookings Institution.

Majgaard, K. and Mingat, A. 2012. *Education in Sub-Saharan Africa: A Comparative Analysis*. Washington, DC, World Bank.

Makuwa, D. K. 2010. The SACMEQ III project: mixed results in achievement. *UNESCO IIEP Newsletter*, Vol. XXVIII, No.3, p. 4.

McKinley, T. and Kyrili, K. 2009. *Is Stagnation of Domestic Revenue in Low-income Countries Inevitable?* London, School of Oriental and African Studies, University of London. (Discussion Paper, 27/09.)

Mitra, S., Posarac, A. and Vick, B. 2011. *Disability and Poverty in Developing Countries: A Snapshot from the World Health Survey*. Washington, DC, World Bank. (Social Protection Working Paper, 1109.)

Namibia Ministry of Education. 2007. *Education and Training Sector Improvement Programme: Programme Document Phase 1 (2006-2011)*. Windhoek, Ministry of Education.

Ncube, M. 2013. *Recognizing Africa's Informal Sector*. Tunis, African Development Bank Group. http:// www.afdb.org/en/blogs/afdb-championing-inclusive-growth-across-africa/post/recognizing-africas-informal-sector-11645/ (Accessed 11 July 2013.)

Nigeria National Bureau of Statistics, UNICEF and United Nations Population Fund. 2013. *Nigeria Multiple Indicator Cluster Survey*. Abuja/New York, Nigeria National Bureau of Statistics/UNICEF/ United Nations Population Fund.

OECD-DAC. 2013. *International Development Statistics: Creditor Reporting System*. Paris, Organisation for Economic Co-operation and Development. http://stats.oecd.org/Index.aspx?datasetcode=CRS1 (Accessed 5 April 2013.)

OECD. 2000. *A System of Health Accounts*. Paris, Organisation of Economic Co-operation and Development.

___. 2008. *Taxation, State Building and Aid*. Paris, Organisation for Economic Co-operation and Development.

___. 2011. *Lessons from PISA for the United States, Strong Performers and Successful Reformers in Education*. Paris, Organisation for Economic Co-operation and Development.

___. 2012a. *2012 DAC Report on Aid Predictability: Survey on Donors' Forward Spending Plans 2012-2015 and Efforts Since HLF-4*. Paris, Organisation for Economic Co-operation and Development.

___. 2012b. *Tax and Development: Aid Modalities for Strengthening Tax Systems*. Paris, Organisation for Economic Co-operation and Development.

___. 2013a. *Aid to Poor Countries Slips Further as Governments Tighten Budgets*. Paris, Organisation for Economic Co-operation and Development. http://www.oecd.org/dac/stats/ aidtopoorcountriesslipsfurtherasgovernmentstightenbudgets.htm (Accessed 9 September 2013.)

___. 2013b. *Education at a Glance 2013*. Paris, Organisation for Economic Co-operation and Development.

___. 2013c. *OECD Skills Outlook 2013: First Results from the Survey of Adult Skills (PIAAC)* Paris, Organisation for Economic Co-operation and Development.

___. 2013d. *Outlook on Aid: Survey on Donors' Forward Spending Plans 2013-2016*. Paris, Organisation for Economic Co-operation and Development.

OECD, Eurostat and WHO. 2011. *A System of Health Accounts: 2011 Edition*. Paris/Luxembourg/ Geneva, Switzerland, Organisation of Economic Co-operation and Development/Eurostat/World Health Organization.

Office for the Coordination of Humanitarian Affairs. 2013. *Financial Tracking Service*. Geneva, Switzerland, United Nations Office for the Coordination of Humanitarian Affairs. http:// fts.unocha.org/pageloader.aspx?page=emerg-emergencies§ion=CE&year=2013. (Accessed 1 March 2013.)

Open Society Foundations, Roma Education Fund and UNICEF. 2011. *Roma Early Childhood Inclusion: Macedonian Report*. London/Budapest/Geneva, Switzerland, Open Society Foundations/Roma Education Fund/UNICEF.

Oxford Poverty and Human Development Initiative. 2013. *Multidimensional Poverty Index Data Tables for 2013*. Oxford, UK, Oxford Poverty and Human Development Initiative, University of Oxford. http://www.ophi.org.uk/multidimensional-poverty-index/mpi-data-bank/mpi-data/ (Accessed 1 May 2013.)

Parmanand, S. 2013. *Few Surpises in New Australian Aid Budget*. Washington, DC, Devex. https://www.devex.com/en/news/few-surprises-in-new-australian-aid-budget/80943 (Accessed 11 July 2013.)

Pasha, A. G. 2010. Can Pakistan get out of the low tax-to-GDP trap? *The Lahore Journal of Economics*, Vol. 15, Supplemental Special Edition, pp. 171–85.

Piccio, L. 2013. *Which Countries are Winners and Losers in Obama's 2014 Aid Budget?* Washington, DC, Devex. www.devex.com/en/news/which-countries-are-winners-and-losers-in-obama-s-2014-aid-budget/80713 (Accessed 12 July 2013.)

Ponce, J. 2010. *Políticas Educativas y Desempeño: Una Evaluación de Impacto de Programas Educativos Focalizados en Ecuador* [Education Policy and Performance: An Evaluation of the Impact of Targeted Educational Programmes in Ecuador]. Quito, Latin American Faculty of Social Sciences.

___. 2011. *Desigualdad del ingreso en Ecuador: un análisis de los años 1990s y 2000s* [Income Inequality in Ecuador: An Analysis of the 1990s and 2000s]. Quito, Latin American Faculty of Social Sciences. (FLACSO Working Paper.)

PREAL and Instituto Desarollo. 2013. *Informe de Progreso Educativo: Paraguay – El Desafío es la Equidad* [Education Progress Report: Paraguay – Equity is the Challenge]. Washington, DC/Asunción, Partnership for Educational Revitalization in the Americas/Institit, Desarollo.

PREAL and Lemann Foundation. 2009. *Overcoming Inertia? A Report Card on Education in Brazil*. Washington, DC/São Paulo, Brazil, Partnership for Educational Revitalization in the Americas/Lemann Foundation.

Publish What You Pay. 2013. *European Union Reaches Deal on Tough Oil, Gas Anti-Corruption Law*. London, Publish What You Pay. www.publishwhatyoupay.org/resources/european-union-reaches-deal-tough-oil-gas-anti-corruption-law (Accessed 11 July 2013.)

Read, T. and Bontoux, V. forthcoming. *Where Have All the Textbooks Gone? The Affordable and Sustainable Provision of Learning and Teaching Materials in Sub-Saharan Africa*. Washington, DC, World Bank.

Republic of Moldova Ministry of Education. 2010. *2011-2015 Consolidated Strategy for Education Development*. Chisinau, Ministry of Education.

Robinson, L. and Barder, O. 2013. Let's not forget that development is more than just CIDA. *The Globe and Mail*, 22 March.

Rwanda Revenue Authority. 2012. *Taxation Background in Rwanda and the Linkage Between a Government's Efforts in Resource Mobilisation and Efficient Service Delivery*. Kigali, Rwanda Revenue Authority.

SACMEQ. 2010. *How Successful Are Textbook Provision Programmes?* Paris, Southern and Eastern Africa Consortium for Monitoring Educational Quality. (Policy Issues Series 6.)

Satriawan, E. 2013. *The Cash Transfer for Poor Students Program: Issues, Reform and Evaluation*. Jakarta, National Team for Acceleration of Poverty Reduction.

Sayed, Y. and Motala, S. 2012. Equity and 'no fee' schools in South Africa: challenges and prospects. *Social Policy and Administration*, Vol. 46, No. 6, pp. 672–87.

Schneider, P., Schott, W., Bhawalkar, M., Nandakumar, A. K., Diop, F. and Butera, D. 2001. *Paying for HIV/AIDS Services: Lessons from National Health Accounts and Community-based Health Insurance in Rwanda, 1998–1999*. Geneva, Switzerland, Joint United Nations Programme on HIV/AIDS.

SITEAL. 2013a. *La Expansión Educativa al Límite: Notas Sobre la Escolarización Básica en América Latina* [Education Expansion at a Limit: Notes on Enrolment in Basic Education in Latin America]. Buenos Aires/Madrid, UNESCO – International Institute for Educational Planning/Organization of Ibero-American States. (Dato Destacado 29.)

___. 2013b. *Sistema de Información de Tendencias Educativas en América Latina* [Information system on education trends in Latin America]. Buenos Aires/Madrid, UNESCO – International Institute for Educational Planning/Organization of Ibero-American States. www.siteal.iipe-oei.org/base_de_datos/consulta (Accessed 2 July 3013.)

Sri Lanka Ministry of Education. 2006. *Education Sector Development Framework and Programme*. Colombo, Ministry of Education.

Stampini, M. and Tornarolli, L. 2012. *The Growth of Conditional Cash Transfers in Latin America and the Caribbean: Did They Go Too Far?* Bonn, Germany, Institute for the Study of Labor. (Policy Paper 49.)

Tax Justice Network. 2012. *Revealed: Global Super-Rich Has at Least $21 Trillion Hidden in Secret Tax Havens*. London, Tax Justice Network.

Taylor, L. 2013. Coalition costings show foreign aid cuts and rely on stopping asylum seekers. *The Guardian,* 5 September.

Teixeira, C., Soares, F. V., Ribas, R., Silva, E. and Hirata, G. 2011. *Externality and Behavioural Change Effects of a Non-randomized CCT programme: Heterogeneous Impact on the Demand for Health and Education*. Brasilia, International Policy Centre for Inclusive Growth. (IPC-IG Working Paper, 82.)

TFYR Macedonia Ministry of Health, Ministry of Education and Science and Ministry of Labour and Social Policy. 2011. *Multiple Indicator Cluster Survey 2011*. Skopje, Ministry of Health/Ministry of Education and Science/Ministry of Labour and Social Policy.

TFYR Macedonia Ministry of Labour and Social Policy. 2010. *Fair Play: A Financially Feasible Plan for Equal Access to Early Childhood Programs in the Republic of Macedonia*. Skopje, Ministry of Labour and Social Policy.

Tran, M. 2013. Tax emerges as crucial issue in post-2015 development talks. *The Guardian,* 25 March.

Turkey Ministry of National Education. 2009. *Milli Egitim Bakanligi 2010–2014 Stratejik Plani* [Ministry of Education Strategic Plan 2010–2014]. Ankara, Strategic Development Department, Ministry of National Education.

___. 2013. *National Education Statistics, Formal Education: 2012–2013*. Ankara, Ministry of National Education.

Twaweza. 2012. *Three Experiments to Improve Learning Outcomes in Tanzania: Delivering Capitation Grants Better and Testing Local Cash on Delivery*. Dar es Salaam, U.R. Tanzania, Twaweza.

Uçan, E. 2013. *Increasing Girls' Secondary Education Attainment in Turkey.* Paper for Global Education Leadership Opportunities 2013, Cambridge, MA., Harvard University.

UIS. 2006. *Education Counts: Benchmarking Progress in 19 WEI Countries: World Education Indicators – 2006*. Montreal, Que., UNESCO Institute for Statistics.

___. 2011. *Financing Education in Sub-Saharan Africa: Meeting the Challenges of Expansion, Equity and Quality*. Montreal, Que.,/Dakar/Paris, UNESCO Institute for Statistics/UNESCO BREDA/UNESCO – International Institute for Education Planning/Pôle de Dakar.

___. 2012. *School and Teaching Resources in Sub-Saharan Africa: Analysis of the 2011 UIS Regional Data Collection on Education*. Montreal, Que., UNESCO Institute for Statistics.

UK House of Commons International Development Committee. 2012. *Tax in Developing Countries: Increasing Resources for Development*. London, House of Commons International Development Committee.

UN. 2013a. *Malawi/Cash Transfers*. New York, United Nations. www.unmultimedia.org/tv/unifeed/2013/06/malawi-cash-transfers (Accessed 2 September 2013.)

___. 2013b. *A New Global Partnership: Eradicate Poverty and Transform Economies Through Sustainable Development – The Report of the High-Level Panel of Eminent Persons on the Post-2015 Development Agenda*. New York, United Nations.

___. 2013c. *Progress Report of the Open Working Group of the General Assembly on Sustainable Development Goals*. New York, United Nations.

UNESCO. 2010. *EFA Global Monitoring Report 2010: Reaching the Marginalized*. Paris, UNESCO.

___. 2012. *EFA Global Monitoring Report 2012: Youth and Skills – Putting Education to Work*. Paris, UNESCO.

___. 2013a. *Children Still Battling to Go to School*. Paris, UNESCO. (Policy Paper, 10.)

___. 2013b. *Education Budgets: A Study of Selected Districts of Pakistan*. Islamabad, UNESCO Islamabad.

___. 2013c. *Education for All is Affordable: By 2015 and Beyond*. Paris, UNESCO. (Policy Paper, 6.)

UNESCO-IBE. 2011. *The former Yugoslav Republic of Macedonia*. Geneva, Switzerland, UNESCO International Bureau of Education. (World Data on Education.)

UNESCO and UNICEF. 2013. *Making Education a Priority in the Post-2015 Development Agenda: Report of the Global Thematic Consultation on Education in the Post-2015 Development Agenda*. Paris/New York, UNESCO/UNICEF.

UNICEF. 2009. *Jordan's Early Childhood Development Initiative: Making Jordan Fit for Children*. Amman, UNICEF Regional Office for the Middle East and North Africa. (Learning Series, 2.)

___. 2013a. *Improving Child Nutrition: The Achievable Imperative for Global Progress*. New York, UNICEF.

___. 2013b. *Syria's Children: A Lost Generation?* Amman, UNICEF Regional Office for the Middle East and North Africa.

___. 2013c. *Syria Conflict Depriving Children of their Education*. New York, UNICEF.

UNICEF, WHO and World Bank. 2013. *Joint Child Malnutrition Estimates*. New York/Geneva, Switzerland/Washington, DC, UNICEF/World Health Organization/World Bank. http://data.worldbank.org/child-malnutrition/compare-regional-prevalence (Accessed 3 October 2013.)

U.R. Tanzania Ministry of Education and Vocational Training. 2011. *Tanzania Education Sector Analysis: Beyond Primary Education, the Quest for Balanced and Efficient Policy Choices for Human Development and Economic Growth*. Dar es Salaam, U.R. Tanzania, Ministry of Education and Vocational Training.

US Department of State. 2013. *Bureau of Educational and Cultural Affairs*. Washington, DC, Department of State. http://eca.state.gov (Accessed 9 September 2013.)

Uwazi. 2010. *Tanzania's Tax Exemptions: Are They Too High and Making Us Too Dependent on Foreign Aid?* Dar es Salaam, U.R. Tanzania, Uwazi at Twaweza. (Policy Brief, TZ.12/2010E.)

Watkins, K. and Alemayehu, W. 2012. *Financing for a Fairer, More Prosperous Kenya: A Review of the Public Spending Challenges and Options for Selected Arid and Semi-arid Counties*. Washington, DC, Center for Universal Education at Brookings Institution. (Working Paper, 6.)

WHO and World Bank. 2011. *World Report on Disability*. Geneva, Switzerland/Washington, DC, World Health Organization/World Bank.

WHO, World Bank and USAID. 2003. *Guide to Producing National Health Accounts: With Special Applications for Low-income and Middle-income Countries*. Geneva, Switzerland/Washington, DC, World Health Organization/World Bank/US Agency for International Development.

World Bank. 2008a. *An African Exploration of the East Asian Education Experience*. Washington, DC, World Bank. (Development Practice in Education.)

___. 2008b. *Nigeria: A Review of the Costs and Financing of Public Education – Volume 2 Main Report*. Washington, DC, World Bank.

___. 2010. *The Education System in Malawi*. Washington, DC, World Bank. (Working Paper, 182.)

___. 2011. *Rwanda Education Country Status Report: Toward Quality Enhancement and Achievement of Universal Nine Year Basic Education*. Washington, DC, World Bank.

___. 2012a. *Philippines: 200,000 More Poor Households Will Have Incentives to Invest in Education and Health of Their Children*. Washington, DC, World Bank. www.worldbank.org/en/news/press-release/2012/12/11/philippines-200000-more-poor-households-incentives-invest-education-health-children (Accessed 2 September 2013.)

___. 2012b. *Towards Gender Equality in Turkey: A Summary Assessment*. Washington, DC, World Bank.

___. 2013a. *2012 Education Year In Review*. Washington, DC, World Bank. (Education Year in Review: Achieving Learning for All.)

___. 2013b. *Armenia: Student Assessment*. Washington, DC, World Bank. (SABER Country Report.)

___. 2013c. *Ethiopia Overview*. Washington, DC, World Bank. www.worldbank.org/en/country/ethiopia/overview (Accessed 12 September 2013.)

___. 2013d. *Liberia at a Glance*. Washington, DC, World Bank. http://devdata.worldbank.org/AAG/lbr_aag.pdf (Accessed 12 September 2013.)

___. 2013e. *Spending More or Spending Better: Improving Education Financing in Indonesia*. Washington, DC, World Bank. www.worldbank.org/en/news/press-release/2013/03/14/spending-more-or-spending-better-improving-education-financing-in-indonesia (Accessed 2 September 2013.)

___. 2013f. *World Development Indicators*. Washington, DC. World Bank. http://data.worldbank.org/data-catalog/world-development-indicators (Accessed 2 September 2013.)

___. 2013h. *Zambia : Student Assessment*. Washington, DC, World Bank. (SABER Country Report.)

Zida, A., Bertone, M. P. and Lorenzetti, L. 2010. *Using National Health Accounts to Inform Policy Change in Burkina Faso*. Bethesda, Md., Health Systems 20/20, Abt Associates Inc. (Policy Brief.)

Part 2: Education transforms lives

Abregú, M. 2001. Barricades or obstacles: the challenges of access to justice. van Puymbroeck, R. V. (ed.), *Comprehensive Legal and Judicial Development: Toward an Agenda for a Just and Equitable Society in the 21st Century*. Washington, DC, World Bank, pp. 53–70.

Afridi, F., Iversen, V. and Sharan, M. R. 2013. *Women Political Leaders, Corruption and Learning: Evidence from a Large Public Program in India*. Bonn, Institute for the Study of Labour. (Discussion Paper, 7212.)

Aisa, R. and Larramona, G. 2012. Household water saving: evidence from Spain. *Water Resources Research*, Vol. 48, No. 12, pp. 1–14.

Alene, A. D. and Manyong, V. M. 2007. The effects of education on agricultural productivity under traditional and improved technology in northern Nigeria: an endogenous switching regression analysis. *Empirical Economics*, Vol. 32, No. 1, pp. 141–59.

Andemariam, S. W. 2011. *Ensuring Access to Justice Through Community Courts in Eritrea*. Rome, International Development Law Organization. (Traditional Justice: Practitioners' Perspectives Working Paper, 3.)

Asfaw, A. and Admassie, A. 2004. The role of education on the adoption of chemical fertiliser under different socioeconomic environments in Ethiopia. *Agricultural Economics*, Vol. 30, No. 3, pp. 215–28.

Aslam, M. 2013. Empowering women: education and the pathways of change. Background paper for *EFA Global Monitoring Report 2013/4*.

Aslam, M., Bari, F. and Kingdon, G. 2012. Returns to schooling, ability and cognitive skills in Pakistan. *Education Economics*, Vol. 20, No. 2, pp. 139–73.

Bandiera, O. and Rasul, I. 2006. Social networks and technology adoption in northern Mozambique. *The Economic Journal*, Vol. 116, No. 514, pp. 869–902.

Barakat, B. and Urdal, H. 2009. *Breaking the Waves? Does Education Mediate the Relationship Between Youth Bulges and Political Violence?* Washington, DC, World Bank. (Policy Research Working Paper, 5114.)

Bardhan, P., Mitra, S., Mookherjee, D. and Sarkar, A. 2009. Local democracy and clientelism: implications for political stability in rural West Bengal. *Economic and Political Weekly*, Vol. 44, No. 9, pp. 46–58.

Bärnighausen, T., Hosegood, V., Timaeus, I. M. and Newell, M.-L. 2007. The socioeconomic determinants of HIV incidence: evidence from a longitudinal, population-based study in rural South Africa. *Aids*, Vol. 21, Supplement 7, pp. S29–S38.

Barro, R. J. and Lee, J.-W. 2013. *Barro-Lee Educational Attainment Dataset*. Seoul, Korea University. www.barrolee.com (Accessed 10 March 2013.)

Baulch, B. and Dat, V. H. 2011. Poverty dynamics in Vietnam, 2002 to 2006. Baulch, B. (ed.), *Why Poverty Persists: Poverty Dynamics in Asia and Africa*. Cheltenham, UK, Edward Elgar, pp. 219–54.

Beaman, L., Chattopadhyay, R., Duflo, E., Pande, R. and Topalova, P. 2009. Powerful women: does exposure reduce bias? *The Quarterly Journal of Economics*, Vol. 124, No. 4, pp. 1497–540.

Beaman, L., Duflo, E., Pande, R. and Topalova, P. 2012. Female leadership raises aspirations and educational attainment for girls: a policy experiment in India. *Science*, Vol. 335, No. 6068, pp. 582–86.

Behrman, J., Murphy, A., Quisumbing, A. and Yount, K. 2009. *Are Returns to Mothers' Human Capital Realized in the Next Generation? The Impact of Mothers' Intellectual Human Capital and Long-run Nutritional Status on Children's Human Capital in Guatemala*. Washington, DC, International Food Policy Research Institute. (Discussion Paper, 850.)

Behrman, J. R., Hoddinott, J., Maluccio, J. and Martorell, R. 2010. Brains versus brawn: labor market returns to intellectual and physical health human capital in a developing country. Washington, DC, International Food Policy Research Institute. (Unpublished.)

Below, T., Artner, A., Siebert, R. and Sieber, S. 2010. *Micro-level Practices to Adapt to Climate Change for African Small-scale Farmers*. Washington, DC, International Food Policy Research Institute. (Discussion Paper, 953.)

Bergh, G. and Melamed, C. 2012. *Inclusive Growth and a Post-2015 Framework*. London, Overseas Development Institute.

Bhalotra, S. and Clarke, D. 2013. Educational attainment and maternal mortality. Background paper for *EFA Global Monitoring Report 2013/4*.
Bhalotra, S., Clots-Figueras, I. and Lyer, L. 2013a. Women's political participation and the female-male literacy differential in India. Background paper for *EFA Global Monitoring Report 2013/4*.
Bhalotra, S., Harttgen, K. and Klasen, S. 2013b. The impact of school fees on the intergenerational transmission of education. Background paper for *EFA Global Monitoring Report 2013/4*.
Bhatta, S. D. and Sharma, S. 2011. The determinants and consequences of chronic and transient poverty in Nepal. Baulch, B. (ed.), *Why Poverty Persists: Poverty Dynamics in Asia and Africa*. Cheltenham, UK, Edward Elgar, pp. 96–144.
Black, R. E., Allen, L. H., Bhutta, Z. A., Caulfield, L. E., De Onis, M., Ezzati, M., Mathers, C. and Rivera, J. 2008. Maternal and child undernutrition: global and regional exposures and health consequences. *The Lancet*, Vol. 371, No. 9608, pp. 243–60.
Bloom, D. E., Canning, D., Fink, G. and Finlay, J. E. 2009. Fertility, female labor force participation, and the demographic dividend. *Journal of Economic Growth*, Vol. 14, No. 2, pp. 79–101.
Borgonovi, F., d'Hombres, B. and Hoskins, B. 2010. Voter turnout, information acquisition and education: evidence from 15 European countries. *The B.E. Journal of Economic Analysis and Policy*, Vol. 10, No. 1, pp. 1–32.
Borgonovi, F. and Miyamoto, K. 2010. Education and civic and social engagement. OECD (ed.), *Improving Health and Social Cohesion through Education*. Paris, Organisation for Economic Co-operation and Development, pp. 65–110.
Botero, J., Ponce, A. and Shleifer, A. 2012. *Education and the Quality of Government*. Cambridge, MA., National Bureau of Economic Research. (NBER Working Paper, 18119.)
Bratton, M., Chu, Y.-H. and Lagos, M. 2010. Who votes? Implications for new democracies. *Taiwan Journal of Democracy*, Vol. 6, No. 1, pp. 107–36.
Bratton, M., Mattes, R. and Gyimah-Boadi, E. 2005. *Public Opinion, Democracy, and Market Reform in Africa*. Cambridge, UK, Cambridge University Press.
Brollo, F. and Troiano, U. 2013. What happens when a woman wins an election? Evidence from close races in Brazil. Cambridge, Mass., Harvard University. (Unpublished.)
Campbell, D. E. 2006. *Why We Vote: How Schools and Communities Shape Our Civic Life*. Princeton, NJ, Princeton University Press.
Carlsson, F. and Johansson-Stenman, O. 2000. Willingness to pay for improved air quality in Sweden. *Applied Economics*, Vol. 32, No. 6, pp. 661–69.
Carreras, M. and Castañeda-Angarita, N. forthcoming. Who votes in Latin America? A test of three theoretical perspectives. *Comparative Political Studies*, forthcoming.
Castelló-Climent, A. 2010. Channels through which human capital inequality influences economic growth. *Journal of Human Capital*, Vol. 4, No. 4, pp. 394–450.
___. 2013. Education and economic growth. Background paper for *EFA Global Monitoring Report 2013/4*.
Castillejo, C. 2009. *Building Accountable Justice in Sierra Leone*. Madrid, Foundation for International Relations and External Dialogue. (Working Paper, 76.)
Child Health Epidemiology Reference Group. 2012. *Underlying Causes of Child Death*. Child Health Epidemiology Reference Group. http://cherg.org/projects/underlying_causes.html (Accessed 18 April 2013.)
Choo, S. and Mokhtarian, P. L. 2004. What type of vehicle do people drive? The role of attitude and lifestyle in influencing vehicle type choice. *Transportation Research Part A: Policy and Practice*, Vol. 38, No. 3, pp. 201–22.
Chzhen, Y. 2013. Education and democratisation: tolerance of diversity, political engagement, and understanding of democracy. Background paper for *EFA Global Monitoring Report 2013/4*.
Cohen, D. and Soto, M. 2007. Growth and human capital: good data, good results. *Journal of Economic Growth*, Vol. 12, No. 1, pp. 51–76.
Colclough, C., Kingdon, G. and Patrinos, H. 2010. The changing pattern of wage returns to education and its implications. *Development Policy Review*, Vol. 28, No. 6, pp. 733–47.
Collier, P. and Hoeffler, A. 2004. Greed and grievance in civil war. *Oxford Economic Papers*, Vol. 56, No. 4, pp. 563–95.
Dalton, R. J. 2008. Citizenship norms and the expansion of political participation. *Political Studies*, Vol. 56, No. 1, pp. 76–98.

de Walque, D. 2007. Does education affect smoking behaviors? Evidence using the Vietnam draft as an instrument for college education. *Journal of Health Economics*, Vol. 26, No. 5, pp. 877–95.
___. 2010. Education, information, and smoking decisions: evidence from smoking histories in the United States, 1940–2000. *Journal of Human Resources*, Vol. 45, No. 3, pp. 682–717.
Dee, T. S. 2004. Are there civic returns to education? *Journal of Public Economics*, Vol. 88, No. 9, pp. 1697–720.
Dercon, S., Hoddinott, J. and Woldehanna, T. 2012. Growth and chronic poverty: evidence from rural communities in Ethiopia. *Journal of Development Studies*, Vol. 48, No. 2, pp. 238–53.
Deressa, T. T., Hassan, R. M., Ringler, C., Alemu, T. and Yesuf, M. 2009. Determinants of farmers' choice of adaptation methods to climate change in the Nile Basin of Ethiopia. *Global Environmental Change*, Vol. 19, No. 2, pp. 248–55.
Di Cesare, M., Khang, Y.-H., Asaria, P., Blakely, T., Cowan, M. J., Farzadfar, F., Guerrero, R., Ikeda, N., Kyobutungi, C. and Msyamboza, K. P. 2013. Inequalities in non-communicable diseases and effective responses. *The Lancet*, Vol. 381, No. 9866, pp. 585–97.
Eichengreen, B., Park, D. and Shin, K. 2013. *Growth Slowdowns Redux: New Evidence on the Middle-income Trap*. Cambridge, MA., National Bureau of Economic Research. (NBER Working Paper, 18673.)
European Commission, EACEA and Eurydice. 2013. *Funding of Education in Europe 2000–2012: The Impact of the Economic Crisis*. Luxembourg, Publications Office of the European Union.
Eurostat. 2013. *Labour Force Survey Series*. Luxembourg, Eurostat. http://epp.eurostat.ec.europa.eu/cache/ITY_SDDS/EN/lfsa_esms.htm (Accessed 2 August 2013.)
Evans, G. and Rose, P. 2007. Support for democracy in Malawi: does schooling matter? *World Development*, Vol. 35, No. 5, pp. 904–19.
___. 2012. Understanding education's influence on support for democracy in sub-Saharan Africa. *Journal of Development Studies*, Vol. 48, No. 4, pp. 498–515.
Ezeh, A. C., Mberu, B. U. and Emina, J. O. 2009. Stall in fertility decline in Eastern African countries: regional analysis of patterns, determinants and implications. *Philosophical Transactions of the Royal Society B: Biological Sciences*, Vol. 364, No. 1532, pp. 2991–3007.
FAO, WFP and IFAD. 2012. *The State of Food Insecurity in the World: Economic Growth is Necessary but not Sufficient to Accelerate Reduction of Hunger and Malnutrition.* Rome, Food and Agriculture Organization of the United Nations.
Fasih, T., Kingdon, G., Patrinos, H., Sakellariou, C. and Soderbom, M. 2012. *Heterogeneous Returns to Education in the Labor Market*. Washington, DC, World Bank. (Policy Research Working Paper, 6170.)
Feinstein, L., Sabates, R., Anderson, T. M., Sorhaindo, A. and Hammond, C. 2006. What are the effects of education on health? Desjardins, R. and Schuller, T. (eds), *Measuring the Effects of Education on Health and Civic Engagement: Proceedings of the Copenhagen Symposium*. Paris, Organisation for Economic Co-operation and Development, pp. 171–354.
Ferrara, I. and Missios, P. 2011. *A Cross-country Study of Waste Prevention and Recycling*. Toronto, Ryerson University. (Department of Economics Working Paper, 28.)
Finkel, S. E., Horowitz, J. and Rojo-Mendoza, R. T. 2012. Civic education and democratic backsliding in the wake of Kenya's post-2007 election violence. *The Journal of Politics*, Vol. 74, No. 1, pp. 52–65.
Finkel, S. E. and Smith, A. E. 2011. Civic education, political discussion, and the social transmission of democratic knowledge and values in a new democracy: Kenya 2002. *American Journal of Political Science*, Vol. 55, No. 2, pp. 417–35.
Fjelde, H. and Østby, G. 2012. Economic inequality and inter-group conflicts in Africa. Oslo, Peace Research Institute Oslo. (Unpublished.)
Flamm, B. 2009. The impacts of environmental knowledge and attitudes on vehicle ownership and use. *Transportation Research Part D: Transport and Environment*, Vol. 14, No. 4, pp. 272–79.
Fox, L. and Sohnesen, T. P. 2012. *Household Enterprises in Sub-Saharan Africa: Why They Matter for Growth, Jobs, and Livelihoods*. Washington, DC, World Bank (Policy Research Working Paper, 6184.)
Frayha, N. 2004. Developing curriculum as a means to bridging national divisions in Lebanon. Tawil, S., Harley, A. and Braslavsky, C. (eds), *Education, Conflict and Social Cohesion*. Geneva, Switzerland, UNESCO International Bureau of Education, pp.159–206.

Fuchs, R., Pamuk, E. and Lutz, W. 2010. Education or wealth: which matters more for reducing child mortality in developing countries? *Vienna Yearbook of Population Research,* Vol. 8, pp. 175–99.

Fullman, N., Burstein, R., Lim, S. S., Medlin, C. and Gakidou, E. 2013. Nets, spray or both? The effectiveness of insecticide-treated nets and indoor residual spraying in reducing malaria morbidity and child mortality in sub-Saharan Africa. *Malaria Journal,* Vol. 12, p. 62.

Gaddis, I. and Klasen, S. 2012. *Economic Development, Structural Change and Women's Labor Force Participation: A Reexamination of the Feminization U Hypothesis*. Göttingen, Germany, Georg-August-Universität Göttingen. (Courant Research Centre Working Paper, 71.)

Gakidou, E. 2013. Education, literacy and health outcomes. Background paper for *EFA Global Monitoring Report 2013/4.*

Gasparini, L., Jaume, D., Serio, M. and Vazquez, E. 2011. *La segregación escolar en Argentina: Reconstruyendo la evidencia* [School segregation in Argentina: Reconstructing the evidence]. La Plata, Argentina, Centre for Distributive, Labor and Social Studies, Universida Nacional de la Plata. (Working Paper, 123.)

GAVI. 2013. *GAVI's Impact.* Geneva, Switzerland, Global Alliance for Vaccines and Immunisation. www.gavialliance.org/about/mission/impact (Accessed 18 April 2013.)

Glaeser, E. L., Ponzetto, G. A. M. and Shleifer, A. 2006. *Why Does Democracy Need Education?* Cambridge, MA., National Bureau of Economic Research. (NBER Working Paper, 12128.)

Green, A., Preston, J. and Sabates, R. 2003. Education, equality and social cohesion: a distributional approach. *Compare,* Vol. 33, No. 4, pp. 453–70.

Greene, D. L. and Plotkin, S. E. 2011. *Reducing Greenhouse Gas Emissions from US Transportation*. Arlington, VA., Pew Center on Global Climate Change.

Grossman, M. 2006. Education and nonmarket outcomes. Hanushek, E. A. and Welch, F. (eds), *Handbook of the Economics of Education*, Vol. 1. Amsterdam, Elsevier, pp. 577–633.

Halperin, D. T., Mugurungi, O., Hallett, T. B., Muchini, B., Campbell, B., Magure, T., Benedikt, C. and Gregson, S. 2011. A surprising prevention success: why did the HIV epidemic decline in Zimbabwe? *PLoS Medicine,* Vol. 8, No. 2, p. e1000414.

Hanushek, E. A. and Woessmann, L. 2008. The role of cognitive skills in economic development. *Journal of Economic Literature,* Vol. 46, No. 3, pp. 607–68.

___. 2012a. Do better schools lead to more growth? Cognitive skills, economic outcomes, and causation. *Journal of Economic Growth,* Vol. 17, No. 4, pp. 267–321.

___. 2012b. GDP projections. Background paper for *EFA Global Monitoring Report 2012.*

Hanushek, E. A. and Zhang, L. 2006. *Quality-consistent Estimates of International Returns to Skill.* Cambridge, MA., National Bureau of Economic Research. (NBER Working Paper, 12664.)

Hargreaves, J. R., Bonell, C. P., Boler, T., Boccia, D., Birdthistle, I., Fletcher, A., Pronyk, P. M. and Glynn, J. R. 2008. Systematic review exploring time trends in the association between educational attainment and risk of HIV infection in sub-Saharan Africa. *Aids,* Vol. 22, No. 3, pp. 403–14.

He, X. F., Cao, H. and Li, F. M. 2007. Econometric analysis of the determinants of adoption of rainwater harvesting and supplementary irrigation technology (RHSIT) in the semiarid Loess Plateau of China. *Agricultural Water Management,* Vol. 89, No. 3, pp. 243–50.

Headey, D. D. 2013. Developmental drivers of nutritional change: a cross-country analysis. *World Development,* Vol. 42, pp. 76–88.

Heston, A., Summers, R. and Aten, B. 2012. *Penn World Table Version 7.1.* University Park, Pa., Center for International Comparisons of Production, Income and Prices at the University of Pennsylvania. https://pwt.sas.upenn.edu/php_site/pwt71/pwt71_form_test.php (Accessed 24 July 2013.)

Hisali, E., Birungi, P. and Buyinza, F. 2011. Adaptation to climate change in Uganda: evidence from micro level data. *Global Environmental Change,* Vol. 21, No. 4, pp. 1245–61.

Hjorth, K. and Fosgerau, M. 2011. Loss aversion and individual characteristics. *Environmental and Resource Economics,* Vol. 49, No. 4, pp. 573–96.

Hoddinott, J., Rosegrant, M. and Torero, M. 2012. *Hunger and Malnutrition*. Copenhagen, Global Copenhagen Consensus.

Hosseinpoor, A. R., Parker, L. A., d'Espaignet, E. T. and Chatterji, S. 2011. Social determinants of smoking in low-and middle-income countries: results from the World Health Survey. *PLoS ONE,* Vol. 6, No. 5, p. e20331.

OECD. 2009. *Green at Fifteen? How 15-year Olds Perform in Environmental Science and Geoscience in PISA 2006*. Paris, Organisation of Economic Co-operation and Development.

___. 2010. *PISA 2009 Results: Overcoming Social Background – Equity in Learning Opportunities and Outcomes*. Paris, Organisation for Economic Co-operation and Development.

___. 2011. *Greening Household Behaviour: The Role of Public Policy*. Paris, Organisation for Economic Co-operation and Development.

___. 2012. *Closing the Gender Gap: Act Now*. Paris, Organisation for Economic Co-operation and Development.

Oommen, T. K. 2009. Development policy and the nature of society: understanding the Kerala model. *Economic and Political Weekly,* Vol. 44, No. 13, pp. 25–31.

Osili, U. O. and Long, B. T. 2008. Does female schooling reduce fertility? Evidence from Nigeria. *Journal of Development Economics,* Vol. 87, No. 1, pp. 57–75.

Østby, G. 2008. Inequalities, the political environment and civil conflict: evidence from 55 developing countries. Stewart, F. (ed.), *Horizontal Inequalities and Conflict: Understanding Group Violence in Multiethnic Societies*. Basingstoke, UK, Palgrave Macmillan, pp. 136–59.

Palipudi, K. M., Gupta, P. C., Sinha, D. N., Andes, L. J., Asma, S. and McAfee, T. 2012. Social determinants of health and tobacco use in thirteen low and middle income countries: evidence from Global Adult Tobacco Survey. *PLoS ONE,* Vol. 7, No. 3, p. e33466.

Pampel, F. C., Denney, J. T. and Krueger, P. M. 2011. Cross-national sources of health inequality: education and tobacco use in the World Health Survey. *Demography,* Vol. 48, No. 2, pp. 653–74.

Pampel, F. C. and Hunter, L. M. 2012. Cohort change, diffusion, and support for environmental spending in the United States. *American Journal of Sociology,* Vol. 118, No. 2, pp. 420–48.

Pawasutipaisit, A. and Townsend, R. M. 2011. Wealth accumulation and factors accounting for success. *Journal of Econometrics,* Vol. 161, No. 1, pp. 56–81.

Pereira, C., Rennó, L. and Samuels, D. 2011. Corruption, campaign finance, and reelection. Power, T. J. and Taylor, M. M. (eds), *Corruption and Democracy in Brazil: the Struggle for Accountability*. Notre Dame, Ind., University of Notre Dame Press, pp. 80–101.

Pettifor, A., Taylor, E., Nku, D., Duvall, S., Tabala, M., Meshnick, S. and Behets, F. 2008. Bed net ownership, use and perceptions among women seeking antenatal care in Kinshasa, Democratic Republic of the Congo (DRC): Opportunities for improved maternal and child health. *BMC Public Health,* Vol. 8, p. 331.

Pintor, R. L. and Gratschew, M. 2002. *Voter Turnout Since 1945: A Global Report*. Stockholm, International Institute for Democracy and Electoral Assistance.

Poortinga, W., Steg, L. and Vlek, C. 2004. Values, environmental concern, and environmental behavior: a study into household energy use. *Environment and Behavior,* Vol. 36, No. 1, pp. 70–93.

Pritchett, L. 2006. Does learning to add up add up? The returns to schooling in aggregate data. Hanushek, E. A. and Welch, F. (eds), *Handbook of the Economics of Education*, Vol. 1. Amsterdam, Elsevier, pp. 635–95.

Radeny, M., van den Berg, M. and Schipper, R. 2012. Rural poverty dynamics in Kenya: structural declines and stochastic escapes. *World Development,* Vol. 40, No. 8, pp. 1577–93.

Rashid, D. A., Smith, L. C. and Rahman, T. 2011. Determinants of dietary quality: evidence from Bangladesh. *World Development,* Vol. 39, No. 12, pp. 2221–31.

Ravallion, M. 2001. Growth, inequality and poverty: looking beyond averages. *World Development,* Vol. 29, No. 11, pp. 1803–15.

Ribas, R. P. and Machado, A. F. 2007. *Distinguishing Chronic Poverty from Transient Poverty in Brazil: Developing a Model for Pseudo-panel Data*. Brasilia, International Poverty Centre (Working Paper, 36.)

Rothstein, B. and Uslaner, E. 2012. *The Roots of Corruption: Mass Education, Economic Inequality and State Building.* for at the American Political Science Association Annual Meeting, New Orleans, La., 30 August – 2 September.

Rudan, I., Boschi-Pinto, C., Biloglav, Z., Mulholland, K. and Campbell, H. 2008. Epidemiology and etiology of childhood pneumonia. *Bulletin of the World Health Organization,* Vol. 86, No. 5, pp. 408–16.

Sabates, R. 2013. Can maternal education hinder, sustain or enhance the benefits of early life interventions? Background paper for *EFA Global Monitoring Report 2013/4*.

Salomon, J. A., Wang, H., Freeman, M. K., Vos, T., Flaxman, A. D., Lopez, A. D. and Murray, C. J. L. 2012. Healthy life expectancy for 187 countries, 1990–2010: a systematic analysis for the Global Burden Disease Study 2010. *The Lancet*, Vol. 380, No. 9859, pp. 2144–62.

Santarelli, E. and Tran, H. T. 2013. The interplay of human and social capital in shaping entrepreneurial performance: the case of Vietnam. *Small Business Economics*, Vol. 40, No. 2, pp. 435–58.

Schulz, W., Ainley, J., Fraillon, J., Kerr, D. and Losito, B. 2010. *ICCS 2009 International Report: Civic Knowledge, Attitudes and Engagement Among Lower Secondary School Students in Thirty-eight Countries*. Amsterdam, International Association for the Evaluation of Educational Achievement.

Semba, R. D., de Pee, S., Sun, K., Sari, M., Akhter, N. and Bloem, M. W. 2008. Effect of parental formal education on risk of child stunting in Indonesia and Bangladesh: a cross-sectional study. *The Lancet*, Vol. 371, No. 9609, pp. 322–28.

Shafiq, M. N. 2010. Do education and income affect support for democracy in Muslim countries? Evidence from the Pew Global Attitudes Project. *Economics of Education Review*, Vol. 29, No. 3, pp. 461–69.

Shapiro, D., Kreider, A., Varner, C. and Sinha, M. 2011. Stalling of fertility transitions and socioeconomic change in the developing world: evidence from the Demographic and Health Surveys. University Park, PA., Pennsylvania State University. (Unpublished.)

Shapiro, J. 2006. Guatemala. Hall, G. and Patrinos, H. A. (eds), *Indigenous Peoples, Poverty, and Human Development in Latin America*. New York, Palgrave Macmillan.

Sharma, A. K., Bhasin, S. and Chaturvedi, S. 2007. Predictors of knowledge about malaria in India. *Journal of Vector Borne Diseases*, Vol. 44, No. 3, pp. 189–97.

Shroff, M. R., Griffiths, P. L., Suchindran, C., Nagalla, B., Vazir, S. and Bentley, M. E. 2011. Does maternal autonomy influence feeding practices and infant growth in rural India? *Social Science and Medicine*, Vol. 73, No. 3, pp. 447–55.

Shuayb, M. 2012. Current models and approaches to social cohesion in secondary education in Lebanon. Shuayb, M. (ed.), *Rethinking Education for Social Cohesion: International Case Studies*. Basingstoke, UK, Palgrave Macmillan, pp. 137–53.

Siri, J. G. 2012. *The Independent Effects of Maternal Education and Household Wealth on Malaria Risk in Children*. Vienna, International Institute for Applied Systems Analysis. (Interim Report, 12-014.)

Sondheimer, R. M. and Green, D. P. 2010. Using experiments to estimate the effects of education on voter turnout. *American Journal of Political Science*, Vol. 54, No. 1, pp. 174–89.

Stallings, R. 2004. *Childhood Morbidity and Treatment Patterns*. Calverton, MD., Opinion Research Corporation Company Macro. (DHS Comparative Studies, 8.)

Stampini, M. and Davis, B. 2006. Discerning transient from chronic poverty in Nicaragua: measurement with a two-period panel data set. *The European Journal of Development Research*, Vol. 18, No. 1, pp. 105–30.

Stern, N. H. 2006. *The Economics of Climate Change: The Stern Review*. London, Her Majesty's Treasury, UK Government.

Subramanian, S. V., Huijts, T. and Avendano, M. 2010. Self-reported health assessments in the 2002 World Health Survey: how do they correlate with education? *Bulletin of the World Health Organization*, Vol. 88, No. 2, pp. 131–38.

Thyne, C. L. 2006. ABC's, 123's, and the golden rule: the pacifying effect of education on civil war, 1980–1999. *International Studies Quarterly*, Vol. 50, No. 4, pp. 733–54.

Tiwari, K. R., Sitaula, B. K., Nyborg, I. L. P. and Paudel, G. S. 2008. Determinants of farmers' adoption of improved soil conservation technology in a middle mountain watershed of central Nepal. *Environmental Management*, Vol. 42, No. 2, pp. 210–22.

UNAIDS. 2012. *Global Report: UNAIDS Report on the Global AIDS Epidemic 2012*. Geneva, Switzerland, Joint United Nations Programme on HIV/AIDS.

Understanding Children's Work. 2012. Youth disadvantage in the labour market: empirical evidence from nine developing countries. Background paper for *EFA Global Monitoring Report 2012*.

___. 2013. Education and employment outcomes. Background paper for *EFA Global Monitoring Report 2013/4*.

Elbadawy, A., Assaad, R., Ahlburg, D. and Levison, D. 2007. Private and group tutoring in Egypt: where is the gender inequality? Cairo, Economic Research Forum. (Working Paper, 0429.)

Engle, P. L., Black, M. M., Behrman, J. R., Cabral de Mello, M., Gertler, P. J., Kapiriri, L., Martorell, R. and Young, M. E. 2007. Strategies to avoid the loss of developmental potential in more than 200 million children in the developing world. *The Lancet*, Vol. 369, No. 9557, pp. 229–42.

Epstein, A. I. and Opolot, S. P. 2012. *Gender Equity through Education (GEE): End of Project Performance Evaluation Report*. Washington, DC, US Agency for International Development.

Erden, F. T. 2009. A course on gender equity in education: does it affect gender role attitudes of preservice teachers? *Teaching and Teacher Education*, Vol. 25, No. 3, pp. 409–14.

European Commission. 2012. *Supporting the Teaching Profession for Better Learning Outcomes: Rethinking Education – Investing in Skills for Better Socio-economic Outcomes*. Strasbourg, France, European Commission.

Evans, P. and Ebersold, S. 2012. Achieving equity in secondary and tertiary education for students with disabilities and learning difficulties. Heyman, J. and Cassola, A. (eds), *Lessons in Educational Equality: Successful Approaches to Intractable Problems Around the World*. Oxford, UK, Oxford University Press, pp. 78–99.

Fairlie, R. W. and Robinson, J. 2013. *Experimental Evidence on the Effects of Home Computers on Academic Achievement Among Schoolchildren*. Cambridge, MA., Abdul Latif Jameel Poverty Action Lab, Massachusetts Institute of Technology.

Farrell, P., Alborz, A., Howes, A. and Pearson, D. 2010. The impact of teaching assistants on improving pupils' academic achievement in mainstream schools: a review of the literature. *Educational Review*, Vol. 62, No. 4, pp. 435–48.

Fehrler, S., Michaelowa, K. and Wechtler, A. 2009. The effectiveness of inputs in primary education: insights from recent student surveys for sub-Saharan Africa. *Journal of Development Studies*, Vol. 45, No. 9, pp. 1545–78.

Forlin, C. 2010. Teacher education for inclusion. Rose, R. (ed.), *Confronting Obstacles to Inclusion: International Responses to Developing Inclusive Education*. Oxford, UK, Routledge, pp. 155–70.

Forlin, C. and Dinh, N. T. 2010. A national strategy for supporting teacher educators to prepare teachers for inclusion. Forlin, C. (ed.), *Teacher Education for Inclusion: Changing Paradigms and Innovative Approaches*. Oxford, UK, Routledge, pp. 34–44.

Forum for African Women Educationalists. 2006. *Experiences in Creating a Conducive Environment for Girls in School*. Nairobi, Forum for African Women Educationalists.

___. 2013. *Gender-responsive Pedagogy*. Nairobi, Forum for African Women Educationalists. www.fawe.org/activities/interventions/GRP/index.php (Accessed 10 June 2013.)

Fyfe, A. 2007. *The Use of Contract Teachers in Developing Countries: Trends and Impact*. Geneva, Switzerland, International Labour Organization.

Gao, F. and Shum, M. S. K. 2010. Investigating the role of bilingual teaching assistants in Hong Kong: an exploratory study. *Educational Research*, Vol. 52, No. 4, pp. 445–56.

Geeves, R. and Bredenberg, K. 2005. *Contract Teachers in Cambodia*. Paris, UNESCO -International Institute for Educational Planning.

Ghana Education Sector Mission. 2013. Draft aide memoire: Ghana education sector mission – pre-identification Ghana secondary education (P145741) Ghana Partnership for Education Grant (P129381-TF013140) May 6–15. Accra, Ghana Ministry of Education.

Ghana Education Service. 2010. *Open and Distance Learning (ODL) Teacher Education to Support Teacher Development in Ghana: the Untrained Teachers Diploma in Basic Education – An Evaluation Report*. Accra, Teacher Education Division, Ghana Education Service.

Ghana Ministry of Education. 2012a. Draft pre-tertiary teacher development and management policy. Accra, Ministry of Education. (Unpublished.)

___. 2012b. *Ghana National Education Assessment: 2011 Findings Report*. Accra, Ministry of Education.

Ghuman, S. and Lloyd, C. 2010. Teacher absence as a factor in gender inequalities in access to primary schooling in rural Pakistan. *Comparative Education Review*, Vol. 54, No. 4, pp. 539–54.

Gilpin, G. A. 2011. Reevaluating the effect of non-teaching wages on teacher attrition. *Economics of Education Review*, Vol. 30, No. 4, pp. 598–616.

Gindin, J. and Finger, L. 2013. Promoting education quality: the role of teacher unions in Latin America. Background paper for *EFA Global Monitoring Report 2013/4*.

Glazerman, S., Mayer, D. P. and Decker, P. T. 2006. Alternative routes to teaching: the impacts of Teach for America on student achievement and other outcomes. *Journal of Policy Analysis and Management*, Vol. 25, No. 1, pp. 75–96.

Glewwe, P., Hanushek, E. A., Humpage, S. D. and Ravina, R. 2011. *School Resources and Educational Outcomes in Developing Countries: a Review of the Literature from 1990 to 2010*. Cambridge, MA., National Bureau of Economic Research. (NBER Working Paper, 17554.)

Glewwe, P., Ilias, N. and Kremer, M. 2010. Teacher incentives. *American Economic Journal: Applied Economics*, Vol. 2, No. 3, pp. 205–27.

Glewwe, P., Kremer, M. and Moulin, S. 2007. *Many Children Left Behind? Textbooks and Test Scores in Kenya*. Cambridge, MA., Abdul Latif Jameel Poverty Action Lab, Massachusetts Institute of Technology.

Glewwe, P. and Maïga, E. 2011. *The Impacts of School Management Reforms in Madagascar: Do the Impacts Vary by Teacher Type?* Cambridge, MA., Abdul Latif Jameel Poverty Action Lab.

Global Partnership for Education. 2012. *Results for Learning Report 2012: Fostering Evidence-based Dialogue to Monitor Access and Quality in Education*. Washington, DC, Global Partnership for Education.

Globalgiving. 2013. *Gender Equity Through Education in South Sudan*. Washington, DC, Globalgiving. www.globalgiving.org/projects/girlseducationsudan (Accessed 23 September 2013.)

Goldhaber, D. and Walch, J. 2012. Strategic pay reform: a student outcomes-based evaluation of Denver's ProComp teacher pay initiative. *Economics of Education Review*, Vol. 31, No. 6, pp. 1067–83.

Gove, A. and Cvelich, P. 2010. *Early Reading: Igniting Education for All – a Report by the Early Grade Learning Community of Practice*. Research Triangle Park, NC, RTI International.

___. 2011. *Early Reading: Igniting Education for All – A Report by the Early Grade Learning Community of Practice, Revised Edition*. Research Triangle Park, NC, RTI International.

Goyal, S. and Pandey, P. 2009. *How Do Government and Private Schools Differ? Findings from Two Large Indian States*. Washington, DC, World Bank.

Greaney, V. and Kellaghan, T. 2008. *National Assessments of Educational Achievement: Assessing National Achievement Levels in Education*. Washington, DC, World Bank.

Guadalupe, C., Leon, J. and Cueto, S. 2013. Charting progress in learning outcomes in Peru using national assessments. Background paper for *EFA Global Monitoring Report 2013/4*.

Guerrero, G., Leon, J., Zapata, M., Sugimaru, C. and Cueto, S. 2012. *What Works to Improve Teacher Attendance in Developing Countries? A Systematic Review*. London, Evidence for Policy and Practice Information and Co-ordinating Centre, Institute of Education, University of London.

Gulpers, E. E. 2013. Teacher accountability in an era of financial scarcity: the case of Jamaican primary education reform. Verger, A., Altinyelken, H. and de Koning, M. (eds), *Global Managerial Education Reforms and Teachers: Emerging Policies, Controversies and Issues in Developing Contexts*. Brussels, Education International Research Institute, pp. 37–54.

Habib, M. 2010. The impact of 2002 national teacher contract policy reform on teacher absenteeism in Lahore, Pakistan. PhD dissertation, Washington, DC., The George Washington University.

Hanushek, E. A. and Rivkin, S. G. 2012. The distribution of teacher quality and implications for policy. *Annual Review of Economics*, Vol. 4, No. 1, pp. 31–57.

Hardman, F. 2012. *Review: Teacher Support and Development Interventions*. London, Save the Children.

Hardman, F., Abd-Kadir, J., Agg, C., Migwi, J., Ndambuku, J. and Smith, F. 2009. Changing pedagogical practice in Kenyan primary schools: the impact of school-based training. *Comparative Education*, Vol. 45, No. 1, pp. 65–86.

Härmä, J. 2009. Can choice promote Education for All? Evidence from growth in private primary schooling in India. *Compare*, Vol. 39, No. 2, pp. 151–65.

___. 2011. *Study of Private Schools in Lagos*. Abuja, UK Department for International Development – Education Sector Support Programme in Nigeria. (Report, LG303.)

Save the Children. 2013. *Literacy Boost*. London, Save the Children. www.savethechildren.org/site/c.8rKLIXMGIpI4E/b.7084483 (Accessed 8 August 2013.)

Schleicher, A. (ed.) 2012. *Preparing Teachers and Developing School Leaders for the 21st Century: Lessons from Around the World*. Paris, Organisation for Economic Co-operation and Development.

SchoolScape and Tamil Nadu Government. 2009. *Activity Based Learning: Effectiveness of ABL Under SSA June 2007–April 2008*. Chennai, India, SchoolScape/Tamil Nadu Government.

Selby, D. and Kagawa, F. 2012. *Disaster Risk Reduction in School Curricula: Case Studies from Thirty Countries*. Paris/Geneva, Switzerland, UNESCO/UNICEF.

Senou, B. M. 2008. Contractualisation de la fonction enseignante et comportement des maîtres au primaire: cas du Bénin [Contractualization of the teaching function and behaviour of primary school teachers: the case of Benin]. Yaoundé, Université de Yaoundé II-SOA. (Unpublished.)

Servas, N. 2012. Responsible citizenship: an education programme in returnee areas of Burundi. Education Above All (ed.), *Education for Global Citizenship*. Doha, Education Above All, pp. 129–40.

Shah, S. F. 2012. Gender inclusion: a neglected aspect of the English textbooks in Pakistan. *International Journal of Social Science and Education,* Vol. 3, No. 1, pp. 118–27.

Singh, R. and Sarkar, S. 2012. *Teaching Quality Counts: How Student Outcomes Relate to Quality of Teaching in Private and Public Schools in India*. Oxford, UK, Young Lives, Department of International Development, University of Oxford.

South African Institute for Distance Education. 2010. *Teacher Education*. Johannesburg, South Africa, South African Institute for Distance Education. www.saide.org.za/Sectors/TeacherEducation/tabid/1453/Default.aspx (Accessed 20 May 2013.)

Spaull, N. 2011. *A Preliminary Analysis of SACMEQ III South Africa*. Matieland, South Africa, Stellenbosch University, Department of Economics. (Stellenbosch Economic Working Papers, 11/11.)

Sprietsma, M. 2007. *Computers as Pedagogical Tools in Brazil: a Pseudo-panel Analysis*. Mannheim, Germany, ZEW Centre for European Economic Research. (Discussion Paper, 07-040.)

Sri Lanka Ministry of Education. 2006. *Education Sector Development Framework and Programme 2006–2010*. Colombo, Ministry of Education.

Sriprakash, A. 2010. Child-centred education and the promise of democratic learning: pedagogic messages in rural Indian primary schools. *International Journal of Educational Development,* Vol. 30, No. 3, pp. 297–304.

Steiner-Khamsi, G. and Kunje, D. 2011. *The Third Approach to Enhancing Teacher Supply in Malawi: Volume I – The UNICEF ESARO Study on Recruitment, Utilization and Retention of Teachers*. Nairobi/Lilongwe, UNICEF. eastern and Southern Africa/UNICEF Malawi.

Steiner-Khamsi, G. and Simelane, I. 2010. *Teachers: Recruitment, Development and Retention in edSwaziland*. Nairobi/Mbabane, UNICEF Eastern and Southern Africa/UNICEF Swaziland.

Stern, J. M. B. and Heyneman, S. P. 2013. Low-fee private schooling: the case of Kenya. Srivastava, P. (ed.), *Low-fee Private Schooling: Aggravating Equity or Mitigating Disadvantage?* Oxford, UK, Symposium Books, pp. 105–28.

Suryadarma, D., Suryahadi, A., Sumarto, S. and Rogers, F. H. 2006. *Improving Student Performance in Public Primary Schools in Developing Countries: Evidence from Indonesia*. Washington, DC, World Bank.

Sutton Trust. 2011. *Improving the Impact of Teachers on Pupil Achievement in the UK: Interim Findings*. London, The Sutton Trust.

Tatto, M. T., Schwille, J., Senk, S. L., Ingvarson, L., Rowley, G., Peck, R., Bankov, K., Rodriguez, M. and Reckase, M. 2012. *Policy, Practice, and Readiness to Teach Primary and Secondary Mathematics in 17 Countries: Findings from the IEA Teacher Education and Development Study in Mathematics (TEDS-M)*. Amsterdam, International Association for the Evaluation of Educational Achievement.

Taylor, S. and Spaull, N. 2013. *The Effects of Rapidly Expanding Primary School Access on Effective Learning: The Case of Southern and Eastern Africa Since 2000*. Matieland, South Africa, University of Stellenbosh. (Stellenbosch Economic Working Papers, 1/13.)

Thomson, S., Hillman, K. and Wernert, N. 2012. *Monitoring Australian Year 8 Student Achievement Internationally: TIMSS 2011*. Melbourne, Australia, Australian Council for Educational Research.

Tooley, J., Dixon, P., Shamsan, Y. and Schagen, I. 2010. The relative quality and cost-effectiveness of private and public schools for low-income families: a case study in a developing country. *School Effectiveness and School Improvement,* Vol. 21, No. 2, pp. 117–44.

Twaweza. 2013. *Form Four Examination Results: Citizens Report on the Learning Crisis in Tanzania*. Dar es Salaam U.R. Tanzania, Uwazi at Twaweza. (Brief, 2.)

UIS. 2012a. *The Global Demand for Primary Teachers: 2012 Update – Projections to Reach Universal Primary Education by 2015*. Montreal, Que., UNESCO Institute for Statistics. (Information Bulletin, 10.)

___. 2012b. *School and Teaching Resources in Sub-Saharan Africa: Analysis of the 2011 UIS Regional Data Collection on Education*. Montreal, Que., UNESCO Institute for Statistics. (Information Bulletin, 9.)

___. 2013. *A Teacher for Every Child: Projecting Global Teacher Needs from 2015 to 2030*. Montreal, Que., UNESCO Institute for Statistics. (UIS Fact Sheet, 27.)

UK Department for Education. 2013. *New Advice to Help Schools Set Performance-related Pay*. London, UK Department for Education. www.gov.uk/government/news/new-advice-to-help-schools-set-performance-related-pay (Accessed 17 July 2013.)

UK Department for Education and School Teachers' Review Body. 2012. *School Teachers' Review Body: 21st Report – 2012*. London, UK Department for Education. www.gov.uk/government/publications/school-teachers-review-body-21st-report-2012# (Accessed 17 July 2013.)

UNESCO. 2010. *EFA Global Monitoring Report 2010: Reaching the Marginalized*. Paris, UNESCO.

___. 2011. *EFA Global Monitoring Report 2011: The Hidden Crisis – Armed Conflict and Education*. Paris, UNESCO.

___. 2012a. *EFA Global Monitoring Report 2012: Youth and Skills – Putting Education to Work*. Paris, UNESCO.

___. 2012b. *Telesecundaria, Mexico: Lower Secondary School Learning with Television Support*. Paris, UNESCO. www.unesco.org/education/educprog/lwf/doc/portfolio/abstract8.htm (Accessed 21 March 2013.)

UNESCO and Education International EFAIDS. 2007. *Supporting HIV-positive Teachers in East and Southern Africa: Technical Consultation Report*. Nairobi/Paris, UNESCO.

UNICEF. 2011. *The Role of Education in Peacebuilding: A Synthesis Report of Findings from Lebanon, Nepal and Sierra Leone*. New York, UNICEF.

United Nations Economic Commission for Latin America and the Caribbean. 2011. *Social Panaroma of Latin America 2011*. Santiago, United Nations Economic Commission for Latin America and the Caribbean.

U.R. Tanzania National Bureau of Statistics. 2010. *Tanzania Disability Survey Report 2008*. Dar es Salaam, U.R. Tanzania National Bureau of Statistics.

USAID. 2008. *Pakistan Teacher Education and Professional Development Programme: Performance Gap Analysis and Training Needs*. Washington, DC, US Agency for International Development.

___. 2010. *Promoting Quality Education in Nicaragua*. Washington, DC, US Agency for International Development.

___. 2012. *Improved Reading Performance in Grade 2: GILO-supported Schools vs. Control Schools*. Washington, DC, US Agency for International Development.

USAID and Education Development Center. 2009. *Radio Instruction to Strengthen Education (RISE) in Zanzibar: Learning Gains Assessment – More Than Child's Play*. Washington, DC/Boston, MA., US Agency for International Development/Educational Development Center, Inc.

US Department of Education. 2010. *A Blueprint for Reform: The Reauthorization of the Elementary and Secondary Education Act*. Washington, DC, Department of Education.

Uwezo Kenya. 2011. *Are Our Children Learning? Annual Learning Assessment Report*. Nairobi, Uwezo.

Uwezo Uganda. 2011. *Are Our Children Learning? Annual Learning Assessment Report*. Kampala, Uwezo.

van der Tuin, M. and Verger, A. 2013. Evaluating teachers in Peru: policy shortfalls and political implications. Verger, A., Altinyelken, H. and de Koning, M. (eds), *Global Managerial Education Reforms and Teachers: Emerging Policies, Controversies and Issues in Developing Contexts*. Brussels, Education International Research Institute, pp. 127–40.

Varly, P. 2010. *The Monitoring of Learning Outcomes in Mali: Language of Instruction and Teachers' Methods in Mali Grade 2 Curriculum Classrooms*. Research Triangle Park, NC, RTI International.

Vavrus, F., Thomas, M. and Bartlett, L. 2011. *Ensuring Quality by Attending to Inquiry: Learner-centered Pedagogy in Sub-Saharan Africa*. Addis Ababa, UNESCO – International Institute for Capacity Building in Africa. (Fundamentals of Teacher Education Development, 4.)

Vegas, E. and Petrow, J. 2007. *Raising Student Learning in Latin America: The Challenge for the 21st Century*. Washington, DC, World Bank.

Vithanapathirana, M. 2006. Adapting the primary mathematics curriculum to the multigrade classroom in rural Sri Lanka. Little, A. W. (ed.), *Education for All and Multigrade Teaching: Challenges and Opportunities*. Dordrecht, the Netherlands, Springer, pp. 127–53.

Voluntary Service Overseas. 2009. *Teaching Matters: A Policy Report on the Motivation and Morale of Teachers in Cambodia*. Kingston upon Thames, UK/Phnom Penh, Voluntary Services Overseas/NGO Education Partnership.

___. 2011. *Teaching Matters: A Policy Report on the Motivation and Morale of Teachers in Cambodia*. Kingston upon Thames, UK, Voluntary Service Overseas. (Paper for the third International Policy Dialogue Forum 13–14 September 2011, Bali, Indonesia.)

Walter, S. L. and Chuo, K. G. 2012. *The Kom Experimental Mother Tongue Education Pilot Project: Report for 2012*. Dallas, Tex., SIL International.

Walton, M. and Banerji, R. 2011. *What Helps Children to Learn? Evaluation of Pratham's Read India Program in Bihar and Uttarakhand*. Cambridge, Mass., Abdul Latif Jameel Poverty Action Lab, Massachusetts Institute of Technology.

Wang, D. and Gao, M. 2013. Educational equality or social mobility: the value conflict between preservice teachers and the Free Teacher Education program in China. *Teaching and Teacher Education*, Vol. 32, pp. 66–74.

Welch, T. 2012. Why Mother Tongue Literacy Isn't Working: Policy, Pedagogy, Parents and Publishing. Address at the Annual General Meeting of the Witswatersrand Council on Education, Wits School of Education, Johannesburg, South Africa 9 October 2012.

Were, E., Rubagiza, J. and Sutherland, R. 2009. *Bridging the Digital Divide? Educational Challenges and Opportunities in Rwanda*. Kigali/Bristol, UK, EdQual. (EdQual Working Paper, 15.)

West, K. L. and Mykerezi, E. 2011. Teachers' unions and compensation: the impact of collective bargaining on salary schedules and performance pay schemes. *Economics of Education Review*, Vol. 30, No. 1, pp. 99–108.

Wildlife and Environment Society of South Africa. 2013. *Eco-Schools Newsletter 16*. Howick, South Africa/Cape Town, South Africa/Copenhagen, Wildlife and Environment Society of South Africa/ World Wildlife Fund South Africa/Eco-Schools.

Wirak, A. and Lexow, J. 2008. *Evaluation of MoE/UNICEF's "Basic Education and Gender Equality Programme" for 2006–2008 Afghanistan*. Kabul/Stockholm, Norwegian Embassy Kabul/Swedish International Development Cooperation Agency.

Woessmann, L. 2011. Cross-country evidence on teacher performance pay. *Economics of Education Review*, Vol. 30, No. 3, pp. 404-18.

World Bank. 2005. *Improving Educational Quality Through Interactive Radio Instruction: A Toolkit for Policy Makers and Planners*. Washington, DC, World Bank. (Africa Human Development Working Paper, 52.)

___. 2009. *Le système éducatif béninois: analyse sectorielle pour une politique éducative plus équilibrée et plus efficace* [The Benin education system: sectoral analysis for a more balanced and effective education policy]. Washington, DC, World Bank. (Africa Region Human Development Working Paper, 165.)

___. 2010a. *The Education System in Malawi*. Washington, DC, World Bank. (Working Paper, 182.)

___. 2010b. *Egypt: Teachers*. Washington, DC, World Bank. (SABER Country Report.)

___. 2010c. *Teacher Early Retirement and Transfer Schemes: Indonesia*. Washington, DC, World Bank. (Policy Brief.)

___. 2011a. *Jordan: Higher Education Development Project*. Washington, DC, World Bank. (Project Performance Assessment Report, 62732.)

___. 2011b. *Republic of Chad Public Expenditure Review Update: Using Public Resources for Economic Growth and Poverty Reduction*. Washington, DC, World Bank. (Poverty Reduction and Economic Management, 3.)

___. 2012a. *Education in the Republic of South Sudan: Status and Challenges for a New System*. Washington, DC, World Bank.

___. 2012b. *The Status of the Education Sector in Sudan*. Washington, DC, World Bank. (Education Sector Review, 66608.)

___. 2012c. *Uganda: Teachers*. Washington, DC, World Bank. (SABER Country Report.)

___. 2013. *Spending More or Spending Better: Improving Education Financing in Indonesia*. Jakarta, World Bank.

Xu, Z., Hannaway, J. and Taylor, C. 2009. *Making a Difference? The Effects of Teach for America in High School*. Washington, DC, National Center for Analysis of Longitudinal Data in Education Research, The Urban Institute.

Yoshikawa, H. K., Myers, R., Bub, K. L., Lugo-Gil, J., Ramos, M. and Knaul, F. 2007. *Early Childhood Education in Mexico: Expansion, Quality Improvement and Curricular Reform*. Florence, Italy, UNICEF Innocenti Research Centre. (Working Paper, 2007-03.)

Zimbabwe Ministries of Education, Sport, Arts and Culture and Higher and Tertiary Education. 2010. Cost and financing of the education sector in Zimbabwe. Harare/Paris/New York, Zimbabwe Ministries of Education, Sport, Arts and Culture and Higher and Tertiary Education/UNESCO/ UNICEF. (Unpublished.)

Index

Note: *Italic* page numbers refer to figures and tables; those in **bold** refer to material in boxes and panels.; ***bold italics*** indicates a figure or table in a box or a panel.

A

D

F

I

J

K

M

N